THE
NELSON
INTRODUCTION
TO LITERATURE
SECOND EDITION

EDITED BY

AL VALLEAU
KWANTLEN UNIVERSITY COLLEGE

JACK FINNBOGASON
KWANTLEN UNIVERSITY COLLEGE

THOMSON
———✳———™
NELSON

Australia   Canada   Mexico   Singapore   Spain   United Kingdom   United States

THOMSON
NELSON

The Nelson Introduction to Literature
Second Edition
by Al Valleau and Jack Finnbogason

Editorial Director and Publisher:
Evelyn Veitch

Executive Editor:
Anne Williams

Acquisitions Editor:
Pam Duprey

Marketing Manager:
Lisa Rahn

Senior Developmental Editor:
Mike Thompson

Production Editor:
Carrie McGregor

Copy Editor:
Erin Moore

Proofreader:
Erin Moore

Production Coordinator:
Hedy Sellers

Creative Director:
Angela Cluer

Interior Design:
Sue Peden

Cover Design:
Concrete Design Communication Inc.

Cover Image:
Ann Cutting/Photonica

Compositor:
Alicja Jamorski

Permissions Coordinator:
Patricia Buckley

Printer:
Transcontinental

National Library of Canada Cataloguing in Publication Data

The Nelson introduction to literature / edited by Jack Finnbogason, Al Valleau. — 2nd ed.

Includes indexes.
ISBN 0-17-641550-5

1. Literature—Collections. I. Finnbogason, Jack, 1942– II. Valleau, Al, 1946– III. Title: Introduction to literature.

PN6014.N345 2004   808.8
C2003-905016-5

Contents

∾

POETRY

ESSAYS

☙

SHORT FICTION

Preface

It is gratifying to be writing a preface for the second edition of *The Nelson Introduction to Literature*. We believe it says that our anthology has found an audience and fulfilled part of our intention. From the outset, we envisioned a compact anthology that could be reasonably priced for students yet contain enough depth to give them diverse reading choices and introduce them to the challenges implicit in reading three genres—poetry, stories, and essays. Enough of you have agreed to allow us a second edition. So let us start by saying thank you to the instructors and students who chose this book.

The first step in creating this second edition was to ask a review team to give us feedback on our selections. Their responses started us on the way to a new table of contents, and in the majority of cases, we followed their advice. What we gained from that review experience was primary, however; we understood how experienced instructors in different areas of Canada saw our book and how it could be improved.

In the end, then, 19 writers from our first edition have been taken out and 18 new writers have been introduced. Poets like Elizabeth Bishop, Adrienne Rich, Alden Nowlan, Marge Piercy, and Billy Collins are here for the first time. Leon Rooke, Richard Ford, Salman Rushdie, and Lisa Moore are new to our Short Fiction offerings. And essayists as diverse as Northrop Frye, Naomi Klein, Dionne Brand, and Ann Hodgman offer new and distinctive perspectives in this second edition. All told, there are 47 new selections for readers of this anthology, a change of more than a quarter from the previous edition's contents. We hope you like the new writers and texts and agree with what we chose to retain from our first edition.

As we said in the preface of the first edition, we wanted to fashion an anthology that would include tradition but also make room for many new voices, well known or not. We drew from the literatures of three countries primarily—Britain, the United States, and Canada, with a special emphasis on Canadian works. This is, after all, a book aimed primarily at Canadian post-secondary institutions. In this second edition, we have kept this basic blueprint and tried to introduce some voices and issues that have gained prominence since the first book was published.

We are also conscious that the anthology will serve as a base text in a course introducing students to literature. To assist that aim, we have retained the chronological ordering of writers and the division of the text into three separate units, one for each of the genres included. The biographies are brief and try to include a comment or two that highlight a feature of the text or texts included from that writer. The notes are minimal and appear only when we think they offer essential information. We have rewritten the Introductions to the three genres and kept them as a feature here. The Glossary of Terms has also been retained, and students and instructors will find the entry on "Literary Analysis" has been re-ordered and one school has been added. These are all features included to help students read with understanding and empathy.

We have added one important new feature in this edition, an essay on how to write literary analysis. It is deliberately brief and tries to give students an overview of the process involved in writing this kind of analysis. We have emphasized the pre-writing phase of the analytic process because we believe that's where students typically don't devote enough time and thought before they attempt a first draft. We even included the means by which students can take more control of an assigned topic and make it their own.

We are also aware that this is the only Canadian anthology of literature in the marketplace that includes a full Instructor's Manual for those who wish to have it as a reference.

But the purpose of the anthology is the same. We prize the achievements of Canadians in creating our multicultural heritage, past and present. And literature is the embodiment of what different individuals in different times and places have felt and thought and written. Here are more than 160 opportunities to share their experiences and become better readers for doing so.

Al Valleau and Jack Finnbogason
Kwantlen University College, Surrey, B.C.
July 2003

Acknowledgments

As mentioned above, we feel fortunate to have this opportunity to create a second edition of this book. Our first thanks go to Marsha, Yit Shang, Loa, Signe, and Genevieve for tolerating what appear to be endless book projects. Loa, Signe, and Genevieve all have their first degrees now and one new poem here was a suggestion from Genevieve, so she's directly in our pages.

We also want to offer special thanks to our review team, who had such a direct early effect on our work. They are: Diana Austin, University of New Brunswick; Elaine Bander, Dawson College; Nancy E. Batty, Red Deer College; Stewart Blott, Vanier College; Jannie Edwards, Grant MacEwan College; Robert Einarsson, Grant MacEwan College; Robert Fleming, Kwantlen University College; Marie-Claude Legault, University of Calgary; Kent Lewis, Capilano College; Greg McSweeney, Dawson College; Phyllis Rozendal, York University; and Goran Stanivukovic, Saint Mary's University. Thank you all for your time, experience, and valuable comments.

Finally, this ends where it began, with the Nelson team that first approved the project, then saw it through. Ann Williams spoke to us first and got things started. We want to extend a special thank you to Mike Thompson, who put up with endless e-mails and constantly forged ahead with good cheer and professional knowledge, keeping the project moving ahead. Finally, it was a real assist to have the aid of Patricia Buckley in rounding up the necessary permissions.

We recently were cleaning up and discovered an envelope and enclosure from Nelson. It was dated 1992. So we have had a special relationship with Nelson for a considerable time now and could not have chosen better people to work with.

Poetry

Introduction to Poetry

Poetry, by its nature, is a chameleon. Depending on its surroundings, poetry takes on different meanings, different colours, and different personas. Poetry reflects the shifting flavours of a culture, its people, its beliefs, its concerns, its humour, its sounds, its rhythms, its images. But poetry is a blend of technique and topic, emotion and reason, order and inventiveness, restraint and freedom. It is no wonder that poetry has always elicited strong reactions, both positive and negative.

Poetry and Music: The Origins

One of the major components of poetic form, the line, is inextricably related to rhythm and metrics, and historically linked to music. The link between poetry and chanting, rhythm, and music cannot be overstated. The moment a person uses cadence to lend emotion and tension to a tale, or repeats patterns to provide emphasis and to help the reciter remember the details of the work, some of the fundamental elements of music are brought into play. Music was essential to the early ballads like "Sir Patrick Spens" and it also defines T.S. Eliot's "Love Song of J. Alfred Prufrock" and Theodore Roethke's "My Papa's Waltz." As Percy Bysshe Shelley pointed out in "A Defence of Poetry," "In the youth of the world, men dance and sing and imitate natural objects, observing in these actions, as in all others, a certain rhythm or order." In fact, the strong link between music and poetry is what distinguishes poetry from prose: whereas prose utilizes the sentence and paragraph as its base units, poetry relies on sound, syllable, cadence, line, and stanza.

Poets on Poetry

But let us allow the poets to speak for themselves in order to sample the range of styles and elements that are important to poetry. In fact, poets' comments can act as a guide to the shifts in poetic taste and style that are a part of that complex we call poetry.

Sir Philip Sidney in "An Apology for Poetry" (1595)

> Poesy therefore is an art of imitation, for so Aristotle termeth it in his word Mimesis, that is to say, a representing, counterfeiting, or figuring forth: to speak metaphorically, a speaking picture: with this end, to teach and delight; of this have been three several kinds ...
> a. imitate the inconceivable excellencies of GOD
> b. deal with matters philosophical: either moral,... or natural
> c. imitate to teach and delight, and to imitate, borrow nothing of what is, hath been, or shall be: but range only reined with learned discretion, into the divine consideration of what may be, and should be.

John Dryden in "Heroic Poetry and Poetic Licence" (1674)

> Imaging is, in itself, the very height and life of poetry. It is, as Longinus describes it, a discourse, which, by a kind of enthusiasm, or extraordinary emotion of the soul, makes it seem to us that we behold those things which the poet paints, so as to be pleased with them, and to admire them.

William Wordsworth in "Preface to Lyrical Ballads" (1802)

> The principal object, then, which I proposed to myself in these poems was to choose incidents and situations from common life, and to relate or describe them throughout, as far as was possible, in a selection of language really used by men; and, at the same time, to throw over them a certain colouring of imagination ...

> ... poetry is the spontaneous overflow of powerful feelings, it takes its origin from emotion recollected in tranquillity ...

Percy Bysshe Shelley in "A Defence of Poetry" (1840)

> But Poets, or those who imagine and express this indestructible order, are not only the authors of language and of music, of the dance and architecture and statuary and painting: they are the institutors of laws, and the founders of civil society and the inventors of the arts of life and the teachers, who draw into a certain propinquity with the beautiful and the true that partial apprehension of the agencies of the invisible world which is called religion.

> Poetry is not like reasoning, a power to be exerted according to the determination of the will. A man cannot say, "I will compose poetry" ... for the mind in creation is as a fading coal which some invisible influence, like an inconstant wind, awakens to transitory brightness ...

Ezra Pound in "A Retrospect" (1913)

> An "image" is that which presents an intellectual and emotional complex in an instant of time.

T.S. Eliot in "Tradition and the Individual Talent" from *Selected Essays* (1932, 1951)

> Consequently, we must believe that "emotion recollected in tranquillity" is an inexact formula. For it is neither emotion, nor recollection, nor, without distortion of meaning, tranquillity. It is a concentration, and a new thing resulting from the concentration ...

T.S. Eliot in "The Music of Poetry" (1942)

> The poet is occupied with frontiers of consciousness beyond which words fail, though meanings still exist. A poem may appear to mean very different things to different readers, [and] from what the author thought he meant.

As for "free verse," I expressed my view twenty-five years ago by saying that no verse is free for the man who wants to do a good job.

Charles Olson in "Projective Verse" (1950)

Let me put it baldly: The two halves are,
the HEAD by way of the EAR to the SYLLABLE
the HEART, by way of the BREATH, to the LINE.

E. E. Cummings in "A Poet's Advice to Students" (1955)

A poet is somebody who feels, and who expresses his feelings through words.
A lot of people think or believe or know they feel—but that's thinking or believing or knowing; not feeling. And poetry is feeling—not knowing or believing or thinking.

Robert Frost in *Selected Letters* (1964)

If I must be classified as a poet, I might be called a Synecdochist, for I prefer the synecdoche in poetry—that figure of speech in which we use a part for the whole.

in Selected Prose (1966)

[I] would as soon write free verse as play tennis with the net down.

P.K. Page in "Traveller, Conjuror, Journeyman" (1970)

[An aural poem] relies for its effect on long silences between words—the silences as significant as the words themselves. If one wants to reproduce this poem on paper one can use the conventions of musical transcription or one can so space the words on the page [so] that the poem becomes ... visual. What is time to the ear becomes space to the eye.

Earle Birney in *The Cow Jumped Over the Moon* (1972)

From a discussion of "premises about the nature of poetry" (2)

1. a poem is an art object, something begun in personal fancy, and developed by a kind of serious play
2. it is therefore unreliable as a source of information about its subject or author, on any rational level

Earle Birney on "Vancouver Lights" (started in 1923, taken up and finished in 1941)

...the visual details were still alive enough to send me back in my imagination to that same ridge to look again at Vancouver's lights—this time with the knowledge that they might, any moment now, be blacked or even bombed out ... by the annihilation that was spreading ever westward." (82)

Seamus Heaney in *Feelings into Words* (1974)

> Implicit in those lines is a view of poetry which I think is also implicit in the few poems I have written that give me any right to be here addressing you: poetry as divination; poetry as revelation of the self to the self, as restoration of the culture to itself ...

> "Digging" in fact, was the name of the first poem I wrote where I thought my feelings got into words, or, to put it more accurately, where I thought my feel had got into words.... This was the first place where I felt I had done more than make an arrangement of words: I felt that I had let down a shaft into real life.

bp Nichol in "Narrative in Language: The Long Poem" (1988)

> Of course the alphabet is a narrative—that movement thru your ABC. And any word you write is a displacement of that primary narrative. So that all writing always deconstructs some given even as it notes another given down.

Lorna Crozier in "Who's Listening?" (1989)

> I throw out the poem like a net and pull things together with thin threads of language that need mending, that need new patterns to catch the light. This is my woman's work, pulling these threads through my voice.

Poetics

Poetics involves a number of elements that can have a sensory impact on the reader/viewer/listener. The major elements of poetry include prosody (metre, rhythm), sound patterns (created by rhyme, assonance, consonance, alliteration), and figurative language (simile, metaphor, image). For more on each of these elements of poetry, see the Glossary of Terms.

Poetry, like music, is auditory: it is meant to be heard. Although oral poetry in the Western tradition goes back to at least 800 B.C., the printing press was not invented until 1456, when Gutenberg first printed the Bible. It is not surprising, then, that the meaning and emotional tone of a poem come alive when the poem is read aloud. Just as musical notation is the abstract representation of what is heard when a piece of music is played, the written form of a poem is only the abstract representation of a complex artistic whole. Read Dylan Thomas's "Fern Hill" or Allen Ginsberg's "A Supermarket in California" and you will hear the poets playing with sound and auditory patterns.

Poetry also depends on image, which can involve all the senses. When images recur, their pattern can take on thematic or even symbolic meaning. An image pattern is one way in which poets communicate with their audience. If you look at isolated images, as in Ezra Pound's "In a Station of the Metro," and complex patterns, as in Shakespeare's Sonnet 18, you discover how imagery makes both individual and cumulative contributions to the texture and meaning of poems.

In poetry, language is chosen carefully for its effect. The unit of meaning in a poem may still be the phrase or the clause, but the unit of rhythm is the line, as Charles Olson points out in the excerpt above.

Design

The dominating conventions in English poetry have been, in succession, syllabic, accentual-syllabic, and free verse. These conventions have also influenced the arrangement of lines that is, in a sense, the element that visually separates poetry from prose. In Anglo-Saxon verse, one line generally followed another in the form called sticchic poetry. As poetry came to rely on a repeated pattern of stresses for its rhythmic base, however, the arrangement of lines into groupings known as stanzas (and therefore strophic poetry) became equally dominant.

Stanzas vary in length according to the poetic form adopted. Traditional forms such as the four-line ballad stanza or the fourteen-line sonnet convention are easily recognized, but others, such as in "Fern Hill," require closer study.

The use of space on the page, the breaking up of words and the spacing of words within a line or between lines, the conventions of indentation, and even the shaping of a poem into a concrete form are also ways that poetic design can influence the emotional or intellectual impact a poem has on the reader. For example, Dorothy Livesay uses indentation and spacing between words in "And Give Us Our Trespasses" to guide our reading. All of these elements of poetry have been affected by the historical development of script, the printing press, the type-writer, and the computer.

Form

One of the essential characteristics of poetry is its compression. In contrast to prose, in which the introductory line encourages the writer to develop detailed description or argumentation, poetry is, for the most part, restricted by form. If you turn to the Glossary of Literary Terms at the end of this book and look up poetic forms, you will see that poetry in English utilizes a number of conventional poetic forms or styles and that these forms have very distinct structural patterns. These conventional forms are also called closed forms, as they abide by set stanzaic patterns, rhyme schemes, and metrics.

Poetry can also utilize what the Modernists called free verse, a form that is, to use Coleridge's term, "organic," as it derives its rhythm, rhyme or lack of rhyme, shape, and length of line from the content or conception of the poem itself. Free verse is not bound by a set line pattern, rhythm, or metrics. This is not to say free verse is poetry without any constraints. T.S. Eliot, as we have already pointed out, in writing on free verse, noted "no verse is free for the man who wants to do a good job." Ironically, both closed and open forms of poetry are demanding. Form, when original or inspired, leads to fresh, imaginative work, but, when uninspired, creates work that is derivative and as aesthetically painful as a bad pop melody.

Content: Traditions and Change

Considering that the earliest poetry, in the form of anonymous ballads and lyrics, was used to recount folk stories, it is not surprising that one of the oldest traditions in poetry is narrative poetry. From the early folk ballads like "Sir Patrick Spens" to the Robin Hood ballads, this tradition allowed people to create local mythology and moral tales that commented on the nature of their lives. The tradition of social commentary and protest has lived on in such poems as Anne Finch's "The Unequal Fetters," which comments on women's place in society; William Blake's "London," which criticizes family, church, and state; Matthew Arnold's "Dover Beach," which sees the fabric of society falling apart; Wilfred Owen's "Strange Meeting," which condemns the glorification of war; Wole Soyinka's "Telephone Conversation," which censures racism; and Marilyn Dumont's "Letter to Sir John A. Macdonald," which comments on the marginalization of Aboriginal people in Canada. Poetry, as a dynamic medium, is continually finding new subjects.

The pastoral tradition, originating in Greek and Roman poetry, is also well represented in Western poetry. The pastoral tradition that looks at elements of rural life as an ideal is represented by Christopher Marlowe's "The Passionate Shepherd to His Love," but elements of the pastoral tradition are also present in Andrew Marvell's "The Garden," Samuel Taylor Coleridge's "Frost at Midnight," John Keats's "To Autumn," and Charles G.D. Roberts's "The Potato Harvest."

Although the topic of love is included in pastoral poetry, as evinced by "The Passionate Shepherd," there is a long tradition of lyrical love poetry that includes some of Shakespeare's sonnets and John Donne's "The Canonization," but that also includes complaints such as Anne Finch's "The Unequal Fetters," Dorothy Livesay's "And Give Us Our Trespasses," and Robert Creeley's "Ballad of the Despairing Husband." In fact, a large part of the poetry written in the last century is lyrical in nature. The poetry is subjective, imaginative, rooted deeply in emotion, and, in most cases, as the word *lyric* suggests, melodic. Dylan Thomas's "Fern Hill," for example, gains its power from its melodic rhythm and its intense emotional appeal.

Besides following these obvious traditions, poetry ranges over the entire human experience. It is possible to find a poem on any topic; indeed, poetry is used playfully, seriously, and mockingly to comment on, criticize, and praise everything we do, from making dinner to making love. Thus, every poem is at the same time traditional and new and iconoclastic. As Irving Layton points out, "Whatever else poetry is freedom."

Geoffrey Chaucer

England ca. 1343–1400

Chaucer's work provides us with a wonderful record of late medieval life, capturing the variety and energy of the fourteenth century in great clarity and colour. Born in London, Chaucer was familiar with the merchants at London Vintry and learned, at an early age, French and Latin; he was also fortunate in being placed, in his early teens, as a page in an aristocratic household. Chaucer's long service at court, in what amounted at the time to the civil service, gave him a rich perspective from which to write. Travels to Italy in 1372 and 1378 acquainted him with the Italian Renaissance and the writings of Dante, Petrarch, and Boccaccio; the new verse forms he encountered in these writings inspired and informed much of his own work. Chaucer remains best known for *The Canterbury Tales*, the stories of a group of pilgrims on a pilgrimage; the "Prologue" of the *Tales* is included here.

General Prologue   1386–1400

Here bygynneth the Book of the Tales of Canterbury.

Whan that Aprill with his shoures soote
The droghte of March hath perced to the roote,
And bathed every veyne in swich licour
Of which vertu engendred is the flour;
5   Whan Zephirus eek with his sweete breeth
Inspired hath in every holt and heeth
The tendre croppes, and the yonge sonne
Hath in the Ram his halve cours yronne,
And smale foweles maken melodye,
10 That slepen al the nyght with open ye
(So priketh hem nature in hir corages);
Thanne longen folk to goon on pilgrimages,
And palmeres for to seken straunge strondes,
To ferne halwes, kowthe in sondry londes;
15 And specially from every shires ende
Of Engelond to Caunterbury they wende,
The hooly blisful martir for to seke,
That hem hath holpen whan that they were seeke.
Bifil that in that seson on a day,
20 In Southwerk at the Tabard as I lay
Redy to wenden on my pilgrymage
To Caunterbury with ful devout courage,
At nyght was come into that hostelrye
Wel nyne and twenty in a compaignye,
25 Of sondry folk, by aventure yfalle

In felaweshipe, and pilgrimes were they alle,
That toward Caunterbury wolden ryde.
The chambres and the stables weren wyde,
And wel we weren esed atte beste.
30   And shortly, whan the sonne was to reste,
So hadde I spoken with hem everichon
That I was of hir felaweshipe anon,
And made forward erly for to ryse,
To take oure wey ther as I yow devyse.
35   But nathelees, whil I have tyme and space,
Er that I ferther in this tale pace,
Me thynketh it acordaunt to resoun
To telle yow al the condicioun
Of ech of hem, so as it semed me,
40   And whiche they weren, and of what degree,
And eek in what array that they were inne;
And at a knyght than wol I first bigynne.
. . . .

Anonymous

Sir Patrick Spens

The king sits in Dumferline town,
    Drinking the blude-reid wine:
"O whar will I get a guid sailor
    To sail this ship of mine?"

5   Up and spak an eldern knicht,
    Sat at the king's richt knee:
"Sir Patrick Spens is the best sailor
    That sails upon the sea."

The king has written a braid letter
10   And signed it wi' his hand,
And sent it to Sir Patrick Spens,
    Was walking on the sand.

The first line that Sir Patrick read,
    A loud lauch lauched he;
15   The next line that Sir Patrick read,
    The tear blinded his ee.

"O wha is this has done this deed,
 This ill deed done to me,
To send me out this time o' the year,
20 To sail upon the sea?

"Make haste, make haste, my mirry men all,
 Our guid ship sails the morn."
"O say na sae, my master dear,
 For I fear a deadly storm.

25 "Late late yestre'en I saw the new moon
  Wi' the auld moon in her arm,
And I fear, I fear, my dear master,
 That we will come to harm."

O our Scots nobles were richt laith[1]
30 To weet their cork-heeled shoon,[2]
But lang owre a' the play were played
 Their hats they swam aboon.

O lang, lang may their ladies sit,
 Wi' their fans into their hand,
35 Or e'er they see Sir Patrick Spens
  Come sailing to the land.

O lang, lang may the ladies stand,
 Wi' their golden kembs in their hair,
Waiting for their ain dear lords,
40 For they'll see thame na mair.

Half o'er, half o'er to Aberdour
 It's fifty fadom deep,
And there lies guid Sir Patrick Spens,
 Wi' the Scots lords at his feet.

The Three Ravens

There were three ravens sat on a tree,
 Down a down, hay down, hay down,
There were three ravens sat on a tree,
 With a down,

---

1 loath
2 shoes

5   There were three ravens sat on a tree,
They were as black as they might be,
   With a down, derry, derry, derry, down, down.

The one of them said to his mate,
"Where shall we our breakfast take?"

10   "Down in yonder green field
There lies a knight slain under his shield.

"His hounds they lie down at his feet,
So well they can their master keep.

"His hawks they fly so eagerly,
15   There's no fowl dare him come nigh."

Down there comes a fallow doe,
As great with young as she might go.

She lifted up his bloody head,
And kissed his wounds that were so red.

20   She got him up upon her back,
And carried him to earthen lake.

She buried him before the prime;
She was dead herself ere evensong time.

God send every gentleman
25   Such hawks, such hounds, and such a lemman.

Western Wind

Western wind, when will thou blow,
   The small rain down can rain?
Christ, if my love were in my arms
   And I in my bed again.

Sir Thomas Wyatt the Elder

England 1503–1542

Born at Allington Castle, Kent, and educated at Cambridge, Sir Thomas Wyatt became a courtier and diplomat who spent much time abroad in the service of his country. Wyatt's life was by no means tranquil; he ended up in prison twice, and, on the second occasion, he lost all his property. Wyatt's poetry was influenced by the Italian sonnet writers, including Petrarch, and he introduced the sonnet into English verse. His poem "They Flee from Me" adopts the sad lover of the Italian sonnet but uses a verse form of seven-line stanzas. It helps to read this poem as it was intended to be read if you sound any "e's" that conclude a line.

They Flee from Me   1557

They flee from me, that sometime did me seek,
With naked foot stalking in my chamber.
I have seen them, gentle, tame, and meek,
That now are wild, and do not remember
5   That sometime they put themselves in danger
To take bread at my hand; and now they range,
Busily seeking with a continual change.

Thankèd be fortune it hath been otherwise,
Twenty times better; but once in special,
10   In thin array, after a pleasant guise,
When her loose gown from her shoulders did fall,
And she me caught in her arms long and small,
Therewithall sweetly did me kiss
And softly said, "Dear heart, how like you this?"

15   It was no dream, I lay broad waking.
But all is turned, thorough my gentleness,
Into a strange fashion of forsaking;
And I have leave to go, of her goodness,
And she also to use newfangleness.
20   But since that I so kindely am servèd,
I fain would know what she hath deservèd.

Sir Walter Ralegh

England 1552–1618

Sir Walter Ralegh, navigator, colonizer of Virginia, and the first to introduce tobacco to Europe, led a life that was far from simple. Nothing illustrates the contradictions of Ralegh's life more than the fact that, despite being a favourite of the crown under Elizabeth I, he was executed during the reign of James I to pacify the Spanish, who lost several men in South America to an English expedition headed but not commanded by Ralegh. Ralegh's "The Nymph's Reply to the Shepherd," a popular poem in its time, was a practical response to the idealized appeal of Marlowe's "The Passionate Shepherd to His Love," which was, in Ralegh's words, "In folly ripe, in reason rotten."

The Nymph's Reply to the Shepherd   1600

If all the world and love were young,
And truth in every shepherd's tongue,
These pretty pleasures might me move
To live with thee and be thy love.

5   Time drives the flocks from field to fold
When rivers rage and rocks grow cold,
And Philomel[1] becometh dumb;
The rest complains of cares to come.

The flowers do fade, and wanton fields
10   To wayward winter reckoning yields;
A honey tongue, a heart of gall,
Is fancy's spring, but sorrow's fall.

Thy gowns, thy shoes, thy beds of roses,
Thy cap, thy kirtle,[2] and thy posies
15   Soon break, soon wither, soon forgotten—
In folly ripe, in reason rotten.

Thy belt of straw and ivy buds,
Thy coral clasps and amber studs,
All these in me no means can move
20   To come to thee and be thy love.

But could youth last and love still breed,
Had joys no date nor age no need,
Then these delights my mind might move
To live with thee and be thy love.

---

1 the nightingale
2 skirt or outer petticoat

Christopher Marlowe

England 1564–1593

Born in Canterbury, Christopher Marlowe achieved his fame as a dramatist, especially for *Tamburlaine*. Marlowe's short life—he was killed at twenty-nine in a tavern brawl—was packed with action. He earned a master of arts degree, acted as a secret agent for the Queen, wrote six plays, and composed incidental poetry, such as the pastoral lyric of invitation included here.

The Passionate Shepherd to His Love   1600

Come live with me and be my love,
And we will all the pleasures prove
That valleys, groves, hills, and fields,
Woods, and steepy mountain yields.

5   And we will sit upon the rocks,
Seeing the shepherds feed their flocks,
By shallow rivers to whose falls
Melodious birds sing madrigals.

And I will make thee beds of roses
10   And a thousand fragrant posies,
A cap of flowers, and a kirtle
Embroidered all with leaves of myrtle;

A gown made of the finest wool
Which from our pretty lambs we pull;
15   Fair lined slippers for the cold,
With buckles of the purest gold;

A belt of straw and ivy buds,
With coral clasps and amber studs:
And if these pleasures may thee move,
20   Come live with me, and be my love.

The shepherds' swains shall dance and sing
For thy delight each May morning:
If these delights thy mind may move,
Then live with me and be my love.

William Shakespeare

England 1564–1616

William Shakespeare, born in Stratford-on-Avon, married Anne Hathaway in 1582 when he was eighteen and she twenty-six. By 1592, he was working as an actor in London and had received payment from Henslowe for his first play *I Henry VI.* By 1594, besides his first plays, Shakespeare had written his poem "Venus and Adonis," produced *The Rape of Lucrece*, and become associated with the Lord Chamberlain's Men, a theatre group that was later known, under James I, as the King's Men. Shakespeare's series of thirty-seven plays ended with *The Tempest* in 1611 and *Henry VIII* in 1613, although *Henry VIII*'s authorship has been disputed. Shakespeare's 154 sonnets, of which three appear here, were first printed in 1609, although he wrote some as much as eleven years earlier. Shakespeare's sonnets use the pattern, introduced by Henry Howard, Earl of Surrey, of three quatrains followed by a couplet that ties together the elements of the first twelve lines with dramatic compression.

Sonnet 18   1609

Shall I compare thee to a summer's day?
Thou art more lovely and more temperate:
Rough winds do shake the darling buds of May,
And summer's lease hath all too short a date:
5   Sometime too hot the eye of heaven shines
And often is his gold complexion dimmed;
And every fair from fair sometimes declines,
By chance or nature's changing course untrimmed;[1]
But thy eternal summer shall not fade,
10   Nor lose possession of that fair thou ow'st;
Nor shall death brag thou wander'st in his shade,
When in eternal lines to time thou grow'st;
   So long as men can breathe, or eyes can see,
   So long lives this, and this gives life to thee.

---

1   put in disordered condition or attire

Sonnet 129   1609

Th' expense of spirit in a waste of shame
Is lust in action;[1] and till action, lust
Is perjured, murd'rous, bloody, full of blame,
Savage, extreme, rude, cruel, not to trust;
5   Enjoyed no sooner but despisèd straight:
Past reason hunted; and no sooner had,
Past reason hated, as a swallowed bait,
On purpose laid to make the taker mad:
Mad in pursuit, and in possession so;
10   Had, having, and in quest to have, extreme;
A bliss in proof and proved, a very woe;
Before, a joy proposed; behind, a dream.
   All this the world well knows; yet none knows well
   To shun the heaven that leads men to this hell.

---

1   line 1 and the first half of 2 = from the idea that sexual orgasm burnt vital energy and shortened life

Sonnet 130   1609

My mistress' eyes are nothing like the sun;
Coral is far more red than her lips' red;
If snow be white, why then her breasts are dun;
If hairs be wires, black wires grow on her head.
5   I have seen roses damasked, red and white,
But no such roses see I in her cheeks;
And in some perfumes is there more delight
Than in the breath that from my mistress reeks.
I love to hear her speak, yet well I know
10   That music hath a far more pleasing sound;
I grant I never saw a goddess go;
My mistress, when she walks, treads on the ground.
   And yet, by heaven, I think my love as rare
   As any she belied with false compare.

John Donne

England 1572–1631

Donne was born Roman Catholic at a time when Catholicism barred him from many opportunities. He attended Oxford, Cambridge, and Lincoln's Inn but failed to complete his education. Donne was a favourite at court until his marriage to Ann More, the seventeen-year-old niece of the powerful Egerton family, gained him imprisonment, followed by dismissal from court service. King James pressured Donne to enter the Anglican ministry, and, in 1615, he accepted a position. Because of his new vocation, Donne's later work, in contrast to his earlier worldly poetry, has a strong religious focus. In 1621, he became dean of St. Paul's Cathedral. Donne's work appeals strongly to the reader's wit and sense of language. He and his followers were later dubbed by John Dryden and Samuel Johnson the metaphysical poets because of their use of fanciful conceits and startling imagery, clearly evident in "The Canonization."

The Canonization   1633

For God's sake hold your tongue, and let me love,
    Or chide my palsy, or my gout,
My five gray hairs, or ruined fortune, flout,
    With wealth your state, your mind with arts improve,
5   Take you a course, get you a place,
        Observe His Honor, or His Grace,
Or the King's real, or his stampèd face
    Contemplate; what you will, approve,
    So you will let me love.

10 Alas, alas, who's injured by my love?
    What merchant's ships have my sighs drowned?
Who says my tears have overflowed his ground?
    When did my colds a forward spring remove?
        When did the heats which my veins fill
15   Add one more to the plaguy bill?
Soldiers find wars, and lawyers find out still
    Litigious men, which quarrels move,
    Though she and I do love.

    Call us what you will, we are made such by love;
20   Call her one, me another fly,
    We're tapers[1] too, and at our own cost die,

---

1   candles connected to the idea that sexual orgasm shortens life

And we in us find the eagle and the dove.
    The phoenix riddle hath more wit
    By us: we two being one, are it.
25 So, to one neutral thing both sexes fit.
    We die and rise the same, and prove
    Mysterious by this love.

We can die by it, if not live by love,
    And if unfit for tomb and hearse
30 Our legend be, it will be fit for verse;
    And if no piece of chronicle we prove,
      We'll build in sonnets pretty rooms;
      As well a well-wrought urn becomes
The greatest ashes, as half-acre tombs,
35   And by these hymns, all shall approve
    Us canonized for love:

And thus invoke us: You whom reverend love
    Made one another's hermitage;
You, to whom love was peace, that now is rage;
40   Who did the whole world's soul contract, and drove
    Into the glasses of your eyes
    (So made such mirrors, and such spies,
That they did all to you epitomize)
    Countries, towns, courts: Beg from above
45   A pattern of your love!

Robert Herrick

England 1591–1674

Born to an affluent London goldsmith, Herrick was fond of writing and talking about literature. He enjoyed the company of Ben Jonson, who helped him develop a stylistic polish. That polish is evident in whimsical poems such as "Delight in Disorder," an archetypal Cavalier poem in which style and wit reflect a gentleman's accomplishments. Herrick took orders in the church and obtained a position in Devonshire. His career was interrupted when Oliver Cromwell came to power, but he returned to the church and Devonshire after the restoration of the monarchy. While in London during Cromwell's reign, Herrick had his only book of poetry printed.

Delight in Disorder   1648

A sweet disorder in the dress
Kindles in clothes a wantonness.
A lawn about the shoulders thrown
Into a fine distractiòn;
5   An erring lace, which here and there
Enthralls the crimson stomacher;
A cuff neglectful, and thereby
Ribbons to flow confusedly;
A winning wave, deserving note,
10   In the tempestuous petticoat;
A careless shoestring, in whose tie
I see a wild civility;
Do more bewitch me than when art
Is too precise in every part.

Dreams   1648

Here we are all, by day; by night, we're hurled
By dreams, each one into a several world.

John Milton

England 1608–1674

Born in Cheapside, London, John Milton was, in his early years, devoted to his studies. After obtaining his degree in 1629, he continued to study European languages for eight years, as well as Latin and Greek. Milton was unhappy with what he saw as corruption in the Anglican Church and slowly moved to Puritanism, eventually becoming Cromwell's foreign secretary when the Puritans took power. When the Restoration brought Charles II back and ousted the Puritans, Milton began work on his epic poem, despite his failing eyesight. *Paradise Lost* was published in 1667; four years later, Milton published his last significant works, *Paradise Regained* and *Samson Agonistes.*

From Paradise Lost, Book 1   1667

Of man's first disobedience, and the fruit
Of that forbidden tree whose mortal taste

Brought death into the world, and all our woe,
With loss of Eden, till one greater Man
5 Restore us, and regain the blissful seat,
Sing, Heavenly Muse,[1] that on the secret top
Of Oreb, or of Sinai, didst inspire
That shepherd who first taught the chosen seed
In the beginning how the heavens and earth
10 Rose out of Chaos: or, if Sion hill[2]
Delight thee more, and Siloa's brook[3] that flowed
Fast by the oracle of God, I thence
Invoke thy aid to my adventurous song,
That with no middle flight intends to soar
15 Above th' Aonian mount,[4] while it pursues
Things unattempted yet in prose or rhyme.
And chiefly thou, O Spirit, that dost prefer
Before all temples th' upright heart and pure,
Instruct me, for thou know'st; thou from the first
20 Wast present, and with mighty wings outspread
Dovelike sat'st brooding on the vast abyss,
And mad'st it pregnant; what in me is dark
Illumine; what is low, raise and support;
That to the height of this great argument
25 I may assert Eternal Providence,
And justify the ways of God to men.
　　　Say first (for Heaven hides nothing from thy view,
Nor the deep tract of Hell), say first what cause
Moved our grand parents, in that happy state,
30 Favored of Heaven so highly, to fall off
From their Creator, and transgress his will
For one restraint, lords of the world besides?
Who first seduced them to that foul revolt?
　　　Th' infernal serpent; he it was, whose guile,
35 Stirred up with envy and revenge, deceived
The mother of mankind, what time his pride
Had cast him out from Heaven, with all his host
Of rebel angels, by whose aid aspiring
To set himself in glory above his peers,
40 He trusted to have equaled the Most High,

---

1 reference to Urania, the muse of astronomy, but here linked to the divine inspiration
   of Moses to write the first five books of the Bible for the Jewish people
2 Sion hill = the Temple Mount in Jerusalem
3 Siloa's brook = a brook on Sion hill; brooks and mountains are both haunts of Muses
4 Aonian mount = belonging to Aonia, which contained the mountains Helicon and
   Cithaeron, sacred to the Muses

If he opposed; and with ambitious aim
Against the throne and monarchy of God
Raised impious war in Heaven and battle proud,
With vain attempt. Him the Almighty Power
45   Hurled headlong flaming from th' ethereal sky
With hideous ruin and combustion down
To bottomless perdition, there to dwell
In adamantine chains and penal fire,
Who durst defy th' Omnipotent to arms.
50   Nine times the space that measures day and night
To mortal men, he with his horrid crew
Lay vanquished, rolling in the fiery gulf
Confounded though immortal. But his doom
Reserved him to more wrath; for now the thought
55   Both of lost happiness and lasting pain
Torments him; round he throws his baleful5 eyes,
That witnessed huge affliction and dismay,
Mixed with obdùrate pride and steadfast hate.
At once, as far as angels ken, he views
60   The dismal situation waste and wild:
A dungeon horrible, on all sides round
As one great furnace flamed; yet from those flames
No light, but rather darkness visible
Served only to discover sights of woe,
65   Regions of sorrow, doleful shades, where peace
And rest can never dwell, hope never comes
That comes to all, but torture without end
Still urges, and a fiery deluge, fed
With ever-burning sulphur unconsumed:
70   Such place Eternal Justice had prepared
For those rebellious; here their prison ordained
In utter darkness and their portion set
As far removed from God and light of Heaven
As from the center thrice to th' utmost pole.
75   O how unlike the place from whence they fell!
There the companions of his fall, o'erwhelmed
With floods and whirlwinds of tempestuous fire,
He soon discerns; and, weltering by his side,
One next himself in power, and next in crime,
80   Long after known in Palestine, and named
Beëlzebub.6 To whom th' arch-enemy,
And thence in Heaven called Satan, with bold words
Breaking the horrid silence thus began:

---

5   willing evil, suffering
6   Beëlzebub = used here as one of the fallen angels, prince of devils, from the Hebrew
baalzbub, lord of the flies

"If thou beëst he—but O how fallen! how changed
85 From him who in the happy realms of light
Clothed with transcendent brightness didst outshine
Myriads, though bright! if he whom mutual league,
United thoughts and counsels, equal hope
And hazard in the glorious enterprise,
90 Joined with me once, now misery hath joined
In equal ruin; into what pit thou seest
From what height fallen, so much the stronger proved
He with his thunder: and till then who knew
The force of those dire arms? Yet not for those,
95 Nor what the potent Victor in his rage
Can else inflict, do I repent or change,
Though changed in outward luster, that fixed mind
And high disdain, from sense of injured merit,
That with the Mightiest raised me to contend,
100 And to the fierce contention brought along
Innumerable force of spirits armed,
That durst dislike his reign, and me preferring,
His utmost power with adverse power opposed
In dubious battle on the plains of Heaven,
105 And shook his throne. What though the field be lost?
All is not lost: the unconquerable will,
And study of revenge, immortal hate,
And courage never to submit or yield:
And what is else not to be overcome?
110 That glory never shall his wrath or might
Extort from me. To bow and sue for grace
With suppliant knee, and deify his power
Who from the terror of this arm so late
Doubted his empire—that were low indeed;
115 That were an ignominy and shame beneath
This downfall; since, by fate, the strength of gods
And this empyreal substance cannot fail;
Since, through experience of this great event,
In arms not worse, in foresight much advanced,
120 We may with more successful hope resolve
To wage by force or guile eternal war,
Irreconcilable to our grand Foe,
Who now triùmphs, and in th' excess of joy
Sole reigning holds the tyranny of Heaven."
125   So spake th' apostate angel, though in pain,
Vaunting aloud, but racked with deep despair;
And him thus answered soon his bold compeer:
"O prince, O chief of many thronèd powers,
That led th' embattled seraphim to war

130   Under thy conduct, and in dreadful deeds
       Fearless, endangered Heaven's perpetual King,
       And put to proof his high supremacy,
       Whether upheld by strength, or chance, or fate!
       Too well I see and rue the dire event
135   That with sad overthrow and foul defeat
       Hath lost us Heaven, and all this mighty host
       In horrible destruction laid thus low,
       As far as gods and heavenly essences
       Can perish: for the mind and spirit remains
140   Invincible, and vigor soon returns,
       Though all our glory extinct, and happy state
       Here swallowed up in endless misery.

Andrew Marvell

England 1621–1678

At twelve, Marvell, a native of Yorkshire, entered Oxford. During Cromwell's tenure, he became John Milton's assistant, and, from 1659 on, he was the member of parliament for Hull. His poetry shows his clever wit and his clear sense of poetics and language. "To His Coy Mistress" echoes other poems on love and sexual conquest and is a good example of the metaphysical *carpe diem* theme; however, the poem's use of hyperbole and descriptions such as "birds of prey" and "tear our pleasures with rough strife" suggest a dark side to the conquest. Marvell's use of opposite forces, irony, and satire are also present in "The Garden."

To His Coy Mistress   1681

     Had we but world enough, and time,
    This coyness, lady, were no crime.
    We would sit down, and think which way
    To walk, and pass our long love's day.
5   Thou by the Indian Ganges' side
    Shouldst rubies find; I by the tide
    Of Humber would complain. I would
    Love you ten years before the Flood,
    And you should, if you please, refuse
10   Till the conversion of the Jews.[1]
    My vegetable love should grow
    Vaster than empires, and more slow;

---

1 According to Christian belief, the Jews would be converted just before the Last Judgment.

An hundred years should go to praise
Thine eyes, and on thy forehead gaze;
15 Two hundred to adore each breast,
But thirty thousand to the rest;
An age at least to every part,
And the last age should show your heart.
For, lady, you deserve this state,
20 Nor would I love at lower rate.
   But at my back I always hear
Time's wingèd chariot hurrying near;
And yonder all before us lie
Deserts of vast eternity.
25 Thy beauty shall no more be found,
Nor, in thy marble vault, shall sound
My echoing song; then worms shall try
That long-preserved virginity,
And your quaint honor turn to dust,
30 And into ashes all my lust:
The grave's a fine and private place,
But none, I think, do there embrace.
   Now therefore, while the youthful hue
Sits on thy skin like morning dew,
35 And while thy willing soul transpires
At every pore with instant fires,
Now let us sport us while we may,
And now, like amorous birds of prey,
Rather at once our time devour
40 Than languish in his slow-chapped² power.
Let us roll all our strength and all
Our sweetness up into one ball,
And tear our pleasures with rough strife
Thorough the iron gates of life:
45 Thus, though we cannot make our sun
Stand still, yet we will make him run.

---

2 slow-jawed, being consumed slowly

The Garden   1681

How vainly men themselves amaze
To win the palm, the oak, or bays,¹
And their incessant labors see
Crowned from some single herb or tree,
5 Whose short and narrow-vergèd shade

---

1 "To win the palm, the oak, or bays" = military, civic, poetic honours

Does prudently their toils upbraid;
While all flowers and all trees do close
To weave the garlands of repose!

Fair Quiet, have I found thee here,
10   And Innocence, thy sister dear?
Mistaken long, I sought you then
In busy companies of men.
Your sacred plants, if here below,
Only among the plants will grow;
15   Society is all but rude,
To this delicious solitude.

No white nor red was ever seen
So amorous as this lovely green.
Fond lovers, cruel as their flame,
20   Cut in these trees their mistress' name:
Little, alas, they know or heed
How far these beauties hers exceed!
Fair trees, wheresoe'er your barks I wound,
No name shall but your own be found.

25   When we have run our passion's heat,
Love hither makes his best retreat.
The gods, that mortal beauty chase,
Still in a tree did end their race:
Apollo hunted Daphne so,
30   Only that she might laurel grow;[2]
And Pan[3] did after Syrinx speed,
Not as a nymph, but for a reed.

What wondrous life in this I lead!
Ripe apples drop about my head;
35   The luscious clusters of the vine
Upon my mouth do crush their wine;
The nectarine and curious peach
Into my hands themselves do reach;
Stumbling on melons as I pass,
40   Insnared with flowers, I fall on grass.

---

2   lines 29–30: Apollo = son of Zeus and Leto, associated with music, archery, prophecy, medicine, and flocks; he chased Daphne, who turned into a laurel bush to escape him.

3   Pan = the god of flocks and herds. His instrument is the pan flute, which consists of eight to ten reeded pipes, called a syrinx after the nymph who escaped Pan by changing into a reed.

Meanwhile the mind, from pleasure less,
Withdraws into its happiness;
The mind, that ocean where each kind
Does straight its own resemblance find;
45 Yet it creates, transcending these,
Far other worlds and other seas,
Annihilating all that's made
To a green thought in a green shade.

Here at the fountain's sliding foot,
50 Or at some fruit tree's mossy root,
Casting the body's vest aside,
My soul into the boughs does glide:
There like a bird it sits and sings,
Then whets and combs its silver wings,
55 And, till prepared for longer flight,
Waves in its plumes the various light.

Such was that happy garden-state,
While man there walked without a mate:
After a place so pure and sweet,
60 What other help could yet be meet!
But 'twas beyond a mortal's share
To wander solitary there:
Two paradises 'twere in one
To live in paradise alone.

65 How well the skillful gardener drew
Of flowers and herbs this dial new,
Where from above the milder sun
Does through a fragrant zodiac run;
And as it works, th' industrious bee
70 Computes its time as well as we!
How could such sweet and wholesome hours
Be reckoned but with herbs and flowers!

Katherine Philips

England/Wales 1632–1664

Born into a prosperous Presbyterian merchant's family in London, Katherine Philips was educated at Mrs. Salmon's Presbyterian School. She and her mother moved to Wales upon her mother's second marriage. Katherine married too and for the next twelve years split her time between Cardigan and London, where her husband was a parliamentarian during the Interregnum. Philips began writing poetry at a young age. The passion that is the central focus of much of her work was praised by her admirers, including her neighbour, Henry Vaughan, and much later, John Keats. She was called by her peers "the Matchless Orinda." "Against Love" shows that not all of Philips's love poetry praised love and its virtues.

Against Love   1664

Hence, Cupid! with your cheating toys.
Your real Griefs, and painted Joys,
Your Pleasure which itself destroys.
Lovers like men in fevers burn and rave,
5   And only what will injure them do crave.
Men's weakness makes Love so severe,
They give him power by their fear,
And make the shackles which they wear.
    Who to another does his heart submit;
10   Makes his own Idol, and then worships it.
Him whose heart is all his own,
Peace and liberty does crown;
He apprehends no killing frown.
    He feels no raptures which are joys diseased,
15   And is not much transported, but still pleased.

Aphra Behn

England 1640–1689

Little is known about Behn's life, although she was one of the most prolific of the Restoration writers and wits, composing more than a dozen plays, a pioneering novel created from letters, and all the other pieces expected of a professional writer. She is believed to have been from East Kent, but no details about her family or her husband have survived. Her writings show that she had been to Surinam and knew the details of the slave trade there; she also acted for Charles II as a spy in Antwerp in the Dutch war. She said she resorted to writing plays to earn money when King Charles was tardy in paying her. Behn offers us a unique and liberal voice in a time not noted for these qualities.

A Song in Dialogue   1691

She[pherd]. Silvi[a], when will you be kind,
    Ah, *Silvi[a]*, when will you be kind.
Sil. When Constancy in Swains[1] I find,
    Ah, when Constancy in Swains I find.
5   *She.* Ah my *Silvia*, you're too Fair,
    E'er to give me cause to change,
   Ah! do not let me then despair,
    For my Heart's not given to range.
Sil. Men will Sigh, Protest, and Weep,
10   Ah! what a coyle[2] with love you'll keep,
   Till our Blushes you o'er-come:
   Ah! till the blessing you have won,
    Which, having once obtain'd, you fly:
   Or if, by chance, you linger on,
15   Can see us Sigh, can see us Dye,
   And Triumph when we are undone.
She. Oh! may my Flocks forget to feed,
    And Wolves into my Sheepfold break:
   May Heaven forget me in my need,
20   And thou disdain me when I speak,
   If ever I thy Love betray,
    Or with false Vows thy faith repay.
Sil. Then take my hand, which ne'er to Swain
    Was render'd, on the score of Love:
25   But, oh! I give it to you with pain,
    For fear you shou'd Inconstant prove.

---

1 Swains = young lovers or suitors
2 coil

Anne Finch

England 1661–1720

Raised in Newbury, Berkshire, Anne Finch, a member of a wealthy, landed family, was a maid of honour at King Charles II's court. She and her husband, Colonel Heneage Finch, retired to an estate in Kent after Charles was forced from the throne. Although suffering from depression after her move, Finch came to love her country estate and wrote poetry about solitude and her country life. Swift was fond of her poetry, and, later, Wordsworth anthologized her work on nature. "The Unequal Fetters" is a good example of Finch's commentary on women's situation in life, a situation she summed up in the lines from her poem "Introduction," in *Miscellany Poems on Several Occasions, Written by a Lady* (1713): "How are we fallen! fallen by mistaken rules, / And education's, more than nature's fools."

The Unequal Fetters   1713

Could we stop the time that's flying
    Or recall it when 'tis past
Put far off the day of dying
    Or make youth for ever last
5   To love would then be worth our cost.

But since we must lose those graces
    Which at first your hearts have won
And you seek for in new faces
    When our spring of life is done
10   It would but urge our ruin on.

Free as Nature's first intention
    Was to make us, I'll be found
Nor by subtle Man's invention
    Yield to be in fetters bound
15   By one that walks a freer round.

Marriage does but slightly tie men
    Whilst close prisoners we remain
They the larger slaves of Hymen[1]
    Still are begging love again
20   At the full length of all their chain.

---

1   the Greek god of marriage

Alexander Pope

England 1688–1744

Alexander Pope is said to be the first English poet to make a living from poetry;
interestingly, the bulk of his income came from his translations of *The Iliad* and
The Odyssey. Pope suffered from tuberculosis of the spine as a child, and it made
him a hunchback less than five feet tall. That fact, plus his Catholicism,
estranged him from the mainstream society of seventeenth-century England.
However, no one more thoroughly mastered the heroic couplet and satire than
did Pope. Anyone wishing to understand the neoclassical spirit should read his
Essay on Criticism and *Essay on Man*. The following excerpt gives the reader some
sense of the neoclassical respect for balance and wit.

From An Essay on Criticism, Part 2   1711

Of all the causes which conspire to blind
Man's erring judgment, and misguide the mind,
What the weak head with strongest bias rules,
Is pride, the never-failing vice of fools.
5   Whatever Nature has in worth denied,
She gives in large recruits[1] of needful pride;
For as in bodies, thus in souls, we find
What wants in blood and spirits swelled with wind:
Pride, where wit fails, steps in to our defense,
10   And fills up all the mighty void of sense.
If once right reason drives that cloud away,
Truth breaks upon us with resistless day.
Trust not yourself: but your defects to know,
Make use of every friend—and every foe.
15   A little learning is a dangerous thing;
Drink deep, or taste not the Pierian spring.[2]
There shallow draughts intoxicate the brain,
And drinking largely sobers us again.
Fired at first sight with what the Muse imparts,
20   In fearless youth we tempt the heights of arts,
While from the bounded level of our mind
Short views we take, nor see the lengths behind;
But more advanced, behold with strange surprise

---

1   supplies

2   spring on Mt. Olympus, home of the Muses, hence an allusion to the place where
    poetic inspiration comes from

New distant scenes of endless science rise!
25 So pleased at first the towering Alps we try,
Mount o'er the vales, and seem to tread the sky,
The eternal snows appear already past,
And the first clouds and mountains seem the last;
But, those attained, we tremble to survey
30 The growing labors of the lengthened way,
The increasing prospect tires our wandering eyes,
Hills peep o'er hills, and Alps on Alps arise!
    A perfect judge will read each work of wit
With the same spirit that its author writ:
35 Survey the whole, nor seek slight faults to find
Where Nature moves, and rapture warms the mind;
Nor lose, for that malignant dull delight,
The generous pleasure to be charmed with wit.
But in such lays as neither ebb nor flow,
40 Correctly cold, and regularly low,
That, shunning faults, one quiet tenor keep,
We cannot blame indeed—but we may sleep.
In wit, as nature, what affects our hearts
Is not the exactness of peculiar parts;
45 'Tis not a lip, or eye, we beauty call,
But the joint force and full result of all.
Thus when we view some well-proportioned dome
(The world's just wonder, and even thine, O Rome!),
No single parts unequally surprise,
50 All comes united to the admiring eyes:
No monstrous height, or breadth, or length appear;
The whole at once is bold and regular.

    . . . .

    Thus critics of less judgment than caprice,
Curious, not knowing, not exact, but nice,
55 Form short ideas, and offend in arts
(As most in manners), by a love to parts.
    Some to conceit alone their taste confine,
And glittering thoughts struck out at every line;
Pleased with a work where nothing's just or fit,
60 One glaring chaos and wild heap of wit.
Poets, like painters, thus unskilled to trace
The naked nature and the living grace,
With gold and jewels cover every part,
And hide with ornaments their want of art.
65   True wit is Nature to advantage dressed,
What oft was thought, but ne'er so well expressed;
Something whose truth convinced at sight we find,
That gives us back the image of our mind.
As shades more sweetly recommend the light,
70 So modest plainness sets off sprightly wit;

For works may have more wit than does them good,
As bodies perish through excess of blood.

. . . .

But most by numbers judge a poet's song,
And smooth or rough with them is right or wrong.
75   In the bright Muse though thousand charms conspire,
Her voice is all these tuneful fools admire,
Who haunt Parnassus[3] but to please their ear,
Not mend their minds; as some to church repair,
Not for the doctrine, but the music there.
80   These equal syllables alone require,
Though oft the ear the open vowels tire,
While expletives[4] their feeble aid do join,
And ten low words oft creep in one dull line:
While they ring round the same unvaried chimes,
85   With sure returns of still expected rhymes;
Where'er you find "the cooling western breeze,"
In the next line, it "whispers through the trees";
If crystal streams "with pleasing murmurs creep,"
The reader's threatened (not in vain) with "sleep";
90   Then, at the last and only couplet fraught
With some unmeaning thing they call a thought,
A needless Alexandrine[5] ends the song
That, like a wounded snake, drags its slow length along.
Leave such to tune their own dull rhymes, and know
95   What's roundly smooth or languishingly slow;
And praise the easy vigor of a line
Where Denham's strength and Waller's[6] sweetness join.
True ease in writing comes from art, not chance,
As those move easiest who have learned to dance.
100   'Tis not enough no harshness gives offense,
The sound must seem an echo to the sense.
Soft is the strain when Zephyr[7] gently blows,
And the smooth stream in smoother numbers flows;
But when loud surges lash the sounding shore,
105   The hoarse, rough verse should like the torrent roar.
When Ajax[8] strives some rock's vast weight to throw,
The line too labors, and the words move slow;
Not so when swift Camilla[9] scours the plain,

---

3   Greek mountain sacred to Muses
4   words used to fill out a sentence or, in poetry, to give a line the right metric length
5   a line with six iambic feet (see line 93)
6   Denham and Waller = shapers of the closed pentameter couplet
7   the west wind or the god of the west wind
8   hero of the Trojan Wars
9   attendant of Diana who was swift of foot

Flies o'er the unbending corn, and skims along the main.
110   Hear how Timotheus'[10] varied lays surprise,
      And bid alternate passions fall and rise!
      While at each change the son of Libyan Jove[11]
      Now burns with glory, and then melts with love;
      Now his fierce eyes with sparkling fury glow,
115   Now sighs steal out, and tears begin to flow:
      Persians and Greeks like turns of nature found
      And the world's victor stood subdued by sound!
      The power of music all our hearts allow,
      And what Timotheus was is Dryden now.

10 musician to Alexander who in Dryden's "Alexander's Feast" is responsible for inspiring
    through his music Alexander's razing of the Persian capital of Persepolis in 331 B.C.
11 Libyan Jove = Alexander the Great

Phillis Wheatley

U.S.A. 1754–1784

Born in Africa, Phillis Wheatley was shipped to Boston as a slave at age seven. When her health faltered, Susanna Wheatley, her owner, educated Phillis and sent her to London. Phillis Wheatley's *Poems on Various Subjects, Religious and Moral* was published in London in 1773. Upon her return to America, Wheatley was freed, and she married John Peters, also a freed slave, in 1778. Wheatley's poem "On Being Brought from Africa to America" illustrated the results of cultural and religious imperialism.

On Being Brought from Africa to America   1773

'Twas mercy brought me from my *Pagan* land,
Taught my benighted[1] soul to understand
That there's a God, that there's a *Saviour* too:
Once I redemption neither sought nor knew.
5   Some view our sable race with scornful eye,
'Their colour is a diabolic dye.'
Remember, *Christians*, *Negroes*, black as *Cain*,
May be refined, and join th' angelic train.

1   intellectually or morally ignorant

William Blake

England 1757–1827

William Blake trained as an engraver and printer in London, but his avocation was writing. In 1794, he brought out his first etched text with drawings, *Songs of Innocence and of Experience*. It is doubtful that Blake made many copies, as he hand-coloured the drawings in his text. Blake's poetry is a sharp contrast to the neoclassical poetry that preceded it. The visionary or prophetic spirit coexists with the social critic in Blake's writing, a juxtaposition that reflects what he called "contraries" in *The Marriage of Heaven and Hell*. The poems here, from *Songs of Innocence and of Experience*, reflect his belief in contraries and his blend of simple diction and complex implication.

The Chimney Sweeper 1789

When my mother died I was very young,
And my father sold me while yet my tongue
Could scarcely cry "'weep!' 'weep!' 'weep!' 'weep!'"
So your chimneys I sweep & in soot I sleep.

5   There's little Tom Dacre, who cried when his head
That curl'd like a lamb's back, was shav'd, so I said,
"Hush, Tom! never mind it, for when your head's bare,
You know that the soot cannot spoil your white hair."

And so he was quiet, & that very night,
10 As Tom was a-sleeping he had such a sight!
That thousands of sweepers, Dick, Joe, Ned, & Jack,
Were all of them lock'd up in coffins of black;

And by came an Angel who had a bright key,
And he open'd the coffins & set them all free;
15 Then down a green plain, leaping, laughing they run,
And wash in a river and shine in the Sun.

Then naked & white, all their bags left behind,
They rise upon clouds, and sport in the wind.
And the Angel told Tom, if he'd be a good boy,
20 He'd have God for his father & never want joy.

And so Tom awoke; and we rose in the dark
And got with our bags & our brushes to work.
Tho' the morning was cold, Tom was happy & warm;
So if all do their duty, they need not fear harm.

The Chimney Sweeper 1794

A little black thing among the snow
Crying "'weep,' 'weep,'" in notes of woe!
"Where are thy father & mother? say?"
"They are both gone up to the church to pray.

5   "Because I was happy upon the heath,
And smil'd among the winter's snow;
They clothed me in the clothes of death,
And taught me to sing the notes of woe.

"And because I am happy, & dance & sing,
10   They think they have done me no injury,
And are gone to praise God & his Priest & King,
Who make up a heaven of our misery."

London 1794

I wander thro' each charter'd street,
Near where the charter'd Thames does flow,
And mark in every face I meet
Marks of weakness, marks of woe.

5   In every cry of every Man,
In every Infant's cry of fear,
In every voice, in every ban,
The mind-forg'd manacles I hear:

How the Chimney-sweeper's cry
10   Every blackning Church appalls,
And the hapless Soldier's sigh
Runs in blood down Palace walls.

But most thro' midnight streets I hear
How the youthful Harlot's curse
15   Blasts the new-born Infant's tear,
And blights with plagues the Marriage hearse.

The Sick Rose 1794

O Rose, thou art sick.
The invisible worm

That flies in the night
In the howling storm

5 Has found out thy bed
Of crimson joy,
And his dark secret love
Does thy life destroy.

William Wordsworth

England 1770–1850

William Wordsworth was born and schooled in the English Lake District, one of
the subjects of his biographical epic, *The Prelude*. He and Samuel Taylor
Coleridge were to remain identified with that area, especially after Wordsworth's
return from France and an unhappy experience with the French Revolution.

The English Romantic movement is often pictured as having its philosophic
roots in the Preface to *Lyrical Ballads*, published in 1795 by Coleridge and
Wordsworth. In that preface, they argued for a new way of seeing and a new
poetics to accompany and convey that vision. Wordsworth's insistence on the
centrality of the imagination as the shaping, creative force both for perception
and writing is a key feature of English Romanticism. "Tintern Abbey" set the
pattern for the "conversation" poem of the Romantics and insists on the imagination's power, whether in immediate experience or in memory. The following
ode equally conveys Wordsworth's faith in the union of human imagination
with a larger force in moments of transcendent vision.

Ode: Intimations of Immortality from Recollections of Early Childhood   1807

The Child is Father of the Man;
And I could wish my days to be
Bound each to each by natural piety.[1]

1

There was a time when meadow, grove, and stream,
The earth, and every common sight,
        To me did seem
        Apparelled in celestial light,
5   The glory and the freshness of a dream.

---

1   concluding lines of Wordsworth's "My Heart Leaps Up"

It is not now as it hath been of yore;—
    Turn wheresoe'er I may,
      By night or day,
The things which I have seen I now can see no more.

2

10   The Rainbow comes and goes,
    And lovely is the Rose,
    The Moon doth with delight
Look round her when the heavens are bare,
    Waters on a starry night
15   Are beautiful and fair;
    The sunshine is a glorious birth;
    But yet I know, where'er I go,
That there hath past away a glory from the earth.

3

    Now, while the birds thus sing a joyous song,
20   And while the young lambs bound
    As to the tabor's[2] sound,
To me alone there came a thought of grief:
A timely utterance gave that thought relief,
    And I again am strong:
25 The cataracts blow their trumpets from the steep;
No more shall grief of mine the season wrong;
I hear the Echoes through the mountains throng,
The Winds come to me from the fields of sleep,
    And all the earth is gay;
30   Land and sea
    Give themselves up to jollity,
    And with the heart of May
    Doth every Beast keep holiday;—
    Thou Child of Joy,
35 Shout round me, let me hear thy shouts, thou happy
    Shepherd-boy!

4

Ye blessed Creatures, I have heard the call
    Ye to each other make; I see
The heavens laugh with you in your jubilee;
    My heart is at your festival,
40   My head hath its coronal,[3]
The fulness of your bliss, I feel—I feel it all.
    Oh evil day! if I were sullen
    While Earth herself is adorning,

---

2 little drum
3 wreath or garland

This sweet May-morning,
45   And the Children are culling
On every side,
In a thousand valleys far and wide,
Fresh flowers; while the sun shines warm,
And the Babe leaps up on his Mother's arm:—
50   I hear, I hear, with joy I hear!
—But there's a Tree, of many, one,
A single Field which I have looked upon,
Both of them speak of something that is gone:
The Pansy at my feet
55   Doth the same tale repeat:
Whither is fled the visionary gleam?
Where is it now, the glory and the dream?

5

Our birth is but a sleep and a forgetting:
The Soul that rises with us, our life's Star,
60   Hath had elsewhere its setting,
And cometh from afar:
Not in entire forgetfulness,
And not in utter nakedness,
But trailing clouds of glory do we come
65   From God, who is our home:
Heaven lies about us in our infancy!
Shades of the prison-house begin to close
Upon the growing Boy,
But He beholds the light, and whence it flows,
70   He sees it in his joy;
The Youth, who daily farther from the east
Must travel, still is Nature's Priest,
And by the vision splendid
Is on his way attended;
75 At length the Man perceives it die away,
And fade into the light of common day.

6

Earth fills her lap with pleasures of her own;
Yearnings she hath in her own natural kind,
And, even with something of a Mother's mind,
80   And no unworthy aim,
The homely Nurse doth all she can
To make her Foster-child, her Inmate Man,
Forget the glories he hath known,
And that imperial palace whence he came.

7

85 Behold the Child among his new-born blisses,
A six years' Darling of a pigmy size!
See, where 'mid work of his own hand he lies,
Fretted by sallies⁴ of his mother's kisses,
With light upon him from his father's eyes!
90 See, at his feet, some little plan or chart,
Some fragment from his dream of human life,
Shaped by himself with newly-learnèd art;
     A wedding or a festival,
     A mourning or a funeral;
95   And this hath now his heart,
     And unto this he frames his song:
       Then will he fit his tongue
To dialogues of business, love, or strife;
     But it will not be long
100 Ere this be thrown aside,
     And with new joy and pride
The little Actor cons another part;
Filling from time to time his "humorous stage"
With all the Persons, down to palsied Age,
105 That Life brings with her in her equipage;
     As if his whole vocation
     Were endless imitation.

8

     Thou, whose exterior semblance doth belie
      Thy Soul's immensity;
110 Thou best Philosopher, who yet dost keep
Thy heritage, thou Eye among the blind,
That, deaf and silent, read'st the eternal deep,
Haunted for ever by the eternal mind,—
     Mighty Prophet! Seer⁵ blest!
115   On whom those truths do rest,
Which we are toiling all our lives to find,
In darkness lost, the darkness of the grave;
Thou, over whom thy Immortality
Broods like the Day, a Master o'er a Slave,
120 A Presence which is not to be put by;
Thou little Child, yet glorious in the might
Of heaven-born freedom on thy being's height,
Why with such earnest pains dost thou provoke
The years to bring the inevitable yoke,
125 Thus blindly with thy blessedness at strife?
Full soon thy Soul shall have her earthly freight,

---

4 sorties, an outburst
5 prophet, one who sees visions (often of the future)

And custom lie upon thee with a weight,
Heavy as frost, and deep almost as life!

9

O joy! that in our embers
130   Is something that doth live,
That nature yet remembers
What was so fugitive!
The thought of our past years in me doth breed
Perpetual benediction: not indeed
135 For that which is most worthy to be blest;
Delight and liberty, the simple creed
Of Childhood, whether busy or at rest,
With new-fledged hope still fluttering in his breast:—
Not for these I raise
140   The song of thanks and praise;
But for those obstinate questionings
Of sense and outward things,
Fallings from us, vanishings;
Blank misgivings of a Creature
145 Moving about in worlds not realised,
High instincts before which our mortal Nature
Did tremble like a guilty Thing surprised:
But for those first affections,
Those shadowy recollections,
150   Which, be they what they may,
Are yet the fountain light of all our day,
Are yet a master light of all our seeing;
Uphold us, cherish, and have power to make
Our noisy years seem moments in the being
155 Of the eternal Silence: truths that wake,
To perish never;
Which neither listlessness, nor mad endeavour,
Nor Man nor Boy,
Nor all that is at enmity with joy,
160 Can utterly abolish or destroy!
Hence in a season of calm weather
Though inland far we be,
Our Souls have sight of that immortal sea
Which brought us hither,
165 Can in a moment travel thither,
And see the Children sport upon the shore,
And hear the mighty waters rolling evermore.

10

Then sing, ye Birds, sing, sing a joyous song!
And let the young Lambs bound
170   As to the tabor's sound!
We in thought will join your throng,

Ye that pipe and ye that play,
Ye that through your hearts to-day
Feel the gladness of the May!
175 What though the radiance which was once so bright
Be now for ever taken from my sight,
Though nothing can bring back the hour
Of splendour in the grass, of glory in the flower;
We will grieve not, rather find
180 Strength in what remains behind;
In the primal sympathy
Which having been must ever be;
In the soothing thoughts that spring
Out of human suffering;
185 In the faith that looks through death,
In years that bring the philosophic mind.

11

And O, ye Fountains, Meadows, Hills, and Groves,
Forebode not any severing of our loves!
Yet in my heart of hearts I feel your might;
190 I only have relinquished one delight
To live beneath your more habitual sway.
I love the Brooks which down their channels fret,
Even more than when I tripped lightly as they;
The innocent brightness of a new-born Day
195 Is lovely yet;
The Clouds that gather round the setting sun
Do take a sober colouring from an eye
That hath kept watch o'er man's mortality;
Another race hath been, and other palms are won.
200 Thanks to the human heart by which we live,
Thanks to its tenderness, its joys, and fears,
To me the meanest flower that blows can give
Thoughts that do often lie too deep for tears.

Samuel Taylor Coleridge

England 1772–1834

Samuel Taylor Coleridge was arguably the central figure in the philosophical
aspect of English Romanticism. From his joint authorship in 1795 of the
"Preface" to *Lyrical Ballads* through to his 1817 publication of *Biographia
Literaria,* Coleridge sought to give Romanticism a philosophical base. Influenced
by German idealist philosophy, he wrote much on the concept and influence of
imagination. Coleridge gave us two of the period's most unusual lyrics in "The
Rime of the Ancient Mariner" and "Kubla Khan." Coleridge always felt that his
writing fell far short of what he had hoped to produce, perhaps because of his
addiction to opium. His "Frost at Midnight" may be compared to Wordsworth's
"Tintern Abbey" as a Romantic conversation poem and is, in a number of ways,
superior. He wrote it after hearing the opening stanzas of Wordsworth's poem.
Note how Coleridge, at the poem's end shifts the focus from himself to his son
and then to nature.

Frost at Midnight   1798

The Frost performs its secret ministry,
Unhelped by any wind. The owlet's cry
Came loud—and hark, again! loud as before.
The inmates of my cottage, all at rest,
5   Have left me to that solitude, which suits
Abstruser musings: save that at my side
My cradled infant slumbers peacefully.
'Tis calm indeed! so calm, that it disturbs
And vexes meditation with its strange
10   And extreme silentness. Sea, hill, and wood,
This populous village! Sea, and hill, and wood,
With all the numberless goings-on of life,
Inaudible as dreams! the thin blue flame
Lies on my low-burnt fire, and quivers not;
15   Only that film, which fluttered on the grate,
Still flutters there, the sole unquiet thing.
Methinks its motion in this hush of nature
Gives it dim sympathies with me who live,
Making it a companionable form,
20   Whose puny flaps and freaks the idling Spirit
By its own moods interprets, everywhere
Echo or mirror seeking of itself,
And makes a toy of Thought.

But O! how oft,
How oft, at school, with most believing mind,
25   Presageful, have I gazed upon the bars,
To watch that fluttering *stranger!*[1] and as oft
With unclosed lids, already had I dreamt
Of my sweet birthplace, and the old church tower,
Whose bells, the poor man's only music, rang
30   From morn to evening, all the hot fair-day,
So sweetly, that they stirred and haunted me
With a wild pleasure, falling on mine ear
Most like articulate sounds of things to come!
So gazed I, till the soothing things, I dreamt,
35   Lulled me to sleep, and sleep prolonged my dreams!
And so I brooded all the following morn,
Awed by the stern preceptor's[2] face, mine eye
Fixed with mock study on my swimming book:
Save if the door half opened, and I snatched
40   A hasty glance, and still my heart leaped up,
For still I hoped to see the *stranger's* face,
Townsman, or aunt, or sister more beloved,
My playmate when we both were clothed alike!

Dear Babe, that sleepest cradled by my side,
45   Whose gentle breathings, heard in this deep calm,
Fill up the interspersèd vacancies
And momentary pauses of the thought!
My babe so beautiful! it thrills my heart
With tender gladness, thus to look at thee,
50   And think that thou shalt learn far other lore,
And in far other scenes! For I was reared
In the great city, pent 'mid cloisters dim,
And saw nought lovely but the sky and stars.
But *thou*, my babe! shalt wander like a breeze
55   By lakes and sandy shores, beneath the crags
Of ancient mountain, and beneath the clouds,
Which image in their bulk both lakes and shores
And mountain crags: so shalt thou see and hear
The lovely shapes and sounds intelligible
60   Of that eternal language, which thy God
Utters, who from eternity doth teach
Himself in all, and all things in himself.

---

1   Coleridge's note for this line: "In all parts of the kingdom these films are called
   strangers and supposed to portend the arrival of some absent friend." "Film" here is
   ash on a fire's grate.
2   teacher's

Great universal Teacher! he shall mold
Thy spirit, and by giving make it ask.

65   Therefore all seasons shall be sweet to thee,
Whether the summer clothe the general earth
With greenness, or the redbreast sit and sing
Betwixt the tufts of snow on the bare branch
Of mossy apple tree, while the nigh thatch
Smokes in the sun-thaw; whether the eave-drops fall
70   Heard only in the trances of the blast,
Or if the secret ministry of frost
Shall hang them up in silent icicles,
Quietly shining to the quiet Moon.

Percy Bysshe Shelley

England 1792–1822

Born into a long line of aristocrats, Shelley was educated to take his place in that conservative tradition. It seems surprising, then, that he was so estranged from his class philosophically. From the time he was expelled from Oxford for co-authoring a pamphlet defending the legitimacy of atheism, Shelley was a rebel, refusing to accept any social forms that he felt were sustained exclusively by authority and tradition. He spent his later years in France and Italy, where he would meet his death by drowning. Shelley's broad range of subjects and poetic forms is evident in his poems "Ode to the West Wind" and "Mont Blanc," as well as in his epics, including *Prometheus Unbound*. "Ozymandias" employs the sonnet form brilliantly in satirizing the human need for power.

Ozymandias[1]   1818

I met a traveller from an antique land,
Who said—"Two vast and trunkless legs of stone
Stand in the desert.... Near them, on the sand,
Half sunk a shattered visage lies, whose frown,
5   And wrinkled lip, and sneer of cold command,
Tell that its sculptor well those passions read

---

1   Ozymandias was the Greek name for Ramses II of Egypt, who lived during the thirteenth century B.C. Diodorus Siculus, the first century B.C. Greek historian, noted that the largest statue in Egypt bore the inscription: "I am Ozymandias, king of kings; if anyone wishes to know what I am and where I lie, let him surpass me in some of my exploits."

Which yet survive, stamped on these lifeless things,
The hand that mocked them, and the heart that fed;
And on the pedestal, these words appear:
10 My name is Ozymandias, King of Kings,
Look on my Works, ye Mighty, and despair!
Nothing beside remains. Round the decay
Of that colossal Wreck, boundless and bare
The lone and level sands stretch far away."

John Keats

England 1795–1821

John Keats, raised in London, studied to be a physician but quickly turned his attention to poetry, consciously pursuing reading and experience that would enhance his poetic gifts. The speed with which he mastered his craft is perhaps unequalled in English poetry. Tuberculosis had killed his mother and his brother, Tom, and in the fall of 1818, began to claim John Keats also. In early 1820, he died in Rome, in vain pursuit of an antidote to his disease in the dry climate of Italy. His 1819 odes are deservedly famous. In them he captures the tension between the ideal and timeless worlds of the imagination and the time-bound, mortal world in which we live. "To Autumn" reflects autumn's twin forces of ripeness and impending death.

To Autumn   1819

1

Season of mists and mellow fruitfulness,
    Close bosom-friend of the maturing sun;
Conspiring with him how to load and bless
    With fruit the vines that round the thatch-eves run;
5   To bend with apples the moss'd cottage-trees,
        And fill all fruit with ripeness to the core;
            To swell the gourd, and plump the hazel shells
        With a sweet kernel; to set budding more,
    And still more, later flowers for the bees,
10 Until they think warm days will never cease,
            For summer has o'er-brimm'd their clammy cells.

2

Who hath not seen thee oft amid thy store?
    Sometimes whoever seeks abroad may find
Thee sitting careless on a granary floor,

15   Thy hair soft-lifted by the winnowing wind;
        Or on a half-reap'd furrow sound asleep,
            Drows'd with the fume of poppies, while thy hook
                Spares the next swath and all its twined flowers:
        And sometimes like a gleaner thou dost keep
20   Steady thy laden head across a brook;
        Or by a cyder-press, with patient look,
            Thou watchest the last oozings hours by hours.

3

        Where are the songs of spring? Ay, where are they?
            Think not of them, thou hast thy music too,—
25   While barred clouds bloom the soft-dying day,
            And touch the stubble-plains[1] with rosy hue;
        Then in a wailful choir the small gnats mourn
            Among the river sallows, borne aloft
                Or sinking as the light wind lives or dies;
30   And full-grown lambs loud bleat from hilly bourn;
        Hedge-crickets sing; and now with treble soft
        The red-breast whistles from a garden-croft;[2]
            And gathering swallows twitter in the skies.

---

1   fields full of cut stalks after harvest
2   small garden enclosure

Ode on a Grecian Urn   1819

1

        Thou still unravish'd bride of quietness,
            Thou foster-child of silence and slow time,
        Sylvan historian, who canst thus express
            A flowery tale more sweetly than our rhyme:
5   What leaf-fring'd legend haunts about thy shape
            Of deities or mortals, or of both,
                In Tempe or the dales of Arcady?[1]
        What men or gods are these? What maidens loth?
        What mad pursuit? What struggle to escape?
10   What pipes and timbrels?[2] What wild ecstasy?

2

        Heard melodies are sweet, but those unheard
            Are sweeter; therefore, ye soft pipes, play on;

---

1   Arcady = state in Greece connected to the pastoral ideal
2   timbrels = tambourines

Not to the sensual ear, but, more endear'd,
    Pipe to the spirit ditties of no tone:
15 Fair youth, beneath the trees, thou canst not leave
    Thy song, nor ever can those trees be bare;
        Bold lover, never, never canst thou kiss,
    Though winning near the goal—yet, do not grieve;
        She cannot fade, though thou hast not thy bliss,
20   For ever wilt thou love, and she be fair!

3

Ah, happy, happy boughs! that cannot shed
    Your leaves, nor ever bid the spring adieu;
And, happy melodist, unwearied,
    For ever piping songs for ever new;
25 More happy love! more happy, happy love!
    For ever warm and still to be enjoy'd,
        For ever panting, and for ever young;
All breathing human passion far above,
    That leaves a heart high-sorrowful and cloy'd,
30   A burning forehead, and a parching tongue.

4

Who are these coming to the sacrifice?
    To what green altar, O mysterious priest,
Lead'st thou that heifer lowing at the skies,
    And all her silken flanks with garlands drest?
35 What little town by river or sea shore,
    Or mountain-built with peaceful citadel,
        Is emptied of this folk, this pious morn?
And, little town, thy streets for evermore
    Will silent be; and not a soul to tell
40   Why thou art desolate, can e'er return.

5

O Attic[3] shape! Fair attitude! with brede[4]
    Of marble men and maidens overwrought,[5]
With forest branches and the trodden weed;
    Thou, silent form, dost tease us out of thought
45 As doth eternity: Cold Pastoral!
    When old age shall this generation waste,
        Thou shalt remain, in midst of other woe
Than ours, a friend to man, to whom thou say'st,
    "Beauty is truth, truth beauty,"—that is all
50   Ye know on earth, and all ye need to know.

---

3 Attica, the region of Greece in which Athens is located
4 brede = a braided pattern
5 overwrought = in bas-relief

Sojourner Truth

U.S.A. 1797–1883

Sojourner Truth was born into slavery in the North, the daughter of slaves belonging to a Dutch-American family. Truth demanded her freedom prior to Emancipation, and she was later involved in a radical form of Methodism. In the 1840s, she lived in a Utopian community in Northampton, Massachusetts, where she met Frederick Douglass and wrote, with assistance, an autobiography. Her address to a women's rights convention in June of 1851, which established her as a feminist and an abolitionist, is reproduced here as a poem.

Ain't I a Woman?   1851

Ain't I a woman?
  Look at me
Look at my arm!
  I have plowed and planted
5   and gathered into barns
    and no man could head me....
And ain't I a woman?
  I could work as much
And eat as much as a man—
10   When I could get it—
And bear the lash as well
  and ain't I a woman?
I have born thirteen children
  and seen most all sold into slavery
15 and when I cried out a mother's grief
   none but Jesus heard me....
And ain't I a woman?...
  If the first woman God ever made
was strong enough to turn the world
20   upside down, all alone
together women ought to be able to turn it
  rightside up again.

Alfred, Lord Tennyson

England 1809–1892

Born in rural Lincolnshire, Alfred Tennyson lived to see England transformed
from a rural to an urban and industrial nation. He became the favoured poet of
the Victorians and served as the nation's poet laureate for forty years. Tennyson
spoke for all Victorians when he grappled with assaults on his religious faith in
In Memoriam, especially with the doubts raised by the "new" sciences of biology
and geology. Nowhere is this struggle more sharply evident than in "In
Memoriam," where Tennyson directly faces the potential fact that the universe is
random rather than a divine creation, governed by a brute struggle for survival
rather than a benevolent order. His slow recovery of a reformed faith forms the
capstone of the poem. One other recurrent theme in Tennyson's early work is
the tension between an art created in isolation from the world and an art that
fully engages the world. In "The Lady of Shalott," Tennyson finds ideal narrative
details to explore this conflict.

The Lady of Shalott   1832, 1842

PART I

On either side the river lie
Long fields of barley and of rye,
That clothe the wold and meet the sky;
And thro' the field the road runs by
5   To many-tower'd Camelot;
And up and down the people go,
Gazing where the lilies blow
Round an island there below,
    The island of Shalott.

10   Willows whiten, aspens quiver,
Little breezes dusk and shiver
Thro' the wave that runs for ever
By the island in the river
    Flowing down to Camelot.
15   Four gray walls, and four gray towers,
Overlook a space of flowers,
And the silent isle imbowers
    The Lady of Shalott.

By the margin, willow-veil'd,
20   Slide the heavy barges trail'd

By slow horses; and unhail'd
The shallop flitteth silken-sail'd
   Skimming down to Camelot:
But who hath seen her wave her hand?
25 Or at the casement seen her stand?
Or is she known in all the land,
   The Lady of Shalott?

Only reapers, reaping early
In among the bearded barley,
30 Hear a song that echoes cheerly
From the river winding clearly,
   Down to tower'd Camelot;
And by the moon the reaper weary,
Piling sheaves in uplands airy,
35 Listening, whispers " 'Tis the fairy
   Lady of Shalott."

PART II

There she weaves by night and day
A magic web with colours gay.
She has heard a whisper say,
40 A curse is on her if she stay
   To look down to Camelot.
She knows not what the curse may be,
And so she weaveth steadily,
And little other care hath she,
45   The Lady of Shalott.

And moving thro' a mirror clear
That hangs before her all the year,
Shadows of the world appear.
There she sees the highway near
50   Winding down to Camelot;
There the river eddy whirls,
And there the surly village-churls,
And the red cloaks of market girls,
   Pass onward from Shalott.

55 Sometimes a troop of damsels glad,
An abbot on an ambling pad,
Sometimes a curly shepherd-lad,
Or long-hair'd page in crimson clad,
   Goes by to tower'd Camelot;
60 And sometimes thro' the mirror blue
The knights come riding two and two:
She hath no loyal knight and true,
   The Lady of Shalott.

But in her web she still delights
65 To weave the mirror's magic sights,
    For often thro' the silent nights
    A funeral, with plumes and lights
        And music, went to Camelot;
    Or when the moon was overhead,
70 Came two young lovers lately wed:
    "I am half sick of shadows," said
        The Lady of Shalott.

Part III

    A bow-shot from her bower-eaves,
    He rode between the barley-sheaves.
75 The sun came dazzling thro' the leaves,
    And flamed upon the brazen greaves
        Of bold Sir Lancelot.
    A red-cross knight for ever kneel'd
    To a lady in his shield,
80 That sparkled on the yellow field,
        Beside remote Shalott.

    The gemmy bridle glitter'd free,
    Like to some branch of stars we see
    Hung in the golden Galaxy.
85 The bridle bells rang merrily
        As he rode down to Camelot;
    And from his blazon'd baldric slung
    A mighty silver bugle hung,
    And as he rode his armor rung,
90   Beside remote Shalott.

    All in the blue unclouded weather
    Thick-jewell'd shone the saddle-leather,
    The helmet and the helmet-feather
    Burn'd like one burning flame together,
95   As he rode down to Camelot;
    As often thro' the purple night,
    Below the starry clusters bright,
    Some bearded meteor, trailing light,
        Moves over still Shalott.

100 His broad clear brow in sunlight glow'd;
        On burnish'd hooves his war-horse trode;
    From underneath his helmet flow'd
    His coal-black curls as on he rode,
        As he rode down to Camelot.
105 From the bank and from the river

He flash'd into the crystal mirror,
"Tirra lirra," by the river
    Sang Sir Lancelot.

    She left the web, she left the loom,
110 She made three paces thro' the room,
    She saw the water-lily bloom,
    She saw the helmet and the plume,
        She look'd down to Camelot.
    Out flew the web and floated wide;
115 The mirror crack'd from side to side;
    "The curse is come upon me," cried
        The Lady of Shalott.

PART IV

    In the stormy east-wind straining,
    The pale yellow woods were waning,
120 The broad stream in his banks complaining,
    Heavily the low sky raining
        Over tower'd Camelot;
    Down she came and found a boat
    Beneath a willow left afloat,
125 And round about the prow she wrote
        The Lady of Shalott.

    And down the river's dim expanse
    Like some bold seër in a trance,
    Seeing all his own mischance—
130 With a glassy countenance
        Did she look to Camelot.
    And at the closing of the day
    She loosed the chain, and down she lay;
    The broad stream bore her far away,
135   The Lady of Shalott.

    Lying, robed in snowy white
    That loosely flew to left and right—
    The leaves upon her falling light—
    Thro' the noises of the night
140   She floated down to Camelot;
    And as the boat-head wound along
    The willowy hills and fields among,
    They heard her singing her last song,
        The Lady of Shalott.

145 Heard a carol, mournful, holy,
    Chanted loudly, chanted lowly,

Till her blood was frozen slowly,
And her eyes were darken'd wholly,
    Turn'd to tower'd Camelot.
150 For ere she reach'd upon the tide
The first house by the water-side,
Singing in her song she died,
    The Lady of Shalott.

Under tower and balcony,
155 By garden-wall and gallery,
A gleaming shape she floated by,
Dead-pale between the houses high,
    Silent into Camelot.
Out upon the wharfs they came,
160 Knight and burgher, lord and dame,
And round the prow they read her name,
    The Lady of Shalott.

Who is this? and what is here?
And in the lighted palace near
165 Died the sound of royal cheer;
And they cross'd themselves for fear,
    All the knights at Camelot:
But Lancelot mused a little space;
He said, "She has a lovely face;
170 God in his mercy lend her grace,
    The Lady of Shalott."

In Memoriam   1850

50

Be near me when my light is low,
    When the blood creeps, and the nerves prick
    And tingle; and the heart is sick,
And all the wheels of being slow.

5 Be near me when the sensuous frame
    Is rack'd with pangs that conquer trust;
    And Time, a maniac scattering dust,
And Life, a Fury slinging flame.

Be near me when my faith is dry,
10   And men the flies of latter spring,
    That lay their eggs, and sting and sing
And weave their petty cells and die.

Be near me when I fade away,
    To point the term of human strife,
15   And on the low dark verge of life
The twilight of eternal day.

51

Do we indeed desire the dead
    Should still be near us at our side?
    Is there no baseness we would hide?
No inner vileness that we dread?

5   Shall he for whose applause I strove,
    I had such reverence for his blame,
    See with clear eye some hidden shame
And I be lessen'd in his love?

I wrong the grave with fears untrue.
10   Shall love be blamed for want of faith?
    There must be wisdom with great Death;
The dead shall look me thro' and thro'.

Be near us when we climb or fall;
    Ye watch, like God, the rolling hours
15   With larger other eyes than ours,
To make allowance for us all.

52

I cannot love thee as I ought,
    For love reflects the thing beloved;
    My words are only words, and moved
Upon the topmost froth of thought.

5   "Yet blame not thou thy plaintive song,"
    The Spirit of true love replied;
    "Thou canst not move me from thy side,
Nor human frailty do me wrong.

"What keeps a spirit wholly true
10   To that ideal which he bears?
    What record? not the sinless years
That breathed beneath the Syrian blue;

"So fret not, like an idle girl,
    That life is dash'd with flecks of sin.
15   Abide: thy wealth is gather'd in,
When Time hath sunder'd shell from pearl."

53

How many a father have I seen,
   A sober man, among his boys,
   Whose youth was full of foolish noise,
Who wears his manhood hale and green;

5   And dare we to this fancy give,
    That had the wild oat not been sown,
    The soil, left barren, scarce had grown
The grain by which a man may live?

Or, if we held the doctrine sound
10   For life outliving heats of youth,
    Yet who would preach it as a truth
To those that eddy round and round?

Hold thou the good: define it well;
   For fear divine Philosophy
15   Should push beyond her mark, and be
Procuress to the Lords of Hell.

54

Oh yet we trust that somehow good
   Will be the final goal of ill,
   To pangs of nature, sins of will,
Defects of doubt, and taints of blood;

5   That nothing walks with aimless feet;
    That not one life shall be destroy'd,
    Or cast as rubbish to the void,
When God hath made the pile complete;

That not a worm is cloven in vain;
10   That not a moth with vain desire
    Is shrivell'd in a fruitless fire,
Or but subserves another's gain.

Behold, we know not anything;
   I can but trust that good shall fall
15   At last—far off—at last, to all,
And every winter change to spring.

So runs my dream; but what am I?
   An infant crying in the night;
   An infant crying for the light,
20   And with no language but a cry.

55

The wish, that of the living whole
  No life may fail beyond the grave,
  Derives it not from what we have
The likest God within the soul?

5 Are God and Nature then at strife,
  That Nature lends such evil dreams?
  So careful of the type she seems,
So careless of the single life,

That I, considering everywhere
10 Her secret meaning in her deeds,
  And finding that of fifty seeds
She often brings but one to bear,

I falter where I firmly trod,
  And falling with my weight of cares
15 Upon the great world's altar-stairs
That slope through darkness up to God,

I stretch lame hands of faith, and grope,
  And gather dust and chaff, and call
  To what I feel is Lord of all,
20 And faintly trust the larger hope.

56

"So careful of the type?" but no.
  From scarpèd[1] cliff and quarried stone
  She cries, "A thousand types are gone;
I care for nothing, all shall go.

5 "Thou makest thine appeal to me.
  I bring to life, I bring to death;
  The spirit does but mean the breath:
I know no more." And he, shall he,

Man, her last work, who seemed so fair,
10 Such splendid purpose in his eyes,
  Who rolled the psalm to wintry skies,
Who built him fanes of fruitless prayer,

---

1 steep, jagged

Who trusted God was love indeed
    And love Creation's final law—
15   Though Nature, red in tooth and claw
    With ravine, shrieked against his creed—

Who loved, who suffered countless ills,
    Who battled for the True, the Just,
    Be blown about the desert dust,
20   Or sealed within the iron hills?

No more? A monster then, a dream,
    A discord. Dragons of the prime,
    That tare[2] each other in their slime,
Were mellow music matched with him.

25   O life as futile, then, as frail!
    O for thy voice to soothe and bless!
    What hope of answer, or redress?
Behind the veil, behind the veil.

---

2   tear

Robert Browning

England 1812–1889

Robert Browning grew up in London and was largely educated at home where he lived until he married at the age of thirty-four. In Victorian England, no love story was better known than the relationship of Browning and Elizabeth Barrett. Perhaps driven by the harsh criticism of his early work, Browning perfected the form of the dramatic monologue, a form that allowed him to withdraw from direct participation in the poem. Browning was particularly fond of imaginatively entering the minds of people who lived on the edge or who were forced to defend central decisions they had made in their lives. It is no accident that Browning's central long poem, *The Ring and the Book*, has murder as its subject, as does "Porphyria's Lover." Such subjects, however, often made the Victorians' response to Browning ambivalent. Browning is regarded by many, including T.S. Eliot, as the first modern poet because of his mastery of human speech in poetry, his use of ambiguity, and his creation of ironic effect.

Porphyria's Lover[1]   1842

The rain set early in tonight,
    The sullen wind was soon awake,
It tore the elm-tops down for spite,
    And did its worst to vex the lake:
5   I listened with heart fit to break.
When glided in Porphyria; straight
    She shut the cold out and the storm,
And kneeled and made the cheerless grate
    Blaze up, and all the cottage warm;
10   Which done, she rose, and from her form
Withdrew the dripping cloak and shawl,
    And laid her soiled gloves by, untied
Her hat and let the damp hair fall,
    And, last, she sat down by my side
15   And called me. When no voice replied,
She put my arm about her waist,
    And made her smooth white shoulder bare,
And all her yellow hair displaced,
    And, stooping, made my cheek lie there,
20   And spread, o'er all, her yellow hair,
Murmuring how she loved me—she
    Too weak, for all her heart's endeavor,
To set its struggling passion free
    From pride, and vainer ties dissever,
25   And give herself to me forever.
But passion sometimes would prevail,
    Nor could tonight's gay feast restrain
A sudden thought of one so pale
    For love of her, and all in vain:
30   So, she was come through wind and rain.
Be sure I looked up at her eyes
    Happy and proud; at last I knew
Porphyria worshiped me: surprise
    Made my heart swell, and still it grew
35   While I debated what to do.
That moment she was mine, mine, fair,
    Perfectly pure and good: I found
A thing to do, and all her hair
    In one long yellow string I wound
40   Three times her little throat around,

---

1 porphyria = a group of genetic disorders associated with abnormal metabolism
   causing in some cases photosensitivity, abdominal pain, neurologic attacks, and mild
   to severe psychiatric disorders. The poem was originally part of a pair of monologues
   published under the title *Madhouse Cells.*

And strangled her. No pain felt she;
    I am quite sure she felt no pain.
As a shut bud that holds a bee,
    I warily oped her lids: again
45   Laughed the blue eyes without a stain.
And I untightened next the tress
    About her neck; her cheek once more
Blushed bright beneath my burning kiss:
    I propped her head up as before,
50   Only, this time my shoulder bore
Her head, which droops upon it still:
    The smiling rosy little head,
So glad it has its utmost will,
    That all it scorned at once is fled,
55   And I, its love, am gained instead!
Porphyria's love: she guessed not how
    Her darling one wish would be heard.
And thus we sit together now,
    And all night long we have not stirred,
60   And yet God has not said a word!

Walt Whitman

U.S.A. 1819–1892

Walt Whitman was born near Huntington, Long Island, across the water from New York City. During his life, he worked as a carpenter, a printer, a nurse (during the American Civil War), and a teacher, although for much of his life he was a journalist and editor in New York. His images of America, traversed by trains and ferries, reflect his vision of an expanding country. His collection of poetry, *Leaves of Grass,* which he continued to rework for thirty-five years, was not greeted warmly in America, although it found favour in Europe. Whitman's most obvious trademarks—his use of American idioms, his freeing of stanzaic length from conventions, his fondness for long lines—are evident in "A Sight in Camp in the Daybreak Gray and Dim," as is his direct experience as a nurse in the Civil War.

A Sight in Camp in the Daybreak Gray and Dim
1865, 1867

A sight in camp in the daybreak gray and dim,
As from my tent I emerge so early sleepless,
As slow I walk in the cool fresh air the path near by the hospital tent,

Three forms I see on stretchers lying, brought out there untended lying,
5   Over each the blanket spread, ample brownish woolen blanket,
Gray and heavy blanket, folding, covering all.

Curious I halt and silent stand,
Then with light fingers I from the face of the nearest the first
just lift the blanket;
10   Who are you elderly man so gaunt and grim, with well-gray'd hair,
and flesh all sunken about the eyes?
Who are you my dear comrade?
Then to the second I step—and who are you my child and darling?
Who are you sweet boy with cheeks yet blooming?

15   Then to the third—a face nor child nor old, very calm, as of
beautiful yellow-white ivory;
Young man I think I know you—I think this face is the face of the
Christ himself,
Dead and divine and brother of all, and here again he lies.

Matthew Arnold

England 1822–1888

Matthew Arnold was born in Laleham, which lies west of London. His father
became headmaster of Rugby School, a prestigious boys' school, and so Arnold
came upon his vocation as a school inspector almost naturally. This work gave
him a view of society that made him both critical of it, and the middle class in particular, and fearful of the sweeping changes that he thought would transform
England negatively. Arnold's concern with the erosion of general beliefs and the
opposition of personal love to social consensus is reflected in "Dover Beach."

Dover Beach   1867

The sea is calm tonight.
The tide is full, the moon lies fair
Upon the straits—on the French coast the light
Gleams and is gone; the cliffs of England stand,
5   Glimmering and vast, out in the tranquil bay.
Come to the window, sweet is the night air!
Only, from the long line of spray
Where the sea meets the moon-blanched land,
Listen! you hear the grating roar
10   Of pebbles which the waves draw back, and fling,

At their return, up the high strand,[1]
Begin, and cease, and then again begin,
With tremulous cadence slow, and bring
The eternal note of sadness in.

15   Sophocles[2] long ago
Heard it on the Aegean, and it brought
Into his mind the turbid ebb and flow
Of human misery; we
Find also in the sound a thought,
20   Hearing it by this distant northern sea.

The Sea of Faith
Was once, too, at the full, and round earth's shore
Lay like the folds of a bright girdle furled.
But now I only hear
25   Its melancholy, long, withdrawing roar,
Retreating, to the breath
Of the night wind, down the vast edges drear
And naked shingles[3] of the world.

Ah, love, let us be true
30   To one another! for the world, which seems
To lie before us like a land of dreams,
So various, so beautiful, so new,
Hath really neither joy, nor love, nor light,
Nor certitude, nor peace, nor help for pain;
35   And we are here as on a darkling plain
Swept with confused alarms of struggle and flight,
Where ignorant armies clash by night.

---

1 margin, high tide mark
2 Greek dramatist, writer of tragedies that examined the relationship between people
    and the divine order of the world
3 pebble-covered beach

Emily Dickinson

U.S.A. 1830–1886

Emily Dickinson spent almost all her life in the confines of her family home in Amherst, Massachusetts. She published only twelve poems in her lifetime, but hundreds of other poems were discovered after her death, stitched into little booklets and punctuated in her own fashion. In total, she left over a thousand poems, their form patterned after the hymns she knew so well. Embedded in these deceptively simple lyrics, however, is extraordinarily dense poetry, which gives itself to the reader only after careful and repeated reading. Dickinson's subjects are most frequently the sights she observed, psychological states, and her musings on death and religion. As 1129 ("Tell all the Truth but tell it slant") implies, she is not always as direct as the reader would prefer to believe. Certainly, 465 ("I heard a fly buzz—when I died") is anything but conventional in its portrait of a dying speaker, and potentially quite radical in its implications.

1129 ("Tell all the Truth but tell it slant") ca. 1868

Tell all the Truth but tell it slant—
Success in Circuit lies
Too bright for our infirm Delight
The Truth's superb surprise

5 As Lightning to the Children eased
With explanation kind
The truth must dazzle gradually
Or every man be blind—

258 ("There's a certain Slant of light") 1878

There's a certain Slant of light,
Winter Afternoons—
That oppresses, like the Heft
Of Cathedral Tunes—

5 Heavenly Hurt, it gives us—
We can find no scar,
But internal difference,
Where the Meanings, are—

None may teach it—Any—
10 'Tis the Seal Despair—

An imperial affliction
Sent us of the Air—

When it comes, the Landscape listens—
Shadows—hold their breath—
15 When it goes, 'tis like the Distance
On the look of Death—

465 ("I heard a Fly buzz—when I died")   1887

I heard a Fly buzz—when I died—
The Stillness in the Room
Was like the Stillness in the Air—
Between the Heaves of Storm—

5 The Eyes around—had wrung them dry—
And Breaths were gathering firm
For that last Onset—when the King
Be witnessed—in the Room—

I willed my Keepsakes—Signed away
10 What portion of me be
Assignable—and then it was
There interposed a Fly—

With Blue—uncertain stumbling Buzz—
Between the light—and me—
15 And then the Windows failed—and then
I could not see to see—

435 ("Much Madness is divinest Sense")   1887

Much Madness is divinest Sense—
To a discerning Eye—
Much Sense—the starkest Madness—
'Tis the Majority

5 In this, as All, prevail—
Assent—and you are sane—
Demur—you're straightway dangerous—
And handled with a Chain—

Christina Rossetti

England 1830–1894

Born in England to an exiled Italian patriot father and an Anglo-Italian mother, Rossetti grew up surrounded by discussions of the politics and culture of the Italian exile community. She became involved in the Anglo-Catholic movement of the Anglican Church and governed her life by religious views, which led her to break off two engagements. Rossetti's sense of self-denial is reflected in her comments on gender and relationships in "An Apple-Gathering."

An Apple-Gathering   1862

I plucked pink blossoms from mine apple tree
   And wore them all that evening in my hair:
Then in due season when I went to see
   I found no apples there.

5 With dangling basket all along the grass
   As I had come I went the selfsame track:
My neighbours mocked me while they saw me pass
   So empty-handed back.

Lilian and Lilias smiled in trudging by,
10   Their heaped-up basket teazed me like a jeer;
Sweet-voiced they sang beneath the sunset sky,
   Their mother's home was near.

Plump Gertrude passed me with her basket full,
   A stronger hand than hers helped it along;
15 A voice talked with her thro' the shadows cool
   More sweet to me than song.

Ah Willie, Willie, was my love less worth
   Than apples with their green leaves piled above?
I counted rosiest apples on the earth
20   Of far less worth than love.

So once it was with me you stooped to talk
   Laughing and listening in this very lane:
To think that by this way we used to walk
   We shall not walk again!

25 I let my neighbours pass me, ones and twos
   And groups; the latest said the night grew chill,
And hastened: but I loitered, while the dews
   Fell fast I loitered still.

Gerard Manley Hopkins

England 1844–1889

Gerard Hopkins was born near London and later attended Oxford, where his teachers included Matthew Arnold, Walter Pater, and Benjamin Jowett. Drawn increasingly to the High Church, Hopkins converted at age twenty to Catholicism and joined the Jesuit order. After serving in working-class parishes in industrial English cities, he was made professor of Greek at University College, Dublin. Fortunately for us, he corresponded regularly with an English poet, Robert Bridges, who published Hopkins's poetry almost thirty years after Hopkins's death. Hopkins's fondness for what he called "sprung rhythm," a kind of accentual verse in which the number of stresses rather than the number of syllables is the ordering principle, gives his poetry a unique texture and syntax. His poems, which almost always deal with the glory of God, are also made complex by their imagery and compression.

God's Grandeur   1918

The world is charged with the grandeur of God.
   It will flame out, like shining from shook foil;
   It gathers to a greatness, like the ooze of oil
Crushed. Why do men then now not reck his rod?
5   Generations have trod, have trod, have trod;
   And all is seared with trade; bleared, smeared with toil;
   And wears man's smudge and shares man's smell: the soil
Is bare now, nor can foot feel, being shod.

   And for all this, nature is never spent;
10   There lives the dearest freshest deep down things;
And though the last lights off the black West went
   Oh, morning, at the brown brink eastward, springs—
Because the Holy Ghost over the bent
   World broods with warm breast and with ah! bright wings.

The Windhover[1]   1918

To Christ our Lord

I caught this morning morning's minion,[2] king-
　　dom of daylight's dauphin,[3] dapple-dawn-drawn Falcon, in his riding
Of the rolling level underneath him steady air, and striding
High there, how he rung upon the rein of a wimpling[4] wing
5　In his ecstasy! then off, off forth on swing,
　　As a skate's heel sweeps smooth on a bow-bend: the hurl and gliding
Rebuffed the big wind. My heart in hiding
Stirred for a bird,—the achieve of, the mastery of the thing!

Brute beauty and valour and act, oh, air, pride, plume, here
10　Buckle![5] AND the fire that breaks from thee then, a billion
Times told lovelier, more dangerous, O my chevalier!

No wonder of it: shéer plód makes plough down sillion[6]
Shine, and blue-bleak embers, ah my dear,
　　Fall, gall[7] themselves, and gash gold-vermilion.

1　small falcon
2　favourite
3　French prince, heir to the throne
4　veiling, enfolding, covering
5　to fasten, to give way, to get to work (as to buckle down to a task); all three meanings
　　apply here
6　ridge between furrows
7　humiliate, rub sore

Sir Charles G.D. Roberts

Canada 1860–1943

Charles G.D. Roberts was born into an Anglican, Loyalist family in New Brunswick
and attended the University of New Brunswick. As writers, Roberts and his cousin,
Bliss Carman, became associated with Archibald Lampman and D.C. Scott. All four
were born in the decade of Canadian Confederation. Like "The Potato Harvest,"
much of Roberts's poetry describes Canadian settings, reflecting his love of the
countryside and his wish to create a Canadian voice for Canadian scenes.

The Potato Harvest   1886

A high bare field, brown from the plough, and borne
   Aslant from sunset; amber wastes of sky
   Washing the ridge; a clamour of crows that fly
In from the wide flats where the spent tides mourn
5 To yon their rocking roosts in pines wind-torn;
   A line of grey snake-fence, that zigzags by
   A pond and cattle; from the homestead nigh
The long deep summonings of the supper horn.

Black on the ridge, against that lonely flush,
10 A cart, and stoop-necked oxen; ranged beside
   Some barrels; and the day-worn harvest folk,
Here emptying their baskets, jar the hush
   With hollow thunders. Down the dusk hillside
   Lumbers the wain; and day fades out like smoke.

Archibald Lampman

Canada 1861–1899

Archibald Lampman grew up in the country near Morpeth on Lake Erie. He
became a scholarship student at Trinity College in Toronto and, after a brief
attempt at teaching high school following his graduation from Trinity, he moved to
Ottawa and worked in the Post Office. Lampman joined the Ottawa Literary and
Scientific Society, and it was through the society that he became friends with
Duncan Campbell Scott. Like Scott, Lampman developed a love for the Canadian
landscape, seeing it as his source of inspiration. Lampman's distaste for the city and
its influence on human civilization is evident in "The City of the End of Things."

The City of the End of Things   1895

Beside the pounding cataracts
Of midnight streams unknown to us
'Tis builded in the leafless tracts
And valleys huge of Tartarus.[1]
5 Lurid and lofty and vast it seems;
It hath no rounded name that rings,

---

1 abyss below Hades

But I have heard it called in dreams
The City of the End of Things.

      Its roofs and iron towers have grown
10 None knoweth how high within the night,
      But in its murky streets far down
      A flaming terrible and bright
      Shakes all the stalking shadows there,
      Across the walls, across the floors,
15 And shifts upon the upper air
      From out a thousand furnace doors;
      And all the while an awful sound
      Keeps roaring on continually,
      And crashes in the ceaseless round
20 Of a gigantic harmony.
      Through its grim depths re-echoing
      And all its weary height of walls,
      With measured roar and iron ring,
      The inhuman music lifts and falls.
25 Where no thing rests and no man is,
      And only fire and night hold sway;
      The beat, the thunder and the hiss
      Cease not, and change not, night nor day.
      And moving at unheard commands,
30 The abysses and vast fires between,
      Flit figures that with clanking hands
      Obey a hideous routine;
      They are not flesh, they are not bone,
      They see not with the human eye,
35 And from their iron lips is blown
      A dreadful and monotonous cry;
      And whoso of our mortal race
      Should find that city unaware,
      Lean Death would smite him face to face,
40 And blanch him with its venomed air:
      Or caught by the terrific spell,
      Each thread of memory snapt and cut,
      His soul would shrivel and its shell
      Go rattling like an empty nut.

45 It was not always so, but once,
      In days that no man thinks upon,
      Fair voices echoed from its stones,
      The light above it leaped and shone:
      Once there were multitudes of men,
50 That built that city in their pride,
      Until its might was made, and then
      They withered age by age and died.

But now of that prodigious race,
Three only in an iron tower,
55 Set like carved idols face to face,
Remain the masters of its power;
And at the city gate a fourth,
Gigantic and with dreadful eyes,
Sits looking toward the lightless north,
60 Beyond the reach of memories;
Fast rooted to the lurid floor,
A bulk that never moves a jot,
In his pale body dwells no more,
Or mind or soul,—an idiot!
65 But sometime in the end those three
Shall perish and their hands be still,
And with the master's touch shall flee
Their incommunicable skill.
A stillness absolute as death
70 Along the slacking wheels shall lie,
And, flagging at a single breath,
The fires shall moulder out and die.
The roar shall vanish at its height,
And over that tremendous town
75 The silence of eternal night
Shall gather close and settle down.
All its grim grandeur, tower and hall,
Shall be abandoned utterly,
And into rust and dust shall fall
80 From century to century;
Nor ever living thing shall grow,
Nor trunk of tree, nor blade of grass;
No drop shall fall, no wind shall blow,
Nor sound of any foot shall pass:
85 Alone of its accursèd state,
One thing the hand of Time shall spare,
For the grim Idiot at the gate
Is deathless and eternal there.

D.C. Scott

Canada 1862–1947

Born into an Ottawa Methodist family who lived both in Ontario and Quebec, Duncan Campbell Scott joined the federal Department of Indian Affairs in 1879. He became the department's deputy superintendent in 1923 and held that position until his retirement in 1932. Scott's work with Aboriginal people and his sense of the Canadian wilderness are reflected in poems such as "The Forsaken." Although Scott can be condemned for some of his actions against Aboriginal people (his part in the banning of the potlatch on the West Coast comes to mind), his writing shows that he was attempting to come to terms with the differences between Euro-Canadian and Aboriginal cultures. Scott's later poems reflect his interest in modernism and his attempt to go beyond nationalist verse while still exploring the struggle for survival.

The Forsaken   1905

I

    Once in the winter
    Out on a lake
    In the heart of the north-land,
    Far from the Fort
5   And far from the hunters,
    A Chippewa woman
    With her sick baby,
    Crouched in the last hours
    Of a great storm.
10 Frozen and hungry,
    She fished through the ice
    With a line of the twisted
    Bark of the cedar,
    And a rabbit-bone hook
15 Polished and barbed;
    Fished with the bare hook
    All through the wild day,
    Fished and caught nothing;
    While the young chieftain
20 Tugged at her breasts,
    Or slept in the lacings
    Of the warm *tikanagan*.[1]

---

1   cradle-board

All the lake-surface
Streamed with the hissing
25 Of millions of iceflakes
Hurled by the wind;
Behind her the round
Of a lonely island
Roared like a fire
30 With the voice of the storm
In the deeps of the cedars.
Valiant, unshaken,
She took of her own flesh,
Baited the fish-hook,
35 Drew in a gray-trout,
Drew in his fellows,
Heaped them beside her,
Dead in the snow.
Valiant, unshaken,
40 She faced the long distance,
Wolf-haunted and lonely,
Sure of her goal
And the life of her dear one:
Tramped for two days,
45 On the third in the morning,
Saw the strong bulk
Of the Fort by the river,
Saw the wood-smoke
Hang soft in the spruces,
50 Heard the keen yelp
Of the ravenous huskies
Fighting for whitefish:
Then she had rest.

II

Years and years after,
55 When she was old and withered,
When her son was an old man
And his children filled with vigour,
They came in their northern tour on the verge of winter,
To an island in a lonely lake.
60 There one night they camped, and on the morrow
Gathered their kettles and birch-bark
Their rabbit-skin robes and their mink-traps,
Launched their canoes and slunk away through the islands,
Left her alone forever,
65 Without a word of farewell,
Because she was old and useless,
Like a paddle broken and warped,

Or a pole that was splintered.
Then, without a sigh,
70 Valiant, unshaken,
She smoothed her dark locks under her kerchief,
Composed her shawl in state,
Then folded her hands ridged with sinews and corded with veins,
Folded them across her breasts spent with the nourishing of children,
75 Gazed at the sky past the tops of the cedars,
Saw two spangled nights arise out of the twilight,
Saw two days go by filled with the tranquil sunshine,
Saw, without pain, or dread, or even a moment of longing:
Then on the third great night there came thronging and thronging
80 Millions of snowflakes out of a windless cloud;
They covered her close with a beautiful crystal shroud,
Covered her deep and silent.
But in the frost of the dawn,
Up from the life below,
85 Rose a column of breath
Through a tiny cleft in the snow,
Fragile, delicately drawn,
Wavering with its own weakness,
In the wilderness a sign of the spirit,
90 Persisting still in the sight of the sun
Till day was done.
Then all light was gathered up by the hand of God and hid in His breast,
Then there was born a silence deeper than silence,
Then she had rest.

William Butler Yeats

Ireland 1865–1939

Born in Dublin, William Butler Yeats is inextricably tied to his country, Ireland.
After early attempts to incorporate Celtic folktales and legends in his poetry,
Yeats, although Anglo-Irish, was drawn into the Irish nationalist movement, in
part because of his love for Maud Gonne, a crusader for a free Ireland. In "Easter
1916," Yeats captures both the sense of waste and the magnificent sacrifice he
discerned in the movement's most violent events. Eventually, he left the movement behind and focused on a national theatre for Ireland, helping to establish
Dublin's Abbey Theatre. Yeats also served as a senator from 1922 to 1928.One
of the duties of a senator was to conduct school inspections, and it is this task
that forms the frame for "Among School Children," his inquiry into the nature
of love and the pains life enacts on us. In "The Circus Animals' Desertion," Yeats
offers his own summary of his poetic career.

The Second Coming[1]   1921

Turning and turning in the widening gyre[2]
The falcon cannot hear the falconer;
Things fall apart; the center cannot hold;
Mere anarchy is loosed upon the world,
5   The blood-dimmed tide is loosed, and everywhere
The ceremony of innocence is drowned;
The best lack all conviction, while the worst
Are full of passionate intensity.
Surely some revelation is at hand;
10   Surely the Second Coming is at hand.
The Second Coming! Hardly are those words out
When a vast image out of *Spiritus Mundi*[3]
Troubles my sight: somewhere in sands of the desert
A shape with lion body and the head of a man,
15   A gaze blank and pitiless as the sun,
Is moving its slow thighs, while all about it
Reel shadows of the indignant desert birds.
The darkness drops again; but now I know
That twenty centuries of stony sleep
20   Were vexed to nightmare by a rocking cradle,
And what rough beast, its hour come round at last,
Slouches towards Bethlehem to be born?

Among School Children   1927

1

I walk through the long schoolroom questioning;
A kind old nun in a white hood replies;
The children learn to cipher and to sing,
To study reading-books and history,
5   To cut and sew, be neat in everything
In the best modern way—the children's eyes
In momentary wonder stare upon
A sixty-year-old smiling public man.

2

I dream of a Ledaean body, bent
10   Above a sinking fire, a tale that she

---

1   the second coming of Christ ends the Christian cycle, but to Yeats the end of the
    Christian cycle is the end of just one of the cycles of civilization

2   spiralling outward in a cone-like shape; another reference to the unwinding of the
    Christian cycle

3   the Spirit of the World, which Yeats felt joins all to a universal subconsciousness

Told of a harsh reproof, or trivial event
That changed some childish day to tragedy—
Told, and it seemed that our two natures blent
Into a sphere from youthful sympathy,
15   Or else, to alter Plato's parable,[1]
Into the yolk and white of the one shell.

3

And thinking of that fit of grief or rage
I look upon one child or t'other there
And wonder if she stood so at that age—
20   For even daughters of the swan can share
Something of every paddler's heritage—
And had that colour upon cheek or hair,
And thereupon my heart is driven wild:
She stands before me as a living child.

4

25   Her present image floats into the mind—
Did Quattrocento finger fashion it
Hollow of cheek as though it drank the wind
And took a mess of shadows for its meat?
And I though never of Ledaean kind[2]
30   Had pretty plumage once—enough of that,
Better to smile on all that smile, and show
There is a comfortable kind of old scarecrow.

5

What youthful mother, a shape upon her lap
Honey of generation had betrayed,
35   And that must sleep, shriek, struggle to escape
As recollection or the drug decide,
Would think her son, did she but see that shape
With sixty or more winters on its head,
A compensation for the pang of his birth,
40   Or the uncertainty of his setting forth?

6

Plato thought nature but a spume that plays
Upon a ghostly paradigm of things;
Solider Aristotle played the taws[3]
Upon the bottom of a king of kings;
45   World-famous golden-thighed Pythagoras

1   A reference in Plato's *Symposium* to love being like the reuniting of separate beings;
Helen's birth as the result of a joining of a swan and a mortal leads to the actual egg
reference.
2   Literally "like Leda," Helen of Troy's daughter, and model for the feminine beauty
Yeats also saw in Maud Gonne.
3   Literally, as his teacher, Aristotle strapped (taws) Alexander, the "King of Kings."

Fingered upon a fiddle-stick or strings
What a star sang and careless Muses heard:
Old clothes upon old sticks to scare a bird.

7

Both nuns and mothers worship images,
50   But those the candles light are not as those
That animate a mother's reveries,
But keep a marble or a bronze repose.
And yet they too break hearts—O Presences
That passion, piety or affection knows,
55   And that all heavenly glory symbolise—
O self-born mockers of man's enterprise;

8

Labour is blossoming or dancing where
The body is not bruised to pleasure soul,
Nor beauty born out of its own despair,
60   Nor blear-eyed wisdom out of midnight oil.
O chestnut-tree, great-rooted blossomer,
Are you the leaf, the blossom, or the bole?
O body swayed to music, O brightening glance,
How can we know the dancer from the dance?

The Circus Animals' Desertion   1939

1

I sought a theme and sought for it in vain,
I sought it daily for six weeks or so.
Maybe at last, being but a broken man,
I must be satisfied with my heart, although
5   Winter and summer till old age began
My circus animals were all on show,
Those stilted boys, that burnished chariot,
Lion and woman and the Lord knows what.

2

What can I but enumerate old themes?
10   First that sea-rider Oisin led by the nose[1]
Through three enchanted islands, allegorical dreams,
Vain gaiety, vain battle, vain repose,
Themes of the embittered heart, or so it seems,
That might adorn old songs or courtly shows;
15   But what cared I that set him on to ride,
I, starved for the bosom of his faery bride?

---

1   Oisin is a legendary Irish hero and Yeats is referring to some of his acts here.

And then a counter-truth filled out its play,
The Countess Cathleen was the name I gave it;
She, pity-crazed, had given her soul away,
20 But masterful Heaven had intervened to save it.
I thought my dear must her own soul destroy,
So did fanaticism and hate enslave it,
And this brought forth a dream and soon enough
This dream itself had all my thought and love.

25 And when the Fool and Blind Man stole the bread
Cuchulain fought the ungovernable sea;[2]
Heart-mysteries there, and yet when all is said
It was the dream itself enchanted me:
Character isolated by a deed
30 To engross the present and dominate memory.
Players and painted stage took all my love,
And not those things that they were emblems of.

3

Those masterful images because complete
Grew in pure mind, but out of what began?
35 A mound of refuse or the sweepings of a street,
Old kettles, old bottles, and a broken can,
Old iron, old bones, old rags, that raving slut
Who keeps the till. Now that my ladder's gone,
I must lie down where all the ladders start,
40 In the foul rag-and-bone shop of the heart.

---

2 This refers again to Irish legends, as does the Countess Cathleen; Cuchulain was a
hero of Ulster legends.

Robert Frost

U.S.A. 1874–1963

For forty years, Robert Frost was America's best-loved poet. At John F. Kennedy's
inauguration, he recited a poem from memory—a rare moment when politics
and literature merged. Born in California, Frost moved to Massachusetts and
then New Hampshire with his mother after his father died. After trying his hand
at teaching, Frost turned to farming in Derry, New Hampshire. Ironically, Frost
had to go to England in 1912 before he was "discovered in the United States."
In interpreting his poetry, the reader has to be careful to distinguish the intent
from the images and action of the surface. Frost is fond of indirection and suggestion as poetic strategies, and uses them here as well as blunt criticism in
"Neither Out Far nor in Deep." The common picture of Frost as some kindly,
aged, New England farmer is contradicted by the harshness of this poem.

Neither Out Far nor In Deep   1936

The people along the sand
All turn and look one way.
They turn their back on the land.
They look at the sea all day.

5   As long as it takes to pass
A ship keeps raising its hull;
The wetter ground like glass
Reflects a standing gull.

The land may vary more;
10   But wherever the truth may be—
The water comes ashore,
And the people look at the sea.

They cannot look out far.
They cannot look in deep.
15   But when was that ever a bar
To any watch they keep?

The Silken Tent   1942

She is as in a field a silken tent
At midday when a sunny summer breeze
Has dried the dew and all its ropes relent,
So that in guys it gently sways at ease,
5   And its supporting central cedar pole,
That is its pinnacle to heavenward
And signifies the sureness of the soul,
Seems to owe naught to any single cord,
But strictly held by none, is loosely bound
10   By countless silken ties of love and thought
To everything on earth the compass round,
And only by one's going slightly taut
In the capriciousness1 of summer air
Is of the slightest bondage made aware.

---

1   unpredictability

Wallace Stevens

U.S.A. 1879–1955

Born in Reading, Pennsylvania, Wallace Stevens went to Harvard University and eventually rose to the position of vice president of the Hartford Insurance Company. His first book of poetry, *Harmonium*, was not published until 1923, when he was already in his forties. His Hartford, Connecticut, base gave him a place from which his imagination could roam freely, seeking sources of order in a disorderly world. This theme plays a part in his enigmatic "The Snow Man." Frequently in Stevens's poems, the mind opposes the brute reality of the physical world and attempts to compose it into a new order.

The Emperor of Ice-Cream   1923

Call the roller of big cigars,
The muscular one, and bid him whip
In kitchen cups concupiscent[1] curds.
Let the wenches dawdle in such dress
5   As they are used to wear, and let the boys
Bring flowers in last month's newspapers.
Let be be finale of seem.
The only emperor is the emperor of ice-cream.

Take from the dresser of deal,[2]
10   Lacking the three glass knobs, that sheet
On which she embroidered fantails once
And spread it so as to cover her face.
If her horny feet protrude, they come
To show how cold she is, and dumb.
15   Let the lamp affix its beam.
The only emperor is the emperor of ice-cream.

---

1   beginning to desire
2   cheap dresser

The Snow Man   1931

One must have a mind of winter
To regard the frost and the boughs
Of the pine-trees crusted with snow;

And have been cold a long time
5   To behold the junipers shagged with ice,
The spruces rough in the distant glitter

Of the January sun; and not to think
Of any misery in the sound of the wind,
In the sound of a few leaves,

10 Which is the sound of the land
Full of the same wind
That is blowing in the same bare place

For the listener, who listens in the snow,
And, nothing himself, beholds
15 Nothing that is not there and the nothing that is.

William Carlos Williams

U.S.A. 1883–1963

William Carlos Williams was born in Rutherford, New Jersey, where he practised
medicine until his late sixties. He began publishing poetry after World War I and
was initially influenced by the imagists. Williams argued throughout his writing
career that American poets must be open enough to imitate the unpredictable
patterns of American speech. Perhaps best known for "The Red Wheelbarrow,"
with its enigmatic series of images supplying all the meaning in response to the
opening "so much depends/upon," Williams could be more direct, as we see in
"The Last Words of My English Grandmother." Here, our expectations about the
images and sentiment associated with an old woman dying are overturned by
unexpected realities.

The Last Words of My English Grandmother   1920

There were some dirty plates
and a glass of milk
beside her on a small table
near the rank, disheveled bed—

5 Wrinkled and nearly blind
she lay and snored
rousing with anger in her tones
to cry for food,

Gimme something to eat—
10 They're starving me—
I'm all right—I won't go
to the hospital. No, no, no

Give me something to eat!
Let me take you
15 to the hospital, I said
and after you are well

you can do as you please.
She smiled, Yes
you do what you please first
20 then I can do what I please—

Oh, oh, oh! she cried
as the ambulance men lifted
her to the stretcher—
Is this what you call

25 making me comfortable?
By now her mind was clear—
Oh you think you're smart
you young people,

she said, but I'll tell you
30 you don't know anything.
Then we started.
On the way

We passed a long row
of elms. She looked at them
35 awhile out of
the ambulance window and said,

What are all those
fuzzy-looking things out there?
Trees? Well, I'm tired
40 of them and rolled her head away.

The Red Wheelbarrow   1923

so much depends
upon

a red wheel
barrow

5 glazed with rain
water

beside the white
chickens.

E. J. Pratt

Canada 1882–1964

Born in Western Bay, Newfoundland, E.J. Pratt, the son of a Methodist minister, lived in a number of outports before attending St. John's Methodist College. In 1907, Pratt entered Canada to study theology, philosophy, and psychology at Victoria College, University of Toronto. In 1919, Pratt was offered an appointment to the English faculty at Victoria College, where he taught until he retired in 1953. "The Prize Cat," like much of his poetry, reveals a keen mind and an interest in irony. Unlike many poets of his time, Pratt wrote a number of long poems, including *Towards the Last Spike* and *The Titanic*, in which he examined massive forces and their interactions.

The Prize Cat   1937

Pure blood domestic, guaranteed,
Soft-mannered, musical in purr,
The ribbon had declared the breed,
Gentility was in the fur.

5   Such feline culture in the gads[1]
No anger ever arched her back—
What distance since those velvet pads
Departed from the leopard's track!

And when I mused how Time had thinned
10   The jungle strains within the cells,
How human hands had disciplined
Those prowling optic parallels;

I saw the generations pass
Along the reflex of a spring,
15   A bird had rustled in the grass,
The tab had caught it on the wing:

Behind the leap so furtive-wild
Was such ignition in the gleam,
I thought an Abyssinian child
20   Had cried out in the whitethroat's[2] scream.

1   claws
2   sparrow

Ezra Pound

U.S.A. 1885–1972

Ezra Pound was born in Idaho and raised in Pennsylvania, where he went to university. In 1908 he left for Europe, where he was to have an influence on modernist writers such as T.S. Eliot, Ernest Hemingway, and James Joyce. On the subject of imagism, Pound noted in "A Retrospect" that "[a]n 'Image' is that which presents an intellectual and emotional complex in an instant of time." Pound's support of Italian fascism landed him in an American disciplinary centre near Pisa at the end of World War II. He was subsequently transferred to the United States, declared unfit to stand trial for treason, and confined to a psychiatric hospital, where he continued to work on his most complex poems, *The Cantos*.

In a Station of the Metro   1916

The apparition of these faces in the crowd;
Petals on a wet, black bough.

The River-Merchant's Wife: A Letter   1915

While my hair was still cut straight across my forehead
I played about the front gate, pulling flowers.
You came by on bamboo stilts, playing horse,
You walked about my seat, playing with blue plums.
5   And we went on living in the village of Chokan:
Two small people, without dislike or suspicion.

At fourteen I married My Lord you.
I never laughed, being bashful.
Lowering my head, I looked at the wall.
10   Called to, a thousand times, I never looked back.

At fifteen I stopped scowling,
I desired my dust to be mingled with yours
For ever and for ever and for ever.
Why should I climb the look out?

15   At sixteen you departed,
You went into far Ku-to-yen, by the river of swirling eddies,
And you have been gone five months.
The monkeys make sorrowful noise overhead.

You dragged your feet when you went out.
20 By the gate now, the moss is grown, the different mosses,
Too deep to clear them away!
The leaves fall early this autumn, in wind.
The paired butterflies are already yellow with August
Over the grass in the West garden;
25 They hurt me. I grow older.
If you are coming down through the narrows of the river Kiang,
Please let me know beforehand,
And I will come out to meet you
   As far as Cho-fu-Sa.

By Rihaku [Li Bai]
A.D. 800

T.S. Eliot

U.S.A./England 1888–1965

Born in St. Louis, Missouri, to an affluent family, T.S. Eliot obtained his M.A. at
Harvard before going abroad in 1914 to study at the Sorbonne and Oxford. In 1927,
he became a British subject and was confirmed in the Anglican Church. Eliot's early
work, such as "The Love Song of J. Alfred Prufrock," focuses on social decay and the
absence of any ordering belief to endow daily life with value. He commented in
"The Metaphysical Poets" that "the poet must become more comprehensive, more
allusive, more indirect, in order to force, to dislocate if necessary, language into his
meaning." His later, more optimistic, vision of history, religion, and humanity,
which first shows itself in "Ash Wednesday" and the "Ariel" poems, published
between 1927 and 1930, is fully realized in "Little Gidding" from *Four Quartets*.

The Love Song of J. Alfred Prufrock   1917

S'io credesse che mia risposta fosse
A persona che mai tornasse al mondo,
Questa fiamma staria senza più scosse.
Ma per ciò giammai di questo fondo
Non tornò vivo alcun, s'i'odo il vero,
Senza tema d'infamia ti rispondo.[1]

---

1 from Dante's *Inferno* (27.61–66). These lines comment on the impossibility of
 returning to life from death. The passage states, in part, "If I thought my answer would
 be to a person who never would return to the world…but since none has returned
 alive from this pit…without fear of infamy, I answer you."

Let us go then, you and I,
When the evening is spread out against the sky
Like a patient etherized upon a table;
Let us go, through certain half-deserted streets,
5   The muttering retreats
Of restless nights in one-night cheap hotels
And sawdust restaurants with oyster shells:
Streets that follow like a tedious argument
Of insidious intent
10   To lead you to an overwhelming question ...
Oh, do not ask, "What is it?"
Let us go and make our visit.

In the room the women come and go
Talking of Michelangelo.

15   The yellow fog that rubs its back upon the windowpanes,
The yellow smoke that rubs its muzzle on the windowpanes
Licked its tongue into the corners of the evening,
Lingered upon the pools that stand in drains,
Let fall upon its back the soot that falls from chimneys,
20   Slipped by the terrace, made a sudden leap,
And seeing that it was a soft October night,
Curled once about the house, and fell asleep.

And indeed there will be time
For the yellow smoke that slides along the street,
25   Rubbing its back upon the windowpanes;
There will be time, there will be time
To prepare a face to meet the faces that you meet;
There will be time to murder and create,
And time for all the works and days[2] of hands
30   That lift and drop a question on your plate;
Time for you and time for me,
And time yet for a hundred indecisions,
And for a hundred visions and revisions,
Before the taking of a toast and tea.

35   In the room the women come and go
Talking of Michelangelo.

And indeed there will be time
To wonder, "Do I dare?" and, "Do I dare?"
Time to turn back and descend the stair,
40   With a bald spot in the middle of my hair—

---

2   works and days = Hesiod's Greek poem about the farming cycle

(They will say: "How his hair is growing thin!")
My morning coat, my collar mounting firmly to the chin,
My necktie rich and modest, but asserted by a simple pin—
(They will say: "But how his arms and legs are thin!")
45 Do I dare
Disturb the universe?
In a minute there is time
For decisions and revisions which a minute will reverse.

     For I have known them all already, known them all—
50 Have known the evenings, mornings, afternoons,
I have measured out my life with coffee spoons;
I know the voices dying with a dying fall
Beneath the music from a farther room.
     So how should I presume?

55   And I have known the eyes already, known them all—
The eyes that fix you in a formulated phrase,
And when I am formulated, sprawling on a pin,
When I am pinned and wriggling on the wall,
Then how should I begin
60 To spit out all the butt-ends of my days and ways?
     And how should I presume?

     And I have known the arms already, known them all—
Arms that are braceleted and white and bare
(But in the lamplight, downed with light brown hair!)
65 Is it perfume from a dress
That makes me so digress?
Arms that lie along a table, or wrap about a shawl.
     And should I then presume?
     And how should I begin?

     . . . . .

70   Shall I say, I have gone at dusk through narrow streets
And watched the smoke that rises from the pipes
Of lonely men in shirt-sleeves, leaning out of windows? ...

I should have been a pair of ragged claws
Scuttling across the floors of silent seas.

     . . . . .

75   And the afternoon, the evening, sleeps so peacefully!
Smoothed by long fingers,
Asleep ... tired ... or it malingers,
Stretched on the floor, here beside you and me.
Should I, after tea and cakes and ices,

80 Have the strength to force the moment to its crisis?
But though I have wept and fasted, wept and prayed,
Though I have seen my head (grown slightly bald) brought in upon a
  platter,
I am no prophet—and here's no great matter;
I have seen the moment of my greatness flicker,
85 And I have seen the eternal Footman hold my coat, and snicker,
And in short, I was afraid.

And would it have been worth it, after all,
After the cups, the marmalade, the tea,
Among the porcelain, among some talk of you and me,
90 Would it have been worth while,
To have bitten off the matter with a smile,
To have squeezed the universe into a ball
To roll it toward some overwhelming question,
To say: "I am Lazarus, come from the dead,
95 Come back to tell you all, I shall tell you all"—
If one, settling a pillow by her head,
    Should say: "That is not what I meant at all.
    That is not it, at all."

And would it have been worth it, after all,
100 Would it have been worth while,
After the sunsets and the dooryards and the sprinkled streets,
After the novels, after the teacups, after the skirts that trail along the
  floor—
And this, and so much more?—
It is impossible to say just what I mean!
105 But as if a magic lantern[3] threw the nerves in patterns on a screen:
Would it have been worth while
If one, settling a pillow or throwing off a shawl,
And turning toward the window, should say:
    "That is not it at all,
110   That is not what I meant, at all."

. . . . .

No! I am not Prince Hamlet, nor was meant to be;
Am an attendant lord, one that will do
To swell a progress, start a scene or two,
Advise the prince; no doubt, an easy tool,
115 Deferential, glad to be of use,
Politic, cautious, and meticulous;
Full of high sentence, but a bit obtuse;
At times, indeed, almost ridiculous—
Almost, at times, the Fool.

---

3   magic lantern = form of image projector using slides

120   I grow old … I grow old …
      I shall wear the bottoms of my trousers rolled.

      Shall I part my hair behind? Do I dare to eat a peach?
      I shall wear white flannel trousers, and walk upon the beach.
      I have heard the mermaids singing, each to each.

125   I do not think that they will sing to me.

      I have seen them riding seaward on the waves
      Combing the white hair of the waves blown back
      When the wind blows the water white and black.

      We have lingered in the chambers of the sea
130   By sea-girls wreathed with seaweed red and brown
      Till human voices wake us, and we drown.

From Four Quartets:
Little Gidding (Part V)   1942

      What we call the beginning is often the end
      And to make an end is to make a beginning.
      The end is where we start from. And every phrase
      And sentence that is right (where every word is at home,
5   Taking its place to support the others,
      The word neither diffident nor ostentatious,
      And easy commerce of the old and the new,
      The common word exact without vulgarity,
      The formal word precise but not pedantic,
10   The complete consort dancing together)
      Every phrase and every sentence is an end and a beginning,
      Every poem an epitaph. And any action
      Is a step to the block, to the fire, down the sea's throat
      Or to an illegible stone: and that is where we start.
15   We die with the dying:
      See, they depart, and we go with them.
      We are born with the dead:
      See, they return, and bring us with them.
      The moment of the rose and the moment of the yew tree
20   Are of equal duration. A people without history
      Is not redeemed from time, for history is a pattern
      Of timeless moments. So, while the light fails
      On a winter's afternoon, in a secluded chapel
      History is now and England.

25 With the drawing of this Love and the voice of this Calling

We shall not cease from exploration
And the end of all our exploring
Will be to arrive where we started
And know the place for the first time.
30 Through the unknown, remembered gate
When the last of earth left to discover
Is that which was the beginning;
At the source of the longest river
The voice of the hidden waterfall
35 And the children in the apple tree
Not known, because not looked for
But heard, half-heard, in the stillness
Between two waves of the sea.
Quick now, here, now, always—
40 A condition of complete simplicity
(Costing not less than everything)
And all shall be well and
All manner of thing shall be well
When the tongues of flame are in-folded
45 Into the crowned knot of fire
And the fire and the rose[1] are one.

---

1 The rose and fire have several layers of meaning, including references to Christ,
beauty, creative energy, and destruction.

Wilfred Owen

England 1893–1918

As his death date shows, Wilfred Owen was a man whose life was cut short by
World War I. Having enlisted in 1916, Owen became a company commander
and was killed in action roughly one week before the war's end. Like other
young men of his generation, a quarter of whom were killed in the Great War,
Owen found his youthful optimism crushed by the brutal realities of trench
warfare. In his poems, he uses haunting and graphic images to capture the
horrors of war. A look at Owen's manuscripts at the Wilfred Owen Multimedia
Digital Archive (http://www.hcu.ox.ac.uk/jtap/) shows how little Owen actually
changed his poems between drafts.

Strange Meeting   1920

It seemed that out of battle I escaped
Down some profound dull tunnel, long since scooped
Through granites which titanic wars had groined.

Yet also there encumbered sleepers groaned,
5   Too fast in thought or death to be bestirred.
Then, as I probed them, one sprang up, and stared
With piteous recognition in fixed eyes,
Lifting distressful hands, as if to bless.
And by his smile, I knew that sullen hall,—
10   By his dead smile I knew we stood in Hell.
With a thousand pains that vision's face was grained;
Yet no blood reached there from the upper ground,
And no guns thumped, or down the flues¹ made moan.
"Strange friend," I said, "here is no cause to mourn."
15   "None," said that other, "save the undone years,
The hopelessness. Whatever hope is yours,
Was my life also; I went hunting wild
After the wildest beauty in the world,
Which lies not calm in eyes, or braided hair,
20   But mocks the steady running of the hour,
And if it grieves, grieves richlier than here.
For by my glee might many men have laughed,
And of my weeping something had been left,
Which must die now. I mean the truth untold,
25   The pity of war, the pity war distilled.
Now men will go content with what we spoiled,
Or, discontent, boil bloody, and be spilled.
They will be swift with swiftness of the tigress.
None will break ranks, though nations trek from progress.
30   Courage was mine, and I had mystery,
Wisdom was mine, and I had mastery:
To miss the march of this retreating world
Into vain citadels that are not walled.
Then, when much blood had clogged their chariot-wheels,
35   I would go up and wash them from sweet wells,
Even with truths that lie too deep for taint.
I would have poured my spirit without stint
But not through wounds; not on the cess of war.
Foreheads of men have bled where no wounds were.

---

1   ducts

40   "I am the enemy you killed, my friend.
      I knew you in this dark: for so you frowned
      Yesterday through me as you jabbed and killed.
      I parried; but my hands were loath and cold.
      Let us sleep now...."

e.e. cummings

U.S.A. 1894–1962

Born in Massachusetts, e.e. (Edward Estlin) cummings began by writing conventional verse, but his experience in World War I and the example of Ezra Pound turned him to more satiric and unconventional themes and styles. Cummings wrote *The Enormous Room* to comment on his absurd experience of being imprisoned over a case of mistaken identity during the war. Cummings, also a painter, was fascinated with what the typewriter could do to expand the range of poetic statement, and his development of a highly personal style of diction and punctuation gave his poetry distinctiveness in both texture and subject. In both "anyone lived in a pretty how town" and "O sweet spontaneous," Cummings's romanticism and original wording lend fresh power to otherwise conventional statements.

anyone lived in a pretty how town   1940

        anyone lived in a pretty how town
        (with up so floating many bells down)
        spring summer autumn winter
        he sang his didn't he danced his did.

5   Women and men(both little and small)
        cared for anyone not at all
        they sowed their isn't they reaped their same
        sun moon stars rain

        children guessed(but only a few
10   and down they forgot as up they grew
        autumn winter spring summer)
        that noone loved him more by more

        when by now and tree by leaf
        she laughed his joy she cried his grief
15   bird by snow and stir by still
        anyone's any was all to her

someones married their everyones
laughed their cryings and did their dance
(sleep wake hope and then)they
20   said their nevers they slept their dream

stars rain sun moon
(and only the snow can begin to explain
how children are apt to forget to remember
with up so floating many bells down)

25   one day anyone died i guess
(and noone stooped to kiss his face)
busy folk buried them side by side
little by little and was by was

all by all and deep by deep
30   and more by more they dream their sleep
noone and anyone earth by april
wish by spirit and if by yes.

Women and men(both dong and ding)
summer autumn winter spring
35   reaped their sowing and went their came
sun moon stars rain

O sweet spontaneous   1923

O sweet spontaneous
earth how often have
the
doting

5   fingers of
prurient philosophers pinched
and
poked

thee
10   , has the naughty thumb
of science prodded
thy

beauty   . how
often have religions taken
15   thee upon their scraggy knees
squeezing and

buffeting thee that thou mightest conceive
gods
    (but
20   true

to the incomparable
couch of death thy
rhythmic
lover

25   thou answerest

them only with

      spring)

F. R. Scott

Canada 1899–1985

Quebec-born Francis R. Scott was part of the McGill group of poets who published an anthology entitled *New Provinces* in 1936. Scott became an expert on
constitutional law and eventually was appointed dean of McGill's Faculty of
Law. A committed socialist, Scott was involved in writing the manifesto of the
Co-operative Commonwealth Federation (CCF), the precursor of the New
Democratic Party. Scott's poetry runs the gamut from satire and invective (he
was the editor of a book of Canadian satire, *The Blasted Pine*) to more traditional lyric themes. Scott's gentle, imaginative side is evident in "Poetry."

Poetry   1954

Nothing can take its place. If I write 'ostrich'
Those who have never seen the bird see it
With its head in the sand and its plumes fluffed with the wind
Like Mackenzie King talking on Freedom of Trade.

5   And if I write 'holocaust', and 'nightingales',
I startle the insurance agents and the virgins
Who belong, by this alchemy, in the same category,
Since both are very worried about their premiums.

A rose and a rose are two roses; a rose is a rose is a rose.
10 Sometimes I have walked down a street marked No Outlet
Only to find that what was blocking my path
Was a railroad track roaring away to the west.

So I know it will survive. Not even the decline of reading
And the substitution of advertising for genuine pornography
15 Can crush the uprush of the mushrooming verb
Or drown the overtone of the noun on its own.

Part V   FORT PROVIDENCE

From Letters from the Mackenzie River   1956

We came out of Beaver Lake
Into swift water,
Past the Big Snye, past Providence Island,
And nosed our barges into shore
5 Till they grated on stones and sand.
Gang planks, thrown to the bank
Were all we had for dock
To drop four tons of freight.

A line of men were squatting
10 Silently above us, straight
Black hair, swarthy skins,
Slavies they call them, who left
Their name on Lake and River.
None of them spoke or moved—
15 Just sat and watched, quietly,
While the white man heaved at his hardware.
Farther on, by themselves,
The women and girls were huddled.

Then we saw Father Denis,
20 Oblate from Rennes, Brittany,
In charge of the only mission.
Young, cheerful, crucifix stuck in his waistband,
He greeted us with friendly warmth,
Would show us the school, his pride.

25 We had seen the school from far off.
It stood four stories high,
Grey, square, isolated,

More fortlike than anything in Fort Providence.
In the entrance hall
30 Walt Disney illustrations for the Kleenex Company
Showed children how to avoid getting colds
By constantly using Kleenex.
The gentle sister in charge,
A Grey Nun from Montreal,
35 Welcomed us in French.
Priests from France, nuns from Quebec,
Taught Slavies (who still speak Indian)
Grades I to VIII, in broken English.

We walked through the crowded class-rooms.
40 No map of Canada or the Territories,
No library or workshop,
Everywhere religious scenes,
Christ and Saints, Stations of the Cross,
Beads hanging from nails, crucifixes,
45 And two kinds of secular art—
Silk-screen prints of the Group of Seven,
And crayon drawings and masks
Made by the younger children,
The single visible expression
50 Of the soul of these broken people.

Upstairs on the second storey
Seventy little cots
Touching end to end
In a room 30 by 40
55 Housed the resident boys
In this firetrap mental gaol.

National Identity   1963

The Canadian Centenary Council
Meeting in le Reine Elizabeth
To seek those symbols
Which will explain ourselves to ourselves
5 Evoke bi-cultural responses
And prove that something called Canada
Really exists in the hearts of all
Handed out to every delegate
At the start of proceedings
10 A portfolio of documents
On the cover of which appeared
In gold letters

not
A Mari Usque Ad Mare
15   not
Dieu Et Mon Droit
not
Je Me Souviens
not
20   *E Pluribus Unum*
but
COURTESY OF COCA-COLA LIMITED

Langston Hughes

U.S.A. 1902–1967

Born in Joplin, Missouri, Langston Hughes lived in Kansas, Illinois, and Ohio before attending Columbia University, New York, in 1921. Hughes became a major figure in the Harlem Renaissance of the 1920s and early 1930s. By then, he had already travelled widely as a merchant seaman and had lived in Rome and Paris for a short time. The publication of *Weary Blues* in 1926 started his poetry career. One of the few poets able to make a living from readings and lectures, Hughes was a pioneer in reading poetry to elementary school students. Through his association with the Harlem Renaissance, he also helped to forge a Black presence in the arts. "Theme for English B" comes much later in Hughes's career but carries the suppressed anger that appears intermittently in his work.

Theme for English B   1951

The instructor said,

Go home and write
a page tonight.
And let that page come out of you—
5   *Then, it will be true.*

I wonder if it's that simple?
I am twenty-two, colored, born in Winston-Salem.
I went to school there, then Durham,[1] then here

---

1   lines 7–8: Winston-Salem, Durham = cities in North Carolina (both are textile manufacturing centres)

to this college on the hill above Harlem.
10   I am the only colored student in my class.
The steps from the hill lead down into Harlem,
through a park, then I cross St. Nicholas,
Eighth Avenue, Seventh, and I come to the Y,
the Harlem Branch Y, where I take the elevator
15   up to my room, sit down, and write this page:

It's not easy to know what is true for you or me
at twenty-two, my age. But I guess I'm what
I feel and see and hear. Harlem, I hear you:
hear you, hear me—we two—you, me, talk on this page.
20   (I hear New York, too.) Me—who?
Well, I like to eat, sleep, drink, and be in love.
I like to work, read, learn, and understand life.
I like a pipe for a Christmas present,
or records—Bessie,[2] bop, or Bach.
25   I guess being colored doesn't make me *not* like
the same things other folks like who are other races.
So will my page be colored that I write?

Being me, it will not be white.
But it will be
30   a part of you, instructor.
You are white—
yet a part of me, as I am a part of you.
That's American.
Sometimes perhaps you don't want to be a part of me.
35   Nor do I often want to be a part of you.
But we are, that's true!
As I learn from you,
I guess you learn from me—
although you're older—and white—
40   and somewhat more free.

This is my page for English B.

---

2   Bessie Smith, the blues singer

Earle Birney

Canada 1904–1995

Earle Birney grew up in Alberta and British Columbia, developing early in his life a respect and love for the Canadian landscape. After spending many years at university, Birney joined the Canadian army and served three years. After World War II, he joined the English faculty at UBC where he remained until his retirement in 1965. An unceasing experimenter, Birney published his first book of verses, *David and Other Poems*, in 1942. In *The Cow That Jumped Over the Moon* (1972), Birney discusses the composition of a number of his poems. Birney's breadth is illustrated by the differences in subject and treatment apparent in "Vancouver Lights" and "The Bear on the Delhi Road." In each, however, the image patterns and narrative frames interact to assist us in understanding the contexts explored, one threatening and defiant, one potentially uplifting.

Vancouver Lights 1941

About me the night   moonless   wimples the mountains
wraps ocean   land   air   and mounting
sucks at the stars   The city   throbbing below
webs the sable peninsula   The golden
5   strands overleap the seajet   by bridge and buoy
vault the shears of the inlet   climb the woods
toward me   falter   and halt   Across to the firefly
haze of a ship on the gulf's erased horizon
roll the lambent spokes of a lighthouse

10   Through the feckless years we have come to the time
when to look on this quilt of lamps is a troubling delight
Welling from Europe's bog   through Africa flowing
and Asia   drowning the lonely lumes on the oceans
tiding up over Halifax   now to this winking
15   outpost comes flooding the primal ink

On this mountain's brutish forehead with terror of space
I stir   of the changeless night and the stark ranges
of nothing   pulsing down from beyond and between
the fragile planets   We are a spark beleaguered
20   by darkness   this twinkle we make in a corner of emptiness
how shall we utter our fear that the black Experimentress
will never in the range of her microscope find it?   Our Phoebus
himself is a bubble that dries on Her slide   while the Nubian
wears for an evening's whim a necklace of nebulae

25 Yet we must speak   we the unique glowworms
Out of the waters and rocks of our little world
we conjured these flames   hooped these sparks
by our will   From blankness and cold we fashioned stars
to our size   and signalled Aldebaran
30 This must we say   whoever may be to hear us
if murk devour   and none weave again in gossamer:

                                    These rays were ours
we made and unmade them   Not the shudder of continents
doused us   the moon's passion   nor crash of comets
35 In the fathomless heat of our dwarfdom   our dream's combustion
we contrived the power   the blast that snuffed us
No one bound Prometheus   Himself he chained
and consumed his own bright liver   O stranger
Plutonian   descendant   or beast in the stretching night—
40 there was light

The Bear on the Delhi Road   1962

Unreal   tall as a myth
by the road the Himalayan bear
is beating the brilliant air
with his crooked arms
5 About him two men   bare
spindly as locusts   leap

One pulls on a ring
in the great soft nose   His mate
flicks   flicks with a stick
10 up at the rolling eyes

They have not led him here
down from the fabulous hills
to this bald alien plain
and the clamorous world   to kill
15 but simply to teach him to dance

They are peaceful both   these spare
men of Kashmir   and the bear
alive is their living   too
If   far on the Delhi way
20 around him galvanic they dance
it is merely to wear   wear
from his shaggy body the tranced

wish forever to stay
only an ambling bear
25 four-footed in berries

It is no more joyous for them
in this hot dust to prance
out of reach of the praying claws
sharpened to paw for ants
30 in the shadows of deodars[1]
It is not easy to free
myth from reality
or rear this fellow up
to lurch   lurch with them
35 in the tranced dancing of men

---

1   A Himalayan cedar tree: the name means "divine tree of the gods."

W.H. Auden

England/U.S.A. 1907–1973

Born in York, Wystan Hugh Auden was educated in Norfolk and Oxford. In the 1930s he forged an association with a group of English poets bound by their Marxist outlook and sense that European culture had been found seriously wanting in World War I and its aftermath. Auden's poetry is characterized by wit, technical experiment, and startling imagery. Although gay, in 1935 Auden married Erica Mann, Thomas Mann's daughter, to allow her to escape the persecution of Jews in Germany. Auden immigrated to the United States at the start of World War II and became an American citizen in 1946. Auden's fondness for employing strong, simple rhythms to explore complex ironies is showcased in "As I Walked Out One Evening." Musée des Beaux Arts" combines Auden's wit and acerbic tone in its presentation of ordinary people's lack of interest in a fabulous event.

Musée des Beaux Arts   1940

About suffering they were never wrong,
The Old Masters: how well they understood
Its human position; how it takes place
While someone else is eating or opening a window or just walking
    dully along;

5 How, when the aged are reverently, passionately waiting
For the miraculous birth, there always must be
Children who did not specially want it to happen, skating
On a pond at the edge of the wood:

They never forgot
10 That even the dreadful martyrdom must run its course
Anyhow in a corner, some untidy spot
Where the dogs go on with their doggy life and the torturer's horse
Scratches its innocent behind on a tree.

In Brueghel's *Icarus*,[1] for instance: how everything turns away
15 Quite leisurely from the disaster; the ploughman may
Have heard the splash, the forsaken cry,
But for him it was not an important failure; the sun shone
As it had to on the white legs disappearing into the green
Water; and the expensive delicate ship that must have seen
20 Something amazing, a boy falling out of the sky,
Had somewhere to get to and sailed calmly on.

---

1 This painting by the Flemish master Pieter Brueghel the Elder shows Icarus
(Daedalus's son, whose wax wings had melted) as a tiny object in the background
falling from the heavens into the sea. (For a different treatment of this myth, see
Lorna Crozier's "Poem about Nothing.")

As I Walked Out One Evening   1940

As I walked out one evening,
   Walking down Bristol Street,
The crowds upon the pavement
   Were fields of harvest wheat.

5 And down by the brimming river
   I heard a lover sing
Under an arch of the railway:
   "Love has no ending.

"I'll love you, dear, I'll love you
10   Till China and Africa meet,
And the river jumps over the mountain
   And the salmon sing in the street.

    "I'll love you till the ocean
      Is folded and hung up to dry,
15 And the seven stars go squawking
      Like geese about the sky.

    "The years shall run like rabbits,
      For in my arms I hold
    The Flower of the Ages,
20   And the first love of the world."

    But all the clocks in the city
      Began to whirr and chime:
    "O let not Time deceive you,
      You cannot conquer Time.

25 In the burrows of the Nightmare
      Where Justice naked is,
    Time watches from the shadow
      And coughs when you would kiss.

    "In headaches and in worry
30   Vaguely life leaks away,
    And Time will have his fancy
      Tomorrow or to-day.

    "Into many a green valley
      Drifts the appalling snow;
35 Time breaks the threaded dances
      And the diver's brilliant bow.

    "O plunge your hands in water,
      Plunge them in up to the wrist;
    Stare, stare in the basin
40   And wonder what you've missed.

    "The glacier knocks in the cupboard,
      The desert sighs in the bed,
    And the crack in the tea-cup opens
      A lane to the land of the dead.

45 "Where the beggars raffle the banknotes
      And the Giant is enchanting to Jack,
    And the Lily-white Boy is a Roarer,
      And Jill goes down on her back.

"O look, look in the mirror,
50   O look in your distress;
Life remains a blessing
    Although you cannot bless.

"O stand, stand at the window
    As the tears scald and start;
55 You shall love your crooked neighbor
    With your crooked heart."

It was late, late in the evening,
    The lovers they were gone;
The clocks had ceased their chiming,
60   And the deep river ran on.

Theodore Roethke

U.S.A. 1908–1963

Theodore Roethke grew up in Saginaw, Michigan, where his family was involved in the greenhouse business. From 1947 until his death in 1963, Roethke taught poetry and writing at the University of Washington. Roethke's attachment to nature shows in his poetry, but it is not a sentimentalized nature. He saw himself as part of a poetic lineage that included writers like Emerson, Thoreau, Whitman, Blake, and Wordsworth, so it is not surprising to see him moving to meditative poetry at the end of his life. "My Papa's Waltz" accurately conveys the speaker's mixed feelings of love, joy, and fear as his father drunkenly dances with him.

My Papa's Waltz   1942

The whiskey on your breath
Could make a small boy dizzy;
But I hung on like death:
Such waltzing was not easy.

5   We romped until the pans
Slid from the kitchen shelf;
My mother's countenance
Could not unfrown itself.

The hand that held my wrist
10   Was battered on one knuckle;
At every step you missed
My right ear scraped a buckle.

You beat time on my head
With a palm caked hard by dirt,
15   Then waltzed me off to bed
Still clinging to your shirt.

Dorothy Livesay

Canada 1909–1996

Dorothy Livesay was born in Winnipeg to two newspaper reporters and educated
at the University of Toronto and the Sorbonne. Livesay's work covers a number
of periods and perspectives. Her poetry from the 1930s reflects the social problems associated with the Canadian Prairies and the politics of the Left. Her later
poetry is, in contrast, reflective, personal, sensual, and confessional. While
Livesay's strong social conscience is apparent in her commentary on sexual and
social roles, her sense of image and metaphor permeates all of her work.

Bartok[1] and the Geranium   1955

    She lifts her green umbrellas
    Towards the pane
    Seeking her fill of sunlight
    Or of rain;
5   Whatever falls
    She has no commentary
    Accepts, extends,
    Blows out her furbelows,
    Her bustling boughs;

10 And all the while he whirls
    Explodes in space,
    Never content with this small room;
    Not even can he be
    Confined to sky
15 But must speed high
    From galaxy to galaxy,
    Wrench from the stars their momentary calm,
    Stir music on the moon.

    She's daylight;
20 He is dark,
    She's heaven's held breath;
    He storms and crackles
    Spits with hell's own spark.

    Yet in this room, this moment now
25 These together breathe and be:

---

1 Béla Bartók (1881–1945), Hungarian pianist and composer

She, essence of serenity,
He in a mad intensity
Soars beyond sight
Then hurls, lost Lucifer,[2]
30   From heaven's height.
And when he's done, he's out:

She lays a lip against the glass
And preens herself in light.

---

2   Satan

And Give Us Our Trespasses   1966

I

Sometimes the room shakes
as the bed did shake
under love
sometimes
5   there's this
      earthquake.

II

As if at midnight
a socket
was plunged in the wall
10   and eyes sprang open.

III

Whenever I speak
      out of turn, is it?
you press your fingers
      against my mouth:
15   "Listen."

I hear only your heartbeat.

IV

My tongue
    is too long
my kiss

20   too short
    inadequate   I shrink
        from perfection.

V

Yet charged—
    your beauty charges me:

25   the receptor trembles

    quivering water
        under the smite
            of sunlight.

VI

The telephone
30   hangs on the wall
    always available
        for transmitting messages:

    why is it
        to lift the receiver
35   is to push the weight
        of a mountain?

VII

Between the impulse to speak
    and the speaking
storms crackle.

40   Forgive us our

        distances.

Elizabeth Bishop

U.S.A. 1911–1979

Elizabeth Bishop was born in Worcester, Massachusetts, but, following her father's death and her mother's mental decline, Bishop spent her childhood living with her maternal grandparents in Great Village, Nova Scotia. Bishop completed her education at Vassar College where, in her final year, she met and became friends with Marianne Moore. Bishop travelled in Europe in the late 1930s, and, in 1942, the same year she befriended Robert Lowell, she met Lota de Macedo Sorares, whom she lived with in Brazil for sixteen years. Bishop won the Pulitzer Prize, the National Book Award, the National Book Critics Circle Award, and the Books Abroad/Neustadt Prize. "The Moose" speaks to the strong influence her childhood summers in Nova Scotia with her maternal grandparents had on her.

The Moose   1976

For Grace Bulmer Bowers

From narrow provinces
of fish and bread and tea,
home of the long tides
where the bay leaves the sea
5   twice a day and takes
the herrings long rides,

where if the river
enters or retreats
in a wall of brown foam
10   depends on if it meets
the bay coming in,
the bay not at home;

where, silted red,
sometimes the sun sets
15   facing a red sea,
and others, veins the flats'
lavender, rich mud
in burning rivulets;

on red, gravelly roads,
20   down rows of sugar maples,
past clapboard farmhouses

and neat, clapboard churches,
bleached, ridged as clamshells,
past twin silver birches,

25   through late afternoon
a bus journeys west,
the windshield flashing pink,
pink glancing off of metal,
brushing the dented flank
30   of blue, beat-up enamel;

down hollows, up rises,
and waits, patient, while
a lone traveller gives
kisses and embraces
35   to seven relatives
and a collie supervises.

Goodbye to the elms,
to the farm, to the dog.
The bus starts. The light
40   grows richer; the fog,
shifting, salty, thin,
comes closing in.

Its cold, round crystals
form and slide and settle
45   in the white hens' feathers,
in gray glazed cabbages,
on the cabbage roses
and lupins like apostles;

the sweet peas cling
50   to their wet white string
on the whitewashed fences;
bumblebees creep
inside the foxgloves,
and evening commences.

55   One stop at Bass River.
Then the Economies—
Lower, Middle, Upper;
Five Islands, Five Houses,
where a woman shakes a tablecloth
60   out after supper.

A pale flickering. Gone.
The Tantramar marshes

and the smell of salt hay.
An iron bridge trembles
65   and a loose plank rattles
but doesn't give way.

On the left, a red light
swims through the dark;
a ship's port lantern.
70   Two rubber boots show,
illuminated, solemn.
A dog gives one bark.

A woman climbs in
with two market bags,
75   brisk, freckled, elderly.
'A grand night. Yes, sir,
all the way to Boston.'
She regards us amicably.

Moonlight as we enter
80   the New Brunswick woods,
hairy, scratchy, splintery;
moonlight and mist
caught in them like lamb's wool
on bushes in a pasture.

85   The passengers lie back.
Snores. Some long sighs.
A dreamy divagation
begins in the night,
a gentle, auditory,
90   slow hallucination. . . .

In the creakings and noises,
an old conversation
—not concerning us,
but recognizable, somewhere,
95   back in the bus:
Grandparents' voices

uninterruptedly
talking, in Eternity:
names being mentioned,
100   things cleared up finally;
what he said, what she said,
who got pensioned;

deaths, deaths and sicknesses;
the year he remarried;
105   the year (something) happened.
She died in childbirth.
That was the son lost
when the schooner foundered.

He took to drink. Yes.
110   She went to the bad.
When Amos began to pray
even in the store and
finally the family had
to put him away.

115   'Yes ...' that peculiar
affirmative. 'Yes ...'
A sharp, indrawn breath,
half groan, half acceptance,
that means 'Life's like that.
120   We know it (also death).'

Talking the way they talked
in the old featherbed,
peacefully, on and on,
dim lamplight in the hall,
125   down in the kitchen, the dog
tucked in her shawl.

Now, it's all right now
even to fall asleep
just as on all those nights
130   —Suddenly the bus driver
stops with a jolt,
turns off his lights.

A moose has come out of
the impenetrable wood
135   and stands there, looms, rather,
in the middle of the road.
It approaches; it sniffs at
the bus's hot hood.

Towering, antlerless,
140   high as a church,
homely as a house
(or, safe as houses).
A man's voice assures us

'Perfectly harmless….'

145   Some of the passengers
      exclaim in whispers,
      childishly, softly,
      'Sure are big creatures.'
      'It's awful plain.'
150   'Look! It's a she!'

      Taking her time,
      she looks the bus over,
      grand, otherworldly.
      Why, why do we feel
155   (we all feel) this sweet
      sensation of joy?

      'Curious creatures,'
      says our quiet driver,
      rolling his r's.
160   'Look at that, would you.'
      Then he shifts gears.
      For a moment longer,

      by craning backward,
      the moose can be seen
165   on the moonlit macadam;
      then there's a dim
      smell of moose, an acrid
      smell of gasoline.

Irving Layton

Canada 1912–

Irving Layton carries a reputation that can seem larger than the man; he has
even acknowledged his occasional assumption of masks: the satyr, the
declaiming rebel, the mystic. Growing up in Montreal after emigrating from
Romania, Layton fell in love with poetry at an early age and was immersed in
the turbulent poetry scene of the 1940s, which marked the beginning of his
association with Louis Dudek and John Sutherland. Layton insists on poetry's
personal and prophetic function. His humour, aggression, and sense of the
world's violence are evident in "Whatever Else Poetry Is Freedom."

Whatever Else Poetry Is Freedom   1958

Whatever else poetry is freedom.
Forget the rhetoric, the trick of lying
All poets pick up sooner or later. From the river,
Rising like the thin voice of grey castratos—the mist;
5   Poplars and pines grow straight but oaks are gnarled;
Old codgers must speak of death, boys break windows;
Women lie honestly by their men at last.

And I who gave my Kate a blackened eye
Did to its vivid changing colours
10   Make up an incredible musical scale;
And now I balance on wooden stilts and dance
And thereby sing to the loftiest casements.
See how with polish I bow from the waist.
Space for these stilts! More space or I fail!

15   And a crown I say for my buffoon's head.
Yet no more fool am I than King Canute,
Lord of our tribe, who scanned and scorned;
Who half-deceived, believed; and, poet, missed
The first white waves come nuzzling at his feet;
20   Then damned the courtiers and the foolish trial
With a most bewildering and unkingly jest.

It was the mist. It lies inside one like a destiny.
A real Jonah it lies rotting like a lung.
And I know myself undone who am a clown
25   And wear a wreath of mist for a crown;
Mist with the scent of dead apples,
Mist swirling from black oily waters at evening,
Mist from the fraternal graves of cemeteries.

It shall drive me to beg my food and at last
30   Hurl me broken I know and prostrate on the road;
Like a huge toad I saw, entire but dead,
That Time mordantly had blacked; O pressed
To the moist earth it pled for entry.
I shall be I say that stiff toad for sick with mist
35   And crazed I smell the odour of mortality.

And Time flames like a paraffin stove
And what it burns are the minutes I live.
At certain middays I have watched the cars
Bring me from afar their windshield suns;
40   What lay to my hand were blue fenders,

The suns extinguished, the drivers wearing sunglasses.
And it made me think I had touched a hearse.

So whatever else poetry is freedom. Let
Far off the impatient cadences reveal
45   A padding for my breathless stilts. Swivel,
O hero, in the fleshy groves, skin and glycerine,
And sing of lust, the sun's accompanying shadow
Like a vampire's wing, the stillness in dead feet—
Your stave brings resurrection, O aggrievèd king.

Dylan Thomas

Wales 1914–1953

Dylan Thomas's American reading tours confirmed his reputation as an inspired
poet-performer with an unforgettable voice. In sharp contrast to the public persona was the solitary Thomas who meticulously revised his lines and was
devoted to his craft. Born in Swansea, Wales, Thomas struggled throughout his
married life to support himself and his family; his readings were but one means
to that end. He brought to poetry surrealism and difficult imagery. If "Fern
Hill" explores the mystery of mortality through the mask of childhood, "Poem
in October" offers a similar thematic journey but this time through the mask of
age; Thomas died just seven years after the poem was published.

Poem in October   1945, 1946

It was my thirtieth year to heaven
Woke to my hearing from harbour and neighbour wood
And the mussel pooled and the heron
Priested shore
5   The morning beckon
With water praying and call of seagull and rook
And the knock of sailing boats on the webbed wall
Myself to set foot
That second
10   In the still sleeping town and set forth.

My birthday began with the water-
Birds and the birds of the winged trees flying my name
Above the farms and the white horses
And I rose
15   In a rainy autumn

And walked abroad in a shower of all my days
High tide and the heron dived when I took the road
     Over the border
       And the gates
20   Of the town closed as the town awoke.

    A springful of larks in a rolling
Cloud and the roadside bushes brimming with whistling
     Blackbirds and the sun of October
       Summery
25   On the hill's shoulder,
Here were fond climates and sweet singers suddenly
Come in the morning where I wandered and listened
     To the rain wringing
       Wind blow cold
30   In the wood faraway under me.

    Pale rain over the dwindling harbour
And over the sea wet church the size of a snail
     With its horns through mist and the castle
       Brown as owls
35   But all the gardens
Of spring and summer were blooming in the tall tales
Beyond the border and under the lark full cloud.
     There could I marvel
       My birthday
40   Away but the weather turned around.

    It turned away from the blithe country
And down the other air and the blue altered sky
     Streamed again a wonder of summer
       With apples
45   Pears and red currants
And I saw in the turning so clearly a child's
Forgotten mornings when he walked with his mother
     Through the parables
       Of sun light
50   And the legends of the green chapels

    And the twice told fields of infancy
That his tears burned my cheeks and his heart moved in mine.
     These were the woods the river and sea
       Where a boy
55   In the listening
Summertime of the dead whispered the truth of his joy
To the trees and the stones and the fish in the tide.
     And the mystery
       Sang alive

60   Still in the water and singingbirds.

     And there could I marvel my birthday
Away but the weather turned around. And the true
     Joy of the long dead child sang burning
          In the sun.
65   It was my thirtieth
Year to heaven stood there then in the summer noon
Though the town below lay leaved with October blood.
        O may my heart's truth
         Still be sung
70   On this high hill in a year's turning.

Fern Hill   1946

Now as I was young and easy under the apple boughs
About the lilting house and happy as the grass was green,
    The night above the dingle starry,
      Time let me hail and climb
5   Golden in the heydeys of his eyes,
And honoured among wagons I was prince of the apple towns
And once below a time I lordly had the trees and leaves
      Trail with daisies and barley
    Down the rivers of the windfall light.

10   And as I was green and carefree, famous among the barns
About the happy yard and singing as the farm was home,
      In the sun that is young once only,
       Time let me play and be
      Golden in the mercy of his means,
15   And green and golden I was huntsman and herdsman, the calves
Sang to my horn, the foxes on the hills barked clear and cold,
       And the sabbath rang slowly
      In the pebbles of the holy streams.

    All the sun long it was running, it was lovely, the hay
20   Fields high as the house, the tunes from the chimneys, was air
      And playing, lovely and watery
        And fire green as grass.
        And nightly under the simple stars
As I rode to sleep the owls were bearing the farm away,
25   All the moon long I heard, blessed among stables, the night-jars

Flying with the ricks,[1] and the horses
Flashing into the dark.

And then to awake, and the farm, like a wanderer white
With the dew, come back, the cock on his shoulder: it was all
30   Shining, it was Adam and maiden,
The sky gathered again
And the sun grew round that very day,
So it must have been after the birth of the simple light
In the first, spinning place, the spellbound horses walking warm
35   Out of the whinnying green stable
On to the fields of praise.

And honoured among foxes and pheasants by the gay house
Under the new made clouds and happy as the heart was long,
In the sun born over and over,
40   I ran my heedless ways,
My wishes raced through the house high hay
And nothing I cared, at my sky blue trades, that time allows
In all his tuneful turning so few and such morning songs
Before the children green and golden
45   Follow him out of grace,

Nothing I cared, in the lamb white days, that time would take me
Up to the swallow thronged loft by the shadow of my hand,
In the moon that is always rising,
Nor that riding to sleep
50   I should hear him fly with the high fields
And wake to the farm forever fled from the childless land.
Oh as I was young and easy in the mercy of his means,
Time held me green and dying
Though I sang in my chains like the sea.

---

1 hayricks or haystacks

P.K. Page

Canada 1916–

Born in Swanage, Dorset, Patricia Kathleen Page was raised and educated in
Calgary. Although best known for her poetry, Page has also written short stories, a
novel, a play, and children's books and has painted under the name P.K. Irwin.
She has lived in numerous places in Canada and in Mexico, Brazil, and Australia
when her husband was in the Canadian diplomatic corps. Page's work is known
for its strong imagery and ever-changing imaginative perspectives. "Stories of
Snow" was inspired by a conversation Page had with a man from Holland. The
title poem from her new anthology *Planet Earth* was chosen by the United Nations
to be read at several international locations as part of the UN project *Dialogue
Among Civilizations Through Poetry*. "A Grain of Sand" uses as its poetic concept the
glosa, a Spanish poetic form that dates back to the fourteenth century, whereby a
poet takes the opening quatrain of another poet's work to, as Page notes, "pay
homage to…poets." In particular, "A Grain of Sand" elicits an interesting comparison between the visionary qualities of her work and William Blake's.

Stories of Snow   1946

Those in the vegetable rain retain
an area behind their sprouting eyes
held soft and rounded with the dream of snow
precious and reminiscent as those globes—
5   souvenir of some never-nether land—
which hold their snow-storms circular, complete,
high in a tall and teakwood cabinet.

In countries where the leaves are large as hands
where flowers protrude their fleshy chins
10   and call their colours,
an imaginary snow-storm sometimes falls
among the lilies.
And in the early morning one will waken
to think the glowing linen of his pillow
15   a northern drift, will find himself mistaken
and lie back weeping.
And there the story shifts from head to head,
of how in Holland, from their feather beds
hunters arise and part the flakes and go
20   forth to the frozen lakes in search of swans—
the snow-light falling white along their guns,
their breath in plumes.
While tethered in the wind like sleeping gulls

ice-boats wait the raising of their wings
25   to skim the electric ice at such a speed
they leap jet strips of naked water,
and how these flying, sailing hunters feel
air in their mouths as terrible as ether.
And on the story runs that even drinks
30   in that white landscape dare to be no colour;
how flasked and water clear, the liquor slips
silver against the hunters' moving hips.
And of the swan in death these dreamers tell
of its last flight and how it falls, a plummet,
35   pierced by the freezing bullet
and how three feathers, loosened by the shot,
descend like snow upon it.
While hunters plunge their fingers in its down
deep as a drift, and dive their hands
40   up to the neck of the wrist
in that warm metamorphosis of snow
as gentle as the sort that woodsmen know
who, lost in the white circle, fall at last
and dream their way to death.

45   And stories of this kind are often told
in countries where great flowers bar the roads
with reds and blues which seal the route to snow—
as if, in telling, raconteurs unlock
the colour with its complement and go
50   through to the area behind the eyes
where silent, unrefractive whiteness lies.

A Grain of Sand[1]   2002

To See a World in a Grain of Sand
And a Heaven in a Wild Flower,
Hold Infinity in the palm of your hand,
And Eternity in an hour.[2]

WILLIAM BLAKE

---

1   "A Grain of Sand" was written for the children's chorus of an oratorio entitled *The Invisible Reality* composed by Derek Holman, and performed at Roy Thomson Hall in 2000.

2   The first four lines of Blake's "Auguries of Innocence," from the second series of *Verses and Fragments* (1800–1810).

Only a fly with its compound eye
an ant, a beetle, a dragonfly
or a child on a beach on a summer day
with time to idle the hours away
5   in the tiniest grain of sand can see
a limitless world of mystery
with suns that circle and stars that shoot
and golden boughs bearing silver fruit.
Can see in a daisy in the grass
10   angels and archangels pass
unfolding wings of dazzling white
to set the darkening earth alight.
See outer space become so small
that the hand of a child could hold it all.
15   Know eons pass, an hour slip by
like a scudding cloud in a windy sky.
With a wink and a blink an age is done.
Old Father Time is a boy again.

To See a World in a Grain of Sand
20   *And a Heaven in a Wild Flower,*
Hold Infinity in the palm of your hand,
And Eternity in an hour.

Margaret Avison

Canada 1918–

Margaret Avison grew up in Galt, Ontario, and Alberta. She has worked in various fields, including librarianship and social work. She has also been the University of Western Ontario's writer-in-residence. Her first collection of poetry, *Winter Sun* (1960), won a Governor General's Award; her recent book *Concrete and Wild Carrot* won the 2003 Griffin Prize for Excellence in Poetry. In her earlier poems, like "Snow," Avison uses imagery to comment on the human condition. Her embracing of Christianity in 1963 is presaged by some of her probing remarks in poems such as "Snow."

Snow   1960

Nobody stuffs the world in at your eyes.
The optic heart must venture: a jail-break
And re-creation. Sedges and wild rice

Chase rivery pewter. The astonished cinders quake
5   With rhizomes. All ways through the electric air
Trundle candy-bright disks; they are desolate
Toys if the soul's gates seal, and cannot bear,
Must shudder under, creation's unseen freight.
But soft, there is snow's legend: colour of mourning
10   Along the yellow Yangtze where the wheel
Spins an indifferent stasis that's death's warning.
Asters of tumbled quietness reveal
Their petals. Suffering this starry blur
The rest may ring your change, sad listener.

Al Purdy

Canada 1918–2000

Al Purdy for the most part lived and worked in Ontario, near Belleville, the setting of many of his poems. He travelled widely, however, and those travels are also frequently reflected in his writings. Purdy's poems are deceptively open; his colloquial diction and tone invite the reader into the subject and/or event that the poem explores. In his poetry, we share in his responses—both playful and serious—to a wide variety of subjects. "Trees at the Arctic Circle" gives us a thoughtful Purdy slowly discovering the paradox behind the "Coward trees" and concluding with self-deprecating lines that perhaps only Purdy would use to end a poem.

Trees at the Arctic Circle   1967

(Salix Cordifolia—Ground Willow)

They are 18 inches long
or even less
crawling under rocks
grovelling among the lichens
5   bending and curling to escape
making themselves small
finding new ways to hide
Coward trees
I am angry to see them
10   like this
not proud of what they are
bowing to weather instead
careful of themselves

worried about the sky
15   afraid of exposing their limbs
like a Victorian married couple
I see tall maples waving green
and oaks like gods in autumn gold
the whole horizon jungle dark
20   and I crouched under that continual night
But these
even the dwarf shrubs of Ontario
mock them
Coward trees

25   And yet—and yet—
their seed pods glow
like delicate grey earrings
their leaves are veined and intricate
like tiny parkas
30   They have about three months
to make sure the species does not die
and that's how they spend their time
unbothered by any human opinion
just digging in here and now
35   sending their roots down down down
And you know it occurs to me
              about 2 feet under
those roots must touch permafrost
ice that remains ice forever
40   and they use it for their nourishment
they use death to remain alive

I see that I've been carried away
in my scorn of the dwarf trees
most foolish in my judgments
45   To take away the dignity
            of any living thing
even tho it cannot understand
            the scornful words
is to make life itself trivial
50   and yourself the Pontifex Maximus
            of nullity
I have been stupid in a poem
I will not alter the poem
but let the stupidity remain permanent
55   as the trees are
in a poem
the dwarf trees of Baffin Island
                Pangnirtung

Philip Larkin

England 1922–1985

Philip Larkin was born in Coventry and became a librarian after studying at
Oxford; for many years, he was the head librarian at the University of Hull.
Larkin published only four small volumes of poetry but was, nevertheless,
widely influential. He opposed the modern fondness for open form and wrote
from the perspective of a disillusioned person in a grim urban landscape devoid
of energy and variety. In "Church Going," his speaker questions the utility of the
church he has stopped at and, indeed, the utility of any faith humans create; in
the end, the speaker arrives at a provincial answer that is far less confident and
assertive than the building that provokes it.

Church Going   1954–55

Once I am sure there's nothing going on
I step inside, letting the door thud shut.
Another church: matting, seats, and stone,
And little books; sprawlings of flowers, cut
5   For Sunday, brownish now; some brass and stuff
Up at the holy end; the small neat organ;
And a tense, musty, unignorable silence,
Brewed God knows how long. Hatless, I take off
My cycle-clips[1] in awkward reverence,

10   Move forward, run my hand around the font.
From where I stand, the roof looks almost new—
Cleaned, or restored? Someone would know: I don't.
Mounting the lectern, I peruse a few
Hectoring large-scale verses, and pronounce
15   "Here endeth" much more loudly than I'd meant.
The echoes snigger briefly. Back at the door
I sign the book, donate an Irish sixpence,[2]
Reflect the place was not worth stopping for.

Yet stop I did: in fact I often do,
20   And always end much at a loss like this,
Wondering what to look for; wondering, too,
When churches fall completely out of use
What we shall turn them into, if we shall keep
A few cathedrals chronically on show,

---

1   clips worn while cycling to stop pant cuffs from getting caught in the bicycle's chain
2   An Irish sixpence was not currency in Britain.

25   Their parchment, plate and pyx[3] in locked cases,
And let the rest rent-free to rain and sheep.
Shall we avoid them as unlucky places?

Or, after dark, will dubious women come
To make their children touch a particular stone;
30   Pick simples[4] for a cancer; or on some
Advised night see walking a dead one?
Power of some sort or other will go on
In games, in riddles, seemingly at random;
But superstition, like belief, must die,
35   And what remains when disbelief has gone?
Grass, weedy pavement, brambles, buttress, sky,

A shape less recognisable each week,
A purpose more obscure. I wonder who
Will be the last, the very last, to seek
40   This place for what it was; one of the crew
That tap and jot and know what rood-lofts[5] were?
Some ruin-bibber[6], randy for antique,
Or Christmas-addict, counting on a whiff
Of gown-and-bands and organ-pipes and myrrh?
45   Or will he be my representative,

Bored, uninformed, knowing the ghostly silt
Dispersed, yet tending to this cross of ground
Through suburb scrub because it held unspilt
So long and equably what since is found
50   Only in separation—marriage, and birth,
And death, and thoughts of these—for which was built
This special shell? For, though I've no idea
What this accoutred frowsty[7] barn is worth,
It pleases me to stand in silence here;

55   A serious house on serious earth it is,
In whose blent air all our compulsions meet,
Are recognised, and robed as destinies.
And that much never can be obsolete,
Since someone will forever be surprising
60   A hunger in himself to be more serious,
And gravitating with it to this ground,
Which, he once heard, was proper to grow wise in,
If only that so many dead lie round.

---

3 communion box
4 medicinal herbs
5 galleries on top of carved screens that separate the nave from the choir
6 tippler, usually of wine; here, with ruin, used figuratively
7 stale-smelling, stuffy mouldy

Robert Creeley

U.S.A. 1926–

Robert Creeley began his life in Arlington, Massachusetts, but has since lived in many places, both in the United States and abroad. In the mid-1950s, he attended Black Mountain College and edited the *Black Mountain Review* with Charles Olson, helping to give a name to the movement of American poetry in which he was a key figure. Creeley believes that poetry should come from all moments, not simply from "high" occasions. He presents the moment in all its smallness and randomness, allowing its emotional intensity to drive the line. His description of poetry as "identity singing" is perfectly reflected in "Ballad of the Despairing Husband."

Ballad of the Despairing Husband   1955

My wife and I lived all alone,
contention was our only bone.
I fought with her, she fought with me,
And things went on right merrily.

5   But now I live here by myself
with hardly a damn thing on the shelf,
and pass my days with little cheer
since I have parted from my dear.

Oh come home soon, I write to her.
10   Go fuck yourself, is her answer.
Now what is that, for Christian word,
I hope she feeds on dried goose turd.

But still I love her, yes I do.
I love her and the children too.
15   I only think it fit that she
should quickly come right back to me.

Ah no, she says, and she is tough
and smacks me down with her rebuff.
Ah no, she says, I will not come
20   after the bloody things you've done.

Oh wife, oh wife—I tell you true,
I never loved no one but you.
I never will, it cannot be
another woman is for me.

25 That may be right, she will say then,
but as for me, there's other men.
And I will tell you I propose
to catch them firmly by the nose.

And I will wear what dresses I choose!
30 And I will dance, and what's to lose!
I'm free of you, you little prick,
and I'm the one can make it stick.

Was this the darling I did love?
Was this that mercy from above
35 did open violets in the spring—
and made my own worn self to sing?

She was. I know. And she is still,
and if I love her? then so I will.
And I will tell her, and tell her right …

40 Oh lovely lady, morning or evening or afternoon.
Oh lovely lady, eating with or without a spoon.
Oh most lovely lady, whether dressed or undressed or partly.
Oh most lovely lady, getting up or going to bed or sitting only.

Oh loveliest of ladies, than whom none is more fair,
45   more gracious, more beautiful.
Oh loveliest of ladies, whether you are just or unjust,
                             merciful, indifferent, or cruel.
Oh most loveliest of ladies, doing whatever, seeing whatever,
                             being whatever.
50 Oh most loveliest of ladies, in rain, in shine, in any weather—

Oh lady, grant me time,
please, to finish my rhyme.

Allen Ginsberg

U.S.A. 1926–1997

Born in Paterson, New Jersey, Allen Ginsberg attended Columbia University. There he met Jack Kerouac, who would lead the beat generation of poets. During the 1950s and 1960s, Ginsberg travelled to Mexico, the Arctic, and Europe, meeting up with other beat poets and developing his spontaneous, jazz-inspired poems in a style he learned from Kerouac. Ginsberg's rhythmic, incantatory verse resonates with emotion as it dwells on the excesses of mainstream American society. His first collection, *Howl and Other Poems* (1956), was seized by U.S. customs and the San Francisco police on the grounds that it was "obscene." In "A Supermarket in California," Ginsberg acknowledges his spiritual affiliation with Walt Whitman, both as a gay man and a chronicler of America's passive acceptance of materialist ideology.

A Supermarket in California   1955

What thoughts I have of you tonight, Walt Whitman, for I walked down the sidestreets under the trees with a headache self-conscious looking at the full moon.

In my hungry fatigue, and shopping for images, I went into the neon
5   fruit supermarket, dreaming of your enumerations!

What peaches and what penumbras![1] Whole families shopping at night! Aisles full of husbands! Wives in the avocados, babies in the tomatoes!

—and you, García Lorca,[2] what were you doing down by the water-
10   melons?

I saw you, Walt Whitman, childless, lonely old grubber, poking among the meats in the refrigerator and eyeing the grocery boys.

I heard you asking questions of each: Who killed the pork chops? What price bananas? Are you my Angel?
15   I wandered in and out of the brilliant stacks of cans following you, and followed in my imagination by the store detective.

We strode down the open corridors together in our solitary fancy tasting artichokes, possessing every frozen delicacy, and never passing the cashier.

20   Where are we going, Walt Whitman? The doors close in a hour. Which way does your beard point tonight?

---

1   partly shaded region
2   Spanish poet

(I touch your book and dream of our odyssey in the supermarket and feel absurd.)

Will we walk all night through solitary streets? The trees add shade
25   to shade, lights out in the houses, we'll both be lonely.

Will we stroll dreaming of the lost America of love past blue automobiles in driveways, home to our silent cottage?

Ah, dear father, graybeard, lonely old courage-teacher, what America did you have when Charon[3] quit poling his ferry and you got out on a
30   smoking bank and stood watching the boat disappear on the black waters of Lethe?

---

3   ferries the dead across the river

Phyllis Webb

Canada 1927–

Born in Victoria, British Columbia, Phyllis Webb taught at the University of British Columbia and then worked for the CBC in Toronto, creating the radio show *Ideas*. For the last thirty years, Webb has resided on Salt Spring Island, off the southeast coast of Vancouver Island, and worked at several universities in Western Canada. "The Days of the Unicorns" shows Webb's concern over how humans have, in their desire to transform the natural world, had a negative impact on their physical environment and their mythology.

The Days of the Unicorns   1980

I remember when the unicorns
roved in herds through the meadow
behind the cabin, and how they would
lately pause, tilting their jewelled
5   horns to the falling sun as we shared
the tensions of private property
and the need to be alone.

Or as we walked along the beach
a solitary delicate beast
10   might follow on his soft paws
until we turned and spoke the words
to console him.

It seemed they were always near
ready to show their eyes and stare

15 us down, standing in their creamy
skins, pink tongues out
for our benevolence.

As if they knew that always beyond
and beyond the ladies were weaving them
20 into their spider looms.

I knew where they slept
and how the grass was bent
by their own wilderness
and I pitied them.

25 It was only yesterday, or seems
like only yesterday when we could
touch and turn and they came
perfectly real into our fictions.
But they moved on with the courtly sun
30 grazing peacefully beyond the story
horns lowering and lifting and
lowering.

I know this is scarcely credible now
as we cabin ourselves in cold
35 and the motions of panic
and our cells destroy each other
performing music and extinction
and the great dreams pass on
to the common good.

Robert Kroetsch

Canada 1927–

Born and raised in Heisler, Alberta, Robert Kroetsch earned a B.A. at the University of Alberta, worked at various jobs in northwest Canada, and moved east to earn an M.A. at the Bread Loaf School of English at Middlebury College, Vermont, and a Ph.D. at the University of Iowa. Kroetsch worked at the State University of New York, Binghamton, before returning to Canada to teach at universities in Lethbridge, Calgary, and Winnipeg. His long poem *Seed Catalogue* has autobiographical and thematic elements that link it to "Stone Hammer Poem" and *The Ledger*. In these poems, Kroetsch playfully examines the world from a central Albertan perspective. In *Seed Catalogue*, for example, he comments that a prairie road is "the shortest distance / between nowhere and nowhere. / This road is a poem."

From Seed Catalogue   1977

1

No. 176—*Copenhagen Market Cabbage:* 'This *new introduction,*
strictly speaking, is in every respect *a thoroughbred,* a *cabbage* of
highest pedigree, and is *creating considerable flurry among profes-*
sional gardeners all *over the world.*'

5   We took the storm windows/off
the south side of the house
and put them on the hotbed.
Then it was spring. Or, no:
then winter was ending.

10   'I wish to say we had lovely success
this summer with the seed purchased
of you. We had the finest Sweet
Corn in the country. and Cabbage
were dandy.
15   —W.W. Lyon, South Junction, Man.

My mother said:
Did you wash your ears?
You could grow cabbages
in those ears.

20   Winter was ending.
This is what happened:
we were harrowing the garden.
You've got to understand this:
I was sitting on the horse.
25   The horse was standing still.
I fell off.

The hired man laughed: how
in hell did you manage to
fall off a horse that was
30   *standing still?*

Bring me the radish seeds,
my mother whispered.

Into the dark of January
the seed catalogue bloomed

35   a winter proposition, if
spring should come, then,

with illustrations:

No. 25—*McKenzie's Improved Golden Wax Bean:* 'THE MOST PRIZED OF
ALL BEANS. *Virtue* is its own reward. We have had many *expressions*
40   from *keen discriminating gardeners extolling our seed* and *this variety.'*

> Beans, beans,
> the musical fruit;
> the more you eat,
> the more you virtue.

45   My mother was marking the first row
with a piece of binder twine, stretched
between two pegs.

The hired man laughed: just
about planted the little bugger.
50   Cover him up and see what grows.
My father didn't laugh. He was puzzled
by any garden that was smaller than a
quarter-section of wheat and summerfallow.

the home place: N.E. 17-42-16-W4th Meridian.

55   the home place: one and a half miles west of Heisler, Alberta,

> on the correction line road
> and three miles south

No trees
around the house.
60   Only the wind.
Only the January snow.
Only the summer sun.
The home place:
a terrible symmetry.

65   *How do you grow a gardener?*

> Telephone Peas
> Garden Gem Carrots
> Early Snowcap Cauliflower
> Perfection Globe Onions
70   Hubbard Squash
> Early Ohio Potatoes

This is what happened—at my mother's wake. This
is a fact—the World Series was in progress. The
Cincinnati Reds were playing the Detroit Tigers.
75 It was raining. The road to the graveyard was barely
passable. The horse was standing still. Bring me
the radish seeds, my mother whispered.

2

My father was mad at the badger: the badger was digging holes in the potato
patch, threatening man and beast with broken limbs (I quote). My father
80 took the double-barrelled shotgun out into the potato patch and waited.

Every time the badger stood up, it looked like a little man, come out of the
ground. Why, my father asked himself—Why would so fine a fellow live
under the ground? Just for the cool of roots? The solace of dark tunnels? The
blood of gophers?

85 My father couldn't shoot the badger. He uncocked the shotgun, came back
to the house in time for breakfast. The badger dug another hole. My father
got mad again. They carried on like that all summer.

> *Love is an amplification*
> *by doing/over and over.*

90 > *Love is a standing up*
> *to the loaded gun.*

> *Love is a burrowing.*

One morning my father actually shot at the badger. He killed a magpie that
was pecking away at a horse turd about fifty feet beyond and to the right of
95 the spot where the badger had been standing.

A week later my father told the story again. In that version he intended to hit the
magpie. Magpies, he explained, are a nuisance. They eat robins' eggs. They're
harder to kill than snakes, jumping around the way they do, nothing but feathers.

Just call me sure-shot,
100 my father added.
    . . . .

4

It arrived in winter, the seed catalogue, on a January
day. It came into town on the afternoon train.

Mary Hauck, when she came west from Bruce County, Ontario,
arrived in town on a January day. She brought along
105   her hope chest.

She was cooking in the Heisler Hotel. The Heisler Hotel
burned down on the night of June 21, 1919. Everything
in between: lost. Everything: an absence

of satin sheets
110   of embroidered pillow cases
of tea towels and English china
of silver serving spoons.

How do you grow a prairie town?

The gopher was the model.
115   Stand up straight:
telephone poles
grain elevators
church steeples.
Vanish, suddenly: the
120   gopher was the model.

How do you grow a past/
to live in

the absence of silkworms
the absence of clay and wattles (whatever the hell
125   they are)
the absence of Lord Nelson
the absence of kings and queens
the absence of a bottle opener, and me with a vicious
attack of the 26 ounce flu
130   the absence of both Sartre and Heidegger
the absence of pyramids
the absence of lions
the absence of lutes, violas and xylophones
the absence of a condom dispenser in the Lethbridge Hotel and
135   me about to screw an old Blood whore. I was
in love.
the absence of the Parthenon, not to mention the Cathédrale de
Chartres
the absence of psychiatrists
140   the absence of sailing ships
the absence of books, journals, daily newspapers and everything
else but the *Free Press Prairie Farmer* and *The
Western Producer*
the absence of gallows (with apologies to Louis Riel)
145   the absence of goldsmiths

the absence of the girl who said that if the Edmonton Eskimos
     won the Grey Cup she'd let me kiss her
     nipples in the foyer of the Palliser Hotel. I
     don't know where she got to.
150   the absence of Heraclitus[1]
     the absence of the Seine, the Rhine, the Danube, the Tiber and
     the Thames. Shit, the Battle River ran dry
     one fall. The Strauss boy could piss across it.
     He could piss higher on a barn wall than any
155   of us. He could piss right clean over the
     principal's new car.
     the absence of ballet and opera
     the absence of Aeneas

How do you grow a prairie town?

160   Rebuild the hotel when it burns down. Bigger. Fill it
     full of a lot of A-1 Hard Northern Bullshitters.

—You ever heard the one about the woman who buried
     her husband with his ass sticking out of the ground
     so that every time she happened to walk by she could
165   give it a swift kick?

—Yeh, I heard it.

5

I planted some melons, just to see what would
     happen. Gophers ate everything.

                    I applied to the Government.
170   I wanted to become a postman,
                    to deliver real words
                    to real people.

                    There was no one to receive
                    my application.

175   I don't give a damn if I do die do die do die do die do die
     do die do die do die do die do die do die do die do die do
     die do die do die do die do die do die do die do die do die
     do

---

1   the Greek philosopher who regarded the universe as a ceaselessly changing conflict of
    opposites

6

180   No. 339—*McKenzie's Pedigreed Early Snowcap Cauliflower:* 'Of the
many *varieties* of *vegetables* in *existence, Cauliflower* is *unquestionably*
one of the *greatest inheritances* of the *present generation, particularly*
Western Canadians. There is *no place* in the *world* where *better cauli-*
flowers can be *grown* than right here in the *West.* The *finest speci-*
185   *mens* we have *ever seen,* larger and of *better quality,* are *annually*
grown here on our *prairies.* Being *particularly* a *high altitude plant* it
thrives to a *point* of *perfection* here, *seldom seen* in *warmer climes.'*

But how do you grow a poet?

   Start: with an invocation
190   invoke—

   His muse is
   his muse/if
   memory is

   and you have
195   no memory then
   no meditation
   no song (shit
   we're up against it)
              how about that girl
200   you felt up in the
              school barn or that
              girl you necked with
              out by Hastings' slough
              and ran out of gas with
205   and nearly froze to
              death with/ or that
              girl in the skating
              rink shack who had on
              so much underwear you
210   didn't have enough
              prick to get past her/
              CCM skates

   Once upon a time in the village of Heisler—

   —Hey, wait a minute.
215   That's a story.

How do you grow a poet?

For appetite: cod-liver
oil.
For bronchitis: mustard
220   plasters.
For pallor and failure to fill
the woodbox: sulphur
& molasses.
For self-abuse: ten Our
225   Fathers & ten Hail Marys.
For regular bowels: Sunny Boy
Cereal.

How do you grow a poet?

'It's a pleasure to advise that I
230   won the First Prize at the Calgary
Horticultural Show … This is my
first attempt. I used your seeds.'

Son, this is a crowbar.
This is a willow fencepost.
235   This is a sledge.
This is a roll of barbed wire.
This is a bag of staples.
This is a claw hammer.

We give form to this land by running
240   a series of posts and three strands
of barbed wire around a quarter-section.

First off I want you to take that
crowbar and drive 1,156 holes
in that gumbo.
245   And the next time you want to
write a poem
we'll start the haying.

How do you grow a poet?

This is a prairie road.
250   This road is the shortest distance
between nowhere and nowhere.
This road is a poem.

Just two miles up the road
you'll find a porcupine
255   dead in the ditch. It was
trying to cross the road.

As for the poet himself
we can find no record
of his having traversed
260   the land/in either direction

no trace of his coming
or going/only a scarred
page, a spoor of wording
a reduction to mere black
265   and white/a pile of rabbit
turds that tells us
all spring long
where the track was

poet ... say uncle.

270   *How?*

Rudy Wiebe: 'You must lay great black steel lines of
fiction, break up that space with huge design and, like
the fiction of the Russian steppes, build a giant
artifact. No song can do that ...'

275   February 14, 1976. Rudy, you
took us there: to the Oldman River
Lorna & Byrna, Ralph & Steve and me
you showed us where
the Bloods surprised the Crees
280   in the next coulee/surprised
them to death. And after
you showed us Rilke's word
Lebensgliedes.[2]

Rudy: Nature thou art.

285   . . . .

10

After the bomb/blossoms   *Poet, teach us*
After the city/falls   *to love our dying.*
After the rider/falls

---

2   of the limbs of life or life link

(the horse

290 standing still)

West is a winter place.
The palimpsest[3] of prairie

under the quick erasure
of snow, invites a flight.

How/do you grow a garden?

(a)

295   No. 3060—*Spencer Sweet Pea:*
Pkt. $.10; oz. $.25;
quarter lb. $.75; half lb. $1.25.

Your sweet peas
climbed the staked
300 chicken wire,
climbing the stretched
binder twine by
the front porch

taught me the smell
305 of morning, the grace
of your tired
hands, the strength
of a noon sun, the
colour of prairie grass

310 taught me the smell
of my sweating armpits.

(b)

How do you a garden grow?
How do you grow a garden?

315 'Dear Sir,
      The longest brome grass I remember seeing was
one night in Brooks. We were on our way up to the Calgary
Stampede, and reached Brooks about 11 pm, perhaps earlier
because there was still a movie on the drive-in screen.
320 We unloaded Cindy, and I remember tying her up to the truck
box and the brome grass was up to her hips. We laid down
in the back of the truck—on some grass I pulled by hand—
and slept for about three hours, then drove into Calgary.

---

3 a piece of writing material on which the original writing has been effaced to make
room for new writing

Amie'

325 (c)

No trees
around the house,
only the wind.
Only the January snow.
330 Only the summer sun.

Adam and Eve got drownded—
Who was left?

Adrienne Rich

U.S.A. 1929–

Born in Baltimore and educated at Radcliffe College, Rich's first book of poetry
was published the year she graduated. She has published over fifteen volumes of
poetry and non-fiction and been the recipient of numerous awards. Rich's commitment to social, sexual, and political justice is evident in much of her work, as
is clear in her August 3, 1997 article "Why I Refused the National Medal for the
Arts," where she writes "I've watched the dismantling of our public education,
the steep rise in our incarceration rates, the demonization of our young black
men, the accusations against our teenage mothers, the selling of health care, …
the export of subsistence-level jobs, … the use of below-minimum-wage prison
labor to break strikes and raise profits, the scapegoating of immigrants, the
denial of dignity and minimal security to our working and poor people."

Power   1978

Living in the earth-deposits of our history

Today a backhoe divulged out of a crumbling flank of earth
one bottle amber perfect a hundred-year-old
cure for fever or melancholy a tonic
5   for living on this earth in the winters of this climate

Today I was reading about Marie Curie:
she must have known she suffered from radiation sickness
her body bombarded for years by the element
she had purified

10 It seems she denied to the end
   the source of the cataracts on her eyes
   the cracked and suppurating skin of her finger-ends
   till she could no longer hold a test-tube or a pencil

   She died a famous woman denying
15 her wounds
   denying
   her wounds came from the same source as her power

Ted Hughes

England 1930–1998

Ted Hughes was born in Mytholmroyd, Yorkshire, and took a degree at
Cambridge, where he studied archaeology, anthropology, and English literature.
While at Cambridge, he met Sylvia Plath, an American poet whom he married
in 1956 and from whom he eventually separated. Hughes was named poet
laureate in 1984. His poetry often examines the violence inherent in the natural
world. Hughes's gift for vivid and memorable imagery is evident in "The
Thought-Fox," a remarkable account of the creative process rendered through
the extended mixing of two domains.

The Thought-Fox   1957

I imagine this midnight moment's forest:
Something else is alive
Beside the clock's loneliness
And this blank page where my fingers move.

5 Through the window I see no star;
Something more near
Though deeper within darkness
Is entering the loneliness:

Cold, delicately as the dark snow,
10 A fox's nose touches twig, leaf;
Two eyes serve a movement, that now
And again now, and now, and now

Sets neat prints into the snow
Between trees, and warily a lame

15 Shadow lags by stump and in hollow
   Of a body that is bold to come

   Across clearings, an eye,
   A widening deepening greenness,
   Brilliantly, concentratedly,
20 Coming about its own business

   Till, with a sudden sharp hot stink of fox
   It enters the dark hole of the head.
   The window is starless still; the clock ticks,
   The page is printed.

Derek Walcott

St. Lucia/Jamaica/Trinidad/U.S.A. 1930–

Derek Walcott was born in the small town of Castries on an isolated island in St. Lucia, and educated there, at St. Mary's College, and at the University of the West Indies, in Jamaica. After graduating, Walcott moved to Trinidad to work. Although he now teaches creative writing and literature at Boston University, he still spends a portion of the year in Trinidad, surrounded by its mix of African, European, and Asian cultures. Walcott received the Nobel Prize for literature in 1992. He is acutely aware of how he—an educated, English-speaking native of the West Indies—carries both the traditions of European English writers and the culture and history of West Indian society. His poem "A Far Cry From Africa" illustrates how these two influences can create contradictions, just as "Central America" illustrates his concern with people and their plight.

A Far Cry From Africa   1962

A wind is ruffling the tawny pelt
Of Africa. Kikuyu,[1] quick as flies
Batten[2] upon the bloodstreams of the veldt.[3]
Corpses are scattered through a paradise.
5 But still the worm, colonel of carrion, cries:

---

1 tribe in Kenya that revolted from 1952 to 1956, recovered land from the Europeans, and attempted to revert to traditional cultural values. In 1963, Kenya gained independence from Britain.
2 thrive at the expense of others
3 Afrikaans for "open country"

'Waste no compassion on these separate dead'
Statistics justify and scholars seize
The salients of colonial policy.
What is that to the white child hacked in bed?
10   To savages, expendable as Jews?

Threshed out by beaters, the long rushes break
In a white dust of ibises whose cries
Have wheeled since civilization's dawn
From the parched river or beast-teeming plain;
15   The violence of beast on beast is read
As natural law, but upright man
Seeks his divinity with inflicting pain.

Delirious as these worried beasts, his wars
Dance to the tightened carcass of a drum,
20   While he calls courage still, that native dread
Of the white peace contracted by the dead.
Again brutish necessity wipes its hands
Upon the napkin of a dirty cause, again
A waste of our compassion, as with Spain.
25   The gorilla wrestles with the superman.

I who am poisoned with the blood of both,
Where shall I turn, divided to the vein?
I who have cursed
The drunken officer of British rule, how choose
30   Between this Africa and the English tongue I love?
Betray them both, or give back what they give?
How can I face such slaughter and be cool?
How can I turn from Africa and live?

Central America   1987

Helicopters are cutlassing the wild bananas.
Between a nicotine thumb and forefinger
brittle faces crumble like tobacco leaves.
Children waddle in vests, their legs bowed,
5   little shrimps curled under their navels.
The old men's teeth are stumps in a charred forest.
Their skins grate like the iguana's.
Their gaze like slate stones.
Women squat by the river's consolations
10   where children wade up to their knees,
and a stick stirs up a twinkling of butterflies.

Up there, in the blue acres
of forest, flies circle their fathers.
In spring, in the upper provinces
15   of the Empire, yellow tanagers
float up trhough the bare branches.
There is no distinction in these distances.

Sylvia Plath

U.S.A. 1932–1963

Born in Boston, Sylvia Plath grew up in an academic environment, as both her parents taught at Boston University. Before she graduated from Smith College, she had already been published in magazines. Plath suffered from clinical depression while still in school. Her only novel, *The Bell Jar,* and a number of her poems give insight into the mental ghosts that haunted her. After studying in England at Cambridge, Plath met and married Ted Hughes, the English poet. Their troubled marriage did not last, and in 1963 Plath committed suicide. "Lady Lazarus" directly addresses her fascination with death, underlined by the speaker's reference to this being a third attempt at suicide. Plath's poems are full of irreconcilable pain, and this one is no exception.

Lady Lazarus   1962

I have done it again.
One year in every ten
I manage it—

A sort of walking miracle, my skin
5   Bright as a Nazi lampshade,
My right foot

A paperweight,
My face a featureless, fine
Jew linen.

10   Peel off the napkin
O my enemy.
Do I terrify?—

The nose, the eye pits, the full set of teeth?
The sour breath
15   Will vanish in a day.

Soon, soon the flesh
The grave cave ate will be
At home on me

And I a smiling woman.
20   I am only thirty.
And like the cat I have nine times to die.

This is Number Three.
What a trash
To annihilate each decade.

25   What a million filaments.
The peanut-crunching crowd
Shoves in to see

Them unwrap me hand and foot—
The big strip tease.
30   Gentlemen, ladies

These are my hands
My knees.
I may be skin and bone,

Nevertheless, I am the same, identical woman.
35   The first time it happened I was ten.
It was an accident.

The second time I meant
To last it out and not come back at all.
I rocked shut

40   As a seashell.
They had to call and call
And pick the worms off me like sticky pearls.

Dying
Is an art, like everything else.
45   I do it exceptionally well.

I do it so it feels like hell.
I do it so it feels real.
I guess you could say I've a call.

It's easy enough to do it in a cell.
50   It's easy enough to do it and stay put.
It's the theatrical

Comeback in broad day
To the same place, the same face, the same brute
Amused shout:

55 'A miracle!'
That knocks me out.
There is a charge

For the eyeing of my scars, there is a charge
For the hearing of my heart—
60 It really goes.

And there is a charge, a very large charge
For a word or touch
Or a bit of blood

Or a piece of my hair or my clothes.
65 So, so, Herr Doktor.
So, Herr Enemy.

I am your opus,
I am your valuable,
The pure gold baby

70 That melts to a shriek.
I turn and burn.
Do not think I underestimate your great concern.

Ash, ash—
You poke and stir.
75 Flesh, bone, there is nothing there—

A cake of soap,
A wedding ring,
A gold filling.

Herr God, Herr Lucifer
80 Beware
Beware.

Out of the ash
I rise with my red hair
And I eat men like air.

Alden Nowlan

Canada   1933–1983

Born in Windsor, Nova Scotia, Alden Nowlan moved to New Brunswick at age
18 after he completed school. Nowlan worked as an editor on newspapers in
Hartland and St. John, and produced his first book of poetry when he was 25.
He won the Governor General's Award for Poetry in 1967 for *Bread, Wine and
Salt* and was the writer-in-residence at the University of New Brunswick for a
number of years. Nowlan's humour and his love of the people in small New
Brunswick communities are obvious in both "The Bull Moose" and "Aunt Jane."

The Bull Moose   1962

Down from the purple mist of trees on the mountain,
lurching through forests of white spruce and cedar,
stumbling through tamarack swamps,
came the bull moose
5   to be stopped at last by a pole-fenced pasture.

Too tired to turn or, perhaps, aware
there was no place left to go, he stood with the cattle.
They, scenting the musk of death, seeing his great head
like the ritual mask of a blood god, moved to the other end
10 of the field, and waited.

The neighbours heard of it, and by afternoon
cars lined the road. The children teased him
with alder switches and he gazed at them
like an old, tolerant collie. The women asked
15 if he could have escaped from a Fair.

The oldest man in the parish remembered seeing
a gelded moose yoked with an ox for plowing.
The young men snickered and tried to pour beer
down his throat, while their girlfriends
20 took their pictures.

And the bull moose let them stroke his tick-ravaged flanks,
let them pry open his jaws with bottles, let a giggling girl
plant a little purple cap
of thistles on his head.

25 When the wardens came, everyone agreed it was a shame
to shoot anything so shaggy and cuddlesome.

He looked like the kind of pet
women put to bed with their sons.

So they held their fire. But just as the sun dropped in the river
30   the bull moose gathered his strength
like a scaffolded king, straightened and lifted his horns
so that even the wardens backed away as they raised their rifles.
When he roared, people ran to their cars. All the young men
leaned on their automobile horns as he toppled.

Aunt Jane   1962

Aunt Jane, of whom I dreamed the nights it thundered,
was dead at ninety, buried at a hundred.
We kept her corpse a decade, hid upstairs,
where it ate porridge, slept and said its prayers.

5   And every night before I went to bed
they took me in to worship with the dead.
Christ Lord, if I should die before I wake,
I pray thee Lord my body take.

Leonard Cohen

Canada 1934–

Leonard Cohen, a native of Montreal, went to McGill University. After finishing his
education, Cohen focused on his writing. His first book of poetry, *Let Us Compare
Mythologies* (1956), inaugurated the McGill Poetry Series, but it was his work
between 1961 and 1966 that brought him to prominence as a poet, songwriter, and
pop performer. Cohen's work reflects some of the earlier macabre images and
themes developed by Irving Layton. The themes of master and slave, beauty and
destruction, saint and loser are interspersed throughout Cohen's work, as is a
strong romantic sensuality, which is present in "You Have the Lovers."

You Have the Lovers   1961

You have the lovers,
they are nameless, their histories only for each other,
and you have the room, the bed and the windows.

Pretend it is a ritual.
5   Unfurl the bed, bury the lovers, blacken the windows,
let them live in that house for a generation or two.
No one dares disturb them.
Visitors in the corridor tip-toe past the long closed door,
they listen for sounds, for a moan, for a song:
10   nothing is heard, not even breathing.
You know they are not dead,
you can feel the presence of their intense love.
Your children grow up, they leave you,
they have become soldiers and riders.
15   Your mate dies after a life of service.
Who knows you? Who remembers you?
But in your house a ritual is in progress:
it is not finished: it needs more people.
One day the door is opened to the lover's chamber.
20   The room has become a dense garden,
full of colours, smells, sounds you have never known.
The bed is smooth as a wafer of sunlight,
in the midst of the garden it stands alone.
In the bed the lovers, slowly and deliberately and silently,
25   perform the act of love.
Their eyes are closed,
as tightly as if heavy coins of flesh lay on them.
Their lips are bruised with new and old bruises.
Her hair and his beard are hopelessly tangled.
30   When he puts his mouth against her shoulder
she is uncertain whether her shoulder
has given or received the kiss.
All her flesh is like a mouth.
He carries his fingers along her waist
35   and feels his own waist caressed.
She holds him closer and his own arms tighten around her.
She kisses the hand beside her mouth.
It is his hand or her hand, it hardly matters,
there are so many more kisses.
40   You stand beside the bed, weeping with happiness,
you carefully peel away the sheets
from the slow-moving bodies.
Your eyes are filled with tears, you barely make out the lovers.
As you undress you sing out, and your voice is magnificent
45   because now you believe it is the first human voice
heard in that room.
The garments you let fall grow into vines.
You climb into bed and recover the flesh.
You close your eyes and allow them to be sewn shut.
50   You create an embrace and fall into it.
There is only one moment of pain or doubt

as you wonder how many multitudes are lying beside your body,
but a mouth kisses and a hand soothes the moment away.

Wole Soyinka

Nigeria 1934–

Born in Abeokuta, Nigeria, to Yoruban parents, Wole Soyinka was educated at the
University College of Ibadan and Leeds University, where he completed a B.A. in
English. Soyinka has written plays, poetry, essays, and novels and, in 1986, was
the first African to win the Nobel Prize for literature. Soyinka was jailed for two
years by the Nigerian military government during the civil war because of his pro-
Biafran stand. After Soyinka protested the cancellation of the elections in Nigeria
in 1993, the government seized his passport. Since then, Soyinka has travelled on
a UN passport, and, in Nigeria, had a death sentence against him both proclaimed
and rescinded. Soyinka's work, as we see in "Telephone Conversation," reflects his
experiences and his strong belief in social justice.

Telephone Conversation   1960

The price seemed reasonable, location
Indifferent. The landlady swore she lived
Off premises. Nothing remained
But self-confession. 'Madam,' I warned,
5   'I hate a wasted journey—I am African.'
Silence. Silenced transmission of
Pressurized good-breeding. Voice, when it came,
Lipstick coated, long gold-rolled
Cigarette-holder pipped. Caught I was, foully.
10 'HOW DARK?'... I had not misheard... 'ARE YOU LIGHT
OR VERY DARK?' Button B. Button A. Stench
Of rancid breath of public hide-and-speak.
Red booth. Red pillar-box. Red double-tiered
Omnibus squelching tar. It *was* real! Shamed
15 By ill-mannered silence, surrender
Pushed dumbfoundment to beg simplification.
Considerate she was, varying the emphasis—
'ARE YOU DARK? OR VERY LIGHT?' Revelation came.
'You mean—like plain or milk chocolate?'
20 Her assent was clinical, crushing in its light
Impersonality. Rapidly, wave-length adjusted,
I chose. 'West African sepia' — and as afterthought,

'Down in my passport.' Silence for spectroscopic
Flight of fancy, till truthfulness changed her accent
25   Hard on the mouthpiece. 'WHAT'S THAT?' conceding
'DON'T KNOW WHAT THAT IS.' 'Like brunette.'
'THAT'S DARK ISN'T IT?' 'Not altogether.
Facially, I am brunette, but madam, you should see
The rest of me. Palm of my hand, soles of my feet
30   Are a peroxide blonde. Friction, caused—
Foolishly madam—by sitting down, has turned
My bottom raven black—One moment madam!'—sensing
Her receiver rearing on the thunderclap
About my ears—'Madam,' I pleaded, 'wouldn't you rather
35   See for yourself?'

George Bowering

Canada 1935–

George Bowering grew up in the Okanagan Valley and left there first to join the
Royal Canadian Air Force and then to attend the University of British Columbia,
from which he graduated in 1963 with an M.A. in English. Bowering, along with
several others studying under Warren Tallman at UBC, was influenced by Black
Mountain poetics. In 1971, after teaching and studying in Eastern Canada,
Bowering returned to teach at Simon Fraser University. Appointed Canada's Poet
Laureate near the end of 2001, Bowering has published over forty books of both
poetry and prose. The two poems here show his gift for irony and for a serious
subtext to that irony.

Grandfather   1962

Grandfather
      Jabez Harry Bowering
strode across the Canadian prairie
hacking down trees
5   and building churches
delivering personal baptist sermons in them
leading Holy holy holy lord god almighty songs in them
red haired man squared off in the pulpit
reading Saul on the road to Damascus at them

10   Left home
         big walled Bristol town
      at age eight

to make a living
buried his stubby fingers in root snarled earth
15   for a suit of clothes and seven hundred gruelly meals a year
taking an anabaptist cane across the back every day
for four years till he was whipped out of England

Twelve years old
and across the ocean alone
20   to apocalyptic Canada
Ontario of bone bending child labor
six years on the road to Damascus till his eyes were blinded
with the blast of Christ and he wandered west
to Brandon among wheat kings and heathen Saturday nights
25   young red haired Bristol boy shoveling coal
in the basement of Brandon college five in the morning

Then built his first wooden church and married
a sick girl who bore two live children and died
leaving several pitiful letters and the Manitoba night

30   He moved west with another wife and built children and churches
Saskatchewan Alberta British Columbia Holy holy holy
lord god almighty
struck his labored bones with pain
and left him a postmaster prodding grandchildren with crutches
35   another dead wife and a glass bowl of photographs
and holy books unopened save the bible by the bed

Till he died the day before his eighty fifth birthday
in a Catholic hospital of sheets white as his hair

Man With Broom   1967

Driving home alone with Angela,
I saw a sad 4:00 a.m. light
in the windows of one room
in a gradeschool by the road.

5   He's alone,
sweeping, looking at the floor
in front of him
maybe twelve more years of school.

Marge Piercy

U.S.A. 1936–

Born and raised in a poor, working-class family in Detroit, Marge Piercy was educated at the University of Michigan and Northwestern. In the 1960s, she became involved first in the anti-war and civil rights movements and then in the women's movement. Her sense of social duty is captured in her poem "To Be of Use" just as her sense of the legacy of having a maternal grandfather who was a union organizer and a maternal great-grandfather who was a rabbi is captured in her remark in "Paths of Resistance" in *Active in Time and History*: "We choose from the infinitely complex past certain stories, certain epochs, certain struggles and battles.... Deciding who we are is intimately associated with who we believe our ancestors ... our precursors are."

To Be of Use   1973

The people I love the best
jump into work head first
without dallying in the shallows
and swim off with sure strokes almost out of sight.
5   They seem to become natives of that element,
the black sleek heads of seals
bouncing like half-submerged balls.

I love people who harness themselves, an ox to a heavy cart,
who pull like water buffalo, with massive patience,
10   who strain in the mud and the muck to move things forward,
who do what has to be done, again and again.

I want to be with people who submerge
in the task, who go into the fields to harvest
and work in a row and pass the bags along,
15   who are not parlor generals and field deserters
but move in common rhythm
when the food must come in or the fire must be put out.

The work of the world is common as mud.
Botched, it smears the hands, crumbles to dust.
20   But the thing worth doing well done
has a shape that satisfies, clean and evident.
Greek amphoras for wine or oil,
Hopi vases that held corn, are put in museums
but you know they were made to be used.
25   The pitcher cries for water to carry
And a person for work that is real.

Michèle Lalonde

Canada 1937–

Born in Montréal, Michèle Lalonde received her B.A. in philosophy at the Université de Montréal. In the 1960s, Lalonde became involved in the debates about Quebec culture, language, and nationalism, and she edited the magazines *Liberté* and *Maintenant,* as well as teaching at l'École nationale de théâtre. In 1982, she became the president of la Fédération internationale des écrivains québécois. The discrimination francophones in Quebec faced is the subject of "Speak White," a poem originally written in a mix of English and French. The expression "speak white" is a dated derogatory remark directed by anglophones at francophones.

Speak White   1969
translated by D.G. Jones

Speak white
it is so lovely to listen to you
speaking of Paradise Lost
or the anonymous, graceful profile trembling in the sonnets of
    Shakespeare

5   We are a rude and stammering people
but we are not deaf to the genius of a language
speak with the accent of Milton and Byron and Shelley and Keats
speak white
and please excuse us if in return
10   we've only our rough ancestral songs
and the chagrin of Nelligan[1]

speak white
speak of places, this and that
speak to us of the Magna Carta
15   of the Lincoln Monument
of the cloudy charm of the Thames
or blossom-time on the Potomac
speak to us of your traditions
We are a people who are none too bright
20   but we are quick to sense
the great significance of crumpets
or the Boston Tea Party

---

1 Émile Nelligan, a popular Quebec poet (1879–1941)

But when you really speak white
when you get down to brass tacks
25 to speak of Better Homes and Gardens
and the high standard of living
and the Great Society
a little louder then speak white

raise your foremen's voices
30 we are a little hard of hearing
we live too close to the machines
and only hear our heavy breathing over the tools
speak white and loud
so we can hear you clearly
35 from Saint Henri to Santo Domingo
yes, what a marvellous language
for hiring and firing
for giving the orders
for fixing the hour to be worked to death
40 and that pause that refreshes
and bucks up the dollar

Speak white
tell us that God is a great big shot
and that we're paid to trust him
45 speak white
speak to us of production, profits and percentages
speak white
it's a rich language
for buying
50 but for selling oneself
but for selling one's soul
but for selling oneself

Ah
speak white
55 big deal
but for telling about
the eternity of a day on strike
for telling the whole
life-story of a nation of caretakers
60 for coming back home in the evening
at the hour when the sun's gone bust in the alleys
for telling you yes the sun does set yes
every day of our lives to the east of your empires
Nothing's as good as a language of oaths
65 our mode of expression none too clean
dirtied with oil and with axle grease

Speak white
feel at home with your words
we are a bitter people
70 but we'd never reproach a soul
for having a monopoly
on how to improve one's speech

In the sweet tongue of Shakespeare
with the accent of Longfellow
75 speak a French purely and atrociously white
as in Viet Nam, in the Congo
speak impeccable German
a yellow star between your teeth
speak Russian speak of the right to rule speak of repression
80 speak white
it's a universal language
we were born to understand it
with its tear-gas phrases
with its billy-club words

85 Speak white
tell us again about freedom and democracy
We know that liberty is a Black word
as misery is Black
as blood is muddied with the dust of Algiers[2] or of Little Rock[3]

90 Speak white
from Westminster to Washington take turns
speak white as on Wall Street
white as in Watts
Be civilized
95 and understand our conventional answer
when you ask us politely
how do you do
and we mean to reply
we're doing all right
100 we're doing fine
we
are not alone

We know now
that we are not alone.

---

2 capital city of Algeria, which achieved independence from France in 1962, following
seven years of war.

3 The United States Supreme Court's decision to desegregate schools in Little Rock,
Arkansas, provoked demonstrations in 1958.

Margaret Atwood

Canada 1939–

Margaret Atwood was born in Ottawa and spent her early life moving between the Canadian Shield, where her entomologist father did research, and various Canadian cities, especially Ottawa and Toronto. After studying at the University of Toronto (Victoria College) and Harvard, Atwood taught at UBC for almost nine years. A poet, novelist, and short-story writer, Atwood has also published works of nonfiction, including the critical study *Survival: A Thematic Guide to Canadian Literature*. In "This is a Photograph of Me," Atwood returns to a theme that recurs in her work: false surfaces and underlying realities.

This is a Photograph of Me   1966

It was taken some time ago.
At first it seems to be
a smeared
print: blurred lines and grey flecks
5   blended with the paper;

then, as you scan
it, you see in the left-hand corner
a thing that is like a branch: part of a tree
(balsam or spruce) emerging
10   and, to the right, halfway up
what ought to be a gentle
slope, a small frame house.

In the background there is a lake,
and beyond that, some low hills.

15   (The photograph was taken
the day after I drowned.

I am in the lake, in the center
of the picture, just under the surface.

It is difficult to say where
20   precisely, or to say
how large or small I am:
the effect of water
on light is a distortion

but if you look long enough,
25   eventually
you will be able to see me.)

Seamus Heaney

Northern Ireland 1939–

Born into a Catholic family in Derry, Northern Ireland, Seamus Heaney graduated from Queen's University, Belfast, and then obtained a teaching diploma. After teaching at a number of universities, including Queen's University and Harvard, Heaney moved to the Republic of Ireland in 1972, but continues to live for part of the year at Harvard. He won the Nobel Prize for literature in 1995. In "Digging," published in Heaney's first book of poetry, *Death of a Naturalist* (1966), Heaney begins the unearthing of his Irish roots, a journey that eventually takes him into Irish folklore and both national and personal history. His gift for arresting and layered imagery is strongly present in "The Haw Lantern."

Digging   1966

Between my finger and my thumb
The squat pen rests; snug as a gun.

Under my window, a clean rasping sound
When the spade sinks into gravelly ground:
5   My father, digging. I look down

Till his straining rump among the flowerbeds
Bends low, comes up twenty years away
Stooping in rhythm through potato drills
Where he was digging.

10   The course boot nestled on the lug, the shaft
Against the inside knee was levered firmly.
He rooted out tall tops, buried the bright edge deep
To scatter new potatoes that we picked
Loving their cool hardness in our hands.

15   By God, the old man could handle a spade.
Just like his old man.

My grandfather cut more turf[1] in a day
Than any other man on Toner's bog.
Once I carried him milk in a bottle
20   Corked sloppily with paper. He straightened up
To drink it, then fell to right away

---

1   peat

Nicking and slicing neatly, heaving sods
Over his shoulder, going down and down
For the good turf. Digging.

25   The cold smell of potato mould, the squelch and slap
Of soggy peat, the curt cuts of an edge
Through living roots awaken in my head.
But I've no spade to follow men like them.

Between my finger and my thumb
30   The squat pen rests.
I'll dig with it.

The Haw Lantern[1]   1987

The wintry haw is burning out of season,
crab of the thorn, a small light for small people,
wanting no more from them but that they keep
the wick of self-respect from dying out,
5   not having to blind them with illumination.

But sometimes when your breath plumes in the frost
it takes the roaming shape of Diogenes[2]
with his lantern, seeking one just man;
so you end up scrutinized from behind the haw
10   he holds up at eye-level on its twig,
and you flinch before its bonded pith and stone,
its blood-prick that you wish would test and clear you,
its pecked-at ripeness that scans you, then moves on.

---

1   In Celtic mythology, the hawthorn tree, which bears a fruit called a haw, is associated
with faeries and the faery realm. However, the Catholic Church, in trying to obliterate
Celtic mythology, linked the hawthorn to bad luck and witches.
2   There is a story that Diogenes of Sinope (fourth century BCE), a cynic and a man who
believed in self-sufficiency, wandered Greece looking for an honest man.

Billy Collins

U.S.A. 1941–

Born in New York City, and currently living in Somers, NY, Billy Collins teaches in the English Department at Lehman College of the City University of New York. He completed his second annual term as the Library of Congress's Poet Laureate Consultant in Poetry in May 2003. Collins is unique as a poet in many ways. His ironic voice can be both disarming and disorienting. As he noted in an April 25, 2002 interview with *The Christian Science Monitor*, "The poem should be taking you somewhere; you should find yourself moved, taken into some wonderful location where the rules of logic have been changed." In 1998, his collection of poems *Picnic, Lightning* became a poetry best seller with sales of over 20,000 copies. Collins asserts "Humor is important [for] there is so much pretentiousness in poetry. Humor is a deflating device, a protective device, a way of trying to defend the self." His gift for absurdity is obvious in "Victoria's Secret."

Victoria's Secret   1998

The one in the upper left-hand corner
is giving me a look
that says I know you are here
and I have nothing better to do
5   for the remainder of human time
than return your persistent but engaging stare.
She is wearing a deeply scalloped
flame-stitch halter top
with padded push-up styling
10   and easy side-zip tap pants.

The one on the facing page, however,
who looks at me over her bare shoulder,
cannot hide the shadow of annoyance in her brow.
You have interrupted me,
15   she seems to be saying,
with your coughing and your loud music.
Now please leave me alone;
let me finish whatever it was I was doing
in my organza-trimmed
20   whisperweight camisole with
keyhole closure and a point d'esprit mesh back.
I wet my thumb and flip the page.
Here, the one who happens to be reclining
in a satin and lace merry widow
25   with an inset lace-up front,

decorated underwire cups and bodice
with lace ruffles along the bottom
and hook-and-eye closure in the back,
is wearing a slightly contorted expression,
30   her head thrust back, mouth partially open,
a confusing mixture of pain and surprise
as if she had stepped on a tack
just as I was breaking down
her bedroom door with my shoulder.

35   Nor does the one directly beneath her
looking particularly happy to see me.
She is arching one eyebrow slightly
as if to say, so what if I am wearing nothing
but this stretch panne velvet bodysuit
40   with a low sweetheart neckline
featuring molded cups and adjustable straps.
Do you have a problem with that?!

The one on the far right is easier to take,
her eyes half-closed
45   as if she were listening to a medley
of lullabies playing faintly on a music box.
Soon she will drop off to sleep,
her head nestled in the soft crook of her arm,
and later she will wake up in her
50   Spandex slip dress with the high side slit,
deep scoop neckline, elastic shirring,
and concealed back zip and vent.

But opposite her,
stretched out catlike on a couch
55   in the warm glow of a paneled library,
is one who wears a distinctly challenging expression,
her face tipped up, exposing
her long neck, her perfectly flared nostrils.
Go ahead, her expression tells me,
60   take off my satin charmeuse gown
with a sheer, jacquard bodice
decorated with a touch of shimmering Lurex.
Go ahead, fling it into the fireplace.
What do I care, her eyes say, we're all going to hell anyway.
65   I have other mail to open,
but I cannot help noticing her neighbor
whose eyes are downcast,
her head ever so demurely bowed to the side
as if she were the model who sat for Coreggio
70   when he painted "The Madonna of St. Jerome,"

only, it became so ungodly hot in Parma
that afternoon, she had to remove
the traditional blue robe
and pose there in his studio
75   in a beautifully shaped satin teddy
with an embossed V-front,
princess seaming to mold the bodice,
and puckered knit detail.

And occupying the whole facing page
80   is one who displays that expression
we have come to associate with photographic beauty.
Yes, she is pouting about something,
all lower lip and cheekbone.
Perhaps her ice cream has tumbled
85   out of its cone onto the parquet floor.
Perhaps she has been waiting all day
for a new sofa to be delivered,
waiting all day in stretch lace hipster
with lattice edging, satin frog closures,
90   velvet scrollwork, cuffed ankles,
flare silhouette, and knotted shoulder straps
available in black, champagne, almond,
cinnabar, plum, bronze, mocha,
peach, ivory, caramel, blush, butter, rose, and periwinkle.
95   It is, of course, impossible to say,
impossible to know what she is thinking,
why her mouth is the shape of petulance.

But this is already too much.
Who has the time to linger on these delicate
100   lures, these once unmentionable things?
Life is rushing by like a mad, swollen river.
One minute roses are opening in the garden
and the next, snow is flying past my window.
Plus the phone is ringing.
105   The dog is whining at the door.
Rain is beating on the roof.
And as always there is a list of things I have to do
before the night descends, black and silky,
and the dark hours begin to hurtle by,
110   before the little doors of the body swing shut
and I ride to sleep, my closed eyes
still burning from all the glossy lights of day.

Sharon Olds

U.S.A. 1942–

Born in San Francisco, Sharon Olds grew up in a strong Calvinist environment. She was educated at Stanford and Columbia University and was the Poet Laureate for the State of New York from 1998–2000. She works in the New York University Graduate Creative Writing Program and was one of the founders of the writing program for the severely physically disabled at Goldwater Hospital in New York. Although, in poems like "35/10," Olds seems to be mining her own experience, she says in an interview in *Salon*, "I don't know if it would feel accurate to me to say that I put myself into my poems.... Someone is seeing, someone is thinking, dreaming, wondering, and remembering, in everyone's poems. Whether there's a speaker that has an explicit 'I' or not, there is some kind of self or spirit or personality."

35/10   1984

Brushing out my daughter's dark
silken hair before the mirror
I see the grey gleaming on my head,
the silver-haired servant behind her. Why is it
5   just as we begin to go
they begin to arrive, the fold in my neck
clarifying as the fine bones of her
hips sharpen? As my skin shows
its dry pitting, she opens like a small
10   pale flower on the tip of a cactus;
as my last chances to bear a child
are falling through my body, the duds among them,
her full purse of eggs, round and
firm as hard-boiled yolks, is about
15   to snap its clasp. I brush her tangled
fragrant hair at bedtime. It's an old
story—the oldest we have on our planet—
the story of replacement.

Michael Ondaatje

Canada 1943–

Michael Ondaatje was born in Sri Lanka but moved to England to live with his mother when he was ten. In 1962, he came to Canada. He attended Bishop's University, the University of Toronto (B.A.), and Queen's University (M.A.). He has taught English at the University of Western Ontario and at York University. Although Ondaatje's first published work was poetry and poems such as "The Cinnamon Peeler" illustrate his strong sense of image and emotion, in recent years he has been best known for his prose. Both *Running in the Family* and *In the Skin of a Lion* were critically acclaimed and his third novel, *The English Patient*, received the Booker Prize for literature and was made into a successful feature film.

The Cinnamon Peeler   1981

If I were a cinnamon peeler
I would ride your bed
and leave the yellow bark dust
on your pillow.

5   Your breasts and shoulders would reek
you could never walk through markets
without the profession of my fingers
floating over you. The blind would
stumble certain of whom they approached
10   though you might bathe
under rain gutters, monsoon.

Here on the upper thigh
at this smooth pasture
neighbour to your hair
15   or the crease
that cuts your back. This ankle.
You will be known among strangers
as the cinnamon peeler's wife.

I could hardly glance at you
20   before marriage
never touch you
—your keen nosed mother, your rough brothers.
I buried my hands
in saffron, disguised them
25   over smoking tar,
helped the honey gatherers ...

*

When we swam once
I touched you in water
and our bodies remained free,
30   you could hold me and be blind of smell.
You climbed the bank and said

    this is how you touch other women
the grass cutter's wife, the lime burner's daughter.
And you searched your arms
35   for the missing perfume
        and knew

    what good is it
to be the lime burner's daughter
left with no trace
40   as if not spoken to in the act of love
as if wounded without the pleasure of a scar.

You touched
your belly to my hands
in the dry air and said
45   I am the cinnamon
peeler's wife. Smell me.

bp Nichol

Canada 1944–1988

Brought up in Vancouver, Winnipeg, and Port Arthur (Thunder Bay), bp Nichol was educated at UBC. After a brief stint teaching grade four, Nichol moved east to Toronto, where he began writing concrete poetry, editing, and teaching creative writing. In 1970, he won the Governor General's Award for poetry. Nichol's most complex work, *The Martyrology*, a multivolume poem, shows his love of language and play. In *The Martyrology*, Nichol deconstructed and reconstructed words in a variety of ways.

Two Words: A Wedding   1978

For Rob and Sheron

There are things you have words for, things you do not
have words for. There are words that encompass all your
feelings & words that encompass none. There are feelings

you have that are like things to you, picked up & placed in
5   the pocket, worn like the cloth the pocket is attached to, like
a skin you live inside of. There is a body of feeling, of
language, of friends; the body politic, the body we are carried
inside of till birth, the body we carry our self inside
of till death, a body of knowledge that tells of an afterlife, a
10 heaven, an unknown everything we have many words for
but cannot encompass. There are relationships between
words & concepts, between things, between life & death,
between friends & family, between each other & some other
other. We wed words to things, people to feelings, speak of
15 a true wedding of the mind & heart, intuition & intellect, &
out of this form our realities. Our realities are wedded one
to another, concepts & people are joined, new people
conceived within that mesh of flesh & realities, are carried
forward in the body of the mother, the family, the bodily
20 love we have for one another. They are creating their own
reality each step of the way, daily, another kind of reality is
born, each new word, person, expanding our vocabulary,
our concepts, new realities are conceived, our old reality
changes, the 'real' grows realer every day. We are marrying
25 the flesh to the flesh, the word to the daily flux of lives we
know & don't know, our friends grow older & marry, raise
children as you once were children with mothers & fathers
of your own, grow older, so many things you still lack
words for, struggle to wed the inner & outer worlds, the self
30 to some other self or selves, confess your love & struggle
with one another, together, conscious there is this word is
you, your name, & that you are yet another thing or things
you will never encompass, never exhaust the possibilities of,
because you are wedded to the flux of life, because we are
35 words and our meanings change.

Alice Walker

U.S.A. 1944–

Alice Walker was born in Eatonton, Georgia, the eighth and last child of a share-cropping family. At the age of twenty-four, she published her first book of poetry, *Once*. Since that time, she has published collections of stories, books of poetry, novels, and a book of essays—*Living By the Word*. Her novel *The Color Purple*, her most famous work, won her the Pulitzer Prize in 1982. Walker's work has consciously addressed the painful issues of Black history in America. In "Women," we see her exploring some of the universal elements of Black female experience.

Women   1970

They were women then
My mama's generation
Husky of voice—Stout of
Step
5   With fists as well as
Hands
How they battered down
Doors
And ironed
10   Starched white
Shirts
How they led
Armies
Headragged Generals
15   Across mined
Fields
Booby-trapped
Ditches
To discover books
20   Desks
A place for us
How they knew what we
Must know
Without knowing a page
25   Of it
Themselves.

Bronwen Wallace

Canada 1945–1989

Bronwen Wallace lived most of her life in her native Kingston, Ontario,
receiving her B.A. and M.A. from Queen's University. Wallace was sensitive to
the problems of class and gender, so it is not surprising that she eventually ran a
shelter for women and children. In "A Simple Poem for Virginia Woolf,"
Wallace starts with the plea for personal space that Woolf made in *A Room of
One's Own*. However, Wallace goes further by pointing out the much more basic
challenges and needs of ordinary women of our time. Before reading "A Simple
Poem for Virginia Woolf," you might benefit from reading Wallace's essay "One
More Woman Talking" in the essay section of this text (see page 285).

A Simple Poem for Virginia Woolf   1983

This started out as a simple poem
for Virginia Woolf   you know the kind
we women writers write these days
in our own rooms
5   on our own time
a salute   a gesture of friendship
a psychological debt
paid off
I wanted it simple
10   and perfectly round
hard as an
egg   I thought
only once I'd said egg
I thought of the smell
15   of bacon grease and dirty frying-pans
and whether there were enough for breakfast
I couldn't help it
I wanted the poem to be carefree and easy
like children playing in the snow
20   I didn't mean to mention
the price of snowsuits or
how even on the most expensive ones
the zippers always snag
just when you're late for work
25   and trying to get the children
off to school on time
a straightforward poem
for Virginia Woolf   that's all
I wanted really
30   not something tangled in
domestic life the way
Jane Austen's novels tangled
with her knitting her embroidery
whatever it was she hid them under
35   I didn't mean to go into all that
didn't intend to get confessional
and tell you how
every time I read a good poem
by a woman writer I'm always peeking
40   behind it trying to see
if she's still married
or has a lover at least
wanted to know what she did
with her kids while she wrote it
45   or whether she had any

and if she didn't if she'd chosen
not to or if she did did she
choose and why   I didn't mean
to bother with that
50 and I certainly wasn't going
to tell you about the time
my best friend was sick in intensive care
and I went down to see her
but they wouldn't let me in
55 because I wasn't her husband
or her father   her mother
I wasn't family
I was just her friend
and the friendship of women
60 wasn't mentioned
in hospital policy
or how I went out and kicked
a dent in the fender of my car
and sat there crying because
65 if she died I wouldn't be able
to tell her how much I loved her
(though she didn't and we laugh
about it now) but that's what got me
started I suppose   wanting to write
70 a gesture of friendship
for a woman for a woman writer
for Virginia Woolf
and thinking I could do it
easily   separating the words
75 from the lives they come from
that's what a good poem should do
after all and I wasn't going to make excuses
for being a woman   blaming years of silence
for leaving us
80 so much to say

This started out as a simple poem
for Virginia Woolf
it wasn't going to mention history
or choices or women's lives
85 the complexities of women's friendships
or the countless gritty details
of an ordinary woman's life
that never appear in poems at all
yet even as I write these words
90 those ordinary details intervene
between the poem I meant to write
and this one   where the delicate faces

of my children   faces of friends
of women I have never even seen
95   glow on the blank pages
and deeper than any silence
press around me
waiting their turn

Tom Wayman

Canada 1945–

Educated at the University of British Columbia, Tom Wayman is a poet, editor, and teacher. His understanding of the dilemma of teaching about literature is evident in his remarks that "school is where we learn to regard literature as though it is insulated from the everyday" and "the literary arts today are one of the last potentially free spaces in modern industrial society." Satire and self-parody dominate the poems "Wayman in Love" and "Did I Miss Anything?" Wayman currently teaches at the University of Calgary.

Wayman in Love   1973

At last Wayman gets the girl into bed.
He is locked in one of those embraces
so passionate his left arm is asleep
when suddenly he is bumped in the back.
5   'Excuse me,' a voice mutters, thick with German.
Wayman and the girl sit up astounded
as a furry gentleman in boots and a frock coat
climbs in under the covers.

'My name is Doktor Marx,' the intruder announces
10   settling his neck comfortably on the pillow.
'I'm here to consider for you the cost of a kiss.'
He pulls out a notepad. 'Let's see now,
we have the price of the mattress, this room must be rented,
your time off work, groceries for two,
15   medical fees in case of accidents....'

'Look,' Wayman says,
'couldn't we do this later?'
The philosopher sighs, and continues: 'You are affected too, Miss.
If you are not working, you are going to resent

20   your dependent position. This will influence
        I assure you, your most intimate moments….'

        'Doctor, please,' Wayman says. 'All we want
        is to be left alone.'
        But another beard, more nattily dressed,
25   is also getting into the bed.
        There is a shifting and heaving of bodies
        as everyone wriggles out room for themselves.
        'I want you to meet a friend from Vienna,'
        Marx says. 'This is Doktor Freud.'

30   The newcomer straightens his glasses,
        peers at Wayman and the girl.
        'I can see,' he begins,
        'that you two have problems….'

Did I Miss Anything?   1991

Question frequently asked by
students after missing a class

Nothing. When we realized you weren't here
we sat with our hands folded on our desks
in silence, for the full two hours

        Everything. I gave an exam worth
5   40 per cent of the grade for this term
        and assigned some reading due today
        on which I'm about to hand out a quiz
        worth 50 per cent.

Nothing. None of the content of this course
10   has value or meaning
        Take as many days off as you like:
        any activities we undertake as a class
        I assure you will not matter either to you or me
        and are without purpose

15   Everything. A few minutes after we began last time
        a shaft of light descended and an angel
        or other heavenly being appeared
        and revealed to us what each woman or man must do
        to attain divine wisdom in this life and
20   the hereafter
        This is the last time the class will meet
        before we disperse to bring this good news to all people on earth

Nothing. When you are not present
how could something significant occur?

25   Everything. Contained in this classroom
is a microcosm of human existence
assembled for you to query and examine and ponder
This is not the only place such an opportunity has been
      gathered

30   but it was one place

And you weren't here

Leona Gom

Canada 1946–

Leona Gom grew up on an isolated farm in northern Alberta, a background that
can be glimpsed in "Survival." She has published five books of poetry, including
Land of Peace, which was awarded the Canadian Authors Association Award in
1980. More recently, Gom's interests have turned to fiction, and she has written
five novels. Her first, *Housebroken*, won the Ethel Wilson Fiction Prize in 1987.
After three novels that were thrillers featuring a hero of mixed Aboriginal and
white heritage, Gom's most recent novel, *Hating Gladys* (2002) explores the
complex manner in which a past can penetrate and haunt a present.

Survival   1984

There was never gentleness.
All this romantic bullshit
about growing up on farms.
All I remember
5 are the pain and death.
When pigs were castrated,
their screams all afternoon
and my father coming in,
the guilty blood all over him.
10 When calves were dehorned,
their desperate bawling
and my mother saying,
"it doesn't really hurt them."
When I saw kittens smashed
15 against the barn walls,

and dogs shot
when they were too old
to herd the cattle,
and chickens
20   with their severed heads
throbbing on the bleeding ground,
and horses shipped
when my father bought a tractor,
and I could bus to school.
25   I learned a lot about necessity,
that things are functional, or die;
and I was not as ill-equipped
as first I thought
to live in cities.

Michael Lassell

USA 1947–

Born and raised in Great Neck, twenty miles along Long Island Sound from New York, Michael Lassell works as a feature editor for *Metropolitan Home* magazine. As a writer, editor, and anthologist, his most recent work includes such wide-ranging books as *Disney on Broadway* (2002), *Elton John and Tim Rice's Aida: The Making of the Broadway Musical* (2000), and *World in Us: Lesbian and Gay Poetry of the Next Wave*, co-edited with Elena Georgiou, (2000). His work also includes *Decade Dance* (1990), which won the Lambda Literary Award, as well as seven other books of poetry and prose. In an interview with Mark Huisman in *Letters From Camp Rehoboth*, he remarks "In other countries today, poems appear in daily newspapers next to the soccer scores. People are sent to jail or elected president for writing those poems." His sense of how poetry can shape social awareness and sensitivity is evident in "How To Watch Your Brother Die."

How To Watch Your Brother Die   1990

For Carl Morse

When the call comes, be calm.
Say to your wife, "My brother is dying. I have to fly
to California."
Try not to be shocked that he already looks like
5   a cadaver.
Say to the young man sitting by your brother's side,

"I'm his brother."
Try not to be shocked when the young man says,
"I'm his lover. Thanks for coming."

10   Listen to the doctor with a steel face on.
Sign the necessary forms.
Tell the doctor you will take care of everything.
Wonder why doctors are so remote.

Watch the lover's eyes as they stare into
15   your brother's eyes as they stare into
space.
Wonder what they see there.
Remember the time he was jealous and
opened your eyebrow with a sharp stick.
20   Forgive him out loud
even if he can't
understand you.
Realize the scar will be
all that's left of him.

25   Over coffee in the hospital cafeteria
say to the lover, "You're an extremely good-looking
young man."
Hear him say,
"I never thought I was good enough looking to
30   deserve your brother."

Watch the tears well up in his eyes. Say,
"I'm sorry, I don't know what it means to be
the lover of another man."
Hear him say,
35   "It's just like a wife, only the commitment is
deeper because the odds against you are so much
greater."
Say nothing, but
take his hand like a brother's.

40   Drive to Mexico for unproved drugs that might
help him live longer.
Explain what they are to the border guard.
Fill with rage when he informs you,
"You can't bring those across."

45   Begin to grow loud.
Feel the lover's hand on your arm
restraining you. See in the guard's eye

how much a man can hate another man.
Say to the lover, "How can you stand it?"
50   Hear him say, "You get used to it."
Think of one of your children getting used to
another man's hatred.

Call your wife on the telephone. Tell her,
"He hasn't much time.
55   I'll be home soon." Before you hang up, say,
"How could anyone's commitment be deeper than
a husband and wife?" Hear her say,
"Please, I don't want to know all the details."

When he slips into an irrevocable coma,
60   hold his lover in your arms while he sobs,
no longer strong. Wonder how much longer
you will be able to be strong.
Feel how it feels to hold a man in your arms
whose arms are used to holding men.
65   Offer God anything to bring your brother back.
Know you have nothing God could possibly want.
Curse God, but do not
abandon Him.

Stare at the face of the funeral director
70   when he tells you he will not
embalm the body for fear of
contamination. Let him see in your eyes
how much a man can hate another man.

Stand beside a casket covered in flowers,
75   white flowers. Say,
"Thank you for coming," to each of several
hundred men
who file past in tears, some of them
holding hands. Know that your brother's life
80   was not what you imagined. Overhear two
mourners say, "I wonder who'll be next?" and
"I don't care anymore,
as long as it isn't you."

Arrange to take an early flight home,
85   his lover will drive you to the airport.
When your flight is announced say,
awkwardly, "If I can do anything, please
let me know." Do not flinch when he says,
"Forgive yourself for not wanting to know him
90   after he told you. He did."

Stop and let it soak in. Say,
"He forgave me, or he knew himself?"
"Both," the lover will say, not knowing what else
to do. Hold him like a brother while he
95 kisses you on the cheek. Think that
you haven't been kissed by a man since
your father died. Think,
"This is no moment not to be strong."

Fly first class and drink Scotch. Stroke
100 your split eyebrow with a finger and
think of your brother alive. Smile
at the memory and think
how your children will feel in your arms,
warm and friendly and without challenge.

Lorna Crozier

Canada 1948–

After a childhood in Swift Current, Saskatchewan, and an early career teaching
high school, Crozier completed an M.A. at the University of Alberta. She has
taught creative writing in several provinces and has published collections of
poetry, first under her married name, Uher, and then under her family name,
Crozier. Crozier's work often has a playfulness about it. Although on the surface
it focuses on what appears to be simple subject matter, its themes are complex.
"Poem about Nothing" is a good example of Crozier's playful yet serious bent.

Poem about Nothing   1985

Zero is the one we didn't understand
at school. Multiplied by anything
it remains nothing.

When I ask my friend
5 the mathematician who studies rhetoric
if zero is a number, he says *yes*
and I feel great relief.

If it were a landscape
it would be a desert.
10 If it had anything to do
with anatomy, it would be

a mouth, a missing limb,
a lost organ.

Ø

15 Zero worms its way
                    between one and one
    and changes everything.

    It is the vowel on a mute tongue,
    the pupil in a blind man's eye,
20 the image
            of the face
    he holds on his fingertips.

Ø

    When you look up
25 from the bottom of a dry well
    zero is what you see,
    the terrible blue of it.

    It is the rope
    you knot around your throat
30 when your heels itch for wings.

    Icarus[1] understood zero
    as he caught the smell
    of burning feathers
    and fell into the sea.

35   Ø

    If you roll zero down a hill
    it will grow,
    swallow the towns, the farms,
    the people at their tables
40 playing tic-tac-toe.

Ø

    When the Cree chiefs
    signed the treaties on the plains
    they wrote *X*
45 beside their names.

    In English, X equals zero.

Ø

---

1 According to Greek myth, Icarus and his father, Daedalus, escaped the labyrinth of
   Knossos by using wings fashioned out of feathers and wax. Icarus ignored his father's
   advice and flew too close to the sun. As a result, his wax wings melted, and he fell
   into the sea and drowned. (See also Auden's "Musée des Beaux Arts.")

I ask my friend
the rhetorician who studies mathematics
50 *What does zero mean and keep it simple.*

He says *Zip.*

Ø

Zero is the pornographer's number.
He orders it through the mail
55 under a false name. It is the number
of the last man on death row,
the number of the girl who jumps
three stories to abort.

Zero starts and ends
60 at the same place. Some compare it
to driving across the Prairies all day
and feeling you've gone nowhere.

Ø Ø Ø

In the beginning God made zero.

Jim Wong-Chu

Canada 1949–

Jim Wong-Chu was born in Hong Kong, came to Canada in 1953, and was educated at the Vancouver Art School. As a young man, he worked in restaurants in the Chinese community in various places in North America. He has since worked as a community organizer, a historian, and a radio broadcaster, and he is one of the founding members of the Asian Canadian Writers Workshop. The following poem, from his 1986 collection *Chinatown Ghosts*, alludes to the untold hardships and deprivations that early settlers from China faced in the place they called "the sea of the golden mountains."

old chinese cemetery kamloops   july 1977

like a child lost
wandering about
touching   feeling
tattered grounds
5 touching   seeing
wooden boards

etched in ink
etched in weather
etched in fading memories
10   etched
faded
forgotten

I walk
on earth
15   above the bones
of a multitude
of golden mountain men
searching for scraps
of memory

20   like a child unloved
his face pressed hard
against the wet window

peering in
for a desperate moment
25   I touch my past

Anne Carson

Canada 1950–

Anne Carson was born and raised in Ontario, and obtained a PhD in Classical Studies from the University of Toronto. She now lives in Montreal and works at McGill University although she has taken time away from McGill to live in the United States at such places as the University of Michigan. There, she worked on the libretto for an opera while teaching a course about the "mystical literature of women." "My Religion," from "The Truth About God" (*Glass, Irony and God*, 1995), is by no means simple. When she opens her poem with "My religion makes no sense/ and does not help me/ therefore I pursue it" readers know that they are going to be challenged by a poet who demands both intellect and a tolerance for ambiguity from her readers.

The Truth About God   1995

MY RELIGION

My religion makes no sense
and does not help me
therefore I pursue it.

When we see
5   how simple it would have been
we will thrash ourselves.

I had a vision
of all the people in the world
who are searching for God

10   massed in a room
on one side
of a partition

that looks
from the other side
15   (God's side)

transparent
but we are blind.
Our gestures are blind.

Our blind gestures continue
20   for some time until finally
from somewhere

on the other side of the partition there we are
looking back at them.
It is far too late.

25   We see how brokenly
how warily
how ill

our blind gestures
parodied
30   what God really wanted

(some simple thing).
The thought of it
(this simple thing)

is like a creature
35   let loose in a room
and battering

to get out.
It batters my soul
with its rifle butt.

Vikram Seth

India 1952–

Vikram Seth is an international citizen, having lived in India, California,
England, and China. Seth has written several novels, including *A Suitable Boy*
(1993) and *An Equal Music* (1999), a book detailing his walk through Sinkiang
and Tibet called *From Heaven Lake* (winner of the Thomas Cook Travel Book
Award for 1983), a novel in verse, and two volumes of poetry. In "Work and
Freedom," he explores the banal and perversely ignorant roots of human evil.

Work and Freedom   1990

Even small events that others might not notice,
I found hard to forget. In Auschwitz truly
I had no reason to complain of boredom.
If an incident affected me too deeply
5   I could not go straight home to my wife and children.
I would ride my horse till the terrible picture faded.
Often at night I would wander through the stables
And seek relief among my beloved horses.
At home my thoughts, often and with no warning,
10   Turned to such things. When I saw my children playing
Or observed my wife's delight over our youngest,
I would walk out and stand beside the transports,
The firepits, crematoriums, or gas chambers.
My wife ascribed my gloom to some annoyance
15   Connected with my work—but I was thinking,
'How long will our happiness last?' I was not happy
Once the mass exterminations had started.

My work, such unease aside, was never-ending,
My colleagues untrustworthy, those above me
20   Reluctant to understand or even to listen—
Yet everyone thought the commandant's life was heaven.

My wife and children, true, were well looked after.
Her garden was a paradise of flowers.
The prisoners, trying no doubt to attract attention,
25 Never once failed in little acts of kindness.
Not one of them, in our house, was badly treated:
My wife would have loved to give the prisoners presents—
And as for the children, they begged for cigarettes for them,
Especially for those who worked in the garden and brought them
30 Tortoises, martens, lizards, cats. Each Sunday
We'd walk to the stables, never omitting the kennels
Where the dogs were kept. My children loved all creatures
But most of all our foal and our two horses.
In summer they splashed in the wading pool, but their greatest
35 Joy was to bathe together with Daddy—who had
Limited hours, alas, for these childish pleasures.
My wife said, 'Think of us, not only the service.'
How could she know what lay so heavily on me?
(It made life hard, this excessive sense of duty.)

40 When Auschwitz was divided, Pohl in a kindly
And quite exceptional gesture gave me the option
—Perhaps as recompense for this last assignment—
To head DK or to run Sachsenhausen.
I had one day to decide. At first the thought of
45 Uprooting myself from Auschwitz made me unhappy,
So involved had I grown in its tasks and troubles.
But in the end I was glad to gain my freedom.

Louise Erdrich

U.S.A. 1954–

Louise Erdrich was born in Little Falls, Minnesota, to an Ojibway mother and a father of Germanic descent. Erdrich, whose parents both worked at an Indian Affairs school in North Dakota, became very involved with Native American land claims. She was educated at Dartmouth College and Johns Hopkins University, and she now teaches at Dartmouth College. In "Dear John Wayne," Erdrich uses an aggressive irony and juxtaposition to reveal how a myth that comforts a majority can harm a minority and spawn unintended and destructive progeny.

Dear John Wayne   1984

August and the drive-in picture is packed.
We lounge on the hood of the Pontiac
surrounded by the slow-burning spirals they sell
at the window, to vanquish the hordes of mosquitoes.
5   Nothing works. They break through the smoke screen for blood.

Always the lookout spots the Indians first,
spread north to south, barring progress.
The Sioux or some other Plains bunch
in spectacular columns, ICBM missiles,[1]
10 their feathers bristling in the meaningful sunset.

The drum breaks. There will be no parlance.
Only the arrows whining, a death-cloud of nerves
swarming down on the settlers
who die beautifully, tumbling like dust weeds
15 into the history that brought us all here
together: this wide screen beneath the sign of the bear.

The sky fills, acres of blue squint and eye
that the crowd cheers. His face moves over us,
a thick cloud of vengeance, pitted
20 like the land that was once flesh. Each rut,
each scar makes a promise: *It is*
not over, this fight, not as long as you resist.

Everything we see belongs to us.

A few laughing Indians fall over the hood
25 slipping in the hot spilled butter.
The eye sees a lot, John, but the heart is so blind.
Death makes us owners of nothing.
He smiles, a horizon of teeth
the credits reel over, and then the white fields

30 again blowing in the true-to-life dark.
The dark films over everything.
We get into the car
scratching our mosquito bites, speechless and small
as people are when the movie is done.
35 We are back in our skins.

---

1   intercontinental ballistic missiles

How can we help but keep hearing his voice,
the flip side of the sound track, still playing:
Come on, boys, we got them
where we want them, drunk, running.
40 *They'll give us what we want, what we need.*
Even his disease was the idea of taking everything.
Those cells, burning, doubling, splitting out of their skins.

Marilyn Dumont

Canada 1955–

Born in Olds, Alberta into a Cree/Métis family, Marilyn Dumont earned a
Master of Fine Arts degree at UBC. She has worked in film and video produc-
tion. A descendant of Louis Riel's military commander, Gabriel Dumont,
Dumont combines her fine sense of language and her concerns about the plight
of Aboriginal Canadians to create a challenging, complex commentary in "The
White Judges" and "Letter to Sir John A. Macdonald," both from her first book,
A Really Good Brown Girl (1996).

The White Judges   1996

We lived in an old schoolhouse, one large room that my father converted into
two storeys with a plank staircase leading to the second floor. A single
window on the south wall created a space that was dimly lit even at midday.
All nine kids and the occasional friend slept upstairs like cadets in rows of
5   shared double beds, ate downstairs in the kitchen near the gas stove and
watched TV near the airtight heater in the adjacent room. Our floors were
worn linoleum and scatter rugs, our walls high and bare except for the family
photos whose frames were crowded with siblings waiting to come of age,
marry or leave. At supper eleven of us would stare down a pot of moose stew,
10   bannock and tea, while outside the white judges sat encircling our house.

And they waited to judge

waited till we ate tripe
watched us inhale its wild vapour
sliced and steaming on our plates,
15   watched us welcome it into our being,
sink our teeth into its rubbery texture
chew and roll each wet and tentacled piece
swallow its gamey juices
until we had become it and it had become us.

20   Or waited till the cardboard boxes
     were anonymously dropped at our door, spilling with clothes
     waited till we ran swiftly away from the windows and doors
     to the farthest room for fear of being seen
     and dared one another to
25   'open it'
     'no you open it'
     'no you'
     someone would open it
     cautiously pulling out a shirt
30   that would be tried on
     then passed around till somebody claimed it by fit
     then sixteen or eighteen hands would be pulling out
     skirts, pants, jackets, dresses from a box transformed now
     into the Sears catalogue.

35   Or the white judges would wait till twilight
     and my father and older brothers
     would drag a bloodstained canvas
     heavy with meat from the truck onto our lawn, and
     my mother would lift and lay it in place
40   like a dead relative,
     praying, coaxing and thanking it
     then she'd cut the thick hair and skin back
     till it lay in folds beside it like carpet

     carving off firm chunks
45   until the marble bone shone out of the red-blue flesh
     long into the truck-headlight-night she'd carve
     talking in Cree to my father and in English to my brothers
     long into the dark their voices talking us to sleep
     while our bellies rested in the meat days ahead.

50   Or wait till the guitars came out
     and the furniture was pushed up against the walls
     and we'd polish the linoleum with our dancing
     till our socks had holes.

     Or wait till a fight broke out
55   and the night would settle in our bones
     and we'd ache with shame
     for having heard or spoken
     that which sits at the edge of our light side
     that which comes but we wished it hadn't
60   like 'settlement' relatives who would arrive at Christmas and
     leave at Easter.

Letter to Sir John A. Macdonald   1996

Dear John: I'm still here and halfbreed,
after all these years
you're dead, funny thing,
that railway you wanted so badly,
5   there was talk a year ago
of shutting it down
and part of it was shut down,
the dayliner at least,
'from sea to shining sea,'
10   and you know, John,
after all that shuffling us around to suit the settlers,
we're still here and Métis.

We're still here
after Meech Lake and
15   one no-good-for-nothin-Indian
holdin-up-the-train,
stalling the 'Cabin syllables /Nouns of settlement,
/. . . steel syntax [and] /The long sentence of its exploitation'[1]
and John, that goddamned railroad never made this a great nation,
20   cause the railway shut down
and this country is still quarreling over unity,
and Riel is dead
but he just keeps coming back
in all the Bill Wilsons yet to speak out of turn or favour
25   because you know as well as I
that we were railroaded
by some steel tracks that didn't last
and some settlers who wouldn't settle
and it's funny we're still here and callin ourselves halfbreed.

---

1   lines from F. R. Scott's "Laurentian Shield"

Armand Garnet Ruffo

Canada 1955–

Armand Garnet Ruffo currently teaches Native literature at Carleton University and previously taught creative writing at the Banff Centre for the Performing Arts and the En'owkin International School of Writing, in Penticton, British Columbia. Ruffo grew up in Northern Ontario and holds a master's degree from the University of Windsor. Ruffo's best-known work reflects his Ojibway heritage and his continuing exploration of the complexities of minority cultures. He has published a collection of poetry entitled *Opening in the Sky* (1994) and a creative biography, *Grey Owl: The Mystery of Archie Belaney* (1997). His plays, stories, and essays have appeared in periodicals and anthologies.

Creating a Country　　1994

They came to North America in search of a new life,
clinging to their few possessions, hungry for prosperity.
They'd had enough poverty and suffering to last a lifetime.
And so they believed with all their hearts
5　　that if they laboured they would all become barons
in a classless society. Patriots were thus born
on both sides of the border. But the process of creating
a country took much longer than most ever imagined.
For there were a myriad of unforeseen obstacles
10　　in this formidable new land. Like mosquitoes and Indians.
Undaunted, the pioneering spirit persisted.

In Canada, Susanna Moodie[1] arrived to take notes.
After writing anti-slavery tracts in England,
she thought it only natural to document the burden
15　　of roughing it in the bush. Susanna shied away
from both mosquitoes and Indians. One day, however,
quite by accident, she met a young Mohawk
whom she thought handsome and for a period flirted
with the notion of what it would be like to be swept away
20　　by him. But she soon tired of such thoughts and nothing ever
became of it. Later she would say neither Indians nor mosquitoes
make good company. She did make it perfectly clear
that she bore no grudge. She believed everything has a place.

1　nineteenth-century writer who wrote about emigrating from Britain and life in
Canada in *Roughing It in the Bush*

Just as she believed her place was across the ocean,
25   but she too had heard stories of golden opportunities.
Lies! She could be heard screaming. Nothing but lies!
Susanna also believed she was turning life into art
and creating the first semblance of culture
in a godforsaken land.
30   It was her only compensation.
When she spoke about her life her eyes rolled in her head
like a ship leaving port. She never gave up the dream
of returning home. Dreamed so hard
that even on her death bed she never stopped
35   talking to herself.

South of the border, Lt. Col. George Armstrong Custer
never once worried about mosquitoes.
It's said that he too was interested in culture
and for this reason carried a gun.
40   He was a soldier, not an artist, and made no pretence
about it. Custer rarely wrote and never spoke
unless formally addressed. Yet, he was a passionate man
who dreamed the same dream every night.
He fancied that he had discovered the final solution.
45   Each night he rounded up all the buffalo
in what is now Montana and shot every last one of them.

As a son of European peasantry, he had heard stories
about what it was like to go hungry.
He also knew Indians could starve
50   just like white people. As a patriot,
he believed his solution was perfectly reasonable.
He also believed American politicians
would see to it that both the buffalo and the Indian
would find a new home
55   on the American nickel.

Susanna Moodie never met General Golden Hair (as Custer
was affectionately called), she never liked Americans anyway.
She was an old lady of 73 when he died young on the plains
of Little Bighorn trying to live out his dream.
60   They say that Custer was singing,
'The Girl I Left Behind Me' the day he headed west.
We know he wasn't singing to Susanna Moodie.
We also know that after hearing what the U.S. Cavalry
was doing south of the border, Susanna thought
65   about the anti-slavery tracts she had written years before
and, for a brief moment, about what had ever become
of her young Mohawk,
if he fared any better.

George Elliott Clarke

Canada 1960–

Born in Windsor Plains, Nova Scotia, George Elliott Clarke, a seventh-generation Canadian, was raised in Halifax and educated at the University of Waterloo, Dalhousie University, and Queen's University. Clarke, who currently teaches world literature in English at the University of Toronto, taught African-American and Canadian literature at Duke University (1994–99) and served as the visiting Seagram's Chair in Canadian Studies at McGill University (1998–99). He produced a two-volume anthology of Black writing from Nova Scotia entitled *Fire on the Water* in 1991–92, *Eyeing the North Star: Directions in African-Canadian Literature* in 1997, and, in 2002, *Odysseys Home: Mapping African-Canadian Literature*, a study of African-Canadian writing. Clarke's own creative work reflects his work on African-Canadian writing and his social consciousness. He won the Governor General's Award for Poetry in 2001 for *Execution Poems*.

Blank Sonnet   1990

The air smells of rhubarb, occasional
Roses, or first birth of blossoms, a fresh,
Undulant hurt, so body snaps and curls
Like flower. I step through snow as thin as script,
5   Watch white stars spin dizzy as drunks, and yearn
To sleep beneath a patchwork quilt of rum.
I want the slow, sure collapse of language
Washed out by alcohol. Lovely Shelley,[1]
I have no use for measured, cadenced verse
10   If you won't read. Icarus-like,[2] I'll fall
Against this page of snow, tumble blackly
Across vision to drown in the white sea
That closes every poem—the white reverse
That cancels the blackness of each image.

1   Shelley Clemence, a female resident of the fictional Whylah Falls, is the beloved of the narrator, known as X.

2.   In Greek mythology, Icarus, son of Daedalus, escaped from Crete on wings his father had made for him. He flew so close to the sun, however, that the wax holding together the wings melted, and he fell into the Aegean Sea.

Casualties   1992

JANUARY 16, 1991[1]

Snow annihilates all beauty
this merciless January.
A white blitzkrieg, Klan—cruel,
arsons and obliterates.

5   Piercing lies numb us to pain.
Nerves and words fail so we
can't feel agony or passion,
so we can't flinch or cry,

when we spy blurred children's
10   charred bodies protruding
from the smoking rubble
of statistics or see a man

stumbling in a blizzard
of bullets. Everything is
15   normal, absurdly normal.
We see, as if through a snow-

storm, darkly. Reporters
rat-a-tat-tat tactics,
stratagems. Missiles bristle
20   behind newspaper lines.

Our minds chill; we weather
the storm, huddle in dreams.
Exposed, though, a woman,
lashed by lightning, repents

25   of her flesh, becomes a living
X-ray, "collateral damage."
The first casualty of war
is language.

---

1   On January 11, 1991, the White House announced that "the Liberation of Kuwait has begun." This poem reflects Clarke's reaction to that announcement.

Nu(is)ance   2001

for Wayde Compton

Jabbering double-crossing doubletalk,
Pale-assed poetasters void my 'blues-caucused,
Raucous lyrics'—too Negroid and rowdy,
While sable, sassy poets preach I ink
5   Too blankly, *comme les blancs*, my bleached-out verse
Bleating too whitey-like—worse—in they ears.
What can I say?
     All this blather about
'Black' and 'white' verse is blackmail and white noise.
10   Cripes! English—fallacious—be finished here!
     I'd rather stutter a bastard's language
Only spoken in gutters, a broken,
Vulgar, Creole screech, loud with bawling, slurring,
Balderdash, cussing, and caterwauling,
15   A corrupt palaver that bankrupts all meeching[1] speech
Because it be literal, guttural *Poetry*,
I.e. *Hubbub*.

---

1   to meech means to steal

Essays

Introduction to the Essay

The modern **essay** has a lengthy history, one that has defined both its limitations and its potential. The name of this genre, derived from the French verb *essayer,* "to attempt," was first applied at the end of the sixteenth century with Michel de Montaigne's publication of his *Essais.* Although the writings of the classical Greek and Roman philosophers could be considered essays, Montaigne was the first to define the essay as the writer's attempt to discuss a single subject, event, or issue. Montaigne insisted that the subject matter of the essay could not be artificially limited, that its structure needed to be flexible to allow the writer to express a range of ideas related to the subject, and that the essential element of the essay was the author's voice.

Today, the essay is defined as nonfiction prose written in the first or third person and intended to be read at a single sitting. The author writes with the intent to inform or persuade the reader, using primarily an expository or argumentative mode but incorporating narration, description, and any other rhetorical techniques to achieve this end. The length of the essay is flexible, but it is generally fewer than twenty pages to allow it to be read at a single sitting.

The essay can be divided into four main styles. Montaigne set the initial standard of the discursive style, which tends to be rambling and loose. In 1597, Francis Bacon created the plain style with the publication of his *Essays,* in which he used deliberately simple, straightforward prose to cultivate clarity. By 1642, with the publication of Thomas Browne's *Religio Medici,* a third style, sometimes called the baroque mode, appeared. Browne's sentences created a rich complexity, with their constant embellishments, diversions, stops and starts, inclusions of unanticipated information, and shift from subject to subject.

Jonathan Swift's use of the essay form for satire created a fourth style, one that enlists mockery, irony, and wit to attack human folly or immorality. In Swift's "A Modest Proposal," the reader will miss the author's intention if he or she assumes that Swift is the speaker; satiric forms require the reader to distinguish the invented persona of the speaker from the author.

Elements of the Essay

Regardless of which style the writer uses, in every essay the writer takes a rhetorical stance, which is made up of two elements, voice and tone. The **tone** is the writer's attitude toward his or her subject, which can encompass the whole range of emotions, from indignation to amusement, love to anger. **Voice** is the writer's character—the way in which the writer hopes the reader will perceive him or her. Therefore, the writer's relationship to the reader creates the author's voice, while the writer's relationship to the chosen subject creates tone. Together, they compose the writer's stance.

Through voice and tone, the essay writer expresses the central argument of the essay, its thesis. A subject alone cannot create a thesis—it is the writer's perspective on that subject that furnishes the thesis. The writer may not begin the essay with an isolated thesis or controlling idea, but the writer's viewpoint must be clear by the end. To support the thesis, the essay writer uses various methods of development, such as narration, description, comparison/contrast, and classification. The essayist rarely uses just one means of development, and instead selects whatever means are necessary to speak powerfully to the reader.

As readers, we respond to the writer's voice and thesis, but much of the delight of an essay lies in its detail. Coupled with our interest in discovering a new perspective on a subject, it is the details that help us remember the essayist's views. The turn of phrase, the vivid images a writer conveys, the examples provided to drive home a point—all of these details create a richness and variety that make an essay memorable.

Reading and Responding to the Essay

Some essays communicate their central premises upon first reading, but others require more effort from the reader. When analyzing an essay, you should create a systematic format for reading and responding. The following are some guidelines you might wish to consider in reading the essays that follow:

1. Try to read the essay twice. It is often difficult to read critically the first time, when you are caught up in enjoyment and appreciation of the writer's skills in communicating. A second reading allows you to be more critical, since the elements of surprise and entertainment have lost some of their original force and you can think more about *how* the writer is developing the thesis.
2. Two or three hours after you first read the essay, try summarizing its controlling idea or ideas in three or four sentences. Then, in point form, list the elements that supported the thesis—the illustrations and evidence. Connect one of these concrete elements to the controlling idea, and explain what the

FIGURE 1 Rhetorical Stance

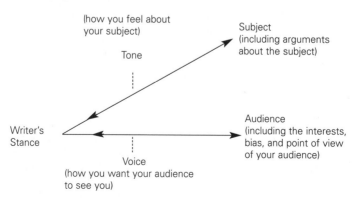

connection is. Allow yourself no more than twenty minutes for this exercise; the point is to test how well the writer communicated the essay's point to you on your first reading.

3. Check your understanding of the writer's structure by copying the first and last paragraphs of the essay, then reproducing from memory the content that lies between these two points. Trying this exercise after one reading and then again after two readings will reveal how much you gain from a second reading. Then, analyze why the writer used a particular means to connect the essay's beginning to the ending.

4. If the essay is argumentative, try to come up with three refutations of its thesis and three confirmations. Which were easier to create? If you found it easier to supply supportive arguments, your sympathy probably lies with the writer's position. Another way to test your understanding of the essay is to furnish three examples that could support the argument and three examples that could negate it. You may wish to attempt this exercise after reading Neil Bissoondath's essay.

5. Ask yourself whether you understand all the references and words in the essay, and look up any that you don't understand.

6. Let the experienced writer help you with your own writing. Select a master sentence from the essay you have just read—one that caught your attention. Analyze the grammar of that sentence, ascertaining the position and relationship of the sentence's main elements. Then, using another subject, try writing a sentence with the same basic grammatical structure. Ask yourself if this is a structure that you frequently employ; if it is not, practise it until its use comes naturally.

Clearly, there is much that we can learn from reading essays. The voice speaking to us may be from another time or culture, it may speak to us of what we know or don't know, it may confirm our assumptions about the world around us, or it may demolish them. To respond fully to the essay, we must read critically, carefully, and passionately.

Plato

Greece ca. 428–348 B.C.

Plato is arguably the most influential philosopher of all time. Born in Athens into an aristocratic family, Plato was a follower of Socrates, the Athenian philosopher. When Socrates was forced by his political enemies to commit suicide, Plato left Athens to travel through the Grecian world. In about 387 B.C., he opened his Academy at Athens, the first school of philosophy, law, and science and the model for our universities today. Plato's writings, all of which have survived, deal with philosophical issues mainly through imagined dialogues. His most famous work, *The Republic*, discusses a utopian society and the nature of human knowledge, justice, and societal institutions. Plato described three types of people in this ethical treatise: the philosopher, whose goal is to achieve wisdom; the hedonist, whose purpose is to experience pleasure; and the man of action, whose aim is to win recognition for his abilities. In "The Allegory of the Cave," Plato uses dialogue to explore the nature and limits of human knowledge.

The Allegory of the Cave   ca. 4th century B.C.

1   And now, I said, let me show in a figure how far our nature is enlightened or unenlightened: Behold! human beings living in an underground den, which has a mouth open towards the light and reaching all along the den; here they have been from their childhood, and have their legs and necks chained so that they cannot move, and can only see before them, being prevented by the chains from turning round their heads. Above and behind them a fire is blazing at a distance, and between the fire and the prisoners there is a raised way; and you will see, if you look, a low wall built along the way, like the screen which marionette players have in front of them, over which they show the puppets.

2   I see.

3   And do you see, I said, men passing along the wall carrying all sorts of vessels, and statues and figures of animals made of wood and stone and various materials, which appear over the wall? Some of them are talking, others silent.

4   You have shown me a strange image, and they are strange prisoners.

5   Like ourselves, I replied; and they see only their own shadows, or the shadows of one another, which the fire throws on the opposite wall of the cave?

6   True, he said; how could they see anything but the shadows if they were never allowed to move their heads?

7   And of the objects which are being carried in like manner they would only see the shadows?

8   Yes, he said.

9   And if they were able to converse with one another, would they not suppose that they were naming what was actually before them?

10   Very true.

11   And suppose further that the prison had an echo which came from the other side, would they not be sure to fancy when one of the passers-by spoke that the voice which they heard came from the passing shadow?

12   No question, he replied.

13   To them, I said, the truth would be literally nothing but the shadows of the images.

14   That is certain.

15   And now look again, and see what will naturally follow if the prisoners are released and disabused of their error. At first, when any of them is liberated and compelled suddenly to stand up and turn his neck round and walk and look towards the light, he will suffer sharp pains; the glare will distress him and he will be unable to see the realities of which in his former state he had seen the shadows; and then conceive some one saying to him, that what he saw before was an illusion, but that now, when he is approaching nearer to being and his eye is turned towards more real existence, he has a clearer vision—what will be his reply? And you may further imagine that his instructor is pointing to the objects as they pass and requiring him to name them—will he not be perplexed? Will he not fancy that the shadows which he formerly saw are truer than the objects which are now shown to him?

16   Far truer.

17   And if he is compelled to look straight at the light, will he not have a pain in his eyes which will make him turn away to take refuge in the objects of vision which he can see, and which he will conceive to be in reality clearer than the things which are now being shown to him?

18   True, he said.

19   And suppose once more, that he is reluctantly dragged up a steep and rugged ascent, and held fast until he is forced into the presence of the sun himself, is he not likely to be pained and irritated? When he approaches the light his eyes will be dazzled and he will not be able to see anything at all of what are now called realities.

20   Not all in a moment, he said.

21   He will require to grow accustomed to the sight of the upper world. And first he will see the shadows best, next the reflections of men and other objects in the water, and then the objects themselves; then he will gaze upon the light of the moon and the stars and the spangled heaven; and he will see the sky and the stars by night better than the sun or the light of the sun by day?

22   Certainly.

23   Last of all he will be able to see the sun, and not mere reflections of him in the water, but he will see him in his own proper place, and not in another; and he will contemplate him as he is.

24   Certainly.

25   He will then proceed to argue that this is he who gives the season and the years, and is the guardian of all that is in the visible world, and in a certain way the cause of all things which he and his fellows have been accustomed to behold?

26   Clearly, he said, he would first see the sun and then reason about him.

27   And when he remembered his old habitation, and the wisdom of the den and his fellow-prisoners, do you not suppose that he would felicitate himself on the change, and pity them?

28   Certainly, he would.

29   And if they were in the habit of conferring honors among themselves on those who were quickest to observe the passing shadows and to remark which of them went before, and which followed after, and which were together; and who were therefore best able to draw conclusions as to the future, do you think that he would care for such honors and glories, or envy the possessors of them? Would he not say with Homer,

Better to be the poor servant of a poor master,

and to endure anything, rather than think as they do and live after their manner?

30   Yes, he said, I think that he would rather suffer anything than entertain these false notions and live in this miserable manner.

31   Imagine once more, I said, such a one coming suddenly out of the sun to be replaced in his old situation; would he not be certain to have his eyes full of darkness?

32   To be sure, he said.

33   And if there were a contest, and he had to compete in measuring the shadows with the prisoners who had never moved out of the den, while his sight was still weak, and before his eyes had become steady (and the time which would be needed to acquire this new habit of sight might be very considerable) would he not be ridiculous? Men would say of him that up he went and down he came without his eyes; and that it was better not even to think of ascending; and if any one tried to loose another and lead him up to the light, let them only catch the offender, and they would put him to death.

34   No question, he said.

35   This entire allegory, I said, you may now append, dear Glaucon, to the previous argument, the prison-house is the world of sight, the light of the fire is the sun, and you will not misapprehend me if you interpret the journey upwards to be the ascent of the soul into the intellectual world according to my poor belief, which, at your desire, I have expressed—whether rightly or wrongly God knows. But, whether true or false, my opinion is that in the world of knowledge the idea of good appears last of all, and is seen only with an effort; and, when seen, is also inferred to be the universal author of all things beautiful and right, parent of light and of the lord of light in this visible world, and the immediate source of reason and truth in the intellectual; and that this is the power upon which he who would act rationally either in public or private life must have his eye fixed.

36   I agree, he said, as far as I am able to understand you.

37   Moreover, I said, you must not wonder that those who attain to this beatific vision are unwilling to descend to human affairs; for their souls are ever hastening into the upper world where they desire to dwell; which desire of theirs is very natural, if our allegory may be trusted.

38   Yes, very natural.

39   And is there anything surprising in one who passes from divine contemplations to the evil state of man, misbehaving himself in a ridiculous manner; if, while his eyes are blinking and before he has become accustomed to the surrounding darkness, he is compelled to fight in courts of law, or in other places, about the images or the shadows of images of justice, and is endeavouring to meet the conceptions of those who have never yet seen absolute justice?

40   Anything but surprising, he replied.

41   Any one who has common sense will remember that the bewilderments of the eyes are of two kinds, and arise from two causes, either from coming out of the light or from going into the light, which is true of the mind's eye, quite as much as of the bodily eye; and he who remembers this when he sees any one whose vision is perplexed and weak, will not be too ready to laugh; he will first ask whether that soul of man has come out of the brighter life, and is unable to see because unaccustomed to the dark, or having turned from darkness to the day is dazzled by excess of light. And he will count the one happy in his condition and state of being, and he will pity the other; or, if he had a mind to laugh at the soul which comes from below into the light, there will be more reason in this than in the laugh which greets him who returns from above out of the light into the den.

42   That, he said, is a very just distinction.

Sir Thomas More

England 1478–1535

Sir Thomas More, who studied at Oxford and the Inns of Court, was one of the best-known writers of the English Renaissance. More's writing and his life reflect the fact that he was divided between the secular and the religious worlds. On the one hand, his interest in works such as *Plato' Republic* shows in his social commentary in *Utopia*. As a humanist, he argued for community ownership of property, a stance that is evident in Utopia. On the other hand, his high moral standards brought him into conflict with Henry VIII's quarrel with the Catholic Church. When Henry wanted to become the head of the Church of England and have it separate from the Catholic Church, More refused to agree to the Act of Succession and Supremacy. This was declared treason, and More was beheaded.

From Utopia   1516

THEIR GOLD AND SILVER

1   For these reasons, therefore, they have accumulated a vast treasure, but they do not keep it like a treasure. I'm really quite ashamed to tell you how they do keep it, because you probably won't believe me. I would not have believed it myself if someone had just told me about it; but I was there, and saw it with my own eyes. As a general rule, the more different anything is from what people are used to, the harder it is to accept. But considering that all their other customs are so unlike ours, a sensible man will not be surprised that they treat gold and silver quite dif-

ferently from the way we do. After all, they never do use money among themselves, but keep it only for a contingency that may or may not actually arise. So in the meanwhile they take care that no one shall overvalue gold and silver, of which money is made, beyond what the metals themselves deserve. Anyone can see, for example, that iron is far superior to either; men could not live without iron, by heaven, any more than without fire or water. But gold and silver have, by nature, no function with which we cannot easily dispense. Human folly has made them precious because they are rare. But in fact nature, like a most indulgent mother, has placed her best gifts out in the open, like air, water, and the earth itself; vain and unprofitable things she has hidden away in remote places.

2   If in Utopia[1] gold and silver were kept locked up in some tower, foolish heads among the common people might concoct a story that the prince and senate were out to cheat ordinary folk and get some advantage for themselves. Of course, the gold and silver might be put into beautiful plate-ware and such rich handiwork, but then in case of necessity the people would not want to give up such articles, on which they had begun to fix their hearts—only to melt them down for soldiers' pay. To avoid these problems they thought of a plan which conforms with their institutions as clearly as it contrasts with our own. Unless one has actually seen it working, their plan may seem incredible, because we prize gold so highly and are so careful about guarding it. With them it's just the other way. While they eat from earthenware dishes and drink from glass cups, finely made but inexpensive, their chamber pots and all their humblest vessels, for use in common halls and even in private homes, are made of gold and silver. The chains and heavy fetters of slaves are also made of these metals. Finally, criminals who are to bear the mark of some disgraceful act are forced to wear golden rings in their ears and on their fingers, golden chains around their necks, even gold crowns on their heads. Thus they hold up gold and silver to scorn in every conceivable way. As a result, if they had to part with their entire supply of these metals, which other people give up with as much agony as if they were being disemboweled, the Utopians feel it no more than the loss of a penny.

3   They pick up pearls by the seashore, diamonds and garnets in certain cliffs, but never go out of set purpose to look for them. If they happen to find some, they polish them and give them to the children, who feel proud and pleased with such gaudy decorations when they are small. But after, when they grow a bit older and notice that only babies like such toys, they lay them aside. The parents don't have to say anything, they simply put these trifles away out of a shamefaced sense that they're no longer suitable, just as our children, when they grow up, put away their marbles, rattles, and dolls.

4   Different customs, different feelings: I never saw the adage better illustrated than in the case of the Anemolian[2] ambassadors, who came to Amaurot while I was there. Because they came to discuss important business, the senate had assembled ahead of time, three citizens from each city. The ambassadors from nearby nations, who had visited Utopia before and knew the local customs, realized that fine clothing was not much respected in that land, silk was despised, and gold a

---

1   More's name for the perfect land

2   from the Greek words for "windy people"

badge of contempt; therefore they always came in the very plainest of their clothes. But the Anemolians, who lived farther off and had had fewer dealings with the Utopians, had heard only that they all dressed alike and very simply; so they took for granted that their hosts had nothing to wear that they didn't put on. Being themselves rather more proud than wise, they decided to dress as splendidly as the very gods, and dazzle the eyes of the poor Utopians with their gaudy garb.

5   Consequently the three ambassadors made a grand entry with a suite of a hundred attendants, all in clothing of many colors, and most in silk. Being noblemen at home, the ambassadors were arrayed in cloth of gold, with heavy gold chains round their necks, gold jewels at their ears and on their fingers, and sparkling strings of pearls and gems on their caps. In fact, they were decked out in all the articles which in Utopia are used to punish slaves, shame wrongdoers, or pacify infants. It was a sight to see how they strutted when they compared their finery with the dress of the Utopians who had poured out into the street to see them pass. But it was just as funny to see how wide they fell of the mark, and how far they were from getting the consideration they expected. Except for a very few Utopians who for some special reason had visited foreign countries, all the onlookers considered this splendid pomp a mark of disgrace. They therefore bowed to the humblest servants as lords, and took the ambassadors, because of their golden chains, to be slaves, passing them by without any reverence at all. You might have seen children, who had themselves thrown away their pearls and gems, nudge their mothers when they saw the ambassadors' jeweled caps, and say: "Look at that big lout, mother, who's still wearing pearls and jewels as if he were a little kid!" But the mother, in all seriousness, would answer, "Quiet, son, I think he is one of the ambassadors' fools."

6   Others found fault with the golden chains as useless because they were so flimsy any slave could break them, and so loose that he could easily shake them off and run away whenever he wanted.

7   But after the ambassadors had spent a couple of days among the Utopians, they learned of the immense amounts of gold which were as thoroughly despised there as they were prized at home. They saw too that more gold and silver went into making chains and fetters for a single runaway slave than into costuming all three of them. Somewhat crestfallen, then, they put away all the finery in which they had strutted so arrogantly; but they saw the wisdom of doing so after they had talked with the Utopians enough to learn their customs and opinions.

MARRIAGE CUSTOMS

8   Women do not marry till they are eighteen, nor men till they are twenty-two. Clandestine premarital intercourse, if discovered and proved, brings severe punishment on both man and woman; and the guilty parties are forbidden to marry for their whole lives, unless the prince by his pardon mitigates the sentence. Also both the father and mother of the household where the offense occurred suffer public disgrace for having been remiss in their duty. The reason they punish this offense so severely is that they suppose few people would join in married love— with confinement to a single partner and all the petty annoyances that married life involves—unless they were strictly restrained from promiscuity.

9   In choosing marriage partners they solemnly and seriously follow a custom which seemed to us foolish and absurd in the extreme. Whether she be widow or virgin, the bride-to-be is shown naked to the groom by a responsible and respectable matron; and similarly, some respectable man presents the groom naked to his prospective bride. We laughed at this custom, and called it absurd; but they were just as amazed at the folly of all other peoples. When men go to buy a colt, where they are risking only a little money, they are so cautious that, though the animal is almost bare, they won't close the deal until saddle and blanket have been taken off, lest there be a hidden sore underneath. Yet in the choice of a mate, which may cause either delight or disgust for the rest of their lives, men are so careless that they leave all the rest of the woman's body covered up with clothes and estimate her attractiveness from a mere handsbreadth of her person, the face, which is all they can see. And so they marry, running great risk of bitter discord, if something in either's person should offend the other. Not all people are so wise as to concern themselves solely with character; even the wise appreciate physical beauty as a supplement to a good disposition. There's no doubt that a deformity may lurk under clothing, serious enough to make a man hate his wife when it's too late to be separated from her. If some disfiguring accident takes place after marriage, each person must bear his own fate; but the Utopians think everyone should be legally protected from deception beforehand.

10   There is extra reason for them to be careful, because in that part of the world, they are the only people who practice monogamy, and because their marriages are seldom terminated except by death, though they do allow divorce for adultery or for intolerably offensive behavior. A husband or wife who is an aggrieved party to such a divorce is granted leave by the senate to take a new mate, but the guilty party suffers disgrace and is permanently forbidden to remarry. They absolutely forbid a husband to put away his wife against her will and without any fault on her part, just because of some bodily misfortune; they think it cruel that a person should be abandoned when most in need of comfort; and they add that old age, since it not only entails disease but is a disease itself, needs more than a precarious fidelity.

11   It happens occasionally that a married couple cannot get along, and have both found other persons with whom they hope to live more harmoniously. After getting approval of the senate, they may then separate by mutual consent and contract new marriages. But such divorces are allowed only after the senators and their wives have carefully investigated the case. Divorce is deliberately made difficult because they know that couples will have a hard time settling down if each has in mind that another new relation is easily available.

12   They punish adulterers with the strictest form of slavery. If both parties were married, both are divorced, and the injured parties may marry one another if they want, or someone else. But if one of the injured parties continues to love such an undeserving spouse, the marriage may go on, provided the innocent person chooses to share in the labor to which every slave is condemned. And sometimes it happens that the repentance of the guilty and the devotion of the innocent party so move the prince to pity that he restores both to freedom. But a second conviction of adultery is punished by death.

RELIGIONS

13   There are different forms of religion throughout the island, and in the different cities as well. Some worship as a god the sun, others the moon, still others one of the planets. There are some who worship a man of past ages, conspicuous either for virtue or glory; they consider him not only a god, but the supreme god. The vast majority of Utopians, however, and among these all the wisest, believe nothing of the sort: they believe in a single power, unknown, eternal, infinite, inexplicable, far beyond the grasp of the human mind, and diffused throughout the universe, not physically, but in influence. Him they call father, and to him alone they attribute the origin, increase, progress, change, and end of all visible things; they do not offer divine honors to any other.

14   Though the other sects differ from this group in various particular doctrines, they all agree in a single main head, that there is one supreme power, the maker and ruler of the universe; in their native tongue they all call him Mithra. Different people define him differently, and each supposes the object of his worship is the special vessel of that great force which all people agree in worshipping. But gradually they are coming to forsake this mixture of superstitions and unite in that one religion which seems more reasonable than any of the others. And there is no doubt that the other religions would have disappeared long ago, had not various unlucky accidents, befalling certain Utopians who were thinking of changing their religion, been interpreted as a sign of divine anger, not chance—as if the deity who was being abandoned were avenging an insult against himself.

15   But after they heard from us the name of Christ, and learned of his teachings, his life, his miracles, and the no less marvelous devotion of the many martyrs whose blood, freely shed, had drawn nations far and near into the Christian fellowship, you would not believe how they were impressed. Either through the secret inspiration of God, or because Christianity seemed very like the belief that most prevails among them, they were well disposed toward it from the start. But I think they were also much influenced by the fact that Christ encouraged his disciples to practice community of goods, and that among the truest groups of Christians, the practice still prevails. Whatever the reason, no small number of them chose to join our communion and were washed in the holy water of baptism.

16   By that time, two of our group had died, and among us four survivors there was, I am sorry to say, no priest. So, though they received instruction in other matters, they still lack those sacraments which in our religion can be administered only by priests. They do, however, understand what these are, and eagerly desire them. In fact, they dispute warmly whether a man chosen from among themselves could be considered a priest without ordination by a Christian bishop. Though they seemed about to select such a person, they had not yet done so when I left.

17   Those who have not accepted Christianity make no effort to restrain others from it, nor do they criticize new converts to it. While I was there, only one of the Christians got into trouble with the law. As soon as he was baptized, he took on himself to preach the Christian religion publicly, with more zeal than discretion. We warned him not to do so, but he soon worked himself up to a pitch where he not only preferred our religion, but condemned all others as profane, leading their impious and sacrilegious followers to the hell-fires they richly deserved. After he had been going on in this style for a long time, they arrested him. He was

tried on a charge, not of despising their religion, but of creating a public disorder, convicted, and sentenced to exile. For it is one of their oldest rules that no one should suffer for his religion.

18   Even before he took over the island, King Utopus had heard that the natives were continually squabbling over religious matters. Actually, he found it easy to conquer the country because the different sects were too busy fighting one another to oppose him. As soon as he had gained the victory, therefore, he decreed that every man might cultivate the religion of his choice, and proselytize for it too, provided he did so quietly, modestly, rationally, and without bitterness toward others. If persuasions failed, no man might resort to abuse or violence, under penalty of exile or slavery.

19   Utopus laid down these rules, not simply for the sake of peace, which he saw was being destroyed by constant quarrels and implacable hatreds, but also for the sake of religion itself. In such matters he was not at all quick to dogmatize, because he suspected that God perhaps likes various forms of worship and has therefore deliberately inspired different men with different views. On the other hand, he was quite sure that it was arrogant folly for anyone to enforce conformity with his own beliefs by threats or violence. He supposed that if one religion is really true and the rest are false, the true one will sooner or later prevail by its own natural strength, if men will only consider the matter reasonably and moderately. But if they try to decide things by fighting and rioting, since the worst men are always most head-strong, the best and holiest religion in the world will be crowded out by foolish superstitions, like grain choked out of a field by thorns and briars. So he left the whole matter open, allowing each person to choose what he would believe. The only exception was a positive and strict law against anyone who should sink so far below the dignity of human nature as to think that the soul perishes with the body, or that the universe is ruled by blind chance, not divine providence.

20   Thus they believe that after this life vices will be punished and virtue rewarded. Anyone who denies this proposition they consider less than a man, since he has degraded the sublimity of his own soul to the base level of a beast's wretched body. Still less will they not even count him as one of their citizens, since he would openly despise all the laws and customs of society, if not prevented by fear. Who can doubt that a man who has nothing to fear but the law, and no hope of life beyond the grave, will do anything he can to evade his country's laws by craft or to break them by vio-lence, in order to gratify his own personal greed? Therefore a man who holds such views is offered no honors, entrusted with no offices, and given no public responsi-bility; he is universally regarded as a low and sordid fellow. Yet they do not punish him, because they are persuaded that no man can choose to believe by a mere act of the will. They do not compel him by threats to dissemble his views, nor do they tol-erate in the matter any deceit or lying, which they detest as next door to deliberate malice. The man may not argue with common people in behalf of his opinion; but in the presence of priests and other important persons, they not only permit but encourage it. For they are confident that in the end his madness will yield to reason.

21   There are some others, in fact no small number of them, who err the other way in supposing that animals too have immortal souls, though not comparable to ours in excellence nor destined to equal felicity. These men are not thought to be evil, their opinion is not considered wholly unreasonable, and so they are not interfered with.

22   Almost all the Utopians are absolutely convinced that man's bliss after death will be enormous and eternal; thus they lament every man's sickness, but mourn over a death only if the man was torn from life wretchedly and against his will. Such behavior they take to be a very bad sign, as if the soul, despairing and conscious of guilt, dreaded death through a secret premonition of punishments to come. Besides, they suppose God can hardly be well pleased with the coming of one who, when he is summoned, does not come gladly, but is dragged off reluctantly and against his will. Such a death fills the onlookers with horror, and they carry off the corpse to the cemetery in melancholy silence. There, after begging God to have mercy on his spirit and to pardon his infirmities, they bury the unhappy man. But when someone dies blithely and full of good hope, they do not mourn for him, but carry the body cheerfully away, singing and commending the dead man's soul to God. They cremate him in a spirit of reverence more than of grief, and erect a tombstone on which the dead man's honors are inscribed. As they go home, they talk of his character and deeds, and no part of his life is mentioned more frequently or more gladly than his joyful death.

23   They think that recollecting the good qualities of a man inspires the living to behave virtuously and is the most acceptable form of honor to the dead. For they think that dead persons are actually present among us, and hear what we say about them, though through the dullness of human sight they remain invisible. Given their state of bliss, the dead must be able to travel freely where they please, and it would be unkind of them to cast off every desire of seeing those friends to whom in life they had been joined by mutual affection and charity. Like other good qualities they think that after death charity is increased rather than diminished in all good men; and thus they believe the dead come frequently among the living, to observe their words and acts. Hence they go about their business the more confidently because of their trust in such protectors; and the belief that their forefathers are physically present keeps men from any secret dishonorable deed.

24   Fortune-telling and other vain, superstitious divinations, such as other peoples take very seriously, they consider ridiculous and contemptible. But they venerate miracles which occur without the help of nature, considering them direct and visible manifestations of the divinity. Indeed, they report that miracles have often occurred in their country. Sometimes in great and dangerous crises they pray publicly for a miracle, which they then anticipate with great confidence, and obtain.

25   They think the investigation of nature and the reverence rising from it are most acceptable to God. There are some people, however, and quite a few of them, who from religious motives reject literary and scientific pursuits, and refuse all leisure, but devote their full time to good works. Only by constant dedication to the offices of charity, these people think, can happiness after death be earned; and so they are always busy. Some tend the sick; others repair roads, clean ditches, rebuild bridges, dig turf, sand, or stones; still others fell trees and cut them up, and transport wood, grain, or other commodities into the cities by wagon. They work for private citizens as well as for the public, and work even harder than slaves. With cheery good will they undertake any task that is so rough, hard, and dirty that most people refuse to tackle it because of the toil, boredom, and frustration involved. While constantly engaged in heavy labor themselves, they procure leisure for others, yet claim no credit for it. They neither criticize the way others

live, nor boast of their own doings. The more they put themselves in the position of slaves, the more highly they are honored by everyone.

26   These people are of two sects. The first are celibates who abstain not only from sex, but also from eating meat, and some from any sort of animal food whatever. They reject all the pleasures of this life as harmful, and look forward only to the joys of the life to come, which they hope to merit by hard labor and all-night vigils. As they hope to attain it soon, they are cheerful and active in the here and now. The other kind are just as fond of hard work, but prefer to marry. They don't despise the comforts of marriage, but think as they owe nature their labor, so they owe children to their country. Unless it interferes with their labor, they avoid no pleasure, and gladly eat meat, precisely because they think it makes them stronger for any sort of heavy work. The Utopians regard the second sort as more sensible, but the first sort as holier. If anyone chose celibacy over marriage and a hard life over a comfortable one on grounds of reason alone, they would laugh at him; but as these men say they are motivated by religion, the Utopians respect and revere them. On no subject are they warier of jumping to conclusions than in this matter of religion. Such then are the men whom in their own language they call Buthrescas, a term which can be translated as "specially religious."

Thomas Hobbes

England 1588–1679

Thomas Hobbes, one of the notable English philosophers of the seventeenth century, was best known for his materialist outlook. Not surprisingly, he fled to France when the civil war broke out in England, preferring to remove himself from the conflict even though he had initially favoured the royalist position. While waiting out the war in France from 1640 to 1651, he wrote *Leviathan*, his best-known work. The secular tone of the book did not sit well with the Puritans, but when Hobbes returned to England, he made peace with Cromwell; ironically, he was subsequently pensioned by Charles II after the Restoration. During the period, Hobbesian materialism became a subject for ministers to attack and skeptics to embrace.

From Leviathan, Part 1   1651

CHAPTER 1. OF SENSE

1   Concerning the thoughts of man, I will consider them first singly and afterwards in train or dependence upon one another. Singly, they are every one a representation or appearance of some quality or other accident of a body without us, which is commonly called an object. Which object worketh on the eyes, ears, and other parts of man's body, and by diversity of working produceth diversity of appearances.

2   The original of them all is that which we call sense. (For there is no conception in a man's mind which hath not at first, totally or by parts, been begotten upon the organs of sense.) The rest are derived from that original.

3   To know the natural cause of sense is not very necessary to the business now in hand, and I have elsewhere written of the same at large. Nevertheless, to fill each part of my present method, I will briefly deliver the same in this place.

4   The cause of sense is the external body or object which presseth the organ proper to each sense, either immediately as in the taste and touch, or mediately, as in seeing, hearing, and smelling; which pressure, by the mediation of nerves and other strings and membranes of the body continued inwards to the brain and heart, causeth there a resistance or counter-pressure or endeavor of the heart to deliver itself; which endeavor, because outward, seemeth to be some matter without. And this seeming or fancy is that which men call sense; and consisteth, as to the eye, in a light or color figured; to the ear, in a sound; to the nostril in an odor; to the tongue and palate in a savor; and to the rest of the body in heat, cold, hardness, softness, and such other qualities as we discern by feeling. All which qualities called "sensible"[1] are, in the object that causeth them, but so many several motions of the matter by which it presseth our organs diversely. Neither, in us that are pressed, are they anything else but diverse motions; for motion produceth nothing but motion. But their appearance to us is fancy, the same waking, that dreaming. And as pressing, rubbing, or striking the eye makes us fancy a light; and pressing the ear produceth a din; so do the bodies also we see or hear produce the same by their strong though unobserved actions. For if those colors and sounds were in the bodies or objects that cause them, they could not be severed from them, as by glasses[2] and in echoes by reflection we see they are; where we know the thing we see is in one place, the appearance in another. And though at some certain distance the real and very object seem invested with the fancy it begets in us, yet still the object is one thing, the image or fancy is another. So that sense in all cases is nothing else but original fancy, caused (as I have said) by the pressure, that is by the motion, of external things upon our eyes, ears, and other organs thereunto ordained.

5   But the philosophy-schools through all the universities of Christendom, grounded upon certain texts of Aristotle, teach another doctrine, and say for the cause of vision, that the thing seen sendeth forth on every side a visible species— in English, a visible show, apparition, or aspect, or a being seen—the receiving whereof into the eye is seeing. And for the cause of hearing, that the thing heard sendeth forth an audible species, that is an audible aspect or audible being seen, which entering at the ear maketh hearing. Nay for the cause of understanding also they say the thing understood sendeth forth intelligible species, that is an intelligible being seen, which coming into the understanding makes us understand. I say not this as disapproving the use of universities, but because I am to speak hereafter of their office in a commonwealth, I must let you see on all occasions by the way what things would be amended in them; amongst which the frequency of insignificant speech is one.

---

1   accessible through the body's senses
2   mirrors

CHAPTER 13. OF THE NATURAL CONDITION OF MANKIND AS CONCERNING THEIR FELICITY AND MISERY

6   Nature hath made men so equal in the faculties of body and mind as that, though there be found one man sometimes manifestly stronger in body or of quicker mind than another, yet when all is reckoned together, the difference between man and man is not so considerable as that one man can thereupon claim to himself any benefit, to which another may not pretend as well as he. For as to the strength of body, the weakest has strength enough to kill the strongest, either by secret machination, or by confederacy with others that are in the same danger with himself.

7   And as to the faculties of the mind—setting aside the arts grounded upon words, and especially that skill of proceeding upon general and infallible rules, called science; which very few have, and but in few things; as being not a native faculty, born with us; nor attained, as prudence, while we look after somewhat else— I find yet a greater equality amongst men than that of strength. For prudence is but experience, which equal time equally bestows on all men, in those things they equally apply themselves unto. That which may perhaps make such equality incredible is but a vain conceit of one's own wisdom, which almost all men think they have in a greater degree than the vulgar[3]—that is, than all men but themselves and a few others, whom by fame, or for concurring with themselves, they approve. For such is the nature of men, that howsoever they may acknowledge many others to be more witty, or more eloquent, or more learned, yet they will hardly believe there be many so wise as themselves; for they see their own wit at hand, and other men's at a distance. But this proveth rather that men are in that point equal, than unequal. For there is not ordinarily a greater sign of the equal distribution of anything than that every man is contented with his share.

8   From this equality of ability ariseth equality of hope in the attaining of our ends. And therefore if any two men desire the same thing, which nevertheless they cannot both enjoy, they become enemies; and in the way to their end (which is principally their own conservation, and sometimes their delectation[4] only) endeavor to destroy or subdue one another. And from hence it comes to pass, that where an invader hath no more to fear than another man's single power, if one plant, sow, build, or possess a convenient seat, others may probably be expected to come prepared with forces united, to dispossess and deprive him, not only of the fruit of his labor, but also of his life or liberty. And the invader again is in the like danger of another.

9   And from this diffidence[5] of one another, there is no way for any man to secure himself so reasonable as anticipation; that is, by force or wiles to master the persons of all men he can, so long, till he see no other power great enough to endanger him; and this is no more than his own conservation requireth, and is generally allowed. Also because there be some, that taking pleasure in contemplating their own power in the acts of conquest, which they pursue farther than their security requires; if others that otherwise would be glad to be at ease within

---

3   the lower classes
4   enjoyment
5   distrust, lack of faith

modest bounds, should not by invasion increase their power, they would not be able long time, by standing only on their defense, to subsist. And by consequence, such augmentation of dominion over men being necessary to a man's conservation, it ought to be allowed him.

10   Again, men have no pleasure, but on the contrary a great deal of grief, in keeping company, where there is no power able to overawe them all. For every man looketh that his companion should value him at the same rate he sets upon himself; and upon all signs of contempt, or undervaluing, naturally endeavors, as far as he dares (which amongst them that have no common power to keep them in quiet, is far enough to make them destroy each other), to extort a greater value from his contemners[6] by damage, and from others by the example.

11   So that in the nature of man, we find three principal causes of quarrel. First, competition; secondly, diffidence; thirdly, glory.

12   The first maketh men invade for gain; the second, for safety; and the third, for reputation. The first use violence to make themselves masters of other men's persons, wives, children, and cattle; the second, to defend them; the third, for trifles, as a word, a smile, a different opinion, and any other sign of undervalue, either direct in their persons, or by reflection in their kindred, their friends, their nation, their profession, or their name.

13   Hereby it is manifest that during the time men live without a common power to keep them all in awe, they are in that condition which is called war; and such a war as is of every man against every man. For war consisteth not in battle only, or the act of fighting, but in a tract of time wherein the will to contend by battle is sufficiently known; and therefore the notion of time is to be considered in the nature of war, as it is in the nature of weather. For as the nature of foul weather lieth not in a shower or two of rain, but in an inclination thereto of many days together; so the nature of war consisteth not in actual fighting, but in the known disposition thereto, during all the time there is no assurance to the contrary. All other time is peace.

14   Whatsoever therefore is consequent to a time of war, where every man is enemy to every man, the same is consequent to the time wherein men live without other security than what their own strength and their own invention shall furnish them withal. In such condition there is no place for industry, because the fruit thereof is uncertain, and consequently no culture of the earth; no navigation, nor use of the commodities that may be imported by sea; no commodious building; no instruments of moving, and removing, such things as require much force; no knowledge of the face of the earth; no account of time; no arts; no letters; no society; and, which is worst of all, continual fear, and danger of violent death; and the life of man, solitary, poor, nasty, brutish, and short.

15   It may seem strange to some man that has not well weighed these things, that nature should thus dissociate and render men apt to invade and destroy one another; and he may therefore, not trusting to this inference, made from the passions, desire perhaps to have the same confirmed by experience. Let him therefore consider with himself, when taking a journey, he arms himself and seeks to go well accompanied; when going to sleep, he locks his doors; when even in his house he locks his chests; and this when he knows there be laws, and public offi-

---

6   condemners

cers, armed, to revenge all injuries shall be done him; what opinion he has of his fellow subjects, when he rides armed; of his fellow citizens, when he locks his doors; and of his children and servants, when he locks his chests. Does he not there as much accuse mankind by his actions, as I do by my words? But neither of us accuse man's nature in it. The desires and other passions of man are in themselves no sin. No more are the actions that proceed from those passions, till they know a law that forbids them, which, till laws be made, they cannot know; nor can any law be made, till they have agreed upon the person that shall make it.

16   It may peradventure be thought there was never such a time nor condition of war as this; and I believe it was never generally so, over all the world; but there are many places where they live so now. For the savage people in many places of America, except the government of small families, the concord whereof dependeth on natural lust, have no government at all and live at this day in that brutish manner as I said before. Howsoever, it may be perceived what manner of life there would be, where there were no common power to fear, by the manner of life which men that have formerly lived under a peaceful government use to degenerate into in a civil war.

17   But though there had never been any time wherein particular men were in a condition of war one against another, yet in all times, kings and persons of sovereign authority, because of their independency, are in continual jealousies, and in the state and posture of gladiators; having their weapons pointing, and their eyes fixed on one another; that is, their forts, garrisons, and guns upon the frontiers of their kingdoms, and continual spies upon their neighbors, which is a posture of war. But because they uphold thereby the industry of their subjects, there does not follow from it that misery which accompanies the liberty of particular men.

18   To this war of every man against every man, this also is consequent: that nothing can be unjust. The notions of right and wrong, justice and injustice, have there no place. Where there is no common power, there is no law; where no law, no injustice. Force and fraud are in war the two cardinal virtues. Justice and injustice are none of the faculties neither of the body nor mind. If they were, they might be in a man that were alone in the world, as well as his senses and passions. They are qualities that relate to men in society, not in solitude. It is consequent also to the same condition that there be no propriety,[7] no dominion, no *mine* and *thine* distinct; but only that to be every man's, that he can get; and for so long as he can keep it. And thus much for the ill condition which man by mere nature is actually placed in; though with a possibility to come out of it, consisting partly in the passions, partly in his reason.

19   The passions that incline men to peace are fear of death, desire of such things as are necessary to commodious living, and a hope by their industry to obtain them. And reason suggesteth convenient articles of peace, upon which men may be drawn to agreement. These articles are they which otherwise are called the Laws of Nature, whereof I shall speak more particularly in the two following chapters.

---

7   property

Jonathan Swift

Ireland 1667–1745

Born into an Anglo-Irish family in Dublin, Jonathan Swift reluctantly became an Anglican cleric yet soon realized his gift for penetrating satire and social criticism in poetry and prose. Swift moved to England in 1688, abandoned his political affiliation with the Liberals, and became involved with the Tories and their journal, *The Examiner.* As a reward, Swift was made dean of St. Patrick's Cathedral, Dublin. Swift's opposition to political and social oppression is central to his essay "A Modest Proposal," in which his naive Anglo-Irish narrator makes outrageous suggestions for how poverty in Ireland can be eliminated.

A Modest Proposal   1729

For Preventing the Children of Poor People in Ireland from Being a Burden to Their Parents or Country, and for Making Them Beneficial to the Public

1   It is a melancholy object to those who walk through this great town or travel in the country, when they see the streets, the roads, and cabin doors, crowded with beggars of the female sex, followed by three, four, or six children, all in rags and importuning every passenger for an alms. These mothers, instead of being able to work for their honest livelihood, are forced to employ all their time in strolling to beg sustenance for their helpless infants, who, as they grow up, either turn thieves for want of work, or leave their dear native country to fight for the Pretender in Spain, or sell themselves to the Barbadoes.[1]

2   I think it is agreed by all parties that this prodigious number of children in the arms, or on the backs, or at the heels of their mothers, and frequently of their fathers, is in the present deplorable state of the kingdom a very great additional grievance; and therefore whoever could find out a fair, cheap, and easy method of making these children sound, useful members of the commonwealth would deserve so well of the public as to have his statue set up for a preserver of the nation.

3   But my intention is very far from being confined to provide only for the children of professed beggars; it is of a much greater extent, and shall take in the whole number of infants at a certain age who are born of parents in effect as little able to support them as those who demand our charity in the streets.

4   As to my own part, having turned my thoughts for many years upon this important subject, and maturely weighed the several schemes of other projectors,

---

1   James Stuart, the son of James II, claimed the throne of England and gained the loyalty of Irish Catholics; Irish immigrants to the West Indies indentured themselves to plantation owners there to escape Ireland's endemic poverty.

I have always found them grossly mistaken in their computation. It is true, a child just dropped from its dam may be supported by her milk for a solar year, with little other nourishment; at most not above the value of two shillings, which the mother may certainly get, or the value in scraps, by her lawful occupation of begging; and it is exactly at one year old that I propose to provide for them in such a manner as instead of being a charge upon their parents or the parish, or wanting food and raiment for the rest of their lives, they shall on the contrary contribute to the feeding and partly to the clothing, of many thousands.

5 　　There is likewise another great advantage in my scheme, that it will prevent those voluntary abortions, and that horrid practice of women murdering their bastard children, alas, too frequent among us, sacrificing the poor innocent babes, I doubt, more to avoid the expense than the shame, which would move tears and pity in the most savage and inhuman breast.

6 　　The number of souls in this kingdom being usually reckoned one million and a half, of these I calculate there may be about two hundred thousand couples whose wives are breeders; from which number I subtract thirty thousand couples who are able to maintain their own children, although I apprehend there cannot be so many under the present distresses of the kingdom; but this being granted, there will remain an hundred and seventy thousand breeders. I again subtract fifty thousand for those women who miscarry, or whose children die by accident or disease within the year. There only remain an hundred and twenty thousand children of poor parents annually born. The question therefore is, how this number shall be reared and provided for, which, as I have already said, under the present situation of affairs, is utterly impossible by all the methods hitherto proposed. For we can neither employ them in handicraft or agriculture; we neither build houses (I mean in the country) nor cultivate land. They can very seldom pick up a livelihood by stealing till they arrive at six years old, except where they are of towardly parts;[2] although I confess they learn the rudiments much earlier, during which time they can however be looked upon only as probationers, as I have been informed by a principal gentleman in the county of Cavan, who protested to me that he never knew above one or two instances under the age of six, even in a part of the kingdom so renowned for the quickest proficiency in that art.

7 　　I am assured by our merchants that a boy or a girl before twelve years old is no salable commodity; and even when they come to this age they will not yield above three pounds, or three pounds and half a crown at most on the Exchange; which cannot turn to account either to the parents or the kingdom, the charge of nutriment and rags having been at least four times that value.

8 　　I shall now therefore humbly propose my own thoughts, which I hope will not be liable to the least objection.

9 　　I have been assured by a very knowing American of my acquaintance in London, that a young healthy child well nursed is at a year old a most delicious, nourishing, and wholesome food, whether stewed, roasted, baked, or boiled; and I make no doubt that it will equally serve in a fricassee or a ragout.

10 　　I do therefore humbly offer it to public consideration that of the hundred and twenty thousand children, already computed, twenty thousand may be reserved for

---

2　exceptionally skilled

breed, whereof only one fourth part to be males, which is more than we allow to sheep, black cattle, or swine; and my reason is that these children are seldom the fruits of marriage, a circumstance not much regarded by our savages, therefore one male will be sufficient to serve four females. That the remaining hundred thousand may at a year old be offered in sale to the persons of quality and fortune through the kingdom, always advising the mother to let them suck plentifully in the last month, so as to render them plump and fat for a good table. A child will make two dishes at an entertainment for friends; and when the family dines alone, the fore or hind quarter will make a reasonable dish, and seasoned with a little pepper or salt will be very good boiled on the fourth day, especially in winter.

11   I have reckoned upon a medium that a child just born will weigh twelve pounds, and in a solar year if tolerably nursed increaseth to twenty-eight pounds.

12   I grant this food will be somewhat dear, and therefore very proper for landlords, who, as they have already devoured most of the parents, seem to have the best title to the children.

13   Infant's flesh will be in season throughout the year, but more plentiful in March, and a little before and after. For we are told by a grave author, an eminent French physician, that fish being a prolific diet, there are more children born in Roman Catholic countries about nine months after Lent than at any other season; therefore, reckoning a year after Lent, the markets will be more glutted than usual, because the number of popish infants is at least three to one in this kingdom; and therefore it will have one other collateral advantage, by lessening the number of Papists among us.

14   I have already computed the charge of nursing a beggar's child (in which list I reckon all cottagers, laborers, and four fifths of the farmers) to be about two shillings per annum, rags included; and I believe no gentleman would repine to give ten shillings for the carcass of a good fat child, which, as I have said, will make four dishes of excellent nutritive meat, when he hath only some particular friend or his own family to dine with him. Thus the squire will learn to be a good landlord, and grow popular among the tenants; the mother will have eight shillings net profit, and be fit for work till she produces another child.

15   Those who are more thrifty (as I must confess the times require) may flay the carcass; the skin of which artificially dressed will make admirable gloves for ladies, and summer boots for fine gentlemen.

16   As to our city of Dublin, shambles[3] may be appointed for this purpose in the most convenient parts of it, and butchers we may be assured will not be wanting; although I rather recommend buying the children alive, and dressing them hot from the knife as we do roasting pigs.

17   A very worthy person, a true lover of his country, and whose virtues I highly esteem, was lately pleased in discoursing on this matter to offer a refinement upon my scheme. He said that many gentlemen of this kingdom, having of late destroyed their deer, he conceived that the want of venison might be well supplied by the bodies of young lads and maidens, not exceeding fourteen years of age nor under twelve, so great a number of both sexes in every county being now ready to starve for want of work and service; and these to be disposed of by their parents,

---

3   portable slaughterhouses

if alive, or otherwise by their nearest relations. But with due deference to so excellent a friend and so deserving a patriot, I cannot be altogether in his sentiments; for as to the males, my American acquaintance assured me from frequent experience that their flesh was generally tough and lean, like that of our schoolboys, by continual exercise, and their taste disagreeable; and to fatten them would not answer the charge. Then as to the females, it would, I think with humble submission, be a loss to the public, because they soon would become breeders themselves: and besides, it is not improbable that some scrupulous people might be apt to censure such a practice (although indeed very unjustly) as a little bordering upon cruelty; which, I confess, hath always been with me the strongest objection against any project, how well soever intended.

18 But in order to justify my friend, he confessed that this expedient was put into his head by the famous Psalmanazar, a native of the island Formosa, who came from thence to London above twenty years ago, and in conversation told my friend that in his country when any young person happened to be put to death, the executioner sold the carcass to persons of quality as a prime dainty; and that in his time the body of a plump girl of fifteen, who was crucified for an attempt to poison the emperor, was sold to his Imperial Majesty's prime minister of state, and other great mandarins of the court, in joints from the gibbet, at four hundred crowns. Neither indeed can I deny that if the same use were made of several plump young girls in this town, who without one single groat to their fortunes cannot stir abroad without a chair, and appear at the playhouse and assemblies in foreign fineries which they never will pay for, the kingdom would not be the worse.

19 Some persons of a desponding spirit are in great concern about that vast number of poor people who are aged, diseased, or maimed, and I have been desired to employ my thoughts what course may be taken to ease the nation of so grievous an encumbrance. But I am not in the least pain upon that matter, because it is very well known that they are every day dying and rotting by cold and famine, and filth and vermin, as fast as can be reasonably expected. And as to the younger laborers, they are now in almost as hopeful a condition. They cannot get work, and consequently pine away for want of nourishment to a degree that if at any time they are accidentally hired to common labor, they have not strength to perform it; and thus the country and themselves are happily delivered from the evils to come.

20 I have too long digressed, and therefore shall return to my subject. I think the advantages by the proposal which I have made are obvious and many, as well as of the highest importance.

21 For first, as I have already observed, it would greatly lessen the number of Papists, with whom we are yearly overrun, being the principal breeders of the nation as well as our most dangerous enemies; and who stay at home on purpose to deliver the kingdom to the Pretender, hoping to take their advantage by the absence of so many good Protestants, who have chosen rather to leave their country than stay at home and pay tithes against their conscience to an Episcopal curate.

22 Secondly, the poorer tenants will have something valuable of their own, which by law may be made liable to distress,[4] and help to pay their landlord's rent, their corn and cattle being already seized and money a thing unknown.

---

4 available for legal seizure

23   Thirdly, whereas the maintenance of an hundred thousand children, from two years old and upwards, cannot be computed at less than ten shillings a piece per annum, the nation's stock will be thereby increased fifty thousand pounds per annum, besides the profit of a new dish introduced to the tables of all gentlemen of fortune in the kingdom who have any refinement in taste. And the money will circulate among ourselves, the goods being entirely of our own growth and manufacture.

24   Fourthly, the constant breeders, besides the gain of eight shillings sterling per annum by the sale of their children, will be rid of the charge of maintaining them after the first year.

25   Fifthly, this food would likewise bring great custom to taverns, where the vintners will certainly be so prudent as to procure the best receipts for dressing it to perfection, and consequently have their houses frequented by all the fine gentlemen, who justly value themselves upon their knowledge in good eating; and a skillful cook, who understands how to oblige his guests, will contrive to make it as expensive as they please.

26   Sixthly, this would be a great inducement to marriage, which all wise nations have either encouraged by rewards or enforced by laws and penalties. It would increase the care and tenderness of mothers toward their children, when they were sure of a settlement for life to the poor babes, provided in some sort by the public, to their annual profit instead of expense. We should see an honest emulation among the married women, which of them could bring the fattest child to the market. Men would become as fond of their wives during the time of their pregnancy as they are now of their mares in foal, their cows in calf, or sows when they are ready to farrow; nor offer to beat or kick them (as is too frequent a practice) for fear of a miscarriage.

27   Many other advantages might be enumerated. For instance, the addition of some thousand carcasses in our exportation of barreled beef, the propagation of swine's flesh, and improvement in the art of making good bacon, so much wanted among us by the great destruction of pigs, too frequent at our tables, which are no way comparable in taste or magnificence to a well-grown, fat, yearling child, which roasted whole will make a considerable figure at a lord mayor's feast or any other public entertainment. But this and many others I omit, being studious of brevity.

28   Supposing that one thousand families in this city would be constant customers for infants' flesh, besides others who might have it at merry meetings, particularly weddings and christenings, I compute that Dublin would take off annually about twenty thousand carcasses, and the rest of the kingdom (where probably they will be sold somewhat cheaper) the remaining eighty thousand.

29   I can think of no one objection that will possibly be raised against this proposal, unless it should be urged that the number of people will be thereby much lessened in the kingdom. This I freely own, and it was indeed one principal design in offering it to the world. I desire the reader will observe, that I calculate my remedy for this one individual kingdom of Ireland and for no other that ever was, is, or I think ever can be upon earth. Therefore let no man talk to me of other expe-

dients: of taxing our absentees at five shillings a pound: of using neither clothes nor household furniture except what is of our own growth and manufacture: of utterly rejecting the materials and instruments that promote foreign luxury: of curing the expensiveness of pride, vanity, idleness, and gaming in our women: of introducing a vein of parsimony, prudence, and temperance: of learning to love our country, in the want of which we differ even from Laplanders and the inhabitants of Topinamboo:5 of quitting our animosities and factions, nor acting any longer like the Jews,6 who were murdering one another at the very moment their city was taken: of being a little cautious not to sell our country and conscience for nothing: of teaching landlords to have at least one degree of mercy toward their tenants: lastly, of putting a spirit of honesty, industry, and skill into our shopkeepers; who, if a resolution could now be taken to buy only our native goods, would immediately unite to cheat and exact upon us in the price, the measure, and the goodness, nor could ever yet be brought to make one fair proposal of just dealing, though often and earnestly invited to it.

30　　Therefore, I repeat, let no man talk to me of these and the like expedients, till he hath at least some glimpse of hope that there will ever be some hearty and sincere attempt to put them in practice.

31　　But as to myself, having been wearied out for many years with offering vain, idle, visionary thoughts, and at length utterly despairing of success, I fortunately fell upon this proposal, which, as it is wholly new, so it hath something solid and real, of no expense and little trouble, full in our own power, and whereby we can incur no danger in disobliging England. For this kind of commodity will not bear exportation, the flesh being of too tender a consistence to admit a long continuance in salt, although perhaps I could name a country7 which would be glad to eat up our whole nation without it.

32　　After all, I am not so violently bent upon my own opinion as to reject any offer proposed by wise men, which shall be found equally innocent, cheap, easy, and effectual. But before something of that kind shall be advanced in contradiction to my scheme, and offering a better, I desire the author or authors will be pleased maturely to consider two points. First, as things now stand, how they will be able to find food and raiment for an hundred thousand useless mouths and backs. And secondly, there being a round million of creatures in human figure throughout this kingdom, whose sole subsistence put into a common stock would leave them in debt two millions of pounds sterling, adding those who are beggars by profession to the bulk of farmers, cottagers, and laborers, with their wives and children who are beggars in effect; I desire those politicians who dislike my overture, and may perhaps be so bold to attempt an answer, that they will first ask the parents of these mortals whether they would not at this day think it a great happiness to have been sold for food at a year old in the manner I prescribe, and thereby have avoided such a perpetual scene of misfortunes as they have since gone through by the oppression of landlords, the impossibility of paying rent without money or trade, the want of common sustenance, with neither house nor clothes

5　Brazil

6　reference to the siege of Jerusalem in A.D. 70 by Titus, a Roman emperor

7　England

to cover them from the inclemencies of the weather, and the most inevitable prospect of entailing the like or greater miseries upon their breed forever.

33   I profess, in the sincerity of my heart, that I have not the least personal interest in endeavoring to promote this necessary work, having no other motive than the public good of my country, by advancing our trade, providing for infants, relieving the poor, and giving some pleasure to the rich. I have no children by which I can propose to get a single penny; the youngest being nine years old, and my wife past childbearing.

Mary Wollstonecraft

England 1759–1797

Mary Wollstonecraft's home was affluent but troubled, chiefly by a father who drank and was subject to violent rages; it is not surprising that she left at nineteen to support herself with positions such as companion, governess, partner in a girls' school, and writer. Her first book to receive acclaim was her response to Edmund Burke's *Reflections on the Revolution in France. A Vindication of the Rights of Men* examined the problems of the English lower classes while attacking Burke's conservative stance. Two years later, she shifted her focus to the problems of her own gender in *A Vindication of the Rights of Woman*. After a spectacularly unfortunate alliance with an American called Gilbert Imlay and two attempts at suicide, Mary Wollstonecraft had a happy, complex, three-year relationship with William Godwin, the philosopher. In 1797, she gave birth to Mary Wollstonecraft Godwin (Mary Shelley) but died ten days later of blood poisoning.

From A Vindication of the Rights of Woman   1792

INTRODUCTION

1   After considering the historic page, and viewing the living world with anxious solicitude, the most melancholy emotions of sorrowful indignation have depressed my spirits, and I have sighed when obliged to confess, that either nature has made a great difference between man and man, or that the civilization which has hitherto taken place in the world has been very partial. I have turned over various books written on the subject of education, and patiently observed the conduct of parents and the management of schools; but what has been the result?—a profound conviction that the neglected education of my fellow-creatures is the grand source of the misery I deplore; and that women, in particular, are rendered weak and wretched by a variety of concurring causes, originating from one hasty conclusion. The conduct and manners of women, in fact, evidently prove that their minds are not in a healthy state; for, like the flowers which are planted in too rich a soil, strength and usefulness are sacrificed to beauty; and the flaunting leaves, after having pleased a

fastidious eye, fade, disregarded on the stalk, long before the season when they ought to have arrived at maturity. —One cause of this barren blooming I attribute to a false system of education, gathered from the books written on this subject by men who, considering females rather as women than human creatures, have been more anxious to make them alluring mistresses than affectionate wives and rational mothers; and the understanding of the sex has been so bubbled[1] by this specious homage, that the civilized women of the present century, with a few exceptions, are only anxious to inspire love, when they ought to cherish a nobler ambition, and by their abilities and virtues exact respect.

2   In a treatise, therefore, on female rights and manners, the works which have been particularly written for their improvement must not be overlooked; especially when it is asserted, in direct terms, that the minds of women are enfeebled by false refinement; that the books of instruction, written by men of genius, have had the same tendency as more frivolous productions; and that, in the true style of Mahometanism, they are treated as a kind of subordinate beings and not as a part of the human species,[2] when improvable reason is allowed to be the dignified distinction which raises men above the brute creation, and puts a natural sceptre in a feeble hand.

3   Yet, because I am a woman, I would not lead my readers to suppose that I mean violently to agitate the contested question respecting the equality or inferiority of the sex; but as the subject lies in my way, and I cannot pass it over without subjecting the main tendency of my reasoning to misconstruction, I shall stop a moment to deliver, in a few words, my opinion. —In the government of the physical world it is observable that the female in point of strength is, in general, inferior to the male. This is the law of nature; and it does not appear to be suspended or abrogated in favour of woman. A degree of physical superiority cannot, therefore, be denied—and it is a noble prerogative! But not content with this natural pre-eminence, men endeavour to sink us still lower, merely to render us alluring objects for a moment; and women, intoxicated by the adoration which men, under the influence of their senses, pay them, do not seek to obtain a durable interest in their hearts, or to become the friends of the fellow creatures who find amusement in their society.

4   I am aware of an obvious inference:—from every quarter have I heard exclamations against masculine women; but where are they to be found? If by this appellation men mean to inveigh against their ardour in hunting, shooting, and gaming, I shall most cordially join in the cry; but if it be against the imitation of many virtues, or, more properly speaking, the attainment of those talents and virtues, the exercise of which ennobles the human character, and which raise females in the scale of animal being, when they are comprehensively termed mankind;—all those who view them with a philosophic eye must, I should think, wish with me, that they may every day grow more and more masculine.

5   This discussion naturally divides the subject. I shall first consider women in the grand light of human creatures, who, in common with men, are placed on

---

1   deluded, misled

2   Europeans mistakenly believed that the Koran, the holy text of the Mohammedans, stated that women had no souls.

this earth to unfold their faculties; and afterwards I shall more particularly point out their peculiar designation.

6   I wish also to steer clear of an error which many respectable writers have fallen into; for the instruction which has hitherto been addressed to women, has rather been applicable to *ladies*, if the little indirect advice, that is scattered through Sandford and Merton,[3] be excepted; but, addressing my sex in a firmer tone, I pay particular attention to those in the middle class, because they appear to be in the most natural state. Perhaps the seeds of false refinement, immorality, and vanity, have ever been shed by the great. Weak, artificial beings, raised above the common wants and affections of their race, in a premature, unnatural manner, undermine the very foundation of virtue, and spread corruption through the whole mass of society! As a class of mankind they have the strongest claim to pity; the education of the rich tends to render them vain and helpless, and the unfolding mind is not strengthened by the practice of those duties which dignify the human character.—They only live to amuse themselves, and by the same law which in nature invariably produces certain effects, they soon only afford barren amusement.

7   But as I purpose taking a separate view of the different ranks of society, and of the moral character of women, in each, this hint is, for the present, sufficient, and I have only alluded to the subject, because it appears to me to be the very essence of an introduction to give a cursory account of the contents of the work it introduces.

8   My own sex, I hope, will excuse me, if I treat them like rational creatures, instead of flattering their *fascinating* graces, and viewing them as if they were in a state of perpetual childhood, unable to stand alone. I earnestly wish to point out in what true dignity and human happiness consists—I wish to persuade women to endeavour to acquire strength, both of mind and body, and to convince them that the soft phrases, susceptibility of heart, delicacy of sentiment, and refinement of taste, are almost synonymous with epithets of weakness, and that those beings who are only the objects of pity and that kind of love, which has been termed its sister, will soon become objects of contempt.

9   Dismissing then those pretty feminine phrases, which the men condescendingly use to soften our slavish dependence, and despising that weak elegancy of mind, exquisite sensibility, and sweet docility of manners, supposed to be the sexual characteristics of the weaker vessel, I wish to shew that elegance is inferior to virtue, that the first object of laudable ambition is to obtain a character as a human being, regardless of the distinction of sex; and that secondary views should be brought to this simple touchstone.

10   This is a rough sketch of my plan; and should I express my conviction with the energetic emotions that I feel whenever I think of the subject, the dictates of experience and reflection will be felt by some of my readers. Animated by this important object, I shall disdain to cull my phrases or polish my style;—I aim at being useful, and sincerity will render me unaffected; for, wishing rather to persuade by the force of my arguments, than dazzle by the elegance of my language, I shall not waste my time in rounding periods,[4] or in fabricating the turgid bombast of artificial feelings, which, coming from the head, never reach the heart. I shall be employed about

---

3 *The History of Sandford and Merton,* a popular children's story, showed a lower-class person as morally superior to an upper-class individual.

4 a carefully crafted, balanced sentence

things, not words!—and, anxious to render my sex more respectable members of society, I shall try to avoid that flowery diction which has slided from essays into novels, and from novels into familiar letters and conversation.

11   These pretty superlatives, dropping glibly from the tongue, vitiate the taste, and create a kind of sickly delicacy that turns away from simple unadorned truth; and a deluge of false sentiments and over-stretched feelings, stifling the natural emotions of the heart, render the domestic pleasures insipid, that ought to sweeten the exercise of those severe duties, which educate a rational and immortal being for a nobler field of action.

12   The education of women has, of late, been more attended to than formerly; yet they are still reckoned a frivolous sex, and ridiculed or pitied by the writers who endeavour by satire or instruction to improve them. It is acknowledged that they spend many of the first years of their lives in acquiring a smattering of accomplishments; meanwhile strength of body and mind are sacrificed to libertine notions of beauty, to the desire of establishing themselves,—the only way women can rise in the world,—by marriage. And this desire making mere animals of them, when they marry they act as such children may be expected to act:—they dress; they paint, and nickname God's creatures.—Surely these weak beings are only fit for a seraglio![5]—Can they be expected to govern a family with judgment, or take care of the poor babes whom they bring into the world?

13   If then it can be fairly deduced from the present conduct of the sex, from the prevalent fondness for pleasure which takes place of ambition and those nobler passions that open and enlarge the soul; that the instruction which women have hitherto received has only tended, with the constitution of civil society, to render them insignificant objects of desire—mere propagators of fools!—if it can be proved that in aiming to accomplish them, without cultivating their understandings, they are taken out of their sphere of duties, and made ridiculous and useless when the short-lived bloom of beauty is over, I presume that *rational* men will excuse me for endeavouring to persuade them to become more masculine and respectable.

14   Indeed the word masculine is only a bugbear: there is little reason to fear that women will acquire too much courage or fortitude; for their apparent inferiority with respect to bodily strength, must render them, in some degree, dependent on men in the various relations of life; but why should it be increased by prejudices that give a sex to virtue, and confound simple truths with sensual reveries?

15   Women are, in fact, so much degraded by mistaken notions of female excellence, that I do not mean to add a paradox when I assert, that this artificial weakness produces a propensity to tyrannize, and gives birth to cunning, the natural opponent of strength, which leads them to play off those contemptible infantile airs that undermine esteem when whilst they excite desire. Let men become more chaste and modest, and if women do not grow wiser in the same ratio it will be clear that they have weaker understandings. It seems scarcely necessary to say, that I now speak of the sex in general. Many individuals have more sense than their male relatives; and, as nothing preponderates where there is a constant struggle for an equilibrium, without it has naturally more gravity, some women govern their husbands without degrading themselves, because intellect will always govern.

---

5   harem

Virginia Woolf

England 1882–1941

Born in London, the daughter of parents who were, historically and profession-
ally, closely connected to the world of writers and literature, Virginia Woolf, like
many women of her time, and in contrast to her two university educated
brothers, was educated at home in her father's library. Woolf is most closely
linked to the group of writers active in Bloomsbury, the area of London around
the British Museum. She was a fine stylistic innovator who is most often
remembered for her contributions to modernist writing. The stream of consciousness narratives of her finer work, such as *The Waves*, testifies how innovative and creative she was with narrative, time sequence, and point of view. Woolf
is also known for her essays and her remarks on women's place in society, as her
essay "Women in Fiction" illustrates.

WOMEN AND FICTION   1929

1   The title of this article can be read in two ways; it may allude to women and the
fiction that they write, or to women and the fiction that is written about them.
The ambiguity is intentional, for in dealing with women as writers, as much elas-
ticity as possible is desirable; it is necessary to leave oneself room to deal with
other things besides their work, so much has that work been influenced by conditions that have nothing whatever to do with art.

2   The most superficial inquiry into women's writing instantly raises a host of
questions. Why, we ask at once, was there no continuous writing done by women
before the eighteenth century? Why did they then write almost as habitually as
men, and in the course of that writing produce, one after another, some of the
classics of English fiction? And why did their art then, and why to some extent
does their art still, take the form of fiction?

3   A little thought will show us that we are asking questions to which we shall
get, as answer, only further fiction. The answer lies at present locked in old diaries,
stuffed away in old drawers, half obliterated in the memories of the aged. It is to
be found in the lives of the obscure—in those almost unlit corridors of history
where the figures of generations of women are so dimly, so fitfully perceived. For
very little is known about women. The history of England is the history of the male
line, not of the female. Of our fathers we know always some fact, some distinction.
They were soldiers or they were sailors; they filled that office or they made that law.
But of our mothers, our grandmothers, our great-grandmothers, what remains?
Nothing but a tradition. One was beautiful; one was red-haired; one was kissed by
a Queen. We know nothing of them except their names and the dates of their marriages and the number of children they bore.

4   Thus, if we wish to know why at any particular time women did this or that, why
they wrote nothing, why on the other hand they wrote masterpieces, it is extremely
difficult to tell. Anyone who should seek among those old papers, who should turn
history wrong side out and so construct a faithful picture of the daily life of the ordi-

nary woman in Shakespeare's time, in Milton's time, in Johnson's time, would not only write a book of astonishing interest, but would furnish the critic with a weapon which he now lacks. The extraordinary woman depends on the ordinary woman. It is only when we know what were the conditions of the average woman's life—the number of her children, whether she had money of her own, if she had a room to herself, whether she had help in bringing up her family, if she had servants, whether part of the housework was her task—it is only when we can measure the way of life and the experience of life made possible to the ordinary woman that we can account for the success or failure of the extraordinary woman as a writer.

5   Strange spaces of silence seem to separate one period of activity from another. There was Sappho and a little group of women all writing poetry on a Greek island six hundred years before the birth of Christ. They fall silent. Then about the year 1000 we find a certain court lady, the Lady Murasaki, writing a very long and beautiful novel in Japan. But in England in the sixteenth century, when the dramatists and poets were most active, the women were dumb. Elizabethan literature is exclusively masculine. Then, at the end of the eighteenth century and in the beginning of the nineteenth, we find women again writing—this time in England—with extraordinary frequency and success.

6   Law and custom were of course largely responsible for these strange inter-missions of silence and speech. When a woman was liable, as she was in the fif-teenth century, to be beaten and flung about the room if she did not marry the man of her parents' choice, the spiritual atmosphere was not favourable to the pro-duction of works of art. When she was married without her own consent to a man who thereupon became her lord and master, 'so far at least as law and custom could make him,' as she was in the time of the Stuarts,[1] it is likely she had little time for writing, and less encouragement. The immense effect of environment and suggestion upon the mind, we in our psychoanalytical age are beginning to realize. Again, with memoirs and letters to help us, we are beginning to understand how abnormal is the effort needed to produce a work of art, and what shelter and what support the mind of the artist requires. Of those facts the lives and letters of men like Keats and Carlyle and Flaubert assure us.

7   Thus it is clear that the extraordinary outburst of fiction in the beginning of the nineteenth century in England was heralded by innumerable slight changes in law and customs and manners. And women of the nineteenth century had some leisure; they had some education. It was no longer the exception for women of the middle and upper classes to choose their own husbands. And it is significant that of the four great women novelists—Jane Austen, Emily Brontë, Charlotte Brontë, and George Eliot—not one had a child, and two were unmarried.

8   Yet, though it is clear that the ban upon writing had been removed, there was still, it would seem, considerable pressure upon women to write novels. No four women can have been more unlike in genius and character than these four. Jane Austen can have had nothing in common with George Eliot; George Eliot was the direct opposite of Emily Brontë. Yet all were trained for the same profession; all, when they wrote, wrote novels.

---

1   The Stuart family occupied the English throne from 1603 to 1714, except for the Cromwellian period of 1649 to 1659.

9   Fiction was, as fiction still is, the easiest thing for a woman to write. Nor is it difficult to find the reason. A novel is the least concentrated form of art. A novel can be taken up or put down more easily than a play or a poem. George Eliot left her work to nurse her father. Charlotte Brontë put down her pen to pick the eyes out of the potatoes. And living as she did in the common sitting-room, surrounded by people, a woman was trained to use her mind in observation and upon the analysis of character. She was trained to be a novelist and not to be a poet.

10   Even in the nineteenth century, a woman lived almost solely in her home and her emotions. And those nineteenth-century novels, remarkable as they were, were profoundly influenced by the fact that the women who wrote them were excluded by their sex from certain kinds of experience. That experience has a great influence upon fiction is indisputable. The best part of Conrad's novels, for instance, would be destroyed if it had been impossible for him to be a sailor. Take away all that Tolstoy knew of war as a soldier, of life and society as a rich young man whose education admitted him to all sorts of experience, and *War and Peace* would be incredibly impoverished.

11   Yet *Pride and Prejudice, Wuthering Heights, Villette,* and *Middlemarch* were written by women from whom was forcibly withheld all experience save that which could be met within a middle-class drawing-room. No first-hand experience of war or seafaring or politics or business was possible for them. Even their emotional life was strictly regulated by law and custom. When George Eliot ventured to live with Mr. Lewes without being his wife, public opinion was scandalized. Under its pressure she withdrew into a suburban seclusion which, inevitably, had the worst possible effects upon her work. She wrote that unless people asked of their own accord to come and see her, she never invited them. At the same time, on the other side of Europe, Tolstoy was living a free life as a soldier, with men and women of all classes, for which nobody censured him and from which his novels drew much of their astonishing breadth and vigour.

12   But the novels of women were not affected only by the necessarily narrow range of the writer's experience. They showed, at least in the nineteenth century, another characteristic which may be traced to the writer's sex. In *Middlemarch* and in *Jane Eyre* we are conscious not merely of the writer's character, as we are conscious of the character of Charles Dickens, but we are conscious of a woman's presence—of someone resenting the treatment of her sex and pleading for its rights. This brings into women's writing an element which is entirely absent from a man's, unless, indeed, he happens to be a working man, a negro, or one who for some other reason is conscious of disability. It introduces a distortion and is frequently the cause of weakness. The desire to plead some personal cause or to make a character the mouthpiece of some personal discontent or grievance always has a distressing effect, as if the spot at which the reader's attention is directed were suddenly twofold instead of single.

13   The genius of Jane Austen and Emily Brontë is never more convincing than in their power to ignore such claims and solicitations and to hold on their way unperturbed by scorn or censure. But it needed a very serene or a very powerful mind to resist the temptation to anger. The ridicule, the censure, the assurance of inferiority in one form or another which were lavished upon women who practised an art, provided such reactions naturally enough. One sees the effect in Charlotte Brontë's indignation, in George Eliot's resignation. Again and again

one finds it in the work of the lesser women writers—in their choice of a subject, in their unnatural self-assertiveness, in their unnatural docility. Moreover, insincerity leaks in almost unconsciously. They adopt a view in deference to authority. The vision becomes too masculine or it becomes too feminine; it loses its perfect integrity and, with that, its most essential quality as a work of art.

14   The great change that has crept into women's writing is, it would seem, a change of attitude. The woman writer is no longer bitter. She is no longer angry. She is no longer pleading and protesting as she writes. We are approaching, if we have not yet reached, the time when her writing will have little or no foreign influence to disturb it. She will be able to concentrate upon her vision without distraction from outside. The aloofness that was once within the reach of genius and originality is only now coming within the reach of ordinary women. Therefore the average novel by a woman is far more genuine and far more interesting today than it was a hundred or even fifty years ago.

15   But it is still true that before a woman can write exactly as she wishes to write, she has many difficulties to face. To begin with, there is the technical difficulty, so simple, apparently; in reality, so baffling—that the very form of the sentence does not fit her. It is a sentence made by men; it is too loose, too heavy, too pompous for a woman's use. Yet in a novel, which covers so wide a stretch of ground, an ordinary and usual type of sentence has to be found to carry the reader on easily and naturally from one end of the book to the other. And this a woman must make for herself, altering and adapting the current sentence until she writes one that takes the natural shape of her thought without crushing or distorting it.

16   But that, after all, is only a means to an end, and the end is still to be reached only when a woman has the courage to surmount opposition and the determination to be true to herself. For a novel, after all, is a statement about a thousand different objects—human, natural, divine; it is an attempt to relate them to each other. In every novel of merit these different elements are held in place by the force of the writer's vision. But they have another order also, which is the order imposed upon them by convention. And as men are the arbiters of that convention, as they have established an order of values in life, so too, since fiction is largely based on life, these values prevail there also to a very great extent.

17   It is probable, however, that both in life and in art the values of a woman are not the values of a man. Thus, when a woman comes to write a novel, she will find that she is perpetually wishing to alter the established values—to make serious what appears insignificant to a man, and trivial what is to him important. And for that, of course, she will be criticized; for the critic of the opposite sex will be genuinely puzzled and surprised by an attempt to alter the current scale of values, and will see in it not merely a difference of view, but a view that is weak, or trivial, or sentimental, because it differs from his own.

18   But here, too, women are coming to be more independent of opinion. They are beginning to respect their own sense of values. And for this reason the subject matter of their novels begins to show certain changes. They are less interested, it would seem, in themselves; on the other hand, they are more interested in other women. In the early nineteenth century, women's novels were largely autobiographical. One of the motives that led them to write was the desire to expose their own suffering, to plead their own cause. Now that this desire is no longer so urgent, women are beginning to explore their own sex, to write of women as

women have never been written of before; for, of course, until very lately, women in literature were the creation of men.

19   Here again there are difficulties to overcome, for, if one may generalize, not only do women submit less readily to observation than men, but their lives are far less tested and examined by the ordinary processes of life. Often nothing tangible remains of a woman's day. The food that has been cooked is eaten; the children that have been nursed have gone out into the world. Where does the accent fall? What is the salient point for the novelist to seize upon? It is difficult to say. Her life has an anonymous character which is baffling and puzzling in the extreme. For the first time, this dark country is beginning to be explored in fiction; and at the same moment a woman has also to record the changes in women's minds and habits which the opening of the professions has introduced. She has to observe how their lives are ceasing to run underground; she has to discover what new colours and shadows are showing in them now that they are exposed to the outer world.

20   If, then, one should try to sum up the character of women's fiction at the present moment, one would say that it is courageous; it is sincere; it keeps closely to what women feel. It is not bitter. It does not insist upon its femininity. But at the same time, a woman's book is not written as a man would write it. These qualities are much commoner than they were, and they give even to second- and third-rate work the value of truth and the interest of sincerity.

21   But in addition to these good qualities, there are two that call for a word more of discussion. The change which has turned the English woman from a nondescript influence, fluctuating and vague, to a voter, a wage-earner, a responsible citizen, has given her both in her life and in her art a turn toward the impersonal. Her relations now are not only emotional; they are intellectual, they are political. The old system which condemned her to squint askance at things through the eyes or through the interests of husband or brother, has given place to the direct and practical interests of one who must act for herself, and not merely influence the acts of others. Hence her attention is being directed away from the personal centre which engaged it exclusively in the past to the impersonal, and her novels naturally become more critical of society, and less analytical of individual lives.

22   We may expect that the office of gadfly[2] to the state, which has been so far a male prerogative, will now be discharged by women also. Their novels will deal with social evils and remedies. Their men and women will not be observed wholly in relation to each other emotionally, but as they cohere and clash in groups and classes and races. That is one change of some importance. But there is another more interesting to those who prefer the butterfly to the gadfly—that is to say, the artist to the reformer. The greater impersonality of women's lives will encourage the poetic spirit, and it is in poetry that women's fiction is still weakest. It will lead them to be less absorbed in facts and no longer content to record with astonishing acuteness the minute details which fall under their own observation. They will look beyond the personal and political relationships to the wider questions which the poet tries to solve—of our destiny and the meaning of life.

23   The basis of the poetic attitude is of course largely founded upon material things. It depends upon leisure, and a little money, and the chance which money and leisure give to observe impersonally and dispassionately. With money and

---

2   an irritating or worrying person

leisure at their service, women will naturally occupy themselves more than has hitherto been possible with the craft of letters. They will make a fuller and a more subtle use of the instrument of writing. Their technique will become bolder and richer.

24   In the past, the virtue of women's writing often lay in its divine spontaneity, like that of the blackbird's song or the thrush's. It was untaught; it was from the heart. But it was also, and much more often, chattering and garrulous—mere talk spilt over paper and left to dry in pools and blots. In future, granted time and books and a little space in the house for herself, literature will become for women, as for men, an art to be studied. Women's gift will be trained and strengthened. The novel will cease to be the dumping-ground for the personal emotions. It will become, more than at present, a work of art like any other, and its resources and its limitations will be explored.

25   From this it is a short step to the practice of the sophisticated arts, hitherto so little practised by women—to the writing of essays and criticisms of history and biography. And that, too, if we are considering the novel, will be of advantage; for besides improving the quality of the novel itself, it will draw off the aliens who have been attracted to fiction by its accessibility while their hearts lay elsewhere. Thus will the novel be rid of those excrescences[3] of history and fact which, in our time, have made it so shapeless.

26   So, if we may prophesy, women in time to come will write fewer novels, but better novels; and not novels only, but poetry and criticism and history. But in this, to be sure, one is looking ahead to that golden, that perhaps fabulous, age when women will have what has so long been denied them—leisure, and money, and a room to themselves.

---

3   abnormal or morbid outgrowths on animal or vegetable bodies

J.B.S. Haldane

England 1892–1964

J.B.S. Haldane was best known for his work on heredity and for championing various controversial causes. An English geneticist and biochemist, he also authored many essays on science and society, in which he attempted to bring together these separate areas of study. As this essay reveals, Haldane had a gift for persuading his readers to think more carefully about subjects that tend to generate emotional, rather than intellectual, responses.

Some Enemies of Science   1928

1   Last week my wife successfully poisoned a number of rats. They were eating the food of our chickens, and would have eaten the smaller of the birds if they had got the chance. Owing to the failure of a more humane poison she found herself compelled

to use phosphorus; which is a slow and, to judge from the experience of the human beings who commit suicide by eating matches, often rather painful means of death.

2   During the same period I killed two rats in the course of experimental work intended to advance medical science. One of them, if we can judge from human experience (and we have no more direct means of evaluating the consciousness of animals), died after a period of rather pleasant delirium like that of alcoholic intoxication. The other had convulsions, and may have been in pain for three or four minutes. I should be very thankful if I knew that I should suffer no more than it did before my death. It therefore seems to me somewhat ridiculous that, whereas my wife is encouraged by the Government and the Press, I should be compelled to apply to the President of the Royal Society and another eminent man of science for signatures to an application to the already overworked Home Secretary, before I can even kill a mouse in a slightly novel manner.

3   It is probably right that some control should be kept over experiments likely to involve severe and prolonged pain to animals; but it is monstrous that with regard to wholly or nearly painless procedures the scientific man should be worse treated than any other member of the community.

4   Under the present law, or, at any rate, under the law as at present interpreted, a license is required for a large number of absolutely painless experiments, and, what is more serious, they can only be performed in a limited number of laboratories. In consequence, the isolated amateur worker, who has played so great a part in the development of British science, is debarred from wide fields of physiology. The sportsman may go out and shoot as many rabbits as he pleases; and if some of them are wounded and escape to die a lingering death in their holes, no blame attaches to him. But if he anaesthetizes one of his own rabbits at home, and opens its abdomen to observe the effect of a drug on its intestines, killing it before it recovers consciousness, he will be lucky if he escapes with a fine.

5   Nor may the doctor, after his day's shooting of unanaesthetized partridges, acquire surgical skill by an operation on an anaesthetized animal, even in a licensed laboratory. He has to practise on human patients. There are, of course, a few operations of human surgery for which animals would furnish relatively little guidance. In the majority of cases, however, they would be of very real value, and have been proved to be so in America. Not only is medical science already greatly hampered by the law, but a constant fight has to be kept up to preserve what possibilities are left it. It is worth while enquiring into the reasons which have led to this state of affairs.

6   There are a few honest anti-vivisectionists. They are, of course, vegetarians; for the painless killing of animals for physiology is no more reprehensible than their killing for meat. They wear canvas shoes, cotton or woollen gloves, and artificial pearls if any. They refuse to sit on leather-covered chairs, or to wear horn-rimmed spectacles. They do not spray their roses, or employ Keating's powder even under the gravest provocation. I have not met any of them, but I am quite prepared to believe that they exist. No one who does not come up to this rather exacting standard can logically demand the total abolition of vivisection. But logic is not the strongest point of the enemies of science.

7   All others who demand the prohibition of experiments on anaesthetized animals are quite definitely hypocrites, engaged in the familiar pursuit of

'Compounding sins they are inclined to
By damning those they have no mind to.'

There are few more disgusting spectacles in our public life than that of the two or three sporting peers who habitually introduce or support Bills to prohibit such experiments. Each of them has caused more pain to animals in a single day's sport than the average physiologist inflicts in a lifetime, and usually for no end except his personal pleasure. For it seems to me that from the ethical point of view a fairly sharp distinction can be drawn between the killing of animals bred for this purpose at considerable expense, which would produce far more food if applied to agriculture; and that of rabbits, hares, and pigeons which must be kept down in the interest of crops and livestock. Personally, since I have realized from my own experience with shell splinters that it is no fun to carry bits of metal about one's person, I would no more shoot a rabbit than kill my bacon for breakfast. But I certainly do not condemn those who do so.

8   We must next consider the relatively small number of anti-vivisectionists who would merely prohibit all painful or possibly painful experiments. Now, the world is so constituted that we cannot avoid inflicting pain on others. I cannot dig in my garden without bisecting a number of earthworms, or drive a car for any time without running over a few of the various animals whose flattened corpses decorate our country roads. But it is our duty, as far as possible, to diminish the amount of pain in the world. The question therefore is whether medical research does this or not.

9   Now, anti-vivisectionist literature distorts both sides of the account. It states that a great deal of severe suffering is inflicted on animals in the name of science, and that there is little or no return for this in the diminution of human and animal suffering. With regard to the first of these assertions I can speak with a certain degree of experience. I have seen numerous experiments on animals, but I have never seen an animal undergoing pain which I would not have been willing to undergo myself for the same object. Why, then, it may be asked, should not all painful experiments be done on human volunteers?

10   There are several reasons why not. One is the very simple fact that many of these experiments possibly or necessarily involve the death of the animal. For example, rats are frequently inoculated under the skin of their sides with transplantable cancers. These are not painful, for the rat does not wince or squeak when the lump is pressed. If it were allowed to die of cancer it would often suffer; for the original tumour or its metastases elsewhere would press on nerves, and one of them would probably start to ulcerate. But before either of these events occurs, all such rats in the laboratory in which I work are killed, and the tumours used for chemical study of inoculation. A man, even if he could legally be used for such a purpose and chloroformed before pain began, would presumably suffer from the anticipation of an early death.

11   Just the same applies to deformity. A rickety child suffers mainly because it cannot take part in the activities of its comrades and is made to realize that it is deformed. A rickety rat has none of these disadvantages, not only because it is probably not self-conscious, but because under laboratory conditions all its acquaintances are rickety too. Finally, there is the question of expense. Human beings cost a lot in board and lodging, and must be compensated for loss of time. If, as in experiments on the effects of small changes in the diet, hundreds of individuals and years of time are needed, this consideration is generally final.

12   However, if we are to believe anti-vivisectionists, animals constantly undergo tortures which no human being would voluntarily endure. I recently received an

illustrated pamphlet, which I should think is fairly typical, describing the sufferings of laboratory animals. There was a picture of an oven in which dogs were slowly heated till they died, while a physiologist watched their agonies through a window. The thought of such cruelty would have made my blood boil, if it had not already been partially boiled in such a chamber on several occasions. Under such circumstances one becomes dizzy long before there is any definite pain, and death, if it occurs, is from heat stroke, not from burning. Personally, I prefer being overheated in a bath. Immersion of all but the head in water kept hot enough just not to be painful, causes loss of consciousness, after a good deal of panting, in about twenty minutes. Hence there is reason to think that a lobster, if put into cold water and heated fairly slowly, feels no pain, which it must certainly do if dropped into boiling water. Probably, however, it would suffer still less if about 2½ per cent of salt were added to the cold water.

13   Then came a picture of a dog's mouth held open by a somewhat brutal-looking contrivance. This was said to be taken from a scientific periodical called the 'Transactions of the Physiological Society.' There is, unfortunately, no such journal, nor could I find the picture in the Proceedings of that body for the date given. Perhaps, therefore, it was the anti-vivisectionist's idea of what an instrument of scientific torture ought to look like. But if I had been a maiden lady with a pet dog and no knowledge either of the facts or the literature of physiology, I might have sent a cheque to one of the ladies and gentlemen who make a living by compiling documents of this kind.

14   In some cases experiments are supposed to be painful out of ignorance rather than malice. A group of experiments by Sir John Bradford, in which parts of the kidneys of dogs were removed under an anaesthetic, are constantly described in parliament as torture. Some of these dogs recovered completely, others died with the symptoms of chronic kidney disease, which in human beings seldom causes any pain worse than a headache. Stone in the kidney can, of course, be very painful, but the dogs were not so treated as to cause them pain of this type, nor did they show any signs of suffering it. As a matter of fact, too, dogs can stand a good deal of wounding without much suffering, so far as one can judge. I know this, not from laboratory experience, but because I have owned a dog whose courage and love affairs constantly led him into fights with larger dogs.

15   A large part of the unhappiness of dogs in English laboratories is directly due to the anti-vivisectionists. In the laboratory where I work there are a number of dogs, each of which, for two or three months in the year, eats certain organic compounds which it transforms in its body. The newly formed compounds are excreted in the urine. To facilitate the collection of urine an operation has been performed on them analogous to circumcision, and not nearly so severe as tail-docking. Of course, an anaesthetic was used. But because the operation has been performed in the cause of science rather than fashion, these dogs are forbidden by law to leave the laboratory. They are exercised in the grounds twice daily, but may not go into the street, and must lead a rather dull life. This regulation is typical of the present law, which is designed quite as much to hamper research as to protect animals.

16   While the large majority of experiments performed annually are nearly painless, a few dozen, which attempt to reproduce a painful human disease, and thus to discover its cause or cure, are as painful as the disease which they imitate, except that when the animal's condition is clearly hopeless it can be killed.

17   I do not think it will be necessary to convince any reader of this book of the value of medical research. It has been the principal cause which renders the worst slum of to day healthier than the palace of a century ago. If that result had been reached by the infliction of appalling torture on millions of animals the ethical justification of this torture would certainly be a matter for discussion. Actually the fate of experimental rats, for example, is no worse than that of pet rats, which generally die from deficient diet or epidemic disease.

18   It remains to consider the psychology of anti-vivisectionists. I think that their most important motive is a hatred of science, which they attack at its weakest point. They hate science partly because they do not understand it, and will not take the trouble to; partly because it is ethically neutral. Many of them feel that disease must be a punishment for sin, and that it could be avoided if we lived according to their own particular prejudices. This view has been taken by most religions, though, of course, Jesus did not share it (John, chap. 9, v. 3). Almost all believe that there is some short cut to health. So a great many simple-lifers, vegetarians, faith-healers, Christian scientists, and so forth, are opposed to medical research, and say that its results are worthless.

19   In some cases anti-vivisection goes with pacifism. The fallacy involved in this association is rather interesting. Non-resistance of human evil is sometimes effective. A certain percentage of human smiters are seriously disconcerted if one turns the other cheek to them. But this kind of method does not work on bacteria, which have no finer feelings. We cannot find out how they behave, and thus acquire power over them, except by experiments on men or animals. This is a very unfortunate fact, but then the universe differs in a great many ways from what we should wish it to be. Medicine continued on non-experimental lines (with a very few exceptions) from the dawn of history till the seventeenth century. And in consequence it remained stationary during thousands of years. If its enemies get their way it will begin to stagnate again.

20   But there is a less respectable side to the anti-vivisectionist mind. During the recent agitation against experiments on dogs I made an offer of £100 (published in the *Daily Mail*) to the National Canine Defence League, if they would produce any evidence for certain libels on the medical profession which they were circulating in order to obtain signatures for a petition. I got no answer from the league, but a number of abusive and most instructive letters.

21   One of them, from E. Hough of Hammersmith, objected to experiments 'on the dear, faithful doggies for the benefit of worthless human beings.' 'I like to think,' she wrote (for I picture the writer as an elderly and soured spinster) 'that God will torture physiologists in a future life. I would not lift a finger to save one of them if he were writhing in agony.' There is, then, a group of anti-vivisectionists who like to think about torture. As they can no longer attend the burning of atheists and witches, they gloat over imaginary stories of animal torture till their blood boils; and then cool it with the thought of physiologists in hell fire. Thanks largely to the psychological mutilation to which our society subjects adults, and more particularly children, the world is over-full of

'Ceux dont le rêve obscur salit tout ce qu'il touche,'[1]

and I suspect that a fair number of them become anti-vivisectionists.

---

1   "Those whose hidden dream stains all that it touches"

22   Those who have benefited by the results of medical research and wish it to continue might do worse than support the Research Defence Society, which carries on a lonely fight against a vast flood of lies. And they should urge the following alterations in the law, none of which would increase animal suffering in the faintest degree. Stray dogs impounded by the police should be used for experiment. This would abolish dog stealing for laboratories, and save the lives of some thousand dogs per year. No licence should be required for experiments on fully anaesthetized animals which are killed under the anaesthetic. Surgeons should be allowed to practise their art under the same conditions. Animals should not be condemned to imprisonment for life because an experiment has been done on them. And in the interests of national economy the number of officials and of Government forms used in the supervision of research should be cut down.

23   At present biological and medical research workers are enormously handicapped by the law and by public opinion. Several hospitals, out of deference to subscribers, do not allow animal experiments. They thus render the rapid diagnosis of various diseases impossible, and kill a certain number of patients annually. And medical teaching is seriously handicapped in the same way. These are some of the reasons why England is less healthy than a number of other European countries. Anti-vivisectionists are responsible for far more deaths per year in England than motor vehicles, smallpox, or typhoid fever.

George Orwell

England 1903–1950

George Orwell, whose real name was Eric Blair, was born in India. Schooled in England, Orwell won a scholarship to Eton. After completing his education at Eton without obtaining the university scholarship that would have enabled him to continue his studies, Orwell returned to the east and became a member of the Imperial Police in Burma. Dissatisfied with his role in colonial life and conscious of the class structure of English society, Orwell embarked on a series of adventures, which he wrote about in *Down and Out in Paris and London* and *Homage to Catalonia*. Orwell's best writing, both as an essayist and as a fiction writer, addresses the social problems he saw around him. *1984* and *Animal Farm* are his most popular attacks on repressive political structures. "Marrakech" is a good example of how Orwell uses description to make his point.

Marrakech   1939

1   As the corpse went past the flies left the restaurant table in a cloud and rushed after it, but they came back a few minutes later.

2   The little crowd of mourners—all men and boys, no women—threaded their way across the market-place between the piles of pomegranates and the taxis and the

camels, wailing a short chant over and over again. What really appeals to the flies is that the corpses here are never put into coffins, they are merely wrapped in a piece of rag and carried on a rough wooden bier on the shoulders of four friends. When the friends get to the burying-ground they hack an oblong hole a foot or two deep, dump the body in it and fling over it a little of the dried-up, lumpy earth, which is like broken brick. No gravestone, no name, no identifying mark of any kind. The burying-ground is merely a huge waste of hummocky earth, like a derelict building-lot. After a month or two no one can even be certain where his own relatives are buried.

3   When you walk through a town like this—two hundred thousand inhabitants, of whom at least twenty thousand own literally nothing except the rags they stand up in—when you see how the people live, and still more how easily they die, it is always difficult to believe that you are walking among human beings. All colonial empires are in reality founded upon that fact. The people have brown faces—besides, there are so many of them! Are they really the same flesh as yourself? Do they even have names? Or are they merely a kind of undifferentiated brown stuff, about as individual as bees or coral insects? They rise out of the earth, they sweat and starve for a few years, and then they sink back into the nameless mounds of the graveyard and nobody notices that they are gone. And even the graves themselves soon fade back into the soil. Sometimes, out for a walk, as you break your way through the prickly pear, you notice that it is rather bumpy underfoot, and only a certain regularity in the bumps tells you that you are walking over skeletons.

4   I was feeding one of the gazelles in the public gardens.

5   Gazelles are almost the only animals that look good to eat when they are still alive, in fact, one can hardly look at their hindquarters without thinking of mint sauce. The gazelle I was feeding seemed to know that this thought was in my mind, for though it took the piece of bread I was holding out it obviously did not like me. It nibbled rapidly at the bread, then lowered its head and tried to butt me, then took another nibble and then butted again. Probably its idea was that if it could drive me away the bread would somehow remain hanging in mid-air.

6   An Arab navvy[1] working on the path nearby lowered his heavy hoe and sidled slowly towards us. He looked from the gazelle to the bread and from the bread to the gazelle, with a sort of quiet amazement, as though he had never seen anything quite like this before. Finally he said shyly in French:

7   "*I* could eat some of that bread."

8   I tore off a piece and he stowed it gratefully in some secret place under his rags. This man is an employee of the Municipality.

9   When you go through the Jewish quarters you gather some idea of what the medieval ghettoes were probably like. Under their Moorish rulers the Jews were only allowed to own land in certain restricted areas, and after centuries of this kind of treatment they have ceased to bother about overcrowding. Many of the streets are a good deal less than six feet wide, the houses are completely windowless, and sore-eyed children cluster everywhere in unbelievable numbers, like clouds of flies. Down the centre of the street there is generally running a little river of urine.

10   In the bazaar huge families of Jews, all dressed in the long black robe and the little black skull-cap, are working in dark fly-infested booths that look like caves. A carpenter sits crosslegged at a prehistoric lathe, turning chair-legs at lightning speed. He

---

1 labourer

works the lathe with a bow in his right hand and guides the chisel with his left foot, and thanks to a lifetime of sitting in this position his left leg is warped out of shape. At his side his grandson, aged six, is already starting on the simpler parts of the job.

11   I was just passing the coppersmiths' booths when somebody noticed that I was lighting a cigarette. Instantly, from the dark holes all round, there was a frenzied rush of Jews, many of them old grandfathers with flowing grey beards, all clamouring for a cigarette. Even a blind man somewhere at the back of one of the booths heard a rumour of cigarettes and came crawling out, groping in the air with his hand. In about a minute I had used up the whole packet. None of these people, I suppose, works less than twelve hours a day, and every one of them looks on a cigarette as a more or less impossible luxury.

12   As the Jews live in self-contained communities they follow the same trades as the Arabs, except for agriculture. Fruit-sellers, potters, silversmiths, blacksmiths, butchers, leatherworkers, tailors, water-carriers, beggars, porters—whichever way you look you see nothing but Jews. As a matter of fact there are thirteen thousand of them, all living in the space of a few acres. A good job Hitler wasn't here. Perhaps he was on his way, however. You hear the usual dark rumours about the Jews, not only from the Arabs but from the poorer Europeans.

13   "Yes, mon vieux,[2] they took my job away from me and gave it to a Jew. The Jews! They're the real rulers of this country, you know. They've got all the money. They control the banks, finance—everything."

14   "But," I said, "isn't it a fact that the average Jew is a labourer working for about a penny an hour?"

15   "Ah, that's only for show! They're all moneylenders really. They're cunning, the Jews."

16   In just the same way, a couple of hundred years ago, poor old women used to be burned for witchcraft when they could not even work enough magic to get themselves a square meal.

17   All people who work with their hands are partly invisible, and the more important the work they do, the less visible they are. Still, a white skin is always fairly conspicuous. In northern Europe, when you see a labourer ploughing a field, you probably give him a second glance. In a hot country, anywhere south of Gibraltar or east of Suez, the chances are that you don't even see him. I have noticed this again and again. In a tropical landscape one's eye takes in everything except the human beings. It takes in the dried-up soil, the prickly pear, the palm tree and the distant mountain, but it always misses the peasant hoeing at his patch. He is the same colour as the earth, and a great deal less interesting to look at.

18   It is only because of this that the starved countries of Asia and Africa are accepted as tourist resorts. No one would think of running cheap trips to the Distressed Areas. But where the human beings have brown skins their poverty is simply not noticed. What does Morocco mean to a Frenchman? An orange-grove or a job in Government service. Or to an Englishman? Camels, castles, palm trees, Foreign Legionnaires, brass trays, and bandits. One could probably live there for years without noticing that for nine-tenths of the people the reality of life is an endless, back-breaking struggle to wring a little food out of an eroded soil.

2   general term of address in conversation

19 Most of Morocco is so desolate that no wild animal bigger than a hare can live on it. Huge areas which were once covered with forest have turned into a treeless waste where the soil is exactly like broken-up brick. Nevertheless a good deal of it is cultivated, with frightful labour. Everything is done by hand. Long lines of women, bent double like inverted capital L's, work their way slowly across the fields, tearing up the prickly weeds with their hands, and the peasant gathering lucerne for fodder pulls it up stalk by stalk instead of reaping it, thus saving an inch or two on each stalk. The plough is a wretched wooden thing, so frail that one can easily carry it on one's shoulder, and fitted underneath with a rough iron spike which stirs the soil to a depth of about four inches. This is as much as the strength of the animals is equal to. It is usual to plough with a cow and a donkey yoked together. Two donkeys would not be quite strong enough, but on the other hand two cows would cost a little more to feed. The peasants possess no harrows, they merely plough the soil several times over in different directions, finally leaving it in rough furrows, after which the whole field has to be shaped with hoes into small oblong patches to conserve water. Except for a day or two after the rare rainstorms there is never enough water. Along the edges of the fields channels are hacked out to a depth of thirty or forty feet to get at the tiny trickles which run through the subsoil.

20 Every afternoon a file of very old women passes down the road outside my house, each carrying a load of firewood. All of them are mummified with age and the sun, and all of them are tiny. It seems to be generally the case in primitive communities that the women, when they get beyond a certain age, shrink to the size of children. One day a poor old creature who could not have been more than four feet tall crept past me under a vast load of wood. I stopped her and put a five-sou piece[3] (a little more than a farthing) into her hand. She answered with a shrill wail, almost a scream, which was partly gratitude but mainly surprise. I suppose that from her point of view, by taking any notice of her, I seemed almost to be violating a law of nature. She accepted her status as an old woman, that is to say as a beast of burden. When a family is travelling it is quite usual to see a father and a grown-up son riding ahead on donkeys, and an old woman following on foot, carrying the baggage.

21 But what is strange about these people is their invisibility. For several weeks, always at about the same time of day, the file of old women had hobbled past the house with their firewood, and though they had registered themselves on my eyeballs I cannot truly say that I had seen them. Firewood was passing—that was how I saw it. It was only that one day I happened to be walking behind them, and the curious up-and–down motion of a load of wood drew my attention to the human being beneath it. Then for the first time I noticed the poor old earth-coloured bodies, bodies reduced to bones and leathery skin, bent double under the crushing weight. Yet I suppose I had not been five minutes on Moroccan soil before I noticed the overloading of the donkeys and was infuriated by it. There is no question that the donkeys are damnably treated. The Moroccan donkey is hardly bigger than a St. Bernard dog, it carries a load which in the British Army would be considered too much for a fifteen-hands mule, and very often its pack-saddle is not taken off its back for weeks together. But what is peculiarly pitiful is that it is the most willing creature on earth, it follows its master like a dog and does not need either bridle or halter. After a dozen years of devoted work it sud-

---

3 five-sou piece and farthing; units of money in France and England, respectively

denly drops dead, whereupon its master tips it into the ditch and the village dogs have torn its guts out before it is cold.

22   This kind of thing makes one's blood boil, whereas—on the whole—the plight of the human beings does not. I am not commenting, merely pointing to a fact. People with brown skins are next door to invisible. Anyone can be sorry for the donkey with its galled back, but it is generally owing to some kind of accident if one even notices the old woman under her load of sticks.

23   As the storks flew northward the Negroes were marching southward—a long, dusty column, infantry, screw-gun batteries, and then more infantry, four or five thousand men in all, winding up the road with a clumping of boots and a clatter of iron wheels.

24   They were Senegalese, the blackest Negroes in Africa, so black that sometimes it is difficult to see whereabouts on their necks the hair begins. Their splendid bodies were hidden in reach-me-down khaki uniforms, their feet squashed into boots that looked like blocks of wood, and every tin hat seemed to be a couple of sizes too small. It was very hot and the men had marched a long way. They slumped under the weight of their packs and the curiously sensitive black faces were glistening with sweat.

25   As they went past a tall, very young Negro turned and caught my eye. But the look he gave me was not in the least the kind of look you might expect. Not hostile, not contemptuous, not sullen, not even inquisitive. It was the shy, wide-eyed Negro look, which actually is a look of profound respect. I saw how it was. This wretched boy, who is a French citizen and has therefore been dragged from the forest to scrub floors and catch syphilis in garrison towns, actually has feelings of reverence before a white skin. He has been taught that the white race are his masters, and he still believes it.

26   But there is one thought which every white man (and in this connection it doesn't matter twopence if he calls himself a socialist) thinks when he sees a black army marching past. "How much longer can we go on kidding these people? How long before they turn their guns in the other direction?"

27   It was curious, really. Every white man there had this thought stowed somewhere or other in his mind. I had it, so had the other onlookers, so had the officers on their sweating chargers and the white N.C.O.'s[4] marching in the ranks. It was a kind of secret which we all knew and were too clever to tell; only the Negroes didn't know it. And really it was like watching a flock of cattle to see the long column, a mile or two miles of armed men, flowing peacefully up the road, while the great white birds drifted over them in the opposite direction, glittering like scraps of paper.

---

4   noncommissioned officers

Northrop Frye

Canada 1912–1991

Born in Sherbrooke, Quebec, Northrop Frye was raised in Moncton, New Brunswick and educated at the University of Toronto, Emmanuel College, and Oxford University. During his academic career, Frye lectured at over 100 universities and received over 30 honorary degrees. His study on William Blake, *Fearful Symmetry* (1947), brought him to prominence, but it was followed by equally important books including *Anatomy of Criticism* (1957), *The Educated Imagination* (1963), *The Bush Garden* (1971), *The Great Code* (1982), and *Words with Power* (1990). His essay "Elementary Teaching," from his collection *The Stubborn Structure* (1970), shows how wide ranging Frye's enquiry was. Here, he focuses on some educators' pitfalls when approaching English studies. In the essay, he attacks such concepts as "effective communication" and asserts "the connections of literature are with the imagination, not with the reason."

Elementary Teaching   1970

1   The first thing that university teachers want to know is: what is important in the pre-university study of literature? Most of us, when we complain about our freshmen, base our complaints on the theme of information or memorized knowledge: our students don't know enough; they haven't read enough: the chronology of literature is a vague haze in their minds; some of them could hardly distinguish Chaucer from Tennyson except by the spelling, and so on. But if students don't have enough information, it is a simple enough matter to supply it or provide the sources of supply. The trouble is that what they learn they learn within a mental structure of habits and assumptions, and university comes much too late in a student's life to alter that structure. For example: many students come to university assuming that convention is the opposite of originality, and is a sign that a poet is superficial and insincere. If they are writing poetry themselves, they are apt to get bristly and aggressive about this assumption. They can't be writing in a convention that all their friends are writing in: they must be conveying unique experiences, because their poems say that they are. Here is a result of illiterate teaching that makes the most scrambled nonsense out of all literary values, yet nothing can really be done about it. We tell them at university that literary sincerity is quite different from personal sincerity, that it can only be developed by craftsmanship working within a convention, and that it is the function of convention to set free the power of expressing emotions, not to provide formulas for ready-made emotions, though it may do this for dull writers. They listen; they understand; they may even believe; but the effect on their mental habits is very like the effect of schoolmarm English on the little boy: "Dar ain't no 'ain't you,' is dey? It's 'aren't you', ain't it?"

2   Or, again, I am at an educational conference listening to a speech by a high authority in the field. I know him to be a good scholar, a dedicated servant of

society, and an admirable person. Yet his speech is a muddy river of clichés, flowing stickily into a delta of banalities at the peroration. The content of the speech does not do justice to his mind: what it does reflect is the state of his literary education. It is not that he has never read good literature, for he has the literary tastes that one would expect a cultivated man to have. But he has never been trained to think rhetorically, to visualize his abstractions, to subordinate logic and sequences to the insights of metaphor and simile, to realize that figures of speech are not the ornaments of language, but the elements of both language and thought. And because his main scholarly interests lie outside literature, he has never been compelled to make up for these deficiencies himself. The result is that he is fluent without being articulate, and cannot break out of an armour of ready-made phrases when he tries to express his real convictions. Once again, nothing can now be done for him: there are no courses in remedial metaphor.

3   The greatest fallacy in the present conception of literary education is the notion that prose is the normal language of ordinary speech, and should form the centre and staple of literary teaching. From prose in this sense we move out to utilitarian English on one side and to the more specialized literary study of poetry on the other. Few subjects can be more futile than a prose-based approach to poetry, an approach which treats poems as documents, to be analysed or summarized or otherwise translated into the language of communication. The root of the fallacy is the assumption that prose represents the only valid form of thought, and that poetry, considered as thought, is essentially decorated or distorted prose. When we suggest that young people try writing poetry, what most of them immediately produce are discontinuous prose statements about their emotions, or what they think their emotions ought to be, when confronted with the outside world. This is not merely because they have been taught to read poetry as a series of statements of this kind—"all that guff about nature," as one freshman expressed it—it is rather that they assume that all verbal expression derives from the attempt to describe something, and that poetry differs from prose, as a mode of thought, in being an attempt to describe subjective emotions.

4   The main principles of a coherently organized curriculum are simple enough, but very different from the one just mentioned. Poetry should be at the centre of all literary training, and literary prose forms the periphery. In a properly constructed curriculum there would be no place for "effective communication" or for any form of utilitarian English. We still have textbooks on effective writing produced by people who have no notion how to write, mainly because they are trying to be effective about it, but one hopes that the market for them will disappear in our time. The styles employed by journalists and advertisers are highly conventionalized rhetorics, in fact practically trade jargons, and have to be learned as separate skills, without much direct reference to literature at all. A literary training is a considerable handicap in trying to understand, for example, the releases of public relations counsels. I am not saying this just to be ironic: I am stating a fact. I remember a New Yorker cartoon of a milkman who found the notice "no milk" on a doorstep, and woke up the household at four in the morning to enquire whether he meant that he had no milk or that he wanted no milk. I suspect that the milkman was a retired teacher of English: certainly he reflects the disadvantages of being sensitive to the nuances of expression. A literary person confronted with most of the verbal technologies of our time is in the

position of a genuinely intelligent student confronted with an intelligence test which grossly oversimplifies its categories and calls for an arbitrary choice of half-truths. He is sure to fail the test simply because he is more intelligent than the creature who designed it. The primary function of education is to make one maladjusted to ordinary society; and literary education makes it more difficult to come to terms with the barbarizing of speech, or what *Finnegans Wake* calls the jinglish janglage.

5   The connections of literature are with the imagination, not with the reason, hence the ideal in literature is one of intensity and power rather than of precision or accuracy, as in science. There can be no intensity without precision, but to aim directly at precision is trying to seize the shadow. Poetry is one of the creative arts, in the context of music and painting, or rhythm and pattern. The rhythmical energy of poetry, its intimate connection with song and dance, is the elementary basis of its appeal, and the primary aspect of it to be presented to children, along with its affinity with the concrete and the sensational, its power of making things vivid by illustration, which has traditionally been expressed in the formula *ut pictura poesis*.

6   I am certainly no expert on the teaching of children, but it seems obvious that all such teaching has to follow the child's own rhythm of thought and development, and not project on him some half-baked adult mystique, whether that mystique claims to derive from the anti-intellectual left or the anti-anti-intellectual right. And it is clear that children recapitulate, as we should expect them to do, the experience of primitive literature, and turn most naturally and easily to the abstract and conventionalized, to riddles, conundrums, and, stylized jingles. The authors of *The Lore and Language of Schoolchildren* quote an unremarkable verse:

> Mrs. White had a fright
> In the middle of the night,
> She saw a ghost eating toast
> Half-way up the lamp post

and append the comment of a nine-year-old critic: "I think what's so clever about this is the way it all rhymes." Later, in speaking of the child's fondness for tongue twisters and multiple puns, they remark: "It takes children a long time before they cease to be amazed that one word can have more than one meaning." One would hope that this amazement would last the rest of their lives. The speech of a small child is full of chanting and singing, and it is clear that the child understands what many adults do not, that verse is a more direct and primitive way of conventionalizing speech than prose is.

7   This principle, that the physical energy and concrete vividness of verse should normally be presented earlier than the more complex and adulterated rhythm of prose, affects the training in both reading and writing. It is difficult to know how a child thinks, but it is less difficult to know how he talks, once one has gained his confidence, and how he talks might afford an educational clue. Any child who has talked to me has addressed me in an uninhibited stream of burble for which the nearest literary counterpart is the last chapter of *Ulysses*. This chapter has no punctuation, and neither has a child's speech. Surely in teaching writing one should begin by trying to channel this free current of verbal energy and start

giving it some precision as it goes along. To teach a child to write as though he were deciphering something from linear B, proceeding from word to phrase, from phrase to sentence, from sentence to paragraph, is to ensure that what he eventually writes will be a dead language. Good writing has to be based on good speech, and good speech is a logical, though complex, development from natural speech. It is a striking feature of our culture that so much creative activity in literature, as in music and painting, should be either explicitly academic or explicitly resistant to education, a culture either of Brahmins or of Dharma bums. In Canada these two aspects of literary culture have reached a curious schizophrenia in which a constant polemic against academic poetry is carried on by poets who are nearly all employed by universities. It seems to me that the source of the feeling that education inhibits spontaneity may be somewhere in the region I have just indicated: in the reversal of the natural rhythms of thought and expression which a prose-based literary education is only too apt to produce.

Basil H. Johnston

Canada 1929–

A member of the Order of Ontario, Basil Johnston was born on the Parry Island Reserve and was educated at Loyola College in Montreal and the Ontario College of Education. He has written widely on Ojibway language and culture in such works as *Ojibway Heritage* (1976), *Indian School Days* (1988), *The Manitous: The Spiritual World of the Ojibway* (1995), and *Honour Earth Mother* (2003). Retired from the Royal Ontario Museum's Department of Ethnology, Johnston is one of only a handful of people fluent in the Ojibway language.

One Generation from Extinction   1991

1   Within the past few years, Gregor Keeshig, Henry Johnston, Resime Akiwenzie, Norman McLeod, and Belva Pitwaniquot died. They all spoke their tribal language, Anishinaubae (Ojibwa). When these elders passed away, so did a portion of the tribal language come to an end as a tree disintegrates by degrees and in stages until it is no more; and, though infants were born to replenish the loss of life, not any of them will learn the language of their grandfathers or grandmothers to keep it alive and to pass it on to their descendants. Thus language dies.

2   In some communities there are no more Gregor Keeshigs, Henry Johnstons, Resime Akiwenzies, Norman McLeods, Belva Pitwaniquots; those remaining have no more affinity to their ancestral language than they do to Swahili or Sanskrit; in other communities the languages may not survive beyond a generation. Some tribal languages are at the edge of extinction, not expected to survive for more than a few years. There remain but three aboriginal languages out of the original fifty-three found in Canada that may survive several more generations.

3   There is cause to lament but it is the native peoples who have the most cause to lament the passing of their languages. They lose not only the ability to express the simplest of daily sentiments and needs but they can no longer understand the ideas, concepts, insights, attitudes, rituals, ceremonies, institutions brought into being by their ancestors; and, having lost the power to understand, cannot sustain, enrich, or pass on their heritage. No longer will they think Indian or feel Indian. And though they may wear 'Indian' jewellery and take part in pow-wows, they can never capture that kinship with and reverence for the sun and the moon, the sky and the water, or feel the lifebeat of Mother Earth or sense the change in her moods; no longer are the wolf, the bear, and the caribou elder brothers but beasts, resources to be killed and sold. They will have lost their identity which no amount of reading can ever restore. Only language and literature can restore the 'Indian-ness.'

4   Now if Canadians of West European or other origin have less cause than 'Indians' to lament the passing of tribal languages and cultures it is because they may not realize that there is more to tribal languages than 'ugh' or 'how' or 'kimu sabi'. At most and at best Euro-Canadians might have read or heard about Raven and Nanabush and Thunderbirds and other 'tricksters'; some may have even studied 'Culture Myths', 'Hero Tales', 'Transformation Tales', or 'Nature Myths and Beast Fables', but these accounts were never regarded as bearing any more sense than 'Little Red Riding Hood' or 'The Three Little Pigs'. Neither language nor literature were ever considered in their natural kinship, which is the only way in which language ought to be considered were its range, depth, force, and beauty to be appreciated.

5   Perhaps our Canadian compatriots of West European origin have more cause to lament the passing of an Indian language than they realize or care to admit. Scholars mourn that there is no one who can speak the Huron language and thus assist scholars in their pursuit of further knowledge about the tribe; scholars mourn that had the Beothuk language survived, so much more would be known about the Beothuk peoples. In mourning the extinction of the language, scholars are implicitly declaring that the knowledge derived from a study of snowshoes, shards, arrowheads, old pipes, shrunken heads and old bones, hunting, fishing, transportation, food preparation, ornamentation, and sometimes ritual is limited. And so it is; material culture can yield only so much.

6   Language is crucial. If scholars are to increase their knowledge and if they are to add depth and width to their studies, they must study a native language and literature. It is not enough to know linguistics or to know a few words or even some phrases or to have access to the Jesuit *Relations*, Chippewa *Exercises*, Ojibwa *Texts*, or a *Dictionary of the Otchipwe Language*. Without a knowledge of the language scholars can never take for granted the accuracy of an interpretation or translation of a passage, let alone a single word; nor can they presume that their articles, tracts, treatises, essays bear the kind of accuracy that scholarship and integrity demand. They would continue to labour under the impression that the word 'manitou' means spirit and that it has no other meaning. Superstitious nonsense, according to the white man. They do not know that the word bears other meanings even more fundamental than 'spirit', such as, and/or pertaining to the deities; of a substance, character, nature, essence, quiddity beyond comprehension and therefore beyond explanation, a mystery; supernatural; potency, potential. What a difference such knowledge might have made in the studies conducted

by Ruth Landes or Thomas B. Leekley, and others on the Anishinaubae tribe. Perhaps, instead of regarding 'Indians' as superstitious for positing 'spirits' in trees or in other inanimate or insensate objects, they might have credited them with insight for having perceived a vital substance or essence that imparted life, form, growth, healing, and strength in all things, beings, and places. They might have understood that the expression 'manitouwan' meant that an object possessed or was infused with an element or a feature that was beyond human ken; they might have understood that 'w'manitouwih' meant that he or she was endowed with extraordinary talents, and that it did not mean that he or she was a spirit.

7   Language is essential. If scholars and writers are to know how 'Indians' perceive and regard certain ideas they must study an 'Indian' language. When an 'Anishinaubae' says that someone is telling the truth, he says 'w'daeb-awae'. But the expression is not just a mere confirmation of a speaker's veracity. It is at the same time a philosophical proposition that, in saying, a speaker casts his words and his voice only as far as his vocabulary and his perception will enable him. In so doing the tribe was denying that there was absolute truth; that the best a speaker could achieve and a listener expect was the highest degree of accuracy. Somehow that one expression 'w'daeb-awae' set the limits of a single statement as well as setting limits on all speech.

8   There was a special regard almost akin to reverence for speech and for the truth. Perhaps it was because words bear the tone of the speaker and may therefore be regarded as belonging to that person; perhaps it is because words have but a fleeting momentary existence in sound and are gone except in memory; perhaps it is because words have not ceased to exist but survive in echo and continue on in infinity; perhaps it is because words are medicine that can heal or injure; perhaps it is because words possess an element of the manitou that enabled them to conjure images and ideas out of nothing, and are the means by which the autissokanuk (muses) inspired men and women. It was not for nothing that the older generation did not solicit the autissokanuk to assist in the genesis of stories or in the composition of chants in seasons other than winter.

9   To instil respect for language the old counselled youth, 'Don't talk too much' (Kegon zaum-doongaen), for they saw a kinship between language and truth. The expression is not without its facetious aspect but in its broader application it was intended to convey to youth other notions implicit in the expression 'Don't talk too much', for the injunction also meant 'Don't talk too often ... Don't talk too long ... Don't talk about those matters that you know nothing about.' Were a person to restrict his discourse, and measure his speech, and govern his talk by what he knew, he would earn the trust and respect of his (her) listeners. Of that man or woman they would say 'w'daeb-awae'. Better still, people would want to hear the speaker again and by so doing bestow upon the speaker the opportunity to speak, for ultimately it is the people who confer the right of speech by their audience.

10   Language was a precious heritage; literature was no less precious. So precious did the tribe regard language and speech that it held those who abused language and speech and truth in contempt and ridicule and withheld from them their trust and confidence. To the tribe the man or woman who rambled on and on, or who let his tongue range over every subject or warp the truth was said to talk in circles in a manner no different from that of a mongrel who, not knowing the source of alarm, barks in circles (w'geewi-animoh). Ever since words and sounds

were reduced to written symbols and have been stripped of their mystery and magic, the regard and reverence for them have diminished in tribal life.

11   As rich and full of meaning as may be individual words and expression, they embody only a small portion of the entire stock and potential of tribal knowledge, wisdom, and intellectual attainment; the greater part is deposited in myths, legends, stories, and in the lyrics of chants that make up the tribe's literature. Therein will be found the essence and the substance of tribal ideas, concepts, insights, attitudes, values, beliefs, theories, notions, sentiments, and accounts of their institutions and rituals and ceremonies. Without language scholars, writers, and teachers will have no access to the depth and width of tribal knowledge and understanding, but must continue to labour as they have done these many years under the impression that 'Indian' stories are nothing more than fairy tales or folklore, fit only for juvenile minds. For scholars and academics Nanabush, Raven, Glooscap, Weesaukeechauk, and other mythological figures will ever remain 'tricksters,' culture heroes, deities whose misadventures were dreamed into being only for the amusement of children. Primitive and pagan and illiterate to boot, 'Indians' could not possibly address or articulate abstract ideas or themes; neither their minds nor their languages could possibly express any idea more complex than taboos, superstitions, and bodily needs.

12   But were ethnologists, anthropologists, linguists, teachers of native children and writers of native literature—yes, even archaeologists—to learn a native language, perhaps they might learn that Nanabush and Raven are not simply 'tricksters' but the caricatured representations of human nature and character in their many facets; perhaps they might give thought to the meaning and sense to be found in Weessaukeetchauk, The Bitter Soul. There is no other way except through language for scholars to learn or to validate their studies, their theories, their theses about the values, ideals or institutions or any other aspect of tribal life; there is no other way by which knowledge of native life can find increase. Not good enough is it to say in hushed tones after a reverential description of a totem pole or the lacing of a snowshoe, 'My, weren't they clever.'

13   Just consider the fate of 'Indian' stories written by those who knew nothing of the language and never did hear any of the stories in their entirety or in their original version but derived everything that they knew of their subject from second, third, and even fourth diluted sources. Is it any wonder then that the stories in *Indian Legends of Canada* by E.E. Clark or in *Manabozho* by T.B. Leekley are so bland and devoid of sense. Had the authors known the stories in their 'Indian' sense and flavour, perhaps they might have infused their versions with more wit and substance. Had the authors known that the creation story as the Anishinaubae understood it to mean was intended to represent in the most dramatic way possible the process of individual development from the smallest portion of talent to be retrieved from the depths of one's being and then given growth by breath of life. Thus a man and woman are to develop themselves, create their own worlds, and shape their being and give meaning to life. Had the authors known this meaning of the Creation Story, perhaps they might have written their accounts in terms more in keeping with the sense and thrust of the story. But not knowing the language nor having heard the story in its original text or state, the authors could not, despite their intentions, impart to their accounts the due weight and perspective the story deserved. The stories were demeaned.

14   With language dead and literature demeaned, 'Indian' institutions are beyond understanding and restoration. Let us turn back the calendar two and a half centuries, to
that period when the 'Indian' languages were spoken in every home, when native literature inspired thought, and when native 'Indian' institutions governed native
'Indian' life. It was then that a native institution caught the imagination of the newcomers to this continent. The men and women who founded a new nation to be
known as the United States of America took as their model for their constitution and
government the principles of government and administration embodied in The
Great Tree of Peace of the Five Nations Confederacy. The institution of The Great
Tree of Peace was not then too primitive nor too alien for study or emulation to the
founders of the United States. In more recent years even the architects of the United
Nations regarded the 'Indian' institution of The Great Tree of Peace not as a primitive organization beneath their dignity and intellect, but rather as an institution of
merit. There exist still 'Indian' institutions that may well serve and benefit this society
and this nation, not as dramatically as did The Great Tree of Peace the United States
of America, but bestow some good as yet undreamed or unimagined. Just how much
good such institutions may confer upon this or some future generation will not be
known unless the 'Indian' languages survive.

15   And what is it that had undermined the vitality of some of the 'Indian' languages and deprived this generation and this society the promise and the benefit
of the wisdom and knowledge embodied in tribal literature?

16   In the case of the Beothuk and their language, the means used were simple
and direct: it was the blade, the bludgeon, and the bullet that were plied in the
destruction of the Beothuk in their sleep, at their table, and in their quiet passage
from home to place of work, until the tribe was no more. The speakers were annihilated; no more was the Beothuk language spoken; whatever their wisdom or
whatever their institutions, the whole of the Beothuk heritage was destroyed.

17   In other instances, instead of bullets, bludgeons, and bayonets, other means
were used to put an end to the speaking of an 'Indian' language. A kick with a police
riding boot administered by a 175-pound man upon the person of an eight-year-
old boy for uttering the language of a savage left its pain for days and its bruise upon
the spirit for life. A boy once kicked was not likely to risk a second or a third. A slap
in the face or a punch to the back of the head delivered even by a small man upon
the person of a small boy left its sting and a humiliation not soon forgotten. And if
a boot or a fist were not administered, then a lash or a yardstick was plied until the
'Indian' language was beaten out. To boot and fist and lash was added ridicule. Both
speaker and his language were assailed. 'What's the use of that language? It isn't
polite to speak another language in the presence of other people. Learn English!
That's the only way you're going to get ahead. How can you learn two languages at
the same time? No wonder kids can't learn anything else. It's a primitive language;
hasn't the vocabulary to express abstract ideas, poor. Say "ugh." Say something in
your language! ... How can you get your tongue around those sounds?' On and on
the comments were made, disparaging, until in too many the language was shamed
into silence and disuse.

18   And how may the federal government assist in the restoration of the native
languages to their former vigour and vitality and enable them to fulfil their
promise?

19   The Government of Canada must finance the establishment of either provincial or regional language institutes to be affiliated with a museum or a university or a provincial native educational organization. The function of the 'institute', to be headed by a native person who speaks, reads, and writes a native language, will be to foster research into language and to encourage the publication of lexicons, dictionaries, grammars, courses, guides, outlines, myths, stories, legends, genealogies, histories, religion, rituals, ceremonies, chants, prayers, and general articles; to tape stories, myths, legends, grammars, teaching guides and outlines and to build a collection of written and oral literature to make same accessible to scholars, teachers, and native institutions; and to duplicate and distribute written and oral literature to the native communities and learning institutions. The native languages deserve to be enshrined in this country's heritage as much as do snowshoes, shards, and arrowheads. Nay! More.

20   But unless the writings, the essays, stories, plays, the papers of scholars, academics, lexicographers, grammarians, etymologists, playwrights, poets, novelists, composers, philosophers are published and distributed, they can never nurture growth in language or literature. Taking into account the market represented by each tribe, no commercial publisher would risk publication of an 'Indian' book. Hence, only the federal government has the means to sponsor publication of an 'Indian text', either through a commercial publisher or through the Queen's Printer. The publication of an 'Indian' book may not be a commercially profitable enterprise, but it would add to the nation's intellectual and literary heritage.

Neil Postman

U.S.A. 1931–2003

Neil Postman's work became widely read and quoted after the publication of *Teaching as a Subversive Activity* in 1969. His critical commentaries on education and, more recently, the effects of the media on society have made him a respected critic of American culture. Having begun his career as an educator associated with the public school system, he is now a professor of media ecology at New York University. "Now ... This" is a chapter from his book *Amusing Ourselves to Death.*

"Now ... This"   1985

1   The American humorist H. Allen Smith once suggested that of all the worrisome words in the English language, the scariest is "uh oh," as when a physician looks at your X-rays, and with knitted brow says, "Uh oh." I should like to suggest that the words which are the title of this chapter are as ominous as any, all the more so because they are spoken without knitted brow—indeed, with a kind of idiot's delight. The phrase, if that's what it may be called, adds to our grammar a new part of speech, a conjunction that does not connect anything to anything but does

the opposite: separates everything from everything. As such, it serves as a compact metaphor for the discontinuities in so much that passes for public discourse in present-day America.

2   "Now ... this" is commonly used on radio and television newscasts to indicate that what one has just heard or seen has no relevance to what one is about to hear or see, or possibly to anything one is ever likely to hear or see. The phrase is a means of acknowledging the fact that the world as mapped by the speeded-up electronic media has no order or meaning and is not to be taken seriously. There is no murder so brutal, no earthquake so devastating, no political blunder so costly—for that matter, no ball score so tantalizing or weather report so threatening—that it cannot be erased from our minds by a newscaster saying, "Now ... this." The newscaster means that you have thought long enough on the previous matter (approximately forty-five seconds), that you must not be morbidly preoccupied with it (let us say, for ninety seconds), and that you must now give your attention to another fragment of news or a commercial.

3   Television did not invent the "Now ... this" world view. As I have tried to show, it is the offspring of the intercourse between telegraphy and photography. But it is through television that it has been nurtured and brought to a perverse maturity. For on television, nearly every half hour is a discrete event, separated in content, context, and emotional texture from what precedes and follows it. In part because television sells its time in seconds and minutes, in part because television must use images rather than words, in part because its audience can move freely to and from the television set, programs are structured so that almost each eight-minute segment may stand as a complete event in itself. Viewers are rarely required to carry over any thought or feeling from one parcel of time to another.

4   Of course, in television's presentation of the "news of the day," we may see the "Now ... this" mode of discourse in its boldest and most embarrassing form. For there, we are presented not only with fragmented news but news without context, without consequences, without value, and therefore without essential seriousness; that is to say, news as pure entertainment.

5   Consider, for example, how you would proceed if you were given the opportunity to produce a television news show for any station concerned to attract the largest possible audience. You would, first, choose a cast of players, each of whom has a face that is both "likable" and "credible." Those who apply would, in fact, submit to you their eight-by-ten glossies, from which you would eliminate those whose countenances are not suitable for nightly display. This means that you will exclude women who are not beautiful or who are over the age of fifty, men who are bald, all people who are overweight or whose noses are too long or whose eyes are too close together. You will try, in other words, to assemble a cast of talking hair-do's. At the very least, you will want those whose faces would not be unwelcome on a magazine cover.

6   Christine Craft has just such a face, and so she applied for a co-anchor position on KMBC-TV in Kansas City. According to a lawyer who represented her in a sexism suit she later brought against the station, the management of KMBC-TV "loved Christine's look." She was accordingly hired in January 1981. She was fired in August 1981 because research indicated that her appearance "hampered viewer acceptance." What exactly does "hampered viewer acceptance" mean? And what does it have to do with the news? Hampered viewer acceptance means the same thing for television

news as it does for any television show: Viewers do not like looking at the performer. It also means that viewers do not believe the performer, that she lacks credibility. In the case of a theatrical performance, we have a sense of what that implies: The actor does not persuade the audience that he or she is the character being portrayed. But what does lack of credibility imply in the case of a news show? What character is a co-anchor playing? And how do we decide that the performance lacks verisimilitude? Does the audience believe that the newscaster is lying, that what is reported did not in fact happen, that something important is being concealed?

7   It is frightening to think that this may be so, that the perception of the truth of a report rests heavily on the acceptability of the newscaster. In the ancient world, there was a tradition of banishing or killing the bearer of bad tidings. Does the television news show restore, in a curious form, this tradition? Do we banish those who tell us the news when we do not care for the face of the teller? Does television countermand the warnings we once received about the fallacy of the ad hominem argument?

8   If the answer to any of these questions is even a qualified "Yes," then here is an issue worthy of the attention of epistemologists. Stated in its simplest form, it is that television provides a new (or, possibly, restores an old) definition of truth: The credibility of the teller is the ultimate test of the truth of a proposition. "Credibility" here does not refer to the past record of the teller for making statements that have survived the rigors of reality-testing. It refers only to the impression of sincerity, authenticity, vulnerability or attractiveness (choose one or more) conveyed by the actor/reporter.

9   This is a matter of considerable importance, for it goes beyond the question of how truth is perceived on television news shows. If on television, credibility replaces reality as the decisive test of truth-telling, political leaders need not trouble themselves very much with reality provided that their performances consistently generate a sense of verisimilitude. I suspect, for example, that the dishonor that now shrouds Richard Nixon results not from the fact that he lied but that on television he looked like a liar. Which, if true, should bring no comfort to anyone, not even veteran Nixon-haters. For the alternative possibilities are that one may look like a liar but be telling the truth; or even worse, look like a truth-teller but in fact be lying.

10   As a producer of a television news show, you would be well aware of these matters and would be careful to choose your cast on the basis of criteria used by David Merrick and other successful impresarios. Like them, you would then turn your attention to staging the show on principles that maximize entertainment value. You would, for example, select a musical theme for the show. All television news programs begin, end, and are somewhere in between punctuated with music. I have found very few Americans who regard this custom as peculiar, which fact I have taken as evidence for the dissolution of lines of demarcation between serious public discourse and entertainment. What has music to do with the news? Why is it there? It is there, I assume, for the same reason music is used in the theater and films—to create a mood and provide a leitmotif for the entertainment. If there were no music—as is the case when any television program is interrupted for a news flash—viewers would expect something truly alarming, possibly life-altering. But as long as the music is there as a frame for the program, the viewer is comforted to believe that there is nothing to be greatly alarmed about; that, in fact, the events that are reported have as much relation to reality as do scenes in a play.

11   This perception of a news show as a stylized dramatic performance whose content has been staged largely to entertain is reinforced by several other features, including the fact that the average length of any story is forty-five seconds. While brevity does not always suggest triviality, in this case it clearly does. It is simply not possible to convey a sense of seriousness about any event if its implications are exhausted in less than one minute's time. In fact, it is quite obvious that TV news has no intention of suggesting that any story *has* any implications, for that would require viewers to continue to think about it when it is done and therefore obstruct their attending to the next story that waits panting in the wings. In any case, viewers are not provided with much opportunity to be distracted from the next story since in all likelihood it will consist of some film footage. Pictures have little difficulty in overwhelming words, and short-circuiting introspection. As a television producer, you would be certain to give both prominence and precedence to any event for which there is some sort of visual documentation. A suspected killer being brought into a police station, the angry face of a cheated consumer, a barrel going over Niagara Falls (with a person alleged to be in it), the President disembarking from a helicopter on the White House lawn—these are always fascinating or amusing, and easily satisfy the requirements of an entertaining show. It is, of course, not necessary that the visuals actually document the point of a story. Neither is it necessary to explain why such images are intruding themselves on public consciousness. Film footage justifies itself, as every television producer well knows.

12   It is also of considerable help in maintaining a high level of unreality that the newscasters do not pause to grimace or shiver when they speak their prefaces or epilogs to the film clips. Indeed, many newscasters do not appear to grasp the meaning of what they are saying, and some hold to a fixed and ingratiating enthusiasm as they report on earthquakes, mass killings and other disasters. Viewers would be quite disconcerted by any show of concern or terror on the part of newscasters. Viewers, after all, are partners with the newscasters in the "Now ... this" culture, and they expect the newscaster to play out his or her role as a character who is marginally serious but who stays well clear of authentic understanding. The viewers, for their part, will not be caught contaminating their responses with a sense of reality, any more than an audience at a play would go scurrying to call home because a character on stage has said that a murderer is loose in the neighborhood.

13   The viewers also know that no matter how grave any fragment of news may appear (for example, on the day I write a Marine Corps general has declared that nuclear war between the United States and Russia is inevitable), it will shortly be followed by a series of commercials that will, in an instant, defuse the import of the news, in fact render it largely banal. This is a key element in the structure of a news program and all by itself refutes any claim that television news is designed as a serious form of public discourse. Imagine what you would think of me, and this book, if I were to pause here, tell you that I will return to my discussion in a moment, and then proceed to write a few words on behalf of United Airlines or the Chase Manhattan Bank. You would rightly think that I had no respect for you and, certainly, no respect for the subject. And if I did this not once but several times in each chapter, you would think the whole enterprise unworthy of your attention. Why, then, do we not think a news show similarly unworthy? The reason, I believe, is that whereas we expect books and even other media (such as film) to maintain a consistency of tone and a continuity of content, we have no

such expectation of television, and especially television news. We have become so accustomed to its discontinuities that we are no longer struck dumb, as any sane person would be, by a newscaster who having just reported that a nuclear war is inevitable goes on to say that he will be right back after this word from Burger King; who says, in other words, "Now … this." One can hardly overestimate the damage that such juxtapositions do to our sense of the world as a serious place. The damage is especially massive to youthful viewers who depend so much on television for their clues as to how to respond to the world. In watching television news, they, more than any other segment of the audience, are drawn into an epistemology based on the assumption that all reports of cruelty and death are greatly exaggerated and, in any case, not to be taken seriously or responded to sanely.

14   I should go so far as to say that embedded in the surrealistic frame of a television news show is a theory of anticommunication, featuring a type of discourse that abandons logic, reason, sequence and rules of contradiction. In aesthetics, I believe the name given to this theory is Dadaism; in philosophy, nihilism; in psychiatry, schizophrenia. In the parlance of the theater, it is known as vaudeville.

15   For those who think I am here guilty of hyperbole, I offer the following description of television news by Robert MacNeil, executive editor and co-anchor of the "MacNeil-Lehrer Newshour." The idea, he writes, "is to keep everything brief, not to strain the attention of anyone but instead to provide constant stimulation through variety, novelty, action, and movement. You are required … to pay attention to no concept, no character, and no problem for more than a few seconds at a time." He goes on to say that the assumptions controlling a news show are "that bite-sized is best, that complexity must be avoided, that nuances are dispensable, that qualifications impede the simple message, that visual stimulation is a substitute for thought, and that verbal precision is an anachronism."

16   Robert MacNeil has more reason than most to give testimony about the television news show as vaudeville act. The "MacNeil-Lehrer Newshour" is an unusual and gracious attempt to bring to television some of the elements of typographic discourse. The program abjures visual stimulation, consists largely of extended explanations of events and in-depth interviews (which even there means only five to ten minutes), limits the number of stories covered, and emphasizes background and coherence. But television has exacted its price for MacNeil's rejection of a show business format. By television's standards, the audience is minuscule, the program is confined to public-television stations, and it is a good guess that the combined salary of MacNeil and Lehrer is one-fifth of Dan Rather's or Tom Brokaw's.

17   If you were a producer of a television news show for a commercial station, you would not have the option of defying television's requirements. It would be demanded of you that you strive for the largest possible audience, and, as a consequence and in spite of your best intentions, you would arrive at a production very nearly resembling MacNeil's description. Moreover, you would include some things MacNeil does not mention. You would try to make celebrities of your newscasters. You would advertise the show, both in the press and on television itself. You would do "news briefs," to serve as an inducement to viewers. You would have a weatherman as comic relief, and a sportscaster whose language is a touch uncouth (as a way of his relating to the beer-drinking common man). You would, in short, package the whole event as any producer might who is in the entertainment business.

18   The result of all this is that Americans are the best entertained and quite likely the least well-informed people in the Western world. I say this in the face of the popular conceit that television, as a window to the world, has made Americans exceedingly well informed. Much depends here, of course, on what is meant by being informed. I will pass over the now tiresome polls that tell us that, at any given moment, 70 percent of our citizens do not know who is the Secretary of State or the Chief Justice of the Supreme Court. Let us consider, instead, the case of Iran during the drama that was called the "Iranian Hostage Crisis." I don't suppose there has been a story in years that received more continuous attention from television. We may assume, then, that Americans know most of what there is to know about this unhappy event. And now, I put these questions to you: Would it be an exaggeration to say that not one American in a hundred knows what language the Iranians speak? Or what the word "Ayatollah" means or implies? Or knows any details of the tenets of Iranian religious beliefs? Or the main outlines of their political history? Or knows who the Shah was, and where he came from?

19   Nonetheless, everyone had an opinion about this event, for in America everyone is entitled to an opinion, and it is certainly useful to have a few when a pollster shows up. But these are opinions of a quite different order from eighteenth- or nineteenth-century opinions. It is probably more accurate to call them emotions rather than opinions, which would account for the fact that they change from week to week, as the pollsters tell us. What is happening here is that television is altering the meaning of "being informed" by creating a species of information that might properly be called *disinformation*. I am using this word almost in the precise sense in which it is used by spies in the CIA or KGB. Disinformation does not mean false information. It means misleading information—misplaced, irrelevant, fragmented or superficial information—information that creates the illusion of knowing something but which in fact leads one away from knowing. In saying this, I do not mean to imply that television news deliberately aims to deprive Americans of a coherent, contextual understanding of their world. I mean to say that when news is packaged as entertainment, that is the inevitable result. And in saying that the television news show entertains but does not inform, I am saying something far more serious than that we are being deprived of authentic information. I am saying we are losing our sense of what it means to be well informed. Ignorance is always correctable. But what shall we do if we take ignorance to be knowledge?

20   Here is a startling example of how this process bedevils us. A *New York Times* article is headlined on February 15, 1983:

REAGAN MISSTATEMENTS GETTING LESS ATTENTION

21   The article begins in the following way:

> President Reagan's aides used to become visibly alarmed at suggestions that he had given mangled and perhaps misleading accounts of his policies or of current events in general. That doesn't seem to happen much anymore.
>
> Indeed, the President continues to make debatable assertions of fact but news accounts do not deal with them as extensively as they once did. In the view of White House officials, the declining news coverage mirrors a *decline in interest by the general public.* (my italics)

22   This report is not so much a news story as a story about the news, and our recent history suggests that it is not about Ronald Reagan's charm. It is about how news is defined, and I believe the story would be quite astonishing to both civil libertarians and tyrants of an earlier time. Walter Lippmann, for example, wrote in 1920: "There can be no liberty for a community which lacks the means by which to detect lies." For all of his pessimism about the possibilities of restoring an eighteenth- and nineteenth-century level of public discourse, Lippmann assumed, as did Thomas Jefferson before him, that with a well-trained press functioning as a lie-detector, the public's interest in a President's mangling of the truth would be piqued, in both senses of that word. Given the means to detect lies, he believed, the public could not be indifferent to their consequences.

23   But this case refutes his assumption. The reporters who cover the White House are ready and able to expose lies, and thus create the grounds for informed and indignant opinion. But apparently the public declines to take an interest. To press reports of White House dissembling, the public has replied with Queen Victoria's famous line: "We are not amused." However, here the words mean something the Queen did not have in mind. They mean that what is not amusing does not compel their attention. Perhaps if the President's lies could be demonstrated by pictures and accompanied by music the public would raise a curious eyebrow. If a movie, like *All the President's Men,* could be made from his misleading accounts of government policy, if there were a break-in of some sort or sinister characters laundering money, attention would quite likely be paid. We do well to remember that President Nixon did not begin to come undone until his lies were given a theatrical setting at the Watergate hearings. But we do not have anything like that here. Apparently, all President Reagan does is *say* things that are not entirely true. And there is nothing entertaining in that.

24   But there is a subtler point to be made here. Many of the President's "misstatements" fall in the category of contradictions—mutually exclusive assertions that cannot possibly both, in the same context, be true. "In the same context" is the key phrase here, for it is context that defines contradiction. There is no problem in someone's remarking that he prefers oranges to apples, and also remarking that he prefers apples to oranges—not if one statement is made in the context of choosing a wallpaper design and the other in the context of selecting fruit for dessert. In such a case, we have statements that are opposites, but not contradictory. But if the statements are made in a single, continuous, and coherent context, then they are contradictions, and cannot both be true. Contradiction, in short, requires that statements and events be perceived as interrelated aspects of a continuous and coherent context. Disappear the context, or fragment it, and contradiction disappears. This point is nowhere made more clear to me than in conferences with my younger students about their writing. "Look here," I say. "In this paragraph you have said one thing. And in that you have said the opposite. Which is it to be?" They are polite, and wish to please, but they are as baffled by the question as I am by the response. "I know," they will say, "but that is *there* and this is *here*." The difference between us is that I assume "there" and "here," "now" and "then," one paragraph and the next to be connected, to be continuous, to be part of the same coherent world of thought. That is the way of typographic discourse, and typography is the universe I'm "coming from," as they say. But they are coming from a different universe of discourse altogether: the "Now … this" world of television. The fundamental assumption of that world is not

coherence but discontinuity. And in a world of discontinuities, contradiction is useless as a test of truth or merit, because contradiction does not exist.

25   My point is that we are by now so thoroughly adjusted to the "Now ... this" world of news—a world of fragments, where events stand alone, stripped of any connection to the past, or to the future, or to other events—that all assumptions of coherence have vanished. And so, perforce, has contradiction. In the context of *no context*, so to speak, it simply disappears. And in its absence, what possible interest could there be in a list of what the President says *now* and what he said *then*? It is merely a rehash of old news, and there is nothing interesting or entertaining in that. The only thing to be amused about is the bafflement of reporters at the public's indifference. There is an irony in the fact that the very group that has taken the world apart should, on trying to piece it together again, be surprised that no one notices much, or cares.

26   For all his perspicacity, George Orwell would have been stymied by this situation; there is nothing "Orwellian" about it. The President does not have the press under his thumb. *The New York Times* and *The Washington Post* are not *Pravda;*[1] the Associated Press is not Tass.[2] And there is no Newspeak[3] here. Lies have not been defined as truth nor truth as lies. All that has happened is that the public has adjusted to incoherence and been amused into indifference. Which is why Aldous Huxley would not in the least be surprised by the story. Indeed, he prophesied its coming. He believed that it is far more likely that the Western democracies will dance and dream themselves into oblivion than march into it, single file and manacled. Huxley grasped, as Orwell did not, that it is not necessary to conceal anything from a public insensible to contradiction and narcoticized by technological diversions. Although Huxley did not specify that television would be our main line to the drug, he would have no difficulty accepting Robert MacNeil's observation that "Television is the *soma*[4] of Aldous Huxley's *Brave New World.*" Big Brother turns out to be Howdy Doody.[5]

27   I do not mean that the trivialization of public information is all accomplished *on* television. I mean that television is the paradigm for our conception of public information. As the printing press did in an earlier time, television has achieved the power to define the form in which news must come, and it has also defined how we shall respond to it. In presenting news to us packaged as vaudeville, television induces other media to do the same, so that the total information environment begins to mirror television.

28   For example, America's newest and highly successful national newspaper, *USA Today,* is modeled precisely on the format of television. It is sold on the street in receptacles that look like television sets. Its stories are uncommonly short, its design leans heavily on pictures, charts and other graphics, some of them printed in various colors. Its weather maps are a visual delight; its sports section includes enough

1   state-run newspaper in the former Soviet Union
2   Russian national news service
3   in *1984,* George Orwell's term for the way in which history and truth are twisted by the state
4   the drug in Huxley's book *Brave New World* that everyone takes and that renders the population passive
5   central figure of a popular children's show on television in the early 1950s

pointless statistics to distract a computer. As a consequence, *USA Today*, which began publication in September 1982, has become the third largest daily in the United States (as of July 1984, according to the Audit Bureau of Circulations), moving quickly to overtake the *Daily News* and the *Wall Street Journal*. Journalists of a more traditional bent have criticized it for its superficiality and theatrics, but the paper's editors remain steadfast in their disregard of typographic standards. The paper's Editor-in-Chief, John Quinn, has said: "We are not up to undertaking projects of the dimensions needed to win prizes. They don't give awards for the best investigative paragraph." Here is an astonishing tribute to the resonance of television's epistemology: In the age of television, the paragraph is becoming the basic unit of news in print media. Moreover, Mr. Quinn need not fret too long about being deprived of awards. As other newspapers join in the transformation, the time cannot be far off when awards will be given for the best investigative sentence.

29   It needs also to be noted here that new and successful magazines such as *People* and *Us* are not only examples of television-oriented print media but have had an extraordinary "ricochet" effect on television itself. Whereas television taught the magazines that news is nothing but entertainment, the magazines have taught television that nothing but entertainment is news. Television programs, such as "Entertainment Tonight," turn information about entertainers and celebrities into "serious" cultural content, so that the circle begins to close: Both the form and content of news become entertainment.

30   Radio, of course, is the least likely medium to join in the descent into a Huxleyan world of technological narcotics. It is, after all, particularly well suited to the transmission of rational, complex language. Nonetheless, and even if we disregard radio's captivation by the music industry, we appear to be left with the chilling fact that such language as radio allows us to hear is increasingly primitive, fragmented, and largely aimed at invoking visceral response; which is to say, it is the linguistic analogue to the ubiquitous rock music that is radio's principal source of income. As I write, the trend in call-in shows is for the "host" to insult callers whose language does not, in itself, go much beyond humanoid grunting. Such programs have little content, as this word used to be defined, and are merely of archeological interest in that they give us a sense of what a dialogue among Neanderthals might have been like. More to the point, the language of radio newscasts has become, under the influence of television, increasingly decontextualized and discontinuous, so that the possibility of anyone's knowing about the world, as against merely knowing *of* it, is effectively blocked. In New York City, radio station WINS entreats its listeners to "Give us twenty-two minutes and we'll give you the world." This is said without irony, and its audience, we may assume, does not regard the slogan as the conception of a disordered mind.

31   And so, we move rapidly into an information environment which may rightly be called trivial pursuit. As the game of that name uses facts as a source of amusement, so do our sources of news. It has been demonstrated many times that a culture can survive misinformation and false opinion. It has not yet been demonstrated whether a culture can survive if it takes the measure of the world in twenty-two minutes. Or if the value of its news is determined by the number of laughs it provides.

Gloria Steinem

U.S.A. 1934–

Gloria Steinem grew up in poverty, travelling around Ohio in a trailer while her father looked for work. She attended Smith College and graduated Phi Beta Kappa in 1956. Following graduation, she travelled for a while, then pursued a career in journalism. Steinem became editor of *Ms.* magazine in 1971 and today is chairperson of Liberty Media for Women, the consortium of feminists that now publishes the magazine. For nine years, Steinem was listed by the *World Almanac* as one of the 25 most influential women in America. Two of her most successful books have been *Outrageous Acts and Everyday Rebellions* (1983) and *Revolution from Within: A Book of Self-Esteem* (1992). "Sex, Lies, and Advertising" appeared in the July/August 1990 issue of *Ms.*

Sex, Lies, and Advertising   1990

1   About three years ago, as *glasnost* was beginning and *Ms.* seemed to be ending, I was invited to a press lunch for a Soviet official. He entertained us with anecdotes about new problems of democracy in his country. Local Communist leaders were being criticized in their media for the first time, he explained, and they were angry.

2   "So I'll have to ask my American friends," he finished pointedly, "how more *subtly* to control the press." In the silence that followed, I said, "Advertising."

3   The reporters laughed, but later, one of them took me aside: How *dare* I suggest that freedom of the press was limited? How dare I imply that his newsweekly could be influenced by ads?

4   I explained that I was thinking of advertising's media-wide influence on most of what we read. Even newsmagazines use "soft" cover stories to sell ads, confuse readers with "advertorials," and occasionally self-censor on subjects known to be a problem with big advertisers.

5   But, I also explained, I was thinking especially of women's magazines. There, it isn't just a little content that's devoted to attracting ads, it's almost all of it. That's why advertisers—not readers—have always been the problem for *Ms.* As the only women's magazine that didn't supply what the ad world euphemistically describes as "supportive editorial atmosphere" or "complementary copy" (for instance, articles that praise food/fashion/beauty subjects to "support" and "complement" food/fashion/beauty ads), *Ms.* could never attract enough advertising to break even.

6   "Oh, *women's* magazines," the journalist said with contempt. "Everybody knows they're catalogs—but who cares? They have nothing to do with journalism."

7   I can't tell you how many times I've had this argument in 25 years of working for many kinds of publications. Except as moneymaking machines—"cash cows" as they are so elegantly called in the trade—women's magazines are rarely taken seriously. Though changes being made by women have been called more far-reaching

than the industrial revolution—and though many editors try hard to reflect some of them in the few pages left to them after all the ad-related subjects have been covered—the magazines serving the female half of this country are still far below the journalistic and ethical standards of news and general interest publications. Most depressing of all, this doesn't even rate an exposé.

8   If *Time* and *Newsweek* had to lavish praise on cars in general and credit General Motors in particular to get GM ads, there would be a scandal—maybe a criminal investigation. When women's magazines from *Seventeen* to *Lear's* praise beauty products in general and credit Revlon in particular to get ads, it's just business as usual.

I

9 When *Ms.* began, we didn't consider *not* taking ads. The most important reason was keeping the price of a feminist magazine low enough for most women to afford. But the second and almost equal reason was providing a forum where women and advertisers could talk to each other and improve advertising itself. After all, it was (and still is) as potent a source of information in this country as news or TV and movie dramas.

10   We decided to proceed in two stages. First, we would convince makers of "people products" used by both men and women but advertised mostly to men— cars, credit cards, insurance, sound equipment, financial services, and the like—that their ads should be placed in a women's magazine. Since they were accustomed to the division between editorial and advertising in news and general interest magazines, this would allow our editorial content to be free and diverse. Second, we would add the best ads for whatever traditional "women's products" (clothes, shampoo, fragrance, food, and so on) that surveys showed *Ms.* readers used. But we would ask them to come in *without* the usual quid pro quo of "complementary copy."

11   We knew the second step might be harder. Food advertisers have always demanded that women's magazines publish recipes and articles on entertaining (preferably ones that name their products) in return for their ads; clothing advertisers expect to be surrounded by fashion spreads (especially ones that credit their designers); and shampoo, fragrance, and beauty products in general usually insist on positive editorial coverage of beauty subjects, plus photo credits besides. That's why women's magazines look the way they do. But if we could break this link between ads and editorial content, then we wanted good ads for "women's products," too.

12   By playing their part in this unprecedented mix of *all* the things our readers need and use, advertisers also would be rewarded: ads for products like cars and mutual funds would find a new growth market; the best ads for women's products would no longer be lost in oceans of ads for the same category; and both would have access to a laboratory of smart and caring readers whose response would help create effective ads for other media as well.

13   I thought then that our main problem would be the imagery in ads themselves. Carmakers were still draping blondes in evening gowns over the hoods like ornaments. Authority figures were almost always male, even in ads for products that only women used. Sadistic, he-man campaigns even won industry praise. (For instance, *Advertising Age* had hailed the infamous Silva Thin cigarette theme, "How

to Get a Woman's Attention: Ignore Her," as "brilliant.") Even in medical journals, tranquilizer ads showed depressed housewives standing beside piles of dirty dishes and promised to get them back to work.

14   Obviously, *Ms.* would have to avoid such ads and seek out the best ones—but this didn't seem impossible. *The New Yorker* had been selecting ads for aesthetic reasons for years, a practice that only seemed to make advertisers more eager to be in its pages. *Ebony* and *Essence* were asking for ads with positive black images, and though their struggle was hard, they weren't being called unreasonable.

15   Clearly, what *Ms.* needed was a very special publisher and ad sales staff. I could think of only one woman with experience on the business side of magazines— Patricia Carbine, who recently had become a vice president of *McCall's* as well as its editor in chief—and the reason I knew her name was a good omen. She had been managing editor at *Look* (really *the* editor, but its owner refused to put a female name at the top of his masthead) when I was writing a column there. After I did an early interview with Cesar Chavez, then just emerging as a leader of migrant labor, and the publisher turned it down because he was worried about ads from Sunkist, Pat was the one who intervened. As I learned later, she had told the publisher she would resign if the interview wasn't published. Mainly because *Look* couldn't afford to lose Pat, it *was* published (and the ads from Sunkist never arrived).

16   Though I barely knew this woman, she had done two things I always remembered: put her job on the line in a way that editors often talk about but rarely do, and been so loyal to her colleagues that she never told me or anyone outside *Look* that she had done so.

17   Fortunately, Pat did agree to leave *McCall's* and take a huge cut in salary to become publisher of *Ms.* She became responsible for training and inspiring generations of young women who joined the *Ms.* ad sales force, many of whom went on to become "firsts" at the top of publishing. When *Ms.* first started, however, there were so few women with experience selling space that Pat and I made the rounds of ad agencies ourselves. Later, the fact that *Ms.* was asking companies to do business in a different way meant our saleswomen had to make many times the usual number of calls—first to convince agencies and then client companies besides—and to present endless amounts of research. I was often asked to do a final ad presentation, or see some higher decision-maker, or speak to women employees so executives could see the interest of women they worked with. That's why I spent more time persuading advertisers than editing or writing for *Ms.* and why I ended up with an unsentimental education in the seamy underside of publishing that few writers see (and even fewer magazines can publish).

18   Let me take you with us through some experiences, just as they happened:

19   • Cheered on by early support from Volkswagen and one or two other car companies, we scrape together time and money to put on a major reception in Detroit. We know U.S. carmakers firmly believe that women choose the upholstery, not the car, but we are armed with statistics and reader mail to prove the contrary: a car is an important purchase for women, one that symbolizes mobility and freedom.

20   But almost nobody comes. We are left with many pounds of shrimp on the table and quite a lot of egg on our face. We blame ourselves for not guessing that there would be a baseball pennant play-off on the same day, but

executives go out of their way to explain they wouldn't have come anyway. Thus begins ten years of knocking on hostile doors, presenting endless documentation, and hiring a full-time saleswoman in Detroit; all necessary before *Ms.* gets any real results.

21   This long saga has a semihappy ending: foreign and, later, domestic carmakers eventually provided *Ms.* with enough advertising to make cars one of our top sources of ad revenue. Slowly, Detroit began to take the women's market seriously enough to put car ads in other women's magazines, too, thus freeing a few pages from the hothouse of fashion-beauty-food ads.

22   But long after figures showed a third, even a half, of many car models being bought by women, U.S. makers continued to be uncomfortable addressing women. Unlike foreign carmakers, Detroit never quite learned the secret of creating intelligent ads that exclude no one, and then placing them in women's magazines to overcome past exclusion. (*Ms.* readers were so grateful for a routine Honda ad featuring rack and pinion steering, for instance, that they sent fan mail.) Even now, Detroit continues to ask, "Should we make special ads for women?" Perhaps that's why some foreign cars still have a disproportionate share of the U.S. women's market.

23 • In the *Ms.* Gazette, we do a brief report on a congressional hearing into chemicals used in hair dyes that are absorbed through the skin and may be carcinogenic. Newspapers report this too, but Clairol, a Bristol-Myers subsidiary that makes dozens of products—a few of which have just begun to advertise in *Ms.*—is outraged. Not at newspapers or newsmagazines, just at us. It's bad enough that *Ms.* is the only women's magazine refusing to provide the usual "complementary" articles and beauty photos, but to criticize one of their categories—*that* is going too far.

24   We offer to publish a letter from Clairol telling its side of the story. In an excess of solicitousness, we even put this letter in the Gazette, not in Letters to the Editors where it belongs. Nonetheless—and in spite of surveys that show *Ms.* readers are active women who use more of almost everything Clairol makes than do the readers of any other women's magazine—*Ms.* gets almost none of these ads for the rest of its natural life.

25   Meanwhile, Clairol changes its hair coloring formula, apparently in response to the hearings we reported.

26 • Our saleswomen set out early to attract ads for consumer electronics: sound equipment, calculators, computers, VCRs, and the like. We know that our readers are determined to be included in the technological revolution. We know from reader surveys that *Ms.* readers are buying this stuff in numbers as high as those of magazines like *Playboy*, or "men 18 to 34," the prime targets of the consumer electronics industry. Moreover, unlike traditional women's products that our readers buy but don't need to read articles about, these are subjects they want covered in our pages. There actually *is* a supportive editorial atmosphere.

27   "But women don't understand technology," say executives at the end of ad presentations. "Maybe not," we respond, "but neither do men—and we all buy it."

28   "If women *do* buy it," say the decision-makers, "they're asking their husbands and boyfriends what to buy first." We produce letters from *Ms.* readers saying how turned off they are when salesmen say things like "Let me know when your husband can come in."

29   After several years of this, we get a few ads for compact sound systems. Some of them come from JVC, whose vice president, Harry Elias, is trying to convince his Japanese bosses that there is something called a women's market. At his invitation, I find myself speaking at huge trade shows in Chicago and Las Vegas, trying to persuade JVC dealers that showrooms don't have to be locker rooms where women are made to feel unwelcome. But as it turns out, the shows themselves are part of the problem. In Las Vegas, the only women around the technology displays are seminude models serving champagne. In Chicago, the big attraction is Marilyn Chambers, who followed Linda Lovelace of *Deep Throat* fame as Chuck Traynor's captive and/or employee. VCRs are being demonstrated with her porn videos.

30   In the end, we get ads for a car stereo now and then, but no VCRs; some IBM personal computers, but no Apple or Japanese ones. We notice that office magazines like *Working Woman* and *Savvy* don't benefit as much as they should from office equipment ads either. In the electronics world, women and technology seem mutually exclusive. It remains a decade behind even Detroit.

31 • Because we get letters from little girls who love toy trains, and who ask our help in changing ads and box-top photos that feature little boys only, we try to get toy-train ads from Lionel. It turns out that Lionel executives *have* been concerned about little girls. They made a pink train, and were surprised when it didn't sell.

32   Lionel bows to consumer pressure with a photograph of a boy *and* a girl— but only on some of their boxes. They fear that, if trains are associated with girls, they will be devalued in the minds of boys. Needless to say, *Ms.* gets no train ads, and little girls remain a mostly unexplored market. By 1986, Lionel is put up for sale.

33   But for different reasons, we haven't had much luck with other kinds of toys either. In spite of many articles on child-rearing; an annual listing of non-sexist, multi-racial toys by Letty Cottin Pogrebin; Stories for Free Children, a regular feature also edited by Letty; and other prizewinning features for or about children, we get virtually no toy ads. Generations of *Ms.* saleswomen explain to toy manufacturers that a larger proportion of *Ms.* readers have preschool children than do the readers of other women's magazines, but this industry can't believe feminists have or care about children.

34 • When *Ms.* begins, the staff decides not to accept ads for feminine hygiene sprays or cigarettes: they are damaging and carry no appropriate health warnings. Though we don't think we should tell our readers what to do, we do think we should provide facts so they can decide for themselves. Since the antismoking lobby has been pressing for health warnings on cigarette ads, we decide to take them only as they comply.

35   Philip Morris is among the first to do so. One of its brands, Virginia Slims, is also sponsoring women's tennis and the first national polls of women's opinions. On the other hand, the Virginia Slims theme, "You've come a long

way, baby," has more than a "baby" problem. It makes smoking a symbol of progress for women.

36   We explain to Philip Morris that this slogan won't do well in our pages, but they are convinced its success with some women means it will work with *all* women. Finally, we agree to publish an ad for a Virginia Slims calendar as a test. The letters from readers are critical—and smart. For instance: Would you show a black man picking cotton, the same man in a Cardin suit, and symbolize the antislavery and civil rights movements by smoking? Of course not. But instead of honoring the test results, the Philip Morris people seem angry to be proven wrong. They take away ads for *all* their many brands.

37   This costs *Ms.* about $250,000 the first year. After five years, we can no longer keep track. Occasionally, a new set of executives listens to *Ms.* saleswomen, but because we won't take Virginia Slims, not one Philip Morris product returns to our pages for the next 16 years.

38   Gradually, we also realize our naiveté in thinking we *could* decide against taking cigarette ads. They became a disproportionate support of magazines the moment they were banned on television, and few magazines could compete and survive without them; certainly not *Ms.*, which lacks so many other categories. By the time statistics in the 1980s showed that women's rate of lung cancer was approaching men's, the necessity of taking cigarette ads has become a kind of prison.

39 • General Mills, Pillsbury, Carnation, DelMonte, Dole, Kraft, Stouffer, Hormel, Nabisco: you name the food giant, we try it. But no matter how desirable the *Ms.* readership, our lack of recipes is lethal.

40   We explain to them that placing foods ads *only* next to recipes associates food with work. For many women, it is a negative that works *against* the ads. Why not place food ads in diverse media without recipes (thus reaching more men, who are now a third of the shoppers in supermarkets anyway), and leave the recipes to specialty magazines like *Gourmet* (a third of whose readers are also men)?

41   These arguments elicit interest, but except for an occasional ad for a convenience food, instant coffee, diet drinks, yogurt, or such extras as avocados and almonds, this mainstay of the publishing industry stays closed to us. Period.

42 • Traditionally, wines and liquors didn't advertise to women: men were thought to make the brand decisions, even if women did the buying. But after endless presentations, we begin to make a dent in this category. Thanks to the unconventional Michel Roux of Carillon Importers (distributors of Grand Marnier, Absolut Vodka, and others), who assumes that food and drink have no gender, some ads are leaving their men's club.

43   Beermakers are still selling masculinity. It takes *Ms.* fully eight years to get its first beer ad (Michelob). In general, however, liquor ads are less stereotyped in their imagery—and far less controlling of the editorial content around them—than are women's products. But given the underrepresentation of other categories, these very facts tend to create a disproportionate number of alcohol ads in the pages of *Ms.* This in turn dismays readers worried about women and alcoholism.

44 • We hear in 1980 that women in the Soviet Union have been producing feminist *samizdat* (underground, self-published books) and circulating them throughout the country. As punishment, four of the leaders have been exiled. Though we are operating on our usual shoestring, we solicit individual contributions to send Robin Morgan to interview these women in Vienna.

45 The result is an exclusive cover story that includes the first news of a populist peace movement against the Afghanistan occupation, a prediction of *glasnost* to come, and a grass-roots, intimate view of Soviet women's lives. From the popular press to women's studies courses, the response is great. The story wins a Front Page award.

46 Nonetheless, this journalistic coup undoes years of efforts to get an ad schedule from Revlon. Why? Because the Soviet women on our cover *are not wearing makeup.*

47 • Four years of research and presentations go into convincing airlines that women now make travel choices and business trips. United, the first airline to advertise in *Ms.*, is so impressed with the response from our readers that one of its executives appears in a film for our ad presentations. As usual, good ads get great results.

48 But we have problems unrelated to such results. For instance: because American Airlines flight attendants include among their labor demands the stipulation that they could choose to have their last names preceded by "Ms." on their name tags—in a long-delayed revolt against the standard, "I am your pilot, Captain Rothgart, and this is your flight attendant, Cindy Sue"— American officials seem to hold the magazine responsible. We get no ads.

49 There is still a different problem at Eastern. A vice president cancels subscriptions for thousands of copies on Eastern flights. Why? Because he is offended by ads for lesbian poetry journals in the *Ms.* Classified. A "family airline," as he explains to me coldly on the phone, has to "draw the line somewhere."

50 It's obvious that *Ms.* can't exclude lesbians and serve women. We've been trying to make that point ever since our first issue included an article by and about lesbians, and both Suzanne Levine, our managing editor, and I were lectured by such heavy hitters as Ed Kosner, then editor of *Newsweek* (and now of *New York Magazine*), who insisted that *Ms.* should "position" itself *against* lesbians. But our advertisers have paid to reach a guaranteed number of readers, and soliciting new subscriptions to compensate for Eastern would cost $150,000, plus rebating money in the meantime.

51 Like almost everything ad-related, this presents an elaborate organizing problem. After days of searching for sympathetic members of the Eastern board, Frank Thomas, president of the Ford Foundation, kindly offers to call Roswell Gilpatrick, a director of Eastern. I talk with Mr. Gilpatrick, who calls Frank Borman, then the president of Eastern. Frank Borman calls me to say that his airline is not in the business of censoring magazines: *Ms.* will be returned to Eastern flights.

52 • Women's access to insurance and credit is vital, but with the exception of Equitable and a few other ad pioneers, such financial services address men. For almost a decade after the Equal Credit Opportunity Act passes in 1974, we try

to convince American Express that women are a growth market—but nothing works.

53   Finally, a former professor of Russian named Jerry Welsh becomes head of marketing. He assumes that women should be cardholders, and persuades his colleagues to feature women in a campaign. Thanks to this 1980s series, the growth rate for female cardholders surpasses that for men.

54   For this article, I asked Jerry Welsh if he would explain why American Express waited so long. "Sure," he said, "they were afraid of having a 'pink' card."

55   • Women of color read *Ms.* in disproportionate numbers. This is a source of pride to *Ms.* staffers, who are also more racially representative than the editors of other women's magazines. But this reality is obscured by ads filled with enough white women to make a reader snowblind.

56   Pat Carbine remembers mostly "astonishment" when she requested African American, Hispanic, Asian, and other diverse images. Marcia Ann Gillespie, a *Ms.* editor who was previously the editor in chief of *Essence,* witnesses ad bias a second time: having tried for *Essence* to get white advertisers to use black images (Revlon did so eventually, but L'Oréal, Lauder, Chanel, and other companies never did), she sees similar problems getting integrated ads for an integrated magazine. Indeed, the ad world often creates black and Hispanic ads only for black and Hispanic media. In an exact parallel of the fear that marketing a product to women will endanger its appeal to men, the response is usually, "But your [white] readers won't identify."

57   In fact, those we are able to get—for instance, a Max Factor ad made for *Essence* that Linda Wachner gives us after she becomes president—are praised by white readers, too. But there are pathetically few such images.

58   • By the end of 1986, production and mailing costs have risen astronomically, ad income is flat, and competition for ads is stiffer than ever. The 60/40 preponderance of edit over ads that we promised to readers becomes 50/50; children's stories, most poetry, and some fiction are casualties of less space; in order to get variety into limited pages, the length (and sometimes the depth) of articles suffers; and, though we do refuse most of the ads that would look like a parody in our pages, we get so worn down that some slip through. ... Still, readers perform miracles. Though we haven't been able to afford a subscription mailing in two years, they maintain our guaranteed circulation of 450,000.

59   Nonetheless, media reports on *Ms.* often insist that our unprofitability must be due to reader disinterest. The myth that advertisers simply follow readers is very strong. Not one reporter notes that other comparable magazines our size (say, *Vanity Fair* or *The Atlantic*) have been losing more money in one year than *Ms.* has lost in 16 years. No matter how much never-to-be-recovered cash is poured into starting a magazine or keeping one going, appearances seem to be all that matter. (Which is why we haven't been able to explain our fragile state in public. Nothing causes ad-flight like the smell of nonsuccess.)

60   My healthy response is anger. My not-so-healthy response is constant worry. Also an obsession with finding one more rescue. There is hardly a night when I don't wake up with sweaty palms and pounding heart, scared that we won't be able to pay the printer or the post office; scared most of all that closing our doors will hurt the women's movement.

61   Out of chutzpah and desperation, I arrange a lunch with Leonard Lauder, president of Estée Lauder. With the exception of Clinique (the brainchild of Carol Phillips), none of Lauder's hundreds of products has been advertised in *Ms.* A year's schedule of ads for just three or four of them could save us. Indeed, as the scion of a family-owned company whose ad practices are followed by the beauty industry, he is one of the few men who could liberate many pages in all women's magazines just by changing his mind about "complementary copy."

62   Over a lunch that costs more than we can pay for some articles, I explain the need for his leadership. I also lay out the record of *Ms.*: more literary and journalistic prizes won, more new issues introduced into the mainstream, new writers discovered, and impact on society than any other magazine; more articles that became books, stories that became movies, ideas that became television series, and newly advertised products that became profitable; and, most important for him, a place for his ads to reach women who aren't reachable through any other women's magazine. Indeed, if there is one constant characteristic of the ever-changing *Ms.* readership, it is their impact as leaders. Whether it's waiting until later to have first babies, or pioneering PABA as sun protection in cosmetics, *whatever* they are doing today, a third to a half of American women will be doing three to five years from now. It's never failed.

63   But, he says, *Ms.* readers are not *our* women. They're not interested in things like fragrance and blush-on. If they were, *Ms.* would write articles about them.

64   On the contrary, I explain, surveys show they are more likely to buy such things than the readers of, say, *Cosmopolitan* or *Vogue*. They're good customers because they're out in the world enough to need several sets of everything: home, work, purse, travel, gym, and so on. They just don't need to read articles about these things. Would he ask a men's magazine to publish monthly columns on how to shave before he advertised Aramis products (his line for men)?

65   He concedes that beauty features are often concocted more for advertisers than readers. But *Ms.* isn't appropriate for his ads anyway, he explains. Why? Because Estée Lauder is selling "a kept-woman mentality."

66   I can't quite believe this. Sixty percent of the users of his products are salaried, and generally resemble *Ms.* readers. Besides, his company has the appeal of having been started by a creative and hardworking woman, his mother, Estée Lauder.

67   That doesn't matter, he says. He knows his customers, and they would *like* to be kept women. That's why he will never advertise in *Ms.*

68   In November 1987, by vote of the Ms. Foundation for Education and Communication (*Ms.*'s owner and publisher, the media subsidiary of the Ms. Foundation for Women), *Ms.* was sold to a company whose officers, Australian feminists Sandra Yates and Anne Summers, raised the investment money in their country that *Ms.* couldn't find in its own. They also started *Sassy* for teenage women.

69   In their two-year tenure, circulation was raised to 550,000 by investment in circulation mailings, and, to the dismay of some readers, editorial features on clothes and new products made a more traditional bid for ads. Nonetheless, ad pages fell below previous levels. In addition, *Sassy*, whose fresh voice and sexual frankness were an unprecedented success with young readers, was targeted by two mothers from Indiana who began, as one of them put it, "calling every Christian organiza-

tion I could think of." In response to this controversy, several crucial advertisers pulled out.

70   Such links between ads and editorial content were a problem in Australia, too, but to a lesser degree. "Our readers pay two times more for their magazines," Anne explained, "so advertisers have less power to threaten a magazine's viability."

71   "I was shocked," said Sandra Yates with characteristic directness. "In Australia, we think you have freedom of the press—but you don't."

72   Since Anne and Sandra had not met their budget's projections for ad revenue, their investors forced a sale. In October 1989, *Ms.* and *Sassy* were bought by Dale Lang, owner of *Working Mother*, *Working Woman*, and one of the few independent publishing companies left among the conglomerates. In response to a request from the original *Ms.* staff—as well as to reader letters urging that *Ms.* continue, plus his own belief that *Ms.* would benefit his other magazines by blazing a trail—he agreed to try the ad-free, reader-supported *Ms.* you hold now and to give us complete editorial control.

II

73 Do you think, as I once did, that advertisers make decisions based on solid research? Well, think again. "Broadly speaking," says Joseph Smith of Oxtoby-Smith, Inc., a consumer research firm, "there is no persuasive evidence that the editorial context of an ad matters."

74   Advertisers who demand such "complementary copy," even in the absence of respectable studies, clearly are operating under a double standard. The same food companies place ads in *People* with no recipes. Cosmetics companies support *The New Yorker* with no regular beauty columns. So where does this habit of controlling the content of women's magazines come from?

75   Tradition. Ever since *Ladies Magazine* debuted in Boston in 1828, editorial copy directed to women has been informed by something other than its readers' wishes. There were no ads then, but in an age when married women were legal minors with no right to their own money, there was another revenue source to be kept in mind: husbands. "Husbands may rest assured," wrote editor Sarah Josepha Hale, "that nothing found in these pages shall cause her [his wife] to be less assiduous in preparing for his reception or encourage her to 'usurp station' or encroach upon prerogatives of men."

76   Hale went on to become the editor of *Godey's Lady's Book*, a magazine featuring "fashion plates": engravings of dresses for readers to take to their seamstresses or copy themselves. Hale added "how to" articles, which set the tone for women's service magazines for years to come: how to write politely, avoid sunburn, and—in no fewer than 1,200 words—how to maintain a goose quill pen. She advocated education for women but avoided controversy. Just as most women's magazines now avoid politics, poll their readers on issues like abortion but rarely take a stand, and praise socially approved lifestyles, Hale saw to it that *Godey's* avoided the hot topics of its day: slavery, abolition, and women's suffrage.

77   What definitively turned women's magazines into catalogs, however, were two events: Ellen Butterick's invention of the clothing pattern in 1863 and the mass manufacture of patent medicines containing everything from colored water

to cocaine. For the first time, readers could purchase what magazines encouraged them to want. As such magazines became more profitable, they also began to attract men as editors. (Most women's magazines continued to have men as top editors until the feminist 1970s.) Edward Bok, who became editor of *The Ladies' Home Journal* in 1889, discovered the power of advertisers when he rejected ads for patent medicines and found that other advertisers canceled in retribution. In the early 20th century, *Good Housekeeping* started its Institute to "test and approve" products. Its Seal of Approval became the grandfather of current "value added" programs that offer advertisers such bonuses as product sampling and department store promotions.

78   By the time suffragists finally won the vote in 1920, women's magazines had become too entrenched as catalogs to help women learn how to use it. The main function was to create a desire for products, teach how to use products, and make products a crucial part of gaining social approval, pleasing a husband, and performing as a homemaker. Some related articles and short stories were included to persuade women to pay for these catalogs. But articles were neither consumerist nor rebellious. Even fiction was usually subject to formula: if a woman had any sexual life outside marriage, she was supposed to come to a bad end.

79   In 1965, Helen Gurley Brown began to change part of that formula by bringing "the sexual revolution" to women's magazines—but in an ad-oriented way. Attracting multiple men required even more consumerism, as the Cosmo Girl made clear, than finding one husband.

80   In response to the workplace revolution of the 1970s, traditional women's magazines—that is, "trade books" for women working at home—were joined by *Savvy*, *Working Woman*, and other trade books for women working in offices. But by keeping the fashion/beauty/entertaining articles necessary to get traditional ads and then adding career articles besides, they inadvertently produced the antifeminist stereotype of Super Woman. The male-imitative, dress-for-success woman carrying a briefcase became the media image of a woman worker, even though a blue-collar woman's salary was often higher than her glorified secretarial sister's, and though women at a real briefcase level are statistically rare. Needless to say, these dress-for-success women were also thin, white, and beautiful.

81   In recent years, advertisers' control over the editorial content of women's magazines has become so institutionalized that it is written into "insertion orders" or dictated to ad salespeople as official policy. The following are recent typical orders to women's magazines:

82   • Dow's Cleaning Products stipulates that ads for its Vivid and Spray 'n Wash products should be adjacent to "children or fashion editorial"; ads for Bathroom Cleaner should be next to "home furnishing/family" features; and so on for other brands. "If a magazine fails for ½ the brands or more," the Dow order warns, "it will be omitted from further consideration."

83   • Bristol-Myers, the parent of Clairol, Windex, Drano, Bufferin, and much more, stipulates that ads be placed next to "a full page of compatible editorial."

84   • S.C. Johnson & Son, makers of Johnson Wax, lawn and laundry products, insect sprays, hair sprays, and so on, orders that its ads *should not be opposite extremely controversial features or material antithetical to the nature/copy of the advertised product.*" (Italics theirs.)

85 • Maidenform, manufacturer of bras and other apparel, leaves a blank for the particular product and states: "The creative concept of the _____ campaign, and the very nature of the product itself appeal to the positive emotions of the reader/consumer. Therefore, it is imperative that all editorial adjacencies reflect that same positive tone. The editorial must not be negative in content or lend itself contrary to the _____ product imagery/message (e.g., *editorial relating to illness, disillusionment, large size fashion, etc.*)." (Italics mine.)

86 • The De Beers diamond company, a big seller of engagement rings, prohibits magazines from placing its ads with "adjacencies to hard news or anti/love-romance themed editorial."

87 • Procter & Gamble, one of this country's most powerful and diversified advertisers, stands out in the memory of Anne Summers and Sandra Yates (no mean feat in this context): its products were not to be placed in *any* issue that included *any* material on gun control, abortion, the occult, cults, or the disparagement of religion. Caution was also demanded in any issue covering sex or drugs, even for educational purposes.

88   Those are the most obvious chains around women's magazines. There are also rules so clear they needn't be written down; for instance, an overall "look" compatible with beauty and fashion ads. Even "real" nonmodel women photographed for a woman's magazine are usually made up, dressed in credited clothes, and retouched out of all reality. When editors do include articles on less-than-cheerful subjects (for instance, domestic violence), they tend to keep them short and unillustrated. The point is to be "upbeat." Just as women in the street are asked, "Why don't you smile, honey?" women's magazines acquire an institutional smile.

89   Within the text itself, praise for advertisers' products has become so ritualized that fields like "beauty writing" have been invented. One of its frequent practitioners explained seriously that "It's a difficult art. How many new adjectives can you find? How much greater can you make a lipstick sound? The FDA restricts what companies can say on labels, but we create illusion. And ad agencies are on the phone all the time pushing you to get their product in. A lot of them keep the business based on how many editorial clippings they produce every month. The worst are products," like Lauder's as the writer confirmed, "with their own name involved. It's all ego."

90   Often, editorial becomes one giant ad. Last November, for instance, *Lear's* featured an elegant woman executive on the cover. On the contents page, we learned she was wearing Guerlain makeup and Samsara, a new fragrance by Guerlain. Inside were full-page ads for Samsara and Guerlain antiwrinkle cream. In the cover profile, we learned that this executive was responsible for launching Samsara and is Guerlain's director of public relations. When the *Columbia Journalism Review* did one of the few articles to include women's magazines in coverage of the influence of ads, editor Frances Lear was quoted as defending her magazine because "this kind of thing is done all the time."

91   Often, advertisers also plunge odd-shaped ads into the text, no matter what the cost to the readers. At *Woman's Day*, a magazine originally founded by a supermarket chain, editor in chief Ellen Levine said, "The day the copy had to rag around a chicken leg was not a happy one."

92   Advertisers are also adamant about where in a magazine their ads appear. When Revlon was not placed as the first beauty ad in one Hearst magazine, for

instance, Revlon pulled its ads from *all* Hearst magazines. Ruth Whitney, editor in chief of *Glamour*, attributes some of these demands to "ad agencies wanting to prove to a client that they've squeezed the last drop of blood out of a magazine." She also is, she says, "sick and tired of hearing that women's magazines are controlled by cigarette ads." Relatively speaking, she's right. To be as censoring as are many advertisers for women's products, tobacco companies would have to demand articles in praise of smoking and expect glamorous photos of beautiful women smoking their brands.

93   I don't mean to imply that the editors I quote here share my objections to ads: most assume that women's magazines have to be the way they are. But it's also true that only former editors can be completely honest. "Most of the pressure came in the form of direct product mentions," explains Sey Chassler, who was editor in chief of *Redbook* from the sixties to the eighties. "We got threats from the big guys, the Revlons, blackmail threats. They wouldn't run ads unless we credited them.

94   "But it's not fair to single out the beauty advertisers because these pressures came from everybody. Advertisers want to know two things: What are you going to charge me? What *else* are you going to do for me? It's a holdup. For instance, management felt that fiction took up too much space. They couldn't put any advertising in that. For the last ten years, the number of fiction entries into the National Magazine Awards had declined.

95   "And pressures are getting worse. More magazines are more bottom-line oriented because they have been taken over by companies with no interest in publishing.

96   "I also think advertisers do this to women's magazines especially," he concluded, "because of the general disrespect they have for women."

97   Even media experts who don't give a damn about women's magazines are alarmed by the spread of this ad-edit linkage. In a climate *The Wall Street Journal* describes as an unacknowledged Depression for media, women's products are increasingly able to take their low standards wherever they go. For instance: newsweeklies publish uncritical stories on fashion and fitness. *The New York Times Magazine* recently ran an article on "firming creams," complete with mentions of advertisers. *Vanity Fair* published a profile of one major advertiser, Ralph Lauren, illustrated by the same photographer who does his ads, and turned the lifestyle of another, Calvin Klein, into a cover story. Even the outrageous *Spy* has toned down since it began to go after fashion ads.

98   And just to make us really worry, films and books, the last media that go directly to the public without having to attract ads first, are in danger, too. Producers are beginning to depend on payments for displaying products in movies, and books are now being commissioned by companies like Federal Express.

99   But the truth is that women's products—like women's magazines—have never been the subjects of much serious reporting anyway. News and general interest publications, including the "style" or "living" sections of newspapers, write about food and clothing as cooking and fashion, and almost never evaluate such products by brand name. Though chemical additives, pesticides, and animal fats are major health risks in the United States, and clothes, shoddy or not, absorb

more consumer dollars than cars, this lack of information is serious. So is ignoring the contents of beauty products that are absorbed into our bodies through our skins, and that have profit margins so big they would make a loan shark blush.

III

100 What could women's magazines be like if they were as free as books? as realistic as newspapers? as creative as films? as diverse as women's lives? We don't know.

101   But we'll only find out if we take women's magazines seriously. If readers were to act in a concerted way to change traditional practices of *all* women's magazines and the marketing of *all* women's products, we could do it. After all, they are operating on our consumer dollars; money that we now control. You and I could:

102 • write to editors and publishers (with copies to advertisers) that we're willing to pay *more* for magazines with editorial independence, but will *not* continue to pay for those that are just editorial extensions of ads;

103 • write to advertisers (with copies to editors and publishers) that we want fiction, political reporting, consumer reporting—whatever is, or is not, supported by their ads;

104 • put as much energy into breaking advertising's control over content as into changing the images in ads, or protesting ads for harmful products like cigarettes;

105 • support only those women's magazines and products that take *us* seriously as readers and consumers.

106   Those of us in the magazine world can also use the carrot-and-stick technique. For instance: pointing out that, if magazines were a regulated medium like television, the demands of advertisers would be against FCC rules. Payola and extortion could be punished. As it is, there are probably illegalities. A magazine's postal rates are determined by the ratio of ad to edit pages, and the former costs more than the latter. So much for the stick.

107   The carrot means appealing to enlightened self-interest. For instance: there are many studies showing that the greatest factor in determining an ad's effectiveness is the credibility of its surroundings. The "higher the rating of editorial believability," concluded a 1987 survey by the *Journal of Advertising Research*, "the higher the rating of the advertising." Thus, an impenetrable wall between edit and ads would also be in the best interest of advertisers.

108   Unfortunately, few agencies or clients hear such arguments. Editors often maintain the false purity of refusing to talk to them at all. Instead, they see ad salespeople who know little about editorial, are trained in business as usual, and are usually paid by commission. Editors might also band together to take on controversy. That happened once when all the major women's magazines did articles in the same month on the Equal Rights Amendment. It could happen again.

109   It's almost three years away from life between the grindstones of advertising pressures and readers' needs. I'm just beginning to realize how edges got smoothed down—in spite of all our resistance.

110   I remember feeling put upon when I changed "Porsche" to "car" in a piece about Nazi imagery in German pornography by Andrea Dworkin—feeling sure Andrea would understand that Volkswagen, the distributor of Porsche and one of our few supportive advertisers, asked only to be far away from Nazi subjects. It's taken me all this time to realize that Andrea was the one with a right to feel put upon.

111   Even as I write this, I get a call from a writer for *Elle*, who is doing a whole article on where women part their hair. Why, she wants to know, do I part mine in the middle?

112   It's all so familiar. A writer trying to make something of a nothing assignment; an editor laboring to think of new ways to attract ads; readers assuming that other women must want this ridiculous stuff; more women suffering for lack of information, insight, creativity, and laughter that could be on these same pages.

113   I ask you: Can't we do better than this?

David Suzuki

Canada 1936–

David Suzuki is a Canadian scientist, broadcaster, and critic of policies that harm or deplete the natural world. He is well known as host of CBC television's *The Nature of Things*. The direction of his scientific and political interests can be seen in the titles of two of his books: *Geoethics: The Clash Between the New Genetics and Human Values* (1989) and *Time to Change: Essays* (1994). In "The Pain of Animals," he argues against our unexamined use of animal subjects to extend our knowledge.

The Pain of Animals   1989

1   Medical technology has taken us beyond the normal barriers of life and death and thereby created unprecedented choices in *human* lives. Until recently, we have taken for granted our right to use other species in any way we see fit. Food, clothing, muscle power have been a few of the benefits we've derived from this exploitation. This tradition has continued into scientific research where animals are studied and "sacrificed" for human benefit. Now serious questions are being asked about our right to do this.

2   Modern biological research is based on a shared evolutionary history of organisms that enables us to extrapolate from one organism to another. Thus, most fundamental concepts in heredity were first shown in fruit flies, molecular genetics began using bacteria and viruses and much of physiology and psychology has been based on studies in mice and rats. But today, as extinction rates have multiplied as a result of human activity, we have begun to ask what right we

have to use all other animate forms simply to increase human knowledge or for profit or entertainment. Underlying the "animal rights" movement is the troubling question of where we fit in the rest of the natural world.

3   When I was young, one of my prized possessions was a BB gun. Dad taught me how to use it safely and I spent many hours wandering through the woods in search of prey. It's not easy to get close enough to a wild animal to kill it with a BB gun, but I did hit a few pigeons and starlings. I ate everything I shot. Then as a teenager, I graduated to a .22 rifle and with it, I killed rabbits and even shot a pheasant once.

4   One year I saw an ad for a metal slingshot in a comic book. I ordered it, and when it arrived, I practised for weeks shooting marbles at a target. I got to be a pretty good shot and decided to go after something live. Off I went to the woods and soon spotted a squirrel minding its own business doing whatever squirrels do. I gave chase and began peppering marbles at it until finally it jumped onto a tree, ran to the top and found itself trapped. I kept blasting away and grazed it a couple of times so it was only a matter of time before I would knock it down. Suddenly, the squirrel began to cry—a piercing shriek of terror and anguish. That animal's wail shook me to the core and I was overwhelmed with horror and shame at what I was doing—for no other reason than conceit with my prowess with a slingshot, I was going to *kill* another being. I threw away the slingshot and my guns and have never hunted again.

5   All my life, I have been an avid fisherman. Fish have always been the main source of meat protein in my family, and I have never considered fishing a sport. But there is no denying that it is exciting to reel in a struggling fish. We call it "playing" the fish, as if the wild animal's desperate struggle for survival is some kind of game.

6   I did "pleasure-fish" once while filming for a television report on the science of fly fishing. We fished a famous trout stream in the Catskill Mountains of New York state where all fish had to be caught and released. The fish I caught had mouths gouged and pocked by previous encounters with hooks. I found no pleasure in it because to me fish are to be caught for consumption. Today, I continue to fish for food, but I do so with a profound awareness that I am a predator of animals possessing well-developed nervous systems that detect pain. Fishing and hunting have forced me to confront the way we exploit other animals.

7   I studied the genetics of fruit flies for twenty-five years and during that time probably raised and killed tens of millions of them without a thought. In the early seventies, my lab discovered a series of mutations affecting behaviour of flies, and this find led us into an investigation of nerves and muscles. I applied for and received research funds to study behaviour in flies on the basis of the *similarity* of their neuromuscular systems to ours. In fact, psychologists and neurobiologists analyse behaviour, physiology and neuroanatomy of guinea pigs, rats, mice and other animals as *models* for human behaviour. So our nervous systems must closely resemble those of other mammals.

8   These personal anecdotes raise uncomfortable questions. What gives us the right to exploit other living organisms as we see fit? How do we know that these other creatures don't feel pain or anguish just as we do? Perhaps there's no problem with fruit flies, but where do we draw the line? I used to rationalize angling because fish are cold-blooded, as if warm-bloodedness indicates some kind of demarcation of brain development or greater sensitivity to pain. But anyone who has watched a fish's frantic fight to escape knows that it exhibits all the manifestations of pain and fear.

9   I've been thinking about these questions again after spending a weekend in the Queen Charlotte Islands watching grey whales close up. The majesty and freedom of these magnificent mammals contrasted strikingly with the appearance of whales imprisoned in aquariums. Currently, the Vancouver Public Aquarium is building a bigger pool for some of its whales. In a radio interview, an aquarium representative was asked whether even the biggest pool can be adequate for animals that normally have the entire ocean to rove. Part of her answer was that if we watched porpoises in the pool, we'd see that "they are quite happy."

10   That woman was projecting human perceptions and emotions on the porpoises. Our ability to empathize with other people and living things is one of our endearing qualities. Just watch someone with a beloved pet, an avid gardener with plants or, for that matter, even an owner of a new car and you will see how readily we can personalize and identify with another living organism or an object. But are we justified in our inferences about captive animals in their cages?

11   Most wild animals have evolved with a built-in need to move freely over vast distances, fly in the air or swim through the ocean. Can a wild animal imprisoned in a small cage or pool, removed from its habitat and forced to conform to the impositions of our demands, ever be considered "happy"?

12   Animal rights activists are questioning our right to exploit animals, especially in scientific research. Scientists are understandably defensive, especially after labs have been broken into, experiments ruined and animals "liberated." But just as I have had to question my hunting and fishing, scientists cannot avoid confronting the issues raised, especially in relation to our closest relatives, the primates.

13   People love to watch monkeys in a circus or zoo and a great deal of the amusement comes from the recognition of ourselves in them. But our relationship with them is closer than just superficial similarities. When doctors at Loma Linda hospital in California implanted the heart of a baboon into the chest of Baby Fae, they were exploiting our close *biological* relationship.

14   Any reports on experimentation with familiar mammals like cats and dogs are sure to raise alarm among the lay public. But the use of primates is most controversial. In September 1987, at the Wildlife Film Festival in Bath, England, I watched a film shot on December 7, 1986, by a group of animal liberationists who had broken into SEMA, a biomedical research facility in Maryland. It was such a horrifying document that many in the audience rushed out after a few minutes. There were many scenes that I could not watch. As the intruders entered the facility, the camera followed to peer past cage doors, opened to reveal the animals inside. I am not ashamed to admit that I wept as baby monkeys deprived of any contact with other animals seized the fingers of their liberators and clung to them as our babies would to us. Older animals cowered in their tiny prisons, shaking from fear at the sudden appearance of people.

15   The famous chimpanzee expert, Jane Goodall, also screened the same film and as a result asked for permission to visit the SEMA facility. This is what she saw (*American Scientist*, November–December 1987):

> Room after room was lined with small, bare cages, stacked one above the other, in which monkeys circled round and round and chimpanzees sat huddled, far gone in depression and despair.

Young chimpanzees, three or four years old, were crammed, two together into tiny cages measuring 57 cm by 57 cm and only 61 cm high. They could hardly turn around. Not yet part of any experiment, they had been confined to these cages for more than three months.

The chimps had each other for comfort, but they would not remain together for long. Once they are infected, probably with hepatitis, they will be separated and placed in another cage. And there they will remain, living in conditions of severe sensory deprivation, for the next several years. During that time they will become insane.

16   Goodall's horror sprang from an intimate knowledge of chimpanzees in their native habitat. There, she has learned, chimps are nothing like the captive animals that we know. In the wild, they are highly social, requiring constant interaction and physical contact. They travel long distances, and they rest in soft beds they make in the trees. Laboratory cages do not provide the conditions needed to fulfill the needs of these social, emotional and highly intelligent animals.

17   Ian Redmond (*BBC Wildlife*, April 1988) gives us a way to understand the horror of what lab conditions do to chimps:

Imagine locking a two- or three-year-old child in a metal box the size of an isolette—solid walls, floor and ceiling, and a glass door that clamps shut, blotting out most external sounds—and then leaving him or her for months, the only contact, apart from feeding, being when the door swings open and masked figures reach in and take samples of blood or tissue before shoving him back and clamping the door shut again. Over the past 10 years, 94 young chimps at SEMA have endured this procedure.

18   Chimpanzees, along with the gorilla, are our closest relatives, sharing ninety-nine per cent of our genes. And it's that biological proximity that makes them so useful for research—we can try out experiments, study infections and test vaccines on them as models for people. And although there are only about 40,000 chimps left in the wild, compared to millions a few decades ago, the scientific demand for more has increased with the discovery of AIDS.

19   No chimpanzee has ever contracted AIDS, but the virus grows in them, so scientists argue that chimps will be invaluable for testing vaccines. On February 19, 1988, the National Institute of Health in the U.S. co-sponsored a meeting to discuss the use of chimpanzees in research. Dr. Maurice Hilleman, Director of the Merck Institute for Therapeutic Research, reported:

We need more chimps.... The chimpanzee is certainly a threatened species and there have been bans on importing the animal into the United States and into other countries, even though ... the chimpanzee is considered to be an agricultural pest in many parts of the world where it exists. And secondly, it's being destroyed by virtue of environmental encroachment—that is, destroying the natural habitat. So these chimpanzees are being eliminated by virtue of their being an agricultural pest and by the fact that their habitat is being destroyed. So why not rescue them? The number of chimpanzees for AIDS research in the United States [is] somewhere in the hundreds and certainly, we need thousands.

20   Our capacity to rationalize our behaviour and needs is remarkable. Chimpanzees have occupied their niche over tens of millennia of biological evolution. *We* are newcomers who have encroached on *their* territory, yet by defining them as *pests* we render them expendable. As Redmond says, "The fact that the chimpanzee is our nearest zoological relative makes it perhaps the unluckiest animal on earth, because what the kinship has come to mean is that we feel free to do most of the things to a chimp that we mercifully refrain from doing to each other."

21   And so the impending epidemic of AIDS confronts us not only with our inhumanity to each other but to other species.

W.H. New

Canada 1938–

In an address at the 2001 CUFA/BC Career Achievement Award Ceremonies, William New, who teaches Canadian and Commonwealth literature at the University of British Columbia and who was raised in Vancouver, noted that his enthusiasm for his fields of study began when in high school he was faced with a textbook question "'Discuss the role of our President." At this point, he become aware of how cultural assumptions imposed upon us from other places can create a colonial mentality and have an impact on the way we see our culture and ourselves. "Giddy Limits" is from his book *Borderlands*, a study that examines the cultural multiplicities of Canada and the metaphoric borders of the country.

Giddy Limits: Canadian Studies and Other Metaphors 1998

1   My title, 'Giddy Limits,' comes from a traveller's dictionary. Specifically, it comes from a dictionary I bought some thirty years ago, when I was about to embark from Harwich on a student trip to Scandinavia. It seemed a reasonable purchase at the time for it was full of the Swedish words for *fish* and *cucumber* and the like— I was certain I could at least eat. But on closer inspection it seems that the book had first been issued sometime in the 1930s and never subsequently revised. So that (for use in the mid-1960s) I now had available to me several Scandinavian equivalents for 1930s slang. I could, if I wished, consult my book, look at the world with all the northern savoir faire I could muster, and utter in smooth Swedish, 'That's the giddy limit!'

2   As it turns out, I never found the opportunity. But in retrospect, I think I was standing on giddy limits during the whole holiday. I had not yet absorbed just how insubstantial a lot of boundaries are, nor how fragile are the structures on which nationalities depend. So there I stood, West Coast Canadian, with a limited sense of the strengths and vulnerabilities of my own country, on the brink of a Europe I'd been trained to identify with civilization. I was testing boundaries of

language, history, space, and expectation—not knowing I was also already crossing boundaries of value, knowledge, permanence, and youth.

3   Why *boundaries?* Because boundaries seem to me to be metaphors more than fixed edges: *signs* of limits more than the limits themselves—but signs of what kind? Perhaps of reach, accessibility, appreciation, understanding, perhaps of size, power, acknowledgment, permission, perhaps of possibility, territoriality, allowance, refusal. There is *borderline*, Russell Brown once remarked about the Canada-US boundary—and there is *borderland*. The one names and divides; the other is psychic, indeterminate, McLuhanesque. Lines of geometry, lines of poetry; lines of sight, lines of enquiry; wonderland, no-man's land; line-ups, line drives.

4   But why *giddy?* Recently I looked up the word in the *Oxford English Dictionary* to trace its history. Two-and-a-half columns' worth of definition told me that it currently means *staggering* or *dizzy, whirling with bewildering rapidity ... flighty, frivolous,* and *inconstant;* once upon a time it meant literally 'elf-possessed' (fr. *gidig,* fr. *ylfig*)—that is, *mad, foolish, insane.* 'Giddy limits,' therefore, are mobile ones: not necessarily where you'll find tidiness and order, but where you'll find uncertainty and exchange, a discourse that moves between elf-possessed and self-possessed, always interrogating where it stands.

5   This interrogation, in the many-headed exercise called Canadian Studies, repeatedly invokes these border metaphors—to isolate a subject, clarify issues, trace changes, and otherwise explain and theorize the nature of nation, convention, position, and power. (Bloodlines, time lines, power lines, pipelines.) One critic suggests that *nationalism* itself is a conceptual limit (Brydon 1995), another that *academic disciplinarity* is (Kuester 1995). For both critics, the danger of such conceptions is that they can come to seem natural, that (by turning into axioms) they can let the borders they impose go unexamined....

6   So the borderlines construct conceptual edges and the borderlands construct territories of translation. But this distinction misleads; borders can work both ways at once, whereas the distinction suggests that a definitive binary resolution is possible. I resist the simplistic rhetoric of *either/or,* and engage with the more difficult rhetoric of *both/and.* To what end, here? In the comments that follow, I propose that the various Canadas that 'Canadian Studies' discuss in large part *derive from*—not just 'use'—various forms of boundary rhetoric. What does this mean? It acknowledges, simply, that boundaries function both as descriptions of concrete agreements *and* as metaphors of relationship and organization.

7   Now as academics, as citizens, as plain consumers of the media, we are in daily contact with metaphors. They shape how we conceptualize the world. But they also designate giddy limits. I want to use these border metaphors (drawing examples primarily from literature, but also from current politics, history, and geography) to talk about some of the issues that currently occupy a lot of Canadians' attention—issues such as regionalism, separatism, multiculturalism, the influence of the United States, and the shifting proximity of Europe and Asia. I want to argue that the paradigms of boundary rhetoric variously construct Canada as a place that *includes,* a place that *excludes,* as a place *divided,* as a place that *distributes* resources and power, and as a place that embraces some ongoing principle of *boundary negotiation.* Each of these paradigms, moreover, assumes a different set of social priorities and social consequences.

8   Consider Martin Kuester's evocative phrase that 'Canada is unthinkable without its border with the U.S.A.' True. The 49th parallel—itself a synecdoche, a rhetorical part standing for the rhetorical whole—at once joins and divides two nation-states, permits contact, influence, choice, trade (hypothetically in two directions), and difference as well.... But is not Canada *also* 'unthinkable' without its *other* borders? The polar border with Russia, the Atlantic border with Europe, the Pacific border with Asia? ...

9   There is a further set of borders implied by that word 'Central' (and its coded alternatives, 'Region' and 'Hinterland'). (One might compare them with the familiar metaphors of linear history: branch and trunk, tributary and main-stream.) A 'Central Canada' so *delineated*—that is, in southern Ontario and Quebec—sits clearly *on one edge* of the country, not in any cartographically con-ventional 'heart.' But the border construction 'Central'—reinforced by demog-raphy—produces a version of Canada that construes the external boundaries of the society (*except* that with the US) as 'peripheral'—not just referentially, as a determination of extent, but also imaginatively, as a determination of social con-sequence....

10   This heartland/hinterland paradigm structures assumptions about norms and variants from the norm—or, more fundamentally, it is the product of a rhetoric of *inclusion and exclusion*. Intrinsically, it uses a boundary metaphor to represent one part of Canada as the 'characteristic' representative of the conceptual whole. In turn, this selectivity produces an illusion of a uniform culture, or at least of a uniform agreement as to what constitutes social priority and social value.

. . . . .

11   Substitute 'national' and 'regional' for 'centre' and 'hinterland' and you can hear such distinctions made daily on the Toronto-centred CBC English-language TV news or the Montreal-centred French-language Radio Canada TV news, both of which construct themselves as 'national,' consigning all else to 'the regions' or treating it as comedy or ignoring it altogether. It turns out that the 'regions' often constitute the leading edge of social thought, not the territorial lags that the rhetoric constructs. But this revelation often goes unacknowledged. If a Jack Hodgins novel is dismissed in Toronto as odd or erratic or magic realist or *regional,* and if a Robertson Davies novel, for all its magical but Ontario-centred oddness, is praised as a *national* voice, what does this say about values and the promulgation of values? And if the values being expressed in *other centres* in the country do not get a national hearing, what does this say about multiculturalism, mobility, diversity, and national culture? One of the things it says is that a familiar rhetoric—such as that of Ontario-Quebec opposition, or that of separation, or that of deficit-reduction, or that of bilingualism, or that of the ostensibly missing Canadian 'identity'—will, if repeated often enough and left unexamined, perhaps especially in the mass media, begin to be accepted as embodying a fixed truth even if not true and not ever adequately understood.

12   Assumptions about a hierarchy of regions are not the only expressions of a rhetoric of inclusion and exclusion in Canada. Religion, politics, gender, class, ethnicity, race, sexuality: each of these categories of experience and discourse also raises questions about the power invested in normative models of appearance, belief, behaviour, and opportunity. Think of how a *dis*ability depends on how we define ability, or how that which is *un*natural hinges on an accepted determina-

tion of what is natural. An exclusive model of Canada, likewise, tends to be nationalist, conservative, and (because it assumes itself to be right) resistant to changes in existing power hierarchies; whoever is thus excluded from the prevailing norm is couched as an exception, an aberration, a 'special interest group' (especially by those who hold power and do not wish to reconsider an entrenched position). Think about the advice I was seriously given from one quarter (and which I rejected) when I became editor of the journal *Canadian Literature* in 1977: 'Don't accept submissions from outside the country'—what would 'Canadian Studies' mean then? Compare this with what critics of 'multiculturalism' sometimes say, critiquing it as subsidized folkdancing, attacking it as though it were a planned *alternative* to 'culture proper,' or, like Neil Bissoondath, characterizing the institutional policy as an officially sanctioned system of *excluding* minorities from having an effective political voice. Even if none of these positions is unassailable, the conventional 'mosaic' metaphor used to describe Canada seems to me to be problematic in this regard, for it produces the illusion of equivalence without facilitating the reality.

13   I am scrutinizing restrictive versions of national possibility here, the terms under which national*ism* is advertised as the same thing as nationhood. These terms return this discussion to the rhetoric of separation, whether of Quebec, of BC, or of the West as some indeterminate whole. Clearly, such phrases as 'Quebeckers believe' or 'Westerners say' construct uniformities that are dubious at best; but the extreme assertions of some adherents of the Parti Québécois or the Cascadia Movement or the Western Canada Concept Party depend on a belief in uniformity. To read separatism again as an *exclusionary* rhetoric is to see how its declarations of difference, while couched as independence (i.e., as necessary in order to restrict outside 'interference' in internal affairs), in fact function the other way around, to preserve the power invested in the idea of uniformity by restricting the inside's access to outside alternatives and information.

. . . . .

14   Clearly, however, using a claim upon difference to justify a claim upon power—us in, you out—seems most justifiable to those who espouse its norms. Sometimes this claim serves community interests, though sometimes it will serve the powerful few rather than the many, increasing disparities rather than diminishing them. When the historical geographer Graeme Wynn speaks of the ' "greed line" of development' expanding across agricultural land, he is criticizing the exclusionary exercise of economic power, that which claims the right to profit as a validation of action. In parallel fashion, the nineteenth-century actions that determined the edges of Indian reserves in Canada imposed the force of civil and military power on cultures that were deemed inferior and presumed to be dying out. The 1907 legislation in the city of Vancouver that prevented persons of Asian origin from owning land or working on government-funded projects provides a third example: an exercise in racial exclusion, openly expressive of a set of prevailing social norms that have, happily, long since been rejected and replaced.

15   The 1942 uprooting of Canadians of Japanese origin from their West Coast homes and businesses, and the selling of their properties at a fraction of their value to local white developers, provides an immediate example of the way racist boundaries recur in Canadian social history. Less familiar, perhaps, is the 1944 federal government policy (recounted on a CBC TV documentary, 28 December

1995) that developed postwar choices for Canadians of Japanese origin; these persons—a category of persons, actually, based entirely on assumptions about racial stock—were to be given two: choices: settle somewhere away from the Coast, or choose to be 'repatriated' to Japan. Louis St. Laurent (according to Mackenzie King's diary) argued in cabinet that there should be no choice at all, because to permit 'Japanese' to stay would permit them to reproduce and dilute the country's racial purity. While the policy that the government actually adopted did not endorse this position, what was not made clear to those who had to choose is that government agencies were treating the choice as a 'loyalty test'— whoever chose Japan was considered potentially traitorous; yet many of these people had emotionally lost their faith in the Canada they considered their home. What was also being ignored in Ottawa was the unlikelihood (without access to their prewar place and property) that postwar jobs would be readily available to people who wanted to stay. Even today the problem of categorical racism continues to reappear. It showed up again in Canada in the hours and weeks following the 1995 Quebec referendum. I think of the *pure laine* megalomania that so informs a fascist demagoguery in some politicians. I think of Jacques Parizeau's referendum-night targeting of *anglais* and *allophone*; of the category 'allophone' itself and its millwheel manifestations in social policy; and I think of this comment attributed to Louise Cousineau, a television critic for *La Presse:* 'The *Anglais* don't want Quebec to separate so as not to inherit our ethnics' (W. Johnson A10).

16   This territorializing of ethnicity follows on the politics of authenticity and its companion claim upon physical territory. *Us, ours, mine, and you people over there.* Place and space turn into metaphors of social and ethical compartmentalization.

· · · · ·

17   The social assumptions that underlie the language of nationhood and nationalism have, of course, changed from decade to decade. Current wisdom questions whether nationalism can ever be creative. It assumes that nationalism privileges uniformity, and asks if the idea of globalism might be preferable. But globalism has its own chequered history, as is readily apparent in the metaphors and practices of imperial expansion, which worked against national independence before they worked for it. The mother-daughter metaphors of imperial family, for example, appealed to a desire for connectedness and tradition, but they always positioned 'maturity' at one remove from an other-centred 'source of civilization.' Relatedly, transplantation and branching tree metaphors invoked an organic relation between art and society—suggesting the possibility of growth and the likelihood of progress—but once again assumed the virtue of a common rootstock as the basis for a global common ground. Given this context, asking who or what is 'Canadian' sometimes leads to simplistic definitions, the sort that would restrict change, or veto it. For there is a way of using mainstream assumptions as closed constructions—'garrisons,' to use Northrop Frye's much-maligned word. There is also a way of using oppositional language as a kind of defensive reply that simply mirrors the exclusiveness of the dominant culture. I am not trying to dismiss the sensibility being expressed here, or the experience from which it derives, but rather to examine the rhetorical strategy it employs.

· · · · ·

18   ...Margaret Atwood's pithy observation, in her introduction to *The New Oxford Book of Canadian Short Stories in English,* is apropos: 'we gave up some time ago

trying to isolate the gene for "Canadianness." [Taking distance and language and cultural variety into account] ... it's kind of difficult to pin such a thing down'. Does this assertion imply that such a thing as 'Canada' cannot or does no longer exist, and that 'Canadian Studies' is implicitly a metaphor for historical nostalgia? Of course not. But the character of 'inclusiveness' does have to be interpreted— not as appropriation, not as a covert exclusion, and not as a vapid willingness to be anything to anybody and accept everything from everybody else, but as a creative process of accommodating to the present: of making conscious choices about what needs still to be valued (honouring connectedness and heritage) as well as about what seems increasingly to need changing. Should we give away the state—which is a still working, if sometimes creaky, set of social agreements— because some people are impatient with it and others are ill-informed? The question begs absurd answers. But cultural statistics are cautionary: 97 percent of film distribution in Canada is controlled outside the country; foreign-controlled publishers and agencies account for 75 percent of Canadian textbook sales; and fourteen foreign-controlled companies were responsible for 66 percent of all new releases and 84 percent of total sales in the recording industry in Canada during 1993-4. The national boundary line is unstable, and not inevitable.

19   Some of this instability emerges from within, of course; it does not all derive from American expansionism or Japanese capital. And such instability is made to seem more real to the degree that people—especially people in the media— passively accept and actively employ the *divisive or separatist* power of boundary-line rhetoric. Now a boundaryline rhetoric usually proves divisive when it is used to express a competition for some sort of control, for under these conditions arguments are characteristically expressed in binary terms. Those who articulated the issues during the recent separatist debate, for example, frequently accepted the terms 'anglophone' and 'francophone' as though they equated with 'Canada' and 'Quebec'. By this means, language was made to seem as though it coincided with territory (which it does not), territory was made to define the limits of culture (which it does not), and the separated elements in the equation *(anglophone* and *francophone, Canada* and *Quebec)* were made to seem as though they did not overlap (which they do). I do not for a moment doubt the emotional commitment that led people to espouse different positions in this debate. What I do wish to emphasize, however, is the degree to which the passion and the politics are alike functions of rhetoric more than they are empirical commodities—though the rhetoric of division can be marketed till it comes to seem 'real', and in Canada *is* being marketed: to whose advantage still being somewhat unclear.

. . . . .

20   The boundary metaphors I have been outlining here are, of course, susceptible to reinterpretation. As I have been using them, they are less categories of analysis than overlapping discourses, and when applied to 'Canadian Studies' they reveal how rhetorical tropes direct (and sometimes subvert) understanding. Inside Canada, a boundary discourse often functions both inclusively and exclusively, as the metaphoric plane on which differing versions of nationhood and nationalism—some with a misconceived faith in the power of definition—declare themselves. Outside Canada, Canadian nationhood is less an emotional issue than the opportunity for a case study. Perhaps a catchall category for disparate disciplinary exercises, perhaps a subcategory of 'American Studies' or 'postcolo-

nialism' or some other territorial 'whole', 'Canada' is seen as a theatre of political experiment, an economic tangent, the site of geological processes, a cartographic challenge, a cultural ferment, a colonial irrelevance, a social alternative, a success *story*. And more besides.

21   These differences, too, can be the subject of analysis, and while they can be simply seen as normal variations in perspective, the differences can mislead us into thinking that we've found answers when all we're doing is reaching academic discipline-bound conclusions. That is no reason to stop looking—looking *for* information and explanations, looking *at* Canada and at how we look at Canada, taking account of the substantive and metaphorical borderlines that remain part of this process. For of course my conclusions are ambivalent as well. I applaud those who have sufficient calm to have learned to appreciate the moment; yet I am wary of those who cannot read the moment in context, who cannot remember history, who refuse to acknowledge it, who have never learned to forget mere rivalry, and who are so infatuated with rules that they cannot ever value uncertainty as a matrix of creation. I am temperamentally opposed to petty restrictions and arbitrary lines; yet I am concerned when I hear some local boundaries construed as irrelevant and national social agreements pronounced as meaningless, *especially* at a time when global communications systems appear to be warming. I am concerned because such faith in the ostensible neutrality of postnational ideologies seems peculiarly narrowing—because it does not take into account the character of the culture of profit, or the limits that master narratives of culture and society can impose on knowledge and learning, and because it does not address the desirability of preserving ethical and aesthetic choices, for the very old, for the very young, and for those of us who mostly find ourselves very in-between.

22   When Linnet Muir, the narrator of Mavis Gallant's 'In Youth Is Pleasure', crosses 'the border to Canada, I expected to sense at once an air of calm and grit and dedication [she writes], but the only changes were from prosperous to shabby, from painted to unpainted, from smiling to dour. I was entering a poorer and a curiously empty country, where the faces of the people gave nothing away.' She was also, however, entering 'a world other people could scarcely envision, let alone attain. It involved giddy risks and changes, stepping off the edge blindfolded, one's hand on nothing more than a birth certificate and a five-dollar bill.' Near the narrative climax of Hodgins's *The Macken Charm*, too, the assembled family clan have just rebuilt an old hotel where they once used to live. It seems an odd, even extravagantly inconsequential act—but, the narrator writes, they are 'giddy with their success, and ready for more': ready, somehow, for whatever comes next.

23   At about the same time as I was leaving for my trip to Scandinavia, those many years ago, a friend of mine was packing to leave for Greece. Whether or not he knew that the buses of Athens—the vehicles of public transport — are called *metaphorai* I do not know; but I do know that he also bought a traveller's dictionary ahead of time and laughed at some of the unlikely phrases it contained. At least they seemed unlikely. One of them said: 'Hello shepherd, call your dog.' A few days later, however, he came over a hill in the Macedonian highlands to find his car almost instantly encircled by a mob of sheep. He braked quickly, paused for a moment, then leaned out the window, phrase book in hand, and in his best Greek calmly said 'Hello shepherd, call your dog!' The road ahead cleared.

24   Those of us who teach and study 'Canadian Studies' sometimes find ourselves in the role of the traveller along such a road—looking for *metaphorai* perhaps—driving through mapped but still unpredictable highlands, with the way ahead unclear. Sometimes we occupy the role of the dog, snapping at the heels of facts, and sometimes, I suspect, the role of the sheep, turning aimlessly, mistaking movement for direction. Often there's no phrase book to turn to, and no shepherd to ask solutions from even if there were. But sometimes we have to be the shepherds ourselves—at least those of us who are citizens of *the real country* of Canada have to—we have to resist the subversive appeal of the binary rhetoric of restriction and division, of ethnic unitariness and reductive commitments to privilege, of exclusiveness and enclosure, of separation and competitive margins. We have, in other words, to accept the need to recognize that some versions of Canadian society are static and others misleading and dangerous, that some are creative, that some preserve choice and promote possibility, and that some are a mix of many expectations and contrary desires; we also have to accept the need at least to try to discriminate among them, both in the present and in the borderland years to come.

Stephen Jay Gould

U.S.A. 1941–2002

Stephen Jay Gould was born in Manhattan; at the age of 26, he completed his Ph.D. at Columbia and subsequently accepted a position at Harvard to teach biology, geology, and the history of science. In 1974, he started publishing a monthly essay in *Natural History* and quickly became one of the most successful interpreters of science to the general public. He has stated that his goal in his essays is to investigate "instructive oddities in nature" and "the enduring themes of evolution." In "Columbus Cracks an Egg," Gould finds a circuitous route to his intended major point about the function of "image breakers" and the profound difference between merely breaking and truly creating.

Columbus Cracks an Egg   1992

Was the great voyager also a heavy-handed trickster?

1   The moment of truth—put up or shut up—has arrived. It is September, and this column has a lead time of three months. I either write about Christopher Columbus now or I miss the opportunity to note the most important quincentennial of my lifetime. Five hundred one just doesn't have that nice, even ring that we associate with celebrations.

2   Obviously, since I have delayed to the last possible moment, I have experienced no burning desire to address this subject. My reluctance does not arise from any doubt about the importance of the event, or of its relevance to natural history,

but only from a widely shared feeling of personal ambivalence toward the value and meaning of Columbus's Bahamian landfall. History is full of horror, and we prefer to commemorate rare moments of light. I did not note, in 1983, the 500th anniversary of Torquemada's leadership of the Spanish Inquisition, so why should I celebrate, nine years later, an expedition that led to even more bloodshed and chauvinism (and was, incidentally, not unrelated to Torquemada's success)?

3   I am scarcely alone in my ambivalence, and this greatest opportunity for a white man's patriotic outburst has been a muted thing indeed. The usual, and entirely valid, reason for subdued acknowledgment arises from the treatment of indigenous peoples by their European conquerors—a panoply ranging from enslavement to genocide, with occasional islands of decency. For a natural historian, the further theme of environmental rape and pillage only adds to the profound feeling of ambiguity. While fully allying myself with these reasons for doubt, I would rather emphasize another set of home-grown factors, all too rarely discussed (and often not even mentioned) in popular statements of reluctance to celebrate.

4   Fourteen hundred ninety-two was an amazing year in Spain, a moment of triple coincidence. We may now be marking Columbus's quincentenary, but 1992 is also the 500th anniversary of military victory over the Moors and of the expulsion of all Jews from Spain—and the three events are complexly intertwined, for this is a causal coincidence, not a fortuitous array of simultaneous happenings. Moreover, Columbus's expedition ranks last in time among the three, and was partly a consequence of the other two, not a prod.

5   The marriage, in 1469, of Ferdinand of Aragon (roughly east Spain) and Isabella of Castile (roughly west Spain) began a train of events that led to both increased power and, in a term now tragically in vogue, to "ethnic purification" for a white and Catholic Spain. Isabella's victory in her war of succession against Afonso V of Portugal, and Ferdinand's accession to the throne of Aragon, following the death of his father, John II, in 1479, established a powerful joint monarchy, committed to the expansion of power and territory and the contraction of the ethnic and religious diversity that had marked the Iberian peninsula for centuries.

6   The Encyclopaedia Britannica's article on Spanish history notes: "With its large Moorish and Jewish populations, medieval Spain was the only multiracial and multireligious country in Western Europe, and much of the development of Spanish civilization in religion, literature, art, and architecture during the later Middle Ages stemmed from this fact" (quoted from the 1980 edition, before contemporary terminology of "political correctness" came into vogue—so don't blame this claim on early 1990s fashion).

7   But the *reyes catolicos* (the Catholic kings), as Ferdinand and Isabella were called, struggled to terminate this diversity and succeeded in the Columbian year of 1492. The campaign against the Moors, who had held power for nearly 800 years and had once ruled almost all of Spain, had been proceeding for centuries. The final conquest of Granada and its Alhambra, with the capitulation and exile of Boabdil, the last Muslim ruler, ended a long process of conquest and removed the last handhold of Islamic temporal power in Western Europe (although the Turks besieged Vienna in 1683). Aided greatly by internecine warfare within the Moorish ruling family, Ferdinand and Isabella prevailed and received the keys to

Granada from Boabdil on January 2, 1492 (in medieval walled cities with gates, keys to towns were more than symbolic). According to legend, the weak ruler (derisively called *el rey chico*, or "the little king," by the Spaniards) took one last look over his shoulder and burst into tears as he departed into exile. His powerful mother responded with the most viciously sexist one-liner in history: "Cry like a woman for what you could not hold as a man."

8   As for the Jews, Ferdinand and Isabella had obtained a papal bull from Sixtus IV for setting up an Inquisition in 1478. (Sixtus later regretted his decision when he understood the ferocity of the institution he had permitted and the ecclesiastical powers that he had given away.) The Inquisition itself—and this is widely misunderstood today—did not persecute professing Jews because it was established to root out heresy *within* Catholicism. Its ardor turned instead to the so-called *conversos*, or Jewish converts to Catholicism, whose successes and large numbers (some 300,000) had frightened the older establishment. In a mixture of parancia and expediency (for the property of those convicted was confiscated and redistributed), the inquisitors searched for "Judaizing practices" among the *conversos* as signs of their insincerity and their conspiracy to usurp the church from within. They used a variety of techniques that became a textbook for such later organizations as the S.S. and K.G.B., including networks of informers (who looked for such signs as failure of *converso* neighbors to buy adequate amounts of pork, or lack of chimney smoke emerging on Saturdays), interrogation with no right to counsel and no opportunity to confront hostile witnesses, and of course, torture and burning.

9   But when Tomás de Torquemada (ironically, from a *converso* family himself) became head of the Inquisition in 1483, he began to badger Ferdinand and Isabella about the professing Jews (who may have numbered close to 200,000). As this well- and long-established community retained such a focal role in arts and commerce, the monarchs were at first reluctant to follow Torquemada's advice. But their growing power and success, particularly in victory over the Moors, boosted their confidence and their narrow piety, and they issued an order for the expulsion of all Jews in the same focal year of 1492. Thus began the diaspora of the Sephardic (Spanish) Jews, first largely into Portugal (where many were killed or forcibly converted in 1498) and thence to more accepting Muslim countries (where many still live today, or at least until recent migration to Israel), and to a few pockets of relative toleration in Europe, notably the Netherlands where, among many others of note, the great philosopher Spinoza lived and worked.

10   A few days after the final departure of the Jews in July, Columbus set sail on August 3. I do not, of course, claim that the eventual, crucial patronage of Ferdinand and Isabella (after so much dithering over so many years) arose directly from their "cleansing" of both Muslim and Jew from their lands, but these prior events of 1492 surely set a climate of narrow piety and aggressive expansionism that greatly boosted support for Columbus's plans. In any case, I cannot, both as a Jew and as a general celebrator of diversity and its cultural benefits, view Spain in 1492 as an object of wholehearted commemoration.

11   And yet, I really don't want to bypass something so important by an almost cowardly silence. I therefore take recourse in two of my own traditions. If I cannot celebrate the broad generality, let me look for a tiny little something about Columbus (which may then cascade by implication to a statement of wider

worth), and let me go, once again, to my intellectual hero Charles Darwin for inspiration.

12   In his autobiography, Darwin writes about his excitement in formulating the principle of natural selection as a young man in 1838. But he then chides himself for having ignored a crucial problem that any evolutionary theory must resolve (we will return to the nature and identification of this problem at the end). Darwin writes:

> But at that time I overlooked one problem of great importance; and it is astonishing to me, except on the principle of Columbus and his egg, how I could have overlooked it and its solution.

13   Now this is a famous quotation in the Darwinian brotherhood; it is cited over and over again, and I have been encountering it throughout my professional life in numerous guises. But something about this statement always bothered me: I didn't understand the reference to Columbus and his egg—and no one ever bothered to explain it by commentary or footnote. As a young man, and with the usual diffidence of those years, I hypothesized my own stupidity and shut up. That is, I assumed that everyone else grasped something I ought to know, and that one day I'd figure it out. Better not embarrass myself by asking. As I got older and learned the ways of the world, I realized that if I didn't comprehend the line, maybe no one else did either—and the fact that every citationist passed by Columbus's egg in silence could just as well signify ignorance as comprehension. Yet Darwin's mention is so off-the-cuff that he, at least, must have regarded Columbus's egg as a schoolboy tale known to all. But times change, and the folk wisdom of one generation may be oblivion to the next. Will our children relish the details of Woody and Mia; do we even remember much about Joe DiMaggio and Marilyn Monroe or Grace Kelly and the Prince of Monaco or Edward VIII and Ms. Simpson?

14   Cambridge, Massachusetts, is a funny place. The town is not so rarified and intellectual as some folks think, but it certainly provides a great advantage if you want to pursue Columbus's egg by the art of survey. I began by asking several of my contemporaries, and not a soul had ever heard of Columbus's egg. So I queried some older American colleagues on the theory that Darwin had cited a former school-boy's tale, now extinct. None of them had a glimmer. As a last effort, I then approached some older colleagues who had spent their childhoods in prewar Europe, conjecturing that Darwin might have cited folk wisdom that never crossed the ocean. I finally got some return, but no solution. Two of my colleagues (neither English, but both continental) remembered such a story but could not recall the details.

15   So I gave up, and Columbus's egg remained in limbo for me—there are, after all, more important matters demanding attention during our short sojourn in this vale of tears. Then, as so often happens, the solution dropped into my lap when I wasn't looking. The scene switches to the spring equinox of 1989. The editorial and letters column of the *New York Times* are buzzing with an exchange about an old (and truly foolish) chestnut—the issue of whether or not one can balance an egg on its end during the equinoxes, but on no other day (now how many of you have encountered that one!). A Mr. Louis Marck—bless his soul—contributed the

following letter on March 26, not only resolving Columbus's egg, but also acknowledging the failure of the story to penetrate our culture:

> In "It's Spring. Go Balance an Egg" (editorial March 19), you say that cheaters "crack the shell to create a flat bottom." According to a tradition strangely unknown in this country, one person who did that very thing, not as a cheater, but to prove a point, was Christopher Columbus.
>
> My German dictionary of quotations places the apocryphal incident in 1493, at a banquet given in honor of Columbus by Cardinal Mendoza. When the difficulty of his voyage of discovery was put into question, Columbus challenged his interlocutors to balance an egg. When they failed, he did it by cracking the shell.
>
> In German, as well as Spanish, "the egg of Columbus" has become proverbial for solving a difficult problem by a surprisingly simple knack or expedient.

16   Fine. A welcome solution. But why have I chosen this obscure item of Columbiana for my essay on this quincentenary? I may not particularly like the man, and I may feel nothing but ambivalence in contemplating his achievements, but I am both too vain and too conscious of duty to blow an essay by mock celebration of a triviality. The image is as colorful as the expression is clichéd: I will not cut off my nose to spite my face. No, I actively like the story of Columbus's egg and find it wonderfully illustrative of an important principle of science and intellectual life in general. Columbus's egg is an emblem for a different kind of ambiguity that we all must face.

17   Did Columbus achieve a fair solution of the puzzle that he himself had set? He asks his dinner companions to balance an egg. They assume that they may not destroy the object as they attempt to stand it on an end—and they fail as the egg rolls back each time. Columbus cracks the shell at its bottom, and the egg stands. I'm sure that he fractured the shell ever so gently—just enough to achieve a sufficiently flat bottom. But he still destroyed the egg. Does the destruction of an object count as a fair solution to a puzzle posed about it? Were Columbus's dinner guests unoriginal, obtuse, or bovine—or were they just properly respectful? And does such respectful-ness always indicate a hidebound resistance to innovation?

18   The story of Columbus's egg is, of course, a metaphor about creativity and its meaning. Any true creator must wield a mallet against an accepted framework. The word *iconoclast*, after all, means "image breaker." We reserve the primary niches in our intellectual pantheon for great iconoclasts: For Galileo, fracturing a limited, earth-centered universe; for Darwin, shattering a system of created, immutable species. Our great intellectual revolutions are never simple infusions of knowledge into a previous void; they are always exercises in destruction and replacement.

19   But the dark figure, the fallen angel of mindless, truly anti-intellectual destruction always waits in the wings, carefully watching any potential episode of iconoclastic creativity, trying to impart the small nudge that pushes a potential intellectual triumph into the abyss of thoughtless destruction. The frenzied mob that cries for the blood of old privilege is no better than the king's polite execu-

tioner. The rabble who cursed and spat at Lavoisier on his way to the guillotine might just as well have been the henchmen of Torquemada tightening the rack or the thumbscrews.

20   Consider the classical example of a "clever" response that overstepped the boundary and substituted thoughtless destruction for genuine resolution—the story of Alexander and the Gordian knot. In 333 B.C. after victories in Asia Minor and as he began a campaign that would defeat Darius and the Persian Empire, Alexander marched to Gordium, the capital of Phrygia (now in central Turkey). There he was shown the famous Gordian knot, an enormously complex configuration (with a hidden end) that lashed the chariot of Gordius, ancient founder of the city, to a pole. According to legend, the man who untied the Gordian knot would conquer all of Asia. Alexander took one look at the knot, drew out his sword, and cut it clean through. (If you don't like tales from antiquity, consider the best modern example from one of the Indiana Jones movies. Jones is challenged by a muscular local hero, who takes out his sword and puts on a long preliminary display by graceful and pyrotechnical brandishing of his preferred weapon. Jones withdraws his gun and promptly plugs his adversary between the eyes.)

21   For that matter, I'm not so sure we should be celebrating the original iconoclasts by incorporating their name in such a favorable way into our language. The iconoclasts objected to veneration of icons or images of human faces, citing an interpretation of the biblical prohibition in the Ten Commandments against worshiping graven images (Exodus 20:4). (Traditional Islamic and Jewish religious art avoids images for the same reason.) The iconoclastic movement twice won power, only to be reversed within the Byzantine Empire during the eighth and ninth centuries. Ironically, the Christian art of Constantinople was ravaged twice—both times by Christians. First, by the iconoclasts during their temporary ascendancy; second, by the armies of the Fourth Crusade who, having failed in their objective of capturing Jerusalem, turned their marauding attention to Christians of another stripe. The Latin rulers of Byzantium (1204–1261) plundered the city, destroyed its art and even melted down most bronze statues for coin. When Mehmed II took Constantinople for the Turks in 1453, he did not engage in the wholesale destruction of Byzantine art, which he admired. Islamic worship precluded veneration of human figures, so when many Christian churches were converted to mosques, the great Byzantine mosaics were often plastered over, rather than ripped apart—and so, thankfully, we may still enjoy them today, as restored in such shrines as Hagia Sophia and the museum of the former Kariye mosque (Saint Savior in Chora under the Byzantines).

22   Alexander's assault upon the Gordian knot remains one of the most ambiguous events in our history or legends. Some have praised Alexander, either for seeking novel solutions apart from expected pathways or simply for taking decisive action when the situation demanded an immediate response. But intellectuals have generally read the story in a deeply negative way, and I must align myself with my own tribe in this case.

23   The quick and violent fix, particularly one that destroys the very object that set the puzzle, must be viewed as the antithesis of our best mental functioning. I do not say that all worthy intellectual activity must follow the silly stereotype of ponderous contemplation (the professor knitting his brow and chewing on the end of his glasses). Brilliant insights are often the antithesis of calm and may be sudden

or even violent. But a revolutionary solution to a problem must at least honor the processes of thought and not belittle our mentality for the sake of expediency.

24   At least I can document this negative use of Alexander's example over several centuries of commentary in my own field of geology. In 1690, Thomas Burnet called for a naturalistic rather than a miraculous interpretation of the Flood by attacking those who would simply attribute the excess water to God's creating power: "They say in short, that God Almighty created waters on purpose to make the deluge, and then annihilated them again. . . . This is to cut the knot when we cannot loose it." And, in one of the most famous passages in all geological writing, Charles Lyell excoriated the miraclemongers with the same image in 1833: "We see the ancient spirit of speculation revived, and a desire manifested to cut, rather than patiently to untie, the Gordian knot."

25   Now I admit that cracking an egg at a banquet may not be so drastic as severing a venerated object at the outset of a war.

26   But Columbus's solution still evokes the whiff of the philistine. Cracking the bottom was clever, but it violated the rules in a manner that strikes me as destructive of a legitimate game.

27   How then shall we define that most precious, yet most elusive, property called creativity? I don't know the answer of course. But we can at least state some properties and specify some criteria. The most historically potent and positive form of creativity must occupy the middle ground between strong respect for accepted norms and accumulated knowledge and Alexander's or Columbus's tactic of destroying rules and objects for an immediate and narrow victory. Maximally useful creativity will surely not arise from the immobilization of the obsessive t-crosser and i-dotter, but the waste and carelessness of a brilliant scholar who refuses to build upon the fruitful work of others, or even acknowledge past tradition (if only to break it), rarely yields much of use either. Let me tell one personal story about a man who, in my opinion, strayed too close to the Columbian end of this spectrum. Many people regard Richard Feynman as the greatest scientific genius of recent times. Perhaps so; as I said, I hardly know what the term means. But I do think that Feynman's antischolarly approach led him to waste a great deal of time, at the very least (and he died too young, with too much undone). Despite his stunning raw mental power, Feynman was a self-proclaimed and vigorous philistine. He simply would not consult anyone else's work or acknowledge that anything already in the literature might be worth his attention. He insisted on working everything out for himself from first principles.

28   One may admire the audacity, but what an inefficient system. The world, after all, is not entirely inhabited by morons, and some conclusions of quality can be found in published sources. Several years ago. I visited CalTech to give a lecture and spent the night in a suite that Einstein had occupied. In the best conceivable follow-up, my host told me the next morning that Richard Feynman wanted to have breakfast with me because he had "figured out some things about evolution" and wanted to discuss them with me (tell them at me would be more accurate, as it turned out). I was delighted, of course, for I had never met the man and knew him only by his incandescent reputation. We sat for three hours, long past closing time for bacon and eggs. I was fascinated but also disturbed.

29   Feynman told me that he had reached some conclusions about evolution that were probably important and no doubt novel—all by reasoning from basic

principles of Darwin's theory of natural selection. Well, he had figured out about half a dozen things, and they were all correct (so far as we know). But I was as dumbstruck as I have ever been in my intellectual life. Every one of his conclusions can be found in chapter one of any elementary evolution textbook. They were all figured out more than a hundred years ago, mostly by Darwin himself. (Feynman, for example, had rediscovered Darwin's principle of sexual selection in both versions of male combat and female choice.) I said to him, "Dick, that's all well and true, but we really do know these things; they are the basis of our science; didn't you ever encounter them in your readings?" He replied that he had read nothing, on purpose.

30   Now Feynman could get away with such an antischolarly approach because he was so brilliant, and because the method had served him well. But he had frittered some time away in this case—and I would certainly not recommend this tactic to ordinary mortals, even highly intelligent and creative ones. My colleague Sid Coleman spoke of Feynman's willful ignorance of past work (quoted by James Gleick, *New York Times Magazine*, September 20, 1992):

> I'm sure Dick thought of that as a virtue, as noble. I don't think it's so. I think it's kidding yourself. Those other guys are not all a collection of yo-yos. Sometimes it would be better to take the recent machinery they have built and not try to rebuild it, like reinventing the wheel. Dick could get away with a lot because he was so goddamn smart.

31   The intellectual version rarely produces real injury, and the cracked egg probably didn't spoil Cardinal Mendoza's dinner. But the destructive side of exploration can cause painful, palpable harm when the object involved is an inhabited land rather than an abstract concept.

32   I must recall the other column I once considered writing for the quincentenary. I wanted to illustrate the biological importance of taxonomic diversity by pointing out that I could personally solve the old debate about Columbus's Bahamian landfall if only he had collected a single *Cerion* shell (they live right at the coastline) as he stepped off the boat. Several islands have been proposed as the spot that Columbus called San Salvador, most historians accept Wailing (now officially called San Salvador), but Cay Sal and several other spots have their defenders. *Cerion*, the focus of my personal research, is a highly diverse land snail with absolutely distinctive populations on each of the proposed islands. A single snail marked "This is the first thing I picked up when I landed on October 12, C. C." would settle the issue forever.

33   But then I thought, what irony! We know the distinctness of each island's *Cerion* because humans have never bothered them, and they have suffered no extinction or transportation. We have not disturbed these snails because they have absolutely no impact upon us: they are not agricultural pests and they taste terrible. They do not fight back; they cannot be enslaved, they know nothing of gold. But humans are exploitable, and their original Bahamian diversity was shattered in the wake of a man whom legend honored because he broke an object to illustrate his ability to manipulate it, and who sailed as emissary of a nation that had just purged the twin sources of its internal diversity.

34   Let us return then, in conclusion, to the subject of Darwin's attention when he cited the story of Columbus and his egg. What was the "one problem of great importance" that he had overlooked? Ironically again, Darwin identified the missing piece in his system as an explanation of *diversity*. Darwin realized that his original (1838) version of natural selection only told how one population might evolve into another of different form, but not how diversity might be produced— that is, how one population might branch into two descendants. He wrote, just after citing Columbus's egg: "The problem is the tendency in organic beings descended from the same stock to diverge in character as they become modified."

35   Darwin now understood that he would not have a complete theory until he could explain the origin of species, the process of making new twigs on life's bush— the source of the stunning variety that is both the glory and the staying power of life on earth. And so Darwin celebrated and sought to explain the very property that Spain had eliminated at home and Columbus diminished abroad—the diversity that is our ballast, our anchor, our only safe mooring in the flood of time. We either preserve this nurturing variety, or ultimately, we may intone a requiem for all humanity with Shakespeare's words for Hamlet (using a Columbian style of fracture): "Now cracks a noble heart. Good night, sweet prince."

Bronwen Wallace

Canada 1945–1989

Bronwen Wallace lived most of her life in her native Kingston, Ontario, receiving her B.A. and M.A. from Queen's University. Wallace was sensitive to the problems of class and gender, so it is not surprising that she eventually ran a shelter for women and children. "One More Woman Talking" reasserts the theme of her poem "A Simple Poem for Virginia Woolf." (See page 167.)

One More Woman Talking   1987

1   I can't separate my personal poetics from the life I am leading or from the events that have brought me to this point in it. But since I can't work my whole life history into a statement of poetics, I'll go straight to one of the high points: a day in May, twenty-one years ago, at Queen's University. On that day, I left a provincial meeting of the Student Union for Peace Action with a number of other women (while the men grumbled that we were being "divisive") to meet and discuss what was then being called The Women's Movement. I think I probably left the room because it seemed to be Theoretically Correct to do so. I'd been in the peace movement / new left for about three years at this point; I'd started to read Marx; I was big on being TC. I had absolutely no idea, however, what we would talk about. And I certainly had no idea, theoretically or otherwise, how much this meeting was going to change my life.

2   What we talked about, in one way or another, for about four hours, were our lives. For me, that meeting represented the first time I had ever been in a room full of women talking *consciously* about their lives, trying to make sense of them, trying to see how the unique and private anecdotes became part of a story that gave each of our lives a public and collective meaning as well.

3   Since then, the majority of my time has been spent listening to women tell the story of their lives in one form or another. I have attended countless meetings to raise consciousness or disrupt beauty contests or plan antinuclear marches; I have listened to women tell about being beaten by husbands or boyfriends; I have held a woman's hand while I gave birth and another's as she lay dying. In being part of these events, I share what is common to many women *and* I also experience them uniquely, as myself. Like every other woman, I come to feminism from my own particular pain and strength and am changed by it as no one else will be ever, while at the same time I participate in events that change us all. The continuing dialectic between these two elements—the public and the private, the unique and the common—is what I enjoy most about living as I do in these particular times.

4   It is also the basis for my poems. I begin with what I have been given: women's stories, women's conversations. Since most of these stories come to me in pretty straightforward, conversational language, that's what I use in the poem. But as I begin to recreate that conversation on the page, I begin to listen to the voice that tells these stories, a voice that is angry sometimes, or frightened, or grieving, or ecstatic. And it becomes the voice I have heard in so many women's conversations, a voice that explores *both* the events in the story itself, *and* something else that lies within those events.

5   This something else is always a mystery for me, since I never know what the poem will discover (just as I never know, in my day-to-day conversations, what any particular woman will discover). For me that everyday language is a sort of safety net, a familiar place in which a deeper, often more dangerous exploration can take place. These stories, because they are women's stories, have never been heard before. For that reason, content, *what happens,* is extremely important in itself *and also* in what it conveys about a new way of looking at the world, of being in the world. What I hear in "ordinary conversation" is that movement that goes on among us. when we feel safe enough or confident enough or loved enough to explore the power within us. This power is so often belittled or denied by the society around us (or by ourselves), but it remains the power by which, in our best moments, we manage to survive and to live, sometimes, with grace. This is what I hear in conversation and what I try to record in my poems. If this sounds like a statement of faith, as much as a statement of poetics, that's because it is.

6   The questions about language which my writing raises have to do primarily with voice, with how to convey this sense of inner discovery at the heart of the most prosaic anecdote. In that sense, my use of everyday language becomes a challenge for me in the poem, as it is in conversation, when we try to convey matters of life-and-death importance with the same words we also use to order a cheeseburger at Harvey's or teach our children how to swim. Sometimes I think the difference is not as great as we like to think, but mostly I just like the challenge.

7   Another challenge, obviously, lies in the fact that the language I am using has been used in the past primarily to tell men's stories or, more accurately, to tell

everyone's stories from a patriarchal point of view. That point of view is embedded in the language itself and one of the questions raised by feminist theory is whether women can speak our piece using it. The following quotation from Xavière Gauthier is a typical representation of the issue:

> Women are, in fact, caught in a real contradiction. Throughout the course of history, they have been mute, and it is doubtless by virtue of this mutism that men have been able to speak and write. As long as women remain silent, they will be outside the historical process. But, if they begin to speak and write *as men do*, they will enter history subdued and alienated; it is a history that, logically speaking, their speech should disrupt.

8   While I definitely experience the problem of the male viewpoint being embedded in language in my own work, I have real difficulty with the way Gauthier (and others who share her view) pose the question and would like to address it in detail. Firstly I am discouraged—almost offended—by Gauthier's use of "they" rather than "we" in talking about women. It seems to privilege a distant stance that implies theory is somehow separate from our lives.

9   Also a problem is the notion of women as mute. I just can't see it. I have no trouble seeing Mr. Historian in his study writing his official Report of the Battle, say, and I have no trouble seeing how the maid brings in his tea and takes it away without a word. In fact, I happen to know that her sister was raped by soldiers after that battle and that her sweetheart was killed in it, I can tell that Mr. H. doesn't even notice her swollen eyes and shaking hands, and I'm darn sure none of this will be part of his Account any more than her gossip with the cook will be. BUT I CANNOT, WILL NOT, BELIEVE THAT SHE WAS MUTE ABOUT IT.

10   Excluded, yes. Mute? Absolutely not!

11   For one thing, we have other records than those of Mr. H.'s: diaries, journals, letters, recipes, the liturgy of the Craft, lace, home-remedies, quilts, poems, essays, and novels, all of which feminist (and other) historians use all the time to develop other histories than the rather limited Patriarchal Record. Why are we judging women by the same standard that has oppressed us?

12   As to women, by their alleged silence, remaining outside the historical process... My Great Aunt Nettie, age ninety-four, is telling me a story. In it her father dies when she is three, leaving her mother alone on a farm with several children. That winter, she discovers she has breast cancer. Since she cannot leave the farmwork, she persuades her doctor to come out, chloroform her on the dining room table, and remove her breast while her oldest daughter holds the oil-lamp. A few days later, she is back in the barn. She goes on living for another ten years.

13   This story, out of all her stories, was the one my great aunt chose to give me at the end of her life. I put it in a poem once. I tell you now. So it becomes History.

14   But—and this is a Great Big But—regardless of what is recorded, the farm exists, the taxes were paid, the kids raised, the crops planted and harvested. My great grandmother can never be *outside* of these. She exists, she persists, she *moves events* as surely as her cells shape my hands, whether they write about her or no. What are we saying about ourselves, about millions of women like her, when we deny her that? Why are we *starting* from a view of history in which women are *always* the victims?

15   And then there is the issue of talking like a man. On the TV, Margaret Thatcher, a woman who "talks like a man" if I ever heard one. But when I say "talks like a man" I really mean "speaks the language of the patriarchy" (and by patriarchy I mean a structure originating in households where the father dominated which is reproduced in society in gender relations, language, ways of seeing, etc.). I'm certainly subdued by and alien to such language. I hear it as the language of *power over*, of estrangement, of a system which separates men from women, adults from children, people from other animals, people from nature, in a way that expresses difference as opposition, us versus them, life versus death, etc. It is a history which we must disrupt, I believe, both logically and passionately, because our survival, as a species, depends on it.

16   I have trouble when the issue is posed in a way which opposes men, *as a gender*, to women, *as a gender*, without any reference to the relationship between gender and power, say. It leaves me with the impression that anyone who uses the same syntax, vocabulary, etc. as persons of the male gender are on the side of the devil. Bad guys/good girls. Oppressor/victim. Same old story, just different sides. It's still, as far as I can hear, the patriarchy talking.

17   Such thinking includes the assumption that "men" and "language" are contained in each other. It's assumed that the patriarchy, that patriarchal language, is a monolith and that women are victimized, determined, totally, by the point of view embedded in it.

18   Such assumptions, if they remain unquestioned, create a situation in which our discussion of women and language becomes a discussion on men and language because it poses all the questions in the same old way, uses the same old methods of setting things up.

19   When I write of disrupting or changing history, I begin with the assumption that *people* can change, that we are not totally determined by, *bespoken* by the culture in which we live. I begin, always, with the power of the personal, the private, the unique in each of us, which resists, survives, and can change the power that our culture has over us. This is what I have learned from the women's movement and what I try to explore in my poems. I believe that when we speak and write of our lives in this way, we also change language, if only because we say things that have never been said before.

20   A woman who tells someone that her husband is beating her and she wants it to stop. A man who admits that he is violent and asks for help in changing. A poet who writes a poem that challenges conventional syntax and grammar. A feminist reading of *Jane Eyre*. A speech by Helen Caldicott. Two women sitting in a bar talking to each other.

21   For me, all of these change *language*. They change what can be said about women's lives because they disrupt the silence which has covered so much. They change what we think about each other in a culture which accepts things as they are and constantly erodes our power to change even ourselves. They challenge our assumption that how we speak or see or think is neutral, *not* culturally determined. They permit even feminists to have a sense of humour. They embrace passion and anger and even hysteria as appropriate responses to the present danger of the planet.

22   I personally believe that language will change—and does change—as women's lives change and not because one way of writing or speaking is theoret-

ically correct. I don't think there is one way of writing and speaking that *is* theoretically correct. I'm excited by some of the language theory that forms the basis
of Gauthier's statement. Some of it I just can't understand. Some of it simply
doesn't correspond with my own experience, either of women or of language.
That's generally how I respond to most theories.

23   What matters to me personally is *being here*, in another room, with another
bunch of women, still talking.

24   I'd like to read a poem at the end of this:

Bones

for Barb

A story of yours got this one going,
so I'm sending it back now, changed of course,
just as each person I love
is a relocation, where I take up
a different place in the world.

The way you told it, it was after midnight,
you coming off the late shift, heading home
in a taxi, a woman driving,
and you ask her if she's ever scared
working these hours and she says, "No, I've got this
to protect me!" reaching under her seat
to pull up (you expected a crowbar,
a tire iron) this eight-inch, stainless steel
shank. "The pin from my mother's thigh,"
she tells you, "I got it when they put
one of those new plastic ones in."

Sometimes when I tell myself this story
I get caught up in logistics,
how the doctor must have delivered the thing
from layers of fat and muscle
into one of those shiny dishes
the nurse is always holding
and then she would have,
what? washed it off? wrapped it in towels?
carried it down to the waiting room, the daughter
sitting there, reading magazines, smoking cigarettes?
It's so improbable, like the foetus
pickled in a jar in the science lab in high school,
though other times it's just
there, natural as the light
that bounces off it,
somebody's mother's thigh bone,
for protection, like her face

in the hall light, rescuing you
from a nightmare.

You told me this
during my visit last year
when I'd just quit working
at the crisis centre, that job
that wrenched me round
until each morning stretched, a pale, dry skin,
over the real colour of the day,
ready to spring at me, like the child
whose hand had been held down
on a red-hot burner
reappearing in the face of a woman
met casually at a cocktail party.
Everywhere I went, my work experience
drew me through confessions I couldn't stop,
and I couldn't stop talking about them
so you had to listen
but, being you, in that way that listening
can be active, when the listener re-enters
the country of her own damage
from a new direction.

This can be like watching someone we love
return from the limits a body can be taken to
— a botched suicide, say, or an accident.
Years, it might be, before the eyes or the hands retrieve enough
to offer as a sign,
what doctors think they can detect
on a CAT scan, some pattern in the cells
to show them, once and for all,
how the mind, like the body, makes shape
of what's left, the terrible knowledge
it labours through, slowly regaining itself.

Though on an X-ray, even the bones show up
as light, a translucence that belies their strength
or renders it immeasurable,
like the distances we count on them to carry us,
right to the end of our lives and back again,
and again.

John Ralston Saul

Canada 1948–

John Ralston Saul has a B.A. in political science, history, and economics from McGill and a Ph.D. from King's College, University of London. His popularity began with the publication in 1992 of his book *Voltaire's Bastards: The Dictatorship of Reason in the West*, in which he criticizes the power elite at the end of the twentieth century. Since that time, Saul has written a number of books, including *The Unconscious Civilization*, winner of the Governor General's Award for nonfiction in 1996, and the novel *The Paradise Eater*, winner of the Premio Lettario Internazionale in 1990. Saul's essays are provocative, asking us to be more critical of society's accepted ideologies. His provocative tone is evident in "The Politics of Common Sense," which is from his 2001 book, *On Equilibrium*.

The Politics of Common Sense   2001

1   Without serious consideration given to common sense, we have difficulty dealing with many of our most basic questions. Homelessness and a persistent increase in poverty among a growing percentage of our populations have accompanied a remarkable increase in financial wealth at the opposite end of the society.

2   This problem will never be absolutely resolved. However, there is the question of how many poor and how extreme the differences. After all, those suffering are those on the edge of normal life. They have been shoved or have fallen off that edge for a whole range of reasons. A successful society, as a strict minimum, sets out to minimize the number cast over into free fall.

3   This can be done with little effort and little money. Often all that is needed for people to keep themselves upon the plateau or to climb back up over the ledge is a few solid, long-term basics such as affordable housing. Instead, the false common sense of utilitarianism has tended to put more money into homeless shelters, emergency services, food banks and drop-in centres. Why? Because managerial societies are desperate to measure crises and responses. Decent housing at the margins is not a measurable solution. Treating those who have fallen over the edge as charitable cases is perfectly calculable. Treating the excluded as excluded fits quite naturally into corporatist societies which do not believe in inclusion or in citizenship as the basis of society's legitimacy.

4   Look at it another way. We know that for decades there has been a continual rise in broken families and in the number of single-parent families. Put the complexity of causes aside. Look instead at their reality. We know that the market has gradually adjusted to the two-income family by increasing the cost of living so that what a family could once support on one income now requires two. The broken or single family is therefore caught in an impossible corner.

5   A sensible approach would therefore be not to punish the failure to meet these conditions; and certainly not to push these people into a humiliating world of charity—public or private—which will scar them for life with a sense of exclu-

sion. Instead, it would make sense to ensure, for example, that the one remaining all-inclusive public structure in most of our democracies—public schools— would be strengthened and rounded out to ensure that meals, after-hour programs and smaller classes picked up on what is missing in many families. Instead, increasing numbers of democracies are trying to apply private-sector models to public education. They attempt to shave off the non-utilitarian elements and to charge for them, as well as for use of the facilities after-hours. The result is a gradual return to mid-nineteenth-century moralism in which those children without must either be left behind or be humiliated by entering a category deserving of charity. Whether public or private, charity indicates a return to societies divided by class. This is ethics denied in favour of moralism; citizens' rights converted into clientism.

6   Take an example at the international level. Images of a famine somewhere out there in the world are brought to our attention. We vibrate with momentary horror and guilt. There is instant consensus—or an intense campaign produces consensus. Action must be taken. Lives must be saved.

7   The reality, however, is that the structure of expert analysis has converted famine into a process. What does that mean? Well, unless there is an established right, our public structures require a proof of 'need' before they feel empowered to act. They require body counts. They can't respond to unsubstantiated warnings. Substantiation may indeed unleash money. But can we wait for a ghoulish audit? "If there aren't enough bodies, there isn't a famine." The whole idea of forethought—a characteristic of shared knowledge—is excluded from this process as unprofessional. Michael Glanz describes famine as a spike which rises above the norm. Through heroic activity governments can push the spike back down, by flying in food, troops, cash. None of which addresses the ongoing causes.

8   It isn't that those responding are unwilling to address the issue of civil wars and landownership. But before they did so, they would have to address key structural problems. For a start, most international aid agencies have one department for dealing with development issues and another for emergency issues such as famine. As if one did not lead to the other.

9   If we really did believe in systems—as opposed to simply dividing up power— we would at least have developed an early-warning system for famines. That would set off a process of anticipation. But such movement on the horizon is considered not sufficiently calculable. Not sufficiently disembodied and utilitarian. Anticipation would suggest an active use of shared knowledge in order to identify what is probable, with action based on probabilities not substantiation. To put it in health-care terms, this would mean building policy around health not sickness.

10   The same could be said about our response to global warming. For every problematic statistic a theoretically rational reply can be made with a reassuring statistic. The North Pole melts and there's an immediate chorus chanting that it has happened before. Specialists say polar ice has reduced by forty per cent in recent years and continues to shrink by four per cent a year. Someone funded to argue the opposite pumps out a reply from an 'independent' source.

11   In an era of utilitarian facts, each side argues its numbers, like little boys caught up in an analytic sandbox struggle. I could add something I have personally seen—the Inuit in Nunavut in the High Arctic are starting to use artificial ice on their unheated hockey arenas. The natural winter season is now too short.

12   A sensible question on hearing all of this would be not: 'what is the truth?' but 'what are the probabilities?' As with war, the stakes are high for the loser. What if it turns out that the Cassandras are right? There might be no turning back by then. Why choose the most optimistic probability and plough on with the blustering self-assurance of false masculinity? "Retreat is not flight;" Sancho Panza said, "nor staying wisdom, when danger outweighs hope." Why not use the sort of prudence which indicates that we are conscious and responsible enough to limit our risks?

13   Or take the question of fish stocks. We know that species after species is in decline. They are sinking to levels which make commercial fishing impossible. Everywhere there are fewer and fewer fishermen on a shrinking number of boats. But still the stocks do not regenerate. There are great all-encompassing theories, but they don't really help us.

14   There are, however, elements which can be separated out as part of the complicated puzzle. For example, although there are a shrinking number of boats, each of them is increasingly large. They are increasingly indiscriminate by nature. The industrial nature of their approach means that, while fishing for a particular species of a particular size, they actually damage smaller fish of the same species, other species of different sizes and even the physical environment.

15   After several years of a virtual cod ban inside various territorial waters, we are suddenly informed that the same factory ships now vacuum the same waters in search of halibut. Many of the new cod are caught by accident. At that point, they are dead, but not counted as a catch. Add to this pattern the fact that fifty per cent of the fish consumed in Europe is now imported. With little left in its own waters, the European Union now pays US$100 million a year to fourteen developing countries in return for vacuuming up their fish.

16   The deregulationists say, 'well look at what a mess government management has already made. How much worse could the market do?' But the mess has been made by disembodied expertise; an expertise shared by the public and private sectors. It produces economic models unrelated to reality and subdivided strategies unable to look at the whole situation. The result is fractured, short-term, clumsy strategies.

17   We know that the factory ships have an unquenchable hunger. They appear modern and efficient. Why then are they so clumsy? Because they are actually the product of late-nineteenth-century industrial production management theory. The Ford assembly-line model.

18   Factory ships are not even in the business of catching fish per se. A high percentage of the catch goes into low-value fish by-products, such as fertilizer. The economic logic is clear: the indiscriminate vacuuming up of fish types for a blunt-ended market uninterested in quality product is far cheaper and more efficient than, for example, catching a halibut for some people who want to eat a halibut. And if the fish stocks are eliminated, well, too bad. The fertilizer market will find another ingredient and the fish eaters will support a larger fish-farm industry. That massive fish-farming produces a whole series of other complex consequences would be described as a separate issue for analysis by a separate group of people.

19   Common sense might suggest that we get our fertilizer elsewhere, because the fish stocks, taken in their own terms, are far more valuable. The cash value of the product is being dangerously devalued by a highly abstract, but old-fashioned, industrial means of production.

20   It might turn out that if you removed the factory-ship model and the fertilizer by-product component, and converted from nets to lines as the highly effective Icelandic industry has, you would actually have protected fish stocks and increased employment in both the fisheries and agriculture. But to do that would require accepting the complexity of common sense as well as life without a series of independently linear resolved questions. And perhaps accepting the advice of the great Haida poet Ghandl: "These will be of use to the last people in the world."

21   You could describe our obsessive overfishing as a sort of institutionalized panic—a terror before the idea of simply looking at all we know, putting it into an integrated consideration and then acting upon the resulting probabilities. You could call our current state a lack of leadership. But that would be a passive response. A way to do nothing. That would be the Tristan and Isolde syndrome. We have taken a love potion and we can but love each other, whatever the catastrophic consequences, until the potion wears off. Then we'll see.

22   This syndrome is not simply pure romanticism. It is an extremely low-level type of ideology. It replaces restraint, which is what common sense provides in a non-moralizing way. The effort needed to be intelligent in an integrated manner is certainly not easy. "But this yoke," Montesquieu said, "seems hard to carry: you would prefer to be subjected to a prince and obey his laws, less demanding than your own standards."

23   Panic is brought on by a denial of shared knowledge. It feeds on the absence of belief in a larger good. And results in an urgent conviction of the absolute necessity of apparently utilitarian, narrow, short-term actions. That means the absolute necessity of selfishness and of self-interest—let's call it selfishness—as the essential human characteristic.

24   What common sense provides is a clear sense that nothing is inevitable; that we belong to a society. Panic of this sort is therefore unnecessary. We are too intelligent for that.

25   What prevents us from acting as if we were that intelligent is our unwillingness to insist upon integrated thought—that is, to act as if we shared knowledge with others in our society.

Dionne Brand

Trinidad/Canada   1953–

Dionne Brand, who was born in Guayguayare, Trinidad moved to Canada in 1970 and received both a B.A. and an M.A. from the University of Toronto. Brand has taught both English and Creative Writing at various post-secondary institutions, directed four films for the NFB, been active in community work and involved with organizations that have focused on civil rights and feminist issues. Of her education as a child, she has remarked, "when I was in elementary and high schools, none of the books we studied were about Black people's lives; they were about Europeans, mostly the British. But I felt that Black people's experiences were as important and as valuable, and needed to be written down and read about." "Imagination, Representation and Culture" echoes Brand's hostility to analysts who see culture as homogenous rather than layered, complex, and diffuse.

Imagination, Representation and Culture 1994

1   Wilson Harris, the Guyanese novelist, writes, 'such a notion as the fabric of the imagination, implies a ... force which imbues the human psyche with flexible and far flung roots in all creatures, all elements, all worlds and constellations, all sciences, all spaces susceptible to visualisation.... Alas we have been conditioned to freeze such an awe-inspiring and wonderful genesis of the imagination into an obsession with binding and homogeneous archetype. Cultural homogeneity ... extrapolates ... an unchanging sanction of identity. Thus pure cultures, so-called, tend to fear or scorn what is mixed or apparently impure.' 'Concepts of invariant identity', Harris says, are the weapons of the oppressor and, in a 'tautology of power', also the oppressed. 'There is comfort in this for those who command the destinies of the human race ... no comfort whatever for those who descend into themselves and seek to breech a one track state of mind—who seek to perceive that every window of changelessness that a culture constructs anew brings back into focus the participation of a fallible humanity.'

2   Harris situates us at the heart of the question, linking the imagination to culture and power as he argues for the rejecting of cultural homogeneity in favour of the 'revisionary potential of imageries and texts'. Let me say that Harris is not arguing for the classic stance of the imagination as a kind of market where a superior intelligence roams around assessing 'lower' forms of culture, tastes their wares, marks them down for correction where necessary or remarks on their quaintness, admires their craft even though primitive, appropriates what it deems useful and ambles along to the next bazaar confident of its own superiority. Rather, he is proposing a stance far more self-searching, far more vulnerable. Dare I say a 'post-colonial' stance, in the true historical meaning of the word. Harris is standing in the middle of the 'great eviscerated landscape' of the new world and calling from the imagination the heterogeneous ancestral memory. Repopulating history with buried and new visions other than those of the dominating cultures.

3   Within Canada, but not only, notions of the imagination, representation and culture rise from their hieroglyphs as charged elements, contested terrain. So much of who we are, how we see ourselves and what we experience is contained in these concepts that they are naturally explosive. The idea of these concepts as given and uncontested spaces, spaces without choice or judgement, spaces free somehow of all we have lived or long to live, free of our material struggles—that these are spaces self-evidently honest or moral, without prejudice or failure, presanctioned, sanctified, unanswerable spaces—this idea is disingenuous. Rather, they are places of wars, ascendancies, claiming grounds, hegemonic strategy. But some of us who are artists, writers, trust that they can also be places of utter fallibility, searches for clarity or complexity, places everlastingly unfinished if we are

lucky, places with the uncomfortable certainty of uncertainty, places of reckoning with other consciousnesses, histories, desires, descriptions, interpretations, visions and visionings.

4   Canada is not (and cannot ever claim to be) a homogeneous culture. It has never been such (not even before recent immigrants, who are accused from time to time of messing up the works), it has never been such despite the exhortations of state power formulated largely by the English and the French to make it so. That very formulation illustrates the cultural battles fought. Even they who call themselves the founding nations contest continuously that homogeneity to the point of threats of secession. If there is any homogeneous element, it is the collective angst over whether we can say there is a Canadian identity. And it is curious for what it says about positionings in the society. Perhaps it is the healthy expression of disease with the power relations, with how the 'we' unravels if we really think about it, with how the 'we' got to be 'we'. Angst aside, however, there is an official Canadianness that functions. It functions to exclude as it functions to define. I will deal with only one exclusion here today. It excludes and evades immigrants, regardless of their length of citizenship, either through race or language, and suggests that they pass a kind of means test of 'Canadianness' over and over again. This test involves the intricate mental trick of forgetting what is called 'their past' despite the fact that their past is their present. The migrant is the only one in the world whose past was a ten-hour flight ago. And that might be interesting for some but only an incredible mind-negating fantasy for others. Their countries of origin become, upon their arrival at Pearson or Dorval, the past. And this past is circumscribed as a tortured and rejected past, regardless of their reasons for migration. All immigration is seen as fleeing a horrible past/place and arriving gratefully at an unblemished present/place. So Canada presents itself as an alluring historyless place, at least not a place charged with a similarly hostile history, even as one is persuaded later that it isn't, as one is presented with the pristine documents of its not-where-you-come-from-but-better morality. One is supposed to empty oneself of the past/place and fill oneself with the present/place—'Canadianness'. And while that prospect might be convenient for some of us fleeing some personal domestic crisis—money, work, hurt or discomfort, guilt, greed, self-interest or at times terrifying political strife—we are not in control of it all and we come full of ourselves—who we were and are and will become. We may crave the boon of forgetfulness, because we are either terrified or disaffected but there it is—all of ourselves bursting the suitcases and trunks, our memories, our histories, our grandness, our pettiness, our sense of hurt, our sense of justice, our love of mangoes or tamarinds, cream or smoked meat, bacalau or chillies, the grease stains on boxes patched with string, the smell of somewhere else escaping our clothing, the pictures wrapped in newspaper, and the promises, the lies, the already untrue, to send money back or send for someone. We are full of ritual or mundane acts, lusts and hatreds, and all not necessarily specific to our places of origin and yes some particular but not unique. The emptying out that this notion of 'Canadianness' or the cultural archetype requires is not only impossible but it seems to me undesirable and unnecessary because it renders the society we enter also empty of the creativity, knowledges, imaginings, dreamings, life experiences that enhance human beings. Impossible because losing memory is losing anchor, losing instances of life, senses, ideas.

Unless these narratives joined other narratives, not in an act of dislocation but as part of the collectivity.

5 And then there is what we replace all this loss with—this idea of Canadianness, which has its permutations and provisions. It strikes me that the one constructed for immigrants prescribes silence as their discourse because immigration is propelled by labour needs (and you can check various immigration acts for verification), such a labour force is not required to take part in the national discourse but take part strictly in labour. So this loss is replaced in effect by work. How it is constructed even for those who fit all of its criteria is also fascinating, contested over regions and origins of regions, Newfoundland to B.C., it is marked by a singular absence striking its very centre—namely, the peoples who predate the English and the French. (Not to omit the Africans, who arrived simultaneously as slaves or reluctant allies of the Europeans.) This absent presence is at the core of Canadian identity, a whole set of people relegated to a present past. An emptying out of the past then, both physical and mental, seems to be crucial to the concept.

6 To digress, there is a way in which this country is divided into not only provinces but also time. A way in which everything that does not emanate from its industrial and populous centre configures itself as ancient or in the past, as if time moves from the centre to the outskirts, from the present to the past, as much as time moves from Toronto to New York as moving from the present into the future. As if mimicking the time zones one flies into night as one flies east. One flies into the past as flying into night suggests, as flying into daylight gives one a sense of flying into the future. But perhaps that is only a useful metaphor for this piece, as I've also experienced night as flying into tomorrow, which is what is really happening flying east. Let us just say that this country has its own distorted rhythms for what has happened here and who lives here, so flying west is flying into what hasn't happened yet and flying east is flying into what happened before. At least for someone who lives in the middle of it. And someone who's lived in the middle of it for only the last twenty-seven years. Someone who is as much a part of it as estranged from it and who is at any one time as alarmed at the social outcomes of these patterns as intrigued by their persistence in the mind of the culture. First Nations peoples are located in the culture as its past and treated as an uncomfortable and unwelcome intrusion in the present.

7 Distributed through the culture and through the Canadian imagination are other archetypes; this imagination contains Indians who are dangerous, threatening, useless, savage or drunk, Indians with old and un-understandable griefs, who have no rights to land but exist on sufferance; it contains Blacks who are immigrant complainers, servants inferior, not entitled because we're not the States, no slavery here, violent young men; it contains Chinese who helped build the railroads but remained foreign and some newcomers who want to buy up all the good neighbourhoods in B.C. and have triads; it contains people of English origin (two kinds— one centrally located, modern, erudite, smart, keepers of the culture; the other folksy, usually from down east, perennially poor, why don't they move, quaint, largely unintelligent and dependent); it contains Italians, labourers and mafiosi; French, a nuisance, they want everything; we can go on and on. Jews, Portuguese, South Asians, all with their particular stereotypes, and then there is wilderness, beer, hockey, the North. These notions embedded in the Canadian imagination and

operating more or less in organising our material life. Contradictory notions too inhabit this imagination, notions of social democracy, social welfare, justice, social equality, these too shape the imagination, finding accommodation and regulating the former cultural stereotypes. The pride, however, in being different from the pariah to the south obfuscates the challenges in destroying the stereotypes and rather enhances them. (Nothing we can do can be as bad.)

8   What could we mean by culture today when the governments of nation-states are exposed as mere managers of corporate interests? The idea that nation-states are somehow manifestations of the common or best will of their inhabitants, that nation-state governments are the keepers of the social welfare, is unravelling as a deep and dangerous deception. If we can say that there is a Canadian culture, we have to say that it is revealed in the process by which the country was created as a nation-state, through conquest, cross-imperialist conflict, capitalist formations and imperatives, a physical border with and against an imperialist power, waves of immigration marked by racial- and labour-need determinations, regional differences and disparities, ethnic concerns and social justice movements. If we can call on a culture, we have to look at how all of these interactions have worked themselves out (through the short history of this nation-state), into a dominant voice claiming to speak for all. A dominant voice that need not of course have all of our consent—our silence or our repressed voice is sufficient.

9   I do not resist the idea of a 'Canadianness' wholly. I resist the particular myth-making process of the Canadian nation-state. I resist the idea that the collectivity is a done deal, a coat to slip on ready-made, a dead thing, a language spoken by only a chosen number or one mouth, a thing that cannot be added to, reassessed, challenged, criticised, changed. And I resist the notion that it is somehow pure and superior.

10   We are asked to coalesce around English and French identities in Canada rather than any true tracings of the make-up of the inhabitants of the country, and we are asked to do so on the basis of an assumption of the right of the people asking us to do so as our cultural superiors, for why would we be here if where we are from was not inferior, socially as well as culturally. This is the culture I resist and I notice instead a becoming. Riding the College or Dundas streetcar, I listen to the sound of voices changing in timbre, sibilances, assonances, cadences, breathiness, finally languages as the streetcar crosses the city from Roncesvalles to Main and beyond—from slow English to Ukrainian to German to West Indian to Tamil to Italian to Portuguese to Nova Scotia African to Nova Scotia English to Cantonese to Vietnamese to corporate and medical silence on University to Cantonese again to Yonge Streetese, which is a glorious mishmash of all, to Regent Park West Indian to Scotian to Vietnamese to working-class English, or is it third-generation white immigrant, to Punjabi to Urdu and banking off to Main. And at night coming back on the subway, coming west, first there are some Anglo punks screaming at each other, 'Fucking A, man. Fucking A', then emptying off a bus from Don Mills some Black punks screaming at each other, 'Ay Trini, ay guy don't fuck with me. Ay, ay guy. Yuh Ras!' then there are some Italian women and some Portuguese women 'querida, querida, querida' and a scream of laughter, they come on near Yonge just off from cleaning offices, then there is a Black nurse and a Filipino nurse come from Wellesley or Mt. Sinai, then University is quiet, then some students all young, all different races, looking worried or doped on,

Wake Ups, coming from the Robarts library, then Black women, Chinese men, young Portuguese women, black lipstick, then Spadina Bathurst Christie, more black lipstick black clothing baggy clothing all races, high schoolers squeezing through the door as it closes. By Lansdowne the Italians and Portuguese are gone, a strung-out couple hesitates and then doesn't take the train, by Jane most of the Africans and Filipinos are gone except those going to Islington to catch a ride to Mississauga or Brampton … and on and on and not all that you can see and hear. I resist the idea of a mono-culture for this. And these sounds and this movement of the train and the bodies gesturing to each other. These people are doing something. Their obligation cannot only be to forget where they came from, denounce themselves, don't complain when they are treated badly because they should just be grateful that they are here. I challenge the notion that all they are doing is remembering old hurts, petrifying old customs and trying to impose their views on an uninvolved landscape. They may well be doing this but not only. Because the compulsion of the immediate shades all of this; generations contest it and hopes shape it. Yes, we are groping and angst-ridden about here and there and lonely for some small hill or some broken bicycle and hate the cold and complain and say after fifty years this would never happen where I come from even though we left when we were ten, but this is the right business of being human I'm afraid. These are also people (by their very presence here) for whom change is not a fearful thing—they have travelled thousands of miles as well as sensibilities, that very act has already changed them, is already a mark of their complete willingness to acknowledge if not welcome the changeable, to leap into other experiences. And this leaping, this faith in landing in other geographies and life experiences, is their crucial gift to the culture. They do not arrive empty, though they arrive with latitude; neither do they enter an empty landscape, a place with no history. The question really is how do people in this country express their collectivity outside the dynamic of a dominating voice (which ends up somehow expressive of those in power) and subordinated voices (which are only afforded certain moments of expression and certain types of expression)? The question is not how do we indoctrinate people into the dominating culture but are these the only forms in which expression might take place?

11 I believe, as Wilson Harris has said, that people have within them layers and layers of experiences, memories consisting of past ages, lost antecedents; that our knowledge inhabits past knowledges and futures and we have to ask ourselves how we tap these to navigate our way in our collectivity. These memories and knowledges exist in history, of course; they are not ahistorical objects, relative and neutral. So we are necessarily mindful that we live in a country, on a continent, a hemisphere, marked by racial genocide, mass migrations, slavery, forced labour, wars but also by great insurrections and also massive hopes. From Toussaint and Bolivar to Malcolm X, Rigoberto Menchu and Oka, all the movements and insurrections in between, where people in this hemisphere wrestle for control of their daily lives.

12 Within the context of our now corporate-run states, the idea of a homogeneous culture in Canada today seems to me not only a dead end (at its most innocent interpretation) but also a hegemonic strategy of capital to produce a 'pure' identity to be filled up with commodities and pumped up to defend economic threat by other corporate-run states. I am not suggesting that the dominating cul-

ture is pure deceit, pure lies. I think that genuine expressions of experiences, ways of seeing, are distilled by state-making practices for which one view of history might be more convenient and beneficial than many views.

13   So what would we make, what would we create, to take Adrienne Rich's line from What Is Found There. What would we create as a more realistic and life-respecting expression of our collectivity? Maybe riding the College streetcar; maybe it is an admission of our history, an admission of our collectivity; maybe it is many stories and not one dominating one.

David Freedman

U.S.A. 1954–

David Freedman is a contributing editor at Forbes ASAP and at *Discover* magazine. He writes on a wide range of topics and has been published in *Wired, The Washington Post, The Boston Globe,* and *Harvard Business Review.* His first book, *The Brainmakers,* was published by Simon and Schuster in 1994; his second book, *At Large: The Strange Case of the World's Biggest Internet Invasion* (1997), was co-authored by Charles C. Mann and also published by Simon and Schuster. In "The Aggressive Egg," he explores, with humour and significant detail, the influence of chauvinism on the supposedly objective science of biology.

The Aggressive Egg   1992

1   Ah, fertilization—that miraculous process to which we all owe our existence. Let's review: first, a wastefully huge swarm of sperm weakly flops along, its members bumping into walls and flailing aimlessly through thick strands of mucus. Eventually, through sheer odds of pinball-like bouncing more than anything else, a few sperm end up close to an egg. As they mill around, the egg selects one and reels it in, pinning it down in spite of its efforts to escape. It's no contest, really. The gigantic, hardy egg yanks this tiny sperm inside, distills out the chromosomes, and sets out to become an embryo. Or would you have put it differently? Until very recently, so would most biologists. For decades they've been portraying sperm as intrepid warriors battling their way to an aging, passive egg that can do little but await the sturdy victor's final, bold plunge. But the first description is closer to the truth, insists Emily Martin, a 47-year-old researcher at Johns Hopkins who has spent the past seven years examining the metaphors used to describe fertilization. Martin is not a biologist; she's a cultural anthropologist. But her efforts to spotlight the male-skewed imagery that permeates our views of reproduction have placed her at the center of a growing debate about how cultural myths can turn into scientific myths, and vice versa.

2   Martin didn't set out to skewer biologists. Actually she was studying biology, among other things, at the University of Michigan in 1965 when a course on Japanese music hooked her on investigating other cultures. After picking up a Ph.D.

in cultural anthropology from Cornell in 1971, she spent nine years traveling back and forth between the United States, Taiwan, and China, where she was studying Chinese rituals and social organization. Then, having done the study of a foreign culture that's traditionally expected of anthropologists, and being pregnant with her first child, she started casting about for a new project closer to home. "Studying your own culture is harder," she says, "because everything seems so normal to you."

3   Not until 1982, while attending a class for expectant parents before the birth of her second child, did Martin stumble on her topic. "It suddenly hit me that the way everyone was talking about their bodies was really weird," she recalls. "It was *the* body, *the* uterus, and *the* contraction—as if these things weren't a part of us. I realized that medical science was in need of some sort of interpretation, and my wedge would be reproductive issues." Martin started off by interviewing dozens of women on their feelings about every aspect of reproduction, from menstruation to menopause. Her book *The Woman in the Body,* published in 1987, explored the relation between images of the body and ideas about oneself. But by 1985 Martin realized that she had been looking at these issues from only one point of view. "I decided to do an ethnographic[1] study in a scientific setting, to see how biologists thought about some of these questions," she says. "Also, I thought I should be including male reproductive processes as well." Fertilization research, she realized, would allow her to cover all the bases.

4   As she began her background studies, Martin was surprised to find that popular literature, textbooks, and even medical journals were crammed with descriptions of warrior sperm and damsel-in-distress eggs. Martin found that classic biology texts, for example, enthused about the human male's "amazing" productivity—some 200 million sperm every hour—while practically complaining over the "waste" of the 2 million immature eggs present in the human female at birth, only some 400 of which the ovaries ever "shed" for possible fertilization, with the rest destined to "degenerate" over the woman's lifetime. "The real mystery," says Martin, "is why the male's vast production of sperm is not seen as wasteful."

5   Less mysterious, in Martin's opinion, was the motivation for such biased language. "Men link potency to strong sperm," she says. "You'd like your sperm to be like you; no wonder everyone believed sperm were torpedoes." In all her searching, Martin came up with only a single depiction of less-than-mighty sperm: Woody Allen's portrayal of a neurotic sperm nervous about his imminent ejaculation in the movie *Everything You Always Wanted to Know About Sex But Were Afraid to Ask.*

6   Woody Allen aside, the durability of the masterful sperm imagery astonished Martin. It continued to dominate the contemporary technical and popular literature despite a growing body of evidence that the egg plays anything but a passive role. From the early 1970s on, studies of the sperm and eggs of many species have revealed that molecules released by the egg are critical to guiding and "activating" the sperm—that is, triggering the sperm to release proteins that help it adhere to the egg. In fact, the egg might just as well be called eager as passive. Among many species of lizards, insects, some crustaceans, and even turkeys, the egg doesn't always wait for the sperm's arrival. It can begin dividing without fertilization, and females can reproduce without sperm at all.

---

1   pertaining to the branch of anthropology that deals with the origin and division of races and cultures

7   Yet none of this had made a dent in biologists' language. "When I asked them about it, they told me I had a point," says Martin. "They claimed the imagery came up only when they needed to explain their research, and not in the lab. But I wanted to know what was really going on."

8   By 1986 Martin had begun hanging out with a team of researchers at Johns Hopkins who were observing sperm mobility in hopes of coming up with a strategy for a new contraceptive. They had started the year before with a simple experiment—measuring human sperm's ability to escape and swim away from a tiny suction pipet[2] placed against the side of the sperm cell's head. To the team's great surprise, the sperm turned out to be feeble swimmers; their heads thrashed from side to side ten times more vigorously than their bodies pushed forward. "It makes sense," says Martin. "The last thing you'd want a sperm to be is a highly effective burrower, because it would end up burrowing into the first obstacle it encountered. You want a sperm that's good at getting away from things."

9   The team went on to determine that the sperm tries to pull its getaway act even on the egg itself, but is held down against its struggles by molecules on the surface of the egg that hook together with counterparts on the sperm's surface, fastening the sperm until the egg can absorb it. Yet even after having revealed the sperm to be an escape artist and the egg to be a chemically active sperm catcher, even after discussing the egg's role in "tethering" the sperm, the research team continued for another three years to describe the sperm's role as actively "penetrating" the egg.

10   Meanwhile, Martin was keeping an eye on two other fertilization groups. They too seemed at times to disregard their own observations when writing about fertilization. Researchers at the University of Wisconsin, for example, described the way sea urchin sperm first make contact with an egg by quickly stringing together protein molecules into a filament that extends out until it reaches the egg. But instead of describing this as an innocuous process of assembly and attachment, the group wrote—in a pioneering paper that otherwise points out the egg's ability to actively "clasp" and "entwine"—that the sperm's filament "shoots out and harpoons" the egg. Likewise, when a researcher at the Roche Institute of Molecular Biology in Nutley, New Jersey, wrote in 1987 of his discovery that mouse eggs carry a molecular structure on their coating that fits inside a complementary structure on the sperm, helping bind the two together, he described the two structures, naturally enough, as a lock and key—but he called the egg's protruding structure the lock and the sperm's engulfing structure the key.

11   Martin doesn't suggest that these researchers willfully distorted their imagery. In fact, she notes that one of the investigators at Johns Hopkins was her politically correct husband, Richard Cone. What's more, Martin concedes that she herself was slow to recognize the disparity between the discoveries at Johns Hopkins and the way the findings were written up. "It didn't strike me for a few years," she says. But innocent or not, she adds, the cultural conditioning these biologists had absorbed early in their careers influenced more than their writing: it skewed their research. "I believe, and my husband believes, and the lab believes, that they would have seen these results sooner if they hadn't had these male-oriented images of sperm. In fact, biologists could have figured out a hundred years ago

---

2   a piece of lab apparatus made from glass and designed to measure, transfer, and absorb fluids

that sperm are weak forward-propulsion units, but it's hard for men to accept the idea that sperm are best at escaping. The imagery you employ guides you to ask certain questions and to not ask certain others."

12   People preparing to dismiss Emily Martin as a humorless feminist have their work cut out for them. At once animated and easygoing in her cramped, cactus-strewn office, Martin chuckles as she goes through an inch-thick file of hapless-egg and macho-sperm imagery clipped from magazines. (In one Gary Larson cartoon, a housewife egg fends off a swarm of sperm trying to get past her by posing as phone repairmen, insurance salesmen, and UPS deliverymen.) "I just think this stuff is a riot," she says. In fact, it's the biologists who seem a little stuffy. Though she usually lectures to students, Martin recalls one lecture she gave to biologists at the Woods Hole Oceanographic Institution in 1990. "It was one of the most painful experiences of my life," she says. "I had gotten to the point where the audience is usually rolling in the aisles, and all I got was stony silence. I could see they were furious. On the other hand, I can understand their feelings; I get defensive when someone criticizes cultural anthropology."

13   One researcher who doesn't bristle at Martin's jabs is Scott Gilbert, a developmental biologist at Swarthmore College. Though he suggests Martin may go a little overboard in stressing the egg's aggressiveness—for example, he prefers to think of the egg as "engaging in a dialog" with the sperm rather than gluing it down—he does believe her views are a vast improvement over the conventional explanation. "Most studies clearly show that the sperm is attracted by the egg and activated by it," says Gilbert. "But if you don't have an interpretation of fertilization that allows you to look at the egg as active, you won't look for the molecules that can prove it. You simply won't find activities that you don't visualize."

14   Now that the discrepancy between experiment and interpretation is being brought out into the open, the professional literature seems to be coming around—although a recent issue of the biology journal *Cell Differentiation and Development* placed on its cover a Prince Charming sperm delivering a wake-up kiss to a long-eyelashed Sleeping Beauty egg. As for the popular press, Gilbert and Martin cite the same recent example as particularly egregious[3]: an article titled "Sperm Wars" that appeared as a cover story in a national science magazine whose name you'd recognize in a minute, which referred to the sperm cell as "a formidable .00024-inch weapon, tipped with a chemical warhead" (see DISCOVER, July 1991). On the other hand, *Developmental Biology*, the most popular college textbook in its subject area, takes great pains to point out the new, equal opportunity view of fertilization. No wonder: Gilbert wrote it.

15   One reason the older interpretation is dying hard is that it tends to be self-reinforcing, not only in suggesting ready-made imagery that can skew observations but also in subtly determining who becomes a biologist in the first place. "This business has stopped certain people from entering the field," says Gilbert. "Why would a woman want to continue if people are telling her she's passive?"

16   Nevertheless, as Martin points out, a growing number of women *are* continuing in biology. But that won't guarantee more evenhanded interpretations. "Scientific training involves a rigorous socialization process that doesn't allow for

---

3   conspicuous for bad taste or quality

different perspectives," she says. "It's hard to say that women biologists are any less guilty of these things than men."

17   Even if biologists do move away from the passive-egg myth, other images are waiting in the wings. These days, says Martin, researchers seem ready to confer a "spider woman" aspect on the egg. "Men have always turned to spider imagery when they are confronted with women who acquire power," she charges. Indeed, her file of magazine clippings contains several images in support of her claim. One striking example: the cartoonish silhouette employed as the emblem of the once-popular *Charlie's Angels* television series, which depicts the three starring female characters, guns and all, unmistakably merged into the eight-limbed shape of a spider.

18   Though Martin is the first to insist that much of the fertilization imagery is good for a laugh, she doesn't mean to let scientists dismiss it all as a big joke. "People say, 'Oh, what difference does it make?' as if this stuff doesn't affect anyone," she says. "But our culture *is* affected by these powerful visual images. We all put so much faith in science, and so much of the negative load lands on women."

19   She notes, as another example, that it's been known since the 1960s that women exposed to toxic chemicals bear children who run a higher risk of serious medical problems. Those findings reinforced the cultural notion that women should be sheltered, and some companies have rules to prevent women of reproductive age from working at jobs that might involve exposure to these chemicals. But only in the past few years have comparable studies shown that men exposed to high levels of lead, vinyl chloride, and about a dozen other chemicals also have children who are at higher risk. "It's the notion of invulnerable sperm," she claims, "that made it take so long for scientists and the public to accept the male role in birth defects and infertility."

20   Martin has recently shifted her focus to metaphors used in other areas of medical research. For example, she says, "when AIDS was seen as affecting only the 'dregs' of society, scientists described it as a monkey virus. Now that well-to-do white women are getting it, all of a sudden researchers are talking about AIDS being an autoimmune disease." There are, of course, other reasons that researchers' language might change, including a growing knowledge of how the AIDS virus in fact wreaks havoc on the host's immune system. Martin is still studying the literature and observing researchers in immunology labs. For now, she concedes, "all you can do is raise a question. It's often impossible to prove causality."

21   Although she is no longer studying fertilization imagery, Martin still lectures on the topic because, she contends, "the work shows that science can have social effects. When we anthropomorphize[4] the egg and sperm, when we turn them into a miniature bride and groom complete with personalities, what effect does this have on abortion legislation? These effects aren't intended by scientists, but they happen. They blend moral and scientific issues together in a way that makes me want to stand up and say something."

22   There's further irony in the traditional metaphors. The notion of fiercely battling, competitive sperm suggests that they're battling each other in a "race" to the egg. In fact, says Cone, they have a hard time making their way through the mucus glop, and like a team of bicyclists they "take turns" up front parting strands of

---

4   attribute human form or personality to animals or things

mucus. So in a sense sperm are cooperative. The egg, on the other hand, is the real competitive loner. Only one matures each month, and the one out in front suppresses the maturation of all the others. The macho image of sperm not only obscures this reality; it actually reverses what's been observed.

23　　Can biased metaphors be eliminated from science? Martin doesn't think so. Even if they could be, she doesn't think that antiseptically neutral language would be desirable. Metaphor is, after all, a powerful vehicle for creative thinking. "The goal shouldn't be to clean the imagery out," she says, "but to be aware that it's there." It also helps, she adds, to be able to take a joke. "Humor takes away the sting," she says, "along with the potential for inculcating harmful ideas."

Neil Bissoondath

Trinidad/Canada 1955–

At the age of eighteen, Neil Bissoondath emigrated from his native Trinidad to Canada, where he went to York University, earned a B.A., and became a teacher. Bissoondath's stories and essays focus on the cultural mix of Canada and the economic and social problems that are often linked to its multiculturalism. His critique, *Selling Illusions: The Cult of Multiculturalism in Canada*, from which "Marginalization" is taken, focuses on the controversies central to multicultural policy in Canada.

Marginalization　1994

1　One never really gets used to the conversation. It will typically go something like this:

"What nationality are you?"
"Canadian."
"No, I mean, what nationality are you *really*?"

There is probably not a person who has emigrated to Canada from a hot, moist country who has not been asked: "Why in the world did you come here, to this cold and beachless land, from *such a beautiful place?*" It is a question simplistic in the asking; it assumes so much. But it is also a question breath-taking in the response; it ignores so much.

2　　Your first thought, as you take a deep breath, is: What does this person, fantasizing about perpetual sunstroke, want to hear? A cry of desperation? *Yes! Yes! God, why have I done this to myself?*

3　　Your second thought is: Don't you read the newspapers? Don't you know what's happening in the world?

4　　And your third thought, in growing desperation, is: Where do I begin?

5   No obvious point of departure offers itself because you know that your reasons for leaving "such a beautiful place" are so complex that your questioner would require a whirlwind tour of history, politics and economics all mixed together with a healthy dose of reality. So you simply plunge ahead, hastily tossing out words—depending on where you come from—like "political corruption," "torture," "violence," "murder," "oppression," and you watch your questioner's eyes glaze over, his gaze grow distant, his face tighten into a barely restrained scepticism. He has seen tourist posters, he has watched "Travel, Travel" on television, he subscribes to *National Geographic*. And you know that your words are competing hopelessly in his head with stylized visions of sun, sea and sand, that your version of reality cannot hope to vanquish the Tropics à la Club Med.

6   Should you manage to complete your answer—and more often than not the reception proves too disheartening halfway through—you frequently run into the stunningly unanswerable: "Yes, but we have all that in Canada, too...."

7   You nod, despite the obscenity of the remark which, in its ignorance, in its heartlessness, devalues so much Third World pain, so much Third World struggle; for to reject this assertion is to lose all hope of convincing your questioner that, in coming here, you have immeasurably improved your lot—and it is suddenly vital that you do so. You need to narrow that gap; you need to prove that your decision to move here was neither whimsical nor erroneous. Yes, you agree, there is political corruption in Canada, and violence and murder—isn't there everywhere?—and the native peoples may have something to say about oppression and torture of a kind, but.... You offer the merest of acknowledgements, for, in the end, the conversation is really about the weather.

8   So you talk about growing up in the hot, moist country. You talk about the heat and the humidity and the sensation of physical oppression. You tell of sitting and reading and, with no greater physical exertion, of sweating like a pig. You tell of laboured breathing, of your energy drained and the soporific effect of the air itself. You dramatize: A hurricane hit the island once ...

9   But winter! comes the response. All that snow, all that slush, the bite of the wind on your nose, ears, teeth: the endless inhumanity of it all!

10   You reveal your perversity: You enjoy winter. No, you don't ski, you haven't quite managed to get the hang of skating, you don't even enjoy watching hockey. But you need less sleep during the winter months, your concentration improves, your productivity goes up, your sense of well-being is sweetened.

11   But you can't go outside in shorts and a T-shirt the way you can in "your" country ...

12   There's no point in explaining that Canada is now your country—you have been distanced from the beginning, seen merely as some exoticism on two legs—so you remark that to go outside in "my" country is often to enter a sunlight strong enough to crisp your skin, a heat so powerful it causes you to shiver even as it sucks your strength out through your pores. So, if you can afford it, you prefer to stay indoors, shut off from the sweltering world in a room defined by shadows and the hum of an air-conditioner.

13   But isn't winter equally imprisoning? Who wants to go out into a world that resembles a freezer gone wild?

14   The point, though, is that with the proper clothing you can, whereas the portable air-conditioner has not yet been invented.

15   But for your questioner, caressing images of coconut trees swaying in the breeze, all of this is beside the point. He has been to the Bahamas or Jamaica or Cuba; he has experienced life in the islands, life lived on the sand.

16   And this is the crux of the problem. Experiencing the tropics only as a two-week visitor, passport and return air-ticket safely tucked away in a pocket, he can afford to speculate on the leavened delights of life in tropical zones. But you grew up there, you consider the experience from a rather different point of view. So the simplistic question brings two completely opposed visions hurtling towards one another. Yet you pursue the answer because the question itself is mildly insulting; it assumes your philosophy of life and your urge to accomplishment are sufficiently shallow that you would choose your country of residence based on mere meteorology.

17   So, despite the beauty left behind, you look fondly on the blowing snow, the frigid wind and the treacherous ice of February. You smile to yourself, you smile at your questioner, for you know that all this, even with its challenge, is symbolic of a greater freedom than you have ever known.

18   Your questioner smiles back and, after a moment of silence, asks what food people eat in "your" country.

19   Pizza, you say. Big Macs, Kentucky Fried Chicken … To be simply Canadian, untinged by the exoticism of elsewhere, seems insufficient, even unacceptable, to many other Canadians. The fact clearly stems, in part, from the simple human attraction to the exotic. But it seems to me that it also has much to do with a wider issue: the uncertainty we feel as a people.

20   We reveal this uncertainty in a variety of ways, including our newly minted concern for traditions, but particularly through that quintessential (and possibly eternal) Canadian question: Who are we? The usual answer—"Well, we're not like the Americans …"—is insufficient: a self-perception cast in the negative can never satisfy (although it can obsess: in John Robert Colombo's *The Dictionary of Canadian Quotations*, "Canada" requires fewer than nine columns while "Canada & the United States" fills more than seventeen).

21   Nor might we be pleased by the impression offered of Canada by Naipaul's Nazruddin[1]: "I felt the place was a hoax. They thought they were part of the West, but really they had become like the rest of us who had run to them for safety. They were like people far away, living on other people's land and off other people's brains, and that was all they thought they should do. That was why they were so bored and dull."

22   American novelist Alison Lurie's take is more personal: "[H]e wasn't hateful, or cruel, or cold-hearted, or neurotic. But he seemed to be … I don't know … a Canadian."

23   There are many visions of us, many answers to that question of who we are, some complimentary, some critical. And so, ourselves lacking a full and vigorous response ("A Canadian," the English essayist J.B. Priestley once remarked, "is lost when he asks himself what a Canadian is.") we search for distinctiveness—exoticism—wherever we can find it. And we find it most readily in our compatriots most recently arrived.

---

1   Nazruddin is a character in V.S. Naipaul's *A Bend in the River.*

24   For people I think of as "professional ethnics"—they who enjoy the role of the exotic and who depend on their exoticism for a sense of self—this is not an unpleasant state of affairs. But for those who would rather be accepted for their individuality, who resent being distinguished only by their differences, it can prove a matter of some irritation, even discomfort. The game of exoticism can cut two ways: it can prevent an individual from being ordinary, and it can prevent that same individual from being accepted.

25   Trudi Hanley, a twenty-one-year-old black woman who works in a field—modelling—where exoticism can reasonably be expected to be an advantage, once spoke to a reporter of the excuses used by those reluctant to hire her: "My nose was too big. I was too black. I was too different. We have enough ethnics. I heard them all."

26   But the finest example of this exclusion remains the sprinter Ben Johnson. Within a shattering twenty-four-hour period in Seoul, Korea, Mr. Johnson was transformed in media reports from being the Canadian who had won Olympic gold through effort to the Jamaican immigrant who had lost it through use of drugs. The only thing swifter than Mr. Johnson's drug-enhanced achievement was his public demotion from "one of us" to "one of them." The exotic multicultural concept of the everlasting immigrant has come to function as an institutional system for the marginalization of the individual: Ben Johnson was, in other words, a Canadian when convenient, an immigrant when not. Had he, success or failure, been accepted as being simply Canadian and not "Jamaican-Canadian," it would have been difficult for anyone to distance him in this way.

27   Thus the weight of the multicultural hyphen, the pressure of the link to exoticism, can become onerous—and instead of its being an anchoring defini-tion, it can easily become a handy form of estrangement. Dr. John Polanyi, born elsewhere, is the *Canadian* Nobel-prize-winning chemist. Michael Ondaatje, born elsewhere, is the *Canadian* Booker-prize-winning novelist. Valery Fabrikant, born elsewhere, is the *Russian émigré* murderer.

28   This hyphen, even when it is there in spirit only, is a curious beast. It appears to mean so much and is yet so often indicative of so little.

29   Ali Sharrif, a Somali immigrant who freelances for *NOW* magazine in Toronto, began wondering why the city's black community had failed to come to the aid of Somalis in conflict with long-time residents of six apartment buildings in Toronto. He telephoned a man identified only as a "well-known Toronto black activist" and was told, "You see, it's hard to place the Somalis. They really are not black in the true sense of the word." He explained that the black community in North America saw Somalis and other people from the Horn of Africa as Muslims and Arabs first, Africans second. Somalis, who to those without the distinguishing eye bear a strong resemblance to Ethiopians, are Muslims but not Arabs, Africans but not black, and in Metro Toronto they find acceptance and support difficult to obtain. Sharrif ends his article on a note that is part plaintive, part angry: "Most of the Somalis I know, casual acquaintances and friends, really want to be part of the black community. But their fate might be that they are considered black, but not black enough to be really black."

30   Too much of this, not enough of that: it is a problem. There are people of African descent, born in the Caribbean, immigrants to Canada, who describe themselves as African-Canadians, a phrase now deemed more acceptable than

"coloured" or even "black." Yet I cannot help wondering how, say, former South African president F.W. de Klerk would be described should events force him to flee his country for a Canadian haven: would he too be an African-Canadian? And what about, say, Muammar al-Qaddafi? Libya too is in Africa. I am uncertain, then, as to the precise meaning of phrases such as African-Canadian or Italian-Canadian or Greek-Canadian, particularly when applied to people whose experience of these foreign lands is most likely historical, touristic or anecdotal: what conclusions are to be drawn from them? Their principal effect, I would suggest, is not to define the word "Canadian" but to mark a distance from it, the hyphen that links them a sign of an acceptable marginalization.

31   If the questions of degree of race and ethnicity, and of that troublesome hyphen, unsettle me, it is because they strike close to home—as they strike close to home for the growing number of Canadians whose personal relationships entail a commingling of ethnicities. It is a realm that must be entered with care, for the very language we use is a minefield of offence.

32   One of my favourite *New Yorker* fillers—those little nuggets of linguistic curios with which the magazine rounds out its articles—concerned a U.S. newspaper that reported on the restructuring program instituted by a faltering company. Not only would the plan save jobs in the long run, the newspaper reported, but it was expected eventually to put the company's books back in the African-American.

33   Back in the *what?*

34   The newspaper subsequently ran a correction explaining that it had meant to say that the company's finances would be back in the—uhh—black. It blamed overzealousness on the part of a copy-editor.

35   The trend to more specific ethnic self-identification is a complex one. What is one to make, for instance, of Sir Peter Ustinov, he of the Russian surname, the British manner (Jacques Parizeau with a sense of humour and no chip on the shoulder) and a family history that ties together influences from Russia, Italy, France, Germany, Switzerland and, by virtue of a great-great-grandmother, Ethiopia (which may qualify him as a person of colour)?

36   A similar deconstruction would make of me an Indian-West-Indian (or, more accurately, an Indian-Trinidadian-West-Indian) by birth and an Indian-Trinidadian-West-Indian-Canadian by choice. My companion's ethnicity is less complex. She would be a Franco-Québécoise-Canadian (barring possible confirmation of a family legend that tells of an infusion of native blood somewhere in the distant past).

37   But what then of our daughter?

38   With her mixture of heritages, should she one day be asked to define her ethnicity, she would be obliged to take a deep breath before replying that she is "a Franco-Québécoise-First Nations-Indian-Trinidadian-West-Indian-Canadian." Or something of the sort. (I am assuming here that the actual order of the ethnicities is not subject to political considerations, but I may be wrong.) I do shudder, though, for the children she may one day have should she choose to have a family with someone of different but equally complex composition.

39   There is an interest here, it seems to me, in a certain simplicity, a simplicity that my daughter might find in moving away from an ethnic concept of self-definition (without abandoning the knowledge of it) towards a self-definition

based on her homeland. But, as I found out after the publication of an article I wrote on the subject, even the word "homeland" is problematic.

40   I had written in the article of the many young men, born and bred in Canada of parents from Croatia, who had returned to that unhappy land to take up arms in its defence. I was puzzled by their actions, concerned about the implications for Canada, saddened by the thought of young men eager to go off to war. The following week, a Montreal writer and editor named François Hébert penned a reply to my piece in which he defended the right of these young men to go to the aid of, as he put it, their homeland. I had not questioned their right, but what struck me in the reply was the defining of Croatia as the "homeland" of these young men.

41   My understanding of the word would have defined Croatia as the homeland of these young men's parents or grandparents, while their homeland would be Canada, the land of their birth and upbringing. I felt that to view their *ancestral* land as their homeland was to wilfully distance them, to make them marginal to the Canadian context. It was to define the belonging of others through the prism of one's own personal and political needs, in a way not very different from the historical view of that young woman on the phone-in show in Washington.

42   To consider the ancestral land as the true homeland is to risk engaging a dizzying absurdity, for it would mean that my homeland is India, a place I have never visited and have little wish to. It would mean that Lucien Bouchard's would be neither Quebec nor Canada but France; Brian Mulroney's would be Ireland, David Suzuki's Japan, Nino Ricci's Italy and so on. Only aboriginals, then, could claim Canada as their homeland—unless it is true that they happen to have migrated here thousands of years ago from another continent, in which case they're out of luck. And what is one to make of the homelands of people like Pierre-Marc Johnson, Claude Ryan, Jeanne Blackburn and others complicated by history?

43   And what of my daughter's homeland? Does she have two, India and France? How much time must go by, then, how many cultural changes are required, before one's homeland is no longer that of one's ancestors? Is there a moment when one stops being, in the eyes of others, an alien, an exile, an immigrant?

44   It seems to me vital that, as unfashionable or as outdated as it may seem in their rush both to claim and to impose narrow ethnicity and tribal exoticism, that my daughter should grow up to think of her homeland as simply Canada and of herself as simply Canadian. In this way, there will be no other "homeland" to which others can wilfully consign—and therefore distance—her, alienating her from the mainstream and thereby withholding her rightful place in the land of her birth.

45   There is also a strong element of marginalization in the Sikh-turban issue. The controversy of turbans in Legion halls and the RCMP is in itself an indication of the failure of multiculturalism programs to go beyond superficiality in explaining us to each other. To view the turban as just another kind of hat, with no significance beyond sheltering the head, is to say that a cross worn on a chain is of no significance beyond a decoration for the neck: it is to reveal a deep ignorance of the ways and beliefs of others. To ban either in any context is to revel in that ignorance and to alienate the wearer by rejecting an intimate and fundamental part of his or her self.

46   The marginalization to which we so easily subject one another comes frequently in times of economic hardship. The stresses of unemployment—the difficulty of the present and the unimaginable idea of a future—create a need for scapegoats: we need something or someone to blame. We can rail against politicians, taxes, corporations—but these are all distant, untouchable.

47   No one is more easily blamed for the lack of opportunity than the obvious "foreigner" cleaning tables in the local doughnut shop or serving behind the counter at McDonald's. Maybe he has brown skin, maybe he speaks with an accent: clearly he is out of place here, filling a paid position that should by rights have gone to a "real" Canadian. All differences, always so close to the surface, are seized upon, turned into objects of ridicule and resentment, the psychology of exoticism once more cutting both ways.

48   Encouraging people to view each other as simply Canadian, discouraging the use of the marginalizing hyphen, would not solve such problems—humans, in times of fear and anger, have a unique ability for seeking out bull's-eyes in each other—but it might help deflect some of the resentment, so that in expressing our pain we do not also alienate our fellow citizens. Differences between people are already obvious enough without their being emphasized through multiculturalism policy and its growing cult of racial and ethnic identity.

Ann Hodgman

U.S.A. 1956–

Ann Hodgman is best known for her work with *Spy* magazine and on children's books. She lives in Washington, Connecticut, and writes regularly for the on-line magazine *Salon*. Forty children's books, two cookbooks, and a number of humour books are testimony to her prodigious writing ability. With co-authors Lise Birnbach and Patty Marx, she has written a series of books sharing the common title, *1,003 Great Things About....* She also plays goal on a women's hockey team. This essay was first published in *Spy* in June 1989, and was included in *Best American Essays*, 1990. Its unusual premise attracts and holds the attention of readers; after an initial sense of revulsion, we learn startling realities about the pet food industry.

No Wonder They Call Me a Bitch   1989

1   I've always wondered about dog food. Is a Gaines-burger really like a hamburger? Can you fry it? Does dog food "cheese" taste like real cheese? Does Gravy Train actually make gravy in the dog's bowl, or is that brown liquid just dissolved crumbs? And exactly what *are* by-products?

2   Having spent the better part of a week eating dog food, I'm sorry to say that I now know the answers to these questions. While my dachshund, Shortie,

watched in agonies of yearning, I gagged my way through can after can of stinky, white-flecked mush and bag after bag of stinky, fat-drenched nuggets. And now I understand exactly why Shortie's breath is so bad.

3   Of course, Gaines-burgers are neither mush nor nuggets. They are, rather, a miracle of beauty and packaging—or at least that's what I thought when I was little. I used to beg my mother to get them for our dogs, but she always said they were too expensive. When I finally bought a box of cheese-flavored Gaines-burgers—after twenty years of longing—I felt deliciously wicked.

4   "Dogs love real beef," the back of the box proclaimed proudly. "That's why Gaines-burgers is the only beef burger for dogs with real beef and no meat by-products!" The copy was accurate: meat by-products did not appear in the list of ingredients. Poultry by-products did, though—right there next to preserved animal fat.

5   One Purina spokesman told me that poultry by-products consist of necks, intestines, undeveloped eggs and other "carcass remnants," but not feathers, heads, or feet. When I told him I'd been eating dog food, he said, "Oh, you're kidding! Oh, *no!*" (I came to share his alarm when, weeks later, a second Purina spokesman said that Gaines-burgers *do* contain poultry heads and feet—but *not* undeveloped eggs.)

6   Up close my Gaines-burger didn't much resemble chopped beef. Rather, it looked—and felt—like a single long, extruded piece of redness that had been chopped into segments and formed into a patty. You could make one at home if you had a Play-Doh Fun Factory.

7   I turned on the skillet. While I waited for it to heat up I pulled out a shred of cheese-colored material and palpated it. Again, like Play-Doh, it was quite malleable. I made a little cheese bird out of it; then I counted to three and ate the bird.

8   There was a horrifying rush of cheddar taste, followed immediately by the dull tang of soybean flour—the main ingredient in Gaines-burgers. Next I tried a piece of red extrusion. The main difference between the meat-flavored and cheese-flavored extrusions is one of texture. The "cheese" chews like fresh Play-Doh, whereas the "meat" chews like Play-Doh that's been sitting out on a rug for a couple of hours.

9   Frying only turned the Gaines-burger black. There was no melting, no sizzling, nor warm meat smells. A cherished childhood illusion was gone. I flipped the patty into the sink, where it immediately began leaking rivulets of red dye.

10   As alarming as the Gaines-burgers were, their soy meal began to seem like an old friend when the time came to try some *canned* dog foods. I decided to try the Cycle foods first. When I opened them, I thought about how rarely I use can openers these days, and I was suddenly visited by a long-forgotten sensation of can-opener distaste. *This* is the kind of unsavory place can openers spend their time when you're not watching! Every time you open a can of, say, Italian plum tomatoes, you infect them with invisible particles of by-product.

11   I had been expecting to see the usual homogenous scrapple inside, but each can of Cycle was packed with smooth, round, oily nuggets. As if someone at Gaines had been tipped off that a human would be tasting the stuff, the four Cycles really were different from one another. Cycle-1, for puppies, is wet and soyish. Cycle-2, for adults, glistens nastily with fat, but it's passably edible—a lot like some canned Swedish meatballs I once got in a Care package at college.

Cycle-3, the "lite" one, for fatties, had no specific flavor; it just tasted like dog food. But at least it didn't make me fat.

12 Cycle-4, for senior dogs, had the smallest nuggets. Maybe old dogs can't open their mouths as wide. This kind was far sweeter than the other three Cycles— almost like baked beans. It was also the only one to contain "dried beef digest," a mysterious substance that the Purina spokesman defines as "enzymes" and my dictionary defined as "the products of digestion."

13 Next on the menu was a can of Kal Kan Pedigree with Chunky Chicken. Chunky *chicken?* There were chunks in the can, certainly—big, purplish-brown chunks. I forked one chunk out (by now I was becoming more callous) and found that while it had no discernible chicken flavor, it wasn't bad except for its texture—like meat loaf with ground-up chicken bones.

14 In the world of canned dog food, a smooth consistency is a sign of low quality—lots of cereal. A lumpy, frightening, bloody, stringy horror is a sign of high quality—lots of meat. Nowhere in the world of wet dog foods was this demonstrated better than in the fanciest I tried—Kal Kan's Pedigree Select Dinners. These came not in a can but in a tiny foil packet with a picture of an imperious Yorkie. When I pulled open the container, juice spurted all over my hand, and the first chunk I speared was trailing a long gray vein. I shrieked and went instead for a plain chunk, which I was able to swallow only after taking a break to read some suddenly fascinating office equipment catalogues. Once again, though, it tasted no more alarming than, say, canned hash.

15 Still, how pleasant it was to turn to *dry* dog food! Gravy Train was the first I tried, and I'm happy to report that it really does make a "thick, rich, real beef gravy" when you mix it with water. Thick and rich, anyway. Except for a lingering rancid-fat flavor, the gravy wasn't beefy, but since it tasted primarily like tap water, it wasn't nauseating either.

16 My poor dachshund just gets plain old Purina Dog Chow, but Purina also makes a dry food called Butcher's Blend that comes in Beef, Bacon & Chicken flavors. Here we see dog food's arcane semiotics at its best: a red triangle with a *T* stamped into it is supposed to suggest beef; a tan curl, chicken; and a brown *S,* a piece of bacon. Only dogs understand these messages. But Butcher's Blend does have an endearing slogan: "Great Meaty Tastes—without bothering the Butcher!" *You know, I wanted to buy some meat, but I just couldn't bring myself to bother the butcher...*

17 Purina O.N.E. ("Optimum Nutritional Effectiveness") is targeted at people who are unlikely ever to worry about bothering a tradesperson. "We chose chicken as a primary ingredient in Purina O.N.E. for several reasonings," the long, long essay on the back of the bag announces. Chief among these reasonings, I'd guess, is the fact that chicken appeals to people who are—you know—*like us.* Although our dogs do nothing but spend eighteen-hour days alone in the apartment, we still want them to be *premium* dogs. We want them to cut down on red meat, too. We also want dog food that comes in a bag with an attractive design, a subtle typeface, and no kitschy pictures of slobbering golden retrievers.

18 Besides that, we want a list of Nutritional Benefits of our dog food—and we get it on O.N.E. One thing I especially like about this list is its constant references to a dog's "hair coat," as in "Beef tallow is good for the dog's skin and hair coat."

(On the other hand, beef tallow merely provides palatability, while the dried beef digest in Cycle provides palatability *enhancement.)*

19   I hate to say it, but O.N.E. was pretty palatable. Maybe that's because it has about 100 percent more fat than, say, Butcher's Blend. Or maybe I'd been duped by the packaging; that's been known to happen before.

20   As with people, dog snacks taste much better than dog meals. They're better looking, too. Take Milk-Bone Flavor Snacks. The loving-hands-at-home prose describing each flavor is colorful; the writers practically choke on their exuberance. Of bacon they say, "It's so good your dog will think it's hot off the frying pan." Of liver: "The only taste your dog wants more than liver—is even more liver!" Of poultry: "All those warm fresh flavors deliciously mixed in one biscuit. Your dog will bark with delight!" And of vegetable: "Gardens of taste! Specially blended to give your dog that vegetable flavor he wants—but can rarely get!"

21   Well, I may be a sucker, but advertising *this* emphatic just doesn't convince me. I lined up all seven flavors of Milk-Bone Flavor Snacks on the floor. Unless my dog's palate is a lot more sensitive than mine—and considering that she steals dirty diapers out of the trash and eats them, I'm loath to think it is—she doesn't detect any more difference in the seven flavors than I did when I tried them.

22   I much preferred Bonz, the hard-baked, bone-shaped snack stuffed with simulated marrow. I liked the bone part, that is; it tasted almost exactly like the cornmeal it was made of. The mock marrow inside was a bit more problematic: in addition to looking like the sludge that collects in the treads of my running shoes, it was bursting with tiny hairs.

23   I'm sure you have a few dog food questions of your own. To save us time, I've answered them in advance.

24   *Q: Are those little cans of Mighty Dog actually branded with the sizzling word?*
A: You should know by now that that kind of thing never happens.
Q: Does chicken-flavored dog food taste like chicken-flavored cat food?
A: To my surprise, chicken cat food was actually a little better—more chickeny. It tasted like inferior canned pâté.
Q: Was there any dog food that you just couldn't bring yourself to try?
A: Alas, it was a can of Mighty Dog called Prime Entree with Bone Marrow. The meat was dark, dark brown, and it was surrounded by gelatin that was almost black. I knew I would die if I tasted it, so I put it outside for the raccoons.

Drew Hayden Taylor

Canada 1962–

Drew Hayden Taylor grew up on the Curve Lake Reserve near Peterborough, Ontario. He went to Seneca College, where he earned an honours diploma in broadcasting, and then began a career in journalism and what he describes as the "television mines, writing scripts for *The Beachcombers*, *Street Legal*, and *North of Sixty*." Taylor has written four plays and several collections of essays, often using humour in his storytelling, as in the piece that follows. In this essay,

Taylor manages to derive comedy and social irony from a subject another writer might have approached only with serious intent; we are constantly surprised by the reactions he provokes in us.

Pretty Like a White Boy: The Adventures of a Blue Eyed Ojibway 1992

1 In this big, huge world, with all its billions and billions of people, it's safe to say that everybody will eventually come across personalities and individuals that will touch them in some peculiar yet poignant way. Individuals that in some way represent and help define who you are. I'm no different, mine was Kermit the Frog. Not just because Natives have a long tradition of savouring Frogs' legs, but because of his music. If you all may remember, Kermit is quite famous for his rendition of 'It's Not Easy Being Green'. I can relate. If I could sing, my song would be 'It's Not Easy Having Blue Eyes in a Brown Eyed Village'.

2 Yes, I'm afraid it's true. The author happens to be a card-carrying Indian. Once you get past the aforementioned eyes, the fair skin, light brown hair, and noticeable lack of cheekbones, there lies the heart and spirit of an Ojibway storyteller. Honest Injun, or as the more politically correct term may be, honest aboriginal.

3 You see, I'm the product of a white father I never knew, and an Ojibway woman who evidently couldn't run fast enough. As a kid I knew I looked a bit different. But, then again, all kids are paranoid when it comes to their peers. I had a fairly happy childhood, frolicking through the bullrushes. But there were certain things that, even then, made me notice my unusual appearance. Whenever we played cowboys and Indians, guess who had to be the bad guy, the cowboy.

4 It wasn't until I left the Reserve for the big bad city that I became more aware of the role people expected me to play, and the fact that physically I didn't fit in. Everybody seemed to have this preconceived idea of how every Indian looked and acted. One guy, on my first day of college, asked me what kind of horse I preferred. I didn't have the heart to tell him 'hobby'.

5 I've often tried to be philosophical about the whole thing. I have both white and red blood in me, I guess that makes me pink. I am a 'Pink' man. Try to imagine this, I'm walking around on any typical Reserve in Canada, my head held high, proudly announcing to everyone 'I am a Pink Man'. It's a good thing I ran track in school.

6 My pinkness is constantly being pointed out to me over and over and over again. 'You don't look Indian?' 'You're not Indian, are you?' 'Really?!?' I got questions like that from both white and Native people, for a while I debated having my Status card tattooed on my forehead.

7 And like most insecure people and specially a blue eyed Native writer, I went through a particularly severe identity crisis at one point. In fact, I admit it, one depressing spring evening, I dyed my hair black. Pitch black.

8 The reason for such a dramatic act, you may ask? Show Business. You see, for the last eight years or so, I've worked in various capacities in the performing arts, and as a result I'd always get calls to be an extra or even try out for an important

role in some Native oriented movie. This anonymous voice would phone, having been given my number, and ask if I would be interested in trying out for a movie. Being a naturally ambitious, curious, and greedy young man, I would always readily agree, stardom flashing in my eyes and hunger pains from my wallet.

9   A few days later I would show up for the audition, and that was always an experience. What kind of experience you may ask? Picture this, the picture calls for the casting of seventeenth-century Mohawk warriors living in a traditional long-house. The casting director calls the name 'Drew Hayden Taylor' and I enter.

10   The casting director, the producer, and the film's director look up from the table and see my face, blue eyes flashing in anticipation. I once was described as a slightly chubby beachboy. But even beachboys have tans. Anyway, there would be a quick flush of confusion, a recheck of the papers, and a hesitant 'Mr. Taylor?' Then they would ask if I was at the right audition. It was always the same. By the way, I never got any of the parts I tried for, except for a few anonymous crowd shots. Politics tells me it's because of the way I look, reality tells me it's probably because I can't act. I'm not sure which is better.

11   It's not just film people either. Recently I've become quite involved in Theatre, Native theatre to be exact. And one cold October day I was happily attending the Toronto leg of a province-wide tour of my first play, *Toronto at Dreamer's Rock*. The place was sold out, the audience very receptive and the performance was wonderful. Ironically one of the actors was also half white.

12   The director later told me he had been talking with the actor's father, an older Non-Native type chap. Evidently he had asked a few questions about me, and how I did my research. This made the director curious and he asked about his interest. He replied 'He's got an amazing grasp of the Native situation for a white person.'

13   Not all these incidents are work related either. One time a friend and I were coming out of a rather upscale bar (we were out YUPPIE watching) and managed to catch a cab. We thanked the cab driver for being so comfortably close on such a cold night, he shrugged and nonchalantly talked about knowing what bars to drive around. 'If you're not careful, all you'll get is drunk Indians.' I hiccuped.

14   Another time this cab driver droned on and on about the government. He started out by criticizing Mulroney, and eventually to his handling of the Oka crisis. This perked up my ears, until he said 'If it were me, I'd have tear-gassed the place by the second day. No more problem.' He got a dime tip. A few incidents like this and I'm convinced I'd make a great undercover agent for one of the Native political organizations.

15   But then again, even Native people have been known to look at me with a fair amount of suspicion. Many years ago when I was a young man, I was working on a documentary on Native culture up in the wilds of Northern Ontario. We were at an isolated cabin filming a trapper woman and her kids. This one particular nine-year-old girl seemed to take a shine to me. She followed me around for two days both annoying me and endearing herself to me. But she absolutely refused to believe that I was Indian. The whole film crew tried to tell her but to no avail. She was certain I was white.

16   Then one day as I was loading up the car with film equipment, she asked me if I wanted some tea. Being in a hurry I declined the tea. She immediately smiled with victory crying out 'See, you're not Indian, all Indians drink tea!'

17   Frustrated and a little hurt I whipped out my Status card and thrust it at her. Now there I was, standing in a Northern Ontario winter, showing my Status card to a nine-year-old non-status Indian girl who had no idea what one was. Looking back, this may not have been one of my brighter moves.

18   But I must admit, it was a Native woman that boiled everything down in one simple sentence. You may know that woman, Marianne Jones from 'The Beachcombers' television series. We were working on a film together out west and we got to gossiping. Eventually we got around to talking about our respective villages. Hers on the Queen Charlotte Islands, or Haida Gwaii as the Haida call them, and mine in central Ontario.

19   Eventually childhood on the Reserve was being discussed and I made a comment about the way I look. She studied me for a moment, smiled, and said 'Do you know what the old women in my village would call you?' Hesitant but curious, I shook my head. 'They'd say you were pretty like a white boy.' To this day I'm still not sure if I like that.

20   Now some may argue that I am simply a Métis with a Status card. I disagree, I failed French in grade 11. And the Métis as everyone knows have their own separate and honourable culture, particularly in western Canada. And of course I am well aware that I am not the only person with my physical characteristics.

21   I remember once looking at a video tape of a drum group, shot on a Reserve up near Manitoulin Island. I noticed one of the drummers seemed quite fairhaired, almost blond. I mentioned this to my girlfriend at the time and she shrugged saying 'Well, that's to be expected. The highway runs right through the Reserve.'

22   Perhaps I'm being too critical. There's a lot to be said for both cultures. For example, on the left hand, you have the Native respect for Elders. They understand the concept of wisdom and insight coming with age.

23   On the white hand, there's Italian food. I mean I really love my mother and family but seriously, does anything really beat good Veal Scallopini? Most of my aboriginal friends share my fondness for this particular brand of food. Wasn't there a warrior at Oka named Lasagna? I found it ironic, though curiously logical, that Columbus was Italian. A connection I wonder?

24   Also Native people have this wonderful respect and love for the land. They believe they are part of it, a mere chain in the cycle of existence. Now, as many of you know, this conflicts with the accepted Judeo-Christian i.e. western view of land management. I even believe somewhere in the first chapters of the Bible it says something about God giving man dominion over Nature. Check it out, Genesis 4:?, 'Thou shalt clear cut.' So I grew up understanding that everything around me is important and alive. My Native heritage gave me that.

25   And again, on the white hand, there's breast implants. Darn clever them white people. That's something Indians would never have invented, seriously. We're not ambitious enough. We just take what the Creator decides to give us, but no, not the white man. Just imagine it, some serious looking white man, and let's face it people, we know it was a man who invented them, don't we? So just imagine some serious looking white doctor sitting around in his laboratory muttering to himself, 'Big tits, big tits, hmm, how do I make big tits?' If it was an Indian, it would be 'Big tits, big tits, white women sure got big tits' and leave it at that.

26   So where does that leave me on the big philosophical scoreboard, what exactly are my choices again; Indians—respect for elders, love of the land. White people—food and big tits. In order to live in both cultures I guess I'd have to find an Indian woman with big tits who lives with her grandmother in a cabin out in the woods and can make Fettuccini Alfredo on a wood stove.

27   Now let me make this clear, I'm not writing this for sympathy, or out of anger, or even some need for self-glorification. I am just setting the facts straight. For as you read this, a new Nation is born. This is a declaration of independence, my declaration of independence.

28   I've spent too many years explaining who and what I am repeatedly, so as of this moment, I officially secede from both races. I plan to start my own separate nation. Because I am half Ojibway, and half Caucasian, we will be called the Occasions. And I of course, since I'm founding the new nation, will be a Special Occasion.

Naomi Klein

Canada 1971–

Born in Montreal, Naomi Klein's book *No Logo: Taking Aim at the Brand Bullies* (2000), from which "Threats and Temps" is taken, has turned Klein into an international spokesperson for anti-globalization. *No Logo* was awarded the Canadian National Business Book Award, and France's Le Prix Médiations. She has followed up *No Logo* with *Fences and Windows: Dispatches from the Front Lines of the Globalization Debate* (2002), a collection of her recent essays on globalization. After publishing *Fences and Windows*, Klein launched the Fences and Windows Fund, a non-profit organization for resisting privatization and corporatization. Klein's work has appeared in *The Globe and Mail*, *The Guardian*, *The Nation*, *The New Statesman*, *Newsweek*, *The New York Times*, *The Village Voice*, and *Ms. Magazine*. *No Logo* has been translated into sixteen languages.

Threats and Temps:
From Working for Nothing to "Free Agent Nation"   2000

1   A sense of impermanence is blowing through the labor force, destabilizing everyone from office temps to high-tech independent contractors to restaurant and retail clerks. Factory jobs are being outsourced, garment jobs are morphing into homework, and in every industry, temporary contracts are replacing full, secure employment. In a growing number of instances, even CEOs are opting for shorter stints at one corporation after another, breezing in and out of different corner offices and purging half the employees as they come and go.

2   Almost every major labor battle of the decade has focused not on wage issues but on enforced casualization, from the United Parcel Service workers' stand against "part-time America" to the unionized Australian dockworkers fighting their replacement by contract workers, to the Canadian autoworkers at Ford and Chrysler striking against the outsourcing of their jobs to non-union factories. All these stories are about different industries doing variations on the same thing: finding ways to cut ties to their workforce and travel light. The underbelly of the shiny "brands, not products" revelation can be seen increasingly in every workplace around the globe. Every corporation wants a fluid reserve of part-timers, temps and freelancers to help it keep overheads down and ride the twists and turns in the market. As British management consultant Charles Handy says, savvy companies prefer to see themselves as "organizers" of collections of contractors, as opposed to "employment organizations:" One thing is certain: offering employment—the steady kind, with benefits, holiday pay, a measure of security and maybe even union representation—has fallen out of economic fashion.

Branded Work: Hobbies, Not Jobs

3   Though an entire class of consumer-goods companies has transcended the need to produce what it sells, so far not even the most weightless multinational has been able to free itself entirely from the burden of employees. Production may be relegated to contractors, but clerks are still needed to sell the brand-name goods at the point of purchase, especially given the growth of branded retail. In the service industry, however, big-brand employers have become artful at dodging most commitments to their employees, expertly fostering the notion that their clerks are somehow not quite legitimate workers, and thus, do not really need or deserve job security, livable wages and benefits.

4   Most of the large employers in the service sector manage their workforce as if their clerks didn't depend on their paychecks for anything essential, such as rent or child support. Instead, retail and service employers tend to view their employees as children: students looking for summer jobs, spending money or a quick stopover on the road to a more fulfilling and better paying career. These are great jobs, in other words, for people who don't really need them. And so the mall and the superstore have given birth to a ballooning subcategory of joke jobs—the frozen-yogurt jerk, the Orange Julius juicer, the Gap greeter, the Prozac-happy Wal-Mart "sales associate"—that are notoriously unstable, low-paying and overwhelmingly part-time.

5   What is distressing about this trend is that over the past two decades, the relative importance of the service sector as a source of jobs has soared. The decline in manufacturing, as well as the waves of downsizing and cutbacks in the public sector, have been met by dramatic growth in the numbers of service-sector jobs to the extent that services and retail now account for 75 percent of total U.S. employment. Today, there are four and a half times as many Americans selling clothes in specialty and, department stores as there are workers stitching and weaving them, and Wal-Mart isn't just the biggest retailer in the world, it is also the largest private employer in the United States.

. . . . .

6   ...Laurie Bonang, who works at Starbucks in Vancouver, British Columbia, told me that "people our age are finally realizing that we get out of university, we're a zillion dollars in debt, and we're working in Starbucks. This isn't how we want to spend the rest of our lives, but for right now the dream job isn't waiting for us anymore.... I was hoping that Starbucks would be a stepping stone to bigger and better things, but unfortunately it's a stepping stone to a big sinkhole."

7   As Bonang told her story, she was painfully aware that she is living out one of the most hackneyed pop-culture clichés of our branded age: this is the stuff of *Saturday Night Live*'s "Gap Girls" skit, circa 1993, in which bored, underemployed mall chicks ask each other: "Didja cinch it?" Or of the Starbucks "baristas" who rattle off long trains of coffee adjectives—grande-decaf-low-fat-moccacino—in movies like *You've Got Mail*....

8   McDonald's and Starbucks staff, meanwhile, frequently earn less than the employees of single-outlet restaurants and cafés, which explains why McDonald's is widely credited for pioneering the throwaway "McJob" that the entire fast-food industry has since moved to emulate. At Britain's McLibel Trial, in which the company contested claims made by two Greenpeace activists about its employment practices, international trade unionist Dan Gallin defined a McJob as "a low skill, low pay, high stress, exhausting and unstable job." Though the activists on trial for libel were found guilty on several counts, in his verdict Chief Justice Rodger Bell ruled that in the matter of McJobs the defendants had a point. The chain has had a negative impact on food-service wages as a whole, he wrote, and the allegation that McDonald's "pays its workers low wages, helping to depress wages for workers in the catering trade in Britain has been proved to be true. It is justified."

9   ...The brand-name multinationals have freed themselves of the burden of providing employees with a living wage. In the malls of North America and England, on the high street, in the food court and at the superstore, they have managed a similar trick. In some cases, particularly in the garment sector, these retailers are the very same companies that are doing business in the export processing zones, meaning that their responsibilities as employers have been sharply reduced at both the production and service ends of the economic cycle. Wal-Mart and the Gap, for instance, contract out their production to EPZs dotting the Southern Hemisphere, where goods are produced mostly by women in their teens and twenties who earn minimum wage or less and live in cramped dorm rooms. Those goods—sweatshirts, baby clothes, toys and Walkmans—are then sold by another workforce, concentrated in the North, which is also largely filled with young people earning approximately minimum wage, most in their teens and early twenties.

10   Though in many ways it is indecent to compare the relative privilege of retail workers at the mall with the abuse and exploitation suffered by zone workers, there is an undeniable pattern at work. In general, the corporations in question have ensured that they do not have to confront the possibility that adults with families are depending on the wages that they pay, whether at the mall or in the zone. Just as factory jobs that once supported families have been reconfigured in the Third World as jobs for teenagers, so have the brand-name clothing companies and restaurant chains given legitimacy to the idea that fast-food and retail-sector jobs are disposable, and unfit for adults.

. . . . .

11   The fact is that the economy needs steady jobs that adults can live on. And it's clear that many people would stay in retail if it paid adult rates the proof being that when the sector does pay decently, it attracts older workers, and the rate of staff turnover falls in line with the rest of the economy. But at the large chains, which seem at least for now to have bottomless resources to build superstores and to sink millions into expanding and synergizing their brands, the idea of paying a living wage is rarely considered. At Borders, where most clerks earn wages in line with other bookstore chains but below the retail average, company president Richard L. Flanagan wrote a letter to all his clerks, addressing the question of whether Borders could pay a "living wage" as opposed to what it reportedly pays now—between US$6.63 and $9.27 an hour. "While the concept is romantically appealing," he wrote, "it ignores the practicalities and realities of our business environment."

12   Much of what makes paying a living wage seem so "romantic" has to do with … rapid expansion. For companies whose business plans depend upon becoming dominant in their market before their nearest competitor beats them to it, new outlets come before workers—even when those workers are a key part of the chain's image. "They expect us to look like a Gap ad, professional, clean and neat all the time, and I can't even pay to do laundry," says Laurie Bonang of Starbucks. "You can buy two grande mocha cappuccinos with my hourly salary." Like millions of her demographic coevals on the payrolls of all-star brands like the Gap, Nike and Barnes & Noble, Bonang is living inside a stunning corporate success story—though you'd never know it from the resignation and anger in her voice. All the brand-name retail workers I spoke with expressed their frustration at helping their stores rake in, to them, unimaginable profits, and then having to watch that profit get funneled into compulsive expansion. Employee wages, meanwhile, stagnate or even decline. At Starbucks in British Columbia new workers faced an actual wage decrease—from Can$7.50 to $7 an hour—during a period when the chain was doubling its profits and opening 350 new stores a year. "I do the banking. I know how much the store pulls in a week," Laurie Bonang says. "They just take all that revenue and open up new stores."

13   Borders clerks also maintain that wages have suffered as a result of rapid growth. They say that their chain used to be a more equitable place to work before the neck-and-neck race with Barnes & Noble took over corporate priorities; there was a profit-sharing program and a biannual 5 percent raise for all workers. "Then came expansion and corresponding cuts," reads a statement from disgruntled employees at a downtown Philadelphia outlet of Borders. "Profit sharing was dropped, raises were cut…"

14   In sharp contrast to the days when corporate employees took pride in their company's growth, seeing it as the result of a successful group effort, many clerks have come to see themselves as being in direct competition with their employers' expansion dreams. "If Borders opened thirty-eight new stores a year instead of forty," reasoned Jason Chappell, sitting next to Brenda Hilbrich on the vinyl seats of our deli booth, "they could afford to give us a nice wage increase. On average it costs $7 million to open a superstore. That's Borders' own figures.…"

15   "But," Brenda interrupted, "if you say that directly to them, they say, 'Well, that's two markets we don't get into."

16   "We have to saturate markets," Chappell said, nodding.

17 "Yeah," Brenda added. "We have to compete with Barnes & Noble."

18 The retail clerks employed by the superchains are only too familiar with the manic logic of expansion.

BUSTING THE McUNION

19 The need to prevent workers from weighing too heavily on the bottom line is the main reason that the branded chains have fought off the recent wave of unionization with such ferocity. McDonald's, for instance, has been embroiled in bribery scandals during German union drives, and over the course of a 1994 union drive in France, ten McDonald's managers were arrested for violating labor laws and trade-union rights. In June 1998, the company fired the two young workers who organized the strike in Macedonia, Ohio. In 1997, when the employees at a Windsor, Ontario, Wal-Mart were about to hold an election on joining a union, a series of not-so-subtle management hints led many workers to believe that if they voted yes their store would be shut down. The Ontario Labour Relations Board reviewed the process and found that the behavior of Wal-Mart managers and supervisors before the vote amounted to "a subtle but extremely effective threat," which caused "the average reasonable employee to conclude that the store would close if the union got in."

20 Other chains have not hesitated to make good on the threat to close. In 1997, Starbucks decided to shut down its Vancouver distribution plant after workers unionized. In February 1998, just as a union certification for a Montreal-area outlet of McDonald's was being reviewed by the Quebec Labour Commission, the franchise owner closed down the outlet. Shortly after the closure, the labor commission accredited the union—cold comfort, since no one works there anymore. Six months later, another McDonald's restaurant was successfully unionized, this one a busy outlet in Squamish. British Columbia, near the Whistler ski resort. The organizers were two teenage girls, one sixteen, the other seventeen. It wasn't about wages, they said—they were just tired of being scolded like children in front of the customers. The outlet remains open, making it the only unionized McDonald's in North America, but at the time of writing, the company was on the verge of having the union decertified. Fighting the battle on the public-relations front, in mid-1999 the fast-food chain launched an international television campaign featuring McDonald's workers serving up shakes and fries under the captions "future lawyer," "future engineer" and so on. Here was the true McDonald's workforce, the company seemed to be saying: happy, contented and just passing through.

. . . . .

21 It is one of the paradoxes of service-sector employment that the more prominent a role it plays in the labor landscape, the more casual service-sector companies became in their attitude toward providing job security. Nowhere is this more in evidence than in the industry's increasing reliance on part-timers. Starbucks, for instance, staffs its outlets almost exclusively with part-timers while only one-third of Kmart's workforce is full-time. Workers at the ill-fated Montreal-area McDonald's cited as their principal reason for unionization the fact that they often couldn't get shifts longer than three hours.

22   In the U.S. the number of part-timers has tripled since 1968, while in Canada, between 1975 and 1997, the growth rate of part-time jobs was nearly three times the rate of full-time jobs. But the problem is not the part-time nature of work per se. In Canada, only one-third of part-timers want but cannot find full-time jobs (which is an increase from one-fifth in the late eighties). In the U.S., only one-quarter want full-time jobs but can't find them. The vast majority of part-timers are students and women, many of whom are juggling childcare and paid work.

· · · · ·

23   Starbucks has been the most innovative in the modern art of supple scheduling. The company has created a software program called Star Labor that allows head office maximum control over the schedules of its clerks down to the minute. With Star Labor, gone is anything as blunt and imprecise as a day or evening shift. The software measures exactly when each latte is sold and by whom, then tailor-makes shifts—often only a few hours long—to maximize coffee-selling efficiency. As Laurie Bonang explains, "They give you an arbitrary skill number from one to nine and they plug in when you're available, how long you've been there, when customers come in and when we need more staff, and the computer spits out your schedule based on that." While Starbucks' breakthrough in "just-in-time" frothing looks great on a spreadsheet, for Steve Emery it meant hauling himself out of bed to start work at 5 a.m., only to leave at 9:30 a.m. after the morning rush had peaked and, according to Star Labor, he was no longer working at maximum efficiency. Wal-Mart has introduced a similar centralized scheduling system, effectively reducing employee hours by pinning them precisely to in-store traffic. "It's done just like we order merchandise," says Wal-Mart CEO David Glass.

· · · · ·

24   Some service-sector companies have made much of the fact that they offer stock options or "profit-sharing" to low-level employees, among them Wal-Mart, which calls its clerks "sales associates"; Borders, which refers to them as "co-owners"; and Starbucks, which prefers the term "partners." Many employees do appreciate these gestures, but others claim that while the workplace democracy schemes sparkle on a corporate Web site, they rarely translate into much of substance. Most part-time workers at Starbucks, for instance, can't afford to buy into the employee stock-option program since their salaries barely cover their expenses. And where profit-sharing schemes are automatic, as at Wal-Mart, workers say their "share" of the $118 billion of annual sales their company hauls in is laughable. Clerks in the Windsor, Ontario, outlet of Wal-Mart, for example, say they only saw an extra $70 during the first three years that their store was open. "Never mind that from the viewpoint of the boardroom, the pension plan's best feature was that it kept 28 million more shares in firm control of company executives," writes *The Wall Street Journal's* Bob Ortega of the Wal-Mart plan. "Most workers *perceived* that they could cash in, so the cost of the plan paid off in spades by helping keep the unions out and the wages low" (italics his).

· · · · ·

Temps: The Rented Worker

25   Rick the Temp isn't just the Great White Hope for unpaid interns. He also represents the pinnacle of another subcategory of New Age workers: the temps. And temps, it must be said, need all the hope they can get. The use of temp labor in the U.S. has increased by 400 percent since 1982 and that growth has been steady. Annual industry revenue among American temp firms has increased by about 20 percent every year since 1992, with the firms pulling in revenues of $58.7 billion in 1998. The mammoth international temp agency Manpower Temporary Services rivals Wal-Mart as the largest private employer in the U.S. According to a 1997 study, 83 percent of the fastest-growing American companies are now outsourcing jobs they once hired people to perform—compared with 64 percent just three years before. In Canada, the Association of Canadian Search, Employment & Staffing Services estimates that more than 75 percent of businesses use the services of the $2 billion Canadian temp industry.

26   The most dramatic growth, however, is taking place not in North America but in Western Europe, where temp agencies are among Europe's fastest-growing companies. In France, Spain, the Netherlands and Germany, hiring workers on long-term temporary contracts has become a well-trampled back entranceway to the labor market, allowing employers to sidestep tough laws that provide generous employee benefits and make firing without just cause far more difficult than in the United States. France, for instance, has become the second-largest temp-services market after the U.S., making up 30 percent of worldwide temp revenue. And though temping accounts for only 2 percent of all the country's jobs, according to France's labor minister, Martine Aubry, "86 per cent of new hires are on short-term contracts." Manpower Europe, an outpost of the U.S.-based temp firm, saw its revenue in Spain jump a staggering 719 percent in just one year, from $6.1 million in 1996 to $50 million in 1997. Italy didn't legalize temp agencies until 1997, but when it did, Manpower Europe rushed in to open thirty-five offices in 1998.

27   Every day, 4.5 million workers are assigned to jobs through temp agencies in Europe and the U.S., but since only 12.5 percent of temps are placed on any given day, the real number of total temporary employees in Europe and the U.S. is closer to 36 million people. More significant than soaring numbers, however, is a major shift under way in the nature of the temporary work industry. Temp agencies are no longer strictly in the business of farming out rent-a-receptionists when the secretary calls in sick. For starters, temps are no longer all that temporary: in the U.S., 29 percent stay at the same posting for a year or more. Their agencies, meanwhile, have become full-service human resource departments for all your no-commitment staffing needs, including accounting, filing, manufacturing and computer services. And according to Bruce Steinberg, director of research at the U.S.-based National Association of Temporary and Staffing Services, "a quiet evolution is taking place throughout the staffing services industry"—rather than renting out workers, the agencies are "providing a complete service solution." What that means is that more companies are contracting out entire functions and divisions—work previously performed in-house—to outside agencies charged not only with staffing but, like the contract factories in the export processing zones, administration and maintenance of the task as well. For instance, in 1993

American Airlines outsourced the ticket counters at twenty-eight U.S. airports to outside agencies. Around 550 ticketing-agent jobs went temp and, in some cases, workers who had earned $40,000 were offered their same jobs back for $16,000. A similar reshuffling took place when UPS decided to turn over its customer-service centers to outside contractors—5,000 employees earning $10 to $12 an hour were replaced with temps earning between $6.50 and $8.

. . . . .

"FREE AGENT NATION"

. . . . .

28   Tom Peters's latest management-guru idea is that just as companies must reach branding nirvana by learning to let go of manufacturing and employment, so must individual workers empower themselves by abandoning the idea of being employees. According to this logic, if we are to be successful in the new economy, all of us must self-incorporate into our very own brand—a Brand Called You. Success in the job market will only come when we retrofit ourselves as consultants and service providers, identify our own Brand You equities and lease ourselves out to targeted projects that will in turn increase our individual portfolio of "braggables." "I call the approach Me Inc.," Peters writes. "You're Chairperson/CEO/Entrepreneur-in-Chief of your own professional service firm." Faith Popcorn, the management guru who came to prominence with her 1991 best-seller, *The Popcorn Report*, goes so far as to recommend that we change our names to better "click" with our carefully designed and marketed brand image. *She* did—her name used to be Faith Plotkin.

29   Even more than Popcorn or Peters, however, it is a man named Daniel H. Pink who is the dean at Brand You U. Pink has seen the growth in temporary and contract work, as well as the rise in self-employment, and has declared the arrival of "Free Agent Nation." Not only is he writing a book by that title, but Pink himself is a proud patriot of the nation. After quitting a prestigious White House job as Al Gore's chief speechwriter, Pink went on a journey in search of fellow "free agents": people who had chosen a life of contracts and freelance gigs over bosses and benefits. What he found, as he relayed in a cover article in *Fast Company*, was the sixties. The citizens of Pink's nation are marketing consultants, headhunters, copywriters and software designers who are all striving to achieve a Zen-like balance of work and personal life. They practice their yoga positions and play with their dogs in their wired home offices, while earning more money—by jumping from one contract to the next—than they did when they were tied to one company and paid a fixed salary. "This is the summer of love revisited, man!" we hear from Bo Rinald, an agent representing a thousand freelance software developers in Silicon Valley. For Pink's free agents, the end of jobs is the baby-boomer dream come true: free-market capitalism without neckties; dropped out of the corporate world in body but plugged-in in spirit. Everyone knows that you can't be a cog in the machine if you work from your living room....

30   A younger—and, of course, hipper—version of Free Agent Nation was articulated in a special work issue of *Details* magazine. For Gen-Xers with MBAs, the future of work is apparently filled with stunningly profitable snowboarding businesses, video-game companies and cool-hunting firms. "Opportunity Rocks!"

crowed the headline of an article that laid out the future of work as a nonstop party of extreme self-employment: "Life without jobs, work without bosses, money without salaries, lives without limits." According to the writer, Rob Lieber, "The time of considering yourself an 'employee' has passed. Now it's time to start thinking of yourself as a service provider, hiring out your skills and services to the highest, or most interesting, bidder."

31   …On the whole, casualization pans out as the worst of both worlds: monotonous work at lower wages, with no benefits or security, and even less control over scheduling.

32   The bottom line is that the advantages and drawbacks of contract and contingency work have a simple correlation to the class of the individuals doing the work: the higher up they are on the income scale, the more chance they have to leverage their comings and goings. The further down they are, the more vulnerable they are to being yanked around and bargained even lower. The top 20 percent of wage earners tend to more or less maintain their high wages whether they are in full-time jobs or on freelance contracts. But according to a 1997 U.S. study, 52 percent of women in nonstandard work arrangements are being paid "poverty-level wages"—compared with only 27.6 percent in the full-time female worker population being paid those low wages. In other words, most nonstandard workers aren't members of Free Agent Nation. According to the study, "58.2 per cent are in the lowest quality work arrangements—jobs with substantial pay penalties and few benefits relative to full-time standard workers." Furthermore, the real wages of temp workers in the U.S. actually went down, on average, by 14.7 percent between 1989 and 1994. In Canada, nonpermanent jobs pay one-third less than permanent jobs, and 30 percent of nonpermanent employees work irregular hours. Clearly, temping puts the most vulnerable workforce further at risk, and no matter what *Details* says, it doesn't rock.

33   Moreover, there is a direct cause-and-effect relationship between the free agents skipping and hopping on the top rungs of the corporate ladder, and the agents hanging off the bottom who have been "freed" of such pesky burdens as security and benefits. Nobody is more liberated, after all, than the CEOs themselves, who, like Nike's cabal of Über-athletes, have formed their own Dream Team to be traded back and forth between companies whenever some star power is needed to boost Wall Street morale. Temp CEOs, as writer Clive Thompson calls them, now shuttle from multinational to multinational, staying for an average term of only five years, collecting multimillion-dollar incentive packages on the way in, and multimillion-dollar golden handshakes on the way out. "Companies are changing executives like baseball managers," says John Challenger, executive vice president of the outplacement firm Challenger, Gray & Christmas. "The replacement will typically arrive like a SWAT team and sweep out the old and restaff with his or her own people." When "Chainsaw" Al Dunlap was appointed CEO of Sunbeam in July 1996, Scott Graham, an analyst at Oppenheimer & Co., commented, "This is like the Lakers signing Shaquille O'Neal."

34   The two extreme poles of workplace transience … work together like a global seesaw. Since the CEO superstars earn their reputation on Wall Street through such kamikaze missions as auctioning off their company's entire manufacturing base or initiating a grandiose merger that will save millions of dollars in job duplication, the more mobile the CEOs become, the more unstable the position

of the broader workforce will be. As Daniel Pink points out, the word "freelance" is derived from the age when mercenary soldiers rented themselves—and their lances—out for battle. "The free lancers roamed from assignment to assignment— killing people for money." Granted it's a little dramatic, but it's not a half-bad job description for today's free-agent executives. In fact, it is the precise reason CEO salaries skyrocketed during the years that layoffs were at their most ruthless. Ira T. Kay, author of *CEO Pay and Shareholder Value*, knows why. Writing in *The Wall Street Journal*, Kay points out that the exorbitant salaries American companies have taken to paying their CEOs is a "crucial factor making the U.S. economy the most competitive in the world" because without juicy bonuses company heads would have "no economic incentive to face up to difficult management decisions, such as layoffs." In other words, as satirist Wayne Grytting retorted, we are "supporting those executive bonuses so we can get … fired."

35   It's a fair enough equation, particularly in the U.S. According to the AFL-CIO, "the CEOs of the 30 companies with the largest announced layoffs saw their salaries, bonuses, and long-term compensation increase by 67.3 per cent." The man responsible for the most layoffs in 1997—Eastman Kodak CEO George Fisher, who cut 20,100 jobs—received an options grant that same year estimated to be worth $60 million. And the highest-paid man in the world in 1997 was Sanford Wiell, who earned $230 million as head of the Travelers Group. The first thing Wiell did in 1998 was announce that Travelers would merge with Citicorp, a move that, while sending stock prices soaring, is expected to throw thousands out of work. In the same spirit, John Smith, the General Motors chairman [who implemented] those 82,000 job cuts … received a $2.54 million bonus in 1997 that was tied to the company's record earnings.

36   There are many others in the business community who, unlike Ira T. Kay, are appalled by the amounts executives have been paying themselves in recent years. In Business *Week*, Jennifer Reingold writes with some disgust, "Good, bad, or indifferent, virtually anyone who spent time in the corner office of a large public company in 1997 saw his or her net worth rise by at least several million." For Reingold, the injustice lies in the fact that CEOs are able to collect raises and bonuses even when their company's stock price drops and shareholders take a hit. For instance, Ray Irani, CEO of Occidental Petroleum, collected $101 million in compensation in 1997, the same year that the company lost $390 million.

37   This camp of market watchers has been pushing for CEO remuneration to be directly linked to stock performance; in other words, "You make us rich, you get a healthy cut. But if we take a hit, then you take one too." Though this system protects stockholders from the greed of ineffective executives, it actually puts ordinary workers at even greater risk, by creating direct incentives for the quick and dirty layoffs that are always sure to rally stock prices and bring on the bonuses. For instance, at Caterpillar—the model of the incentive-driven corporation—executives get paid in stocks that have consistently been inflated by massive plant closures and worker wage rollbacks. What is emerging out of this growing trend of tying executive pay to stock performance is a corporate culture so damaged that workers must often be fired or shortchanged for the boss to get paid.

38   This last point raises the most interesting question of all, I think, about the long-term effect of the brand-name multinationals' divestment of the jobs business. From Starbucks to Microsoft, from Caterpillar to Citibank, the correlation

between profit and job growth is in the process of being severed. As Buzz Hargrove, president of the Canadian Auto Workers, says. "Workers can work harder, their employers can be more successful, but—and downsizing and outsourcing are only one example—the link between overall economic success and the guaranteed sharing in that success is weaker than ever before." We know what this means in the short term: record profits, giddy shareholders and no seats left in business class. But what does it mean in the slightly longer term? What of the workers who fell off the payroll, whose bosses are voices on the phone at employment agencies, who lost their reason to take pride in their company's good fortune? Is it possible that the corporate sector, by fleeing from jobs, is unwittingly pouring fuel on the fire of its own opposition movement?

Short Fiction

Introduction to Short Fiction

Why do we read stories? Is it because we remember being read to as children and our joy in that experience? Is it because it is the cheapest way to take a trip, to travel to another world and spend time there with other people? Or do we simply enjoy guessing where a story will go and seeing if we are right? Whatever the reason, people have been reading stories in one form or another for centuries and are likely to go on reading them for many more.

The short story belongs to the genre of fiction. When we read a story, therefore, we are experiencing it as a shaped or created narrative whose design is intended to help us experience life more richly, more completely. Almost always, a story will comment, directly or obliquely, on the nature of the world we live in.

As we become more experienced readers of stories, we should also acquire a fuller and more critical language we can apply to stories to articulate our understanding of them. That vocabulary requires us first to break a story into its parts (the basic task of analysis), but we should not forget, while we are conducting our analysis, that a story communicates to us as a whole and that breaking it into parts is something we do simply for convenience. The intention behind analyzing the elements of stories is always to make us better readers of whole stories.

The first element of a story that engages us is the **plot**. Every reader wants to know what happens next. In fact, some stories engage us on only that level; for that reason, we are disinclined to reread a mystery until we have had enough time to forget the plot's details. We may define plot as the sequence of actions that compose the story, with a beginning and an end and a number of actions in between. Some contemporary fiction has abandoned this traditional form, but, for our purposes, let us assume that a plot is a sequence of events. There are a number of ways to analyze plot.

In her story "Happy Endings," Margaret Atwood focuses on the element of plot and how changing a plot affects the characters and other elements of the story. In effect, Atwood is attacking plot as one of the most obvious elements of narration when she cynically suggests at the end of her story that plot is "just one thing after another, a what and a what and a what." Inadvertently, even though she suggests that the supporting elements of "how and why" are more important to a story, with "Happy Endings," she does illustrate how altering the events in a plotline changes the basic elements of the characters themselves and how, even when an author may not change the nature of the characters, a change in events does have a strong impact on the characters, the theme, and all else in the story. In effect, she has inadvertently illustrated the interdependency of the elements of fiction.

Aristotle gave us an approach when he defined plot as the arrangement of incidents and suggested that a plot traced a completed change in the central character. He went further and said that the change could happen on the level of situation, character, or thought, meaning that the central character's fortune could improve or decline (situation), his or her character could be altered for good or ill (character), or his or her understanding of the world could be revised (thought). Therefore, we can classify plots as plots of action, character, or thought according to the nature of the change accomplished by the plot. Using this approach requires us to ask:

- Has the central character experienced a change because of the action?
- Can we describe that change as occurring principally on the level of situation? of character? of thought?
- Can we therefore describe this plot as an action plot? a character plot? a thought plot?

A second approach to plot, the mythological approach, draws from the assumption that there are no new plots, that every "new" plot is, in fact, a reworking of an existing plot. The premise of this approach is that all the primary plot forms are available to us in the mythologies of earlier cultures. For Western readers, the main mythological sources are the Greek, Roman, and Norse myths; they furnish us with what Jung would call the archetypal forms of plots. In this approach, we need to ask which archetypal plot form is buried in the plot we are reading. Is "The Birthmark" an initiation plot? Something else? The mythological critic asks us to read plots for their resemblance to the archetypal experiences we read about in myths.

A third approach to plot sees it as a contest between a protagonist and an antagonist. Generally, the protagonist (meaning "positive agent/actor") is human, but the antagonist ("negative agent") may or may not be. Once the contest (or "agon") is complete, the story is over. It is also possible to have an open ending, where the resolution of the contest is unclear or undecided. The contest view of plot is sometimes described as having three forms of competition or conflict: human versus nature, human versus human, and human versus self. Clearly, it is most applicable to a plot that has a clear contest in it. Yet the definition of contest may not be as simple as we initially think. Who or what is the antagonist in "The Boat"? "The Birthmark"?

Besides plot, we respond equally to **character** as a primary part of any story; indeed, one definition of plot is "character in action." As we begin to read a story, we focus on the people in it and on what they are doing. Essentially, we learn about any character in one of five ways.

The first avenue of information about a **character** in a story is action. As Timothy Findley said in *The Wars*, "we are what we do." This category includes both action and reaction: we judge the characters in a story from both the acts they initiate and their reactions to acts initiated by others. What, for instance, do we infer from Miss Brill's final act in Katherine Mansfield's story of the same name? It is important to remember, as well, that a character's doing nothing, or responding passively, nevertheless reveals important dimensions about him or her.

A second external conduit of information about character is his or her physical presence and gestures. Often, a writer helps us to get to know a character by describing the character's body and dress and typical gestures.

A third external means of revealing character is through report—the statements other characters make about a character. When including these in our understanding of a fictional person, we must, of course, factor in the possibility of bias. Does the person reporting on the character have any reason to report inaccurately?

The fourth external means of describing character is through dialogue and scene. As characters interact, we are afforded a deeper glimpse into their motivation and personality. A few scenes in "A Good Man Is Hard to Find" are sufficient to convey to us fundamental differences between the grandmother and Bailey.

Fiction allows us a fifth channel of information about character denied us in life—access to the internal consciousness of a character. Either through a first-person or third-person selective omniscient point of view, the writer lets us enter a person's mind and know that person with an intimacy we could never expect to gain in reality. Joyce Carol Oates, in her story in this volume, allows us a penetrating view of why the anonymous protagonist chooses to return home at the end and what she has learned about the world from her brutal experience; that view is significantly enriched by first-person narration. The five channels of information about character in stories, therefore, let us know a story's characters extremely well.

There are some additional critical terms that aid us in gaining this understanding. The English writer E.M. Forster defined two character types: the round character and the flat character. A flat character is one who is not presented in depth; we get to know this character from only a few characteristics, and he or she lacks the capacity to surprise us. A round character, conversely, has psychological depth and substance, an ability to change in response to what she or he learns and experiences, and an ability to surprise us. There are two related terms applied to character in fiction that draw similar distinctions to the ones outlined in Forster's terms. Characters can be described as static or dynamic according to their ability to change.

Another dimension of stories is **point of view**. As a critical term, point of view means the angle of narration, or the way the story is told. Central to point of view is the issue of distance. When you read a story, a relationship is created among four centres. There is, first, the reader, yourself; you are reading about characters in a narrative. Second, there is the writer who created the narrative. The third centre is the narrator, who provides your window on the action, the means by which you are informed of what is happening. The fourth centre is the characters and their actions. They are the centre that you are principally interested in as you read the story. The key elements of distance are established by the writer's choice of an inside or an outside narrator; inside narrators place us close to characters, whereas outside narrators keep us at a distance. In the first case, our sympathy is strongly engaged; in the second, our judgement is given more emphasis.

Theoretically, a writer has three choices available when it comes to choosing a narrator for a story: first person, second person, and third person. For example, a story could begin "I walked to the door" (first person), "You walked to the door" (second person), or "She walked to the door" (third person).

A useful distinction to be made among these **narrative angles** is the difference between inside and outside narrators. First-person narrators are inside narrators because they must be *in* the story, as part of the action. This is an advantage and a disadvantage for the writer. Perhaps the major strength of inside narrators is the intimacy and drama they bring to the action and to our reception of that action. As we read, we literally become those narrators; their eyes and ears are ours, and what happens to them happens to us. Unconsciously, unless the writer does something to alienate us from the narrative speaker, we will identify with that speaker and extend him or her our sympathy. For this reason, inside narrators are generally not as reliable as outside narrators; because they are part of the action they describe, they are drawn frequently to interpret that action for us in a self-interested way. We must pay special attention to how far we can extend our trust to inside narrators.

The writer can also create two kinds of inside narrators—the witness narrator and the protagonist narrator. We see a witness narrator as more reliable because such a narrator is less intimately involved in the action and its outcome and is less inclined to be biased in presenting that action. The protagonist narrator, on the other hand, is more dramatic and more intimately involved in the action.

With an outside narrator, who is not directly involved in the action, reliability automatically increases, as does distance. We are further from the action because it is being filtered through an outside narrator. As a result, our judgement of what is happening is increased, and our sympathy for the characters is decreased. There are three kinds of outside narrators, and each reflects variations on narrative distance.

The omniscient narrator stays outside the action and thus retains complete freedom in space and time; the term "omniscient" captures this god-like position. Nineteenth-century writers sometimes participated directly in the story; for example, in "The Birthmark," Hawthorne sometimes appears to address us directly. This form is called editorial omniscience.

The limited omniscient narrator is still an outside narrator but one who can enter the consciousness of one or more characters. The limit to the number of characters whose consciousnesses are part of the narrative acts as a filter through which the story is generated. When we read in a story, "She walked to the door. She was still troubled by what had happened that morning and wondered whether she had done the right thing," we can immediately see the shift out of omniscient mode into limited omniscient; "She walked" is omniscient, whereas "She was still troubled" is limited omniscient because we have to be in the character's mind to know how she felt. The chief advantage of the limited omniscient option is that it supplies some of the intimacy of first-person narration in a third-person narrator. That advantage comes, however, at the cost of the narrator's ability to move freely through space and time and with the limitation of seeing only through a character or several characters.

Another option in the outside narrative mode is the objective, or camera, narrator. In this case, the writer accepts the limitation of a narrator who can report only physical observations, or what a camera would see if it were recording a scene. This form of narration is completely impersonal; we never enter a character's consciousness or share a judgement with the narrator. Instead, we build our understanding of the story from the physical reports we get on action, dialogue, and setting.

Point of view is therefore one of the key choices a writer makes in creating a narrative. That choice will dictate how close the reader feels to characters, how bound or free the narrator will be in relaying the story, and how reliable the narrator will appear to us. It may even influence the sequence of the action.

A further dimension of a story, the structure, is chiefly a product of the handling of time. Generally, the writer has three choices. A story can be told in linear time; in this case, the story begins at the beginning and moves forward in time until the capping action, as in "The Birthmark." A story can also be narrated *in medias res*. In this mode, the story starts in the middle or at some advanced point and employs flashbacks or other means of exposition to move us back in time and then up to the present, from which point it can proceed to its finish. Finally, the writer can start a story at the end, as in "The Boat," then take us back to the beginning and trace the way forward in time to the starting point. In each case, we should ask why the writer chose a particular structure and how that structure relates to the story's purpose or intent.

Stories also occur in a particular time and space, which leads us to another element of narratives, the **setting**. The setting of a story includes the physical dimensions of place and time. We should first ask whether the setting is strictly literal or whether it has symbolic dimensions. In the latter case, we should expect some clues from the writer that an element of setting has more than literal value, usually in the form of repetition or emphasis. Settings with symbolic value obviously pose a more sophisticated reading challenge. In many stories, however, one or more elements are symbolic, such as the boat and the kitchen window in "The Boat," Aylmer's lab in "The Birthmark," and the carved ivory rose in "To Set Our House in Order."

A second facet of setting is culture. Culture is a product of a society in a particular space and at a particular time. We will miss what is happening in "The Boarding House" if we fail to consider the culture of Dublin at the beginning of the twentieth century; in particular, we have to reconstruct the complex sexual politics of the time and consider the issues of class that bear on the story. If we do not understand this feature of the setting in Joyce's story, we will fail to understand who is seducing whom and for what reason. Setting, therefore, requires careful and critical reading from us as we try to understand a story.

But analysis is not enough; we cannot rest simply because we have looked carefully at the parts of a fiction and tried to understand the significance of each part. We must, in the end, return to **synthesis** and see the story as a whole, estimate its significance, and discover its meaning. The term **theme** is often employed to capture our sense of a story's overall purpose. While not an entirely satisfactory term, it does allow us to attempt a general statement about the central meaning of a story. If a theme is the unifying centre of a story, the end to which all the details point, we need to know how to express it and defend our interpretation.

First, we need to be able to distinguish between the subject and the theme of a story. Generally, articulating a theme means examining two elements, the subject of the story and the perspective on that subject created by the story. We cannot say that the theme of "The Boat" is guilt, for this statement isolates the subject but says nothing about the perspective on that subject created by the story. We need to add a second element, a description of the perspective on the subject that arises from reading the story. We can say, therefore, that the theme of "The Boat" is the paralyzing and incapacitating effects of guilt; now our statement has two parts, a subject and a position on that subject, the two parts required in a defensible theme.

Having arrived at a tentative statement of a story's theme, we need to test that statement and defend its validity. In doing so, it is useful to apply one of the following tests.

The first test is the principle of **economy**. This principle suggests that simpler explanations are preferable to more complex explanations, as long as they are able to offer a sufficient interpretation. Is there a simpler explanation? Does it offer as complete and satisfying an explanation as the first theme statement?

The second is the test of **comprehensiveness**. Such a test requires that the articulated theme be capable of explaining the role and contribution of all parts of the story, not just some parts. We can apply the test easily enough by selecting parts and asking if the theme statement we have chosen is able to explain that part.

A third test, similar to the second, is the test of **consistency**. Does the theme we have selected seem consistent with the title? with any and all symbols in the story? with the actions of each and every character? A theme must pass the consistency test to be defensible.

Finally, we might ask where we can find the theme of a story. Unfortunately, the answer is not a simple one. Authors do not simply select a theme and start writing. Authors just tell stories as well as they can; frequently, they are uncomfortable responding to a direct question about a story's "meaning."

Nevertheless, it is reasonable for us, as readers, to try to articulate what we took the central idea, purpose, or tension of a story to be. We can look at certain parts of a story for help. Titles are frequently helpful; writers select titles with care, knowing that the average reader will take the title as a pointer toward the story's significance. Beginnings and endings of stories also are emphatic positions and may offer some help by revealing a story's focus. Equally, central effects such as symbols or the actions of the protagonist at the story's end can be seen as pointers that assist the reader in understanding the theme of the work.

A second or third reading of a story will allow us to explore how the story was put together and how it exerted its force on us. And being critical and attentive readers, who are knowledgeable about the ways stories work, will allow us all of the joys of discovery that stories can bring.

Nathaniel Hawthorne

U.S.A. 1804–1864

Nathaniel Hawthorne was born in Salem, Massachusetts, on July 4; after spending his later childhood in Maine, he took his degree at Bowdoin College. *Twice-Told Tales*, which he published while in his mid-twenties, signalled the arrival of a major talent. Hawthorne is best known for his novel *The Scarlet Letter* (1850), though he wrote four others. Hawthorne's stories explore the dark legacy given American culture by the Puritans; here, through a subtle and complex use of symbolism and allegory, he sketches the steps by which Aylmer destroys the woman he loves in a misguided belief that she can be made perfect.

The Birthmark   1843

1   In the latter part of the last century there lived a man of science, an eminent proficient in every branch of natural philosophy, who not long before our story opens had made experience of a spiritual affinity more attractive than any chemical one. He had left his laboratory to the care of an assistant, cleared his fine countenance from the furnace smoke, washed the stain of acids from his fingers, and persuaded a beautiful woman to become his wife. In those days, when the comparatively recent discovery of electricity and other kindred mysteries of Nature seemed to open paths into the region of miracle, it was not unusual for the love of science to rival the love of woman in its depth and absorbing energy. The higher intellect, the imagination, the spirit, and even the heart might all find their congenial ailment in pursuits which, as some of their ardent votaries believed, would ascend from one step of powerful intelligence to another, until the philosopher should lay his hand on the secret of creative force and perhaps make new worlds for himself. We know not whether Aylmer possessed this degree of faith in man's ultimate control over Nature. He had devoted himself, however, too unreservedly to scientific studies ever to be weaned from them by any second passion. His love for his young wife might prove the stronger of the two; but it could only be by intertwining itself with his love of science and uniting the strength of the latter to his own.

2   Such a union accordingly took place, and attended with truly remarkable consequences and a deeply impressive moral. One day, very soon after their marriage, Aylmer sat gazing at his wife with a trouble in his countenance that grew stronger until he spoke.

3   "Georgiana," said he, "has it never occurred to you that the mark upon your cheek might be removed?"

4   "No, indeed," said she, smiling; but, perceiving the seriousness of his manner, she blushed deeply. "To tell you the truth, it has been so often called a charm that I was simple enough to imagine it might be so."

5   "Ah, upon another face perhaps it might," replied her husband; "but never on yours. No, dearest Georgiana, you came so nearly perfect from the hand of Nature that this slightest possible defect, which we hesitate whether to term a defect or a beauty, shocks me, as being the visible mark of earthly imperfection."

6   "Shocks you, my husband!" cried Georgiana, deeply hurt; at first reddening with momentary anger, but then bursting into tears. "Then why did you take me from my mother's side? You cannot love what shocks you!"

7   To explain this conversation it must be mentioned that in the centre of Georgiana's left cheek there was a singular mark, deeply interwoven, as it were, with the texture and substance of her face. In the usual state of her complexion— a healthy though delicate bloom—the mark wore a tint of deeper crimson, which imperfectly defined its shape amid the surrounding rosiness. When she blushed it gradually became more indistinct, and finally vanished amid the triumphant rush of blood that bathed the whole cheek with its brilliant glow. But if any shifting motion caused her to turn pale there was the mark again, a crimson stain upon the snow, in what Aylmer sometimes deemed an almost fearful distinctness. Its shape bore not a little similarity to the human hand, though of the smallest pygmy size. Georgiana's lovers were wont to say that some fairy at birth hour had laid her tiny hand upon the infant's cheek, and left this impress there in token of the magic endowments that were to give her such sway over all hearts. Many a desperate swain would have risked life for the privilege of pressing his lips to the mysterious hand. It must not be concealed, however, that the impression wrought by this fairy sign manual varied exceedingly, according to the difference of temperament in the beholders. Some fastidious persons—but they were exclusively of her own sex—affirmed that the bloody hand, as they chose to call it, quite destroyed the effect of Georgiana's beauty, and rendered her countenance even hideous. But it would be as reasonable to say that one of those small blue stains which sometimes occur in the purest statuary marble would convert the Eve of Powers[1] to a monster. Masculine observers, if the birthmark did not heighten their admiration, contented themselves with wishing it away, that the world might possess one living specimen of ideal loveliness without the semblance of a flaw. After his marriage—for he thought little or nothing of the matter before—Aylmer discovered that this was the case with himself.

8   Had she been less beautiful,—if Envy's self could have found aught else to sneer at,—he might have felt his affection heightened by the prettiness of this mimic hand, now vaguely portrayed, now lost, now stealing forth again and glimmering to and fro with every pulse of emotion that throbbed within her heart; but seeing her otherwise so perfect, he found this one defect grow more and more intolerable with every moment of their united lives. It was the fatal flaw of humanity which Nature, in one shape or another, stamps ineffaceably on all her productions, either to imply that they are temporary and finite, or that their perfection must be wrought by toil and pain. The crimson hand expressed the ineludible gripe in which mortality clutches the highest and purest of earthly mould, degrading them into kindred with the lowest, and even with the very brutes, like whom their visible frames return to dust. In this manner, selecting it

---

1   a statue of Eve in white marble sculpted by American artist Hiram Powers

as the symbol of his wife's liability to sin, sorrow, decay, and death, Aylmer's sombre imagination was not long in rendering the birthmark a frightful object, causing him more trouble and horror than ever Georgiana's beauty, whether of soul or sense, had given him delight.

9   At all the seasons which should have been their happiest he invariably, and without intending it, nay, in spite of a purpose to the contrary, reverted to this one disastrous topic. Trifling as it at first appeared, it so connected itself with innumerable trains of thought and modes of feeling that it became the central point of all. With the morning twilight Aylmer opened his eyes upon his wife's face and recognized the symbol of imperfection; and when they sat together at the evening hearth his eyes wandered stealthily to her cheek, and beheld, flickering with the blaze of the wood fire, the spectral hand that wrote mortality where he would fain have worshipped. Georgiana soon learned to shudder at his gaze. It needed but a glance with the peculiar expression that his face often wore to change the roses of her cheek into a deathlike paleness, amid which the crimson hand was brought strongly out, like a bas-relief of ruby on the whitest marble.

10   Late one night, when the lights were growing dim so as hardly to betray the stain on the poor wife's cheek, she herself, for the first time, voluntarily took up the subject.

11   "Do you remember, my dear Aylmer," said she, with a feeble attempt at a smile, "have you any recollection, of a dream last night about this odious hand?"

12   "None! none whatever!" replied Aylmer, starting; but then he added, in a dry, cold tone, affected for the sake of concealing the real depth of his emotion, "I might well dream of it; for, before I fell asleep, it had taken a pretty firm hold of my fancy."

13   "And you did dream of it?" continued Georgiana, hastily; for she dreaded lest a gush of tears should interrupt what she had to say. "A terrible dream! I wonder that you can forget it. Is it possible to forget this one expression?—'It is in her heart now; we must have it out!' Reflect, my husband; for by all means I would have you recall that dream."

14   The mind is in a sad state when Sleep, the all-involving, cannot confine her spectres within the dim region of her sway, but suffers them to break forth, affrighting this actual life with secrets that perchance belong to a deeper one. Aylmer now remembered his dream. He had fancied himself with his servant Aminadab, attempting an operation for the removal of the birthmark; but the deeper went the knife, the deeper sank the hand, until at length its tiny grasp appeared to have caught hold of Georgiana's heart; whence, however, her husband was inexorably resolved to cut or wrench it away.

15   When the dream had shaped itself perfectly in his memory, Aylmer sat in his wife's presence with a guilty feeling. Truth often finds its way to the mind close muffled in robes of sleep, and then speaks with uncompromising directness, of matters in regard to which we practise an unconscious self-deception during our waking moments. Until now he had not been aware of the tyrannizing influence acquired by one idea over his mind, and of the lengths which he might find in his heart to go for the sake of giving himself peace.

16   "Aylmer," resumed Georgiana, solemnly, "I know not what may be the cost to both of us to rid me of this fatal birthmark. Perhaps its removal may cause

cureless deformity; or it may be the stain goes as deep as life itself. Again: do we know that there is a possibility, on any terms, of unclasping the firm gripe of this little hand which was laid upon me before I came into the world?"

17   "Dearest Georgiana, I have spent much thought upon the subject," hastily interrupted Aylmer. "I am convinced of the perfect practicability of its removal."

18   "If there be the remotest possibility of it," continued Georgiana, "let the attempt be made at whatever risk. Danger is nothing to me; for life, while this hateful mark makes me the object of your horror and disgust,—life is a burden which I would fling down with joy. Either remove this dreadful hand, or take my wretched life! You have deep science. All the world bears witness of it. You have achieved great wonders. Cannot you remove this little, little mark, which I cover with the tips of two small fingers? Is this beyond your power, for the sake of your own peace, and to save your poor wife from madness?"

19   "Noblest, dearest, tenderest wife," cried Aylmer, rapturously, "doubt not my power. I have already given this matter the deepest thought—thought which might almost have enlightened me to create a being less perfect than yourself. Georgiana, you have led me deeper than ever into the heart of science. I feel myself fully competent to render this dear cheek as faultless as its fellow; and then, most beloved, what will be my triumph when I shall have corrected what Nature left imperfect in her fairest work! Even Pygmalion,[2] when his sculptured woman assumed life, felt not greater ecstasy than mine will be."

20   "It is resolved, then," said Georgiana, faintly smiling. "And, Aylmer, spare me not, though you should find the birthmark take refuge in my heart at last."

21   Her husband tenderly kissed her cheek—her right cheek—not that which bore the impress of the crimson hand.

22   The next day Aylmer apprised his wife of a plan that he had formed whereby he might have opportunity for the intense thought and constant watchfulness which the proposed operation would require; while Georgiana, likewise, would enjoy the perfect repose essential to its success. They were to seclude themselves in the extensive apartments occupied by Aylmer as a laboratory, and where, during his toilsome youth, he had made discoveries in the elemental powers of Nature that had roused the admiration of all the learned societies in Europe. Seated calmly in this laboratory, the pale philosopher had investigated the secrets of the highest cloud region and of the profoundest mines; he had satisfied himself of the causes that kindled and kept alive the fires of the volcano; and had explained the mystery of fountains, and how it is that they gush forth, some so bright and pure, and others with such rich medicinal virtues, from the dark bosom of the earth. Here, too, at an earlier period, he had studied the wonders of the human frame, and attempted to fathom the very process by which Nature assimilates all her precious influences from earth and air, and from the spiritual world, to create and foster man, her masterpiece. The latter pursuit, however, Aylmer had long laid aside in unwilling recognition of the truth—against which all seekers sooner or later stumble—that our great creative Mother, while she amuses us with apparently working in the broadest sunshine, is yet severely

2   in Greek legend, the King of Cyprus, who grew infatuated with a statue of a woman and convinced Aphrodite to turn it into a human woman, whom he then married

careful to keep her own secrets, and, in spite of her pretended openness, shows us nothing but results. She permits us, indeed, to mar, but seldom to mend, and, like a jealous patentee,[3] on no account to make. Now, however, Aylmer resumed these half-forgotten investigations; not, of course, with such hopes or wishes as first suggested them; but because they involved much physiological truth and lay in the path of his proposed scheme for the treatment of Georgiana.

23 As he led her over the threshold of the laboratory, Georgiana was cold and tremulous. Aylmer looked cheerfully into her face, with intent to reassure her, but was so startled with the intense glow of the birthmark upon the whiteness of her cheek that he could not restrain a strong convulsive shudder. His wife fainted.

24 "Aminadab! Aminadab!" shouted Aylmer, stamping violently on the floor.

25 Forthwith there issued from an inner apartment a man of low stature, but bulky frame, with shaggy hair hanging about his visage, which was grimed with the vapors of the furnace. This personage had been Aylmer's underworker during his whole scientific career, and was admirably fitted for that office by his great mechanical readiness, and the skill with which, while incapable of comprehending a single principle, he executed all the details of his master's experiments. With his vast strength, his shaggy hair, his smoky aspect, and the indescribable earthiness that incrusted him, he seemed to represent man's physical nature; while Aylmer's slender figure, and pale, intellectual face, were no less apt a type of the spiritual element.

26 "Throw open the door of the boudoir, Aminadab," said Alymer, "and burn a pastil."

27 "Yes, master," answered Aminadab, looking intently at the lifeless form of Georgiana; and then he muttered to himself, "If she were my wife, I'd never part with that birthmark."

28 When Georgiana recovered consciousness she found herself breathing an atmosphere of penetrating fragrance, the gentle potency of which had recalled her from her deathlike faintness. The scene around her looked like enchantment. Aylmer had converted those smoky, dingy, sombre rooms, where he had spent his brightest years in recondite pursuits, into a series of beautiful apartments not unfit to be the secluded abode of a lovely woman. The walls were hung with gorgeous curtains, which imparted the combination of grandeur and grace that no other species of adornment can achieve; and as they fell from the ceiling to the floor, their rich and ponderous folds, concealing all angles and straight lines, appeared to shut in the scene from infinite space. For aught Georgiana knew, it might be a pavilion among the clouds. And Aylmer, excluding the sunshine, which would have interfered with his chemical processes, had supplied its place with perfumed lamps, emitting flames of various hue, but all uniting in a soft, impurpled radiance. He now knelt by his wife's side, watching her earnestly, but without alarm; for he was confident in his science, and felt that he could draw a magic circle round her within which no evil might intrude.

29 "Where am I? Ah, I remember," said Georgiana, faintly; and she placed her hand over her cheek to hide the terrible mark from her husband's eyes.

---

3 one who holds a patent

30   "Fear not, dearest!" exclaimed he. "Do not shrink from me! Believe me, Georgiana, I even rejoice in this single imperfection, since it will be such a rapture to remove it."

31   "Oh, spare me!" sadly replied his wife. "Pray do not look at it again. I can never forget that convulsive shudder."

32   In order to soothe Georgiana, and, as it were, to release her mind from the burden of actual things, Aylmer now put in practice some of the light and playful secrets which science had taught him among its profounder lore. Airy figures, absolutely bodiless ideas, and forms of unsubstantial beauty came and danced before her, imprinting their momentary footsteps on beams of light. Though she had some indistinct idea of the method of these optical phenomena, still the illusion was almost perfect enough to warrant the belief that her husband possessed sway over the spiritual world. Then again, when she felt a wish to look forth from her seclusion, immediately, as if her thoughts were answered, the procession of external existence flitted across a screen. The scenery and the figures of actual life were perfectly represented, but with that bewitching yet indescribable difference which always makes a picture, an image, or a shadow so much more attractive than the original. When wearied of this, Aylmer bade her cast her eyes upon a vessel containing a quantity of earth. She did so, with little interest at first; but was soon startled to perceive the germ of a plant shooting upward from the soil. Then came the slender stalk; the leaves gradually unfolded themselves; and amid them was a perfect and lovely flower.

33   "It is magical!" cried Georgiana. "I dare not touch it."

34   "Nay, pluck it," answered Aylmer,—"pluck it, and inhale its brief perfume while you may. The flower will wither in a few moments and leave nothing save its brown seed vessels; but thence may be perpetuated with a race as ephemeral as itself."

35   But Georgiana had no sooner touched the flower than the whole plant suffered a blight, its leaves turning coal-black as if by the agency of fire.

36   "There was too powerful a stimulus," said Aylmer, thoughtfully.

37   To make up for this abortive experiment, he proposed to take her portrait by a scientific process of his own invention. It was to be effected by rays of light striking upon a polished plate of metal. Georgiana assented; but, on looking at the result, was affrighted to find the features of the portrait blurred and indefinable; while the minute figure of a hand appeared where the cheek should have been. Aylmer snatched the metallic plate and threw it into a jar of corrosive acid.

38   Soon, however, he forgot these mortifying failures. In the intervals of study and chemical experiment he came to her flushed and exhausted, but seemed invigorated by her presence, and spoke in glowing language of the resources of his art. He gave a history of the long dynasty of the alchemists, who spent so many ages in quest of the universal solvent by which the golden principle might be elicited from all things vile and base. Aylmer appeared to believe that, by the plainest scientific logic, it was altogether within the limits of possibility to discover this long-sought medium; "but," he added, "a philosopher who should go deep enough to acquire the power would attain too lofty a wisdom to stoop to the exercise of it." Not less singular were his opinions in regard to the elixir vitae.[4]

---

4   literally, the waters of life

He more than intimated that it was at his option to concoct a liquid that should prolong life for years, perhaps interminably; but that it would produce a discord in Nature which all the world, and chiefly the quaffer of the immortal nostrum, would find cause to curse.

39   "Aylmer, are you in earnest?" asked Georgiana, looking at him with amazement and fear. "It is terrible to possess such power, or even to dream of possessing it."

40   "O, do not tremble, my love," said her husband. "I would not wrong either you or myself by working such inharmonious effects upon our lives; but I would have you consider how trifling, in comparison, is the skill requisite to remove this little hand."

41   At the mention of the birthmark, Georgiana, as usual, shrank as if a red-hot iron had touched her cheek.

42   Again Aylmer applied himself to his labors. She could hear his voice in the distant furnace room giving directions to Aminadab, whose harsh, uncouth, misshapen tones were audible in response, more like the grunt or growl of a brute than human speech. After hours of absence, Aylmer reappeared and proposed that she should now examine his cabinet of chemical products and natural treasures of the earth. Among the former he showed her a small vial, in which, he remarked, was contained the gentle yet most powerful fragrance, capable of impregnating all the breezes that blow across a kingdom. They were of inestimable value, the contents of that little vial; and, as he said so, he threw some of the perfume into the air and filled the room with piercing and invigorating delight.

43   "And what is this?" asked Georgiana, pointing to a small crystal globe containing a gold-colored liquid. "It is so beautiful to the eye that I could imagine it the elixir of life."

44   "In one sense it is," replied Aylmer, "or rather, the elixir of immortality. It is the most precious poison that ever was concocted in this world. By its aid I could apportion the lifetime of any mortal at whom you might point your finger. The strength of the dose would determine whether he were to linger out years, or drop dead in the midst of a breath. No king on his guarded throne could keep his life if I, in my private station, should deem the welfare of millions justified me in depriving him of it."

45   "Why do you keep such a terrific drug?" inquired Georgiana in horror.

46   "Do not mistrust me, dearest," said her husband, smiling; "its virtuous potency is yet greater than its harmful one. But see! here is a powerful cosmetic. With a few drops of this in a vase of water, freckles may be washed away as easily as the hands are cleansed. A stronger infusion would take the blood out of the cheek, and leave the rosiest beauty a pale ghost."

47   "Is it with this lotion that you intend to bathe my cheek?" asked Georgiana, anxiously.

48   "Oh, no," hastily replied her husband; "this is merely superficial. Your case demands a remedy that shall go deeper."

49   In his interviews with Georgiana, Aylmer generally made minute inquiries as to her sensations, and whether the confinement of the rooms and the temperature of the atmosphere agreed with her. These questions had such a particular drift that Georgiana began to conjecture that she was already subjected to certain physical influences, either breathed in with the fragrant air or taken with her

food. She fancied likewise, but it might be altogether fancy, that there was a stirring up of her system—a strange, indefinite sensation creeping through her veins, and tingling, half painfully, half pleasurably, at her heart. Still, whenever she dared to look into the mirror, there she beheld herself pale as a white rose and with the crimson birthmark stamped upon her cheek. Not even Aylmer now hated it so much as she.

50   To dispel the tedium of the hours which her husband found it necessary to devote to the process of combination and analysis, Georgiana turned over the volumes of his scientific library. In many dark old tomes she met with chapters full of romance and poetry. They were the works of the philosophers of the middle ages, such as Albertus Magnus, Cornelius Agrippa, Paracelsus, and the famous friar[5] who created the prophetic Brazen Head. All these antique naturalists stood in advance of their centuries, yet were imbued with some of their credulity, and therefore were believed, and perhaps imagined themselves to have acquired from the investigation of Nature a power above Nature, and from physics a sway over the spiritual world. Hardly less curious and imaginative were the early volumes of the Transactions of the Royal Society, in which the members, knowing little of the limits of natural possibility, were continually recording wonders or proposing methods whereby wonders might be wrought.

51   But to Georgiana, the most engrossing volume was a large folio from her husband's own hand, in which he had recorded every experiment of his scientific career, its original aim, the methods adopted for its development, and its final success or failure, with the circumstances to which either event was attributable. The book, in truth, was both the history and emblem of his ardent, ambitious, imaginative, yet practical and laborious life. He handled physical details as if there were nothing beyond them; yet spiritualized them all and redeemed himself from materialism by his strong and eager aspiration towards the infinite. In his grasp the veriest clod of earth assumed a soul. Georgiana, as she read, reverenced Aylmer and loved him more profoundly than ever, but with a less entire dependence on his judgment than heretofore. Much as he had accomplished, she could not but observe that his most splendid successes were almost invariably failures, if compared with the ideal at which he aimed. His brightest diamonds were the merest pebbles, and felt to be so by himself, in comparison with the inestimable gems which lay hidden beyond his reach. The volume, rich with achievements that had won renown for its author, was yet as melancholy a record as ever mortal hand had penned. It was the sad confession and continual exemplification of the shortcomings of the composite man, the spirit burdened with clay and working in matter, and of the despair that assails the higher nature at finding itself so miserably thwarted by the earthly part. Perhaps every man of genius, in whatever sphere, might recognize the image of his own experience in Aylmer's journal.

52   So deeply did these reflections affect Georgiana that she laid her face upon the open volume and burst into tears. In this situation she was found by her husband.

53   "It is dangerous to read in a sorcerer's books," said he with a smile, though his countenance was uneasy and displeased. "Georgiana, there are pages in that

---

5   a reference to the reputed creation, by a thirteenth-century English friar called Roger Bacon, of a brass head that could speak and supposedly had immense knowledge

volume which I can scarcely glance over and keep my senses. Take heed lest it prove detrimental to you."

54   "It has made me worship you more than ever," said she.

55   "Ah, wait for this one success," rejoined he, "then worship me if you will. I shall deem myself hardly unworthy of it. But come, I have sought you for the luxury of your voice. Sing to me, dearest."

56   So she poured out the liquid music of her voice to quench the thirst of his spirit. He then took his leave with a boyish exuberance of gayety, assuring her that her seclusion would endure but a little longer, and that the result was already certain. Scarcely had he departed when Georgiana felt irresistibly impelled to follow him. She had forgotten to inform Aylmer of a symptom which for two or three hours past had begun to excite her attention. It was a sensation in the fatal birthmark, not painful, but which induced a restlessness throughout her system. Hastening after her husband, she intruded for the first time into the laboratory.

57   The first thing that struck her eye was the furnace, that hot and feverish worker, with the intense glow of its fire, which by the quantities of soot clustered above it seemed to have been burning for ages. There was a distilling apparatus in full operation. Around the room were retorts, tubes, cylinders, crucibles, and other apparatus of chemical research. An electrical machine stood ready for immediate use. The atmosphere felt oppressively close, and was tainted with gaseous odors which had been tormented forth by the processes of science. The severe and homely simplicity of the apartment, with its naked walls and brick pavement, looked strange, accustomed as Georgiana had become to the fantastic elegance of her boudoir. But what chiefly, indeed almost solely, drew her attention, was the aspect of Aylmer himself.

58   He was pale as death, anxious and absorbed, and hung over the furnace as if it depended upon his utmost watchfulness whether the liquid which it was distilling should be the draught of immortal happiness or misery. How different from the sanguine and joyous mien that he had assumed for Georgiana's encouragement!

59   "Carefully now, Aminadab; carefully, thou human machine, carefully, thou man of clay," muttered Aylmer, more to himself than his assistant. "Now, if there be a thought too much or too little, it is all over."

60   "Ho! ho!" mumbled Aminadab. "Look, master! look!"

61   Aylmer raised his eyes hastily, and at first reddened, then grew paler than ever, on beholding Georgiana. He rushed towards her and seized her arm with a gripe that left the print of his fingers upon it.

62   "Why do you come hither? Have you no trust in your husband?" cried he, impetuously. "Would you throw the blight of that fatal birthmark over my labors? It is not well done. Go, prying woman! go!"

63   "Nay, Aylmer," said Georgiana with the firmness of which she possessed no stinted endowment, "it is not you that have a right to complain. You mistrust your wife; you have concealed the anxiety with which you watch the development of this experiment. Think not so unworthily of me, my husband. Tell me all the risk we run, and fear not that I shall shrink; for my share in it is far less than your own."

64   "No, no, Georgiana!" said Aylmer, impatiently; "it must not be."

65   "I submit," replied she, calmly. "And, Aylmer, I shall quaff whatever draught you bring me; but it will be on the same principle that would induce me to take a dose of poison if offered by your hand."

66   "My noble wife," said Aylmer, deeply moved, "I knew not the height and depth of your nature until now. Nothing shall be concealed. Know, then, that this crimson hand, superficial as it seems, has clutched its grasp into your being with a strength of which I had no previous conception. I have already administered agents powerful enough to do aught except to change your entire physical system. Only one thing remains to be tried. If that fail us we are ruined."

67   "Why did you hesitate to tell me this?" asked she.

68   "Because, Georgiana," said Aylmer, in a low voice, "there is danger."

69   "Danger? There is but one danger—that this horrible stigma shall be left upon my cheek!" cried Georgiana. "Remove it, remove it, whatever be the cost, or we shall both go mad!"

70   "Heaven knows your words are too true," said Aylmer, sadly. "And now, dearest, return to your boudoir. In a little while all will be tested."

71   He conducted her back and took leave of her with a solemn tenderness which spoke far more than his words how much was now at stake. After his departure Georgiana became rapt in musings. She considered the character of Aylmer and did it completer justice than at any previous moment. Her heart exulted, while it trembled, at his honorable love—so pure and lofty that it would accept nothing less than perfection nor miserably make itself contented with an earthlier nature than he had dreamed of. She felt how much more precious was such a sentiment than that meaner kind which would have borne with the imperfection for her sake, and have been guilty of treason to holy love by degrading its perfect idea to the level of the actual; and with her whole spirit she prayed that, for a single moment, she might satisfy his highest and deepest conception. Longer than one moment she well knew it could not be; for his spirit was ever on the march, ever ascending, and each instant required something that was beyond the scope of the instant before.

72   The sound of her husband's footsteps aroused her. He bore a crystal goblet containing a liquor colorless as water, but bright enough to be the draught of immortality. Aylmer was pale; but it seemed rather the consequence of a highly-wrought state of mind and tension of spirit than of fear or doubt.

73   "The concoction of the draught has been perfect," said he, in answer to Georgiana's look. "Unless all my science have deceived me, it cannot fail."

74   "Save on your account, my dearest Aylmer," observed his wife, "I might wish to put off this birthmark of mortality by relinquishing mortality itself in preference to any other mode. Life is but a sad possession to those who have attained precisely the degree of moral advancement at which I stand. Were I weaker and blinder, it might be happiness. Were I stronger, it might be endured hopefully. But, being what I find myself, methinks I am of all mortals the most fit to die."

75   "You are fit for heaven without tasting death!" replied her husband. "But why do we speak of dying? The draught cannot fail. Behold its effect upon this plant."

76   On the window seat there stood a geranium diseased with yellow blotches which had overspread all its leaves. Aylmer poured a small quantity of the liquid upon the soil in which it grew. In a little time, when the roots of the plant had

taken up the moisture, the unsightly blotches began to be extinguished in a living verdure.

77   "There need no proof," said Georgiana, quietly. "Give me the goblet. I joyfully stake all upon your word."

78   "Drink, then, thou lofty creature!" exclaimed Aylmer, with fervid admiration. "There is no taint of imperfection on thy spirit. Thy sensible frame, too, shall soon be all perfect."

79   She quaffed the liquid and returned the goblet to his hand.

80   "It is grateful," said she, with a placid smile. "Methinks it is like water from a heavenly fountain; for it contains I know not what of unobtrusive fragrance and deliciousness. It allays a feverish thirst that had parched me for many days. Now, dearest, let me sleep. My earthly senses are closing over my spirit like the leaves around the heart of a rose at sunset."

81   She spoke the last words with a gentle reluctance, as if it required almost more energy than she could command to pronounce the faint and lingering syllables. Scarcely had they loitered through her lips ere she was lost in slumber. Aylmer sat by her side, watching her aspect with the emotions proper to a man the whole value of whose existence was involved in the process now to be tested. Mingled with this mood, however, was the philosophic investigation characteristic of the man of science. Not the minutest symptom escaped him. A heightened flush of the cheek, a slight irregularity of breath, a quiver of the eyelid, a hardly perceptible tremor through the frame,—such were the details which, as the moments passed, he wrote down in his folio volume. Intense thought had set its stamp upon every previous page of that volume; but the thoughts of years were all concentrated upon the last.

82   While thus employed, he failed not to gaze often at the fatal hand, and not without a shudder. Yet once, by a strange and unaccountable impulse, he pressed it with his lips. His spirit recoiled, however, in the very act; and Georgiana, out of the midst of her deep sleep, moved uneasily and murmured as if in remonstrance. Again Aylmer resumed his watch. Nor was it without avail. The crimson hand, which at first had been strongly visible upon the marble paleness of Georgiana's cheek, now grew more faintly outlined. She remained not less pale than ever; but the birthmark, with every breath that came and went lost somewhat of its former distinctness. Its presence had been awful; its departure was more awful still. Watch the stain of the rainbow fading out of the sky, and you will know how that mysterious symbol passed away.

83   "By Heaven! it is well nigh gone!" said Aylmer to himself, in almost irrepressible ecstasy. "I can scarcely trace it now. Success! success! And now it is like the faintest rose color. The lightest flush of blood across her cheek would overcome it. But she is so pale!"

84   He drew aside the window curtain and suffered the light of natural day to fall into the room and rest upon her cheek. At the same time he heard a gross, hoarse chuckle, which he had long known as his servant Aminadab's expression of delight.

85   "Ah, clod! ah, earthly mass!" cried Aylmer, laughing in a sort of frenzy, "you have served me well! Matter and spirit—earth and heaven—have both done their part in this! Laugh, thing of the senses! You have earned the right to laugh."

86   These exclamations broke Georgiana's sleep. She slowly unclosed her eyes and gazed into the mirror which her husband had arranged for that purpose. A faint smile flitted over her lips when she recognized how barely perceptible was now that crimson hand which had once blazed forth with such disastrous brilliancy as to scare away all their happiness. But then her eyes sought Aylmer's face with a trouble and anxiety that he could by no means account for.

87   "My poor Aylmer!" murmured she.

88   "Poor? Nay, richest, happiest, most favored!" exclaimed he. "My peerless bride, it is successful! You are perfect!"

89   "My poor Aylmer," she repeated, with a more than human tenderness, "you have aimed loftily; you have done nobly. Do not repent that, with so high and pure a feeling, you have rejected the best the earth could offer. Aylmer, dearest Aylmer, I am dying!"

90   Alas! it was too true! The fatal hand had grappled with the mystery of life, and was the bond by which an angelic spirit kept itself in union with a mortal frame. As the last crimson tint of the birthmark—that sole token of human imperfection—faded from her cheek, the parting breath of the now perfect woman passed into the atmosphere, and her soul, lingering a moment near her husband, took its heavenward flight. Then a hoarse, chuckling laugh was heard again! Thus ever does the gross fatality of earth exult in its invariable triumph over the immortal essence which, in this dim sphere of half development, demands the completeness of a higher state. Yet, had Aylmer reached a profounder wisdom, he need not thus have flung away the happiness which would have woven his mortal life of the selfsame texture with the celestial. The momentary circumstance was too strong for him; he failed to look beyond the shadowy scope of time, and, living once for all in eternity, to find the perfect future in the present.

James Joyce

Ireland 1882–1941

Born in Dublin, Joyce was educated at Jesuit schools and then at University College, Dublin, where he received a degree in modern languages. Joyce spent most of his life after graduation abroad in Paris, Trieste, and Zurich with Nora Barnacle, whom he married in 1931. Although he did most of his writing after he left Ireland, Dublin was the focal point of his work. Joyce's mocking treatment of sexual matters outraged society and made it difficult for Joyce to get much of his work published. "The Boarding House" is from his first published work, *Dubliners*, which focused on different aspects of what Joyce saw as the chaotic condition of Ireland and the world.

The Boarding House 1914

1   Mrs. Mooney was a butcher's daughter. She was a woman who was quite able to keep things to herself: a determined woman. She had married her father's foreman, and opened a butcher's shop near Spring Gardens. But as soon as his father-in-law was dead Mr. Mooney began to go to the devil. He drank, plundered the till, ran headlong into debt. It was no use making him take the pledge: he was sure to break out again a few days after. By fighting his wife in the presence of customers and by buying bad meat he ruined his business. One night he went for his wife with the cleaver, and she had to sleep in a neighbour's house.

2   After that they lived apart. She went to the priest and got a separation from him, with care of the children. She would give him neither money nor food nor house-room; and so he was obliged to enlist himself as a sheriff's man. He was a shabby stooped little drunkard with a white face and a white moustache and white eyebrows, pencilled above his little eyes, which were pink-veined and raw; and all day long he sat in the bailiff's room, waiting to be put on a job. Mrs. Mooney, who had taken what remained of her money out of the butcher business and set up a boarding house in Hardwicke Street, was a big imposing woman. Her house had a floating population made up of tourists from Liverpool and the Isle of Man and, occasionally, *artistes* from the music halls. Its resident population was made up of clerks from the city. She governed the house cunningly and firmly, knew when to give credit, when to be stern and when to let things pass. All the resident young men spoke of her as *The Madam*.

3   Mrs. Mooney's young men paid fifteen shillings a week for board and lodgings (beer or stout at dinner excluded). They shared in common tastes and occupations and for this reason they were very chummy with one another. They discussed with one another the chances of favourites and outsiders. Jack Mooney, the Madam's son, who was clerk to a commission agent in Fleet Street, had the reputation of being a hard case. He was fond of using soldiers' obscenities: usually he came home in the small hours. When he met his friends he had always a good one to tell them and he was always sure to be on to a good thing—that is to say, a likely horse or a likely *artiste*. He was also handy with the mits and sang comic songs. On Sunday nights there would often be a reunion in Mrs. Mooney's front drawingroom. The music-hall *artistes* would oblige; and Sheridan played waltzes and polkas and vamped accompaniments. Polly Mooney, the Madam's daughter, would also sing. She sang:

> *I'm a ... naughty girl.*
> *You needn't sham:*
> *You know I am.*

4   Polly was a slim girl of nineteen; she had light soft hair and a small full mouth. Her eyes, which were grey with a shade of green through them, had a habit of glancing upwards when she spoke with anyone, which made her look like a little perverse madonna. Mrs. Mooney had first sent her daughter to be a typist in a corn-factor's office, but as a disreputable sheriff's man used to come every other day to the office, asking to be allowed to say a word to his daughter, she had taken

her daughter home again and set her to do housework. As Polly was very lively, the intention was to give her the run of the young men. Besides, young men like to feel that there is a young woman not very far away. Polly, of course, flirted with the young men, but Mrs. Mooney, who was a shrewd judge, knew that the young men were only passing the time away: none of them meant business. Things went on so for a long time, and Mrs. Mooney began to think of sending Polly back to type-writing, when she noticed that something was going on between Polly and one of the young men. She watched the pair and kept her own counsel.

5   Polly knew that she was being watched, but still her mother's persistent silence could not be misunderstood. There had been no open complicity between mother and daughter, no open understanding, but though people in the house began to talk of the affair, still Mrs. Mooney did not intervene. Polly began to grow a little strange in her manner and the young man was evidently per-turbed. At last, when she judged it to be the right moment, Mrs. Mooney inter-vened. She dealt with moral problems as a cleaver deals with meat: and in this case she had made up her mind.

6   It was bright Sunday morning of early summer, promising heat, but with a fresh breeze blowing. All the windows of the boarding house were open and the lace curtains ballooned gently towards the street beneath the raised sashes. The belfry of George's Church sent out constant peals and worshippers, singly or in groups, traversed the little circus[1] before the church, revealing their purpose by their self-contained demeanour no less than by the little volumes in their gloved hands. Breakfast was over in the boarding house, and the table of the breakfast-room was covered with plates on which lay yellow streaks of eggs with morsels of bacon-fat and bacon-rind. Mrs. Mooney sat in the straw armchair and watched the servant Mary remove the breakfast things. She made Mary collect the crusts and pieces of broken bread to help to make Tuesday's bread pudding. When the table was cleared, the broken bread collected, the sugar and butter safe under lock and key, she began to reconstruct the interview which she had had the night before with Polly. Things were as she had suspected: she had been frank in her questions and Polly had been frank in her answers. Both had been somewhat awkward, of course. She had been made awkward by her not wishing to receive the news in too cavalier a fashion or to seem to have connived, and Polly had been made awkward not merely because allusions of that kind always made her awkward, but also because she did not wish it to be thought that in her wise innocence she had divined the intention behind her mother's tolerance.

7   Mrs. Mooney glanced instinctively at the little gilt clock on the mantelpiece as soon as she had become aware through her reverie that the bells of George's Church had stopped ringing. It was seventeen minutes past eleven: she would have lots of time to have the matter out with Mr. Doran and then catch short twelve[2] at Marlborough Street. She was sure she would win. To begin with, she had all the weight of social opinion on her side: she was an outraged mother. She had allowed him to live beneath her roof, assuming that he was a man of honour,

---

1   an open space in a town where several streets converge
2   the briefest Sunday mass, enabling Mrs. Mooney to keep up appearances with a min-
    imum outlay of time

and he had simply abused her hospitality. He was thirty-four or thirty-five years of age, so that youth could not be pleaded as his excuse; nor could ignorance be his excuse, since he was a man who had seen something of the world. He had simply taken advantage of Polly's youth and inexperience: that was evident. The question was: What reparation would he make?

8   There must be reparation made in such cases. It is all very well for the man: he can go his ways as if nothing had happened, having had his moment of pleasure, but the girl has to bear the brunt. Some mothers would be content to patch up such an affair for a sum of money; she had known cases of it. But she would not do so. For her only one reparation could make up for the loss of her daughter's honour: marriage.

9   She counted all her cards again before sending Mary up to Mr. Doran's room to say that she wished to speak with him. She felt sure she would win. He was a serious young man, not rakish or loud-voiced like the others. If it had been Mr. Sheridan or Mr. Meade or Bantam Lyons, her task would have been much harder. She did not think he would face publicity. All the lodgers in the house knew something of the affair; details had been invented by some. Besides, he had been employed for thirteen years in a great Catholic wine-merchant's office, and publicity would mean for him, perhaps, the loss of his sit. Whereas if he agreed all might be well. She knew he had a good screw[3] for one thing, and she suspected he had a bit of stuff put by.

10   Nearly the half-hour! She stood up and surveyed herself in the pier-glass. The decisive expression of her great florid face satisfied her, and she thought of some mothers she knew who could not get their daughters off their hands.

11   Mr. Doran was very anxious indeed this Sunday morning. He had made two attempts to shave, but his hand had been so unsteady that he had been obliged to desist. Three days' reddish beard fringed his jaws, and every two or three minutes a mist gathered on his glasses so that he had to take them off and polish them with his pocket-handkerchief. The recollection of his confession of the night before was a cause of acute pain to him; the priest had drawn out every ridiculous detail of the affair, and in the end had so magnified his sin that he was almost thankful at being afforded a loophole of reparation. The harm was done. What could he do now but marry her or run away? He could not brazen it out. The affair would be sure to be talked of, and his employer would be certain to hear of it. Dublin is such a small city: everyone knows everyone else's business. He felt his heart leap warmly in his throat as he heard in his excited imagination old Mr. Leonard calling out in his rasping voice: "*Send Mr. Doran here, please.*"

12   All his long years of service gone for nothing! All his industry and diligence thrown away! As a young man he had sown his wild oats, of course; he had boasted of his free-thinking and denied the existence of God to his companions in public-houses. But that was all passed and done with ... nearly. He still bought a copy of *Reynolds Newspaper* every week, but he attended to his religious duties, and for nine-tenths of the year lived a regular life. He had money enough to settle

---

3   "screw" and "bit of stuff": money, savings

down on; it was not that. But the family would look down on her. First of all there was her disreputable father, and then her mother's boarding house was beginning to get a certain fame. He had a notion that he was being had. He could imagine his friends talking of the affair and laughing. She *was* a little vulgar; sometimes she said *"I seen"* and *"If I had've known".* But what would grammar matter if he really loved her? He could not make up his mind whether to like her or despise her for what she had done. Of course he had done it too. His instinct urged him to remain free, not to marry. Once you are married you are done for, it said.

13   While he was sitting helplessly on the side of the bed in shirt and trousers, she tapped lightly at his door and entered. She told him all, that she had made a clean breast of it to her mother and that her mother would speak with him that morning. She cried and threw her arms round his neck, saying:

14   "O, Bob! Bob! What am I to do? What am I to do at all?"

15   She would put an end to herself, she said.

16   He comforted her feebly, telling her not to cry, that it would be all right, never fear. He felt against his shirt the agitation of her bosom.

17   It was not altogether his fault that it had happened. He remembered well, with the curious patient memory of the celibate, the first casual caresses her dress, her breath, her fingers had given him. Then late one night as he was undressing for bed she had tapped at his door, timidly. She wanted to relight her candle at his, for hers had been blown out by a gust. It was her bath night. She wore a loose open combing-jacket of printed flannel. Her white instep shone in the opening of her furry slippers and the blood glowed warmly behind her perfumed skin. From her hands and wrists too as she lit and steadied her candle a faint perfume arose.

18   On nights when he came in very late it was she who warmed up his dinner. He scarcely knew what he was eating feeling her beside him alone, at night, in the sleeping house. And her thoughtfulness! If the night was anyway cold or wet or windy there was sure to be a little tumbler of punch ready for him. Perhaps they could be happy together....

19   They used to go upstairs together on tiptoe, each with a candle, and on the third landing exchange reluctant good nights. They used to kiss. He remembered well her eyes, the touch of her hand and his delirium....

20   But delirium passes. He echoed her phrase, applying it to himself: *"What am I to do?"* The instinct of the celibate warned him to hold back. But the sin was there; even his sense of honour told him that reparation must be made for such a sin.

21   While he was sitting with her on the side of the bed Mary came to the door and said that the missus wanted to see him in the parlour. He stood up to put on his coat and waistcoat, more helpless than ever. When he was dressed he went over to her to comfort her. It would be all right, never fear. He left her crying on the bed and moaning softly: *"O my God!"*

22   Going down the stairs his glasses became so dimmed with moisture that he had to take them off and polish them. He longed to ascend through the roof and fly away to another country where he would never hear again of his trouble, and yet a force pushed him downstairs step by step. The implacable faces of his employer and of the Madam stared upon his discomfiture. On the last flight of stairs he passed Jack Mooney who was coming up from the pantry nursing two bottles of *Bass*.[4] They

---

4   a brand of English beer

saluted coldly; and the lover's eyes rested for a second or two on a thick bulldog face and a pair of thick short arms. When he reached the foot of the staircase he glanced up and saw Jack regarding him from the door of the return-room.

23   Suddenly he remembered the night when one of the music-hall *artistes*, a little blond Londoner, had made a rather free allusion to Polly. The reunion had been almost broken up on account of Jack's violence. Everyone tried to quiet him. The music-hall *artiste*, a little paler than usual, kept smiling and saying that there was no harm meant: but Jack kept shouting at him that if any fellow tried that sort of game on with *his* sister he'd bloody well put his teeth down his throat, so he would.

24   Polly sat for a little time on the side of the bed, crying. Then she dried her eyes and went over to the looking-glass. She dipped the end of the towel in the water-jug and refreshed her eyes with the cool water. She looked at herself in profile and readjusted a hairpin above her ear. Then she went back to the bed again and sat at the foot. She regarded the pillows for a long time and the sight of them awakened in her mind secret amiable memories. She rested the nape of her neck against the cool iron bed-rail and fell into a reverie. There was no longer any perturbation visible on her face.

25   She waited on patiently, almost cheerfully, without alarm, her memories gradually giving place to hopes and visions of the future. Her hopes and visions were so intricate that she no longer saw the white pillows on which her gaze was fixed or remembered that she was waiting for anything.

26   At last she heard her mother calling. She started to her feet and ran to the banisters.

27   —Polly! Polly!

28   —Yes, mamma?

29   —Come down, dear. Mr. Doran wants to speak to you.

30   Then she remembered what she had been waiting for.

Stephen Leacock

Canada 1869–1944

Stephen Leacock moved from England to a farm near Lake Simcoe, Ontario, when he was six. Leacock obtained a B.A. from the University of Toronto and a Ph.D. from the University of Chicago. He then became a member of the department of economics and political science at McGill University. In 1910, Leacock published his first comic piece, *Literary Lapses,* which became very popular in Canada, England, and the United States. His third book, *Sunshine Sketches of a Small Town,* from which "The Marine Excursion of the Knights of Pythias" comes, is set in the fictional town of Mariposa, which was modelled on Orillia, Ontario, the site of Leacock's summer residence. Leacock's humour has a quintessential self-mocking tendency that we now see as central to Canadian humour.

The Marine Excursion of the Knights of Pythias   1912

1   Half-past six on a July morning! The *Mariposa Belle* is at the wharf, decked in flags, with steam up ready to start.

2   Excursion day!

3   Half-past six on a July morning, and Lake Wissanotti lying in the sun as calm as glass. The opal colours of the morning light are shot from the surface of the water.

4   Out on the lake the last thin threads of the mist are clearing away like flecks of cotton wool.

5   The long call of the loon echoes over the lake. The air is cool and fresh. There is in it all the new life of the land of the silent pine and the moving waters. Lake Wissanotti in the morning sunlight! Don't talk to me of the Italian lakes, or the Tyrol or the Swiss Alps. Take them away. Move them somewhere else. I don't want them.

6   Excursion Day, at half-past six of a summer morning! With the boat all decked in flags and all the people in Mariposa on the wharf, and the band in peaked caps with big cornets tied to their bodies ready to play at any minute! I say! Don't tell me about the Carnival of Venice and the Delhi Durbar. Don't! I wouldn't look at them. I'd shut my eyes! For light and colour give me every time an excursion out of Mariposa down the lake to the Indian's Island out of sight in the morning mist. Talk of your Papal Zouaves and your Buckingham Palace Guard! I want to see the Mariposa band in uniform and the Mariposa Knights of Pythias with their aprons and their insignia and their picnic baskets and their five-cent cigars!

7   Half-past six in the morning, and all the crowd on the wharf and the boat due to leave in half an hour. Notice it!—in half an hour. Already she's whistled twice (at six, and at six fifteen), and at any minute now, Christie Johnson will step into the pilot house and pull the string for the warning whistle that the boat will leave in half an hour. So keep ready. Don't think of running back to Smith's Hotel for the sandwiches. Don't be fool enough to try to go up to the Greek Store, next to Netley's, and buy fruit. You'll be left behind for sure if you do. Never mind the sandwiches and the fruit! Anyway, here comes Mr Smith himself with a huge basket of provender that would feed a factory. There must be sandwiches in that. I think I can hear them clinking. And behind Mr Smith is the German waiter from the caff with another basket—undubitably lager beer; and behind him, the bartender of the hotel, carrying nothing, as far as one can see. But of course if you know Mariposa you will understand that why he looks so nonchalant and empty-handed is because he has two bottles of rye whisky under his linen duster. You know, I think, the peculiar walk of a man with two bottles of whisky in the inside pockets of a linen coat. In Mariposa, you see, to bring beer to an excursion is quite in keeping with public opinion. But, whisky—well, one has to be a little careful.

8   Do I say that Mr Smith is here? Why, everybody's here. There's Hussell, the editor of the *Newspacket*, wearing a blue ribbon on his coat, for the Mariposa Knights of Pythias are, by their constitution, dedicated to temperance;[1] and

---

1   the name given to the movement aimed at prohibiting the public sale of liquor

there's Henry Mullins, the manager of the Exchange Bank, also a Knight of Pythias, with a small flask of Pogram's Special in his hip pocket as a sort of amendment to the constitution. And there's Dean Drone, the Chaplain of the Order, with a fishing-rod (you never saw such green bass as lie among the rocks at Indian's Island), and with a trolling line in case of maskinonge, and a landing-net in case of pickerel, and with his eldest daughter, Lilian Drone, in case of young men. There never was such a fisherman as the Rev. Rupert Drone.

ॐ

9　Perhaps I ought to explain that when I speak of the excursion as being of the Knights of Pythias, the thing must not be understood in any narrow sense. In Mariposa practically everybody belongs to the Knights of Pythias just as they do to everything else. That's the great thing about the town and that's what makes it so different from the city. Everybody is in everything.

10　　You should see them on the seventeenth of March, for example, when every-body wears a green ribbon and they're all laughing and glad—you know what the Celtic nature is—and talking about Home Rule.[2]

11　　On St Andrew's Day every man in town wears a thistle and shakes hands with everybody else, and you see the fine old Scotch honesty beaming out of their eyes.

12　　And on St George's Day!—well, there's no heartiness like the good old English spirit, after all; why shouldn't a man feel glad that he's an Englishman?

13　　Then on the Fourth of July there are stars and stripes flying over half the stores in town, and suddenly all the men are seen to smoke cigars, and to know all about Roosevelt and Bryan and the Philippine Islands.[3] Then you learn for the first time that Jeff Thorpe's people came from Massachusetts and that his uncle fought at Bunker Hill (anyway Jefferson will swear it was in Dakota all right enough); and you find that George Duff has a married sister in Rochester and that her husband is all right; in fact, George was down there as recently as eight years ago. Oh, it's the most American town imaginable is Mariposa—on the fourth of July.

14　　But wait, just wait, if you feel anxious about the solidity of the British con-nexion, till the twelfth of the month, when everybody is wearing an orange streamer in his coat and the Orangemen (every man in town) walk in the big pro-cession. Allegiance! Well, perhaps you remember the address they gave to the Prince of Wales on the platform of the Mariposa station as he went through on his tour to the west. I think that pretty well settled that question.

15　　So you will easily understand that of course everybody belongs to the Knights of Pythias and the Masons and Oddfellows, just as they all belong to the Snow Shoe Club and the Girls' Friendly Society.

2　the Irish fight for independence from England

3　a reference to the debate about imperial expansion in the United States in 1898; through a war with Spain, America took Cuba, Hawaii, and the Phillippines. Theodore Roosevelt was the secretary of the Navy at the time. He later became presi-dent after McKinley's assassination. William Jennings Bryan was the unsuccessful Democratic candidate for president who ran against McKinley in 1896 and 1900.

16   And meanwhile the whistle of the steamer has blown again for a quarter to seven—loud and long this time, for anyone not here now is late for certain, unless he should happen to come down in the last fifteen minutes.

17   What a crowd upon the wharf and how they pile onto the steamer! It's a wonder that the boat can hold them all. But that's just the marvellous thing about the *Mariposa Belle.*

18   I don't know—I have never known—where the steamers like the *Mariposa Belle* come from. Whether they are built by Harland and Wolff of Belfast, or whether, on the other hand, they are not built by Harland and Wolff of Belfast, is more than one would like to say offhand.

19   The *Mariposa Belle* always seems to me to have some of these strange properties that distinguish Mariposa itself. I mean, her size seems to vary so. If you see her there in the winter, frozen in the ice beside the wharf with a snowdrift against the windows of the pilot house, she looks a pathetic little thing the size of a butternut. But in the summer time, especially after you've *been* in Mariposa for a month or two, and have paddled alongside of her in a canoe, she gets larger and taller, and with a great sweep of black sides, till you see no difference between the *Mariposa Belle* and the *Lusitania.*[4] Each one is a big steamer and that's all you can say.

20   Nor do her measurements help you much. She draws about eighteen inches forward, and more than that—at least half an inch more, astern, and when she's loaded down with an excursion crowd she draws a good two inches more. And above the water—why, look at all the decks on her! There's the deck you walk onto, from the wharf, all shut in, with windows along it, and the after cabin with the long table, and above that the deck with all the chairs piled upon it, and the deck in front where the band stand round in a circle, and the pilot house is higher than that, and above the pilot house is the board with the gold name and the flag pole and the steel ropes and the flags; and fixed in somewhere on the different levels is the lunch counter where they sell the sandwiches, and the engine room, and down below the deck level, beneath the water line, is the place where the crew sleep. What with steps and stairs and passages and piles of cordwood for the engine—oh, no, I guess Harland and Wolff didn't build her. They couldn't have.

21   Yet even with a huge boat like the *Mariposa Belle*, it would be impossible for her to carry all of the crowd that you see in the boat and on the wharf. In reality, the crowd is made up of two classes—all of the people in Mariposa who are going on the excursion and all those who are not. Some come for the one reason and some for the other.

22   The two tellers of the Exchange Bank are both there standing side by side. But one of them—the one with the cameo pin and the long face like a horse—is going, and the other—with the other cameo pin and the face like another horse—is not. In the same way, Hussell of the *Newspacket* is going, but his brother, beside him, isn't. Lilian Drone is going, but her sister can't; and so on all through the crowd.

---

4   one of the largest ships of its time, sunk during World War I

23   And to think that things should look like that on the morning of a steamboat accident.

24   How strange life is!

25   To think of all these people so eager and anxious to catch the steamer, and some of them running to catch it, and so fearful that they might miss it—the morning of a steamboat accident. And the captain blowing his whistle, and warning them so severely that he would leave them behind—leave them out of the accident! And everybody crowding so eagerly to be in the accident.

26   Perhaps life is like that all through.

27   Strangest of all to think, in a case like this, of the people who were left behind, or in some way or other prevented from going, and always afterwards told of how they had escaped being on board the *Mariposa Belle* that day!

28   Some of the instances were certainly extraordinary.

29   Nivens, the lawyer, escaped from being there merely by the fact that he was away in the city.

30   Towers, the tailor, only escaped owing to the fact that, not intending to go on the excursion he had stayed in bed till eight o'clock and so had not gone. He narrated afterwards that waking up that morning at half-past five, he had thought of the excursion and for some unaccountable reason had felt glad that he was not going.

∾

31   The case of Yodel, the auctioneer, was even more inscrutable. He had been to the Oddfellows' excursion on the train the week before and to the Conservative picnic the week before that, and had decided not to go on this trip. In fact, he had not the least intention of going. He narrated afterwards how the night before someone had stopped him on the corner of Nippewa and Tecumseh Streets (he indicated the very spot) and asked: 'Are you going to take in the excursion tomorrow?' and he had said, just as simply as he was talking when narrating it: 'No.' And ten minutes after that, at the corner of Dalhousie and Brock Streets (he offered to lead a party of verification to the precise place) somebody else had stopped him and asked: 'Well, are you going on the steamer trip tomorrow?' Again he had answered: 'No,' apparently almost in the same tone as before.

32   He said afterwards that when he heard the rumour of the accident it seemed like the finger of Providence, and he fell on his knees in thankfulness.

33   There was the similar case of Morison (I mean the one in Glover's hardware store that married one of the Thompsons). He said afterwards that he had read so much in the papers about accidents lately—mining accidents, and aeroplanes and gasoline—that he had grown nervous. The night before his wife had asked him at supper: 'Are you going on the excursion?' He had answered: 'No, I don't think I feel like it,' and had added: 'Perhaps your mother might like to go.' And the next evening just at dusk, when the news ran through the town, he said the first thought that flashed through his head was: 'Mrs Thompson's on that boat.'

34 He told this right as I say it—without the least doubt or confusion. He never for a moment imagined she was on the *Lusitania* or the *Olympic* or any other boat. He knew she was on this one. He said you could have knocked him down where he stood. But no one had. Not even when he got halfway down—on his knees, and it would have been easier still to knock him down or kick him. People do miss a lot of chances.

35 Still, as I say, neither Yodel nor Morison nor anyone thought about there being an accident until just after sundown when they—

36 Well, have you ever heard the long booming whistle of a steamboat two miles out on the lake in the dusk, and while you listen and count and wonder, seen the crimson rockets going up against the sky and then heard the fire bell ringing right there beside you in the town, and seen the people running to the town wharf?

37 That's what the people of Mariposa saw and felt that summer evening as they watched the Mackinaw lifeboat go plunging out into the lake with seven sweeps to a side and the foam clear to the gunwale with the lifting stroke of fourteen men!

38 But, dear me, I am afraid that this is no way to tell a story. I suppose the true art would have been to have said nothing about the accident till it happened. But when you write about Mariposa, or hear of it, if you know the place, it's all so vivid and real, that a thing like the contrast between the excursion crowd in the morning and the scene at night leaps into your mind and you must think of it.

ᕲ

39 But never mind about the accident—let us turn back again to the morning.

40 The boat was due to leave at seven. There was no doubt about the hour—not only seven, but seven sharp. The notice in the *Newspacket* said: 'The boat will leave sharp at seven'; and the advertising posters on the telegraph poles on Missinaba Street that began, 'Ho, for Indian's Island!' ended up with the words: 'Boat leaves at seven sharp.' There was a big notice on the wharf that said: 'Boat leaves sharp on time.'

41 So at seven, right on the hour, the whistle blew loud and long, and then at seven-fifteen three short peremptory blasts, and at seven-thirty one quick angry call—just one—and very soon after that they cast off the last of the ropes and the *Mariposa Belle* sailed off in her cloud of flags, and the band of the Knights of Pythias, timing it to a nicety, broke into the 'Maple Leaf for Ever!'

42 I suppose that all excursions when they start are much the same. Anyway, on the *Mariposa Belle* everybody went running up and down all over the boat with deck chairs and camp stools and baskets, and found places, splendid places to sit, and then got scared that there might be better ones and chased off again. People hunted for places out of the sun and when they got them swore that they weren't going to freeze to please anybody; and the people in the sun said that they hadn't paid fifty cents to get roasted. Others said that they hadn't paid fifty cents to get covered with cinders, and there were still others who hadn't paid fifty cents to get shaken to death with the propeller.

43   Still, it was all right presently. The people seemed to get sorted out into the places on the boat where they belonged. The women, the older ones, all gravitated into the cabin on the lower deck and by getting round the table with needlework, and with all the windows shut, they soon had it, as they said themselves, just like being at home.

44   All the young boys and the toughs and the men in the band got down on the lower deck forward, where the boat was dirtiest and where the anchor was and the coils of rope.

45   And upstairs on the after deck there were Lilian Drone and Miss Lawson, the high-school teacher, with a book of German poetry—Gothey5 I think it was—and the bank teller and the young men.

46   In the centre, standing beside the rail, were Dean Drone and Dr Gallagher, looking through binocular glasses at the shore.

47   Up in front on the little deck forward of the pilot house was a group of the older men, Mullins and Duff and Mr Smith in a deck chair, and beside him Mr Golgotha Gingham, the undertaker of Mariposa, on a stool. It was part of Mr Gingham's principles to take in an outing of this sort, a business matter, more or less—for you never know what may happen at these water parties. At any rate, he was there in a neat suit of black, not, of course, his heavier or professional suit, but a soft clinging effect as of burnt paper that combined gaiety and decorum to a nicety.

∼

48   'Yes,' said Mr Gingham, waving his black glove in a general way towards the shore, 'I know the lake well, very well. I've been pretty much all over it in my time.'

49   'Canoeing?' asked somebody.

50   'No,' said Mr Gingham, 'not in a canoe.' There seemed a peculiar and quiet meaning in his tone.

51   'Sailing, I suppose,' said somebody else.

52   'No,' said Mr Gingham. 'I don't understand it.'

53   'I never knowed that you went onto the water at all, Gol,' said Mr Smith, breaking in.

54   'Ah, not now,' explained Mr Gingham; 'it was years ago, the first summer I came to Mariposa. I was on the water practically all day. Nothing like it to give a man an appetite and keep him in shape.'

55   'Was you camping?' asked Mr Smith.

56   'We camped at night,' assented the undertaker, 'but we put in practically the whole day on the water. You see, we were after a party that had come up here from the city on his vacation and gone out in a sailing canoe. We were dragging. We were up every morning at sunrise, lit a fire on the beach and cooked breakfast, and then we'd light our pipes and be off with the net for a whole day. It's a great life,' concluded Mr Gingham wistfully.

57   'Did you get him?' asked two or three together.

58   There was a pause before Mr Gingham answered.

---

5   a misspelling/mispronunciation of Goethe, a German poet

59   'We did,' he said '—down in the reeds past Horseshoe Point. But it was no use. He turned blue on me right away.'

60   After which Mr Gingham fell into such a deep reverie that the boat had steamed another half-mile down the lake before anybody broke the silence again. Talk of this sort—and after all what more suitable for a day on the water?—beguiled the way.

∾

61   Down the lake, mile by mile over the calm water, steamed the *Mariposa Belle*. They passed Poplar Point where the high sand-banks are with all the swallows' nests in them, and Dean Drone and Dr Gallagher looked at them alternately through the binocular glasses, and it was wonderful how plainly one could see the swallows and the banks and the shrubs—just as plainly as with the naked eye.

62   And a little farther down they passed the Shingle Beach, and Dr Gallagher, who knew Canadian history, said to Dean Drone that it was strange to think that Champlain had landed there with his French explorers three hundred years ago; and Dean Drone, who didn't know Canadian history, said it was stranger still to think that the hand of the Almighty had piled up the hills and rocks long before that; and Dr Gallagher said it was wonderful how the French had found their way through such a pathless wilderness; and Dean Drone said that it was wonderful also to think that the Almighty had placed even the smallest shrub in its appointed place. Dr Gallagher said it filled him with admiration. Dean Drone said it filled him with awe. Dr Gallagher said he'd been full of it ever since he was a boy and Dean Drone said so had he.

63   Then a little further, as the *Mariposa Belle* steamed on down the lake, they passed the Old Indian Portage where the great grey rocks are; and Dr Gallagher drew Dean Drone's attention to the place where the narrow canoe track wound up from the shore to the woods, and Dean Drone said he could see it perfectly well without the glasses.

64   Dr Gallagher said that it was just here that a party of five hundred French had made their way with all their baggage and accoutrements across the rocks of the divide and down to the Great Bay. And Dean Drone said that it reminded him of Xenophon[6] leading his ten thousand Greeks over the hill passes of Armenia down to the sea. Dr Gallagher said that he had often wished he could have seen and spoken to Champlain, and Dean Drone said how much he regretted to have never known Xenophon.

65   And then after that they fell to talking of relics and traces of the past, and Dr Gallagher said that if Dean Drone would come round to his house some night he would show him some Indian arrow heads that he had dug up in his garden. And Dean Drone said that if Dr Gallagher would come round to the rectory any afternoon he would show him a map of Xerxes'[7] invasion of Greece. Only he must come some time between the Infant Class and the Mothers' Auxiliary.

---

6   Greek historian, soldier, and essayist (ca. 430–355 B.C.), whose works contribute greatly to our knowledge of Greece and Persia in fourth century B.C.

7   Xerxes (ca. 519–465 B.C.) was King of Persia for the last twenty-one years of his life.

66   So presently they both knew that they were blocked out of one another's houses for some time to come, and Dr Gallagher walked forward and told Mr Smith, who had never studied Greek, about Champlain crossing the rock divide.

67   Mr Smith turned his head and looked at the divide for half a second and then said he had crossed a worse one up north back of the Wahnipitae and that the flies were Hades—and then went on playing freezeout poker with the two juniors in Duff's bank.

68   So Dr Gallagher realized that that's always the way when you try to tell people things, and that as far as gratitude and appreciation goes one might as well never read books or travel anywhere or do anything.

69   In fact, it was at this very moment that he made up his mind to give the arrows to the Mariposa Mechanics' Institute—they afterwards became, as you know, the Gallagher Collection. But, for the time being, the doctor was sick of them and wandered off round the boat and watched Henry Mullins showing George Duff how to make a John Collins without lemons, and finally went and sat down among the Mariposa band and wished that he hadn't come.

70   So the boat steamed on and the sun rose higher and higher, and the freshness of the morning changed into the full glare of noon, and pretty soon the *Mariposa Belle* had floated out onto the lake again and they went on to where the lake began to narrow in at its foot, just where the Indian's Island is—all grass and trees and with a log wharf running into the water. Below it the Lower Ossawippi runs out of the lake, and quite near are the rapids, and you can see down among the trees the red brick of the power house and hear the roar of the leaping water.

71   The Indian's Island itself is all covered with trees and tangled vines, and the water about it is so still that it's all reflected double and looks the same either way up. Then when the steamer's whistle blows as it comes into the wharf, you hear it echo among the trees of the island, and reverberate back from the shores of the lake.

72   The scene is all so quiet and still and unbroken, that Miss Cleghorn—the sallow girl in the telephone exchange, that I spoke of—said she'd like to be buried there. But all the people were so busy getting their baskets and gathering up their things that no one had time to attend to it.

73   I mustn't even try to describe the landing and the boat crunching against the wooden wharf and all the people running to the same side of the deck and Christie Johnson calling out to the crowd to keep to the starboard and nobody being able to find it. Everyone who has been on a Mariposa excursion knows all about that.

74   Nor can I describe the day itself and the picnic under the trees. There were speeches afterwards, and Judge Pepperleigh gave such offence by bringing in Conservative politics that a man called Patriotus Canadiensis wrote and asked for some of the invaluable space of the *Mariposa Times-Herald* and exposed it.

75   I should say that there were races too, on the grass on the open side of the island, graded mostly according to ages—races for boys under thirteen and girls over nineteen and all that sort of thing. Sports are generally conducted on that plan in Mariposa. It is realized that a woman of sixty has an unfair advantage over a mere child.

76   Dean Drone managed the races and decided the ages and gave out the prizes; the Wesleyan minister helped, and he and the young student, who was relieving in the Presbyterian Church, held the string at the winning point.

77   They had to get mostly clergymen for the races because all the men had wandered off, somehow, to where they were drinking lager beer out of two kegs stuck on pine logs among the trees.

78   But if you've ever been on a Mariposa excursion you know all about these details anyway.

79   So the day wore on and presently the sun came through the trees on a slant and the steamer whistle blew with a great puff of white steam and all the people came straggling down to the wharf and pretty soon the *Mariposa Belle* had floated out onto the lake again and headed for the town, twenty miles away.

∿

80   I suppose you have often noticed the contrast there is between an excursion on its way out in the morning and what it looks like on the way home.

81   In the morning everybody is so restless and animated and moves to and from all over the boat and asks questions. But coming home, as the afternoon gets later and later and the sun sinks below the hills, all the people seem to get so still and quiet and drowsy.

82   So it was with the people on the *Mariposa Belle*. They sat there on the benches and the deck chairs in little clusters, and listened to the regular beat of the propeller and almost dozed off asleep as they sat. Then when the sun set and the dusk drew on, it grew almost dark on the deck and so still that you could hardly tell there was anyone on board.

83   And if you had looked at the steamer from the shore or from one of the islands, you'd have seen the row of lights from the cabin windows shining on the water and the red glare of the burning hemlock from the funnel, and you'd have heard the soft thud of the propeller miles away over the lake.

84   Now and then, too, you could have heard them singing on the steamer—the voices of the girls and the men blended into unison by the distance, rising and falling in long-drawn melody: 'O—Can-a-da—O—Can-a-da.'

85   You may talk as you will about the intoning choirs of your European cathedrals, but the sound of 'O Can-a-da', borne across the waters of a silent lake at evening is good enough for those of us who know Mariposa.

86   I think that it was just as they were singing like this: 'O—Can-a-da', that word went round that the boat was sinking.

87   If you have ever been in any sudden emergency on the water, you will understand the strange psychology of it—the way in which what is happening seems to become known all in a moment without a word being said. The news is transmitted from one to the other by some mysterious process.

88   At any rate, on the *Mariposa Belle* first one and then the other heard that the steamer was sinking. As far as I could ever learn the first of it was that George Duff, the bank manager, came very quietly to Dr Gallagher and asked him if he thought that the boat was sinking. The doctor said no, that he had thought so earlier in the day but that he didn't now think that she was.

89   After that Duff, according to his own account, had said to Macartney, the lawyer, that the boat was sinking, and Macartney said that he doubted it very much.

90   Then somebody came to Judge Pepperleigh and woke him up and said that there was six inches of water in the steamer and that she was sinking. And Pepperleigh said it was perfect scandal and passed the news on to his wife and she said that they had no business to allow it and that if the steamer sank that was the last excursion she'd go on.

91   So the news went all round the boat and everywhere the people gathered in groups and talked about it in the angry and excited way that people have when a steamer is sinking on one of the lakes like Lake Wissanotti.

92   Dean Drone, of course, and some others were quieter about it, and said that one must make allowances and that naturally there were two sides to everything. But most of them wouldn't listen to reason at all. I think, perhaps, that some of them were frightened. You see the last time but one that the steamer had sunk, there had been a man drowned and it made them nervous.

93   What? Hadn't I explained about the depth of Lake Wissanotti? I had taken it for granted that you knew; and in any case parts of it are deep enough, though I don't suppose in this stretch of it from the big reed beds up to within a mile of the town wharf, you could find six feet of water in it if you tried. Oh, pshaw! I was not talking about a steamer sinking in the ocean and carrying down its screaming crowds of people into the hideous depths of green water. Oh, dear me, no! That kind of thing never happens on Lake Wissanotti.

94   But what does happen is that the *Mariposa Belle* sinks every now and then, and sticks there on the bottom till they get things straightened up.

95   On the lakes round Mariposa, if a person arrives late anywhere and explains that the steamer sank, everybody understands the situation.

96   You see when Harland and Wolff built the *Mariposa Belle*, they left some cracks in between the timbers that you fill up with cotton waste every Sunday. If this is not attended to, the boat sinks. In fact, it is part of the law of the province that all the steamers like the *Mariposa Belle* must be properly corked—I think that is the word—every season. There are inspectors who visit all the hotels in the province to see that it is done.

97   So you can imagine now that I've explained it a little straighter, the indignation of the people when they knew that the boat had come uncorked and that they might be stuck out there on a shoal or a mud-bank half the night.

98   I don't say either that there wasn't any danger; anyway, it doesn't feel very safe when you realize that the boat is settling down with every hundred yards that she goes, and you look over the side and see only the black water in the gathering night.

99   Safe! I'm not sure now that I come to think of it that it isn't worse than sinking in the Atlantic. After all, in the Atlantic there is wireless telegraphy, and a lot of trained sailors and stewards. But out on Lake Wissanotti—far out, so that you can only just see the lights of the town away off to the south—when the propeller comes to a stop—and you can hear the hiss of steam as they start to rake out the engine fires to prevent an explosion—and when you turn from the red glare that comes from the furnace doors as they open them, to the black dark that is gathering over the lake—and there's a night wind beginning to run among the rushes—and you see the men going forward to the roof of the pilot house to send up the rockets to rouse the town—safe? Safe yourself, if you like; as for me, let me once get back into Mariposa again, under the night shadow of the maple trees, and this shall be the last, last time I'll go on Lake Wissanotti.

100   Safe! Oh, yes! Isn't it strange how safe other people's adventures seem after they happen? But you'd have been scared, too, if you'd been there just before the steamer sank, and seen them bringing up all the women on to the top deck.

101   I don't see how some of the people took it so calmly; how Mr Smith, for instance, could have gone on smoking and telling how he'd had a steamer 'sink on him' on Lake Nipissing and a still bigger one, a side-wheeler, sink on him in Lake Abbitibbi.

102   Then, quite suddenly, with a quiver, down she went. You could feel the boat sink, sink—down, down—would it never get to the bottom? The water came flush up to the lower deck, and then—thank heaven—the sinking stopped and there was the *Mariposa Belle* safe and tight on a reed bank.

103   Really, it made one positively laugh! It seemed so queer and, anyway, if a man has a sort of natural courage, danger makes him laugh. Danger? pshaw! fiddlesticks! everybody scouted the idea. Why, it is just the little things like this that give zest to a day on the water.

104   Within half a minute they were all running round looking for sandwiches and cracking jokes and talking of making coffee over the remains of the engine fires.

∾

105   I don't need to tell at length how it all happened after that.

106   I suppose the people on the *Mariposa Belle* would have had to settle down there all night or till help came from the town, but some of the men who had gone forward and were peering out into the dark said that it couldn't be more than a mile across the water to Miller's Point. You could almost see it over there to the left—some of them, I think, said 'off on the port bow,' because you know when you get mixed up in these marine disasters, you soon catch the atmosphere of the thing.

107   So pretty soon they had the davits swung out over the side and were lowering the old lifeboat from the top deck into the water.

108   There were men leaning out over the rail of the *Mariposa Belle* with lanterns that threw the light as they let her down, and the glare fell on the water and the reeds. But when they got the boat lowered, it looked such a frail, clumsy thing as one saw it from the rail above, that the cry was raised: 'Women and children first!' For what was the sense, if it should turn out that the boat wouldn't even hold women and children, of trying to jam a lot of heavy men into it?

109   So they put in mostly women and children and the boat pushed out into the darkness so freighted down it would hardly float.

110   In the bow of it was the Presbyterian student who was relieving the minister, and he called out that they were in the hands of Providence. But he was crouched and ready to spring out of them at the first moment.

111   So the boat went and was lost in the darkness except for the lantern in the bow that you could see bobbing on the water. Then presently it came back and they sent another boat till pretty soon the decks began to thin out and everybody got impatient to be gone.

112   It was about the time that the third boat-load put off that Mr Smith took a bet with Mullins for twenty-five dollars, that he'd be home in Mariposa before the people in the boats had walked round the shore.

113   No one knew just what he meant, but pretty soon they saw Mr Smith disappear down below the lowest part of the steamer with a mallet in one hand and a big bundle of marline in the other.

114   They might have wondered more about it, but it was just at this time that they heard the shouts from the rescue boat—the big Mackinaw lifeboat—that had put out from the town with fourteen men at the sweeps when they saw the first rockets go up.

115   I suppose there is always something inspiring about a rescue at sea, or on the water.

116   After all, the bravery of the lifeboat man is the true bravery—expended to save life, not to destroy it.

117   Certainly they told for months after of how the rescue boat came out to the *Mariposa Belle*.

118   I suppose that when they put her in the water the lifeboat touched it for the first time since the old Macdonald Government placed her on Lake Wissanotti.

119   Anyway, the water poured in at every seam. But not for a moment—even with two miles of water between them and the steamer—did the rowers pause for that.

120   By the time they were halfway there the water was almost up to the thwarts, but they drove her on. Panting and exhausted (for mind you, if you haven't been in a fool boat like that for years, rowing takes it out of you), the rowers stuck to their task. They threw the ballast over and chucked into the water the heavy cork jackets and lifebelts that encumbered their movements. There was no thought of turning back. They were nearer to the steamer than the shore.

121   'Hang to it, boys,' called the crowd from the steamer's deck, and hang they did.

122   They were almost exhausted when they got them; men leaning from the steamer threw them ropes and one by one every man was hauled aboard just as the lifeboat sank under their feet.

123   Saved! by heaven, saved by one of the smartest pieces of rescue work ever seen on the lake.

124   There's no use describing it; you need to see rescue work of this kind by lifeboats to understand it.

125   Nor were the lifeboat crew the only ones that distinguished themselves.

126   Boat after boat and canoe after canoe had put out from Mariposa to the help of the steamer. They got them all.

127   Pupkin, the other bank teller with a face like a horse, who hadn't gone on the excursion—as soon as he knew that the boat was signalling for help and that Miss Lawson was sending up rockets—rushed for a row boat, grabbed an oar (two would have hampered him)—and paddled madly out into the lake. He struck right out into the dark with the crazy skiff almost sinking beneath his feet. But they got him. They rescued him. They watched him, almost dead with exhaustion, make his way to the steamer, where he was hauled up with ropes. Saved! Saved!

∾

128 They might have gone on that way half the night, picking up the rescuers, only, at the very moment when the tenth load of people left for the shore—just as suddenly and saucily as you please, up came the *Mariposa Belle* from the mud bottom and floated.

129 *Floated?*

130 Why, of course she did. If you take a hundred and fifty people off a steamer that has sunk, and if you get a man as shrewd as Mr Smith to plug the timber seams with mallet and marline, and if you turn ten bandsmen of the Mariposa band onto your hand pump on the bow of the lower decks—float? why, what else can she do?

131 Then, if you stuff in hemlock into the embers of the fire that you were raking out, till it hums and crackles under the boiler, it won't be long before you hear the propeller thud—thudding at the stern again, and before the long roar of the steam whistle echoes over to the town.

132 And so the *Mariposa Belle*, with all steam up again and with the long train of sparks careering from the funnel, is heading for the town.

133 But no Christie Johnson at the wheel in the pilot house this time.

134 'Smith! Get Smith!' is the cry.

135 Can he take her in? Well, now! Ask a man who has had steamers sink on him in half the lakes from Temiscaming to the Bay, if he can take her in? Ask a man who has run a York boat down the rapids of the Moose when the ice is moving, if he can grip the steering wheel of the *Mariposa Belle*? So there she steams safe and sound to the town wharf!

136 Look at the lights and the crowds! If only the federal census taker could count us now! Hear them calling and shouting back and forward from the deck to the shore! Listen! There is the rattle of the shore ropes as they get them ready, and there's the Mariposa band—actually forming in a circle on the upper deck just as she docks, and the leader with his baton—one—two—ready now—
'O CAN-A-DA!'

Frederick Philip Grove

Canada 1879–1948

Grove's early life is obscure because of conflicts between his own account of it and that of his biographers. What is clear is that he emigrated from Germany to Canada and settled in Manitoba, where he taught between 1912 and 1929, eventually becoming the principal of a school in Gladstone. Grove then left teaching and moved to Ontario, where he lived on a farm near Simcoe. Grove wrote seven novels, a collection of stories, a book of essays and speeches, and two autobiographical works. His four prairie novels are arguably his best work and reflect a bleak realism, well suited to the difficult environment of the prairies. In "Snow," an unforgiving landscape is both a home and a killer.

Snow 1932

1 Towards morning the blizzard had died down, though it was still far from day-light. Stars without number blazed in the dark-blue sky which presented that brilliant and uncompromising appearance always characterizing, on the northern plains of America, those nights in the dead of winter when the thermometer dips to its lowest levels.

2 In the west, Orion was sinking to the horizon. It was between five and six o'clock.

3 In the bush-fringe of the Big Marsh, sheltered by thick but bare bluffs of aspens, stood a large house, built of logs, white-washed, solid—such as a settler who is still single would put up only when he thinks of getting married. It, too, looked ice-cold, frozen in the night. Not a breath stirred where it stood; a thin thread of whitish smoke, reaching up to the level of the tree-tops, seemed to be suspended into the chimney rather than to issue from it.

4 Through the deep snow of the yard, newly packed, a man was fighting his way to the door. Arrived there, he knocked and knocked, first tapping with his knuckles, then hammering with his fists.

5 Two, three minutes passed. Then a sound awoke in the house, as of some-body stirring, getting out of bed.

6 The figure on the door-slab—a medium-sized, slim man in sheepskin and high rubber boots into which his trousers were tucked, with the ear-flaps of his cap pulled down—stood and waited, bent over, hands thrust into the pockets of the short coat, as if he wished to shrink into the smallest possible space so as to offer the smallest possible surface to the attack of the cold. In order to get rid of the dry, powdery snow which filled every crease in his foot-gear and trousers, he stamped his feet. His chin was drawn deep into the turned-up collar on whose points his breath had settled in the form of a thick layer of hoar frost.

7 At last a bolt was withdrawn inside.

8 The face of a man peered out, just discernible in the starlight.

9 Then the door was opened; in ominous silence the figure from the outside entered, still stamping its feet.

10 Not a word was spoken till the door had been closed. Then a voice sounded through the cold and dreary darkness of the room.

11 "Redcliff hasn't come home. He went to town about noon and expected to get back by midnight. We're afraid he's lost."

12 The other man, quite invisible in the dark, had listened, his teeth chattering with the cold. "Are you sure he started out from town?"

13 "Well," the new-comer answered hesitatingly, "one of the horses came to the yard."

14 "One of his horses?"

15 "Yes. One of those he drove. The woman worked her way to my place to get help."

16 The owner of the house did not speak again. He went, in the dark, to the door in the rear and opened it. There, he groped about for matches, and, finding them, lighted a lamp. In the room stood a big stove, a coal-stove of the self-feeder type; but the fuel used was wood. He opened the drafts and shook the grate clear of

ashes; there were two big blocks of spruce in the fire-box, smouldering away for the night. In less than a minute they blazed up.

17   The new-comer entered, blinking in the light of the lamp, and looked on. Before many minutes the heat from the stove began to tell.

18   "I'll call Bill," the owner of the house said. He was himself of medium height or only slightly above it, but of enormous breadth of shoulder: a figure built for lifting loads. By his side the other man looked small, weakly, dwarfed.

19   He left the room and, returning through the cold bare hall in front, went upstairs.

20   A few minutes later a tall, slender, well-built youth bolted into the room where the new-comer was waiting. Bill, Carroll's hired man, was in his underwear and carried his clothes, thrown in a heap over his arm. Without loss of time, but jumping, stamping, swinging his arms, he began at once to dress.

21   He greeted the visitor. "Hello, Mike! What's that Abe tells me? Redcliff got lost?"

22   "Seems that way," Mike said listlessly.

23   "By gringo," Bill went on. "I shouldn't wonder. In that storm! I'd have waited in town. Wouldn't catch me going over the marsh in that kind of weather!"

24   "Didn't start till late in the afternoon," Mike Sobotski said in his shivering way.

25   "No. And didn't last long, either," Bill agreed while he shouldered into his overalls. "But while she lasted…"

26   At this moment Abe Carroll, the owner of the farm, re-entered, with sheep-skin, fur cap, and long, woollen scarf on his arm. His deeply lined, striking, square face bore a settled frown while he held the inside of his sheep-skin to the stove to warm it up. Then, without saying a word, he got deliberately into it.

27   Mike Sobotski still stood bent over, shivering, though he had opened his coat, and, on his side of the stove, was catching all the heat it afforded.

28   Abe, with the least motion needed to complete dressing, made for the door. In passing Bill, he flung out an elbow which touched the young man's arm. "Come on," he said; and to the other, pointing to the stove, "Close the drafts."

29   A few minutes later a noise as of rearing and snorting horses in front of the house …

30   Mike, buttoning up his coat and pulling his mitts over his hands, went out.

31   They mounted three unsaddled horses. Abe leading, they dashed through the new drifts in the yard and out through the gate to the road. Here, where the shelter of the bluffs screening the house was no longer effective, a light but freshening breeze from the north-west made itself felt as if fine little knives were cutting into the flesh of their faces.

32   Abe dug his heels into the flank of his rearing mount. The horse was unwilling to obey his guidance, for Abe wanted to leave the road and to cut across wild land to the south-west.

33   The darkness was still inky-black, though here and there, where the slope of the drifts slanted in the right direction, starlight was dimly reflected from the snow. The drifts were six, eight, in places ten feet high; and the snow was once more crawling up their flanks, it was so light and fine. It would fill the tracks in half an hour. As the horses plunged through, the crystals dusted up in clouds, flying aloft over horses and riders.

34   In less than half an hour they came to a group of two little buildings, of logs, that seemed to squat on their haunches in the snow. Having entered the yard through a gate, they passed one of the buildings and made for the other, a little stable; their horses snorting, they stopped in its lee.

35   Mike dismounted, throwing the halter-shank of his horse to Bill. He went to the house, which stood a hundred feet or so away. The shack was even smaller than the stable, twelve by fifteen feet perhaps. From its flue-pipe a thick, white plume of smoke blew to the south-east.

36   Mike returned with a lantern; the other two sprang to the ground; and they opened the door to examine the horse which the woman had allowed to enter.

37   The horse was there, still excited, snorting at the leaping light and shadows from the lantern, its eyes wild, its nostrils dilated. It was covered with white frost and fully harnessed, though its traces were tied up to the back-band.

38   "He let him go," said Mike, taking in these signs. "Must have stopped and unhitched him."

39   "Must have been stuck in a drift," Bill said, assenting.

40   "And tried to walk it," Abe added.

41   For a minute or so they stood silent, each following his own gloomy thoughts. Weird, luminous little clouds issued fitfully from the nostrils of the horse inside.

42   "I'll get the cutter," Abe said at last.

43   "I'll get it," Bill volunteered. "I'll take the drivers along. We'll leave the filly here in the stable."

44   "All right."

45   Bill remounted, leading Abe's horse. He disappeared into the night.

46   Abe and Mike, having tied the filly and the other horse in their stalls, went out, closed the door and turned to the house.

47   There, by the light of a little coal-oil lamp, they saw the woman sitting at the stove, pale, shivering, her teeth a-chatter, trying to warm her hands, which were cold with fever, and looking with lack-lustre eyes at the men as they entered.

48   The children were sleeping; the oldest, a girl, on the floor, wrapped in a blanket and curled up like a dog; four others in one narrow bed, with hay for a mattress, two at the head, two at the foot; the baby on, rather than in, a sort of cradle made of a wide board slung by thin ropes to the pole-roof of the shack.

49   The other bed was empty and unmade. The air was stifling from a night of exhalations.

50   "We're going to hunt for him," Mike said quietly. "We've sent for a cutter. He must have tried to walk."

51   The woman did not answer. She sat and shivered.

52   "We'll take some blankets," Mike went on. "And some whisky if you've got any in the house."

53   He and Abe were standing by the stove, opposite the woman, and warming their hands, their mitts held under their arm-pits.

54   The woman pointed with a look to a home-made little cupboard nailed to the wall and apathetically turned back to the stove. Mike went, opened the door of the cupboard, took a bottle from it, and slipped it into the pocket of his sheep-skin. Then he raised the blankets from the empty bed, rolled them roughly into a bundle, dropped it, and returned to the stove where, with stiff fingers, he fell to rolling a cigarette.

55   Thus they stood for an hour or so.

56   Abe's eye was fastened on the woman. He would have liked to say a word of comfort, of hope. What was there to be said?

57   She was the daughter of a German settler in the bush, some six or seven miles north-east of Abe's place. Her father, an oldish, unctuous, bearded man had, some ten years ago, got tired of the hard life in the bush where work meant clearing, picking stones, and digging stumps. He had sold his homestead and bought a prairie-farm, half a section, on crop-payments, giving notes for the equipment which he needed to handle the place. He had not been able to make it 'a go'. His bush farm had fallen back on his hands; he had lost his all and returned to the place. He had been counting on the help of his two boys—big, strapping young fellows who were to clear much land and raise crops which would lift the debt. But the boys had refused to go back to the bush; they could get easy work in town. Ready money would help. But the ready money had melted away in their hands. Redcliff, the old people's son-in-law, had been their last hope. They were on the point of losing even their bush farm. Here they might perhaps still have found a refuge for their old age—though Redcliff's homestead lay on the sand-flats bordering on the marsh where the soil was thin, dreadfully thin; it drifted when the scrub-brush was cleared off. Still, with Redcliff living, this place had been a hope. What were they to do if he was gone? And this woman, hardly more than a girl, in spite of her six children!

58   The two tiny, square windows of the shack began to turn grey.

59   At last Abe, thinking he heard a sound, went to the door and stepped out. Bill was there; the horses were shaking the snow out of their pelts; one of them was pawing the ground.

60   Once more Abe opened the door and gave Mike a look for a signal. Mike gathered the bundle of blankets into his arms, pulled on his mitts, and came out.

61   Abe reached for the lines; but Bill objected.

62   "No. Let me drive. I found something."

63   And as soon as the two older men had climbed in, squeezing into the scant space on the seat, he clicked his tongue.

64   "Get up there!" he shouted, hitting the horses' backs with his lines. And with a leap they darted away.

65   Bill turned, heading back to the Carroll farm. The horses plunged, reared, snorted, and then, throwing their heads, shot along in a gallop, scattering snow-slabs right and left and throwing wing-waves of the fresh, powdery snow, especially on the lee side. Repeatedly they tried to turn into the wind, which they were cutting at right angles. But Bill plied the whip and guided them expertly.

66   Nothing was visible anywhere; nothing but the snow in the first grey of dawn. Then, like enormous ghosts, or like evanescent apparitions, the trees of the bluff were adumbrated behind the lingering veils of the night.

67   Bill turned to the south, along the straight trail which bordered Abe Carroll's farm. He kept looking out sharply to right and left. But after a while he drew his galloping horses in.

68   "Whoa!" he shouted, tearing at the lines in see-saw fashion. And when the rearing horses came to a stop, excited and breathless, he added, "I've missed it." He turned.

69   "What is it?" Abe asked.

70 "The other horse," Bill answered. "It must have had the scent of our yard. It's dead … frozen stiff."

71 A few minutes later he pointed to a huge white mound on top of a drift to the left. "That's it," he said, turned the horses into the wind, and stopped.

72 To the right, the bluffs of the farm slowly outlined themselves in the morning greyness.

73 The two older men alighted and, with their hands, shovelled the snow away. There lay the horse, stiff and cold, frozen into a rocklike mass.

74 "Must have been here a long while," Abe said.

75 Mike nodded. "Five, six hours." Then he added, "Couldn't have had the smell of the yard. Unless the wind has turned."

76 "It has," Abe answered and pointed to a fold in the flank of the snow-drift which indicated that the present drift had been superimposed on a lower one whose longitudinal axis ran to the north-east.

77 For a moment longer they stood and pondered.

78 Then Abe went back to the cutter and reached for the lines. "I'll drive," he said.

79 Mike climbed in.

80 Abe took his bearings, looking for landmarks. They were only two or three hundred feet from his fence. That enabled him to estimate the exact direction of the breeze. He clicked his tongue. "Get up!"

81 And the horses, catching the infection of a dull excitement, shot away. They went straight into the desert of drifts to the west, plunging ahead without any trail, without any landmark in front to guide them.

82 They went for half an hour, an hour, and longer.

83 None of the three men said a word. Abe knew the sand-flats better than any other; Abe reasoned better than they. If anyone could find the missing man, it was Abe.

84 Abe's thought ran thus. The horse had gone against the wind. It would never have done so without good reason; that reason could have been no other than a scent to follow. If that was so, however, it would have gone in as straight a line as it could. The sand-flats stretched away to the south-west for sixteen miles with not a settlement, not a farm but Redcliff's. If Abe managed to strike that line of the scent, it must take him to the point whence the horses had started.

85 Clear and glaring, with an almost indifferent air, the sun rose to their left.

86 And suddenly they saw the wagon-box of the sleigh sticking out of the snow ahead of them.

87 Abe stopped, handed Bill the lines, and got out. Mike followed. Nobody said a word.

88 The two men dug the tongue of the vehicle out of the snow and tried it. This was part of the old, burnt-over bush land south of the sand-flats. The sleigh was tightly wedged in between several charred stumps which stuck up through the snow. That was the reason why the man had unhitched the horses and turned them loose. What else, indeed, could he have done?

89 The box was filled with a drift which, toward the tail-gate, was piled high, for there three bags of flour were standing on end and leaning against a barrel half-filled with small parcels the interstices between which were packed with mealy snow.

90   Abe waded all around the sleigh, reconnoitring; and as he did so, wading at the height of the upper edge of the wagon-box, the snow suddenly gave way beneath him; he broke in; the drift was hollow.

91   A suspicion took hold of him; with a few quick reaches of his arm he demolished the roof of the drift all about.

92   And there, in the hollow, lay the man's body as if he were sleeping, a quiet expression, as of painless rest, on his face. His eyes were closed; a couple of bags were wrapped about his shoulders. Apparently he had not even tried to walk! Already chilled to the bone, he had given in to that desire for rest, for shelter at any price, which overcomes him who is doomed to freeze.

93   Without a word the two men carried him to the cutter and laid him down on the snow.

94   Bill, meanwhile, had unhitched the horses and was hooking them to the tongue of the sleigh. The two others looked on in silence. Four times the horses sprang, excited because Bill tried to make them pull with a sudden twist. The sleigh did not stir.

95   "Need an axe," Mike said at last, "to cut the stumps. We'll get the sleigh later."

96   Mike hitched up again and turned the cutter. The broken snowdrifts through which they had come gave the direction.

97   Then they laid the stiff, dead body across the floor of their vehicle, leaving the side doors open, for it protruded both ways. They themselves climbed up on the seat and crouched down, so as not to put their feet on the corpse.

98   Thus they returned to Abe Carroll's farm where, still in silence, they deposited the body in the granary.

99   That done, they stood for a moment as if in doubt. Then Bill unhitched the horses and took them to the stable to feed.

100   "I'll tell the woman," said Mike. "Will you go tell her father?"

101   Abe nodded. "Wait for breakfast," he added.

102   It was ten o'clock; and none of them had eaten since the previous night.

103   On the way to Altmann's place in the bush drifts were no obstacles to driving. Drifts lay on the marsh, on the open sand-flats.

104   Every minute of the time Abe, as he drove along, thought of that woman in the shack: the woman, alone, with six children, and with the knowledge that her man was dead.

105   Altmann's place in the bush looked the picture of peace and comfort: a large log-house of two rooms. Window-frames and door were painted green. A place to stay with, not to leave....

106   When Abe knocked, the woman, whom he had seen but once in his life, at the sale where they had lost their possessions, opened the door—an enormously fat woman, overflowing her clothes. The man, tall, broad, with a long, rolling beard, now grey, stood behind her, peering over her shoulder. A visit is an event in the bush!

107   "Come in," he said cheerfully when he saw Abe. "What a storm that was!"

108   Abe entered the kitchen which was also dining- and living-room. He sat down on the chair which was pushed forward for him and looked at the two old people, who remained standing.

109   Suddenly, from the expression of his face, they anticipated something of his message. No use dissembling.

110   "Redcliff is dead," he said. "He was frozen to death last night on his way from town."

111   The two old people also sat down; it looked as if their knees had given way beneath them. They stared at him, dumbly, a sudden expression of panic fright in their eyes.

112   "I thought you might want to go to your daughter," Abe added sympathetically.

113   The man's big frame seemed to shrink as he sat there. All the unctuousness and the conceit of the handsome man dwindled out of his bearing. The woman's eyes had already filled with tears.

114   Thus they remained for two, three minutes.

115   Then the woman folded her fat, pudgy hands; her head sank low on her breast; and she sobbed, "God's will be done!"

Katherine Mansfield

New Zealand/England 1888–1923

Born in Wellington, New Zealand, Katherine Mansfield was educated in New Zealand and London, England. She returned to England in 1908, two years after she had finished her education. Although she had an unhappy first marriage, Mansfield met and eventually married the editor John Middleton Murry. Mansfield wrote her best stories, often focusing on the individual and society, in the short, productive period between 1916 and her death from tuberculosis in January 1923. "Miss Brill" is typical of the restraint and focused detail that are the strengths of Mansfield's work.

Miss Brill   1922

1   Although it was so brilliantly fine—the blue sky powdered with gold and great spots of light like white wine splashed over the Jardins Publiques—Miss Brill was glad that she had decided on her fur. The air was motionless, but when you opened your mouth there was just a faint chill, like a chill from a glass of iced water before you sip, and now and again a leaf came drifting—from nowhere, from the sky. Miss Brill put up her hand and touched her fur. Dear little thing! It was nice to feel it again. She had taken it out of its box that afternoon, shaken out the moth powder, given it a good brush, and rubbed the life back into the dim little eyes. "What has been happening to me?" said the sad little eyes. Oh, how sweet it was to see them snap at her again from the red eiderdown!… But the nose, which was of some black composition, wasn't at all firm. It must have had a knock, somehow. Never mind—a little dab of black sealing-wax when the time came—when it was absolutely necessary…. Little rogue! Yes, she really felt like that about it. Little rogue biting its tail just by her left ear. She could have taken it off and laid it on her lap and stroked it. She felt a tingling

in her hands and arms, but that came from walking, she supposed. And when she breathed, something light and sad—no, not sad, exactly—something gentle seemed to move in her bosom.

2   There were a number of people out this afternoon, far more than last Sunday. And the band sounded louder and gayer. That was because the Season had begun. For although the band played all the year round on Sundays, out of season it was never the same. It was like some one playing with only the family to listen; it didn't care how it played if there weren't any strangers present. Wasn't the conductor wearing a new coat, too? She was sure it was new. He scraped with his foot and flapped his arms like a rooster about to crow, and the bandsmen sitting in the green rotunda blew out their cheeks and glared at the music. Now there came a little "flutey" bit—very pretty!—a little chain of bright drops. She was sure it would be repeated. It was; she lifted her head and smiled.

3   Only two people shared her "special" seat: a fine old man in a velvet coat, his hands clasped over a huge carved walking stick, and a big old woman, sitting upright, with a roll of knitting on her embroidered apron. They did not speak. This was disappointing, for Miss Brill always looked forward to the conversation. She had become really quite expert, she thought, at listening as though she didn't listen, at sitting in other people's lives just for a minute while they talked round her.

4   She glanced, sideways, at the old couple. Perhaps they would go soon. Last Sunday, too, hadn't been as interesting as usual. An Englishman and his wife, he wearing a dreadful Panama hat and she button boots. And she'd gone on the whole time about how she ought to wear spectacles; she knew she needed them; but that it was no good getting any; they'd be sure to break and they'd never keep on. And he'd been so patient. He'd suggest everything—gold rims, the kind that curved round your ears, little pads inside the bridge. No, nothing would please her. "They'll always be sliding down my nose!" Miss Brill had wanted to shake her.

5   The old people sat on the bench, still as statues. Never mind, there was always the crowd to watch. To and fro, in front of the flower beds and the band rotunda, the couples and groups paraded, stopped to talk, to greet, to buy a handful of flowers from the old beggar who had his tray fixed to the railings. Little children ran among them, swooping and laughing; little boys with big white silk bows under their chins, little girls, little French dolls, dressed up in velvet and lace. And sometimes a tiny staggerer came suddenly rocking into the open from under the trees, stopped, stared, as suddenly sat down "flop," until its small high-stepping mother, like a young hen, rushed scolding to its rescue. Other people sat on the benches and green chairs, but they were nearly always the same, Sunday after Sunday, and—Miss Brill had often noticed—there was something funny about nearly all of them. They were odd, silent, nearly all old, and from the way they stared they looked as though they'd just come from dark little rooms or even— even cupboards!

6   Behind the rotunda the slender trees with yellow leaves down drooping, and through them just a line of sea, and beyond the blue sky with gold-veined clouds.

7   Tum-tum-tum tiddle-um! tiddle-um! tum tiddley-um tum ta! blew the band.

8   Two young girls in red came by and two young soldiers in blue met them, and they laughed and paired and went off arm-in-arm. Two peasant women with funny straw hats passed, gravely, leading beautiful smoke-colored donkeys. A cold, pale nun hurried by. A beautiful woman came along and dropped her bunch of violets,

and a little boy ran after to hand them to her, and she took them and threw them away as if they'd been poisoned. Dear me! Miss Brill didn't know whether to admire that or not! And now an ermine toque and a gentleman in gray met just in front of her. He was tall, stiff, dignified, and she was wearing the ermine toque she'd bought when her hair was yellow. Now everything, her hair, her face, even her eyes, was the same color as the shabby ermine, and her hand, in its cleaned glove, lifted to dab her lips, was a tiny yellowish paw. Oh, she was so pleased to see him— delighted! She rather thought they were going to meet that afternoon. She described where she'd been—everywhere, here, there, along by the sea. The day was so charming—didn't he agree? And wouldn't he, perhaps?... But he shook his head, lighted a cigarette, slowly breathed a great deep puff into her face, and, even while she was still talking and laughing, flicked the match away and walked on. The ermine toque was alone; she smiled more brightly than ever. But even the band seemed to know what she was feeling and played more softly, played ten-derly, and the drum beat, "The Brute! The Brute!" over and over. What would she do? What was going to happen now? But as Miss Brill wondered, the ermine toque turned, raised her hand as though she'd seen some one else, much nicer, just over there, and pattered away. And the band changed again and played more quickly, more gayly than ever, and the old couple on Miss Brill's seat got up and marched away, and such a funny old man with long whiskers hobbled along in time to the music and was nearly knocked over by four girls walking abreast.

9   Oh, how fascinating it was! How she enjoyed it! How she loved sitting here, watching it all! It was like a play. It was exactly like a play. Who could believe the sky at the back wasn't painted? But it wasn't till a little brown dog trotted on solemn and then slowly trotted off, like a little "theater" dog, a little dog that had been drugged, that Miss Brill discovered what it was that made it so exciting. They were all on the stage. They weren't only the audience, not only looking on; they were acting. Even she had a part and came every Sunday. No doubt somebody would have noticed if she hadn't been there; she was part of the performance after all. How strange she'd never thought of it like that before! And yet it explained why she made such a point of starting from home at just the same time each week—so as not to be late for the performance—and it also explained why she had quite a queer, shy feeling at telling her English pupils how she spent her Sunday after-noons. No wonder! Miss Brill nearly laughed out loud. She was on the stage. She thought of the old invalid gentleman to whom she read the newspaper four after-noons a week while he slept in the garden. She had got quite used to the frail head on the cotton pillow, the hollowed eyes, the open mouth and the high pinched nose. If he'd been dead she mightn't have noticed for weeks; she wouldn't have minded. But suddenly he knew he was having the paper read to him by an actress! "An actress!" The old head lifted; two points of light quivered in the old eyes. "An actress—are ye?" And Miss Brill smoothed the newspaper as though it were the manuscript of her part and said gently: "Yes, I have been an actress for a long time."

10   The band had been having a rest. Now they started again. And what they played was warm, sunny, yet there was just a faint chill—a something, what was it?—not sadness—no, not sadness—a something that made you want to sing. The tune lifted, the light shone; and it seemed to Miss Brill that in another moment all of them, all the whole company, would begin singing. The young ones, the laughing ones who were moving together, they would begin, and the men's voices

very resolute and brave, would join them. And then she too, she too, and the others on the benches—they would come in with a kind of accompaniment—something low, that scarcely rose or fell, something so beautiful—moving…. And Miss Brill's eyes filled with tears and she looked smiling at all the other members of the company. Yes, we understand, we understand, she thought—though what they understood she didn't know.

11 Just at that moment a boy and a girl came and sat down where the old couple had been. They were beautifully dressed; they were in love. The hero and the heroine, of course, just arrived from his father's yacht. And still soundlessly singing still with that trembling smile, Miss Brill prepared to listen.

12 "No, not now," said the girl. "Not here, I can't."

13 "But why? Because of that stupid old thing at the end there?" asked the boy. "Why does she come here at all—who wants her? Why doesn't she keep her silly old mug at home?"

14 "It's her fu-fur which is so funny," giggled the girl. "It's exactly like a fried whiting."[1]

15 "Ah, be off with you!" said the boy in an angry whisper. Then: "Tell me, ma petite chère—"

16 "No, not here," said the girl. "Not *yet*."

17 On her way home she usually bought a slice of honeycake at the baker's. It was her Sunday treat. Sometimes there was an almond in her slice, sometimes not. It made a great difference. If there was an almond it was like carrying home a tiny present—a surprise—something that might very well not have been there. She hurried on the almond Sundays and struck the match for the kettle in quite a dashing way.

18 But today she passed the baker's by, climbed the stairs, went into the little dark room—her room like a cupboard—and sat down on the red eiderdown. She sat there for a long time. The box that the fur came out of was on the bed. She unclasped the necklet quickly; quickly, without looking, laid it inside. But when she put the lid on she thought she heard something crying.

---

1 a small, white-fleshed fish common in Europe

F. Scott Fitzgerald

U.S.A. 1896–1940

F. Scott Fitzgerald was irrevocably connected to the 1920s, a decade characterized by conspicuous consumption, an unquestioning belief that things could only keep getting better, and a conviction that the world belonged to the young and the beautiful. Fitzgerald and his wife, Zelda, were two of those beautiful people. When the decade of excess ended with the crash of 1929, which ushered in the Depression, Fitzgerald's mystic connection to his audience also ended. His 1930s novels were not as successful; he had, in a sense, reached his peak with *The Great Gatsby*, a novel that perfectly captured American optimism and the corrupting materialism nourishing it. In "The Lost Decade," Fitzgerald employs a fictional technique he used with more complex force in *Gatsby*, a naive even ignorant narrator in a counterpointed dialogue with a man who has left innocence far behind him.

The Lost Decade   1939

1   All sorts of people come into the offices of the newsweekly and Orrison Brown had all sorts of relations with them. Outside of office hours he was "one of the editors"—during work time he was simply a curly-haired man who a year before had edited the Dartmouth *Jack-0-Lantern* and was now only too glad to take the undesirable assignments around the office, from straightening out illegible copy to playing call boy without the title.

2   He had seen this visitor go into the editor's office—a pale, tall man of forty with blond statuesque hair and a manner that was neither shy nor timid, nor otherworldly like a monk, but something of all three. The name on his card, Louis Trimble, evoked some vague memory, but having nothing to start on, Orrison did not puzzle over it—until a buzzer sounded on his desk, and previous experience warned him that Mr. Trimble was to be his first course at lunch.

3   "Mr. Trimble—Mr. Brown," said the Source of all luncheon money. "Orrison—Mr. Trimble's been away a long time. Or he *feels* it's a long time— almost twelve years. Some people would consider themselves lucky to've missed the last decade."

4   "That's so," said Orrison.

5   "I can't lunch today," continued his chief. "Take him to Voisin or 21 or anywhere he'd like. Mr. Trimble feels there're lots of things he hasn't seen."

6   Trimble demured politely.

7   "Oh, I can get around."

8   "I know it, old boy. Nobody knew this place like you did once—and if Brown tries to explain the horseless carriage just send him back here to me. And you'll be back yourself by four, won't you?"

9   Orrison got his hat.

10   "You've been away ten years?" he asked while they went down in the elevator.

11   "They'd begun the Empire State Building," said Trimble. "What does that add up to?"

12   "About 1928. But as the chief said, you've been lucky to miss a lot." As a feeler he added, "Probably had more interesting things to look at."

13   "Can't say I have."

14   They reached the street and the way Trimble's face tightened at the roar of traffic made Orrison take one more guess.

15   "You've been out of civilization?"

16   "In a sense." The words were spoken in such a measured way that Orrison

concluded this man wouldn't talk unless he wanted to—and simultaneously wondered if he could have possibly spent the thirties in a prison or an insane asylum.

17   "This is the famous 21," he said. "Do you think you'd rather eat somewhere else?"

18   Trimble paused, looking carefully at the brownstone house.

19   "I can remember when the name 21 got to be famous," he said, "about the same year as Moriarity's." Then he continued almost apologetically, "I thought we might walk up Fifth Avenue about five minutes and eat wherever we happened to be. Some place with young people to look at."

20   Orrison gave him a quick glance and once again thought of bars and grey walls and bars; he wondered if his duties included introducing Mr. Trimble to complaisant girls. But Mr. Trimble didn't look as if that was in his mind—the dominant expression was of absolute and deep-seated curiosity and Orrison attempted to connect the name with Admiral Byrd's hideout at the South Pole or flyers lost in Brazilian jungles. He was, or he had been, quite a fellow—that was obvious. But the only definite clue to his environment—and to Orrison the clue that led nowhere—was his countryman's obedience to the traffic lights and his predilection for walking on the side next to the shops and not the street. Once he stopped and gazed into a haberdasher's window.

21   "Crêpe ties," he said. "I haven't seen one since I left college."

22   "Where'd you go?"

23   "Massachusetts Tech."

24   "Great place."

25   "I'm going to take a look at it next week. Let's eat somewhere along here—" They were in the upper Fifties "—you choose."

26   There was a good restaurant with a little awning just around the corner.

27   "What do you want to see most?" Orrison asked, as they sat down.

28   Trimble considered.

29   "Well—the back of people's heads," he suggested. "Their necks—how their heads are joined to their bodies. I'd like to hear what those two little girls are saying to their father. Not exactly what they're saying but whether the words float or submerge, how their mouths shut when they've finished speaking. Just a matter of rhythm—Cole Porter came back to the States in 1928 because he felt there were new rhythms around."

30   Orrison was sure he had his clue now, and with nice delicacy did not pursue it by a millimetre—even suppressing a sudden desire to say there was a fine concert in Carnegie Hall tonight.

31   "The weight of spoons," said Trimble, "so light. A little bowl with a stick attached. the cast in that waiter's eye. I knew him once but he wouldn't remember me."

32   But as they left the restaurant the same waiter looked at Trimble rather puzzled as if he almost knew him. When they were outside Orrison laughed:

33   "After ten years people will forget."

34   "Oh, I had dinner there last May—" He broke off in an abrupt manner.

35   It was all kind of nutsy, Orrison decided—and changed himself suddenly into a guide.

36   "From here you can get a good candid focus on Rockefeller Centre," he pointed out with spirit "—and the Chrysler Building and the Armistead Building, the daddy of all the new ones."

37   "The Armistead Building," Trimble rubber-necked obediently. "Yes—I designed it."

38   Orrison shook his head cheerfully—he was used to going out with all kinds of people. But that stuff about having been in the restaurant last May...

39   He paused by the brass entablature in the cornerstone of the building. "Erected 1928," it said.

40   Trimble nodded.

41   "But I was taken drunk that year—every-which-way drunk. So I never saw it before now."

42   "Oh." Orrison hesitated. "Like to go in now?"

43   "I've been in it—lots of times. But I've never seen it. And now it isn't what I want to see. I wouldn't ever be able to see it now. I simply want to see how people walk and what their clothes and shoes and hats are made of. And their eyes and hands. Would you mind shaking hands with me?"

44   "Not at all, sir."

45   "Thanks. Thanks. That's very kind. I suppose it looks strange—but people will think we're saying good-bye. I'm going to walk up the avenue for a while, so we *will* say good-bye. Tell your office I'll be in at four."

46   Orrison looked after him when he started out, half expecting him to turn into a bar. But there was nothing about him that suggested or ever had suggested drink.

47   "Jesus!" he said to himself. "Drunk for ten years."

48   He felt suddenly of the texture of his own coat and then he reached out and pressed his thumb against the granite of the building by his side.

Flannery O'Connor

U.S.A. 1925–1964

O'Connor spent the first thirteen years of her life in Savannah, Georgia, and then moved inland with her family to a farm in Millidgeville. She left to pursue a fine arts degree at the University of Iowa while publishing stories in magazines. In late 1950, she was diagnosed with lupus, a progressive and degenerative disease that attacks the body's tissues. Her illness forced her to return to the family farm, where she died at the age of thirty-nine. A devout Catholic until her death, she deliberately employed grotesque characters and incidents to convey her spiritual vision through shocking images. O'Connor once said you had to shout for the deaf to hear and draw large pictures for the blind. "A Good Man Is Hard to Find" is an excellent example of her ability to shock for thematic intent.

A Good Man Is Hard to Find   1953

1   The grandmother didn't want to go to Florida. She wanted to visit some of her connections in east Tennessee and she was seizing at every chance to change Bailey's mind. Bailey was the son she lived with, her only boy. He was sitting on the edge of his chair at the table, bent over the orange sports section of the *Journal*. "Now look here, Bailey," she said, "see here, read this," and she stood with one hand on her thin hip and the other rattling the newspaper at his bald head. "Here this fellow that calls himself The Misfit is aloose from the Federal Pen and headed toward Florida and you read here what it says he did to these people. Just you read it. I wouldn't take my children in any direction with a criminal like that aloose in it. I couldn't answer to my conscience if I did."

2   Bailey didn't look up from his reading so she wheeled around then and faced the children's mother, a young woman in slacks, whose face was as broad and innocent as a cabbage and was tied around with a green head-kerchief that had two points on the top like rabbit's ears. She was sitting on the sofa, feeding the baby his apricots out of a jar. "The children have been to Florida before," the old lady said. "You all ought to take them somewhere else for a change so they would see different parts of the world and be broad. They never have been to east Tennessee."

3   The children's mother didn't seem to hear her but the eight-year-old boy, John Wesley, a stocky child with glasses, said, "If you don't want to go to Florida, why dontcha stay at home?" He and the little girl, June Star, were reading the funny papers on the floor.

4   "She wouldn't stay at home to be queen for a day," June Star said without raising her yellow head.

5   "Yes and what would you do if this fellow, The Misfit, caught you?" the grandmother said.

6   "I'd smack his face," John Wesley said.

7   "She wouldn't stay at home for a million bucks," June Star said. "Afraid she'd miss something. She has to go everywhere we go."

8   "All right, Miss," the grandmother said. "Just remember that the next time you want me to curl your hair."

9   June Star said her hair was naturally curly.

10   The next morning the grandmother was the first one in the car, ready to go. She had her big black valise that looked like the head of a hippopotamus in one corner, and underneath it she was hiding a basket with Pitty Sing, the cat, in it. She didn't intend for the cat to be left alone in the house for three days because he would miss her too much and she was afraid he might brush against one of the gas burners and accidentally asphyxiate himself. Her son, Bailey, didn't like to arrive at a motel with a cat.

11   She sat in the middle of the back seat with John Wesley and June Star on either side of her. Bailey and the children's mother and the baby sat in front and they left Atlanta at eight forty-five with the mileage on the car at 55890. The grandmother wrote this down because she thought it would be interesting to say how many miles they had been when they got back. It took them twenty minutes to reach the outskirts of the city.

12 The old lady settled herself comfortably, removing her white cotton gloves and putting them up with her purse on the shelf in front of the back window. The children's mother still had on slacks and still had her hair tied up in a green kerchief, but the grandmother had on a navy blue straw sailor hat with a bunch of white violets on the brim and a navy blue dress with a small white dot in the print. Her collars and cuffs were white organdy trimmed with lace and at her neckline she had pinned a purple spray of cloth violets containing a sachet. In case of an accident, anyone seeing her dead on the highway would know at once that she was a lady.

13 She said she thought it was going to be a good day for driving, neither too hot nor too cold, and she cautioned Bailey that the speed limit was fifty-five miles an hour and that the patrolmen hid themselves behind billboards and small clumps of trees and sped out after you before you had a chance to slow down. She pointed out interesting details of the scenery: Stone Mountain;[1] the blue granite that in some places came up to both sides of the highway; the brilliant red clay banks slightly streaked with purple; and the various crops that made rows of green lace-work on the ground. The trees were full of silver-white sunlight and the meanest of them sparkled. The children were reading comic magazines and their mother had gone back to sleep.

14 "Let's go through Georgia fast so we won't have to look at it much," John Wesley said.

15 "If I were a little boy," said the grandmother, "I wouldn't talk about my native state that way. Tennessee has the mountains and Georgia has the hills."

16 "Tennessee is just a hillbilly dumping ground," John Wesley said, "and Georgia is a lousy state too."

17 "You said it," June Star said.

18 "In my time," said the grandmother, folding her thin veined fingers, "children were more respectful of their native states and their parents and everything else. People did right then. Oh look at the cute little pickaninny!" she said and pointed to a Negro child standing in the door of a shack. "Wouldn't that make a picture, now?" she asked and they all turned and looked at the little Negro out of the back window. He waved.

19 "He didn't have any britches on," June Star said.

20 "He probably didn't have any," the grandmother explained. "Little niggers in the country don't have things like we do. If I could paint, I'd paint that picture," she said.

21 The children exchanged comic books.

22 The grandmother offered to hold the baby and the children's mother passed him over the front seat to her. She set him on her knee and bounced him and told him about the things they were passing. She rolled her eyes and screwed up her mouth and stuck her leathery thin face into his smooth bland one. Occasionally he gave her a faraway smile. They passed a large cotton field with five or six graves fenced in the middle of it, like a small island. "Look at the graveyard!" the grandmother said, pointing it out. "That was the old family burying ground. That belonged to the plantation."

---

1 the Georgia mountain, east of Atlanta, that has, sculpted on its face, three Southern Civil War heroes: Jefferson Davis, Stonewall Jackson, and Robert E. Lee

23   "Where's the plantation?" John Wesley asked.

24   "Gone With the Wind," said the grandmother. "Ha. Ha."

25   When the children finished all the comic books they had brought, they opened the lunch and ate it. The grandmother ate a peanut butter sandwich and an olive and would not let the children throw the box and the paper napkins out the window. When there was nothing else to do they played a game by choosing a cloud and making the other two guess what shape it suggested. John Wesley took one the shape of a cow and June Star guessed a cow and John Wesley said, no, an automobile, and June Star said he didn't play fair, and they began to slap each other over the grandmother.

26   The grandmother said she would tell them a story if they would keep quiet. When she told a story, she rolled her eyes and waved her head and was very dramatic. She said once when she was a maiden lady she had been courted by a Mr. Edgar Atkins Teagarden from Jasper, Georgia. She said he was a very good-looking man and a gentleman and that he brought her a watermelon every Saturday afternoon with his initials cut in it, E.A.T. Well, one Saturday, she said, Mr. Teagarden brought the watermelon and there was nobody at home and he left it on the front porch and returned in his buggy to Jasper, but she never got the watermelon, she said, because a nigger boy ate it when he saw the initials, E.A.T.!

27   This story tickled John Wesley's funny bone and he giggled and giggled but June Star didn't think it was any good. She said she wouldn't marry a man that just brought her a watermelon on Saturday. The grandmother said she would have done well to marry Mr. Teagarden because he was a gentleman and had bought Coca-Cola stock when it first came out and that he had died only a few years ago, a very wealthy man.

28   They stopped at The Tower for barbecued sandwiches. The Tower was a part stucco and part wood filling station and dance hall set in a clearing outside of Timothy. A fat man named Red Sammy Butts ran it and there were signs stuck here and there on the building and for miles up and down the highway saying, TRY RED SAMMY'S FAMOUS BARBECUE. NONE LIKE FAMOUS RED SAMMY'S! RED SAM! THE FAT BOY WITH THE HAPPY LAUGH. A VETERAN! RED SAMMY'S YOUR MAN!

29   Red Sammy was lying on the bare ground outside The Tower with his head under a truck while a gray monkey about a foot high, chained to a small china-berry tree, chattered nearby. The monkey sprang back into the tree and got on the highest limb as soon as he saw the children jump out of the car and run toward him.

30   Inside, The Tower was a long dark room with a counter at one end and tables at the other and dancing space in the middle. They all sat down at a board table next to the nickelodeon[2] and Red Sam's wife, a tall burnt-brown woman with hair and eyes lighter than her skin, came and took their order. The children's mother put a dime in the machine and played "The Tennessee Waltz," and the grand-mother said that tune always made her want to dance. She asked Bailey if he would like to dance but he only glared at her. He didn't have a naturally sunny disposition like she did and trips made him nervous. The grandmother's brown

---

2   a jukebox

eyes were very bright. She swayed her head from side to side and pretended she was dancing in her chair. June Star said play something she could tap to so the children's mother put in another dime and played a fast number and June Star stepped out onto the dance floor and did her tap routine.

31 "Ain't she cute?" Red Sam's wife said, leaning over the counter. "Would you like to come be my little girl?"

32 "No I certainly wouldn't," June Star said. "I wouldn't live in a broken-down place like this for a million bucks!" and she ran back to the table.

33 "Ain't she cute?" the woman repeated, stretching her mouth politely.

34 "Ain't you ashamed?" hissed the grandmother.

35 Red Sam came in and told his wife to quit lounging on the counter and hurry up with these people's order. His khaki trousers reached just to his hip bones and his stomach hung over them like a sack of meal swaying under his shirt. He came over and sat down at a table nearby and let out a combination sigh and yodel. "You can't win," he said. "You can't win," and he wiped his sweating red face off with a gray handkerchief. "These days you don't know who to trust," he said. "Ain't that the truth?"

36 "People are certainly not nice like they used to be," said the grandmother.

37 "Two fellers come in here last week," Red Sammy said, "driving a Chrysler. It was a old beat-up car but it was a good one and these boys looked all right to me. Said they worked at the mill and you know I let them fellers charge the gas they bought? Now why did I do that?"

38 "Because you're a good man!" the grandmother said at once.

39 "Yes'm, I suppose so," Red Sam said as if he were struck with this answer.

40 His wife brought the orders, carrying the five plates all at once without a tray, two in each hand and one balanced on her arm. "It isn't a soul in this green world of God's that you can trust," she said. "And I don't count nobody out of that, not nobody," she repeated, looking at Red Sammy.

41 "Did you read about that criminal, The Misfit, that's escaped?" asked the grandmother.

42 "I wouldn't be a bit surprised if he didn't attact this place right here," said the woman. "If he hears about it being here, I wouldn't be none surprised to see him. If he hears it's two cent in the cash register, I wouldn't be a-tall surprised if he ..."

43 "That'll do," Red Sam said. "Go bring these people their Co'-Colas," and the woman went off to get the rest of the order.

44 "A good man is hard to find," Red Sammy said. "Everything is getting terrible. I remember the day you could go off and leave your screen door unlatched. Not no more."

45 He and the grandmother discussed better times. The old lady said that in her opinion Europe was entirely to blame for the way things were now. She said the way Europe acted you would think we were made of money and Red Sam said it was no use talking about it, she was exactly right. The children ran outside into the white sunlight and looked at the monkey in the lacy chinaberry tree. He was busy catching fleas on himself and biting each one carefully between his teeth as if it were a delicacy.

46 They drove off again into the hot afternoon. The grandmother took catnaps and woke up every five minutes with her own snoring. Outside of Toombsboro

she woke up and recalled an old plantation that she had visited in this neighborhood once when she was a young lady. She said the house had six white columns across the front and that there was an avenue of oaks leading up to it and two little wooden trellis arbors on either side in front where you sat down with your suitor after a stroll in the garden. She recalled exactly which road to turn off to get to it. She knew that Bailey would not be willing to lose any time looking at an old house, but the more she talked about it, the more she wanted to see it once again and find out if the little twin arbors were still standing. "There was a secret panel in this house," she said craftily, not telling the truth but wishing that she were, "and the story went that all the family silver was hidden in it when Sherman came through[3] but it was never found ..."

47 "Hey!" John Wesley said. "Let's go see it! We'll find it! We'll poke all the woodwork and find it! Who lives there? Where do you turn off at? Hey, Pop, can't we turn off there?"

48 "We never have seen a house with a secret panel!" June Star shrieked. "Let's go to the house with the secret panel! Hey Pop, can't we go see the house with the secret panel!"

49 "It's not far from here, I know," the grandmother said. "It wouldn't take over twenty minutes."

50 Bailey was looking straight ahead. His jaw was as rigid as a horseshoe. "No," he said.

51 The children began to yell and scream that they wanted to see the house with the secret panel. John Wesley kicked the back of the front seat and June Star hung over her mother's shoulder and whined desperately into her ear that they never had any fun even on their vacation, that they could never do what THEY wanted to do. The baby began to scream and John Wesley kicked the back of the seat so hard that his father could feel the blows in his kidney.

52 "All right!" he shouted and drew the car to a stop at the side of the road. "Will you all shut up? Will you all just shut up for one second? If you don't shut up, we won't go anywhere."

53 "It would be very educational for them," the grandmother murmured.

54 "All right," Bailey said, "but get this: this is the only time we're going to stop for anything like this. This is the one and only time."

55 "The dirt road that you have to turn down is about a mile back," the grandmother directed. "I marked it when we passed."

56 "A dirt road," Bailey groaned.

57 After they had turned around and were headed toward the dirt road, the grandmother recalled other points about the house, the beautiful glass over the front doorway and the candle-lamp in the hall. John Wesley said that the secret panel was probably in the fireplace.

58 "You can't go inside this house," Bailey said. "You don't know who lives there."

---

3 a reference to General Sherman's brutal march through Georgia in 1864 during the Civil War; Sherman was a general on the Union side

59   "While you all talk to the people in front, I'll run around behind and get in a window," John Wesley suggested.

60   "We'll all stay in the car," his mother said.

61   They turned onto the dirt road and the car raced roughly along in a swirl of pink dust. The grandmother recalled the times when there were no paved roads and thirty miles was a day's journey. The dirt road was hilly and there were sudden washes in it and sharp curves on dangerous embankments. All at once they would be on a hill, looking down over the blue tops of trees for miles around, then the next minute, they would be in a red depression with the dust-coated trees looking down on them.

62   "This place had better turn up in a minute," Bailey said, "or I'm going to turn around."

63   The road looked as if no one had traveled on it for months.

64   "It's not much farther," the grandmother said and just as she said it, a horrible thought came to her. The thought was so embarrassing that she turned red in the face and her eyes dilated and her feet jumped up, upsetting her valise in the corner. The instant the valise moved, the newspaper top she had over the basket under it rose with a snarl and Pitty Sing, the cat, sprang onto Bailey's shoulder.

65   The children were thrown to the floor and their mother, clutching the baby, was thrown out the door onto the ground; the old lady was thrown into the front seat. The car turned over once and landed right-side-up in a gulch off the side of the road. Bailey remained in the driver's seat with the cat—gray-striped with a broad white face and an orange nose—clinging to his neck like a caterpillar.

66   As soon as the children saw they could move their arms and legs, they scrambled out of the car, shouting, "We've had an ACCIDENT!" The grandmother was curled up under the dashboard, hoping she was injured so that Bailey's wrath would not come down on her all at once. The horrible thought she had had before the accident was that the house she had remembered so vividly was not in Georgia but in Tennessee.

67   Bailey removed the cat from his neck with both hands and flung it out the window against the side of a pine tree. Then he got out of the car and started looking for the children's mother. She was sitting against the side of the red gutted ditch, holding the screaming baby, but she only had a cut down her face and a broken shoulder. "We've had an ACCIDENT!" the children screamed in a frenzy of delight.

68   "But nobody's killed," June Star said with disappointment as the grandmother limped out of the car, her hat still pinned to her head but the broken front brim standing up at a jaunty angle and the violet spray hanging off the side. They all sat down in the ditch, except the children, to recover from the shock. They were all shaking.

69   "Maybe a car will come along," said the children's mother hoarsely.

70   "I believe I have injured an organ," said the grandmother, pressing her side, but no one answered her. Bailey's teeth were clattering. He had on a yellow sport shirt with bright blue parrots designed in it and his face was as yellow as the shirt. The grandmother decided that she would not mention that the house was in Tennessee.

71   The road was about ten feet above and they could see only the tops of the trees on the other side of it. Behind the ditch they were sitting in there were more

woods, tall and dark and deep. In a few minutes they saw a car some distance away on top of a hill, coming slowly as if the occupants were watching them. The grandmother stood up and waved both her arms dramatically to attract their attention. The car continued to come on slowly, disappeared around a bend and appeared again, moving even slower, on top of the hill they had gone over. It was a big black battered hearse-like automobile. There were three men in it.

72   It came to a stop just over them and for some minutes, the driver looked down with a steady expressionless gaze to where they were sitting, and didn't speak. Then he turned his head and muttered something to the other two and they got out. One was a fat boy in black trousers and a red sweat shirt with a silver stallion embossed on the front of it. He moved around on the right side of them and stood staring, his mouth partly open in a kind of loose grin. The other had on khaki pants and a blue striped coat and a gray hat pulled down very low, hiding most of his face. He came around slowly on the left side. Neither spoke.

73   The driver got out of the car and stood by the side of it, looking down at them. He was an older man than the other two. His hair was just beginning to gray and he wore silver-rimmed spectacles that gave him a scholarly look. He had a long creased face and didn't have on any shirt or undershirt. He had on blue jeans that were too tight for him and was holding a black hat and a gun. The two boys also had guns.

74   "We've had an ACCIDENT!" the children screamed.

75   The grandmother had the peculiar feeling that the bespectacled man was someone she knew. His face was as familiar to her as if she had known him all her life but she could not recall who he was. He moved away from the car and began to come down the embankment, placing his feet carefully so that he wouldn't slip. He had on tan and white shoes and no socks, and his ankles were red and thin. "Good afternoon," he said. "I see you all had you a little spill?"

76   "We turned over twice!" said the grandmother.

77   "Oncet," he corrected. "We seen it happen. Try their car and see will it run, Hiram," he said quietly to the boy with the gray hat.

78   "What you got that gun for?" John Wesley asked. "Whatcha gonna do with that gun?"

79   "Lady," the man said to the children's mother, "would you mind calling them children to sit down by you? Children make me nervous. I want all you all to sit down right together there where you're at."

80   "What are you telling US what to do for?" June Star asked.

81   Behind them the line of woods gaped like a dark open mouth. "Come here," said their mother.

82   "Look here now," Bailey began suddenly, "we're in a predicament. We're in ..."

83   The grandmother shrieked. She scrambled to her feet and stood staring. "You're The Misfit!" she said. "I recognized you at once!"

84   "Yes'm," the man said, smiling slightly as if he were pleased in spite of himself to be known, "but it would have been better for all of you, lady, if you hadn't of reckernized me."

85   Bailey turned his head sharply and said something to his mother that shocked even the children. The old lady began to cry and The Misfit reddened.

86   "Lady," he said, "don't you get upset. Sometimes a man says things he don't mean. I don't reckon he meant to talk to you thataway."

87 "You wouldn't shoot a lady, would you?" the grandmother said and removed a clean handkerchief from her cuff and began to slap at her eyes with it.

88 The Misfit pointed the toe of his shoe into the ground and made a little hole and then covered it up again. "I would hate to have to," he said.

89 "Listen," the grandmother almost screamed, "I know you're a good man. You don't look a bit like you have common blood. I know you must come from nice people!"

90 "Yes ma'am," he said, "finest people in the world." When he smiled he showed a row of strong white teeth. "God never made a finer woman than my mother and my daddy's heart was pure gold," he said. The boy with the red sweat shirt had come around behind them and was standing with his gun at his hip. The Misfit squatted down on the ground. "Watch them children, Bobby Lee," he said. "You know they make me nervous." He looked at the six of them huddled together in front of him and he seemed to be embarrassed as if he couldn't think of anything to say. "Ain't a cloud in the sky," he remarked, looking up at it. "Don't see no sun but don't see no cloud neither."

91 "Yes, it's a beautiful day," said the grandmother. "Listen," she said, "you shouldn't call yourself The Misfit because I know you're a good man at heart. I can just look at you and tell."

92 "Hush!" Bailey yelled. "Hush! Everybody shut up and let me handle this!" He was squatting in the position of a runner about to spring forward but he didn't move.

93 "I pre-chate that, lady," The Misfit said and drew a little circle in the ground with the butt of his gun.

94 "It'll take a half a hour to fix this here car," Hiram called, looking over the raised hood of it.

95 "Well, first you and Bobby Lee get him and that little boy to step over yonder with you," The Misfit said, pointing to Bailey and John Wesley. "The boys want to ast you something," he said to Bailey. "Would you mind stepping back in them woods there with them?"

96 "Listen," Bailey began, "we're in a terrible predicament! Nobody realizes what this is," and his voice cracked. His eyes were as blue and intense as the parrots in his shirt and he remained perfectly still.

97 The grandmother reached up to adjust her hat brim as if she were going to the woods with him but it came off in her hand. She stood staring at it and after she let it fall on the ground. Hiram pulled Bailey up by the arm as if he were assisting an old man. John Wesley caught hold of his father's hand and Bobby Lee followed. They went off toward the woods and just as they reached the dark edge, Bailey turned and supporting himself against a gray naked pine trunk, he shouted, "I'll be back in a minute, Mamma, wait on me!"

98 "Come back this instant!" his mother shrilled but they all disappeared into the woods.

99 "Bailey Boy!" the grandmother called in a tragic voice but she found she was looking at The Misfit squatting on the ground in front of her. "I just know you're a good man," she said desperately. "You're not a bit common!"

100 "Nome, I ain't a good man," The Misfit said after a second as if he had considered her statement carefully, "but I ain't the worst in the world neither. My

daddy said I was a different breed of dog from my brothers and sisters. 'You know,' Daddy said, 'it's some that can live their whole life out without asking about it and it's others has to know why it is, and this boy is one of the latters. He's going to be into everything!'" He put on his black hat and looked up suddenly and then away deep into the woods as if he were embarrassed again. "I'm sorry I don't have on a shirt before you ladies," he said, hunching his shoulders slightly. "We buried our clothes that we had on when we escaped and we're just making do until we can get better. We borrowed these from some folks we met," he explained.

101   "That's perfectly all right," the grandmother said. "Maybe Bailey has an extra shirt in his suitcase."

102   "I'll look and see terrectly," The Misfit said.

103   "Where are they taking him?" the children's mother screamed.

104   "Daddy was a card himself," The Misfit said. "You couldn't put anything over on him. He never got in trouble with the Authorities though. Just had the knack of handling them."

105   "You could be honest too if you'd only try," said the grandmother. "Think how wonderful it would be to settle down and live a comfortable life and not have to think about somebody chasing you all the time."

106   The Misfit kept scratching in the ground with the butt of his gun as if he were thinking about it. "Yes'm, somebody is always after you," he murmured.

107   The grandmother noticed how thin his shoulder blades were just behind his hat because she was standing up looking down on him. "Do you ever pray?" she asked.

108   He shook his head. All she saw was the black hat wiggle between his shoulder blades. "Nome," he said.

109   There was a pistol shot from the woods, followed closely by another. Then silence. The old lady's head jerked around. She could hear the wind move through the tree tops like a long satisfied insuck of breath. "Bailey Boy!" she called.

110   "I was a gospel singer for a while," The Misfit said. "I been most everything. Been in the arm service, both land and sea, at home and abroad, been twict married, been an undertaker, been with the railroads, plowed Mother Earth, been in a tornado, seen a man burnt alive oncet," and he looked up at the children's mother and the little girl who were sitting close together, their faces white and their eyes glassy; "I even seen a woman flogged," he said.

111   "Pray, pray," the grandmother began, "pray, pray ..."

112   "I never was a bad boy that I remember of," The Misfit said in an almost dreamy voice, "but somewheres along the line I done something wrong and got sent to the penitentiary. I was buried alive," and he looked up and held her attention to him by a steady stare.

113   "That's when you should have started to pray," she said. "What did you do to get sent up to the penitentiary that first time?"

114   "Turn to the right, it was a wall," The Misfit said, looking up again at the cloudless sky. "Turn to the left, it was a wall. Look up it was a ceiling, look down it was a floor. I forget what I done, lady. I set there and set there, trying to remember what it was I done and I ain't recalled it to this day. Oncet in a while, I would think it was coming to me, but it never come."

115   "Maybe they put you in by mistake," the old lady said vaguely.

116   "Nome," he said. "It wasn't no mistake. They had the papers on me."

117   "You must have stolen something," she said.

118   The Misfit sneered slightly. "Nobody had nothing I wanted," he said. "It was a head-doctor at the penitentiary said what I had done was kill my daddy but I known that for a lie. My daddy died in nineteen ought nineteen of the epidemic flu and I never had a thing to do with it. He was buried in the Mount Hopewell Baptist churchyard and you can go there and see for yourself."

119   "If you would pray," the old lady said, "Jesus would help you."

120   "That's right," The Misfit said.

121   "Well then, why don't you pray?" she asked trembling with delight suddenly.

122   "I don't want no hep," he said. "I'm doing all right by myself."

123   Bobby Lee and Hiram came ambling back from the woods. Bobby Lee was dragging a yellow shirt with bright blue parrots in it.

124   "Thow me that shirt, Bobby Lee," The Misfit said. The shirt came flying at him and landed on his shoulder and he put it on. The grandmother couldn't name what the shirt reminded her of. "No, lady," The Misfit said while he was buttoning it up, "I found out the crime don't matter. You can do one thing or you can do another, kill a man or take a tire off his car, because sooner or later you're going to forget what it was you done and just be punished for it."

125   The children's mother had begun to make heaving noises as if she couldn't get her breath. "Lady," he asked, "would you and that little girl like to step off yonder with Bobby Lee and Hiram and join your husband?"

126   "Yes, thank you," the mother said faintly. Her left arm dangled helplessly and she was holding the baby, who had gone to sleep, in the other. "Hep that lady up, Hiram," The Misfit said as she struggled to climb out of the ditch, "and Bobby Lee, you hold onto that little girl's hand."

127   "I don't want to hold hands with him," June Star said. "He reminds me of a pig."

128   The fat boy blushed and laughed and caught her by the arm and pulled her off into the woods after Hiram and her mother.

129   Alone with The Misfit, the grandmother found that she had lost her voice. There was not a cloud in the sky nor any sun. There was nothing around her but woods. She wanted to tell him that he must pray. She opened and closed her mouth several times before anything came out. Finally she found herself saying, "Jesus. Jesus," meaning, Jesus will help you, but the way she was saying it, it sounded as if she might be cursing.

130   "Yes'm," The Misfit said as if he agreed. "Jesus thown everything off balance. It was the same case with Him as with me except He hadn't committed any crime and they could prove I had committed one because they had the papers on me. Of course," he said, "they never shown me my papers. That's why I sign myself now. I said long ago, you get you a signature and sign everything you do and keep a copy of it. Then you'll know what you done and you can hold up the crime to the punishment and see do they match and in the end you'll have something to prove you ain't been treated right. I call myself The Misfit," he said, "because I can't make what all I done wrong fit what all I gone through in punishment."

131   There was a piercing scream from the woods, followed closely by a pistol report. "Does it seem right to you, lady, that one is punished a heap and another ain't punished at all?"

132   "Jesus!" the old lady cried. "You've got good blood! I know you wouldn't shoot a lady! I know you come from nice people! Pray! Jesus, you ought not to shoot a lady. I'll give you all the money I've got!"

133   "Lady," The Misfit said, looking beyond her far into the woods, "there never was a body that give the undertaker a tip."

134   There were two more pistol reports and the grandmother raised her head like a parched old turkey hen crying for water and called, "Bailey Boy, Bailey Boy!" as if her heart would break.

135   "Jesus was the only One that ever raised the dead," The Misfit continued, "and He shouldn't have done it. He thown everything off balance. If He did what He said, then it's nothing for you to do but thow away everything and follow Him, and if He didn't, then it's nothing for you to do but enjoy the few minutes you got left the best way you can—by killing somebody or burning down his house or doing some other meanness to him. No pleasure but meanness," he said and his voice had become almost a snarl.

136   "Maybe He didn't raise the dead," the old lady mumbled, not knowing what she was saying and feeling so dizzy that she sank down in the ditch with her legs twisted under her.

137   "I wasn't there so I can't say He didn't," The Misfit said. "I wisht I had of been there," he said, hitting the ground with his fist. "It ain't right I wasn't there because if I had of been there I would of known. Listen lady," he said in a high voice, "if I had of been there I would of known and I wouldn't be like I am now." His voice seemed about to crack and the grandmother's head cleared for an instant. She saw the man's face twisted close to her own as if he were going to cry and she murmured, "Why you're one of my babies. You're one of my own children!" She reached out and touched him on the shoulder. The Misfit sprang back as if a snake had bitten him and shot her three times through the chest. Then he put his gun down on the ground and took off his glasses and began to clean them.

138   Hiram and Bobby Lee returned from the woods and stood over the ditch, looking down at the grandmother who half sat and half lay in a puddle of blood with her legs crossed under her like a child's and her face smiling up at the cloudless sky.

139   Without his glasses, The Misfit's eyes were red-rimmed and pale and defenseless-looking. "Take her off and thow her where you thown the others," he said, picking up the cat that was rubbing itself against his leg.

140   "She was a talker, wasn't she?" Bobby Lee said, sliding down the ditch with a yodel.

141   "She would of been a good woman," The Misfit said, "if it had been somebody there to shoot her every minute of her life."

142   "Some fun!" Bobby Lee said.

143   "Shut up, Bobby Lee," The Misfit said. "It's no real pleasure in life."

Margaret Laurence

Canada 1926–1987

Margaret Wemys was born in Neepawa, Manitoba, went to school there, and attended United College (now the University of Winnipeg). After graduation, she met and married Jack Laurence, an engineer whose work took them first to England and then to Africa, where they stayed for eight years. Laurence's career as a writer started in Africa with the publication of *A Tree of Poverty* (1954) and *The Tomorrow-Tamer* (1963). After returning to Canada, Laurence separated from her husband and moved to England, where she published her first three Manitoba novels set in Manawaka, a fictional town reminiscent of Neepawa. Laurence returned to Canada in 1969 and eventually settled in Lakefield, Ontario. In 1974, she wrote *The Diviners*, which ended the Manawaka sequence begun by *The Stone Angel*. Laurence's work explores the intricate connections among self, family, culture, and environment, a theme evident in "To Set Our House in Order."

To Set Our House in Order   1970

1   When the baby was almost ready to be born, something went wrong and my mother had to go into hospital two weeks before the expected time. I was wakened by her crying in the night, and then I heard my father's footsteps as he went downstairs to phone. I stood in the doorway of my room, shivering and listening, wanting to go to my mother but afraid to go lest there be some sight there more terrifying than I could bear.

2   "Hello—Paul?" my father said, and I knew he was talking to Dr. Cates. "It's Beth. The waters have broken, and the fetal position doesn't seem quite—well, I'm only thinking of what happened the last time, and another like that would be—I wish she were a little huskier, damn it—she's so—no, don't worry, I'm quite all right. Yes, I think that would be the best thing. Okay, make it as soon as you can, will you?"

3   He came back upstairs, looking bony and dishevelled in his pyjamas, and running his fingers through his sand-coloured hair. At the top of the stairs, he came face to face with Grandmother MacLeod, who was standing there in her quilted black satin dressing gown, her slight figure held straight and poised, as though she were unaware that her hair was bound grotesquely like white-feathered wings in the snare of her coarse night-time hairnet.

4   "What is it, Ewen?"

5   "It's all right, Mother. Beth's having—a little trouble. I'm going to take her into the hospital. You go back to bed."

6   "I told you," Grandmother MacLeod said in her clear voice, never loud, but distinct and ringing like the tap of a sterling teaspoon on a crystal goblet, "I did tell you, Ewen, did I not, that you should have got a girl in to help her with the housework? She would have rested more."

7   "I couldn't afford to get anyone in," my father said. "If you thought she should've rested more, why didn't you ever—oh God, I'm out of my mind tonight—just go back to bed, Mother, please. I must get back to Beth."

8   When my father went down to the front door to let Dr. Cates in, my need overcame my fear and I slipped into my parents' room. My mother's black hair, so neatly pinned up during the day, was startlingly spread across the white pillowcase. I stared at her, not speaking, and then she smiled and I rushed from the doorway and buried my head upon her.

9   "It's all right, honey," she said. "Listen, Vanessa, the baby's just going to come a little early, that's all. You'll be all right. Grandmother MacLeod will be here."

10   "How can she get the meals?" I wailed, fixing on the first thing that came to mind. "She never cooks. She doesn't know how."

11   "Yes, she does," my mother said. "She can cook as well as anyone when she has to. She's just never had to very much, that's all. Don't worry—she'll keep everything in order, and then some."

12   My father and Dr. Cates came in, and I had to go, without ever saying anything I had wanted to say. I went back to my own room and lay with the shadows all around me. I listened to the night murmurings that always went on in that house, sounds which never had a source, rafters and beams contracting in the dry air, perhaps, or mice in the walls, or a sparrow that had flown into the attic through the broken skylight there. After a while, although I would not have believed it possible, I slept.

13   The next morning I questioned my father. I believed him to be not only the best doctor in Manawaka, but also the best doctor in the whole of Manitoba, if not in the entire world, and the fact that he was not the one looking after my mother seemed to have something sinister about it.

14   "But it's always done that way, Vanessa," he explained. "Doctors never attend members of their own family. It's because they care so much about them, you see, and—"

15   "And what?" I insisted, alarmed at the way he had broken off. But my father did not reply. He stood there, and then he put on that difficult smile with which adults seek to conceal pain from children. I felt terrified, and ran to him, and he held me tightly.

16   "She's going to be fine," he said. "Honestly she is. Nessa, don't cry—"

17   Grandmother MacLeod appeared beside us, steel-spined despite her apparent fragility. She was wearing a purple silk dress and her ivory pendant. She looked as though she were all ready to go out for afternoon tea.

18   "Ewen, you're only encouraging the child to give way," she said. "Vanessa, big girls of ten don't make such a fuss about things. Come and get your breakfast. Now, Ewen, you're not to worry. I'll see to everything."

19   Summer holidays were not quite over, but I did not feel like going out to play with any of the kids. I was very superstitious, and I had the feeling that if I left the house, even for a few hours, some disaster would overtake my mother. I did not, of course, mention this feeling to Grandmother MacLeod, for she did not believe in the existence of fear, or if she did, she never let on. I spent the morning morbidly, in seeking hidden places in the house. There were many of these—odd-shaped nooks under the stairs, small and loosely nailed-up doors at the back of clothes closets, leading to dusty tunnels and forgotten recesses in the heart of the

house where the only things actually to be seen were drab oil paintings stacked upon the rafters, and trunks full of outmoded clothing and old photograph albums. But the unseen presences in these secret places I knew to be those of every person, young or old, who had ever belonged to the house and had died, including Uncle Roderick who got killed on the Somme, and the baby who would have been my sister if only she had managed to come to life. Grandfather MacLeod, who had died a year after I was born, was present in the house in more tangible form. At the top of the main stairs hung the mammoth picture of a darkly uniformed man riding upon a horse whose prancing stance and dilated nostrils suggested that the battle was not yet over, that it might indeed continue until Judgment Day. The stern man was actually the Duke of Wellington,[1] but at the time I believed him to be my grandfather MacLeod, still keeping an eye on things.

20   We had moved in with Grandmother MacLeod when the Depression got bad and she could no longer afford a housekeeper, but the MacLeod house never seemed like home to me. Its dark red brick was grown over at the front with Virginia creeper that turned crimson in the fall, until you could hardly tell brick from leaves. It boasted a small tower in which Grandmother MacLeod kept a weedy collection of anaemic ferns. The verandah was embellished with a profusion of wrought-iron scrolls, and the circular rose-window upstairs contained glass of many colours which permitted an outlooking eye to see the world as a place of absolute sapphire or emerald, or if one wished to look with a jaundiced eye, a hateful yellow. In Grandmother MacLeod's opinion, their features gave the house style.

21   Inside, a multitude of doors led to rooms where my presence, if not actually forbidden, was not encouraged. One was Grandmother MacLeod's bedroom, with its stale and old-smelling air, the dim reek of medicines and lavender sachets. Here resided her monogrammed dresser silver, brush and mirror, nail-buffer and button hook and scissors, none of which must even be fingered by me now, for she meant to leave them to me in her will and intended to hand them over in the same flawless and unused condition in which they had always been kept. Here, too, were the silver-framed photographs of Uncle Roderick—as a child, as a boy, as a man in his Army uniform. The massive walnut spool bed had obviously been designed for queens or giants, and my tiny grandmother used to lie within it all day when she had migraine, contriving somehow to look like a giant queen.

22   The living room was another alien territory where I had to tread warily, for many valuable objects sat just-so on tables and mantelpiece, and dirt must not be tracked in upon the blue Chinese carpet with its birds in eternal motionless flight and its water-lily buds caught forever just before the point of opening. My mother was always nervous when I was in this room.

23   "Vanessa, honey," she would say, half apologetically, "why don't you go and play in the den, or upstairs?"

24   "Can't you leave her, Beth?" my father would say. "She's not doing any harm."

25   "I'm only thinking of the rug," my mother would say, glancing at Grandmother MacLeod, "and yesterday she nearly knocked the Dresden[2] shepherdess off the mantel. I mean, she can't help it, Ewen, she has to run around—"

---

1   famous nineteenth-century British general who opposed Napoleon; hero of the Battle of Waterloo

2   a china figurine; Dresden china was highly valued

26   "Goddamn it, I know she can't help it," my father would growl, glaring at the smirking face of the Dresden shepherdess.

27   "I see no need to blaspheme, Ewen," Grandmother MacLeod would say quietly, and then my father would say he was sorry, and I would leave.

28   The day my mother went to the hospital, Grandmother MacLeod called me at lunch-time, and when I appeared, smudged with dust from the attic, she looked at me distastefully as though I had been a cockroach that had just crawled impertinently out of the woodwork.

29   "For mercy's sake, Vanessa, what have you been doing with yourself? Run and get washed this minute. Here, not that way—you use the back stairs, young lady. Get along now. Oh—your father phoned."

30   I swung around. "What did he say? How is she? Is the baby born?"

31   "Curiosity killed a cat," Grandmother MacLeod said, frowning. "I cannot understand Beth and Ewen telling you all these things at your age. What sort of vulgar person you'll grow up to be, I dare not think. No, it's not born yet. Your mother's just the same. No change."

32   I looked at my grandmother, not wanting to appeal to her, but unable to stop myself. "Will she—will she be all right?"

33   Grandmother MacLeod straightened her already-straight back. "If I said definitely yes, Vanessa, that would be a lie, and the MacLeods do not tell lies, as I have tried to impress on you before. What happens is God's will. The Lord giveth, and the Lord taketh away."

34   Appalled, I turned away so she would not see my face and my eyes. Surprisingly, I heard her sigh and felt her papery white and perfectly manicured hand upon my shoulder.

35   "When your Uncle Roderick got killed," she said, "I thought I would die. But I didn't die, Vanessa."

36   At lunch, she chatted animatedly, and I realised she was trying to cheer me in the only way she knew.

37   "When I married your Grandfather MacLeod," she related, "he said to me, 'Eleanor, don't think because we're going to the prairies that I expect you to live roughly. You're used to a proper house, and you shall have one.' He was as good as his word. Before we'd been in Manawaka three years, he'd had this place built. He earned a good deal of money in his time, your grandfather. He soon had more patients than either of the other doctors. We ordered our dinner service and all our silver from Birks' in Toronto. We had resident help in those days, of course, and never had less than twelve guests for dinner parties. When I had a tea, it would always be twenty or thirty. Never any less than half a dozen different kinds of cake were ever served in this house. Well, no one seems to bother much these days. Too lazy, I suppose."

38   "Too broke," I suggested. "That's what Dad says."

39   "I can't bear slang," Grandmother MacLeod said. "If you mean hard up, why don't you say so? It's mainly a question of management anyway. My accounts were always in good order, and so was my house. No unexpected expenses that couldn't be met, no fruit cellar running out of preserves before the winter was over. Do you know what my father used to say to me when I was a girl?"

40   "No," I said. "What?"

41   "God loves Order," Grandmother MacLeod replied with emphasis. "You remember that, Vanessa. God loves Order—he wants each one of us to set our house in order. I've never forgotten those words of my father's. I was a MacInnes before I got married. The MacInnes is a very ancient clan, the lairds of Morven and the constables of the Castle of Kinlochaline. Did you finish that book I gave you?"

42   "Yes," I said. Then, feeling some additional comment to be called for, "It was a swell book, Grandmother."

43   This was somewhat short of the truth. I had been hoping for her cairngorm brooch on my tenth birthday, and had received instead the plaid-bound volume entitled *The Clans and Tartans of Scotland*. Most of it was too boring to read, but I had looked up the motto of my own family and those of some of my friends' families. *Be then a wall of brass. Learn to suffer. Consider the end. Go carefully.* I had not found any of these slogans reassuring. What with Mavis Duncan learning to suffer, and Laura Kennedy considering the end, and Patsy Drummond going carefully, and I spending my time in being a wall of brass, it did not seem to me that any of us were going to lead very interesting lives. I did not say this to Grandmother MacLeod.

44   "The MacInnes motto is *Pleasure Arises from Work*," I said.

45   "Yes," she agreed proudly. "And an excellent motto it is, too. One to bear in mind."

46   She rose from the table, rearranging on her bosom the looped ivory beads that held the pendant on which a fullblown ivory rose was stiffly carved.

47   "I hope Ewen will be pleased," she said.

48   "What at?"

49   "Didn't I tell you?" Grandmother MacLeod said. "I hired a girl this morning, for the housework. She's to start tomorrow."

50   When my father got home that evening, Grandmother MacLeod told him her good news. He ran one hand distractedly across his forehead.

51   "I'm sorry, Mother, but you'll just have to unhire her. I can't possibly pay anyone."

52   "It seems distinctly odd," Grandmother MacLeod snapped, "that you can afford to eat chicken four times a week."

53   "Those chickens," my father said in an exasperated voice, "are how people are paying their bills. The same with the eggs and the milk. That scrawny turkey that arrived yesterday was for Logan MacCardney's appendix, if you must know. We probably eat better than any family in Manawaka, except Niall Cameron's. People can't entirely dispense with doctors or undertakers. That doesn't mean to say I've got any cash. Look, Mother, I don't know what's happening with Beth. Paul thinks he may have to do a Caesarean. Can't we leave all this? Just leave the house alone. Don't touch it. What does it matter?"

54   "I have never lived in a messy house, Ewen," Grandmother MacLeod said, "and I don't intend to begin now."

55   "Oh Lord," my father said. "Well, I'll phone Edna, I guess, and see if she can give us a hand, although God knows she's got enough, with the Connor house and her parents to look after."

56   "I don't fancy having Edna Connor in to help," Grandmother MacLeod objected.

57   "Why not?" my father shouted. "She's Beth's sister, isn't she?"

58 "She speaks in such a slangy way," Grandmother MacLeod said. "I have never believed she was a good influence on Vanessa. And there is no need for you to raise your voice to me, Ewen, if you please."

59 I could barely control my rage. I thought my father would surely rise to Aunt Edna's defence. But he did not.

60 "It'll be all right," he soothed her. "She'd only be here for part of the day, Mother. You could stay in your room."

61 Aunt Edna strode in the next morning. The sight of her bobbed black hair and her grin made me feel better at once. She hauled out the carpet sweeper and the weighted polisher and got to work. I dusted while she polished and swept, and we got through the living room and front hall in next to no time.

62 "Where's her royal highness, kiddo?" she enquired.

63 "In her room," I said. "She's reading the catalogue from Robinson & Cleaver."

64 "Good Glory, not again?" Aunt Edna cried. "The last time she ordered three linen tea-clothes and two dozen serviettes. It came to fourteen dollars. Your mother was absolutely frantic. I guess I shouldn't be saying this."

65 "I knew anyway," I assured her. "She was at the lace handkerchiefs section when I took up her coffee."

66 "Let's hope she stays there. Heaven forbid she should get onto the banqueting cloths. Well, at least she believes the Irish are good for two things—manual labour and linen-making. She's never forgotten Father used to be a blacksmith, before he got the hardware store. Can you beat it? I wish it didn't bother Beth."

67 "Does it?" I asked, and immediately realised this was a wrong move, for Aunt Edna was suddenly scrutinising me.

68 "We're making you grow up before your time," she said. "Don't pay any attention to me, Nessa. I must've got up on the wrong side of the bed this morning."

69 But I was unwilling to leave the subject.

70 "All the same," I said thoughtfully, "Grandmother MacLeod's family were the lairds of Morven and the constables of the Castle of Kinlochaline. I bet you didn't know that."

71 Aunt Edna snorted, "Castle, my foot. She was born in Ontario, just like your Grandfather Connor, and her father was a horse doctor. Come on, kiddo, we'd better shut up and get down to business here."

72 We worked in silence for a while.

73 "Aunt Edna—" I said at last, "what about Mother? Why won't they let me go and see her?"

74 "Kids aren't allowed to visit maternity patients. It's tough for you, I know that. Look, Nessa, don't worry. If it doesn't start tonight, they're going to do the operation. She's getting the best of care."

75 I stood there, holding the feather duster like a dead bird in my hands. I was not aware that I was going to speak until the words came out.

76 "I'm scared," I said.

77 Aunt Edna put her arms around me, and her face looked all at once stricken and empty of defences.

78 "Oh, honey, I'm scared, too," she said.

79   It was this way that Grandmother MacLeod found us when she came stepping lightly down into the front hall with the order in her hand for two dozen lace-bordered handkerchiefs of pure Irish linen.

80   I could not sleep that night, and when I went downstairs, I found my father in the den. I sat down on the hassock beside his chair, and he told me about the operation my mother was to have the next morning. He kept on saying it was not serious nowadays.

81   "But you're worried," I put in, as though seeking to explain why I was.

82   "I should at least have been able to keep from burdening you with it," he said in a distant voice, as though to himself. "If only the baby hadn't got itself twisted around—"

83   "Will it be born dead, like the little girl?"

84   "I don't know," my father said. "I hope not."

85   "She'd be disappointed, wouldn't she, if it was?" I said bleakly, wondering why I was not enough for her.

86   "Yes, she would," my father replied. "She won't be able to have any more, after this. It's partly on your account that she wants this one, Nessa. She doesn't want you to grow up without a brother or sister."

87   "As far as I'm concerned, she didn't need to bother," I retorted angrily.

88   My father laughed. "Well, let's talk about something else, and then maybe you'll be able to sleep. How did you and Grandmother make out today?"

89   "Oh, fine, I guess. What was Grandfather MacLeod like, Dad?"

90   "What did she tell you about him?"

91   "She said he made a lot of money in his time."

92   "Well, he wasn't any millionaire," my father said, "but I suppose he did quite well. That's not what I associate with him, though."

93   He reached across to the bookshelf, took out a small leather-bound volume and opened it. On the pages were mysterious marks, like doodling, only much neater and more patterned.

94   "What is it?" I asked.

95   "Greek," my father explained. "This is a play called *Antigone*. See, here's the title in English. There's a whole stack of them on the shelves there. *Oedipus Rex. Electra. Medea.* They belonged to your Grandfather MacLeod. He used to read them often."

96   "Why?" I enquired, unable to understand why anyone would pore over those undecipherable signs.

97   "He was interested in them," my father said. "He must have been a lonely man, although it never struck me that way at the time. Sometimes a thing only hits you a long time afterwards."

98   "Why would he be lonely?" I wanted to know.

99   "He was the only person in Manawaka who could read these plays in the original Greek," my father said. "I don't suppose many people, if anyone, had even read them in English translations. Maybe he would have liked to be a classical scholar—I don't know. But his father was a doctor, so that's what he was. Maybe he would have liked to talk to somebody about these plays. They must have meant a lot to him."

100   It seemed to me that my father was talking oddly. There was a sadness in his voice that I had never heard before, and I longed to say something that would make him feel better, but I could not, because I did not know what was the matter.
"Can you read this kind of writing?" I asked hesitantly.

101   My father shook his head. "Nope. I was never very intellectual, I guess. Rod was always brighter than I, in school, but even he wasn't interested in learning Greek. Perhaps he would've been later, if he'd lived. As a kid, all I ever wanted to do was go into the merchant marine."

102   "Why didn't you, then?"

103   "Oh well," my father said offhandedly, "a kid who'd never seen the sea wouldn't have made much of a sailor. I might have turned out to be the seasick type."

104   I had lost interest now that he was speaking once more like himself.

105   "Grandmother MacLeod was pretty cross today about the girl," I remarked.

106   "I know," my father nodded. "Well, we must be as nice as we can to her, Nessa, and after a while she'll be all right."

107   Suddenly I did not care what I said.

108   "Why can't she be nice to us for a change?" I burst out. "We're always the ones who have to be nice to her."

109   My father put his hand down and slowly tilted my head until I was forced to look at him.

110   "Vanessa," he said, "she's had troubles in her life which you really don't know much about. That's why she gets migraine sometimes and has to go to bed. It's not easy for her these days, either—the house is still the same, so she thinks other things should be, too. It hurts her when she finds they aren't."

111   "I don't see—" I began.

112   "Listen," my father said, "you know we were talking about what people are interested in, like Grandfather MacLeod being interested in Greek plays? Well, your grandmother was interested in being a lady, Nessa, and for a long time it seemed to her that she was one."

113   I thought of the Castle of Kinlochaline, and of horse doctors in Ontario.

114   "I didn't know—" I stammered.

115   "That's usually the trouble with most of us," my father said. "You go on up to bed now. I'll phone tomorrow from the hospital as soon as the operation's over."

116   I did sleep at last, and in my dreams I could hear the caught sparrow fluttering in the attic, and the sound of my mother crying, and the voices of the dead children.

117   My father did not phone until afternoon. Grandmother MacLeod said I was being silly, for you could hear the phone ringing all over the house, but nevertheless I refused to move out of the den. I had never before examined my father's books, but now, at a loss for something to do, I took them out one by one and read snatches here and there. After I had been doing this for several hours, it dawned on me that most of the books were of the same kind. I looked again at the titles.

118   *Seven-League Boots. Arabia Deserta. The Seven Pillars of Wisdom. Travels in Tibet. Count Lucknor the Sea Devil.* And a hundred more. On a shelf by themselves were copies of the *National Geographic* magazine, which I looked at often enough, but

never before with the puzzling compulsion which I felt now, as though I were on the verge of some discovery, something which I had to find out and yet did not want to know. I riffled through the picture-filled pages. Hibiscus and wild orchids grew in a soft-petalled confusion. The Himalayas stood lofty as gods, with the morning sun on their peaks of snow. Leopards snarled from the vined depths of a thousand jungles. Schooners buffeted their white sails like the wings of giant angels against the great sea winds.

119   "What on earth are you doing?" Grandmother MacLeod enquired waspishly from the doorway. "You've got everything scattered all over the place. Pick it all up this minute, Vanessa, do you hear?"

120   So I picked up the books and magazines, and put them all neatly away, as I had been told to do.

121   When the telephone finally rang, I was afraid to answer it. At last I picked it up. My father sounded faraway, and the relief in his voice made it unsteady.

122   "It's okay, honey. Everything's fine. The boy was born alive and kicking after all. Your mother's pretty weak, but she's going to be all right."

123   I could hardly believe it. I did not want to talk to anyone. I wanted to be by myself, to assimilate the presence of my brother, towards whom, without ever having seen him yet, I felt such tenderness and such resentment.

124   That evening, Grandmother MacLeod approached my father, who, still dazed with the unexpected gift of neither life now being threatened, at first did not take her seriously when she asked what they planned to call the child.

125   "Oh, I don't know. Hank, maybe, or Joe. Fauntleroy, perhaps."

126   She ignored his levity.

127   "Ewen," she said. "I wish you would call him Roderick."

128   My father's face changed. "I'd rather not."

129   "I think you should," Grandmother MacLeod insisted, very quietly, but in a voice as pointed and precise as her silver nail-scissors.

130   "Don't you think Beth ought to decide?" my father asked.

131   "Beth will agree if you do."

132   My father did not bother to deny something that even I knew to be true. He did not say anything. Then Grandmother MacLeod's voice, astonishingly, faltered a little.

133   "It would mean a great deal to me," she said.

134   I remembered what she had told me—*When your Uncle Roderick got killed, I thought I would die. But I didn't die.* All at once, her feeling for that unknown dead man became a reality for me. And yet I held it against her, as well, for I could see that it had enabled her to win now.

135   "All right," my father said tiredly. "We'll call him Roderick."

136   Then, alarmingly, he threw back his head and laughed.

137   "Roderick Dhu!" he cried. "That's what you'll call him, isn't it? Black Roderick. Like before. Don't you remember? As though he were a character out of Sir Walter Scott, instead of an ordinary kid who—"

138   He broke off, and looked at her with a kind of desolation in his face.

139   "God, I'm sorry, Mother," he said. "I had no right to say that."

140   Grandmother MacLeod did not flinch, or tremble, or indicate that she felt anything at all.

141   "I accept your apology, Ewen," she said.

142 My mother had to stay in bed for several weeks after she arrived home. The baby's cot was kept in my parents' room, and I could go in and look at the small creature who lay there with his tightly closed fists and his feathery black hair. Aunt Edna came in to help each morning, and when she had finished the housework, she would have coffee with my mother. They kept the door closed, but this did not prevent me from eavesdropping, for there was an air register in the floor of the spare room, which was linked somehow with the register in my parents' room. If you put your ear to the iron grille, it was almost like a radio.

143 "Did you mind very much, Beth?" Aunt Edna was saying.

144 "Oh, it's not the name I mind," my mother replied. "It's just the fact that Ewen felt he had to. You know that Rod had only had the sight of one eye, didn't you?"

145 "Sure, I knew. So what?"

146 "There was only a year and a half between Ewen and Rod," my mother said, "so they often went around together when they were youngsters. It was Ewen's air-rifle that did it."

147 "Oh Lord," Aunt Edna said heavily. "I suppose she always blamed him?"

148 "No, I don't think it was so much that, really. It was how he felt himself. I think he even used to wonder sometimes if—but people shouldn't let themselves think like that, or they'd go crazy. Accidents do happen, after all. When the war came, Ewen joined up first. Rod should never have been in the Army at all, but he couldn't wait to get in. He must have lied about his eyesight. It wasn't so very noticeable unless you looked at him closely, and I don't suppose the medicals were very thorough in those days. He got in as a gunner, and Ewen applied to have him in the same company. He thought he might be able to watch out for him, I guess, Rod being—at a disadvantage. They were both only kids. Ewen was nineteen and Rod was eighteen when they went to France. And then the Somme. I don't know, Edna, I think Ewen felt that if Rod had had proper sight, or if he hadn't been in the same outfit and had been sent somewhere else—you know how people always think these things afterwards, not that it's ever a bit of use. Ewen wasn't there when Rod got hit. They'd lost each other somehow, and Ewen was looking for him, not bothering about anything else, you know, just frantically looking. Then he stumbled across him quite by chance. Rod was still alive, but—"

149 "Stop it, Beth," Aunt Edna said. "You're only upsetting yourself."

150 "Ewen never spoke of it to me," my mother went on, "until once his mother showed me the letter he'd written to her at the time. It was a peculiar letter, almost formal, saying how gallantly Rod had died, and all that. I guess I shouldn't have, but I told him she'd shown it to me. He was very angry that she had. And then, as though for some reason he were terribly ashamed, he said—*I had to write something to her, but men don't really die like that, Beth. It wasn't that way at all.* It was only after the war that he decided to come back and study medicine and go into practice with his father."

151 "Had Rod meant to?" Aunt Edna asked.

152 "I don't know," my mother said slowly. "I never felt I should ask Ewen that."

153 Aunt Edna was gathering up the coffee things, for I could hear the clash of cups and saucers being stacked on the tray.

154 "You know what I heard her say to Vanessa once, Beth? *The MacLeods never tell lies.* Those were her exact words. Even then, I didn't know whether to laugh or cry."

155   "Please, Edna—" my mother sounded worn out now. "Don't."

156   "Oh Glory," Aunt Edna said remorsefully, "I've got all the delicacy of a two-ton truck. I didn't mean Ewen, for heaven's sake. That wasn't what I meant at all. Here, let me plump up your pillows for you."

157   Then the baby began to cry, so I could not hear anything more of interest. I took my bike and went out beyond Manawaka, riding aimlessly along the gravel highway. It was late summer, and the wheat had changed colour, but instead of being high and bronzed in the fields, it was stunted and dessicated, for there had been no rain again this year. But in the bluff where I stopped and crawled under the barbed wire fence and lay stretched out on the grass, the plentiful poplar leaves were turning to luminous yellow and shone like church windows in the sun. I put my head down very close to the earth and looked at what was going on there. Grasshoppers with enormous eyes ticked and twitched around me, as though the dry air were perfect for their purposes. A ladybird laboured mightily to climb a blade of grass, fell off, and started all over again, seeming to be unaware that she possessed wings and could have flown up.

158   I thought of the accidents that might easily happen to a person—or, of course, might not happen, might happen to somebody else. I thought of the dead baby, my sister, who might as easily have been I. Would she, then, have been lying here in my place, the sharp grass making its small toothmarks on her brown arms, the sun warming her to the heart? I thought of the leather-bound volumes of Greek, and the six different kinds of iced cakes that used to be offered always in the MacLeod house, and the pictures of leopards and green seas. I thought of my brother, who had been born alive after all, and now had been given his life's name.

159   I could not really comprehend these things, but I sensed their strangeness, their disarray. I felt that whatever God might love in this world, it was certainly not order.

Ursula Le Guin

U.S.A. 1929–

Ursula Le Guin, the daughter of an anthropologist and a folklorist, was born in Berkeley, California. She was educated at Radcliffe and Columbia. While best known for her science fiction, Le Guin has published poetry, children's books, travel essays, and essays reflecting her commitments to feminist, environmental, and social issues. She currently lives in Seattle. Her connection to the Pacific Northwest is glimpsed in the title of her story "The Ones Who Walk Away From Omelas," in which the name at the end is a reversal of Salem, O(regon). In this story, as in much of her other work, Le Guin asks us to think about what we might stand for morally, about what we might sanction to guarantee our own comfort and security.

The Ones Who Walk Away From Omelas   1973

1   With a clamor of bells that set the swallows soaring, the Festival of Summer came to the city, Omelas, bright-towered by the sea. The rigging of the boats in harbor sparkled with flags. In the streets between houses with red roofs and painted walls, between old moss-grown gardens and under avenues of trees, past great parks and public buildings, processions moved. Some were decorous: old people in long stiff robes of mauve and grey, grave master workmen, quiet, merry women carrying their babies and chatting as they walked. In other streets the music beat faster, a shimmering of gong and tambourine, and the people went dancing, the procession was a dance. Children dodged in and out, their high calls rising like the swallows' crossing flights over the music and the singing. All the processions wound towards the north side of the city, where on the great water-meadow called the Green Fields boys and girls, naked in the bright air, with mud-stained feet and ankles and long, lithe arms, exercised their restive horses before the race. The horses wore no gear at all but a halter without bit. Their manes were braided with streamers of silver, gold, and green. They flared their nostrils and pranced and boasted to one another; they were vastly excited, the horse being the only animal who has adopted our ceremonies as his own. Far off to the north and west the mountains stood up half encircling Omelas on her bay. The air of morning was so clear that the snow still crowning the Eighteen Peaks burned with white-gold fire across the miles of sunlit air, under the dark blue of the sky. There was just enough wind to make the banners that marked the racecourse snap and flutter now and then. In the silence of the broad green meadows one could hear the music winding through the city streets, farther and nearer and ever approaching, a cheerful faint sweetness of the air that from time to time trembled and gathered together and broke out into the great joyous clanging of the bells.

2   Joyous! How is one to tell about joy? How describe the citizens of Omelas?

3   They were not simple folk, you see, though they were happy. But we do not say the words of cheer much any more. All smiles have become archaic. Given a description such as this one tends to make certain assumptions. Given a description such as this one tends to look next for the King, mounted on a splendid stallion and surrounded by his noble knights, or perhaps in a golden litter borne by great-muscled slaves. But there was no king. They did not use swords, or keep slaves. They were not barbarians. I do not know the rules and laws of their society, but I suspect that they were singularly few. As they did without monarchy and slavery, so they also got on without the stock exchange, the advertisement, the secret police, and the bomb. Yet I repeat that these were not simple folk, not dulcet shepherds, noble savages, bland utopians. They were not less complex than us. The trouble is that we have a bad habit, encouraged by pedants and sophisticates, of considering happiness as something rather stupid. Only pain is intellectual, only evil interesting. This is the treason of the artist: a refusal to admit the banality of evil and the terrible boredom of pain. If you can't lick 'em, join 'em. If it hurts, repeat it. But to praise despair is to condemn delight, to embrace violence is to lose hold of everything else. We have almost lost hold; we can no longer describe a happy man, nor make any celebration of joy. How can I tell you about the people of Omelas? They were not naïve and happy children—though their children were,

in fact, happy. They were mature, intelligent, passionate adults whose lives were not wretched. O miracle! but I wish I could describe it better. I wish I could convince you. Omelas sounds in my words like a city in a fairy tale, long ago and far away, once upon a time. Perhaps it would be best if you imagined it as your own fancy bids, assuming it will rise to the occasion, for certainly I cannot suit you all. For instance, how about technology? I think that there would be no cars or helicopters in and above the streets; this follows from the fact that the people of Omelas are happy people. Happiness is based on a just discrimination of what is necessary, what is neither necessary nor destructive, and what is destructive. In the middle category, however—that of the unnecessary but undestructive, that of comfort, luxury, exuberance, etc.—they could perfectly well have central heating, subway trains, washing machines, and all kinds of marvelous devices not yet invented here, floating light-sources, fuelless power, a cure for the common cold. Or they could have none of that: it doesn't matter. As you like it. I incline to think that people from towns up and down the coast have been coming in to Omelas during the last days before the Festival on very fast little trains and double-decked trams and that the train station of Omelas is actually the handsomest building in town, though plainer than the magnificent Farmers' Market. But even granted trains, I fear that Omelas so far strikes some of you as goody-goody. Smiles, bells, parades, horses, bleh. If so, please add an orgy. If an orgy would help, don't hesitate. Let us not, however, have temples from which issue beautiful nude priests and priestesses already half in ecstasy and ready to copulate with any man or woman, lover or stranger, who desires union with the deep godhead of the blood, although that was my first idea. But really it would be better not to have any temples in Omelas—at least, not manned temples. Religion yes, clergy no. Surely the beautiful nudes can just wander about, offering themselves like divine soufflés to the hunger of the needy and the rapture of the flesh. Let them join the processions. Let tambourines be struck above the copulations, and the glory of desire be proclaimed upon the gongs, and (a not unimportant point) let the offspring of these delightful rituals be beloved and looked after by all. One thing I know there is none of in Omelas is guilt. But what else should there be? I thought at first there were no drugs, but that is puritanical. For those who like it, the faint insistent sweetness of *drooz* may perfume the ways of the city, drooz which first brings a great lightness and brilliance to the mind and limbs, and then after some hours a dreamy languor, and wonderful visions at last of the very arcana and inmost secrets of the Universe, as well as exciting the pleasure of sex beyond all belief; and it is not habit-forming. For more modest tastes I think there ought to be beer. What else, what else belongs in the joyous city? The sense of victory, surely, the celebration of courage. But as we did without clergy, let us do without soldiers. The joy built upon successful slaughter is not the right kind of joy; it will not do; it is fearful and it is trivial. A boundless and generous contentment, a magnanimous triumph felt not against some outer enemy but in communion with the finest and fairest in the souls of all men everywhere and the splendor of the world's summer: this is what swells the hearts of the people of Omelas, and the victory they celebrate is that of life. I really don't think many of them need to take *drooz*.

4   Most of the processions have reached the Green Fields by now. A marvelous smell of cooking goes forth from the red and blue tents of the provisioners. The faces of small children are amiably sticky; in the benign grey beard of a man a

couple of crumbs of rich pastry are entangled. The youths and girls have mounted their horses and are beginning to group around the starting line of the course. An old woman, small, fat, and laughing, is passing out flowers from a basket, and tall young men wear her flowers in their shining hair. A child of nine or ten sits at the edge of the crowd, alone, playing on a wooden flute. People pause to listen, and they smile, but they do not speak to him, for he never ceases playing and never sees them, his dark eyes wholly rapt in the sweet, thin magic of the tune.

5   He finishes, and slowly lowers his hands holding the wooden flute.

6   As if that little private silence were the signal, all at once a trumpet sounds from the pavilion near the starting line: imperious, melancholy, piercing. The horses rear on their slender legs, and some of them neigh in answer. Sober-faced, the young riders stroke the horses' necks and soothe them, whispering, "Quiet, quiet, there my beauty, my hope...." They begin to form in rank along the starting line. The crowds along the racecourse are like a field of grass and flowers in the wind. The Festival of Summer has begun.

7   Do you believe? Do you accept the festival, the city, the joy? No? Then let me describe one more thing.

8   In a basement under one of the beautiful public buildings of Omelas, or perhaps in the cellar of one of its spacious private homes, there is a room. It has one locked door, and no window. A little light seeps in dustily between cracks in the boards, secondhand from a cobwebbed window somewhere across the cellar. In one corner of the little room a couple of mops, with stiff, clotted, foul-smelling heads, stand near a rusty bucket. The floor is dirt, a little damp to the touch, as cellar dirt usually is. The room is about three paces long and two wide: a mere broom closet or disused tool room. In the room a child is sitting. It could be a boy or a girl. It looks about six, but actually is nearly ten. It is feeble-minded. Perhaps it was born defective, or perhaps it has become imbecile through fear, malnutrition, and neglect. It picks its nose and occasionally fumbles vaguely with its toes or genitals, as it sits hunched in the corner farthest from the bucket and the two mops. It is afraid of the mops. It finds them horrible. It shuts its eyes, but it knows the mops are still standing there; and the door is locked; and nobody will come. The door is always locked; and nobody ever comes, except that sometimes—the child has no understanding of time or interval—sometimes the door rattles terribly and opens, and a person, or several people, are there. One of them may come in and kick the child to make it stand up. The others never come close, but peer in at it with frightened, disgusted eyes. The food bowl and the water jug are hastily filled, the door is locked, the eyes disappear. The people at the door never say anything, but the child, who has not always lived in the tool room, and can remember sunlight and its mother's voice, sometimes speaks. "I will be good," it says. "Please let me out. I will be good!" They never answer. The child used to scream for help at night, and cry a good deal, but now it only makes a kind of whining, "eh-haa, eh-haa," and it speaks less and less often. It is so thin there are no calves to its legs; its belly protrudes; it lives on a half-bowl of corn meal and grease a day. It is naked. Its buttocks and thighs are a mass of festered sores, as it sits in its own excrement continually.

9   They all know it is there, all the people of Omelas. Some of them have come to see it, others are content merely to know it is there. They all know that it has to be there. Some of them understand why, and some do not, but they all under-

stand that their happiness, the beauty of their city, the tenderness of their friendships, the health of their children, the wisdom of their scholars, the skill of their makers, even the abundance of their harvest and the kindly weathers of their skies, depend wholly on this child's abominable misery.

10   This is usually explained to children when they are between eight and twelve, whenever they seem capable of understanding; and most of those who come to see the child are young people, though often enough an adult comes, or comes back, to see the child. No matter how well the matter has been explained to them, these young spectators are always shocked and sickened at the sight. They feel disgust, which they had thought themselves superior to. They feel anger, outrage, impotence, despite all the explanations. They would like to do something for the child. But there is nothing they can do. If the child were brought up into the sunlight out of that vile place, if it were cleaned and fed and comforted, that would be a good thing, indeed; but if it were done, in that day and hour all the prosperity and beauty and delight of Omelas would wither and be destroyed. Those are the terms. To exchange all the goodness and grace of every life in Omelas for that single, small improvement: to throw away the happiness of thousands for the chance of the happiness of one: that would be to let guilt within the walls indeed.

11   The terms are strict and absolute; there may not even be a kind word spoken to the child.

12   Often the young people go home in tears, or in a tearless rage, when they have seen the child and faced this terrible paradox. They may brood over it for weeks or years. But as time goes on they begin to realize that even if the child could be released, it would not get much good of its freedom: a little vague pleasure of warmth and food, no doubt, but little more. It is too degraded and imbecile to know any real joy. It has been afraid too long ever to be free of fear. Its habits are too uncouth for it to respond to humane treatment. Indeed, after so long it would probably be wretched without walls about it to protect it, and darkness for its eyes, and its own excrement to sit in. Their tears at the bitter injustice dry when they begin to perceive the terrible justice of reality and to accept it. Yet it is their tears and anger, the trying of their generosity and the acceptance of their helplessness, which are perhaps the true source of the splendor of their lives. Theirs is no vapid, irresponsible happiness. They know that they, like the child, are not free. They know compassion. It is the existence of the child, and their knowledge of its existence, that makes possible the nobility of their architecture, the poignancy of their music, the profundity of their science. It is because of the child that they are so gentle with children. They know that if the wretched one were not there snivelling in the dark, the other one, the flute-player, could make no joyful music as the young riders line up in their beauty for the race in the sunlight of the first morning of summer.

13   Now do you believe in them? Are they not more credible? But there is one more thing to tell, and this is quite incredible.

14   At times one of the adolescent girls or boys who go to see the child does not go home to weep or rage, does not, in fact, go home at all. Sometimes also a man or woman much older falls silent for a day or two, and then leaves home. These people go out into the street, and walk down the street alone. They keep walking, and walk straight out of the city of Omelas, through the beautiful gates. They keep walking across the farmlands of Omelas. Each one goes alone, youth or girl, man

or woman. Night falls; the traveler must pass down the village streets, between the houses with yellow-lit windows, and on out into the darkness of the fields. Each alone, they go west or north, towards the mountains. They go on. They leave Omelas, they walk ahead into the darkness, and they do not come back. The place they go towards is a place even less imaginable to most of us than the city of happiness. I cannot describe it at all. It is possible that it does not exist. But they seem to know where they are going, the ones who walk away from Omelas.

Chinua Achebe

Nigeria 1930–

A devout Christian and a member of the Igbo tribe, Achebe grew up in Ogidi in eastern Nigeria. He learned English when he was eight. After graduating from the University College of Ibadan, Achebe worked in radio, becoming the director of external broadcasting for Nigeria. During the political and religious crisis that led to civil war in Nigeria and caused the deaths of over one million people, Achebe retreated to the Igbo region of the country, which declared itself the independent Republic of Biafra. With the defeat of the Biafran Republican Movement and the installation of a military dictatorship in Nigeria, Achebe left the country. Achebe's sense of the bias in books written by Europeans about Africa fuelled his belief that Africans must tell their own stories in their own voice. *Things Fall Apart*, his first novel, follows the disintegration of village life in Nigeria with the advent of European colonialism. In this novel, the folk tale "Why the Tortoise's Shell Is Not Smooth" is told before European law, religion, and culture break the bonds of village society.

Why the Tortoise's Shell Is Not Smooth   1958

1   Low voices, broken now and again by singing, reached Okonkwo from his wives' huts as each woman and her children told folk stories. Ekwefi and her daughter, Ezinma, sat on a mat on the floor. It was Ekwefi's turn to tell a story.

2   "Once upon a time," she began, "all the birds were invited to a feast in the sky. They were very happy and began to prepare themselves for the great day. They painted their bodies with red cam wood and drew beautiful patterns on them with dye.

3   "Tortoise saw all these preparations and soon discovered what it all meant. Nothing that happened in the world of the animals ever escaped his notice; he was full of cunning. As soon as he heard of the great feast in the sky his throat began to itch at the very thought. There was a famine in those days and Tortoise had not eaten a good meal for two moons. His body rattled like a piece of dry stick in his empty shell. So he began to plan how he would go to the sky."

4   "But he had no wings," said Ezinma.

5   "Be patient," replied her mother. "That is the story. Tortoise had no wings, but he went to the birds and asked to be allowed to go with them.

6   "'We know you too well,' said the birds when they had heard him. 'You are full of cunning and you are ungrateful. If we allow you to come with us you will soon begin your mischief.'

7   "'You do not know me,' said Tortoise. 'I am a changed man. I have learned that a man who makes trouble for others is also making it for himself.'

8   "Tortoise had a sweet tongue, and within a short time all the birds agreed that he was a changed man, and they each gave him a feather, with which he made two wings.

9   "At last the great day came and Tortoise was the first to arrive at the meeting place. When all the birds had gathered together, they set off in a body. Tortoise was very happy as he flew among the birds, and he was soon chosen as the man to speak for the party because he was a great orator.

10   "'There is one important thing which we must not forget,' he said as they flew on their way. 'When people are invited to a great feast like this, they take new names for the occasion. Our hosts in the sky will expect us to honor this age-old custom.'

11   "None of the birds had heard of this custom but they knew that Tortoise, in spite of his failings in other directions, was a widely traveled man who knew the customs of different peoples. And so they each took a new name. When they had all taken, Tortoise also took one. He was to be called *All of you.*

12   "At last the party arrived in the sky and their hosts were very happy to see them. Tortoise stood up in his many-colored plumage and thanked them for their invitation. His speech was so eloquent that all the birds were glad they had brought him, and nodded their heads in approval of all he said. Their hosts took him as the king of the birds, especially as he looked somewhat different from the others.

13   "After kola nuts had been presented and eaten, the people of the sky set before their guests the most delectable dishes Tortoise had ever seen or dreamed of. The soup was brought out hot from the fire and in the very pot in which it had been cooked. It was full of meat and fish. Tortoise began to sniff aloud. There was pounded yam and also yam pottage cooked with palm oil and fresh fish. There were also pots of palm wine. When everything had been set before the guests, one of the people of the sky came forward and tasted a little from each pot. He then invited the birds to eat. But Tortoise jumped to his feet and asked: 'For whom have you prepared this feast?'

14   "'For all of you,' replied the man.

15   "Tortoise turned to the birds and said: 'You remember that my name is *All of you.* The custom here is to serve the spokesman first and the others later. They will serve you when I have eaten.'

16   "He began to eat and the birds grumbled angrily. The people of the sky thought it must be their custom to leave all the food for their king. And so Tortoise ate the best part of the food and then drank two pots of palm wine, so that he was full of food and drink and his body grew fat enough to fill out his shell.

17   "The birds gathered round to eat what was left and to peck at the bones he had thrown all about the floor. Some of them were too angry to eat. They chose

to fly home on an empty stomach. But before they left each took back the feather he had lent to Tortoise. And there he stood in his hard shell full of food and wine but without any wings to fly home. He asked the birds to take a message for his wife, but they all refused. In the end Parrot, who had felt more angry than the others, suddenly changed his mind and agreed to take the message.

18   "'Tell my wife,' said Tortoise, 'to bring out all the soft things in my house and cover the compound with them so that I can jump down from the sky without very great danger.'

19   "Parrot promised to deliver the message, and then flew away. But when he reached Tortoise's house he told his wife to bring out all the hard things in the house. And so she brought out her husband's hoes, machetes, spears, guns, and even his cannon. Tortoise looked down from the sky and saw his wife bringing things out, but it was too far to see what they were. When all seemed ready he let himself go. He fell and fell and fell until he began to fear that he would never stop falling. And then like the sound of his cannon he crashed on the compound."

20   "Did he die?" asked Ezinma.

21   "No," replied Ekwefi. "His shell broke into pieces. But there was a great medicine man in the neighborhood. Tortoise's wife sent for him and he gathered all the bits of shell and stuck them together. That is why Tortoise's shell is not smooth."

Timothy Findley

Canada 1930–2002

Timothy Findley spent his early years in Toronto, an experience he draws on in works such as "Stones" and *The Wars*. After high school, Findley pursued an acting career on stage and television. It was while he was in England studying drama at London's Central School that he began writing fiction. Findley has written in many genres, including advertisements, radio reports, stories, scripts, and novels; his last novel was *Pilgrim* (2000). He died in France in June of 2002. He won the Governor General's Award for *The Wars* (1977), a novel that uses complex frames to explore the concepts of heroism and sacrifice. The terrible experience of war also supplies a context for "Stones," but here the focus is divided between the man damaged by war and the family he is connected to, and whom he, in turn, damages.

Stones   1988

1   We lived on the outskirts of Rosedale, over on the wrong side of Yonge Street. This was the impression we had, at any rate. Crossing the streetcar tracks put you in another world.

2   One September, my sister, Rita, asked a girl from Rosedale over to our house after school. Her name was Allison Pritchard and she lived on Cluny Drive. When my mother telephoned to see if Allison Pritchard could stay for supper, Mrs Pritchard said she didn't think it would be appropriate. That was the way they talked in Rosedale: very polite; oblique and cruel.

3   Over on our side—the west side—of Yonge Street, there were merchants—and this, apparently, made the difference to those whose houses were in Rosedale. People of class were not meant to live in the midst of commerce.

4   Our house was on Gibson Avenue, a cul-de-sac with a park across the road. My bedroom window faced a hockey rink in winter and a football field in summer. Cy, my brother, was a star in either venue. I was not. My forte, then, was the tricycle.

5   Up at the corner, there was an antique store on one side and a variety shop on the other. In the variety shop, you could spend your allowance on penny candy, Eskimo pies and an orange drink I favoured then called *Stubby. Stubby* came in short, fat bottles and aside from everything else—the thick orange flavour and the ginger in the bubbles—there was something wonderfully satisfying in the fact that it took both hands to hold it up to your lips and tip it down your throat.

6   Turning up Yonge Street, beyond the antique store, you came to The Women's Bakery, Adam's Grocery, Oskar Schickel, the butcher and Max's Flowers. We were Max's Flowers. My mother and my father wore green aprons when they stood behind the counter or went back into the cold room where they made up wreaths for funerals, bouquets for weddings and corsages for dances at the King Edward Hotel. Colonel Matheson, retired, would come in every morning on his way downtown and pick out a boutonnière from the jar of carnations my mother kept on the counter near the register. Once, when I was four, I caused my parents untold embarrassment by pointing out that Colonel Matheson had a large red growth on the end of his nose. The 'growth' was nothing of the sort, of course, but merely the result of Colonel Matheson's predilection for gin.

7   Of the pre-war years, my overall memory is one of perfect winters, heavy with snow and the smell of coal- and wood-smoke mingling with the smell of bread and cookies rising from The Women's Bakery. The coal-smoke came from our furnaces and the wood-smoke—mostly birch and maple—came to us from the chimneys of Rosedale, where it seemed that every house must have a fireplace in every room.

8   Summers all smelled of grass being cut in the park and burning tar from the road crews endlessly patching the potholes in Yonge Street. The heat of these summers was heroic and the cause of many legends. Mister Schickel, the butcher, I recall once cooked an egg on the sidewalk outside his store. My father, who was fond of Mister Schickel, made him a bet of roses it could not be done. I think Mister Schickel's part of the bet was pork chops trimmed of excess fat. When the egg began to sizzle, my father slapped his thigh and whistled and he sent my sister, Rita, in to get the flowers. Mister Schickel, however, was a graceful man and when he placed his winnings in the window of his butcher shop, he also placed a card that read: *Thanks to Max's Flowers one dozen roses.*

9   The Great Depression held us all in thrall, but its effects on those of us who were used to relative poverty—living on the west side on Yonge Street—were not

so debilitating as they were on the far side in Rosedale. The people living there regarded money as something you had—as opposed to something you went out and got—and they were slower to adjust to what, for them, was the unique experience of deprivation.

10   I remember, too, that there always seemed to be a tramp at the door: itinerants asking if—for the price of a meal, or the meal itself—they could carry out the ashes, sweep the walks or pile the baskets and pails in which my father brought his flowers from the market and the greenhouse.

11   Our lives continued in this way until about the time I was five—in August of 1939. Everyone's life, I suppose, has its demarcation lines—its latitudes and longitudes passing through time. Some of these lines define events that everyone shares—others are confined to personal—even to secret lives. But the end of summer 1939 is a line drawn through the memory of everyone who was then alive. We were all about to be pitched together into a melting pot of violence from which a few of us would emerge intact and the rest of us would perish.

12   My father joined the army even before the war had started. He went downtown one day and didn't come back till after suppertime. I noticed that he hadn't taken the truck but had ridden off on the streetcar. I asked my mother why he had worn his suit on a weekday and she replied *because today is special.* But that was all she said.

13   At the table, eating soufflé and salad, my brother, Cy—who was nine years old that summer—talked about the World's Fair in New York City and pictures he'd seen of the future in magazines. The Great World's Fair was a subject that had caught all our imaginations with its demonstrations of new appliances, aeroplanes and motor cars. Everything was 'streamlined' in 1939; everything designed with swept-back lines as if we were all preparing to shoot off into space. Earlier that summer, the King and Queen of England had come to Canada, riding on a streamlined train whose blue-painted engine was sleek and slim as something in a silver glove. In fact, the King and Queen had arrived in Toronto just up Yonge Street from where we lived. We got permission from the Darrow family, who lived over Max's Flowers, to stand on the roof and watch the parade with its Mounties in scarlet and its Black Watch Band and the King and Queen, all blue and white and smiling, sitting in an open Buick called a *McLaughlin—built,* according to Cy, *right here in Canada!* For one brief moment while all these symbols of who we were went marching past, the two communities—one on either side of Yonge Street—were united in a surge of cheering and applause. But after the King and Queen were gone, the ribbon of Yonge Street divided us again. It rained.

14   Now, Cy and Rita were arguing over the remnants in the soufflé dish. Cy held the classic belief that what was in the dish was his by virtue of his being the eldest child. He also held the classic belief that girls were meant to be second in everything. Rita, who was always hungry but never seemed to gain an ounce, held none of these beliefs and was capable of fighting Cy for hours on end when our parents weren't present. With Mother at the table, however, the argument was silenced by her announcement that the soufflé dish and all the delicious bits of cheese and egg that clung to its sides would be set aside for our father.

15   Then—or shortly thereafter—our father did indeed arrive, but he said he wasn't hungry and he wanted to be left alone with Mother.

16   In half an hour the children were called from the kitchen where we had been doing the dishes and scooping up the remains of the meal. I—the child my mother called *The Rabbit*—had been emptying the salad bowl, stuffing my mouth with lettuce, tomatoes and onion shards and nearly choking in the process. We all went into the sitting-room with food on our lips and tea towels in our hands: Father's three little Maxes—Cy and Rita and Ben. He looked at us then, as he always did, with a measure of pride he could never hide and a false composure that kept his lips from smiling, but not his eyes. I look back now on that moment with some alarm when I realize my father was only twenty-seven years old—an age I have long survived and doubled.

17   'Children, I have joined the army,' he said—in his formal way, as if we were his customers. 'I am going to be a soldier.'

18   Our mother had been weeping before we entered the room, but she had dried her eyes because she never allowed us to witness her tears. Now, she was smiling and silent. After a moment, she left the room and went out through the kitchen into the garden where, in the twilight, she found her favourite place and sat in a deck-chair amidst the flowers.

19   Cy, for his part, crowed with delight and yelled with excitement. He wanted to know if the war would last until he was a man and could join our father at the front.

20   Father, I remember, told him the war had not yet begun and the reason for his enlistment was precisely so that Cy and I could not be soldiers. 'There will be no need for that,' he said.

21   Cy was immensely disappointed. He begged our father to make the war go on till 1948, when he would be eighteen.

22   Our father only laughed at that.

23   'The war,' he said, 'will be over in 1940.'

24   I went out then and found our mother in the garden.

25   'What will happen to us while he's away?' I asked.

26   'Nothing,' she said. And then she said: 'come here.'

27   I went and leaned against her thigh and she put her arm around my shoulder and I could smell the roses somewhere behind us. It was getting dark.

28   'Look up there,' she said. 'The stars are coming out. Why don't you count them?'

29   This was her way of distracting me whenever my questions got out of hand. Either she told me to count the stars or go outside and dig for China. *There's a shovel in the shed,* she would tell me. *You get started and I will join you.* Just as if we would be in China and back by suppertime.

30   But that night in August, 1939, I wasn't prepared to bite. I didn't want to dig for China and I didn't want to count the stars. I'd dug for China so many times and had so many holes in the yard that I knew I would never arrive; it was much too far and, somehow, she was making a fool of me. As for the stars: 'I counted them last night,' I told her. 'And the night before.'

31   'Oh?' she said—and I felt her body tense, though she went on trying to inject a sense of ease when she spoke. 'So tell me,' she said. 'How many are there?'

32   'Twelve,' I said.

33   'Ah,' she said. And sighed. 'Just twelve. I thought there might be more than twelve.'

34   'I mean twelve zillion,' I said with great authority.
35   'Oh,' she said. 'I see. And you counted them all?'
36   'Unh-hunh.'
37   For a moment she was quiet. And then she said: 'what about that one there?'
38   One week later, the war began. But my father had already gone.

39   On the 14th of February, 1943, my father was returned. He came back home from the war. He did this on a Sunday and I recall the hush that fell upon our house, as indeed it seemed to have fallen over all the city. Only the sparrows out in the trees made sound.

40   We had gone downtown to the Exhibition Grounds to meet him. The journey on the streetcar took us over an hour, but Mother had splurged and hired a car and driver to take us all home. The car, I remember, embarrassed me. I was afraid some friend would see me being driven—sitting up behind a chauffeur.

41   A notice had come that told us the families of all returning soldiers would be permitted to witness their arrival. I suspect the building they used for this was the one now used to house the Royal Winter Fair and other equestrian events. I don't remember what it was called and I'm not inclined to inquire. It was enough that I was there that once—and once remains enough.

42   We sat in the bleachers, Cy and Rita and Mother and me, and there was a railing holding us back. There must have been over a thousand people waiting to catch a glimpse of someone they loved—all of them parents, children or wives of the men returning. I was eight years old that February—almost nine and feeling I would never get there. Time was like a field of clay and all the other children I knew appeared to have cleared it in a single bound while I was stuck in the mud and barely able to lift my feet. I hated being eight and dreaded being nine. I wanted to be ten—the only dignified age a child could be, it seemed to me. Cy, at ten, had found a kind of silence I admired to the point of worship. Rita, who in fact was ten that year and soon to be eleven, had also found a world of silence in which she kept her self secreted—often behind closed doors. Silence was a sign of valour.

43   The occasion was barely one for public rejoicing. The men who were coming home were mostly casualties whose wounds, we had been warned, could be distressing and whose spirit, we had equally been warned, had been damaged in long months of painful recuperation. Plainly, it was our job to lift their spirits and to deny the severity of their wounds. Above all else, they must not be allowed to feel they could not rejoin society at large. A man with no face must not be stared at.

44   Our father's wounds were greater by far than we had been told. There was not a mark on his body, but—far inside—he had been destroyed. His mind had been severely damaged and his spirit had been broken. No one had told me what this might have made of him. No one had said *he may never be kind again*. No one had said *he will never sleep again without the aid of alcohol*. No one had said *he will try to kill your mother*. No one had said *you will not be sure it's him when you see him*. Yet all these things were true.

45   I had never seen a military parade without a band. The effect was eerie and upsetting. Two or three officers came forward into the centre of the oval. Somebody started shouting commands and a sergeant-major, who could not yet be seen, was heard outside the building counting off the steps.

46   I wanted drums. I wanted bugles. Surely this ghostly, implacable sound of marching feet in the deadening sand was just a prelude to everyone standing up and cheering and the music blaring forth. But, no. We all stood up, it is true, the minute the first of the columns rounded the wooden corner of the bleachers and came into sight. But no one uttered a sound. One or two people threw their hands up over their mouths—as if to stifle cries—but most of us simply stood there—staring in disbelief.

47   Nurses came with some of the men, supporting them. Everyone was pale in the awful light—and the colours of their wounds and bruises were garish and quite unreal. There was a predominance of yellow flesh and dark maroon scars and of purple welts and blackened scabs. Some men wore bandages—some wore casts and slings. Others used canes and crutches to support themselves. A few had been the victims of fire, and these wore tight, blue skull-caps and collarless shirts and their faces and other areas of uncovered skin were bright with shining ointments and dressings.

48   It took a very great while for all these men and women—perhaps as many as two hundred of them—to arrive inside the building and make their way into the oval. They were being lined up in order of columns—several long lines, and each line punctuated here and there with attendant nurses. The voices of the sergeant-major and of the adjutant who was taking the parade were swallowed up in the dead acoustics, and—far above us—pigeons and sparrows moved among the girders and beams that supported the roof. I still had not seen Father.

49   At last, because my panic was spreading out of control, I tugged my mother's elbow and whispered that I couldn't see him. Had there been a mistake and he wasn't coming at all?

50   'No,' she told me—looking down at me sideways and turning my head with her ungloved fingers. 'There he is, there,' she said. 'But don't say anything, yet. He may not know we're here.'

51   My father's figure could only be told because of his remarkable height. He was six feet four and had always been, to me, a giant. But now his height seemed barely greater than the height of half a dozen other men who were gathered out in the sand. His head was bowed, though once or twice he lifted his chin when he heard the commands. His shoulders, no longer squared, were rounded forward and dipping towards his centre. His neck was so thin I thought that someone or something must have cut over half of it away. I studied him solemnly and then looked up at my mother.

52   She had closed her eyes against him because she could not bear to look.

53   Later on that night, when everyone had gone to bed but none of us had gone to sleep, I said to Cy: 'what is it?'

54   'What?'

55   'That's happened to Dad ...'

56   Cy didn't answer for a moment and then he said: 'Dieppe.'

57   I didn't understand. I thought it was a new disease.

58   We were told the next day not to mention at school that our father had come back home. Nothing was said about why it must be kept a secret. That was a bitter disappointment. Other children whose fathers had returned from overseas were always

the centre of attention. Teachers, beaming smiles and patting heads, would congratulate them just as if they had won a prize. Classmates pestered them with questions: What does he look like? Have you seen his wounds? How many Germans did he kill? But we had none of this. All we got was: *what did you do on the weekend?*

59   *Nothing.*

60   All day Monday, Father remained upstairs. Our parents' bedroom was on the second floor directly over the sitting-room. Also, directly underneath the bedroom occupied by Cy and me. We had heard our mother's voice long into the night, apparently soothing him, telling him over and over again that everything was going to be all right.

61   We could not make out her words, but the tone of her voice was familiar. Over time, she had sat with each of us, deploying her comforts in all the same cadences and phrases, assuring us that pains and aches and sicknesses would pass.

62   Because we could not afford to lose the sale of even one flower—neither the single rose bought once a week by Edna Holmes to cheer her ailing sister, nor the daily boutonnière of Colonel Matheson—our mother had persuaded Mrs. Adams, the grocer's wife, to tend the store while she 'nipped home' once every hour to see to Father's needs. It was only later that we children realized what those needs entailed. He was drinking more or less constantly in every waking hour, and our mother's purpose was first to tempt him with food—which he refused—and then to make certain that his matches and cigarettes did not set fire to the house.

63   On the Wednesday, Father emerged from his shell around two o'clock in the afternoon. We were all at school, of course, and I have only the account of what follows from my mother. When she returned at two, Mother found that Father had come down into the hallway, fully dressed in civilian clothes. He had already donned his greatcoat when she arrived. She told me that, at first, he had seemed to be remarkably sober. He told her he wanted to go outside and walk in the street. He wanted to go and see the store, he said.

64   'But you can't wear your greatcoat, David,' she told him.

65   'Why?'

66   'Because you're in civilian dress. You know that's not allowed. A man was arrested just last week.'

67   'I wasn't here last week,' said my father.

68   'Nevertheless,' my mother told him, 'this man was arrested because it is not allowed.'

69   'But I'm a soldier!' my father yelled.

70   My mother had to play this scene with all the care and cunning she could muster. The man who had been arrested had been a deserter. All that winter, desertions had been increasing and there had been demonstrations of overt disloyalty. People had shouted *down with the King!* and had booed the Union Jack. There were street gangs of youths who called themselves *Zombies*[1] and they hung around the Masonic Temple on Yonge Street and the Palais Royale at Sunnyside. Some of these young men were in uniform, members of the Home Guard: reserves who had been promised, on joining up, they would not be sent overseas. They may have disapproved of the war, but they did not disapprove of fighting. They waited outside the dancehalls, excessively defensive of their manhood, challenging the servicemen who

---

1   the derogatory term applied to conscientious objectors during World War I

were dancing inside to *come out fighting and show us your guts!* Men had been killed in such encounters and the encounters had been increasing. The government was absolutely determined to stamp these incidents out before they spread across the country. These were the darkest hours of the war and morale, both in and out of the Forces, was at its lowest ebb. If my father had appeared on the street with his military greatcoat worn over his civilian clothes, it would have been assumed he was a *Zombie* or a deserter and he would have been arrested instantly. Our neighbours would have turned him in, no matter who he was. Our patriotism had come to that.

71   'I don't have a civilian overcoat,' my father said. 'And don't suggest that I put on my uniform, because I won't. My uniform stinks of sweat and I hate it.'

72   'Well, you aren't going out like that,' my mother said. 'That's all there is to it. Why not come to the kitchen and I'll fix you a sandwich....'

73   'I don't want a goddamned sandwich,' my father yelled at her. 'I want to see the store!'

74   At this point, he tore off his greatcoat and flung it onto the stairs. And then, before my mother could prevent him, he was out the door and running down the steps.

75   My mother—dressed in her green shop apron and nothing but a scarf to warm her—raced out after him.

76   What would the neighbours think? What would the neighbours say? How could she possibly explain?

77   By the time she had reached the sidewalk, my father had almost reached the corner. But, when she got to Yonge Street, her fears were somewhat allayed. My father had not gone into Max's Flowers but was standing one door shy of it, staring into the butcher's window.

78   'What's going on here?' he said, as my mother came abreast of him.

79   Mother did not know what he meant.

80   'Where is Mister Schickel, Lily?' he asked her.

81   She had forgotten that, as well.

82   'Mister Schickel has left,' she told him—trying to be calm—trying to steer my father wide of the butcher's window and in towards their own front stoop.

83   'Left?' my father shouted. 'He's only just managed to pay off his mortgage! And who the hell is this imposter, Reilly?'

84   'Reilly?'

85   'Arthur Reilly the bloody butcher!' My father pointed at and read the sign that had replaced *Oskar Schickel, Butcher* in the window.

86   'Mister Reilly has been there most of the winter, David. Didn't I write and tell you that?' She knew very well she hadn't.

87   My father blinked at the meagre cuts of rationed meat displayed beyond the glass and said: 'what happened to Oskar, Lily? Tell me.'

88   And so, she had to tell him, like it or not.

89   Mister Schickel's name was disagreeable—stuck up there on Yonge Street across from Rosedale—and someone from Park Road had thrown a stone through the window.

90   There. It was said.

91   'But Oskar wasn't a German,' my father whispered. 'He was a Canadian.'

92   'But his name was German, David.'

93   My father put his fingers against the glass and did not appear to respond to what my mother had said.

94   At last, my mother pulled at his arm. 'Why not come back home,' she said. 'You can come and see the shop tomorrow.'

95   My father, while my mother watched him, concentrated very hard and moved his finger over the dusty glass of Oskar Schickel's store.

96   'What are you doing, David?'

97   'Nothing,' said my father. 'Setting things right, that's all.'

98   Then he stepped back and said to her: 'now—we'll go home.'

99   What he had written was:

100   *Oskar Schickel: Proprietor in absentia.*

101   Mother said that Mrs Reilly rushed outside as soon as they had reached the corner and she washed the window clean.

102   This was the only remaining decent thing my father did until the day he died.

103   The rest was all a nightmare.

104   I had never seen Dieppe. I had seen its face in photographs. I had read all the books and heard all the stories. The battle, of which my father had been a victim, had taken place in August of 1942—roughly six months before he was returned to us. Long since then, in my adult years, I have seen that battle, or seen its parts, through the medium of documentary film. It was only after Cy and Rita had vetted these films that I was able to watch. Till then, I had been afraid I would catch my father's image unawares—fearful that somehow our eyes would meet in that worst of moments. I couldn't bear the thought of seeing him destroyed. So, I had seen all this—the photographs, the books, the films—but I had never seen the town of Dieppe itself until that day in May of 1987 when I took my father's ashes there to scatter them.

105   Before I can begin this ending, I have to make it clear that the last thing I want to provoke is the sentimental image of a wind-blown stretch of rocky beach with a rainbow of ashes arching over the stones and blowing out to sea. If you want that image, let me tell you that had been the way it was when Cy, my brother, and Rita, my sister, and I went walking, wading into the ocean south of Lunenburg, Nova Scotia—where our mother had been born—to cast her ashes into the air above the Atlantic. Then there was almost music and we rejoiced because our mother had finally gained her freedom from a life that had become intolerable. But in Dieppe, when I shook my father's ashes out of their envelope, there was no rejoicing. None.

106   I felt, in fact, as if I had brought the body of an infidel into a holy place and laid it down amongst the true believers. Still, this was what my father had wanted—and how could I refuse him? Neither Cy nor Rita would do it for him. *Gone,* they had said. *Good riddance.*

107   And so it fell to me.

108   I was always the least informed. I was always the most inquisitive. During my childhood, nobody told me—aside from the single word *Dieppe*—what it was that had happened to my father. And yet, perhaps because I knew the least and because I was the youngest and seemed the most naïve and willing, it was more than often me he focused on.

109   His tirades would begin in silence—the silence we had been warned of when he first returned. He would sit at the head of the table, eating a piece of fish and drinking from a glass of beer. The beer was always dark in colour. Gold.

110   Our dining-room had a window facing west. Consequently, winter sunsets in particular got in his eyes.

111   *Curtain*, he would say at his plate—and jab his fork at me.

112   If I didn't understand because his mouth was full, my mother would reach my sleeve and pull it with her fingers. *The curtain, Ben,* she would say. *Your father's eyes.*

113   *Yes, ma'am.* Down I'd get and pull the curtain.

114   Then, no sooner would I be reseated than my father—still addressing his plate—would mumble *lights*. And I would rise and turn on the lights. Then, when I was back at last in my chair, he would look at me and say, without apparent rancour, *why don't you tell me to shove the goddamn curtain up my ass?*

115   You will understand my silence in response to this if you understand that— before he went away—the worst my father had ever said in our presence had been *damn* and *hell*. The ultimate worst had been *Christ!* when he'd nearly sliced his finger off with a knife. Then, however, he hadn't known that anyone was listening. And so, when he started to talk this way—and perhaps especially at table—it paralyzed me.

116   Cy or Mother would sometimes attempt to intervene, but he always cut them off with something worse than he'd said to me. Then he would turn his attention back in my direction and continue. He urged me to refuse his order, then to upbraid him, finally to openly defy him—call him the worst of the words he could put in my mouth and hit him. Of course, I never did any of these things, but the urging, the cajoling and ultimately the begging never ceased.

117   One night, he came into the bedroom where I slept in the bunk-bed over Cy and he shouted at me *why don't you fight back?* Then he dragged my covers off and threw me onto the floor against the bureau. All this was done in the dark, and after my mother had driven me down in the truck to the Emergency Ward of Wellesley Hospital, the doctors told her that my collar-bone was broken. I heard my mother saying *yes, he fell out of bed.*

118   Everyone—even I—conspired to protect him. The trouble was, my father had no wish to protect himself. At least, it seemed that way until a fellow veteran of Dieppe turned up one day in the shop and my father turned on him with a pair of garden shears and tried to drive him back onto Yonge Street. Far from being afraid of my father, the other man took off his jacket and threw it in my father's face and all the while he stood there, the man was yelling at my father: *Coward! Coward! Yellow Bastard!*

119   Then, he turned around and walked away. The victor.

120   Thinking for sure the police would come, my mother drew the blind and closed the shop for the rest of the day.

121   But that was not the end of it. She gathered us together out on the porch and Cy was told to open a can of pork and beans and to make what our mother called a *passel of toast*. He and Rita and I were to eat this meal in the kitchen, after which Cy, who'd been handed a dollar bill my mother had lifted from the till, was to take us down to the Uptown Theatre where an Abbott and Costello film was playing. All these ordinary things we did. Nonetheless, we knew that our father had gone mad.

122   It was summer then and when the movie was over, I remember Cy and Rita and I stood on the street and the sidewalks gave off heat and the air around us smelled of peanuts and popcorn and Cy said: 'I don't think it's safe to go home

just yet.' For almost an hour, we wandered on Yonge Street, debating what we should do and, at last, we decided we would test the waters by going and looking at the house and listening to see if there was any yelling.

123   Gibson Avenue only has about twenty houses, most of them semi-detached—and all of them facing south and the park. The porches and the stoops that night were filled with our neighbours drinking beer from coffee cups and fanning themselves with paper plates and folded bits of the *Daily Star*. They were drinking out of cups—you could smell the beer—because the law back then forbade the public consumption, under any circumstance, of alcohol. Whatever you can hide does not exist.

124   Passing, we watched our neighbours watching us—the Matlocks and the Wheelers and the Conrads and the Bolts—and we knew they were thinking *there go the Max kids and David Max, their father, tried to kill a man today in his store with gardening shears.*...

125   'Hello, Cy.'

126   'Hello.'

127   'Ben. Rita.'

128   'Hi.'

129   'Good-night...'

130   We went and stood together on the sidewalk out in front of our house.

131   Inside, everything seemed to be calm and normal. The lights were turned on in their usual distribution—most of them downstairs. The radio was playing. Someone was singing *Praise the Lord and Pass the Ammunition*.

132   Cy went up the steps and turned the handle. He was brave—but I'd always known that. Rita and I were told to wait on the porch.

133   Two minutes passed—or five—or ten—and finally Cy returned. He was very white and his voice was dry, but he wasn't shaking and all he said was: 'you'd best come in. I'm calling the police.'

134   Our father had tried to kill our mother with a hammer. She was lying on the sofa and her hands were broken because she had used them trying to fend off the blows.

135   Father had disappeared. The next day, he turned himself in because, as he told the doctors, he had come to his senses. He was kept for a year and a half—almost until the war was over—at the Asylum of the Insane on Queen Street. None of us children was allowed to visit him there—but our mother went to see him six months after he had been committed. She told me they sat in a long, grey room with bars on all the windows. My father wore a dressing gown and hadn't shaved. Mother said he couldn't look her in the eyes. She told him that she forgave him for what he had done. But my father never forgave himself. My mother said she never saw his eyes again.

136 Two weeks after our father had tried to kill our mother, a brick was thrown through the window of Max's Flowers. On the brick, a single word was printed in yellow chalk.

137   *Murderer.*

138   Mother said: 'there's no way around this, now. I'm going to have to explain.'

139   That was how we discovered what had gone wrong with our father at Dieppe.

140   Our mother had known this all along, and I still have strong suspicions Cy had found it out and maybe Rita before our mother went through the formal procedure of sitting us down and telling us all together. Maybe they had thought I was just too young to understand. Maybe Cy and maybe Rita hadn't known. Maybe they had only guessed. At any rate, I had a very strong sense that I was the only one who received our mother's news in a state of shock.

141   Father had risen, since his enlistment in 1939, all the way up from an NCO to the rank of captain. Everyone had adored him in the army. He was what they called a natural leader. His men were particularly fond of him and they would, as the saying goes, have followed him anywhere. Then came Dieppe. All but a handful of those who went into battle there were Canadians. This was our Waterloo.[2] Our Gettysburg.

142   There isn't a single history book you can read—there isn't a single man who was there who won't tell you—there isn't a single scrap of evidence in any archive to suggest that the battle of Dieppe was anything but a total and appalling disaster. Most have called it a slaughter.

143   Dieppe is a port and market town on the coast of Normandy in northern France. In 1942, the British High Command had chosen it to be the object of a practice raid in preparation for the invasion of Europe. The allies on every front were faltering, then. A gesture was needed, and even the smallest of victories would do.

144   And so, on the 19th of August, 1942, the raid on Dieppe had taken place— and the consequent carnage had cost the lives of over a thousand Canadians. Over two thousand were wounded or taken prisoner. Five thousand set out; just over one thousand came back.

145   My father never left his landing craft.

146   He was to have led his men ashore in the second wave of troops to follow the tanks—but, seeing the tanks immobilized, unable to move because the beaches were made of stone and the stones had jammed the tank tracks—and seeing the evident massacre of the first wave of troops whose attempt at storming the shore had been repulsed by machine-gun fire from the cliffs above the town—my father froze in his place and could not move. His men—it is all too apparent—did not know what to do. They had received no order to advance and yet, if they stayed, they were sitting ducks.

147   In the end, though a handful escaped by rushing forward into the water, the rest were blown to pieces when their landing craft was shelled. In the meantime, my father had recovered enough of his wits to crawl back over the end of the landing craft, strip off his uniform and swim out to sea where he was taken on board a British destroyer sitting offshore.

148   The destroyer, H.M.S. *Berkley*, was ultimately hit and everyone on board, including my father—no one knowing who he was—was transferred to another ship before the *Berkley* was scuttled where she sat. My father made it all the way back to England, where his burns and wounds were dressed and where he

---

2   a reference to the 1815 Battle of Waterloo and the Civil War Battle of Gettysburg, both battles of great cultural significance to the British and the Americans respectively

debated taking advantage of the chaos to disappear, hoping that, in the long run, he would be counted among the dead.

149   His problem was, his conscience had survived. He stayed and, as a conse-quence, he was confronted by survivors who knew his story. He was dishon-ourably discharged and sent home to us. Children don't understand such things. The only cowards they recognize are figures cut from comic books or seen on movie screens.

150   Fathers cannot be cowards.

151   It is impossible.

ᔐ

152   His torment and his grief were to lead my father all the way to the grave. He left our mother, in the long run, though she would not have wished him to do so and he lived out his days in little bars and back-street beer parlours, seeking whatever solace he could find with whores and derelicts whose stories might have matched his own. The phone would ring and we would dread it. Either it was him or news of him—either his drunken harangue or the name of his most recent jail.

153   He died in the Wellesley Hospital, the place where I was born—and when he was dying he asked to see his children. Cy and Rita 'could not be reached,' but I was found—where he'd always found me—sitting within yelling distance. Perhaps this sounds familiar to other children—of whatever age—whose parents, whether one of them or both of them, have made the mistake of losing faith too soon in their children's need to love.

154   I would have loved a stone.

155   If only he had known.

156   He sensed it, maybe, in the end. He told me he was sorry for everything—and meant it. He told me the names of all his men and he said he had walked with them all through hell, long since their deaths, to do them honour. He hoped they would understand him, now.

157   I said they might.

158   He asked if his ashes could be put with theirs.

159   *Why not*, I thought. *A stone among stones.*

160   The beaches at Dieppe can throw you off balance. The angle at which they slope into the water is both steep and dangerous. At high tide you can slide into the waves and lose your footing before you've remembered how to swim. The stones are treacherous. But they are also beautiful.

161   My father's ashes were contraband. You can't just walk about with someone's remains, in whatever form, in your suitcase. Stepping off the *Sealink* ferry, I carried my father in an envelope addressed to myself in Canada. This was only in case I was challenged. There was hardly more than a handful of him there. I had thrown the rest of him into the English Channel as the coast of Normandy was coming into view. It had been somewhat more than disconcerting to see the interest his ashes caused amongst the gulls and other sea birds. I had hoped to dispose of him in a private way, unnoticed. But a woman with two small children came and stood beside me at the railing and I heard her explain that *this nice gentleman is taking*

care of our feathered friends. I hoped that, if my father was watching, he could laugh. I had to look away.

162   The ferry arrived in the early afternoon and—once I had booked myself into La Présidence Hotel—I went for a walk along the promenade above the sea-wall. It being May, the offshore breeze was warm and filled with the faintest scent of apple trees in bloom.

163   I didn't want to relive the battle. I hadn't come to conjure ghosts. But the ghosts and the battle are palpable around you there, no matter what your wishes are. The sound of the tide rolling back across the stones is all the cue you need to be reminded of that summer day in 1942. I stood that evening, resting my arms along the wall and thinking *at last, my father has come ashore.*

164   In the morning, before the town awoke, I got up in the dark and was on the beach when the sun rose inland beyond the cliffs. I wore a thick woollen sweater, walking shorts and a pair of running shores. The envelope was in my pocket.

165   The concierge must have thought I was just another crazy North American off on my morning run. He grunted as I passed and I pretended not to know that he was there. Out on the beach, I clambered over retaining walls and petrified driftwood until I felt I was safely beyond the range of prying eyes.

166   The stones at Dieppe are mostly flint—and their colours range from white through yellow to red. The red stones look as if they have been washed in blood and the sight of them takes your breath away. I hunkered down above them, holding all that remained of my father in my fist. He felt like a powdered stone— pummelled and broken.

167   I let him down between my fingers, feeling him turn to paste—watching him divide and disappear.

168   He is dead and he is gone.

169   Weekends, our parents used to take us walking under the trees on Crescent Road. This was on the Rosedale side of Yonge Street. My brother Cy and I were always dressed in dark blue suits whose rough wool shorts would chafe against our thighs. Our knee socks—also blue—were turned down over thick elastic garters. Everything itched and smelled of Sunday. Cy had cleats on his shoes because he walked in such a way as to wear his heels *to the bone,* as my mother said—and causing much expense. The cleats made a wondrous clicking noise and you could always hear him coming. I wanted cleats, but I was refused because, no matter how I tried, I couldn't walk like that.

170   The houses sat up neat as pins beyond their lawns—blank-eyed windows, steaming chimneys—havens of wealth and all the mysteries of wealth.

171   Father often walked behind us. I don't know why. Mother walked in front with Rita. Rita always wore a dress that was either red or blue beneath her princess coat and in the wintertime she wore a sort of woollen cloche that was tied with a knitted string beneath her chin. Her Mary Jane shoes were just like Shirley Temple's shoes[3]—which, for a while, was pleasing to Rita; then it was not. Rita always had an overpowering sense of image.

---

3   Shirley Temple was a child star in Hollywood movies in the 1930s and, to a more limited extent, 1940s.

172   After the advent of our father's return, she said from the corner of her mouth one Sunday as we walked on Crescent Road that she and Cy and I had been named as if we were manufactured products: *Cy Max Office Equipment; Rita Max Household Appliances* and *Ben Max Watches*. This, she concluded, was why our father had always walked behind us. Proudly, he was measuring our performance. Now, he had ceased to walk behind us and our mother led us forward dressed in black.

173   *Tick. Tick. Tick.* That's me. The Ben Max Watch.

174   I have told our story. But I think it best—and I like it best—to end with all of us moving there beneath the trees in the years before the war. Mister and Mrs. David Max out walking with their children any Sunday afternoon in any kind of weather but the rain.

175   Colonel Matheson, striding down his walk, is caught and forced to grunt acknowledgement that we are there. He cannot ignore us, after all. We have seen him every weekday morning, choosing his boutonnière and buying it from us.

Alice Munro

Canada 1931–

Alice Munro grew up in Wingham, Ontario, and attended the University of Western Ontario. After two years of study, she married and moved to B.C., where she lived for twenty years. She won the Governor General's award in 1968 for her collection *Dance of the Happy Shades*. Since 1972, she has lived in Clinton in western Ontario. Most recently, Munro won the Giller Prize for her collection *The Love of a Good Woman* (1998). In the title story of her 1974 collection, *Something I've Been Meaning to Tell You*, as in many of Munro's stories, what is not overtly stated is central to a complete understanding of the story. The complexity of human relationships and events, both present and past, in Munro's writing often leaves the reader to fill in the blanks to give closure to her story. "Something I've Been Meaning to Tell You" challenges the reader to examine the narrator's story carefully in order to understand the full import of the title and the story's closing sentence.

Something I've Been Meaning to Tell You   1974

1   "Anyway he knows how to fascinate the women," said Et to Char. She could not tell if Char went paler, hearing this, because Char was pale in the first place as anybody could get. She was like a ghost now, with her hair gone white. But still beautiful, she couldn't lose it.

2   "No matter to him the age or the size," Et pressed on. "It's natural to him as breathing, I guess. I only hope the poor things aren't taken in by it."

3   "I wouldn't worry," Char said.

4   The day before, Et had taken Blaikie Noble up on his invitation to go along on one of his tours and listen to his spiel. Char was asked too, but of course she didn't go. Blaikie Noble ran a bus. The bottom part of it was painted red and the top part was striped, to give the effect of an awning. On the side was painted: LAKESHORE TOURS, INDIAN GRAVES, LIMESTONE GARDENS, MILLIONAIRE'S MANSION, BLAIKIE NOBLE, DRIVER, GUIDE. Blaikie had a room at the hotel, and he also worked on the grounds, with one helper, cutting grass and clipping hedges and digging the borders. What a comedown, Et had said at the beginning of the summer when they first found out he was back. She and Char had known him in the old days.

5   So Et found herself squeezed into his bus with a lot of strangers, though before the afternoon was over she had made friends with a number of them and had a couple of promises of jackets needing letting out, as if she didn't have enough to do already. That was beside the point, the thing on her mind was watching Blaikie.

6   And what did he have to show? A few mounds with grass growing on them, covering dead Indians, a plot full of odd-shaped, grayish-white, dismal-looking limestone things—far-fetched imitations of plants (there could be the cemetery, if that was what you wanted)—and an old monstrosity of a house built with liquor money. He made the most of it. A historical discourse on the Indians, then a scientific discourse on the Limestone. Et had no way of knowing how much of it was true. Arthur would know. But Arthur wasn't there; there was nobody there but silly women, hoping to walk beside Blaikie to and from the sights, chat with him over their tea in the Limestone Pavilion, looking forward to having his strong hand under their elbows, the other hand brushing somewhere around the waist, when he helped them down off the bus ("I'm not a tourist," Et whispered sharply when he tried it on her).

7   He told them the house was haunted. The first Et had ever heard of it, living ten miles away all her life. A woman had killed her husband, the son of the millionaire, at least it was believed she had killed him.

8   "How?" cried some lady, thrilled out of her wits.

9   "Ah, the ladies are always anxious to know the means," said Blaikie, in a voice like cream, scornful and loving. "It was a slow—poison. Or that's what they said. This is all hearsay, all local gossip." (*Local my foot,* said Et to herself.) "She didn't appreciate his lady friends. The wife didn't. No."

10   He told them the ghost walked up and down in the garden, between two rows of blue spruce. It was not the murdered man who walked, but the wife, regretting. Blaikie smiled ruefully at the busload. At first Et had thought his attentions were all false, an ordinary commercial flirtation, to give them their money's worth. But gradually she was getting a different notion. He bent to each woman he talked to— it didn't matter how fat or scrawny or silly she was—as if there was one thing in her he would like to find. He had a gentle and laughing but ultimately serious, narrowing look (was that the look men finally had when they made love, that Et would never see?) that made him seem to want to be a deep-sea diver diving down, down through all the emptiness and cold and wreckage to discover the one thing he had set his heart on, something small and precious, hard to locate, as a ruby maybe on the ocean floor. That was a look she would like to have described to Char. No doubt Char had seen it. But did she know how freely it was being distributed?

❧

11   Char and Arthur had been planning a trip that summer to see Yellowstone Park and the Grand Canyon, but they did not go. Arthur suffered a series of dizzy spells just at the end of school, and the doctor put him to bed. Several things were the matter with him. He was anemic, he had an irregular heartbeat, there was trouble with his kidneys. Et worried about leukemia. She woke at night, worrying.

12   "Don't be silly," said Char serenely, "He's overtired."

13   Arthur got up in the evenings and sat in his dressing gown. Blaikie Noble came to visit. He said his room at the hotel was a hole above the kitchen, they were trying to steam-cook him. It made him appreciate the cool of the porch. They played the games that Arthur loved, schoolteacher's games. They played a geography game, and they tried to see who could make the most words out of the name Beethoven. Arthur won. He got thirty-four. He was immensely delighted.

14   "You'd think you'd found the Holy Grail," Char said.

15   They played "Who Am I?" Each of them had to choose somebody to be—real or imaginary, living or dead, human or animal—and the others had to try to guess it in twenty questions. Et got who Arthur was on the thirteenth question. Sir Galahad.

16   "I never thought you'd get it so soon."

17   "I thought back to Char saying about the Holy Grail."

18   "*My strength is as the strength of ten,*" said Blaikie Noble, "*Because my heart is pure.* I didn't know I remembered that."

19   "You should have been King Arthur," Et said. "King Arthur is your namesake."

20   "I should have. King Arthur was married to the most beautiful woman in the world."

21   "Ha," said Et. "We all know the end of that story."

22   Char went into the living room and played the piano in the dark.

23   *The flowers that bloom in the spring, tra-la,*
        Have nothing to do with the case....

24   When Et arrived, out of breath, that past June, and said, "Guess who I saw downtown on the street?" Char, who was on her knees picking strawberries, said, "Blaikie Noble."

25   "You've seen him."

26   "No," said Char. "I just knew. I think I knew by your voice.

27   A name that had not been mentioned between them for thirty years. Et was too amazed then to think of the explanation that came to her later. Why did it need to be a surprise to Char? There was a postal service in this country, there had been all along.

28   "I asked him about his wife," she said. "The one with the dolls." (As if Char wouldn't remember.) "He says she died a long time ago. Not only that. He married another one and she's dead. Neither could have been rich. And where is all the Nobles' money, from the hotel?"

29   "We'll never know," said Char, and ate a strawberry.

❧

30   The hotel had just recently been opened up again. The Nobles had given it up in the twenties and the town had operated it for a while as a hospital. Now some people from Toronto had bought it, renovated the dining room, put in a cocktail lounge, reclaimed the lawns and garden, though the tennis court seemed to be beyond repair. There was a croquet set put out again. People came to stay in the summers, but they were not the sort of people who used to come. Retired couples. Many widows and single ladies. Nobody would have walked a block to see them get off the boat, Et thought. Not that there was a boat any more.

31   That first time she met Blaikie Noble on the street she had made a point of not being taken aback. He was wearing a creamy suit and his hair, that had always been bleached by the sun, was bleached for good now, white.

32   "Blaikie. I knew either it was you or a vanilla ice-cream cone. I bet you don't know who I am."

33   "You're Et Desmond and the only thing different about you is you cut off your braids." He kissed her forehead, nervy as always.

34   "So you're back visiting old haunts," said Et, wondering who had seen that.

35   "Not visiting. Haunting." He told her then how he had got wind of the hotel opening up again, and how he had been doing this sort of thing, driving tour buses, in various places, in Florida and Banff. And when she asked he told her about his two wives. He never asked was she married, taking for granted she wasn't. He never asked if Char was, till she told him.

❧

36   Et remembered the first time she understood that Char was beautiful. She was looking at a picture taken of them, of Char and herself and their brother who was drowned. Et was ten in the picture, Char fourteen and Sandy seven, just a couple of weeks short of all he would ever be. Et was sitting in an armless chair and Char was behind her, arms folded on the chair-back, with Sandy in his sailor suit cross-legged on the floor—or marble terrace, you would think, with the effect made by what had been nothing but a dusty, yellowing screen, but came out in the picture a pillar and draped curtain, a scene of receding poplars and mountains. Char had pinned her front hair up for the picture and was wearing a bright blue, ankle-length silk dress—of course the color did not show—with complicated black velvet piping. She was smiling slightly, with great composure. She could have been eighteen, she could have been twenty-two. Her beauty was not of the fleshy timid sort most often featured on calendars and cigar boxes of the period, but was sharp and delicate, intolerant, challenging.

37   Et took a long look at this picture and then went and looked at Char, who was in the kitchen. It was washday. The woman who came to help was pulling clothes through the wringer, and their mother was sitting down resting and staring through the screen door (she never got over Sandy, nobody expected her to). Char was starching their father's collars. He had a tobacco and candy store on the Square and wore a fresh collar every day. Et was prepared to find that some metamorphosis had taken place, as in the background, but it was not so. Char, bending over the starch basin, silent and bad-humored (she hated washday, the

heat and steam and flapping sheets and chugging commotion of the machine—in fact, she was not fond of any kind of housework), showed in her real face the same almost disdainful harmony as in the photograph. This made Et understand, in some not entirely welcome way, that the qualities of legend were real, that they surfaced where and when you least expected. She had almost thought beautiful women were a fictional invention. She and Char would go down to watch the people get off the excursion boat, on Sundays, walking up to the Hotel. So much white it hurt your eyes, the ladies' dresses and parasols and the men's summer suits and Panama hats, not to speak of the sun dazzling on the water and the band playing But looking closely at those ladies, Et found fault. Coarse skin or fat behind or chicken necks or dull nests of hair, probably ratted. Et did not let anything get by her, young as she was. At school she was respected for her self-possession and her sharp tongue. She was the one to tell you if you had been at the blackboard with a hole in your stocking or a ripped hem. She was the one who imitated (but in a safe corner of the schoolyard, out of earshot, always) the teacher reading "The Burial of Sir John Moore."

38   All the same it would have suited her better to have found one of those ladies beautiful, not Char. It would have been more appropriate. More suitable than Char in her wet apron with her cross expression, bent over the starch basin. Et was a person who didn't like contradictions, didn't like things out of place, didn't like mysteries or extremes.

39   She didn't like the bleak notoriety of having Sandy's drowning attached to her, didn't like the memory people kept of her father carrying the body up from the beach. She could be seen at twilight, in her gym bloomers, turning cartwheels on the lawn of the stricken house. She made a wry mouth, which nobody saw, one day in the park when Char said, "That was my little brother who was drowned."

∾

40   The park overlooked the beach. They were standing there with Blaikie Noble, the hotel owner's son, who said, "Those waves can be dangerous. Three or four years ago there was a kid drowned."

41   And Char said—to give her credit, she didn't say it tragically, but almost with amusement, that he should know so little about Mock Hill people—"That was my little brother who was drowned."

42   Blaikie Noble was not any older than Char—if he had been, he would have been fighting in France—but he had not had to live all his life in Mock Hill. He did not know the real people there as well as he knew the regular guests at his father's hotel. Every winter he went with his parents to California, on the train. He had seen the Pacific surf. He had pledged allegiance to their flag. His manners were democratic, his skin was tanned. This was at a time when people were not usually tanned as a result of leisure, only work. His hair was bleached by the sun. His good looks were almost as notable as Char's but his were corrupted by charm, as hers were not.

43   It was the heyday of Mock Hill and all the other towns around the lakes, of all the hotels which in later years would become Sunshine Camps for city children, T.B. sanatoriums, barracks for R.A.F. training pilots in World War II. The

white paint on the hotel was renewed every spring, hollowed-out logs filled with flowers were set on the railings, pots of flowers swung on chains above them. Croquet sets and wooden swings were set out on the lawns, the tennis court rolled. People who could not afford the hotel, young workingmen, shop clerks and factory girls from the city, stayed in a row of tiny cottages, joined by lattice-work that hid their garbage pails and communal outhouses, stretching far up the beach. Girls from Mock Hill, if they had mothers to tell them what to do, were told not to walk out there. Nobody told Char what to do, so she walked along the boardwalk in front of them in the glaring afternoon, taking Et with her for company. The cottages had no glass in their windows, they had only propped-up wooden shutters that were closed at night. From the dark holes came one or two indistinct, sad or drunk invitations, that was all. Char's looks and style did not attract men, perhaps intimidated them. All through high school in Mock Hill she had not one boy friend. Blaikie Noble was her first, if that was what he was.

44   What did this affair of Char's and Blaikie Noble's amount to, in the summer of 1918? Et was never sure. He did not call at the house, at least not more than once or twice. He was kept busy, working at the hotel. Every afternoon he drove an open excursion wagon, with an awning on top of it, up the lakeshore road, taking people to look at the Indian graves and the limestone garden and to glimpse through the trees the Gothic stone mansion, built by a Toronto distiller and known locally as Grog Castle. He was also in charge of the variety show the hotel put on once a week, with a mixture of local talent, recruited guests, and singers and comedians brought in especially for the performance.

45   Late mornings seemed to be the time he and Char had. "Come on," Char would say, "I have to go downtown," and she would in fact pick up the mail and walk part way round the Square before veering off into the park. Soon Blaikie Noble would appear from the side door of the hotel and come bounding up the steep path. Sometimes he would not even bother with the path but jump over the back fence, to amaze them. None of this, the bounding or jumping, was done the way some boy from Mock Hill High School might have done it, awkwardly yet naturally. Blaikie Noble behaved like a man imitating a boy; he mocked himself but was graceful, like an actor.

46   "Isn't he stuck on himself?" said Et to Char, watching. The position she had taken up right away on Blaikie was that she didn't like him.

47   "Of course he is," said Char.

48   She told Blaikie. "Et says you're stuck on yourself."

49   "What did you say?"

50   "I told her you had to be, nobody else is."

51   Blaikie didn't mind. He had taken the position that he liked Et. He would with a quick tug loosen and destroy the arrangement of looped-up braids she wore. He told them things about the concert artists. He told them the Scottish ballad singer was a drunk and wore corsets, that the female impersonator even in his hotel room donned a blue nightgown with feathers, that the lady ventrilo-quist talked to her dolls—they were named Alphonse and Alicia—as if they were real people, and had them sitting up in bed one on each side of her.

52   "How would you know that?" Char said.

53   "I took her up her breakfast."

54   "I thought you had maids to do that."

55 "The morning after the show I do it. That's when I hand them their pay envelope and give them their walking papers. Some of them would stay all week if you didn't inform them. She sits up in bed trying to feed them bits of bacon and talking to them and doing them answering back, you'd have a fit if you could see."

56 "She's cracked I guess," Char said peacefully.

ॐ

57 One night that summer Et woke up and remembered she had left her pink organdy dress on the line, after handwashing it. She thought she heard rain, just the first few drops. She didn't, it was just leaves rustling, but she was confused, waking up like that. She thought it was far on in the night, too, but thinking about it later she decided it might have been only around midnight. She got up and went downstairs, turned on the back kitchen light, and let herself out the back door, and standing on the stoop pulled the clothesline towards her. Then almost under her feet, from the grass right beside the stoop, where there was a big lilac bush that had grown and spread, untended, to the size of a tree, two figures lifted themselves, didn't stand or even sit up, just roused their heads as if from bed, still tangled together some way. The back kitchen light didn't shine directly out but lit the yard enough for her to see their faces. Blaikie and Char.

58 She never did get a look at what state their clothes were in, to see how far they had gone or were going. She wouldn't have wanted to. To see their faces was enough for her. Their mouths were big and swollen, their cheeks flattened, coarsened, their eyes holes. Et left her dress, she fled into the house and into her bed where she surprised herself by falling asleep. Char never said a word about it to her next day. All she said was, "I brought your dress in, Et. I thought it might rain." As if she had never seen Et out there pulling on the clothesline. Et wondered. She knew if she said, "You saw me," Char would probably tell her it had been a dream. She let Char think she had been fooled into believing that, if that was what Char was thinking. That way, Et was left knowing more; she was left knowing what Char looked like when she lost her powers, abdicated. Sandy drowned, with green stuff clogging his nostrils, couldn't look more lost than that.

ॐ

59 Before Christmas the news came to Mock Hill that Blaikie Noble was married. He had married the lady ventriloquist, the one with Alphonse and Alicia. Those dolls, who wore evening dress and had sleek hairdos in the style of Vernon and Irene Castle, were more clearly remembered than the lady herself. The only thing people recalled for sure about her was that she could not have been under forty. A nineteen-year-old boy. It was because he had not been brought up like other boys, had been allowed the run of the hotel, taken to California, let mix with all sorts of people. The result was depravity, and could have been predicted.

60 Char swallowed poison. Or what she thought was poison. It was laundry blueing. The first thing she could reach down from the shelf in the back kitchen. Et came home after school—she had heard the news at noon, from Char herself in fact, who had laughed and said, "Wouldn't that kill you?"—and she found

Char vomiting into the toilet. "Go get the Medical Book," Char said to her, 'A terrible involuntary groan came out of her. "Read what it says about poison." Et went instead to phone the doctor. Char came staggering out of the bathroom holding the bottle of bleach they kept behind the tub. "If you don't put up the phone I'll drink the whole bottle," she said in a harsh whisper. Their mother was presumably asleep behind her closed door.

61   Et had to hang up the phone and look in the ugly old book where she had read long ago about childbirth and signs of death, and had learned about holding a mirror to the mouth. She was under the mistaken impression that Char had been drinking from the bleach bottle already, so she read all about that. Then she found it was the blueing. Blueing was not in the book, but it seemed the best thing to do would be to induce vomiting, as the book advised for most poisons— Char was at it already, didn't need to have it induced—and then drink a quart of milk. When Char got the milk down she was sick again.

62   "I didn't do this on account of Blaikie Noble," she said between spasms. "Don't you ever think that. I wouldn't be such a fool. A pervert like him. I did it because I'm sick of living."

63   "What are you sick of about living?" said Et sensibly when Char had wiped her face.

64   "I'm sick of this town and all the stupid people in it and Mother and her dropsy and keeping house and washing sheets every day. I don't think I'm going to vomit any more. I think I could drink some coffee. It says coffee."

65   Et made a pot and Char got out two of the best cups. They began to giggle as they drank.

66   "I'm sick of Latin," Et said. "I'm sick of Algebra. I think I'll take blueing."
67   "Life is a burden," Char said. "O Life, where is thy sting?"
68   "O Death. O Death, where is thy sting?"
69   "Did I say Life? I meant Death. O Death, where is thy sting? Pardon me."

ॐ

70   One afternoon Et was staying with Arthur while Char shopped and changed books at the Library. She wanted to make him an eggnog, and she went searching in Char's cupboard for the nutmeg. In with the vanilla and the almond extract and the artificial rum she found a small bottle of a strange liquid. Zinc phosphide. She read the label and turned it around in her hands. A rodenticide. Rat poison, that must mean. She had not known Char and Arthur were troubled with rats. They kept a cat, old Tom, asleep now around Arthur's feet. She unscrewed the top and sniffed at it, to know what it smelled like. Like nothing. Of course. It must taste like nothing too, or it wouldn't fool the rats.

71   She put it back where she had found it. She made Arthur his eggnog and took it in and watched him drink it. A slow poison. She remembered that from Blaikie's foolish story. Arthur drank with an eager noise, like a child, more to please her, she thought, than because he was so pleased himself. He would drink anything you handed him. Naturally.

72   "How are you these days, Arthur?"
73   "Oh, Et. Some days a bit stronger, and then I seem to slip back. It takes time."

74   But there was none gone, the bottle seemed full. What awful nonsense. Like something you read about, Agatha Christie. She would mention it to Char and Char would tell her the reason.

75   "Do you want me to read to you?" she asked Arthur, and he said yes. She sat by the bed and read to him from a book about the Duke of Wellington. He had been reading it by himself but his arms got tired holding it. All those battles, and wars, and terrible things, what did Arthur know about such affairs, why was he so interested? He knew nothing. He did not know why things happened, why people could not behave sensibly. He was too good. He knew about history but not about what went on, in front of his eyes, in his house, anywhere. Et differed from Arthur in knowing that something went on, even if she could not understand why; she differed from him in knowing there were those you could not trust.

76   She did not say anything to Char after all. Every time she was in the house she tried to make some excuse to be alone in the kitchen, so that she could open the cupboard and stand on tiptoe and look in, to see it over the tops of the other bottles, to see that the level had not gone down. She did think maybe she was going a little strange, as old maids did; this fear of hers was like the absurd and harmless fears young girls sometimes have, that they will jump out a window, or strangle a baby, sitting in its buggy. Though it was not her own acts she was frightened of.

❧

77   Et looked at Char and Blaikie and Arthur, sitting on the porch, trying to decide if they wanted to go in and put the light on and play cards. She wanted to convince herself of her silliness. Char's hair, and Blaikie's too, shone in the dark. Arthur was almost bald now and Et's own hair was thin and dark. Char and Blaikie seemed to her the same kind of animal—tall, light, powerful, with a dangerous luxuriance. They sat apart but shone out together. Lovers. Not a soft word, as people thought, but cruel and tearing. There was Arthur in the rocker with a quilt over his knees, foolish as something that hasn't grown its final, most necessary, skin. Yet in a way the people like Arthur were the most trouble-making of all.

78   "I love my love with an R, because he is ruthless. His name is Rex, and he lives in a—restaurant."

79   "I love my love with an A, because he is absentminded. His name is Arthur, and he lives in an ashcan."

80   "Why Et," Arthur said. "I never suspected. But I don't know if I like about the ashcan."

81   "You would think we were all twelve years old," said Char.

❧

82   After the blueing episode Char became popular. She became involved in the productions of the Amateur Dramatic Society and the Oratorio Society, although she was never much of an actress or a singer. She was always the cold and beautiful heroine in the plays, or the brittle exquisite young society woman. She learned to smoke, because of having to do it onstage. In one play Et never forgot, she was a statue. Or rather, she played a girl who had to pretend to be a statue, so that a young man fell in love with her and later discovered, to his confusion and

perhaps disappointment, that she was only human. Char had to stand for eight minutes perfectly still on stage, draped in white crepe and showing the audience her fine indifferent profile. Everybody marveled at how she did it.

83   The moving spirit behind the Amateur Dramatic Society and the Oratorio Society was a high school teacher new to Mock Hill, Arthur Comber. He taught Et history in her last year. Everybody said he gave her A's because he was in love with her sister, but Et knew it was because she worked harder than she ever had before; she learned the History of North America as she had never learned anything in her life. Missouri Compromise. Mackenzie to the Pacific, 1793. She never forgot.

84   Arthur Comber was thirty or so, with a high bald forehead, a red face in spite of not drinking (that later paled) and a clumsy, excited manner. He knocked a bottle of ink off his desk and permanently stained the History Room floor. "Oh dear, oh dear," he said, crouching down to the spreading ink, flapping at it with his handkerchief. Et imitated that. "Oh dear, oh dear!" "Oh good heavens!" All his flustery exclamations and miscalculated gestures. Then, when he took her essay at the door, his red face shining with eagerness, giving her work and herself such a welcome, she felt sorry. That was why she worked so hard, she thought, to make up for mocking him.

85   He had a black scholar's gown he wore over his suit, to teach in. Even when he wasn't wearing it, Et could see it on him. Hurrying along the street to one of his innumerable, joyfully undertaken obligations, flapping away at the Oratorio singers, jumping on stage—so the whole floor trembled—to demonstrate something to the actors in a play, he seemed to her to have those long ridiculous crow's wings flapping after him, to be as different from other men, as absurd yet intriguing, as the priest from Holy Cross. Char made him give up the gown altogether, after they were married. She had heard that he tripped in it, running up the steps of the school. He had gone sprawling. That finished it, she ripped it up.

86   "I was afraid one of these days you'd, really get hurt."

87   But Arthur said, "Ah. You thought I looked like a fool."

88   Char didn't deny it, though his eyes on her, his wide smile, were begging her to. Her mouth twitched at the corners, in spite of herself. Contempt. Fury. Et saw, they both saw, a great wave of that go over her before she could smile at him and say, "Don't be silly." Then her smile and her eyes were trying to hold on to him, trying to clutch onto his goodness (which she saw, as much as anybody else did, ' but which finally only enraged her, Et believed, like everything else about him, like his sweaty forehead and his galloping optimism), before that boiling wave could come back again, altogether carry her away.

89   Char had a miscarriage during the first year of her marriage and was sick for a long time afterwards. She was never pregnant again. Et by this time was not living in the house; she had her own place on the Square, but she was there one time on washday, helping Char haul the sheets off the line. Their parents were both dead by that time—their mother had died before and their father after the wedding—but it looked to Et like sheets for two beds.

90   "It gives you plenty of wash."

91   "What does?"

92   "Changing sheets like you do."

93   Et was often there in the evening, playing rummy with Arthur while Char, in the other room, picked at the piano in the dark. Or talking and reading library books with Char, while Arthur marked his papers. Arthur walked her home.

"Why do you have to go off and live by yourself anyway?" he scolded her. "You ought to come back and live with us."

94   "Three's a crowd."

95   "It wouldn't be for long. Some man is going to come along some day and fall hard."

96   "If he was such a fool as to do that I'd never fall for him, so we'd be back where we started."

97   "I was a fool that fell for Char, and she ended up having me."

98   Just the way he said her name indicated that Char was above, outside, all ordinary considerations—a marvel, a mystery. No one could hope to solve her, they were lucky just being allowed to contemplate her. Et was on the verge of saying, "She swallowed blueing once over a man that wouldn't have her," but she thought what would be the good of it, Char would only seem more splendid to him, like a heroine out of Shakespeare. He squeezed Et's waist as if to stress their companionable puzzlement, involuntary obeisance, before her sister. She felt afterwards the bumpy pressure of his fingers as if they had left dents just above where her skirt fastened. It had felt like somebody absent-mindedly trying out the keys of a piano.

∞

99   Et had set up in the dressmaking business. She had a long narrow room on the Square, once a shop, where she did all her fitting, sewing, cutting, pressing and, behind a curtain, her sleeping and cooking. She could lie in bed and look at the squares of pressed tin on her ceiling, their flower pattern, all her own. Arthur had not liked her taking up dressmaking because he thought she was too smart for it. All the hard work she had done in History had given him an exaggerated idea of her brains. "Besides," she told him, "it takes more brains to cut and fit, if you do it right, than to teach people about the War of 1812. Because, once you learn that, it's learned and isn't going to change you. Whereas every article of clothing you make is an entirely new proposition."

100   "Still it's a surprise," said Arthur, "to see the way you settle down."

101   It surprised everybody, but not Et herself. She made the change easily, from a girl turning cartwheels to a town fixture. She drove the other dressmakers out of business. They had been meek, unimportant creatures anyway, going around to people's houses, sewing in back rooms and being grateful for meals. Only one serious rival appeared in all Et's years, and that was a Finnish woman who called herself a designer. Some people gave her a try, because people are never satisfied, but it soon came out she was all style and no fit. Et never mentioned her, she let people find out for themselves; but afterwards, when this woman had left town and gone to Toronto—where, from what Et had seen on the streets, nobody knew a good fit from a bad—Et did not restrain herself. She would say to a customer she was fitting, "I see you're still wearing that herringbone my foreigner friend tacked together for you. I saw you on the street."

102   "Oh, I know," the woman would say. "But I do have to wear it out."

103   "You can't see yourself from behind anyway, what's the difference."

104   Customers took this kind of thing from Et, came to expect it, even. She's a terror, they said about her, Et's a terror. She had them at a disadvantage, she had them in their slips and corsets. Ladies who looked quite firm and powerful, out-

side, were here immobilized, apologetic, exposing such trembly, meek-looking thighs squeezed together by corsets, such long sad breast creases, bellies blown up and torn by children and operations.

105   Et always closed her front curtains tight, pinning the crack.

106   "That's to keep the men from peeking."

107   Ladies laughed nervously.

108   "That's to keep Jimmy Saunders from stumping over to get an eyeful."

109   Jimmy Saunders was a World War I veteran who had a little shop next to Et's, harness and leather goods.

110   "Oh, Et. Jimmy Saunders has a wooden leg."

111   "He hasn't got wooden eyes. Or anything else that I know of."

112   "Et you're terrible."

ᴔ

113   Et kept Char beautifully dressed. The two steadiest criticisms of Char, in Mock Hill, were that she dressed too elegantly, and that she smoked. It was because she was a teacher's wife that she should have refrained from doing either of these things, but Arthur of course let her do anything she liked, even buying her a cigarette holder so she could look like a lady in a magazine. She smoked at a high school dance, and wore a backless satin evening dress, and danced with a boy who had got a high school girl pregnant, and it was all the same to Arthur. He did not get to be Principal. Twice the school board passed him over and brought in somebody from outside, and when they finally gave him the job, in 1942, it was only temporarily and because so many teachers were away at war.

114   Char fought hard all these years to keep her figure. Nobody but Et and Arthur knew what effort that cost her. Nobody but Et knew it all. Both of their parents had been heavy, and Char had inherited the tendency, though Et was always as thin as a stick. Char did exercises and drank a glass of warm water before every meal. But sometimes she went on eating binges. Et had known her to eat a dozen cream puffs one after the other, a pound of peanut brittle, or a whole lemon meringue pie. Then pale and horrified she took down Epsom salts, three or four or five times the prescribed amount. For two or three days she would be sick, dehydrated, purging her sins, as Et said. During these periods she could not look at food. Et would have to come and cook Arthur's supper. Arthur did not know about the pie or the peanut brittle or whatever it was, or about the Epsom salts. He thought she had gained a pound or two and was going through a fanatical phase of dieting. He worried about her.

115   "What is the difference, what does it matter?" he would say to Et. "She would still be beautiful."

116   "She won't do herself any harm," said Et, enjoying her food, and glad to see that worry hadn't put him off his. She always made him good suppers.

ᴔ

117   It was the week before the Labor Day weekend. Blaikie had gone to Toronto, for a day or two he said.

118   "It's quiet without him," said Arthur.

119   "I never noticed he was such a conversationalist," Et said.

120   "I only mean in the way that you get used to somebody."

121   "Maybe we ought to get unused to him," said Et.

122   Arthur was unhappy. He was not going back to the school; he had obtained a leave of absence until after Christmas. Nobody believed he would go back then.

123   "I suppose he has his own plans for the winter," he said.

124   "He may have his own plans for right now. You know I have my customers from the hotel. I have my friends. Ever since I went on that excursion, I hear things."

125   She never knew where she got the inspiration to say what she said, where it came from. She had not planned it at all, yet it came so easily, believably.

126   "I hear he's taken up with a well-to-do woman down at the hotel."

127   Arthur was the one to take an interest, not Char.

128   "A widow?"

129   "Twice, I believe. The same as he is. And she has the money from both. It's been suspected for some time and she was talking about it openly. He never said anything, though. He never said anything to you, did he, Char?"

130   "No," said Char.

131   "I heard this afternoon that now he's gone, and she's gone. It wouldn't be the first time he pulled something like this. Char and I remember."

132   Then Arthur wanted to know what she meant and she told him the story of the lady ventriloquist, remembering even the names of the dolls, though of course she left out all about Char. Char sat through this, even contributing a bit.

133   "They might come back but my guess is they'd be embarrassed. He'd be embarrassed. He'd be embarrassed to come here, anyway."

134   "Why?" said Arthur, who had cheered up a little through the ventriloquist story. "We never set down any rule against a man getting married."

135   Char got up and went into the house. After a while they heard the sound of the piano.

ᘓ

136   The question often crossed Et's mind in later years—what did she mean to do about this story when Blaikie got back? For she had no reason to believe he would not come back. The answer was that she had not made any plans at all. She had not planned anything. She supposed she might have wanted to make trouble between him and Char—make Char pick a fight with him, her suspicions roused even if rumors had not been borne out, make Char read what he might do again in the light of what he had done before. She did not know what she wanted. Only to throw things into confusion, for she believed then that somebody had to, before it was too late.

137   Arthur made as good a recovery as could be expected at his age, he went back to teaching history to the senior classes, working half-days until it was time for him to retire. Et kept up her own place on the Square and tried to get up and do some cooking and cleaning for Arthur, as well. Finally, after he retired, she moved back into the house, keeping the other place only for business purposes. "Let people jaw all they like," she said. "At our age."

138   Arthur lived on and on, though he was frail and slow. He walked down to the Square once a day, dropped in on Et, went and sat in the park. The hotel closed down and was sold again. There was a story that it was going to be opened up and used as a rehabilitation center for drug addicts, but the town got up a petition and that fell through. Eventually it was torn down.

139   Et's eyesight was not as good as it used to be, she had to slow down. She had to turn people away. Still she worked, every day. In the evenings Arthur watched television or read, but she sat out on the porch, in the warm weather, or in the dining room in winter, rocking and resting her eyes. She came and watched the news with him, and made him his hot drink, cocoa or tea.

℘

140   There was no trace of the bottle. Et went and looked in the cupboard as soon as she could—having run to the house in response to Arthur's early morning call, and found the doctor, old McClain, coming in at the same time. She ran out and looked in the garbage, but she never found it. Could Char have found the time to bury it? She was lying on the bed, fully and nicely dressed, her hair piled up. There was no fuss about the cause of death as there is in stories. She had complained of weakness to Arthur the night before, after Et had gone, she had said she thought she was getting the flu. So the old doctor said heart, and let it go. Nor could Et ever know. Would what was in that bottle leave a body undisfigured, as Char's was? Perhaps what was in the bottle was not what it said. She was not even sure that it had been there that last evening, she had been too carried away with what she was saying to go and look, as she usually did. Perhaps it had been thrown out earlier and Char had taken something else, pills maybe. Perhaps it really was her heart. All that purging would have weakened anybody's heart.

141   Her funeral was on Labor Day and Blaikie Noble came, cutting out his bus tour. Arthur in his grief had forgotten about Et's story, was not surprised to see Blaikie there. He had come back to Mock Hill on the day Char was found. A few hours too late, like some story. Et in her natural confusion could not remember what it was. Romeo and Juliet, she thought later. But Blaikie of course did not do away with himself afterwards, he went back to Toronto. For a year or two he sent Christmas cards, then was not heard of any more. Et would not be surprised if her story of his marrying had not come true in the end. Only her timing was mistaken.

142   Sometimes Et had it on the tip of her tongue to say to Arthur, "There's something I've been meaning to tell you." She didn't believe she was going to let him die without knowing. He shouldn't be allowed. He kept a picture of Char on his bureau. It was the one taken of her in her costume for that play, where she played the statue-girl. But Et let it go, day to day. She and Arthur still played rummy and kept up a bit of garden, along with raspberry canes. If they had been married, people would have said they were very happy.

Leon Rooke

U.S.A./Canada 1934–

Born in Roanoke, North Carolina, Rooke completed a B.A. at the University of
North Carolina in 1957. Rooke has published novels, short stories, and plays, as
well as writing as a critic and editor, but with over 300 short stories published and
fifty in process, short stories dominate his output. He moved from the U.S.A. to
Canada in 1969 and has since received the Governor General's Award in 1983 for
his novel *Shakespeare's Dog*. His novel *A Good Baby* was made into a feature film in
2000. Rooke's "A Bolt of White Cloth" is often thought of as the quintessential
example of Canadian magical realism, a form most often associated with Mexico's
Fuentes and South American writers such as Borges and García Márquez, but also
having its roots in Proust, Kafka, and surrealism. Magical realism, as Bruce Taylor
suggests, occurs in writing when "the fantastic co-exists with reality and is simply
accepted as a part of that reality."

A Bolt of White Cloth   1984

1   A man came by our road carrying an enormous bolt of white cloth on his back.
Said he was from the East. Said whoever partook of this cloth would come to
know true happiness. Innocence without heartbreak, he said, if that person
proved worthy. My wife fingered his cloth, having in mind something for new
curtains. It was good quality, she said. Beautifully woven, of a fine, light texture,
and you certainly couldn't argue with the color.

2   "How much is it?" she asked.

3   "Before I tell you that," the man said, "you must tell me truthfully if you've
ever suffered."

4   "Oh, I've suffered," she said. "I've known suffering of some description every
day of my natural life."

5   I was standing over by the toolshed, with a big smile. My wife is a real joker,
who likes nothing better than pulling a person's leg. She's known hardships, this
and that upheaval, but nothing I would call down-and-out suffering. Mind you,
I don't speak for her. I wouldn't pretend to speak for another person.

6   This man with the bolt of cloth, however, he clearly had no sense of my
wife's brand of humor. She didn't get an itch of a smile out of him. He kept the
cloth neatly balanced on his shoulder, wincing a little from the weight and from
however far he'd had to carry it, staring hard and straight at my wife the whole
time she fooled with him, as if he hoped to peer clear through to her soul. His
eyes were dark and brooding and hollowed out some. He was like no person
either my wife or me had ever seen before.

7   "Yes," he said, "but suffering of what kind?"

8   "Worse than I hope forever to carry, I'll tell you that," my wife said. "But why
are you asking me these questions? I like your cloth and if the price is right I
mean to buy it."

9   "You can only buy my cloth with love," he said.

10   We began right then to understand that he was some kind of oddity. He was not like anybody we'd ever seen and he didn't come from around here. He'd come from a place we'd never heard of, and if that was the East, or wherever, then he was welcome to it.

11   "Love?" she said. "Love? There's love and there's love, mister. What kind are you talking about?" She hitched a head my way, rolling her eyes, as if to indicate that if it was passionate love he was talking about then he'd first have to do something with me. He'd have to get me off my simmer and onto full boil. That's what she was telling him, with this mischief in her eyes.

12   I put down my pitchfork about here, and strolled nearer. I liked seeing my wife dealing with difficult situations. I didn't want to miss anything. My life with that woman has been packed with the unusual. Unusual circumstances, she calls them. Any time she's ever gone out anywhere without me, whether for a day or an hour or for five minutes, she's come back with whopping good stories about what she's seen and heard and what's happened to her. She's come back with reports on these unusual circumstances, these little adventures in which so many people have done so many extraordinary things or behaved in such fabulous or foolish ways. So what was rare this time, I thought, was that it had come visiting. She hadn't had to go out and find it.

13   "Hold these," my wife told me. And she put this washtub of clothes in my hands, and went back to hanging wet pieces on the line, which is what she'd been doing when this man with the bolt of cloth ventured up into our yard.

14   "Love," she told him. "You tell me what kind I need, if I'm to buy that cloth. I got good ears and I'm listening."

15   The man watched her stick clothespins in her mouth, slap out a good wide sheet, and string it up. He watched her hang two of these, plus a mess of towels, and get her mouth full again before he spoke. He looked about the unhappiest I've ever seen any man look. He didn't have any joy in him. I wondered why he didn't put down that heavy bolt of cloth, and why he didn't step around into a spot of shade. The sun was lick-killing bright in that yard. I was worried he'd faint.

16   "The ordinary kind," he said. "Your ordinary kind of love will buy this cloth."

17   My wife flapped her wash and laughed. He was really tickling her. She was having herself a wonderful time.

18   "What's ordinary?" she said. "I've never known no ordinary love."

19   He jumped right in. He got excited just for a second.

20   "The kind such as might exist between the closest friends," he said. "The kind such as might exist between a man and his wife or between parents and children or for that matter the love a boy might have for his dog. That kind of love."

21   "I've got that," she said. "I've had all three. Last year this time I had me a fourth, but it got run over. Up on the road there, by the tall trees, by a man in a red car who didn't even stop."

22   "That would have been your cat," he said. "I don't know much about cats."

23   I put down the washtub. My wife let her arms drop. We looked at him, wondering how he knew about that cat. Then I laughed, for I figured someone down the road must have told him of my wife's mourning over that cat. She'd dug it a grave under the grapevine and said sweet words over it. She sorely missed that cat.

24   "What's wrong with loving cats?" she asked him. "Or beasts of the fields? I'm surprised at you."

25   The man shifted his burden and worked one shoe into the ground. He stared off at the horizon. He looked like he knew he'd said something he shouldn't.

26   She pushed me out of the way. She wanted to get nearer to him. She had something more to say.

27   "Now listen to me," she said. "I've loved lots of things in my life. Lots and lots. "Him!" she said (pointing at me), "it" (pointing at our house), "them!" (pointing to the flower beds), "that!" (pointing to the sky), "those" (pointing to the woods), "this" (pointing to the ground)—"practically everything! There isn't any of it I've hated, and not much I've been indifferent to. Including cats. So put that in your pipe and smoke it."

28   Then swooping up her arms and laughing hard, making it plain she bore no grudge but wasn't just fooling.

29   Funny thing was, hearing her say it, I felt the same way. It, them, that, those—they were all beautiful. I couldn't deny it was love, I was feeling.

30   The man with the cloth had turned each—way she'd pointed. He'd staggered a time or two but he'd kept up. In fact, it struck me that he'd got a little ahead of her. That he knew where her arm was next going. Some trickle of pleasure was showing in his face. And something else—was happening, something I'd never seen. He had his face lifted up to this burning sun. It was big and orange, that sun, and scorching-hot, but he was staring smack into it. He wasn't blinking or squinting. His eyes were wide open.

31   Madness or miracle, I couldn't tell which.

32   He strode over to a parcel of good grass.

33   "I believe you mean it," he said. "How much could you use?"

34   He placed the bolt of white cloth down on the grass and pulled out shiny scissors from his back pocket.

35   "I bet he's blind," I whispered to my wife. "I bet he's got false eyes."

36   My wife shushed me. She wasn't listening. She had her excitement hat on; her unusual circumstances look. He was offering free cloth for love, ordinary love, and she figured she'd go along with the gag.

37   How much?

38   "Oh," she said, "maybe eight yards. Maybe ten. It depends on how many windows I end up doing, plus what hang I want, plus the pleating I'm after."

39   "You mean to make these curtains yourself?" he asked. He was already down on his knees, smoothing the bolt. Getting set to roll it out.

40   "Why, sure," she said. "I don't know who else would do it for me. I don't know who else I would ask."

41   He nodded soberly, not thinking about it. "That's so," he said casually. "Mend your own fences first." He was perspiring in the sun, and dishevelled, as though he'd been on the road a long time. His shoes had big holes in them and you could see the blistered soles of his feet, but he had an air of exhilaration now. His hair fell down over his eyes and he shoved the dark locks back. I got the impression that some days he went a long time between customers; that he didn't find cause to give away this cloth every day.

42   He got a fair bit unrolled. It certainly did look like prime goods, once you saw it spread out on the grass in that long expanse.

43 "It's so pretty!" my wife said. "Heaven help me, but I think it is prettier than grass!"

44 "It's pretty, all right," he said. "It's a wing-dinger. Just tell me when to stop," he said. "Just shout yoo-hoo."

45 "Hold up a minute," she said. "I don't want to get greedy. I don't want you rolling off more than we can afford."

46 "You can afford it," he said.

47 He kept unrolling. He was up past the well house by now, whipping it off fast, though the bolt didn't appear to be getting any smaller. My wife had both hands up over her mouth. Half of her wanted to run into the house and get her purse so she could pay; the other half wanted to stay and watch this man unfurl his beautiful cloth. She whipped around to me, all agitated.

48 "I believe he means it," she said. "He means us to have this cloth. What do I do?"

49 I shook my head. This was her territory. It was the kind of adventure constant to her nature and necessary to her well-being.

50 "Honey," I said, "you deal with it."

51 The sun was bright over everything: It was whipping-hot. There wasn't much wind but I could hear the clothes flapping on the line. A woodpecker had himself a tree somewhere and I could hear him pecking. The sky was wavy blue. The trees seemed to be swaying.

52 He was up by the front porch now, still unrolling. It surprised us both that he could move so fast.

53 "Yoo-hoo," my wife said. It was no more than a peep, the sound you might make if a butterfly lands on your ear.

54 "Wait," he said. "One thing. One question I meant to ask. All this talk of love; your it, your those and them, it slipped my mind."

55 "Let's hear it," my wife said. "Ask away." It seemed to me that she spoke out of a trance. That she was as dazzled as I was.

56 "You two got no children," he said. "Why is that? You're out here on this nice farm, and no children to your name. Why is that?"

57 We hadn't expected this query from him. It did something to the light in the yard and how we saw it. It was as if some giant dark bird had fluttered between us and the sun. Without knowing it, we sidled closer to each other. We fumbled for the other's hand. We stared off every which way. No one on our road had asked that question in a long, long time; they hadn't asked it in some years.

58 "We're not able," we said. Both of us spoke at the same time. It seemed to me that it was my wife's voice which carried; mine was some place down in my chest, and dropping, as if it meant to crawl on the ground.

59 "We're not able," we said. That time it came out pure, without any grief to bind it. It came out the way we long ago learned how to say it.

60 "Oh," he said. "I see." He mumbled something else. He kicked the ground and took a little walk back and forth. He seemed angry, though not at us. "Wouldn't you know it?" he said. "Wouldn't you know it?"

61 He swore a time or two. He kicked the ground. He surely didn't like it.

62 "We're over that now," my wife said. "We're past that caring."

63 "I bet you are," he said. "You're past that little misfortune."

64   He took to unrolling his bolt again, working with his back to the sun. Down on his knees, scrambling, smoothing the material. Sweating and huffing. He was past the front porch now, and still going, getting on toward that edge where the high weeds grew.

65   "About here, do you think?" he asked.

66   He'd rolled off about fifty yards.

67   My wife and I slowly shook our heads, not knowing what to think.

68   "Say the word," he told us. "I can give you more if more is what you want."

69   "I'd say you were giving us too much," my wife said. "I'd say we don't need nearly that much."

70   "Never mind that," he said. "I'm feeling generous today."

71   He nudged the cloth with his fingers and rolled off a few yards more. He would have gone on unwinding his cloth had the weeds not stopped him. He stood and looked back over the great length he had unwound.

72   "Looks like a long white road, don't it?" he said. "You could walk that road and your feet never get dirty."

73   My wife clenched my hand; it was what we'd both been thinking.

74   SnipSnipSnip. He began snipping. His scissors raced over the material. SnipSnipSnip. The cloth was sheared clear and clean of his bolt, yet it seemed to me the size of that bolt hadn't lessened any. My wife saw it too.

75   "He's got cloth for all eternity," she said. "He could unroll that cloth till doomsday."

76   The man laughed. We were whispering this, but way up by the weeds he heard us. "There's doom and there's doom," he said. "Which doomsday?"

77   I had the notion he'd gone through more than one. That he knew the picture from both sides.

78   "It is smart as grass," he said. "Smarter. It never needs watering." He chuckled at that, spinning both arms. Dancing a little. "You could make nighties out of this," he said. "New bedsheets. Transform your whole bedroom."

79   My wife made a face. She wasn't too pleased, talking nighties with another man.

80   Innocence without heartbreak, I thought. That's what we're coming to.

81   He nicely rolled up the cloth he'd sheared off and presented it to my wife. "I hope you like it," he said. "No complaints yet. Maybe you can make yourself a nice dress as well. Maybe two or three. Make him some shirts. I think you'll find there's plenty here."

82   "Goodness, it's light," she said.

83   "Not if you've been carrying it long as I have," he said. He pulled a blue bandanna from his pocket and wiped his face and neck. He ran his hand through his hair and slicked it back. He looked up at the sky. His dark eyes seemed to have cleared up some. They looked less broody now. "Gets hot," he said, "working in this sun. But a nice day. I'm glad I found you folks home."

84   "Oh, we're most always home," my wife said.

85   I had to laugh at that. My wife is forever gallivanting over the countryside, checking up on this person and that, taking them her soups and jams and breads.

86   "We're homebodies, us two."

87   She kept fingering the cloth and sighing over it. She held it up against her cheek and with her eyes closed rested herself on it. The man hoisted his own bolt

back on his shoulder; he seemed ready to be going. I looked at my wife's closed lids, at the soft look she had.

88   I got trembly, fearful of what might happen if that cloth didn't work out.

89   "Now look," I said to him, "what's wrong with this cloth? Is it going to rot inside a week? Tomorrow is some other stranger going to knock on our door saying we owe him a hundred or five hundred dollars for this cloth? Mister, I don't understand you," I said.

90   He hadn't bothered with me before; now he looked me dead in the eye. "I can't help being a stranger," he said. "If you never set eyes on me before, I guess that's what I would have to be. Don't you like strangers? Don't you trust them?"

91   My wife jumped in. Her face was fiery, like she thought I had wounded him. "We like strangers just fine," she said. "We've helped out many a-one. No, I can't say our door has ever been closed to whoever it is comes by. Strangers can sit in our kitchen just the same as our friends."

92   He smiled at her but kept his stern look for me. "As to your questions," he said, "you're worried about the golden goose, I can see that. Fair enough. No, your cloth will not rot. It will not shred, fade or tear. Nor will it ever need cleaning, either. This cloth requires no upkeep whatsoever. Though a sound heart helps. A sweet disposition, too. Innocence without heartbreak, as I told you. And your wife, if it's her making the curtains or making herself a dress, she will find it to be an amazingly easy cloth to work with. It will practically do the job itself. No, I don't believe you will ever find you have any reason to complain of the quality of that cloth."

93   My wife had it up to her face again. She had her face sunk in it.

94   "Goodness," she said. "it's soft! It smells so fresh. It's like someone singing a song to me."

95   The man laughed. "It is soft," he said. "But it can't sing a note, or has never been known to."

96   It was my wife singing. She had this little hum under her breath.

97   "This is the most wonderful cloth in the world," she said.

98   He nodded. "I can't argue with you on that score," he said. Then he turned again to me. "I believe your wife is satisfied," he said. "But if you have any doubts, if you're worried someone is going to knock on your door tomorrow asking you for a hundred or five hundred dollars, I suppose I could write you up a guarantee. I could give you a PAID IN FULL."

99   He was making me feel ashamed of myself. They both were. "No, no," I said, "if she's satisfied then I am. And I can see she's tickled pink. No, I beg your pardon. I meant no offense."

100   "No offense taken," he said.

101   But his eyes clouded a token. He gazed off at our road and up along the stand of trees and his eyes kept roaming until they snagged the sun. He kept his eyes there, unblinking, open, staring at the sun. I could see the red orbs reflected in his eyes.

102   "There is one thing," he said.

103   I caught my breath and felt my wife catch hers. The hitch? A hitch, after all? Coming so late?

104   We waited.

105   He shuffled his feet. He brought out his bandanna and wiped his face again. He stared at the ground.

106   "Should you ever stop loving," he said, "you shall lose this cloth and all else. You shall wake up one morning and it and all else will no longer be where you left it. It will all be gone and you will not know where you are. You will not know what to do with yourself. You will wish you had never been born."

107   My wife's eyes went saucer-size.

108   He had us in some kind of spell.

109   Hocus-pocus, I thought. He is telling us some kind of hocus-pocus. Yet I felt my skin shudder; I felt the goose bumps rise.

110   "That's it?" my wife said. "That's the only catch?"

111   He shrugged. "That's it," he said. "Not much, is it? Not a whisper of menace for a pair such as yourselves."

112   My wife's eyes were gauzed over; there was a wetness in them.

113   "Hold on," she said. "Don't you be leaving yet. Hold this, honey."

114   She put the cloth in my arms. Then she hastened over to the well, pitched the bucket down, and drew it up running over with fresh water.

115   "Here," she said, coming back with a good dipperful. "Here's a nice drink of cool water. You need it on a day like this."

116   The man drank. He held the dipper in both hands, with the tips of his fingers, and drained the dipper dry, then wiped his chin with the back of his hand.

117   "I did indeed," he said. "That's, very tasty water. I thank you."

118   "That's good water," she said. "That well has been here lo a hundred years. You could stay on for supper," she said. "It's getting on toward that time and I have a fine stew on the stove, with plenty to spare."

119   "That's kind of you," he said back, "and I'm grateful. But I'd best pass on up your road while there's still daylight left, and see who else might have need of this cloth."

120   My wife is not normally a demonstrative woman, not in public. Certainly not with strangers. You could have knocked me over with a feather when she up and kissed him full on the mouth, with a nice hug to boot.

121   "There's payment," she said, "if our money's no good."

122   He blushed, trying to hide his pleasure. It seemed to me she had him wrapped around her little finger . . . or the other way around.

123   "You kiss like a woman," he said. "Like one who knows what kissing is for, and can't hardly stop herself."

124   It was my wife's turn to blush.

125   I took hold of her hand and held her down to grass, because it seemed to me another kiss or two and she'd fly right away with him.

126   He walked across the yard and up by the well house, leaving by the same route he had come. Heading for the road. At the turn, he spun around and waved.

127   "You could try the Hopkins place!" my wife called. "There's a fat woman down that road got a sea of troubles. She could surely use some of that cloth."

128   He smiled and again waved. Then we saw his head and his bolt of white cloth bobbing along the weeds as he took the dips and rises in the road. Then he went on out of sight.

129   "There's that man with some horses down that road!" my wife called. "You be careful of him!"

130   It seemed we heard some sound come back, but whether it was his we couldn't say.

131   My wife and I stood a long time in the yard, me holding the dipper and watching her, while she held her own bolt of cloth in her arms, staring off to where he'd last been.

132   Then she sighed dreamily and went inside.

133   I went on down to the barn and looked after the animals. Getting my feeding done. I talked a spell to them. Talking to animals is soothing to me, and they like it too. They pretend to stare at the walls or the floor as they're munching their feed down, but I know they listen to me. We had us an unusual circumstances chat. "That man with the cloth," I said. "Maybe you can tell me what you make of him."

134   In no time at all I heard my wife excitedly calling me. She was standing out on the back doorstep, with this incredulous look.

135   "I've finished," she said. "I've finished the windows. Nine windows. It beats me how."

136   I started up to the house. Her voice was all shaky. Her face flushed, flinging her arms about. Then she got this new look on.

137   "Wait!" she said. "Stay there! Give me ten minutes!"

138   And she flung herself back inside, banging the door. I laughed. It always gave me a kick how she ordered me around.

139   I got the milk pail down under the cow. Before I'd touched and drained all four teats she was calling again.

140   "Come look, come look, oh come look!"

141   She was standing in the open doorway, with the kitchen to her back. Behind her, through the windows, I could see the streak of a red sunset and how it lit up the swing of trees. But I wasn't looking there. I was looking at her. Looking and swallowing hard and trying to remember how a body produced human speech. I had never thought of white as a color she could wear. White, it pales her some. It leaves her undefined and washes out what parts I like best. But she looked beautiful now. In her new dress she struck me down to my bootstraps. She made my chest break.

142   "Do you like it?" she said.

143   I went running up to her. I was up against her, hugging her and lifting her before she'd even had a chance to get set. I'd never held on so tightly or been so tightly held back.

144   Truth is, it was the strangest thing. Like we were both so innocent we hadn't yet shot up out of new ground.

145   "Come see the curtains," she whispered. "Come see the new sheets. Come see what else I've made. You'll see it all. You'll see how our home has been transformed."

146   I crept inside. There was something holy about it. About it and about us and about those rooms and the whole wide world. Something radiant. Like you had to put your foot down easy and hold it down or you'd float on up.

147   "That's it," she said. "That's how I feel too."

148   That night in bed, trying to figure it out, we wondered how Ella Mae down the road had done. How the people all along our road had made out.

149   "No worry," my wife said. "That man will have found a bonanza around here. There's heaps of decent people in this neck of the woods."
150   "Wonder where he is now?" we said.
151   "Wonder where he goes next?"
152   "Where he gets that cloth?"
153   "Who he is?"
154   We couldn't get to sleep, wondering about that.

Rudy Wiebe

Canada 1934–

Born in northern Saskatchewan in a Mennonite community, Rudy Wiebe was educated at the University of Alberta, the University of Tübingen in Germany, the University of Manitoba, and the Mennonite Brethren Bible College. He has taught English at a Mennonite liberal arts college and at the University of Alberta. Wiebe's work comes back to two subjects: the Mennonite community in which he grew up and the Aboriginal and Métis communities. Moral, cultural, and historical issues are common to much of his writing. "Where Is the Voice Coming From?" illustrates the writer's problems when faced with cultural biases.

Where Is the Voice Coming From?   1982

1   The problem is to make the story.

2   One difficulty of this making may have been excellently stated by Teilhard de Chardin: "We are continually inclined to isolate ourselves from the things and events which surround us ... as though we were spectators, not elements, in what goes on." Arnold Toynbee does venture, "For all that we know, Reality is the undifferentiated unity of the mystical experience," but that need not here be considered. This story ended long ago; it is one of finite acts, of orders, or elemental feelings and reactions, of obvious legal restrictions and requirements.

3   Presumably all the parts of the story are themselves available. A difficulty is that they are, as always, available only in bits and pieces. Though the acts themselves seem quite clear, some written reports of the acts contradict each other. As if these acts were, at one time, too well-known; as if the original nodule of each particular fact had from somewhere received non-factual accretions; or even more, as if, since the basic facts were so clear perhaps there were a larger number of facts than any one reporter, or several, or even any reporter had ever attempted to record. About facts that are simply told by this mouth to that ear, of course, even less can be expected.

4   An affair seventy-five years old should acquire some of the shiny transparency of an old man's skin. It should.

5   Sometimes it would seem that it would be enough—perhaps more than enough—to hear the names only. The grandfather One Arrow; the mother Spotted Calf; the father Sounding Sky; the wife (wives rather, but only one of them seems to have a name, though their fathers are Napaise, Kapahoo, Old Dust, The Rump)—the one wife named, of all things, Pale Face; the cousin Going-Up-To-Sky; the brother-in-law (again, of all things) Dublin. The names of the police sound very much alike; they all begin with Constable or Corporal or Sergeant, but here and there an Inspector, then a Superintendent and eventually all the resonance of an Assistant Commissioner echoes down. More, Herself: Victoria, by the Grace of God, etc., etc., QUEEN, defender of the Faith, etc., etc.; and witness "Our Right Trusty and Right Well-Beloved Cousin and Councillor the Right Honourable Sir John Campbell Hamilton-Gordon, Earl of Aberdeen; Viscount Formartine, Baron Haddo, Methlic, Tarves and Kellie in the Peerage of Scotland; Viscount Gordon of Aberdeen, County of Aberdeen in the Peerage of the United Kingdom; Baronet of Nova Scotia, Knight Grand Cross of Our Most Distinguished Order of Saint Michael and Saint George, etc., Governor General of Canada." And of course himself: in the award proclamation named "Jean-Baptiste" but otherwise known only as Almighty Voice.

6   But hearing cannot be enough; not even hearing all the thunder of A Proclamation: "Now Hear Ye that a reward of FIVE HUNDRED DOLLARS will be paid to any person or persons who will give such information as will lead ... (etc. etc.) this Twentieth day of April, in the year of Our Lord one thousand eight hundred and ninety-six, and the Fifty-ninth year of Our Reign ..." etc. and etc.

7   Such hearing cannot be enough. The first item to be seen is the piece of white bone. It is almost triangular, slightly convex—concave actually as it is positioned at this moment with its corners lightly raised—graduating from perhaps a strong eighth to a weak quarter of an inch in thickness, its scattered pore structure varying between larger and smaller on its perhaps polished, certainly shiny surface. Precision is difficult since the glass showcase is at least thirteen inches deep and therefore an eye cannot be brought as close as the minute inspection of such a small, though certainly quite adequate, sample of skull would normally require. Also, because of the position it cannot be determined whether the several hairs, well over a foot long, are still in some manner attached to it or not.

8   The seven-pounder cannon can be seen standing almost shyly between the showcase and the interior wall. Officially it is known as a gun, not a cannon, and clearly its bore is not large enough to admit a large man's fist. Even if it can be believed that this gun was used in the 1885 Rebellion[1] and that on the evening of Saturday, May 29, 1897 (while the nine-pounder, now unidentified, was in the process of arriving with the police on the special train from Regina), seven shells (all that were available in Prince Albert at that time) from it were sent shrieking into the poplar bluffs as night fell, clearly such shelling could not and would not disembowel the whole earth. Its carriage is now nicely lacquered, the perhaps oak spokes of its petite wheels (little higher than a knee) have been recently scraped, puttied and varnished; the brilliant burnish of its brass breeching testifies with what meticulous care charmen and women have used nationally advertised cleaners and restorers.

---

1   the rebellion led by Louis Riel that was quelled by the Canadian army and that eventually led to Riel's execution

9   Though it can also be seen, even a careless glance reveals that the same concern has not been expended on the one (of two) .44 calibre 1866 model Winchesters apparently found at the last in the pit with Almighty Voice. It is also preserved in a glass case; the number 1536735 is still, though barely, distinguishable on the brass cartridge section just below the brass saddle ring. However, perhaps because the case was imperfectly sealed at one time (though sealed enough not to warrant disturbance now), or because of simple neglect, the rifle is obviously spotted here and there with blotches of rust and the brass itself reveals discolorations almost like mildew. The rifle bore, the three long strands of hair themselves, actually bristle with clots of dust. It may be that this museum cannot afford to be as concerned as the other; conversely, the disfiguration may be something inherent in the items themselves.

10   The small building which was the police guardroom at Duck Lake, Saskatchewan Territory, in 1895 may also be seen. It had subsequently been moved from its original place and used to house small animals, chickens perhaps, or pigs—such as a woman might be expected to have under her responsibility. It is, of course, now perfectly empty, and clean so that the public may enter with no more discomfort than a bend under the doorway and a heavy encounter with disinfectant. The door-jamb has obviously been replaced; the bar network at one window is, however, said to be original; smooth still, very smooth. The logs inside have been smeared again and again with whitewash, perhaps paint, to an insistent point of identity-defying characterlessness. Within the small rectangular box of these logs not a sound can be heard from the streets of the, probably dead, town.

Hey Injun you'll get hung
for stealing that steer
Hey Injun for killing that government cow you'll get three weeks on the woodpile
Hey Injun

The place named Kinistino seems to have disappeared from the map but the Minnechinass Hills have not. Whether they have ever been on a map is doubtful but they will, of course, not disappear from the landscape as long as the grass grows and the rivers run. Contrary to general report and belief, the Canadian prairies are rarely, if ever, flat and the Minnechinass (spelled five different ways and translated sometimes as "The Outside Hill," sometimes as "Beautiful Bare Hills") are dissimilar from any other of the numberless hills that everywhere block out the prairie horizon. They are bare; poplars lie tattered along their tops, almost black against the straw-pale grass and sharp green against the grey soil of the plowing laid in half-mile rectangular blocks upon their western slopes. Poles holding various wires stick out of the fields, back down the bend of the valley; what was once a farmhouse is weathering into the cultivated earth. The poplar bluff where Almighty Voice made his stand has, of course, disappeared.

11   The policemen he shot and killed (not the ones he wounded, of course) are easily located. Six miles east, thirty-nine miles north in Prince Albert, the English Cemetery. Sergeant Colin Campbell Colebrook, North West Mounted Police Registration Number 605, lies presumably under a gravestone there. His name is seventeenth in a very long "list of non-commissioned officers and men who have died in the service since the inception of the force." The date is October 29, 1895,

and the cause of death is anonymous: "Shot by escaping Indian prisoner near Prince Albert." At the foot of this grave are two others: Constable John R. Kerr, No. 3040, and Corporal C. H. S. Hockin, No. 3106. Their cause of death on May 28, 1897 is even more anonymous, but the place is relatively precise: "Shot by Indians at Min-etch-inass Hills, Prince Albert District."

12   The gravestone, if he has one, of the fourth man Almighty Voice killed is more difficult to locate. Mr. Ernest Grundy, postmaster at Duck Lake in 1897, apparently shut his window the afternoon of Friday, May 28, armed himself, rode east twenty miles, participated in the second charge into the bluff at about 6:30 p.m., and on the third sweep of that charge was shot dead at the edge of the pit. It would seem that he thereby contributed substantially not only to the Indians' bullet supply, but his clothing warmed them as well.

13   The burial place of Dublin and Going-Up-To-Sky is unknown, as is the grave of Almighty Voice. It is said that a Métis named Henry Smith lifted the latter's body from the pit in the bluff and gave it to Spotted Calf. The place of burial is not, of course, of ultimate significance. A gravestone is always less evidence than a triangular piece of skull, provided it is large enough.

14   Whatever further evidence there is to be gathered may rest on pictures. There are, presumably, almost numberless pictures of the policemen in the case, but the only one with direct bearing is one of Sergeant Colebrook who apparently insisted on advancing to complete an arrest after being warned three times that if he took another step he would be shot. The picture must have been taken before he joined the force; it reveals him a large-eared young man, hair brush-cut and ascot tie, his eyelids slightly drooping, almost hooded under thick brows. Unfortunately a picture of Constable R. C. Dickson, into whose charge Almighty Voice was apparently committed in that guardroom and who after Colebrook's death was convicted of negligence, sentenced to two months hard labour and discharged, does not seem to be available.

15   There are no pictures to be found of either Dublin (killed early by rifle fire) or Going-Up-To-Sky (killed in the pit), the two teen-age boys who gave their ultimate fealty to Almighty Voice. There is, however, one said to be of Almighty Voice, Junior. He may have been born to Pale Face during the year, two hundred and twenty-one days that his father was a fugitive. In the picture he is kneeling before what could be a tent, he wears striped denim overalls and displays twin babies whose sex cannot be determined from the double-laced dark bonnets they wear. In the supposed picture of Spotted Calf and Sounding Sky, Sounding Sky stands slightly before his wife; he wears a white shirt and a striped blanket folded over his left shoulder in such a manner that the arm in which he cradles a long rifle cannot be seen. His head is thrown back; the rim of his hat appears as a black half-moon above eyes that are pressed shut in, as it were, profound concentration; above a mouth clenched thin in a downward curve. Spotted Calf wears a long dress, a sweater which could also be a man's dress coat, and a large fringed and embroidered shawl which would appear distinctly Dukhobor in origin if the scroll patterns on it were more irregular. Her head is small and turned slightly towards her husband so as to reveal her right ear. There is what can only be called a quizzical expression on her crumpled face; it may be she does not understand what is happening and that she would have asked a question, perhaps of her hus-

band, perhaps of the photographers, perhaps even of anyone, anywhere in the world if such questioning were possible for an Indian woman.

16   There is one final picture. That is one of Almighty Voice himself. At least it is purported to be of Almighty Voice himself. In the Royal Canadian Mounted Police Museum on the Barracks Grounds just off Dewdney Avenue in Regina, Saskatchewan, it lies in the same showcase, as a matter of fact immediately beside that triangular piece of skull. Both are unequivocally labelled, and it must be assumed that a police force with a world-wide reputation would not label *such* evidence incorrectly. But here emerges an ultimate problem in making the story.

17   There are two official descriptions of Almighty Voice. The first reads: "Height about five feet, ten inches, slight build, rather good looking, a sharp hooked nose with a remarkably flat point. Has a bullet scar on the left side of his face about 1½ inches long running from near corner of mouth towards ear. The scar cannot be noticed when his face is painted but otherwise is plain. Skin fair for an Indian." The second description is on the Award Proclamation: "About twenty-two years old, five feet ten inches in height, weight about eleven stone, slightly erect, neat small feet and hands; complexion inclined to be fair, wavy dark hair to shoulders, large dark eyes, broad forehead, sharp features and parrot nose with flat tip, scar on left cheek running from mouth towards ear, feminine appearance."

18   So run the descriptions that were, presumably, to identify a well-known fugitive in so precise a manner that an informant could collect five hundred dollars—a considerable sum when a police constable earned between one and two dollars a day. The nexus of the problems appears when these supposed official descriptions are compared to the supposed official picture. The man in the picture is standing on a small rug. The fingers on his left hand touch a curved Victorian settee, behind him a photographer's backdrop of scrolled patterns merges to vaguely paradisiacal trees and perhaps a sky. The moccasins he wears make it impossible to deduce whether his feet are "neat small." He may be five feet, ten inches tall, may weigh eleven stone, he certainly is "rather good looking" and, though it is a frontal view, it may be that the point of his long and flaring nose could be "remarkably flat." The photograph is slightly over-illuminated and so the unpainted complexion could be "inclined to be fair"; however, nothing can be seen of a scar, the hair is not wavy and shoulder-length but hangs almost to the waist in two thick straight braids worked through with beads, fur, ribbons and cords. The right hand that holds the corner of the blanket-like coat in position is large and, even in the high illumination, heavily veined. The neck is concealed under coiled beads and the forehead seems more low than "broad."

19   Perhaps, somehow, these picture details could be reconciled with the official description if the face as a whole were not so devastating.

20   On a cloth-backed sheet two feet by two and one-half feet in size, under the Great Seal of the Lion and the Unicorn, dignified by the names of the Deputy of the Minister of Justice, the Secretary of State, the Queen herself and all the heaped detail of her "Right Trusty and Right Well-beloved Cousin," this description concludes: "feminine appearance." But the pictures: any face of history, any believed face that the world acknowledges as *man*—Socrates, Jesus, Attila, Genghis Khan, Mahatma Gandhi, Joseph Stalin—no believed face is more *man* than this face. The mouth, the nose, the clenched brows, the eyes—the eyes are large, yes, and dark,

but even in this watered-down reproduction of unending reproductions of that original, a steady look into those eyes cannot be endured. It is a face like an axe.

21   It is now evident that the de Chardin statement quoted at the beginning has relevance only as it proves itself inadequate to explain what has happened. At the same time, the inadequacy of Aristotle's much more famous statement becomes evident: "The true difference [between the historian and the poet] is that one relates what *has* happened, the other what *may* happen." These statements cannot explain the storymaker's activity since, despite the most rigid application of impersonal investigation, the elements of the story have now run me aground. If ever I could, I can no longer pretend to objective, omnipotent disinterestedness. I am no longer *spectator* of what *has* happened or what *may* happen: I am become *element* in what is happening at this very moment.

22   For it is, of course, I myself who cannot endure the shadows on that paper which are those eyes. It is I who stand beside this broken veranda post where two corner shingles have been torn away, where barbed wire tangles the dead weeds on the edge of this field. The bluff that sheltered Almighty Voice and his two friends has not disappeared from the slope of the Minnechinass, no more than the sound of Constable Dickson's voice in that guardhouse is silent. The sound of his speaking is there even if it has never been recorded in an official report:

> *hey injun you'll get*
> *hung*
> *for stealing that steer*
> *hey injun for killing that government*
> *cow you'll get three*
> *weeks on the woodpile hey injun*

The unknown contradictory words about an unprovable act that move a boy to defiance, an implacable Cree warrior long after the three-hundred-and-fifty-year war is ended, a war already lost the day the Cree watch Cartier hoist his guns ashore at Hochelaga and they begin the long retreat west; these words of incomprehension, of threatened incomprehensible law are there to be heard just as the unmoving tableau of the three-day siege is there to be seen on the slopes of the Minnechinass. Sounding Sky is somewhere not there, under arrest, but Spotted Calf stands on a shoulder of the Hills a little to the left, her arms upraised to the setting sun. Her mouth is open. A horse rears, riderless, above the scrub willow at the edge of the bluff, smoke puffs, screams tangle in rifle barrage, there are wounds, somewhere. The bluff is so green this spring, it will not burn and the ragged line of seven police and two civilians is staggering through, faces twisted in rage, terror, and rifles sputter. Nothing moves. There is no sound of frogs in the night; twenty-seven policemen and five civilians stand in cordon at thirty-yard intervals and a body also lies in the shelter of a gully. Only a voice rises from the bluff:

> *We have fought well*
> *You have died like braves*
> *I have worked hard and am hungry*
> *Give me food*

but nothing moves. The bluff lies, a bright green island on the grassy slope surrounded by men hunched forward rigid over their long rifles, men clumped out of rifle-range, thirty-five men dressed as for fall hunting on a sharp spring day, a small gun positioned on a ridge above. A crow is falling out of the sky into the bluff, its feathers sprayed as by an explosion. The first gun and the second gun are in position, the beginning and end of the bristling surround of thirty-five Prince Albert Volunteers, thirteen civilians and fifty-six policemen in position relative to the bluff and relative to the unnumbered whites astride their horses, standing up in their carts, staring and pointing across the valley, in position relative to the bluff and the unnumbered Indians squatting silent along the higher ridges of the Hills, motionless mounds, faceless against the Sunday morning sunlight edging between and over them down along the tree tips, down into the shadows of the bluff. Nothing moves. Beside the second gun the red-coated officer has flung a handful of grass into the motionless air, almost to the rim of the red sun.

23   And there is a voice. It is an incredible voice that rises from among the young poplars ripped of their spring bark, from among the dead somewhere lying there, out of the arm-deep pit shorter than a man a voice rises over the exploding smoke and thunder of guns that reel back in their positions, worked over, serviced by the grimed motionless men in bright coats and glinting buttons, a voice so high and clear, so unbelievably high and strong in its unending wordless cry.

24   The voice of "Gitchie-Manitou Wayo"—interpreted as "voice of the Great Spirit"—that is, The Almighty Voice. His death chant no less incredible in its beauty than in its incomprehensible happiness.

25   I say "wordless cry" because that is the way it sounds to me. I could be more accurate if I had a reliable interpreter who would make a reliable interpretation. For I do not, of course, understand the Cree myself.

Alistair MacLeod

Canada 1936–

Alistair MacLeod lived in small towns in Saskatchewan and Alberta until the age of ten, when his family moved back to Cape Breton. MacLeod had a protracted university education, eventually gaining a Ph.D. from Notre Dame in 1968. He taught at the University of Indiana before joining the English and Creative Writing faculty at the University of Windsor, where he stayed until his recent retirement. In 1999 MacLeod published his first novel, *No Great Mischief*, to great acclaim. Previous to it, MacLeod had published only two collections of stories, *The Lost Salt Gift of Blood* (1976) and *As Birds Bring Forth the Sun* (1986), both of which won international attention. In "The Boat," MacLeod explores the crippling influence of guilt on a man who could not perfectly serve either his mother or his father.

The Boat 1976

1 There are times even now, when I awake at four o'clock in the morning with the terrible fear that I have overslept, when I imagine that my father is waiting for me in the room below the darkened stairs or that the shorebound men are tossing pebbles against my window while blowing their hands and stomping their feet impatiently on the frozen steadfast earth. There are times when I am half out of bed and fumbling for socks and mumbling for words before I realize that I am foolishly alone, that no one waits at the base of the stairs and no boat rides restlessly in the waters by the pier.

2 At such times only the grey corpses on the overflowing ashtray beside my bed bear witness to the extinction of the latest spark and silently await the crushing out of the most recent of their fellows. And then because I am afraid to be alone with death, I dress rapidly, make a great to do about clearing my throat, turn on both faucets in the sink and proceed to make loud splashing intellectual noises. Later I go out and walk the mile to the all night restaurant.

3 In the winter it is a very cold walk and there are often tears in my eyes when I arrive. The waitress usually gives a sympathetic little shiver and says, "Boy, it must be really cold out there, you got tears in your eyes."

4 "Yes," I say, "it sure is; it really is."

5 And then the three or four of us who are always in such places at such times make uninteresting little protective chit chat until the dawn reluctantly arrives. Then I swallow the coffee which is always bitter and leave with a great busy rush because by that time I have to worry about being late and whether I have a clean shirt and whether my car will start and about all the other countless things one must worry about when he teaches at a great Midwestern university. And I know then that that day will go by as have all the days of the past ten years, for the call and the voices and the shapes and the boat were not really there in the early morning's darkness and I have all kinds of comforting reality to prove it. They are only shadows and echoes, the animals a child's hands make on the wall by lamplight, and the voices from the rain barrel; the cuttings from an old movie made in the black and white of long ago.

6 I first became conscious of the boat in the same way and at almost the same time that I became aware of the people it supported. My earliest recollection of my father is a view from the floor of gigantic rubber boots and then of being suddenly elevated and having my face pressed against the stubble of his cheek, and of how it tasted of salt and of how he smelled of salt from his red-soled rubber boots to the shaggy whiteness of his hair.

7 When I was very small, he took me for my first ride in the boat. I rode the half-mile from our house to the wharf on his shoulders and I remember the sound of his rubber boots galumphing along the gravel beach, the tune of the indecent little song he used to sing, and the odour of the salt.

8 The floor of the boat was permeated with the same odour and in its constancy I was not aware of change. In the harbour we made our little circle and returned. He tied the boat by its painter, fastened the stern to its permanent anchor and lifted me high over his head to the solidity of the wharf. Then he climbed up the

little iron ladder that led to the wharf's cap, placed me once more upon his shoulders and galumphed off again.

9   When we returned to the house everyone made a great fuss over my precocious excursion and asked, "How did you like the boat?" "Were you afraid in the boat?" "Did you cry in the boat?" They repeated "the boat" at the end of all their questions and I knew it must be very important to everyone.

10   My earliest recollection of my mother is of being alone with her in the mornings while my father was away in the boat. She seemed to be always repairing clothes that were "torn in the boat," preparing food "to be eaten in the boat" or looking for "the boat" through our kitchen window which faced upon the sea. When my father returned about noon, she would ask, "Well, how did things go in the boat today?" It was the first question I remember asking: "Well, how did things go in the boat today?" "Well, how did things go in the boat today?"

11   The boat in our lives was registered at Port Hawkesbury. She was what Nova Scotians called a Cape Island boat and was designed for the small inshore fishermen who sought the lobsters of the spring and the mackerel of summer and later the cod and haddock and hake. She was thirty-two feet long and nine wide, and was powered by an engine from a Chevrolet truck. She had a marine clutch and a high speed reverse gear and was painted light green with the name *Jenny Lynn* stencilled in black letters on her bow and painted on an oblong plate across her stern. Jenny Lynn had been my mother's maiden name and the boat was called after her as another link in the chain of tradition. Most of the boats that berthed at the wharf bore the names of some female member of their owner's household.

12   I say this now as if I knew it all then. All at once, all about boat dimensions and engines, and as if on the day of my first childish voyage I noticed the difference between a stencilled name and a painted name. But of course it was not that way at all, for I learned it all very slowly and there was not time enough.

13   I learned first about our house which was one of about fifty which marched around the horseshoe of our harbour and the wharf which was its heart. Some of them were so close to the water that during a storm the sea spray splashed against their windows while others were built farther along the beach as was the case with ours. The houses and their people, like those of the neighbouring towns and villages, were the result of Ireland's discontent and Scotland's Highland Clearances and America's War of Independence. Impulsive emotional Catholic Celts who could not bear to live with England and shrewd determined Protestant Puritans who, in the years after 1776, could not bear to live without.

14   The most important room in our house was one of those oblong old-fashioned kitchens headed by a wood- and coal-burning stove. Behind the stove was a box of kindlings and beside it a coal scuttle. A heavy wooden table with leaves that expanded or reduced its dimensions stood in the middle of the floor. There were five wooden home-made chairs which had been chipped and hacked by a variety of knives. Against the east wall, opposite the stove, there was a couch which sagged in the middle and had a cushion for a pillow, and above it a shelf which contained matches, tobacco, pencils, odd fish-hooks, bits of twine, and a tin can filled with bills and receipts. The south wall was dominated by a window which faced the sea and on the north there was a five foot board which bore a variety of clothes hooks and the burdens of each. Beneath

the board there was a jumble of odd footwear, mostly of rubber. There was also, on this wall, a barometer, a map of the marine area and a shelf which held a tiny radio. The kitchen was shared by all of us and was a buffer zone between the immaculate order of ten other rooms and the disruptive chaos of the single room that was my father's.

15   My mother ran her house as her brothers ran their boats. Everything was clean and spotless and in order. She was tall and dark and powerfully energetic. In later years she reminded me of the women of Thomas Hardy, particularly Eustacia Vye,[1] in a physical way. She fed and clothed a family of seven children, making all of the meals and most of the clothes. She grew miraculous gardens and magnificent flowers and raised broods of hens and ducks. She would walk miles on berry picking expeditions and hoist her skirts to dig for clams when the tide was low. She was fourteen years younger than my father, whom she had married when she was twenty-six and had been a local beauty for a period of ten years. My mother was of the sea as were all of her people, and her horizons were the very literal ones she scanned with her dark and fearless eyes.

16   Between the kitchen clothes rack and barometer, a door opened into my father's bedroom. It was a room of disorder and disarray. It was as if the wind which so often clamoured about the house succeeded in entering this single room and after whipping it into turmoil stole quietly away to renew its knowing laughter from without.

17   My father's bed was against the south wall. It always looked rumpled and unmade because he lay on top of it more than he slept within any folds it might have had. Beside it, there was a little brown table. An archaic goose-necked reading light, a battered table radio, a mound of wooden matches, one or two packages of tobacco, a deck of cigarette papers and an overflowing ashtray cluttered its surface. The brown larvae of tobacco shreds and the grey flecks of ash covered both the table and the floor beneath it. The once-varnished surface of the table was disfigured by numerous black scars and gashes inflicted by the neglected burning cigarettes of many years. They had tumbled from the ashtray unnoticed and branded their statements permanently and quietly into the wood until the odour of their burning caused the snuffing out of their lives. At the bed's foot there was a single window which looked upon the sea.

18   Against the adjacent wall there was a battered bureau and beside it there was a closet which held his single ill-fitting serge suit, the two or three white shirts that strangled him and the square black shoes that pinched. When he took off his more friendly clothes, the heavy woollen sweaters, mitts and socks which my mother knitted for him and the woollen and doeskin shirts, he dumped them unceremoniously on a single chair. If a visitor entered the room while he was lying on the bed, he would be told to throw the clothes on the floor and take their place upon the chair.

19   Magazines and books covered the bureau and competed with the clothes for domination of the chair. They further overburdened the heroic little table and lay on top of the radio. They filled a baffling and unknowable cave beneath the bed, and in the corner of the bureau they spilled from the walls and grew up from the floor.

---

1   a strong female character in Thomas Hardy's *The Return of the Native*

20   The magazines were the most conventional: *Time, Newsweek, Life, Maclean's, Family Herald, Reader's Digest*. They were the result of various cut-rate subscriptions or the gift subscriptions associated with Christmas, "the two whole years for only $3.50."

21   The books were more varied. There were a few hard-cover magnificents and bygone Book-of-the-Month wonders and some were Christmas or birthday gifts. The majority of them, however, were used paperbacks which came from those second-hand book stores which advertise in the backs of magazines: "Miscellaneous Used Paperbacks 10¢ Each." At first he sent for them himself, although my mother resented the expense, but in later years they came more and more often from my sisters who had moved to the cities. Especially at first they were very weird and varied. Mickey Spillane and Ernest Haycox vied with Dostoyevsky and Faulkner, and the Penguin Poets edition of Gerard Manley Hopkins arrived in the same box as a little book on sex technique called *Getting the Most Out of Love*. The former had been assiduously annotated by a very fine hand using a very blue-inked fountain pen while the latter had been studied by someone with very large thumbs, the prints of which were still visible in the margins. At the slightest provocation it would open almost automatically to particularly graphic and well-smudged pages.

22   When he was not in the boat, my father spent most of his time lying on the bed in his socks, the top two buttons of his trousers undone, his discarded shirt on the ever-ready chair and the sleeves of the woollen Stanfield underwear, which he wore both summer and winter, drawn half way up to his elbows. The pillows propped up the whiteness of his head and the goose-necked lamp illuminated the pages in his hands. The cigarettes smoked and smouldered on the ashtray and on the table and the radio played constantly, sometimes low and sometimes loud. At midnight and at one, two, three and four, one could sometimes hear the radio, his occasional cough, the rustling thud of a completed book being tossed to the corner heap, or the movement necessitated by his sitting on the edge of the bed to roll the thousandth cigarette. He seemed never to sleep, only to doze, and the light shone constantly from his window to the sea.

23   My mother despised the room and all it stood for and she had stopped sleeping in it after I was born. She despised disorder in rooms and in houses and in hours and in lives, and she had not read a book since high school. There she had read *Ivanhoe* and considered it a colossal waste of time. Still the room remained, like a solid rock of opposition in the sparkling waters of a clear deep harbour, opening off the kitchen where we really lived our lives, with its door always open and its contents visible to all.

24   The daughters of the room and of the house were very beautiful. They were tall and willowy like my mother and had her fine facial features set off by the reddish copper-coloured hair that had apparently once been my father's before it turned to white. All of them were very clever in school and helped my mother a great deal about the house. When they were young they sang and were very happy and very nice to me because I was the youngest and the family's only boy.

25   My father never approved of their playing about the wharf like the other children, and they went there only when my mother sent them on an errand. At such times they almost always overstayed, playing screaming games of tag or hide-and-seek in and about the fishing shanties. They piled traps and tubs of trawl, shouting

down to the perch that swam languidly about the wharf's algae-covered piles, or jumping in and out of the boats that tugged gently at their lines. My mother was never uneasy about them at such times and when her husband criticized her she would say, "Nothing will happen to them there," or "They could be doing worse things in worse places."

26   By about the ninth or tenth grade my sisters one by one discovered my father's bedroom and then the change would begin. Each would go into the room one morning when he was out. She would go with the ideal hope of imposing order or with the more practical objective of emptying the ashtray, and later she would be found spellbound by the volume in her hand. My mother's reaction was always abrupt, bordering on the angry. "Take your nose out of that trash and come and do your work," she would say, and once I saw her slap my youngest sister so hard that the print of her hand was scarletly emblazoned upon her daughter's cheek while the broken-spined paperback fluttered uselessly to the floor.

27   Thereafter my mother would launch a campaign against what she had discovered but could not understand. At times although she was not overly religious she would bring in God to bolster her arguments, saying, "In the next world God will see to those who waste their lives reading useless books when they should be about their work." Or without theological aid, "I would like to know how books help anyone to live a life." If my father were in, she would repeat the remarks louder than necessary, and her voice would carry into this room where he lay upon his bed. His usual reaction was to turn up the volume of the radio, although that action in itself betrayed the success of the initial thrust.

28   Shortly after my sisters began to read the books, they grew restless and lost interest in darning socks and baking bread, and all of them eventually went to work as summer waitresses in the Sea Food Restaurant. The restaurant was run by a big American concern from Boston and catered to the tourists that flooded the area during July and August. My mother despised the whole operation. She said the restaurant was not run by "our people," and "our people" did not eat there, and that it was run by outsiders for outsiders.

29   "Who are these people anyway?" she would ask, tossing back her dark hair, "and what do they, though they go about with their cameras for a hundred years, know about the way it is here, and what do they care about me and mine, and why should I care about them?"

30   She was angry that my sisters should even conceive of working in such a place and more angry when my father made no move to prevent it, and she was worried about herself and about her family and about her life. Sometimes she would say softly to her sisters, "I don't know what's the matter with my girls. It seems none of them are interested in any of the right things." And sometimes there would be bitter savage arguments. One afternoon I was coming in with three mackerel I'd been given at the wharf when I heard her say, "Well I hope you'll be satisfied when they come home knocked up and you'll have had your way."

31   It was the most savage thing I'd ever heard my mother say. Not just the words but the way she said them, and I stood there in the porch afraid to breathe for what seemed like the years from ten to fifteen, feeling the damp moist mackerel with their silver glassy eyes growing clammy against my leg.

32   Through the angle in the screen door I saw my father who had been walking into his room wheel around on one of his rubber-booted heels and look at her

with his blue eyes flashing like clearest ice beneath the snow that was his hair. His usually ruddy face was drawn and grey, reflecting the exhaustion of a man of sixty-five who had been working in those rubber boots for eleven hours on an August day, and for a fleeting moment I wondered what I would do if he killed my mother while I stood there in the porch with those three foolish mackerel in my hand. Then he turned and went into his room and the radio blared forth the next day's weather forecast and I retreated under the noise and returned again, stamping my feet and slamming the door too loudly to signal my approach. My mother was busy at the stove when I came in, and did not raise her head when I threw the mackerel in a pan. As I looked into my father's room, I said, "Well, how did things go in the boat today?" and he replied, "Oh not too badly, all things considered." He was lying on his back and lighting the first cigarette and the radio was talking about the Virginia coast.

33   All of my sisters made good money on tips. They bought my father an electric razor which he tried to use for a while and they took out even more magazine subscriptions. They bought my mother a great many clothes of the type she was very fond of, the wide-brimmed hats and the brocaded dresses, but she locked them all in trunks and refused to wear any of them.

34   On one August day my sisters prevailed upon my father to take some of their restaurant customers for an afternoon ride in the boat. The tourists with their expensive clothes and cameras and sun glasses awkwardly backed down the iron ladder at the wharf's side to where my father waited below, holding the rocking *Jenny Lynn* in snug against the wharf with one hand on the iron ladder and steadying his descending passengers with the other. They tried to look both prim and wind-blown like the girls in the Pepsi-Cola ads and did the best they could, sitting on the thwarts where the newspapers were spread to cover the splattered blood and fish entrails, crowding to one side so that they were in danger of capsizing the boat, taking the inevitable pictures or merely trailing their fingers through the water of their dreams.

35   All of them liked my father very much and, after he brought them back from their circles in the harbour, they invited him to their rented cabins which were located high on a hill overlooking the village to which they were so alien. He proceeded to get very drunk up there with the beautiful view and the strange company and the abundant liquor, and late in the afternoon he began to sing.

36   I was just approaching the wharf to deliver my mother's summons when he began, and the familiar yet unfamiliar voice that rolled down from the cabins made me feel as I had never felt before in my young life or perhaps as I had always felt without really knowing it, and I was ashamed yet proud, young yet old and saved yet forever lost, and there was nothing I could do to control my legs which trembled nor my eyes which wept for what they could not tell.

37   The tourists were equipped with tape recorders and my father sang for more than three hours. His voice boomed down the hill and bounced off the surface of the harbour, which was an unearthly blue on that hot August day, and was then reflected to the wharf and the fishing shanties where it was absorbed amidst the men who were baiting their lines for the next day's haul.

38   He sang all the old sea chanties which had come across from the old world and by which men like him had pulled ropes for generations, and he sang the East Coast sea songs which celebrated the sealing vessels of Northumberland Strait and

the long liners of the Grand Banks and of Anticosti, Sable Island, Grand Manan, Boston Harbor, Nantucket and Block Island. Gradually he shifted to the seemingly unending Gaelic drinking songs with their twenty or more verses and inevitable refrains, and the men in the shanties smiled at the coarseness of some of the verses and at the thought that the singer's immediate audience did not know what they were applauding nor recording to take back to staid old Boston. Later as the sun was setting he switched to the laments and the wild and haunting Gaelic war songs of those spattered Highland ancestors he had never seen, and when his voice ceased, the savage melancholy of three hundred years seemed to hang over the peaceful harbour and the quiet boats and the men leaning in the doorways of their shanties with their cigarettes glowing in the dusk and the women looking to the sea from their open windows with their children in their arms.

39 When he came home he threw the money he had earned on the kitchen table as he did with all his earnings but my mother refused to touch it and the next day he went with the rest of the men to bait his trawl in the shanties. The tourists came to the door that evening and my mother met them there and told them that her husband was not in although he was lying on the bed only a few feet away with the radio playing and the cigarette upon his lips. She stood in the doorway until they reluctantly went away.

40 In the winter they sent him a picture which had been taken on the day of the singing. On the back it said, "To Our Ernest Hemingway" and the "Our" was underlined. There was also an accompanying letter telling how much they had enjoyed themselves, how popular the tape was proving and explaining who Ernest Hemingway was. In a way it almost did look like one of those unshaven, taken-in-Cuba pictures of Hemingway. He looked both massive and incongruous in the setting. His bulky fisherman's clothes were too big for the green and white lawn chair in which he sat, and his rubber boots seemed to take up all of the well-clipped grass square. The beach umbrella jarred with his sunburned face and because he had already been singing for some time, his lips which chapped in the winds of spring and burned in the water glare of summer had already cracked in several places, producing tiny flecks of blood at their corners and on the whiteness of his teeth. The bracelets of brass chain which he wore to protect his wrists from chafing seemed abnormally large and his broad leather belt had been slackened and his heavy shirt and underwear were open at the throat revealing an uncultivated wilderness of white chest hair bordering on the semi-controlled stubble of his neck and chin. His blue eyes had looked directly into the camera and his hair was whiter than the two tiny clouds which hung over his left shoulder. The sea was behind him and its immense blue flatness stretched out to touch the arching blueness of the sky. It seemed very far away from him or else he was so much in the foreground that he seemed too big for it.

41 Each year another of my sisters would read the books and work in the restaurant. Sometimes they would stay out quite late on the hot summer nights and when they came up the stairs my mother would ask them many long and involved questions which they resented and tried to avoid. Before ascending the stairs they would go into my father's room and those of us who waited above could hear them throwing his clothes off the chair before sitting on it or the squeak of the bed as they sat on its edge. Sometimes they would talk to him a

long time, the murmur of their voices blending with the music of the radio into a mysterious vapour-like sound which floated softly up the stairs.

42   I say this again as if it all happened at once and as if all of my sisters were of identical ages and like so many lemmings going into another sea and, again, it was of course not that way at all. Yet go they did, to Boston, to Montreal, to New York with the young men they met during the summers and later married in those far-away cities. The young men were very articulate and handsome and wore fine clothes and drove expensive cars and my sisters, as I said, were very tall and beautiful with their copper-coloured hair and were tired of darning socks and baking bread.

43   One by one they went. My mother had each of her daughters for fifteen years, then lost them for two and finally forever. None married a fisherman. My mother never accepted any of the young men, for in her eyes they seemed always a combination of the lazy, the effeminate, the dishonest and the unknown. They never seemed to do any physical work and she could not comprehend their luxurious vacations and she did not know whence they came nor who they were. And in the end she did not really care, for they were not of her people and they were not of her sea.

44   I say this now with a sense of wonder at my own stupidity in thinking I was somehow free and would go on doing well in school and playing and helping in the boat and passing into my early teens while streaks of grey began to appear in my mother's dark hair and my father's rubber boots dragged sometimes on the pebbles of the beach as he trudged home from the wharf. And there were but three of us in the house that had at one time been so loud.

45   Then during the winter that I was fifteen he seemed to grow old and ill at once. Most of January he lay upon the bed, smoking and reading and listening to the radio while the wind howled about the house and the needle-like snow blistered off the ice-covered harbour and the doors flew out of people's hands if they did not cling to them like death.

46   In February when the men began overhauling their lobster traps he still did not move, and my mother and I began to knit lobster trap headings in the evenings. The twine was as always very sharp and harsh, and blisters formed upon our thumbs and little paths of blood soaked quietly down between our fingers while the seals that had drifted down from distant Labrador wept and moaned like human children on the ice-floes of the Gulf.

47   In the daytime my mother's brother who had been my father's partner as long as I could remember also came to work upon the gear. He was a year older than my mother and was tall and dark and the father of twelve children.

48   By March we were very far behind and although I began to work very hard in the evenings I knew it was not hard enough and that there were but eight weeks left before the opening of the season on May first. And I knew that my mother worried and my uncle was uneasy and that all of our very lives depended on the boat being ready with her gear and two men, by the date of May the first. And I knew then that *David Copperfield* and *The Tempest* and all those friends I had dearly come to love must really go forever. So I bade them all good-bye.

49   The night after my first full day at home and after my mother had gone upstairs he called me into his room where I sat upon the chair beside his bed. "You will go back tomorrow," he said simply.

50   I refused then, saying I had made my decision and was satisfied.

51   "That is no way to make a decision," he said, "and if you are satisfied I am not. It is best that you go back." I was almost angry then and told him as all children do that I wished he would leave me alone and stop telling me what to do.

52   He looked at me a long time then, lying there on the same bed on which he had fathered me those sixteen years before, fathered me his only son, out of who knew what emotions when he was already fifty-six and his hair had turned to snow. Then he swung his legs over the edge of the squeaking bed and sat facing me and looked into my own dark eyes with his of crystal blue and placed his hand upon my knee. "I am not telling you to do anything," he said softly, "only asking you."

53   The next morning I returned to school. As I left, my mother followed me to the porch and said, "I never thought a son of mine would choose useless books over the parents that gave him life."

54   In the weeks that followed he got up rather miraculously and the gear was ready and the *Jenny Lynn* was freshly painted by the last two weeks of April when the ice began to break up and the lonely screaming gulls returned to haunt the silver herring as they flashed within the sea.

55   On the first day of May the boats raced out as they had always done, laden down almost to the gunwales with their heavy cargoes of traps. They were almost like living things as they plunged through the waters of the spring and manoeuvred between the still floating icebergs of crystal white and emerald green on their way to the traditional grounds that they sought out every May. And those of us who sat that day in the high school on the hill, discussing the water imagery of Tennyson, watched them as they passed back and forth beneath us until by afternoon the piles of traps which had been stacked upon the wharf were no longer visible but were spread about the bottom of the sea. And the *Jenny Lynn* went too, all day, with my uncle tall and dark, like a latter-day Tashtego[2] standing at the tiller with his legs wide apart and guiding her deftly between the floating pans of ice and my father in the stern standing in the same way with his hands upon the ropes that lashed the cargo to the deck. And at night my mother asked, "Well, how did things go in the boat today?"

56   And the spring wore on and the summer came and school ended in the third week of June and the lobster season on July first and I wished that the two things I loved so dearly did not exclude each other in a manner that was so blunt and too clear.

57   At the conclusion of the lobster season my uncle said he had been offered a berth on a deep sea dragger and had decided to accept. We all knew that he was leaving the *Jenny Lynn* forever and that before the next lobster season he would buy a boat of his own. He was expecting another child and would be supporting fifteen people by the next spring and could not chance my father against the family that he loved.

58   I joined my father then for the trawling season, and he made no protest and my mother was quite happy. Through the summer we baited the tubs of trawl in the afternoon and set them at sunset and revisited them in the darkness of the early morning. The men would come tramping by our house at four A.M. and we would join them and walk with them to the wharf and be on our way before the sun rose out of the ocean where it seemed to spend the night. If I was not up they

---

2   a character in Herman Melville's *Moby Dick*

would toss pebbles to my window and I would be very embarrassed and tumble downstairs to where my father lay fully clothed atop his bed, reading his book and listening to his radio and smoking his cigarette. When I appeared he would swing off his bed and put on his boots and be instantly ready and then we would take the lunches my mother had prepared the night before and walk off toward the sea. He would make no attempt to wake me himself.

59   It was in many ways a good summer. There were few storms and we were out almost every day and we lost a minimum of gear and seemed to land a maximum of fish and I tanned dark and brown after the manner of my uncles.

60   My father did not tan—he never tanned—because of his reddish complexion, and the salt water irritated his skin as it had for sixty years. He burned and reburned over and over again and his lips still cracked so that they bled when he smiled, and his arms, especially the left, still broke out into the oozing saltwater boils as they had ever since as a child I had first watched him soaking and bathing them in a variety of ineffectual solutions. The chafe-preventing bracelets of brass linked chain that all the men wore about their wrists in early spring were his the full season and he shaved but painfully and only once a week.

61   And I saw then, that summer, many things that I had seen all my life as if for the first time and I thought that perhaps my father had never been intended for a fisherman either physically or mentally. At least not in the manner of my uncles; he had never really loved it. And I remembered that, one evening in his room when we were talking about *David Copperfield*, he had said that he had always wanted to go to the university and I had dismissed it then in the way one dismisses his father's saying he would like to be a tight-rope walker, and we had gone on to talk about the Peggottys and how they loved the sea.

62   And I thought then to myself that there were many things wrong with all of us and all our lives and I wondered why my father, who was himself an only son, had not married before he was forty and then I wondered why he had. I even thought that perhaps he had had to marry my mother and checked the dates on the flyleaf of the Bible where I learned that my oldest sister had been born a prosaic eleven months after the marriage, and I felt myself then very dirty and debased for my lack of faith and for what I had thought and done.

63   And then there came into my heart a very great love for my father and I thought it was very much braver to spend a life doing what you really do not want rather than selfishly following forever your own dreams and inclinations. And I knew then that I could never leave him alone to suffer the iron-tipped harpoons which my mother would forever hurl into his soul because he was a failure as a husband and a father who had retained none of his own. And I felt that I had been very small in a little secret place within me and that even the completion of high school was for me a silly shallow selfish dream.

64   So I told him one night very resolutely and very powerfully that I would remain with him as long as he lived and we would fish the sea together. And he made no protest but only smiled through the cigarette smoke that wreathed his bed and replied, "I hope you will remember what you've said."

65   The room was now so filled with books as to be almost Dickensian, but he would not allow my mother to move or change them and he continued to read them, sometimes two or three a night. They came with great regularity now, and there were more hard covers, sent by my sisters who had gone so long ago and

now seemed so distant and so prosperous, and sent also pictures of small red-haired grandchildren with baseball bats and dolls which he placed upon his bureau and which my mother gazed at wistfully when she thought no one would see. Red-haired grandchildren with baseball bats and dolls who would never know the sea in hatred or in love.

66   And so we fished through the heat of August and into the cooler days of September when the water was so clear we could almost see the bottom and the white mists rose like delicate ghosts in the early morning dawn. And one day my mother said to me, "You have given added years to his life."

67   And we fished on into October when it began to roughen and we could no longer risk night sets but took our gear out each morning and returned at the first sight of the squalls; and on into November when we lost three tubs of trawl and the clear blue water turned to a sullen grey and the trochoidal waves rolled rough and high and washed across our bows and decks as we ran within their troughs. We wore heavy sweaters now and the awkward rubber slickers and the heavy woollen mitts which soaked and froze into masses of ice that hung from our wrists like the limbs of gigantic monsters until we thawed them against the exhaust pipe's heat. And almost every day we would leave for home before noon, driven by the blasts of the northwest wind, coating our eyebrows with ice and freezing our eyelids closed as we leaned into a visibility that was hardly there, charting our course from the compass and the sea, running with the waves and between them but never confronting their towering might.

68   And I stood at the tiller now, on these homeward lunges, stood in the place and in the manner of my uncle, turning to look at my father and to shout over the roar of the engine and the slop of the sea to where he stood in the stern, drenched and dripping with the snow and the salt and the spray and his bushy eyebrows caked in ice. But on November twenty-first, when it seemed we might be making the final run of the season, I turned and he was not there and I knew even in that instant that he would never be again.

69   On November twenty-first the waves of the grey Atlantic are very high and the waters are very cold and there are no signposts on the surface of the sea. You cannot tell where you have been five minutes before and in the squalls of snow you cannot see. And it takes longer than you would believe to check a boat that has been running before a gale and turn her ever so carefully in a wide and stupid circle, with timbers creaking and straining, back in the face of the storm. And you know it is useless and that your voice does not carry the length of the boat and that even if you knew the original spot, the relentless waves would carry such a burden perhaps a mile or so by the time you could return. And you know also, the final irony, that your father like your uncles and all the men that form your past, cannot swim a stroke.

70   The lobster beds off the Cape Breton coast are still very rich and now, from May to July, their offerings are packed in crates of ice, and thundered by the gigantic transport trucks, day and night, through New Glasgow, Amherst, Saint John and Bangor and Portland and into Boston where they are tossed still living into boiling pots of water, their final home.

71   And though the prices are higher and the competition tighter, the grounds to which the *Jenny Lynn* once went remain untouched and unfished as they have for the last ten years. For if there are no signposts on the sea in storm there are certain ones in calm and the lobster bottoms were distributed in calm before any

of us can remember and the grounds my father fished were those his father fished before him and there were others before and before and before. Twice the big boats have come from forty and fifty miles, lured by the promise of the grounds, and strewn the bottom with their traps and twice they have returned to find their buoys cut adrift and their gear lost and destroyed. Twice the Fisheries Officer and the Mounted Police have come and asked many long and involved questions and twice they have received no answers from the men leaning in the doors of their shanties and the women standing at their windows with their children in their arms. Twice they have gone away saying, "There are no legal boundaries in the Marine area"; "No one can own the sea"; "Those grounds don't wait for anyone."

72 　　But the men and the women, with my mother dark among them, do not care for what they say, for to them the grounds are sacred and they think they wait for me.

73 　　It is not an easy thing to know that your mother lives alone on an inadequate insurance policy and that she is too proud to accept any other aid. And that she looks through her lonely window onto the ice of winter and the hot flat calm of summer and the rolling waves of fall. And that she lies awake in the early morning's darkness when the rubber boots of the men scrunch upon the gravel as they pass beside her house on their way down to the wharf. And she knows that the footsteps never stop, because no man goes from her house, and she alone of all the Lynns has neither son or son-in-law that walks toward the boat that will take him to the sea. And it is not an easy thing to know that your mother looks upon the sea with love and on you with bitterness because the one has been so constant and the other so untrue.

74 　　But neither is it easy to know that your father was found on November twenty-eighth, ten miles to the north and wedged between two boulders at the base of the rock-strewn cliffs where he had been hurled and slammed so many many times. His hands were shredded ribbons as were his feet which had lost their boots to the suction of the sea, and his shoulders came apart in our hands when we tried to move him from the rocks. And the fish had eaten his testicles and the gulls had pecked out his eyes and the white-green stubble of his whiskers had continued to grow in death, like the grass on graves, upon the purple, bloated mass that was his face. There was not much left of my father, physically, as he lay there with the brass chains on his wrists and the seaweed in his hair.

Joyce Carol Oates

U.S.A. 1938–

Born in Lockport, New York, Oates gained degrees from Syracuse University and the University of Wisconsin before beginning her literary career. A prolific writer, she has one of the highest outputs of contemporary artists, publishing over thirty prose titles, including novels, short story collections, and three thrillers written under the pseudonym Rosalind Smith. Oates is deeply interested in the psychological and sociological motivation behind human acts, an interest that is prominent in the following story, which manages simultaneously to explore racial and generational divisions and the decaying urban landscape that is the setting for these divisions. Oates makes us pay equal attention to how a story is made and structured with her unusual title and headings.

How I Contemplated the World from the Detroit House of Correction and Began My Life Over Again   1965

Notes for an essay for an English class at Baldwin Country Day School; Poking around in debris; Disgust and curiosity; A revelation of the meaning of life; A happy ending ...

I   EVENTS

1. The girl (myself) is walking through Branden's,[1] that excellent store. Suburb of a large famous city that is a symbol for large famous American cities. The event sneaks up on the girl, who believes she is herding it along with a small fixed smile, a girl of fifteen, innocently experienced. She dawdles in a certain style by a counter of costume jewelry. Rings, earrings, necklaces. Prices from $5 to $50, all within reach. All ugly. She eases over to the glove counter, where everything is ugly too. In her close-fitted coat with its black fur collar she contemplates the luxury of Branden's, which she has known for many years: its many mild pale lights, easy on the eye and the soul, its elaborate tinkly decorations, its women shoppers with their excellent shoes and coats and hairdos, all dawdling gracefully, in no hurry.

    Who was ever in a hurry here?

2. The girl seated at home. A small library, paneled walls of oak. Someone is talking to me. An earnest, husky, female voice drives itself against my ears, nervous, frightened, groping around my heart, saying, "If you wanted gloves, why didn't you say so? Why didn't you ask for them?" That store, Branden's, is owned by Raymond Forrest who lives on Du Maurier Drive. We live on Sioux Drive. Raymond Forrest. A handsome man? An ugly man? A man of fifty or sixty, with gray hair, or a man of forty with earnest, courteous eyes, a good golf game; who is Raymond Forrest, this man who is my salvation? Father has been talking to him. Father is not his physician; Dr. Berg is his physician. Father and Dr. Berg refer patients to each other. There is a connection, Mother plays bridge with ... On Mondays and Wednesdays our maid Billie works at ... The strings draw together in a cat's cradle, making a net to save you when you fall. ...

3. *Harriet Arnold's.* A small shop, better than Branden's. Mother in her black coat, I in my close-fitted blue coat. Shopping. Now look at this, isn't this cute, do you want this, why don't you want this, try this on, take this with you to

---

the fitting room, take this also, what's wrong with you, what can I do for you, why are you so strange...? "I wanted to steal but not to buy," I don't tell her. The girl droops along in her coat and gloves and leather boots, her eyes scan the horizon, which is pastel pink and decorated like Branden's, tasteful walls and modern ceilings with graceful glimmering lights.

4. Weeks later, the girl at a bus stop. Two o'clock in the afternoon, a Tuesday; obviously she has walked out of school.

5. The girl stepping down from a bus. Afternoon, weather changing to colder. Detroit. Pavement and closed-up stores; grillwork over the windows of a pawnshop. What is a pawnshop, exactly?

II CHARACTERS

1. The girl stands five feet five inches tall. An ordinary height. Baldwin Country Day School draws them up to that height. She dreams along the corridors and presses her face against the Thermoplex glass. No frost or steam can ever form on that glass. A smudge of grease from her forehead ... could she be boiled down to grease? She wears her hair loose and long and straight in suburban teen-age style, 1968. Eyes smudged with pencil, dark brown. Brown hair. Vague green eyes. A pretty girl? An ugly girl? She sings to herself under her breath, idling in the corridor, thinking of her many secrets (the thirty dollars she once took from the purse of a friend's mother, just for fun, the basement window she smashed in her own house just for fun) and thinking of her brother who is at Susquehanna Boys' Academy, an excellent preparatory school in Maine, remembering him unclearly ... he has long manic hair and a squeaking voice and he looks like one of the popular teen-age singers of 1968, one of those in a group, *The Certain Forces, The Way Out, The Maniacs Responsible*. The girl in her turn looks like one of those fieldsful of girls who listen to the boys' singing, dreaming and mooning restlessly, breaking into high sullen laughter, innocently experienced.

2. The mother. A Midwestern woman of Detroit and suburbs. Belongs to the Detroit Athletic Club. Also the Detroit Golf Club. Also the Bloomfield Hills Country Club. The Village Women's Club at which lectures are given each winter on Genet and Sartre and James Baldwin,[2] by the Director of the Adult Education Program at Wayne State University ... The Bloomfield Art Association. Also the Founders Society of the Detroit Institute of Arts. Also ... Oh, she is in perpetual motion, this lady, hair like blown-up gold and finer than gold, hair and fingers and body of inestimable grace. Heavy weighs the gold on the back of her hairbrush and hand mirror. Heavy heavy the candlesticks in the dining room. Very heavy is the big car, a Lincoln, long and black, that on one cool autumn day split a squirrel's body in two unequal parts.

3. The father. Dr. _____. He belongs to the same clubs as #2. A player of squash and golf; he has a golfer's umbrella of stripes. Candy stripes. In his mouth nothing turns to sugar, however; saliva works no miracles here. His doctoring is of the

---

2 Jean Genet and Jean-Paul Sartre were French writers; James Baldwin was an American writer.

slightly sick. The sick are sent elsewhere (to Dr. Berg?), the deathly sick are sent back for more tests and their bills are sent to their homes, the unsick are sent to Dr. Coronet (Isabel, a lady), an excellent psychiatrist for unsick people who angrily believe they are sick and want to do something about it. If they demand a male psychiatrist, the unsick are sent by Dr. _____ (my father) to Dr. Lowenstein, a male psychiatrist, excellent and expensive, with a limited practice.

4. Clarita. She is twenty, twenty-five, she is thirty or more? Pretty, ugly, what? She is a woman lounging by the side of a road, in jeans and a sweater, hitch-hiking, or she is slouched on a stool at a counter in some roadside diner. A hard line of jaw. Curious eyes. Amused eyes. Behind her eyes processions move, funeral pageants, cartoons. She says, "I never can figure out why girls like you bum around down here. What are you looking for anyway?" An odor of tobacco about her. Unwashed underclothes, or no underclothes, unwashed skin, gritty toes, hair long and falling into strands, not recently washed.

5. Simon. In this city the weather changes abruptly, so Simon's weather changes abruptly. He sleeps through the afternoon. He sleeps through the morning. Rising, he gropes around for something to get him going, for a cigarette or a pill to drive him out to the street, where the temperature is hovering around 35°. Why doesn't it drop? Why, why doesn't the cold clean air come down from Canada; will he have to go up into Canada to get it? Will he have to leave the Country of his Birth and sink into Canada's frosty fields...? Will the F.B.I. (which he dreams about constantly) chase him over the Canadian border on foot, hounded out in a blizzard of broken glass and horns...?

"Once I was Huckleberry Finn," Simon says, "but now I am Roderick Usher."[3] Beset by frenzies and fears, this man who makes my spine go cold, he takes green pills, yellow pills, pills of white and capsules of dark blue and green ... he takes other things I may not mention, for what if Simon seeks me out and climbs into my girl's bedroom here in Bloomfield Hills and strangles me, what then...? (As I write this I begin to shiver. Why do I shiver? I am now sixteen and sixteen is not an age for shivering.) It comes from Simon, who is always cold.

III   WORLD EVENTS

Nothing.

IV   PEOPLE & CIRCUMSTANCES CONTRIBUTING TO THIS DELINQUENCY

Nothing.

V   SIOUX DRIVE

George, Clyde G. 240 Sioux. A manufacturer's representative; children, a dog, a wife. Georgian with the usual columns. You think of the White House, then of Thomas

---

3 Huck Finn is the protagonist of Mark Twain's novel *The Adventures of Huckleberry Finn;* Usher is the protagonist in Edgar Allan Poe's story, "The Fall of the House of Usher."

Jefferson, then your mind goes blank on the white pillars and you think of nothing. Norris, Ralph W. 246 Sioux. Public relations. Colonial. Bay window, brick, stone, concrete, wood, green shutters, sidewalk, lantern, grass, trees, blacktop drive, two children, one of them my classmate Esther (Esther Norris) at Baldwin. Wife, cars. Ramsey, Michael D. 250 Sioux. Colonial. Big living room, thirty by twenty-five, fireplaces in living room, library, recreation room, paneled walls wet bar five bathrooms five bedrooms two lavatories central air conditioning automatic sprinkler automatic garage door three children one wife two cars a breakfast room a patio a large fenced lot fourteen trees a front door with a brass knocker never knocked. Next is our house. Classic contemporary. Traditional modern. Attached garage, attached Florida room, attached patio, attached pool and cabana, attached roof. A front door mail slot through which pour *Time Magazine, Fortune, Life, Business Week,* the *Wall Street Journal,* the *New York Times,* the *New Yorker,* the *Saturday Review, M.D., Modern Medicine, Disease of the Month* ... and also. ... And in addition to all this, a quiet sealed letter from Baldwin saying: *Your daughter is not doing work compatible with her performance on the Stanford-Binet* ... And your son is not doing well, not well at all, very sad. Where is your son anyway? Once he stole trick-and-treat candy from some six-year-old kids, he himself being a robust ten. The beginning. Now your daughter steals. In the Village Pharmacy she made off with, yes she did, don't deny it, she made off with a copy of *Pageant Magazine* for no reason, she swiped a roll of Life Savers in a green wrapper and was in no need of saving her life or even in need of sucking candy; when she was no more than eight years old she stole, don't blush, she stole a package of Tums only because it was out on the counter and available, and the nice lady behind the counter (now dead) said nothing. ... Sioux Drive. Maples, oaks, elms. Diseased elms cut down. Sioux Drive runs into Roosevelt Drive. Slow, turning lanes, not streets, all drives and lanes and ways and passes. A private police force. Quiet private police, in unmarked cars. Cruising on Saturday evenings with paternal smiles for the residents who are streaming in and out of houses, going to and from parties, a thousand parties, slightly staggering, the women in their furs alighting from automobiles bought of Ford and General Motors and Chrysler, very heavy automobiles. No foreign cars. Detroit. In 275 Sioux, down the block in that magnificent French-Normandy mansion, lives _____ himself, who has the C _____ account itself, imagine that! Look at where he lives and look at the enormous trees and chimneys, imagine his many fireplaces, imagine his wife and children, imagine his wife's hair, imagine her fingernails, imagine her bathtub of smooth clean glowing pink, imagine their embraces, his trouser pockets filled with odd coins and keys and dust and peanuts, imagine their ecstasy on Sioux Drive, imagine their income tax returns, imagine their little boy's pride in his experimental car, a scaled down C _____, as he roars round the neighborhood on the sidewalks frightening dogs and Negro maids, oh imagine all these things, imagine everything, let your mind roar out all over Sioux Drive and Du Maurier Drive and Roosevelt Drive and Ticonderoga Pass and Burning Bush Way and Lincolnshire Pass and Lois Lane.

When spring comes, its winds blow nothing to Sioux Drive, no odors of hollyhocks or forsythia, nothing Sioux Drive doesn't already possess, everything is planted and performing. The weather vanes, had they weather vanes, don't have to turn with the wind, don't have to contend with the weather. There is no weather.

VI DETROIT

There is always weather in Detroit. Detroit's temperature is always 32°. Fast-falling temperatures. Slow-rising temperatures. Wind from the north-northeast four to forty miles an hour, small-craft warnings, partly cloudy today and Wednesday changing to partly sunny through Thursday ... small warnings of frost, soot warnings, traffic warnings, hazardous lake conditions for small craft and swimmers, restless Negro gangs, restless cloud formations, restless temperatures aching to fall out the very bottom of the thermometer or shoot up over the top and boil everything over in red mercury.

Detroit's temperature is 32°. Fast-falling temperatures. Slow-rising temperatures. Wind from the north-northeast four to forty miles an hour. ...

VII EVENTS

1. The girl's heart is pounding. In her pocket is a pair of gloves! In a plastic bag! Airproof breathproof plastic bag, gloves selling for twenty-five dollars on Branden's counter! In her pocket! Shoplifted!... In her purse is a blue comb, not very clean. In her purse is a leather billfold (a birthday present from her grandmother in Philadelphia) with snapshots of the family in clean plastic windows, in the billfold are bills, she doesn't know how many bills. ... In her purse is an ominous note from her friend Tykie *What's this about Joe H. and the kids hanging around at Louise's Sat. night? You heard anything?...* passed in French class. In her purse is a lot of dirty yellow Kleenex, her mother's heart would break to see such very dirty Kleenex, and at the bottom of her purse are brown hairpins and safety pins and a broken pencil and a ballpoint pen (blue) stolen from somewhere forgotten and a purse-size compact of Cover Girl Make-Up, Ivory Rose. ... Her lipstick is Broken Heart, a corrupt pink; her fingers are trembling like crazy; her teeth are beginning to chatter; her insides are alive; her eyes glow in her head; she is saying to her mother's astonished face *I want to steal but not to buy.*

2. At Clarita's. Day or night? What room is this? A bed, a regular bed, and a mattress on the floor nearby. Wallpaper hanging in strips. Clarita says she tore it like that with her teeth. She was fighting a barbaric tribe that night, high from some pills; she was battling for her life with men wearing helmets of heavy iron and their faces no more than Christian crosses to breathe through, every one of those bastards looking like her lover Simon, who seems to breathe with great difficulty through the slits of mouth and nostrils in his face. Clarita has never heard of Sioux Drive. Raymond Forrest cuts no ice with her, nor does the C_____ account and its millions; Harvard Business School could be at the corner of Vernor and 12th Street for all she cares, and Vietnam might have sunk by now into the Dead Sea under its tons of debris, for all the amazement she could show ... her face is overworked, overwrought, at the age of twenty (thirty?) it is already exhausted but fanciful and ready for a laugh. Clarita says mournfully to me *Honey somebody is going to turn you out let me give you warning.* In a movie shown on late television Clarita is not a mess like this but a nurse, with short neat hair and a dedicated look, in love with her

doctor and her doctor's patients and their diseases, enamored of needles and sponges and rubbing alcohol.... Or no: she is a private secretary. Robert Cummings is her boss. She helps him with fantastic plots, the canned audience laughs, no, the audience doesn't laugh because nothing is funny, instead her boss is Robert Taylor and they are not boss and secretary but husband and wife, she is threatened by a young starlet, she is grim, handsome, wifely, a good companion for a good man.... She is Claudette Colbert.[4] Her sister too is Claudette Colbert. They are twins, identical. Her husband Charles Boyer is a very rich handsome man and her sister, Claudette Colbert, is plotting her death in order to take her place as the rich man's wife, no one will know because they are *twins*.... All these marvelous lives Clarita might have lived, but she fell out the bottom at the age of thirteen. At the age when I was packing my overnight case for a slumber party at Toni Deshield's she was tearing filthy sheets off a bed and scratching up a rash on her arms.... Thirteen is uncommonly young for a white girl in Detroit, Miss Brock of the Detroit House of Correction said in a sad newspaper interview for the *Detroit News*, fifteen and sixteen are more likely. Eleven, twelve, thirteen are not surprising in colored ... they are more precocious. What can we do? Taxes are rising and the tax base is falling. The temperature rises slowly but falls rapidly. Everything is falling out the bottom, Woodward Avenue is filthy, Livernois Avenue is filthy! Scraps of paper flutter in the air like pigeons, dirt flies up and hits you right in the eye, oh Detroit is breaking up into dangerous bits of newspaper and dirt, watch out....

Clarita's apartment is over a restaurant. Simon her lover emerges from the cracks at dark. Mrs. Olesko, a neighbor of Clarita's, an aged white wisp of a woman, doesn't complain but sniffs with contentment at Clarita's noisy life and doesn't tell the cops, hating cops, when the cops arrive. I should give more fake names, more blanks, instead of telling all these secrets. I myself am a secret; I am a minor.

3. My father reads a paper at a medical convention in Los Angeles. There he is, on the edge of the North American continent, when the unmarked detective put his hand so gently on my arm in the aisle of Branden's and said, "Miss, would you like to step over here for a minute?"

And where was he when Clarita put her hand on my arm, that very dark sulphurous aching day in Detroit, in the company of closed-down barber shops, closed-down diners, closed-down movie houses, homes, windows, basements, faces ... she put her hand on my arm and said, "Honey, are you looking for somebody down here?"

And was he home worrying about me, gone for two weeks solid, when they carried me off...? It took three of them to get me in the police cruiser, so they said, and they put more than their hands on my arm.

4. I work on this lesson. My English teacher is Mr. Forest, who is from Michigan State. Not handsome, Mr. Forest, and his name is plain, unlike Raymond Forrest's, but he is sweet and rodentlike, he has conferred with the principal and my parents, and everything is fixed ... treat her as if nothing has hap-

---

4 Hollywood actors popular in the 1930s and 1940s.

pened, a new start, begin again, only sixteen years old, what a shame, how did it happen?—nothing happened, nothing could have happened, a slight physiological modification known only to a gynecologist or to Dr. Coronet. I work on my lesson. I sit in my pink room. I look around the room with my sad pink eyes. I sigh, I dawdle, I pause, I eat up time, I am limp and happy to be home, I am sixteen years old suddenly, my head hangs heavy as a pumpkin on my shoulders, and my hair has just been cut by Mr. Faye at the Crystal Salon and is said to be very becoming.

(Simon too put his hand on my arm and said, "Honey, you have got to come with me," and in his six-by-six room we got to know each other. Would I go back to Simon again? Would I lie down with him in all that filth and craziness? Over and over again,

a Clarita is being betrayed in front of a Cunningham Drug Store she is nervously eyeing a colored man who may or may not have money, or a nervous white boy of twenty with sideburns and an Appalachian look, who may or may not have a knife hidden in his jacket pocket, or a husky red-faced man of friendly countenance who may or may not be a member of the Vice Squad out for an early twilight walk.)

I work on my lesson for Mr. Forest. I have filled up eleven pages. Words pour out of me and won't stop. I want to tell everything ... what was the song Simon was always humming, and who was Simon's friend in a very new trench coat with an old high school graduation ring on his finger...? Simon's bearded friend? When I was down too low for him, Simon kicked me out and gave me to him for three days, I think, on Fourteenth Street in Detroit, an airy room of cold cruel drafts with newspapers on the floor.... Do I really remember that or am I piecing it together from what they told me? Did they tell the truth? Did they know much of the truth?

VIII   CHARACTERS

1. Wednesdays after school, at four; Saturday mornings at ten. Mother drives me to Dr. Coronet. Ferns in the office, plastic or real, they look the same. Dr. Coronet is queenly, an elegant nicotine-stained lady who would have studied with Freud had circumstances not prevented it, a bit of a Catholic, ready to offer you some mystery if your teeth will ache too much without it. Highly recommended by Father! Forty dollars an hour, Father's forty dollars! Progress! Looking up! Looking better! That new haircut is so becoming, says Dr. Coronet herself, showing how normal she is for a woman with an I.Q. of 180 and many advance degrees.

2. Mother. A lady in a brown suede coat. Boots of shiny black material, black gloves, a black fur hat. She would be humiliated could she know that of all the people in the world it is my ex-lover Simon who walks most like her ... self-conscious and unreal, listening to distant music, a little bowlegged with craftiness....

3. Father. Tying a necktie. In a hurry. On my first evening home he put his hand on my arm and said, "Honey, we're going to forget all about this."

4. Simon. Outside, a plane is crossing the sky, in here we're in a hurry. Morning. It must be morning. The girl is half out of her mind, whimpering and vague; Simon her dear friend is wretched this morning ... he is wretched with morning itself ... he forces her to give him an injection with that needle she knows is filthy, she had a dread of needles and surgical instruments and the odor of things that are to be sent into the blood, thinking somehow of her father.... This is a bad morning, Simon says that his mind is being twisted out of shape, and so he submits to the needle that he usually scorns and bites his lip with his yellowish teeth, his face going very pale. *Ah baby!* he says in his soft mocking voice, which with all women is a mockery of love, *do it like this—Slowly*—And the girl, terrified, almost drops the precious needle but manages to turn it up to the light from the window ... is it an extension of herself then? She can give him this gift then? *I wish you wouldn't do this to me,* she says, wise in her terror, because it seems to her that Simon's danger—in a few minutes he may be dead—is a way of pressing her against him that is more powerful than any other embrace. She has to work over his arm, the knotted corded veins of his arm, her forehead wet with perspiration as she pushes and releases the needle, staring at that mixture of liquid now stained with Simon's bright blood.... When the drug hits him she can feel it herself, she feels that magic that is more than any woman can give him, striking the back of his head and making his face stretch as if with the impact of a terrible sun.... She tries to embrace him but he pushes her aside and stumbles to his feet. *Jesus Christ,* he says....

5. Princess, a Negro girl of eighteen. What is her charge? She is closed-mouthed about it, shrewd and silent, you know that no one had to wrestle her to the sidewalk to get her in here; she came with dignity. In the recreation room she sits reading *Nancy Drew and the Jewel Box Mystery*, which inspires in her face tiny wrinkles of alarm and interest: what a face! Light brown skin, heavy shaded eyes, heavy eyelashes, a serious sinister dark brow, graceful fingers, graceful wristbones, graceful legs, lips, tongue, a sugar-sweet voice, a leggy stride more masculine than Simon's and my mother's, decked out in a dirty white blouse and dirty white slacks; vaguely nautical is Princess' style.... At breakfast she is in charge of clearing the table and leans over me, saying, *Honey you sure you ate enough?*

6. The girl lies sleepless, wondering. Why here, why not there? Why Bloomfield Hills and not jail? Why jail and not her pink room? Why downtown Detroit and not Sioux Drive? What is the difference? Is Simon all the difference? The girl's head is a parade of wonders. She is nearly sixteen, her breath is marvelous with wonders, not long ago she was coloring with crayons and now she is smearing the landscape with paints that won't come off and won't come off her fingers either. She says to the matron *I am not talking about anything,* not because everyone has warned her not to talk but because, because she will not talk; because she won't say anything about Simon, who is her secret. And she says to the matron, *I won't go home,* up until that night in the lavatory when everything was changed.... "No, I won't go home I want to stay here," she says, listening to her own words with amazement, thinking that weeds might climb everywhere over that marvelous $180,000 house and dinosaurs might return to muddy the beige carpeting, but never never will she reconcile four o'clock in the morning

in Detroit with eight o'clock breakfasts in Bloomfield Hills. ... oh, she aches still for Simon's hands and his caressing breath, though he gave her little pleasure, he took everything from her (five-dollar bills, ten-dollar bills, passed into her numb hands by men and taken out of her hands by Simon) until she herself was passed into the hands of other men, police, when Simon evidently got tired of her and her hysteria.... *No, I won't go home, I don't want to be bailed out.* The girl thinks as a *Stubborn and Wayward Child* (one of several charges lodged against her), and the matron understands her crazy white-rimmed eyes that are seeking out some new violence that will keep her in jail, should someone threaten to let her out. Such children try to strangle the matrons, the attendants, or one another ... they want the locks locked forever, the doors nailed shut ... and this girl is no different up until that night her mind is changed for her....

IX   THAT NIGHT

Princess and Dolly, a little white girl of maybe fifteen, hardy however as a sergeant and in the House of Correction for armed robbery, corner her in the lavatory at the farthest sink and the other girls look away and file out to bed, leaving her. God, how she is beaten up! Why is she beaten up? Why do they pound her, why such hatred? Princess vents all the hatred of a thousand silent Detroit winters on her body, this girl whose body belongs to me, fiercely she rides across the Midwestern plains on this girl's tender bruised body ... revenge on the oppressed minorities of America! revenge on the slaughtered Indians! revenge on the female sex, on the male sex, revenge on Bloomfield Hills, revenge revenge....

X   DETROIT

In Detroit, weather weighs heavily upon everyone. The sky looms large. The horizon shimmers in smoke. Downtown the buildings are imprecise in the haze. Perpetual haze. Perpetual motion inside the haze. Across the choppy river is the city of Windsor, in Canada. Part of the continent has bunched up here and is bulging outward, at the tip of Detroit; a cold hard rain is forever falling on the expressways.... Shoppers shop grimly, their cars are not parked in safe places, their windshields may be smashed and graceful ebony hands may drag them out through their shatterproof smashed windshields, crying, *Revenge for the Indians!* Ah, they all fear leaving Hudson's and being dragged to the very tip of the city and thrown off the parking roof of Cobo Hall, that expensive tomb, into the river....

XI   CHARACTERS WE ARE FOREVER ENTWINED WITH

1. Simon drew me into his tender rotting arms and breathed gravity into me. Then I came to earth, weighed down. He said, *You are such a little girl,* and he weighed me down with his delight. In the palms of his hands were teeth marks from his previous life experiences. He was thirty-five, they said. Imagine Simon in this room, in my pink room: he is about six feet tall and stoops slightly, in a feline cautious way, always thinking, always on guard,

with his scuffed light suede shoes and his clothes that are anyone's clothes, slightly rumpled ordinary clothes that ordinary men might wear to not-bad jobs. Simon has fair long hair, curly hair, spent languid curls that are like ... exactly like the curls of wood shavings to the touch, I am trying to be exact ... and he smells of unheated mornings and coffee and too many pills coating his tongue with a faint green-white scum.... Dear Simon, who would be panicked in this room and in this house (right now Billie is vacuuming next door in my parents' room; a vacuum cleaner's roar is a sign of all good things), Simon who is said to have come from a home not much different from this, years ago, fleeing all the carpeting and the polished banisters ... Simon has a deathly face, only desperate people fall in love with it. His face is bony and cautious, the bones of his cheeks prominent as if with the rigidity of his ceaseless thinking, plotting, for he has to make money out of girls to whom money means nothing, they're so far gone they can hardly count it, and in a sense money means nothing to him either except as a way of keeping on with his life. *Each Day's Proud Struggle*, the title of a novel we could read at jail.... Each day he needs a certain amount of money. He devours it. It wasn't love he uncoiled in me with his hollowed-out eyes and his courteous smile, that remnant of a prosperous past, but a dark terror that needed to press itself flat against him, or against another man ... but he was the first, he came over to me and took my arm, a claim. We struggled on the stairs and I said, *Let me loose, you're hurting my neck, my face,* it was such a surprise that my skin hurt where he rubbed it, and afterward we lay face to face and he breathed everything into me. In the end I think he turned me in.

2.   Raymond Forrest. I just read this morning that Raymond Forrest's father, the chairman of the board at _____, died of a heart attack on a plane bound for London. I would like to write Raymond Forrest a note of sympathy. I would like to thank him for not pressing charges against me one hundred years ago, saving me, being so generous ... well, men like Raymond Forrest are generous men, not like Simon. I would like to write him a letter telling of my love, or of some other emotion that is positive and healthy. Not like Simon and his poetry, which he scrawled down when he was high and never changed a word ... but when I try to think of something to say, it is Simon's language that comes back to me, caught in my head like a bad song, it is always Simon's language:

> *There is no reality only dreams*
> *Your neck may get snapped when you wake*
> *My love is drawn to some violent end*
> *She keeps wanting to get away*
> *My love is heading downward*
> *And I am heading upward*
> *She is going to crash on the sidewalk*
> *And I am going to dissolve into the clouds*

XII EVENTS

1. Out of the hospital, bruised and saddened and converted, with Princess' grunts still tangled in my hair ... and Father in his overcoat, looking like a prince himself, come to carry me off. Up the expressway and out north to home. Jesus Christ, but the air is thinner and cleaner here. Monumental houses. Heartbreaking sidewalks, so clean.

2. Weeping in the living room. The ceiling is two stories high and two chandeliers hang from it. Weeping, weeping, though Billie the maid is *probably listening*. I will never leave home again. Never. Never leave home. Never leave this home again, never.

3. Sugar doughnuts for breakfast. The toaster is very shiny and my face is distorted in it. Is that my face?

4. The car is turning in the driveway. Father brings me home. Mother embraces me. Sunlight breaks in movieland patches on the roof of our traditional-contemporary home, which was designed for the famous automotive stylist whose identity, if I told you the name of the famous car he designed, you would all know, so I can't tell you because my teeth chatter at the thought of being sued ... or having someone climb into my bedroom window with a rope to strangle me.... The car turns up the blacktop drive. The house opens to me like a doll's house, so lovely in the sunlight, the big living room beckons to me with its walls falling away in a delirium of joy at my return, Billie the maid is *no doubt* listening from the kitchen as I burst into tears and the hysteria Simon got so sick of. Convulsed in Father's arms, I say I will never leave again, never, why did I leave, where did I go, what happened, my mind is gone wrong, my body is one big bruise, my backbone was sucked dry, it wasn't the men who hurt me and Simon never hurt me but only those girls ... my God, how they hurt me ... I will never leave home again.... The car is perpetually turning up the drive and I am perpetually breaking down in the living room and we are perpetually taking the right exit from the expressway (Lahser Road) and the wall of the rest room is perpetually banging against my head and perpetually are Simon's hands moving across my body and adding everything up and so too are Father's hands on my shaking bruised back, far from the surface of my skin on the surface of my good blue cashmere coat (dry-cleaned for my release).... I weep for all the money here, for God in gold and blue carpeting, for the beauty of chandeliers and the miracle of a clean polished gleaming toaster and faucets that run both hot and cold water, and I tell them, *I will never leave home, this is my home, I love everything here, I am in love with everything here....*
   I am home.

Margaret Atwood

Canada 1939–

Margaret Atwood was born in Ottawa and spent her early life on the Canadian Shield, where her zoologist father did research, and in various Canadian cities, especially Ottawa and Toronto. After an academic career at the University of Toronto (Victoria College) and Harvard University, Atwood taught at the University of British Columbia for almost nine years. Atwood's writing has ranged from poetry to novels and essays. In her work, the themes of sexual politics, power in relationships, victimization, the Cartesian split, feminist perspectives, and love form a rich stew. "Happy Endings" reveals her talent for satire.

Happy Endings   1983

John and Mary meet.
What happens next?
If you want a happy ending, try A.

A. John and Mary fall in love and get married. They both have worthwhile and remunerative jobs which they find stimulating and challenging. They buy a charming house. Real estate values go up. Eventually, when they can afford live-in help, they have two children, to whom they are devoted. The children turn out well. John and Mary have a stimulating and challenging sex life and worthwhile friends. They go on fun vacations together. They retire. They both have hobbies which they find stimulating and challenging. Eventually they die. This is the end of the story.

B. Mary falls in love with John but John doesn't fall in love with Mary. He merely uses her body for selfish pleasure and ego gratification of a tepid kind. He comes to her apartment twice a week and she cooks him dinner, you'll notice that he doesn't even consider her worth the price of a dinner out, and after he's eaten the dinner he fucks her and after that he falls asleep, while she does the dishes so he won't think she's untidy, having all those dirty dishes lying around and puts on fresh lipstick so she'll look good when he wakes up, but when he wakes up he doesn't even notice, he puts on his socks and his shorts and his pants and his shirt and his tie and his shoes, the reverse order from the one in which he took them off. He doesn't take off Mary's clothes, she takes them off herself, she acts as if she's dying for it every time, not because she likes sex exactly, she doesn't, but she wants John to think she does because if they do it often enough surely he'll get used to her, he'll come to depend on her and they will get married, but John goes out the door with hardly so much as a good-night and three days later he turns up at six o'clock and they do the whole thing over again.

Mary gets run-down. Crying is bad for your face, everyone knows that and so does Mary but she can't stop. People at work notice. Her friends tell her John is a rat, a pig, a dog, he isn't good enough for her, but she can't believe it. Inside John, she thinks, is another John, who is much nicer. This other John will emerge like a butterfly from a cocoon, a Jack from a box, a pit from a prune, if the first John is only squeezed enough.

One evening John complains about the food. He has never complained about the food before. Mary is hurt.

Her friends tell her they've seen him in a restaurant with another woman, whose name is Madge. It's not even Madge that finally gets to Mary: it's the restaurant. John has never taken Mary to a restaurant. Mary collects all the sleeping pills and aspirins she can find, and takes them and a half bottle of sherry. You can see what kind of a woman she is by the fact that it's not even whiskey. She leaves a note for John. She hopes he'll discover her and get her to the hospital in time and repent and then they can get married, but this fails to happen and she dies.

John marries Madge and everything continues as in A.

C. John, who is an older man, falls in love with Mary, and Mary, who is only twenty-two, feels sorry for him because he's worried about his hair falling out. She sleeps with him even though she's not in love with him. She met him at work. She's in love with someone called James, who is twenty-two and not yet ready to settle down.

John on the contrary settled down long ago: this is what is bothering him. John has a steady, respectable job and is getting ahead in his field, but Mary isn't impressed by him, she's impressed by James, who has a motorcycle and a fabulous record collection. But James is often away on his motorcycle, being free. Freedom isn't the same for girls, so in the meantime Mary spends Thursday evenings with John. Thursdays are the only days John can get away.

John is married to a woman called Madge and they have two children, a charming house which they bought just before the real estate values went up, and hobbies which they find stimulating and challenging, when they have the time. John tells Mary how important she is to him, but of course he can't leave his wife because a commitment is a commitment. He goes on about this more than is necessary and Mary finds it boring, but older men can keep it up longer so on the whole she has a fairly good time.

One day James breezes in on his motorcycle with some top-grade California hybrid and James and Mary get higher than you'd believe possible and they climb into bed. Everything becomes very underwater, but along comes John, who has a key to Mary's apartment. He finds them stoned and entwined. He's hardly in any position to be jealous, considering Madge, but nevertheless he's overcome with despair. Finally he's middle-aged, in two years he'll be bald as an egg and he can't stand it. He purchases a handgun, saying he needs it for target practice—this is the thin part of the plot, but it can be dealt with later—and shoots the two of them and himself.

Madge, after a suitable period of mourning, marries an understanding man called Fred and everything continues as in A, but under different names.

D. Fred and Madge have no problems. They get along exceptionally well and are good at working out any little difficulties that may arise. But their charming house is by the seashore and one day a giant tidal wave approaches. Real estate values go down. The rest of the story is about what caused the tidal wave and how they escape from it. They do, though thousands drown, but Fred and

Madge are virtuous and lucky. Finally on high ground they clasp each other, wet and dripping and grateful, and continue as in A.

E. Yes, but Fred has a bad heart. The rest of the story is about how kind and understanding they both are until Fred dies. Then Madge devotes herself to charity work until the end of A. If you like, it can be "Madge," "cancer," "guilty and confused," and "bird watching."

F. If you think this is all too bourgeois, make John a revolutionary and Mary a counterespionage agent and see how far that gets you. Remember, this is Canada. You'll still end up with A, though in between you may get a lustful brawling saga of passionate involvement, a chronicle of our times, sort of.

You'll have to face it, the endings are the same however you slice it. Don't be deluded by any other endings, they're all fake, either deliberately fake, with malicious intent to deceive, or just motivated by excessive optimism if not by downright sentimentality.

The only authentic ending is the one provided here.
John and Mary die. John and Mary die. John and Mary die.

So much for endings. Beginnings are always more fun. True connoisseurs, however, are known to favor the stretch in between, since it's the hardest to do anything with.

That's about all that can be said for plots, which anyway are just one thing after another, a what and a what and a what.

Now try How and Why.

Raymond Carver

U.S.A. 1939–1988

Raymond Carver was born in Oregon, and he and his family moved to Yakima, Washington, when he was three. Carver grew up there and was a married father of two by the time he was twenty. After graduating as an English major from Humboldt State College, he began graduate work at the University of Iowa Writer's Workshop but did not finish. He took a job editing textbooks while continuing to publish stories and poems. His stories frequently focus on less privileged people and their difficulties in life. Carver's stories are haunting tales of alienation and responses to, or struggles against, that alienation. "Cathedral" is the title story of one of his five collections and notable for the way the narrator reaches a moment of spiritual insight we are not expecting.

Cathedral   1981

1 This blind man, an old friend of my wife's, he was on his way to spend the night. His wife had died. So he was visiting the dead wife's relatives in Connecticut. He called my wife from his in-laws'. Arrangements were made. He would come by train, a five-hour trip, and my wife would meet him at the station. She hadn't seen him since she worked for him one summer in Seattle ten years ago. But she and the blind man had kept in touch. They made tapes and mailed them back and forth. I wasn't enthusiastic about his visit. He was no one I knew. And his being blind bothered me. My idea of blindness came from the movies. In the movies, the blind moved slowly and never laughed. Sometimes they were led by seeing-eye dogs. A blind man in my house was not something I looked forward to.

2 That summer in Seattle she had needed a job. She didn't have any money. The man she was going to marry at the end of the summer was in officers' training school. He didn't have any money, either. But she was in love with the guy, and he was in love with her, etc. She'd seen something in the paper: HELP WANTED— *Reading to Blind Man*, and a telephone number. She phoned and went over, was hired on the spot. She'd worked with this blind man all summer. She read stuff to him, case studies, reports, that sort of thing. She helped him organize his little office in the county social-service department. They'd become good friends, my wife and the blind man. How do I know these things? She told me. And she told me something else. On her last day in the office, the blind man asked if he could touch her face. She agreed to this. She told me he touched his fingers to every part of her face, her nose—even her neck! She never forgot it. She even tried to write a poem about it. She was always trying to write a poem. She wrote a poem or two every year, usually after something really important had happened to her.

3 When we first started going out together, she showed me the poem. In the poem, she recalled his fingers and the way they had moved around over her face. In the poem, she talked about what she had felt at the time, about what went through her mind when the blind man touched her nose and lips. I can remember I didn't think much of the poem. Of course, I didn't tell her that. Maybe I just don't understand poetry. I admit it's not the first thing I reach for when I pick up something to read.

4 Anyway, this man who'd first enjoyed her favors, the officer-to-be, he'd been her childhood sweetheart. So okay. I'm saying that at the end of the summer she let the blind man run his hands over her face, said goodbye to him, married her childhood etc., who was now a commissioned officer, and she moved away from Seattle. But they'd kept in touch, she and the blind man. She made the first contact after a year or so. She called him up one night from an Air Force base in Alabama. She wanted to talk. They talked. He asked her to send him a tape and tell him about her life. She did this. She sent the tape. On the tape, she told the blind man about her husband and about their life together in the military. She told the blind man she loved her husband but she didn't like it where they lived and she didn't like it that he was a part of the military-industrial thing. She told the blind man she'd written a poem and he was in it. She told him that she was writing a poem about what it was like to be an Air Force officer's wife. The poem wasn't finished yet. She was still writing it. The blind man made a tape. He sent

her the tape. She made a tape. This went on for years. My wife's officer was posted to one base and then another. She sent tapes from Moody AFB, McGuire, McConnell, and finally Travis, near Sacramento, where one night she got to feeling lonely and cut off from people she kept losing in that moving-around life. She got to feeling she couldn't go it another step. She went in and swallowed all the pills and capsules in the medicine chest and washed them down with a bottle of gin. Then she got into a hot bath and passed out.

5   But instead of dying, she got sick. She threw up. Her officer—why should he have a name? he was the childhood sweetheart, and what more does he want?— came home from somewhere, found her, and called the ambulance. In time, she put it all on a tape and sent the tape to the blind man. Over the years, she put all kinds of stuff on tapes and sent the tapes off lickety-split. Next to writing a poem every year, I think it was her chief means of recreation. On one tape, she told the blind man she'd decided to live away from her officer for a time. On another tape, she told him about her divorce. She and I began going out, and of course she told her blind man about it. She told him everything, or so it seemed to me. Once she asked me if I'd like to hear the latest tape from the blind man. This was a year ago. I was on the tape, she said. So I said okay, I'd listen to it. I got us drinks and we settled down in the living room. We made ready to listen. First she inserted the tape into the player and adjusted a couple of dials. Then she pushed a lever. The tape squeaked and someone began to talk in this loud voice. She lowered the volume. After a few minutes of harmless chitchat, I heard my own name in the mouth of this stranger, this blind man I didn't even know! And then this: "From all you've said about him, I can only conclude—" But we were interrupted, a knock at the door, something, and we didn't ever get back to the tape. Maybe it was just as well. I'd heard all I wanted to.

6   Now this same blind man was coming to sleep in my house.

7   "Maybe I could take him bowling," I said to my wife. She was at the draining board doing scalloped potatoes. She put down the knife she was using and turned around.

8   "If you love me," she said, "you can do this for me. If you don't love me, okay. But if you had a friend, any friend, and the friend came to visit, I'd make him feel comfortable." She wiped her hands with the dish towel.

9   "I don't have any blind friends," I said.

10   "You don't have *any* friends," she said. "Period. Besides," she said, "goddamn it, his wife's just died! Don't you understand that? The man's lost his wife!"

11   I didn't answer. She'd told me a little about the blind man's wife. Her name was Beulah, Beulah! That's a name for a colored woman.

12   "Was his wife a Negro?" I asked.

13   "Are you crazy?" my wife said. "Have you just flipped or something?" She picked up a potato. I saw it hit the floor, then roll under the stove. "What's wrong with you?" she said. "Are you drunk?"

14   "I'm just asking," I said.

15   Right then my wife filled me in with more detail than I cared to know. I made a drink and sat at the kitchen table to listen. Pieces of the story began to fall into place.

16   Beulah had gone to work for the blind man the summer after my wife had stopped working for him. Pretty soon Beulah and the blind man had themselves a church wedding. It was a little wedding—who'd want to go to such a wedding in the first place?—just the two of them, plus the minister and the minister's wife. But

it was a church wedding just the same. It was what Beulah had wanted, he'd said. But even then Beulah must have been carrying the cancer in her glands. After they had been inseparable for eight years—my wife's word, *inseparable*—Beulah's health went into a rapid decline. She died in a Seattle hospital room, the blind man sitting beside the bed and holding on to her hand. They'd married, lived and worked together, slept together—had sex, sure—and then the blind man had to bury her. All this without his having ever seen what the goddamned woman looked like. It was beyond my understanding. Hearing this, I felt sorry for the blind man for a little bit. And then I found myself thinking what a pitiful life this woman must have led. Imagine a woman who could never see herself as she was seen in the eyes of her loved one. A woman who could go on day after day and never receive the smallest compliment from her beloved. A woman whose husband could never read the expression on her face, be it misery or something better. Someone who could wear makeup or not—what difference to him? She could, if she wanted, wear green eye-shadow around one eye, a straight pin in her nostril, yellow slacks and purple shoes, no matter. And then to slip off into death, the blind man's hand on her hand, his blind eyes streaming tears—I'm imagining now—her last thought maybe this: that he never even knew what she looked like, and she on an express to the grave. Robert was left with a small insurance policy and half of a twenty-peso Mexican coin. The other half of the coin went into the box with her. Pathetic.

17   So when the time rolled around, my wife went to the depot to pick him up. With nothing to do but wait—sure, I blamed him for that—I was having a drink and watching the TV when I heard the car pull into the drive. I got up from the sofa with my drink and went to the window to have a look.

18   I saw my wife laughing as she parked the car. I saw her get out of the car and shut the door. She was still wearing a smile. Just amazing. She went round to the other side of the car to where the blind man was already starting to get out. This blind man, feature this, he was wearing a full beard! A beard on a blind man! Too much, I say. The blind man reached into the back seat and dragged out a suitcase. My wife took his arm, shut the car door, and, talking all the way, moved him down the drive and then up the steps to the front porch. I turned off the TV. I finished my drink, rinsed the glass, dried my hands. Then I went to the door.

19   My wife said, "I want you to meet Robert. Robert, this is my husband. I've told you all about him." She was beaming. She had this blind man by his coat sleeve.

20   The blind man let go of his suitcase and up came his hand.

21   I took it. He squeezed hard, held my hand, and then he let it go.

22   "I feel like we've already met," he boomed.

23   "Likewise," I said. I didn't know what else to say. Then I said, "Welcome. I've heard a lot about you." We began to move then, a little group, from the porch into the living room, my wife guiding him by the arm. The blind man was carrying his suitcase in his other hand. My wife said things like, "To your left here, Robert. That's right. Now watch it, there's a chair. That's it. Sit down right here. This is the sofa. We just bought this sofa two weeks ago."

24   I started to say something about the old sofa. I'd liked that old sofa. But I didn't say anything. Then I wanted to say something else, small-talk, about the scenic ride along the Hudson. How going *to* New York, you should sit on the right-hand side of the train, and coming *from* New York, the left-hand side.

25   "Did you have a good train ride?" I said. "Which side of the train did you sit on, by the way?"

26   "What a question, which side!" my wife said. "What's it matter which side?" she said.

27   "I just asked," I said.

28   "Right side," the blind man said. "I hadn't been on a train in nearly forty years. Not since I was a kid. With my folks. That's been a long time. I'd nearly forgotten the sensation. I have winter in my beard now," he said. "So I've been told, anyway. Do I look distinguished, my dear?" the blind man said to my wife.

29   "You look distinguished, Robert," she said. "Robert," she said. "Robert, it's just so good to see you."

30   My wife finally took her eyes off the blind man and looked at me. I had the feeling she didn't like what she saw. I shrugged.

31   I've never met, or personally known, anyone who was blind. This blind man was late forties, a heavy-set, balding man with stooped shoulders, as if he carried great weight there. He wore brown slacks, brown shoes, a light-brown shirt, a tie, a sports coat. Spiffy. He also had this full beard. But he didn't use a cane and he didn't wear dark glasses. I'd always thought dark glasses were a must for the blind. Fact was, I wished he had a pair. At first glance, his eyes looked like anyone else's eyes. But if you looked close, there was something different about them. Too much white in the iris, for one thing, and the pupils seemed to move around in the sockets without his knowing it or being able to stop it. Creepy. As I stared at his face, I saw the left pupil turn in toward his nose while the other made an effort to keep in one place. But it was only an effort, for that eye was on the roam without his knowing it or wanting it to be.

32   I said, "Let me get you a drink. What's your pleasure? We have a little of everything. It's one of our pastimes."

33   "Bub, I'm a Scotch man myself," he said fast enough in this big voice.

34   "Right," I said. Bub! "Sure you are. I knew it."

35   He let his fingers touch his suitcase, which was sitting alongside the sofa. He was taking his bearings. I didn't blame him for that.

36   "I'll move that up to your room," my wife said.

37   "No, that's fine," the blind man said loudly. "It can go up when I go up."

38   "A little water with the Scotch?" I said.

39   "Very little," he said.

40   "I knew it," I said.

41   He said, "Just a tad. The Irish actor, Barry Fitzgerald? I'm like that fellow. When I drink water, Fitzgerald said, I drink water. When I drink whiskey, I drink whiskey." My wife laughed. The blind man brought his hand up under his beard. He lifted his beard slowly and let it drop.

42   I did the drinks, three big glasses of Scotch with a splash of water in each. Then we made ourselves comfortable and talked about Robert's travels. First the long flight from the West Coast to Connecticut, we covered that. Then from Connecticut up here by train. We had another drink concerning that leg of the trip.

43   I remembered having read somewhere that the blind didn't smoke because, as speculation had it, they couldn't see the smoke they exhaled. I thought I knew that much and that much only about blind people. But this blind man smoked his cigarette down to the nubbin and then lit another one. This blind man filled his ashtray and my wife emptied it.

44   When we sat down at the table for dinner, we had another drink. My wife heaped Robert's plate with cube steak, scalloped potatoes, green beans. I buttered him up two slices of bread. I said, "Here's bread and butter for you." I swallowed some of my drink. "Now let us pray," I said, and the blind man lowered his head. My wife looked at me, her mouth agape. "Pray the phone won't ring and the food doesn't get cold," I said.

45   We dug in. We ate everything there was to eat on the table. We ate like there was no tomorrow. We didn't talk. We ate. We scarfed. We grazed that table. We were into serious eating. The blind man had right away located his foods, he knew just where everything was on his plate. I watched with admiration as he used his knife and fork on the meat. He'd cut two pieces of meat, fork the meat into his mouth, and then go all out for the scalloped potatoes, the beans next, and then he'd tear off a hunk of buttered bread and eat that. He'd follow this up with a big drink of milk. It didn't seem to bother him to use his fingers once in a while, either.

46   We finished everything, including half a strawberry pie. For a few moments, we sat as if stunned. Sweat beaded on our faces. Finally, we got up from the table and left the dirty plates. We didn't look back. We took ourselves into the living room and sank into our places again. Robert and my wife sat on the sofa. I took the big chair. We had us two or three more drinks while they talked about the major things that had come to pass for them in the past ten years. For the most part, I just listened. Now and then I joined in. I didn't want him to think I'd left the room, and I didn't want her to think I was feeling left out. They talked of things that had happened to them—to them!—these past ten years. I waited in vain to hear my name on my wife's sweet lips: "And then my dear husband came into my life"—something like that. But I heard nothing of the sort. More talk of Robert. Robert had done a little of everything, it seemed, a regular blind jack-of-all-trades. But most recently he and his wife had had an Amway[1] distributorship, from which, I gathered, they'd earned their living, such as it was. The blind man was also a ham radio operator. He talked in his loud voice about conversations he'd had with fellow operators in Guam, in the Philippines, in Alaska, and even in Tahiti. He said he'd have a lot of friends there if he ever wanted to go visit those places. From time to time, he'd turn his blind face toward me, put his hand under his beard, ask me something. How long had I been in my present position? (Three years.) Did I like my work? (I didn't.) Was I going to stay with it? (What were the options?) Finally, when I thought he was beginning to run down, I got up and turned on the TV.

47   My wife looked at me with irritation. She was heading toward a boil. Then she looked at the blind man and said, "Robert, do you have a TV?"

48   The blind man said, "My dear, I have two TVs. I have a color set and a black-and-white thing, an old relic. It's funny, but if I turn the TV on, and I'm always turning it on, I turn on the color set. It's funny, don't you think?"

49   I didn't know what to say to that. I had absolutely nothing to say to that. No opinion. So I watched the news program and tried to listen to what the announcer was saying.

50   "This is a color TV," the blind man said. "Don't ask me how, but I can tell."

51   "We traded up a while ago," I said.

---

1 a marketing company using a pyramid of individual representatives to sell its products

52   The blind man had another taste of his drink. He lifted his beard, sniffed it, and let it fall. He leaned forward on the sofa. He positioned his ashtray on the coffee table, then put the lighter to his cigarette. He leaned back on the sofa and crossed his legs at the ankles.

53   My wife covered her mouth, and then she yawned. She stretched. She said, "I think I'll go upstairs and put on my robe. I think I'll change into something else. Robert, you make yourself comfortable," she said.

54   "I'm comfortable," the blind man said.

55   "I want you to feel comfortable in this house," she said.

56   "I am comfortable," the blind man said.

57   After she'd left the room, he and I listened to the weather report and then to the sports roundup. By that time, she'd been so long I didn't know if she was going to come back. I thought she might have gone to bed. I wished she'd come back downstairs. I didn't want to be left alone with a blind man. I asked him if he wanted another drink, and he said sure. Then I asked if he wanted to smoke some dope with me. I said I'd just rolled a number. I hadn't, but I planned to do so in about two shakes.

58   "I'll try some with you," he said.

59   "Damn right," I said. "That's the stuff."

60   I got our drinks and sat down on the sofa with him. Then I rolled us two fat numbers. I lit one and passed it. I brought it to his fingers. He took it and inhaled.

61   "Hold it as long as you can," I said. I could tell he didn't know the first thing.

62   My wife came back downstairs wearing her pink robe and her pink slippers.

63   "What do I smell?" she said.

64   "We thought we'd have us some cannabis," I said.

65   My wife gave me a savage look. Then she looked at the blind man and said, "Robert, I didn't know you smoked."

66   He said, "I do now, my dear. There's a first time for everything. But I don't feel anything yet."

67   "This stuff is pretty mellow," I said. "This stuff is mild. It's dope you can reason with," I said. "It doesn't mess you up."

68   "Not much it doesn't, bub," he said, and laughed.

69   My wife sat on the sofa between the blind man and me. I passed her the number. She took it and toked and then passed it back to me. "Which way is this going?" she said. Then she said, "I shouldn't be smoking this. I can hardly keep my eyes open as it is. That dinner did me in. I shouldn't have eaten so much."

70   "It was the strawberry pie," the blind man said. "That's what did it," he said, and he laughed his big laugh. Then he shook his head.

71   "There's more strawberry pie," I said.

72   "Do you want some more, Robert?" my wife said.

73   "Maybe in a little while," he said.

74   We gave our attention to the TV. My wife yawned again. She said, "Your bed is made up when you feel like going to bed, Robert. I know you must have had a long day. When you're ready to go to bed, say so." She pulled his arm. "Robert?"

75   He came to and said, "I've had a real nice time. This beats tapes, doesn't it?"

76   I said, "Coming at you," and I put the number between his fingers. He inhaled, held the smoke, and then let it go. It was like he'd been doing it since he was nine years old.

77   "Thanks, bub," he said. "But I think this is all for me. I think I'm beginning to feel it," he said. He held the burning roach out for my wife.

78   "Same here," she said. "Ditto. Me, too." She took the roach and passed it to me. "I may just sit here for a while between you two guys with my eyes closed. But don't let me bother you, okay? Either one of you. If it bothers you, say so. Otherwise, I may just sit here with my eyes closed until you're ready to go to bed," she said. "Your bed's made up, Robert, when you're ready. It's right next to our room at the top of the stairs. We'll show you up when you're ready. You wake me up now, you guys, if I fall asleep." She said that and then she closed her eyes and went to sleep.

79   The news program ended. I got up and changed the channel. I sat back down on the sofa. I wished my wife hadn't pooped out. Her head lay across the back of the sofa, her mouth open. She'd turned so that her robe had slipped away from her legs, exposing a juicy thigh. I reached to draw her robe back over her, and it was then that I glanced at the blind man. What the hell! I flipped the robe open again.

80   "You say when you want some strawberry pie," I said.

81   "I will," he said.

82   I said, "Are you tired? Do you want me to take you up to your bed? Are you ready to hit the hay?"

83   "Not yet," he said. "No, I'll stay up with you, bub. If that's all right. I'll stay up until you're ready to turn in. We haven't had a chance to talk. Know what I mean? I felt like me and her monopolized the evening." He lifted his beard and he let it fall. He picked up his cigarettes and his lighter.

84   "That's all right," I said. Then I said, "I'm glad for the company."

85   And I guess I was. Every night I smoked dope and stayed up as long as I could before I fell asleep. My wife and I hardly ever went to bed at the same time. When I did go to sleep, I had these dreams. Sometimes I'd wake up from one of them, my heart going crazy.

86   Something about the church and the Middle Ages was on the TV. Not your run-of-the-mill TV fare. I wanted to watch something else. I turned to the other channels. But there was nothing on them, either. So I turned back to the first channel and apologized.

87   "Bub, it's all right," the blind man said. "It's fine with me. Whatever you want to watch is okay. I'm always learning something. Learning never ends. It won't hurt me to learn something tonight. I got ears," he said.

88   We didn't say anything for a time. He was leaning forward with his head turned at me, his right ear aimed in the direction of the set. Very disconcerting. Now and then his eyelids drooped and then they snapped open again. Now and then he put his fingers into his beard and tugged, like he was thinking about something he was hearing on the television.

89   On the screen, a group of men wearing cowls was being set upon and tormented by men dressed in skeleton costumes and men dressed as devils. The men dressed as devils wore devil masks, horns, and long tails. This pageant was part of a procession. The Englishman who was narrating the thing said it took place in Spain once a year. I tried to explain to the blind man what was happening.

90   "Skeletons," he said. "I know about skeletons," he said, and he nodded.

91   The TV showed this one cathedral. Then there was a long, slow look at another one. Finally, the picture switched to the famous one in Paris, with its

flying buttresses and its spires reaching up to the clouds. The camera pulled away to show the whole of the cathedral rising above the skyline.

92   There were times when the Englishman who was telling the thing would shut up, would simply let the camera move around over the cathedrals. Or else the camera would tour the countryside, men in fields walking behind oxen. I waited as long as I could. Then I felt I had to say something. I said, "They're showing the outside of this cathedral now. Gargoyles. Little statues carved to look like monsters. Now I guess they're in Italy. Yeah, they're in Italy. There's paintings on the walls of this one church."

93   "Are those fresco paintings, bub?" he asked, and he sipped from his drink.

94   I reached for my glass. But it was empty. I tried to remember what I could remember. "You're asking me are those frescoes?" I said. "That's a good question. I don't know."

95   The camera moved to a cathedral outside Lisbon. The differences in the Portuguese cathedral compared with the French and Italian were not that great. But they were there. Mostly the interior stuff. Then something occurred to me, and I said, "Something has occurred to me. Do you have any idea what a cathedral is? What they look like, that is? Do you follow me? If somebody says cathedral to you, do you have any notion what they're talking about? Do you know the difference between that and a Baptist church, say?"

96   He let the smoke dribble from his mouth. "I know they took hundreds of workers fifty or a hundred years to build," he said. "I just heard the man say that, of course. I know generations of the same families worked on a cathedral. I heard him say that, too. The men who began their life's work on them, they never lived to see the completion of their work. In that wise, bub, they're no different from the rest of us, right?" He laughed. Then his eyelids drooped again. His head nodded. He seemed to be snoozing. Maybe he was imagining himself in Portugal. The TV was showing another cathedral now. This one was in Germany. The Englishman's voice droned on. "Cathedrals," the blind man said. He sat up and rolled his head back and forth. "If you want the truth, bub, that's about all I know. What I just said. What I heard him say. But maybe you could describe one to me? I wish you'd do it. I'd like that. If you want to know, I really don't have a good idea."

97   I stared hard at the shot of the cathedral on the TV. How could I even begin to describe it? But say my life depended on it. Say my life was being threatened by an insane guy who said I had to do it or else.

98   I stared some more at the cathedral before the picture flipped off into the countryside. There was no use. I turned to the blind man and said, "To begin with, they're very tall." I was looking around the room for clues. "They reach way up. Up and up. Toward the sky. They're so big, some of them, they have to have these supports. To help hold them up, so to speak. These supports are called buttresses. They remind me of viaducts, for some reason. But maybe you don't know viaducts, either? Sometimes the cathedrals have devils and such carved into the front. Sometimes lords and ladies. Don't ask me why this is," I said.

99   He was nodding. The whole upper part of his body seemed to be moving back and forth.

100   "I'm not doing so good, am I?" I said.

101   He stopped nodding and leaned forward on the edge of the sofa. As he listened to me, he was running his fingers through his beard. I wasn't getting

through to him, I could see that. But he waited for me to go on just the same. "They're really big," I said. "They're massive. They're built of stone. Marble, too, sometimes. In those olden days, when they built cathedrals, men wanted to be close to God. In those olden days, God was an important part of everyone's life. You could tell this from their cathedral-building. I'm sorry," I said, "but it looks like that's the best I can do for you. I'm just no good at it."

102   "That's all right, bub," the blind man said. "Hey, listen. I hope you don't mind my asking you: Can I ask you something? Let me ask you a simple question, yes or no. I'm just curious and there's no offense. You're my host. But let me ask if you are in any way religious? You don't mind my asking?"

103   I shook my head. He couldn't see that, though. A wink is the same as a nod to blind man. "I guess I don't believe in it. In anything. Sometimes it's hard. You know what I'm saying?"

104   "Sure, I do," he said.

105   "Right," I said.

106   The Englishman was still holding forth. My wife sighed in her sleep. She drew a long breath and went on with her sleeping.

107   "You'll have to forgive me," I said. "But I can't tell you what a cathedral looks like. It just isn't in me to do it. I can't do any more than I've done."

108   The blind man sat very still, his head down, as he listened to me.

109   I said, "The truth is, cathedrals don't mean anything special to me. Nothing. Cathedrals. They're something to look at on late-night TV. That's all they are."

110   It was then that the blind man cleared his throat. He brought something up. He took a handkerchief from his back pocket. Then he said, "I get it, bub. It's okay. It happens. Don't worry about it," he said. "Hey, listen to me. Will you do me a favor? I got an idea. Why don't you find us some heavy paper? And a pen. We'll do something. We'll draw one together. Get us a pen and some heavy paper. Go on, bub, get the stuff," he said.

111   So I went upstairs. My legs felt like they didn't have any strength in them. They felt like they did after I'd done some running. In my wife's room, I looked around. I found some ballpoints in a little basket on her table. And then I tried to think where to look for the kind of paper he was talking about.

112   Downstairs in the kitchen, I found a shopping bag with onion skins in the bottom of the bag. I emptied the bag and shook it. I brought it into the living room and sat down with it near his legs. I moved some things, smoothed the wrinkles from the bag, spread it out on the coffee table.

113   The blind man got down from the sofa and sat next to me on the carpet.

114   He ran his fingers over the paper. He went up and down the sides of the paper. The edges, even the edges. He fingered the corners.

115   "All right," he said. "All right, let's do her."

116   He found my hand, the hand with the pen. He closed his hand over my hand. "Go ahead, bub, draw," he said. "Draw. You'll see. I'll follow along with you. It'll be okay. Just begin now like I'm telling you. You'll see. Draw," the blind man said.

117   So I began. First I drew a box that looked like a house. It could have been the house I lived in. Then I put a roof on it. At either end of the roof, I drew spires. Crazy.

118   "Swell," he said. "Terrific. You're doing fine," he said. "Never thought anything like this could happen in your lifetime, did you, bub? Well, it's a strange life, we all know that. Go on now. Keep it up."

119   I put in windows with arches. I drew flying buttresses. I hung great doors. I couldn't stop. The TV station went off the air. I put down the pen and closed and opened my fingers. The blind man felt around over the paper. He moved the tips of his fingers over the paper, all over what I had drawn, and he nodded.

120   "Doing fine," the blind man said.

121   I took up the pen again, and he found my hand. I kept at it. I'm no artist. But I kept drawing just the same.

122   My wife opened up her eyes and gazed at us. She sat up on the sofa, her robe hanging open. She said, "What are you doing? Tell me, I want to know."

123   I didn't answer her.

124   The blind man said, "We're drawing a cathedral. Me and him are working on it. Press hard," he said to me. "That's right. That's good," he said. "Sure. You got it, bub. I can tell. You didn't think you could. But you can, can't you? You're cooking with gas now. You know what I'm saying? We're going to have us something here in a minute. How's the old arm?" he said. "Put some people in there now. What's a cathedral without people?"

125   My wife said, "What's going on? Robert, what are you doing? What's going on?"

126   "It's all right," he said to her. "Close your eyes now," the blind man said to me.

127   I did it. I closed them just like he said.

128   "Are they closed?" he said. "Don't fudge."

129   "They're closed," I said.

130   "Keep them that way," he said. He said, "Don't stop now. Draw."

131   So we kept on with it. His fingers rode my fingers as my hand went over the paper. It was like nothing else in my life up to now.

132   Then he said, "I think that's it. I think you got it," he said. "Take a look. What do you think?"

133   But I had my eyes closed. I thought I'd keep them that way for a little longer. I thought it was something I ought to do.

134   "Well?" he said. "Are you looking?"

135   My eyes were still closed. I was in my house. I knew that. But I didn't feel like I was inside anything.

136   "It's really something," I said.

Thomas King

U.S.A./Canada 1943–

Thomas King, who is of Cherokee and Greek-German descent, grew up in California and attended the University of Utah, earning a Ph.D. in history and literature. In 1980, he moved to Alberta to teach Native studies at the University of Lethbridge. Currently, he is a member of the English department at the University of Guelph. King's work has a particular focus on Aboriginal concerns. His fiction includes *Medicine River, Green Grass, Running Water,* and *Truth and Bright Water,* and a collection of short stories, *One Good Story, That One.* King's use of parody and the concept of the trickster to lampoon mainstream cultural views gives his work a critical tone that has a broad appeal.

The Garden Court Motor Motel   2001

1   SUNDAY. AND THE TRAIN IS LATE.

2   Sonny stands at the edge of the pool at the GARDEN COURT MOTOR MOTEL scooping bugs out of the water with the long-handled net and waits for the train to come chug-chug-chugging along. So he can hear Uncle HOLIE blow the train's horn. So he can wave to all the passengers on their way to the coast. Water in the pool is sure blue. Blue and cool. Maybe he'll take his shirt off. But he isn't going to get in. No, sir. No sky-blue water for him. Even if the clouds don't come and cool things off, he isn't fool enough for that.

3   He's the smart one.

4   There are three bugs on the net. Dead. All the bugs he pulls out of the pool are dead. When DAD was a boy, there were fish in the pool. That's what DAD says, and he knows everything.

5   Sonny knows everything, too. He knows all about sky-blue pool water and dead bugs. You can't swim in the pool. You can't swim in the pool unless you rent a room. Those are the rules, and ADAM and EVE and all their kids come by on vacation in a brand new Winnebago, pull up to the office and say, pretty please, aren't going to get in the water until there's up-front money and the key deposit. That's the way things are. Like it or hike it.

6   Sonny steps on a crack. Step on a crack, break your mother's back. Cracks in the concrete. Cracks in the white stucco. Cracks in the black asphalt. Cracks in the fifty-foot sign with the flashing neon-red ball that blinks "GARDEN COURT MOTOR MOTEL" and "Welcome." And it's new.

7   Cracks in the windows. Cracks in the walls. Cracks hiding at the bottom of the pool where Sonny can't get at them.

8   Don't worry about the cracks, DAD tells Sonny. After a while, you don't even notice them.

9   The GARDEN COURT MOTOR MOTEL. Parking for long-haul truckers. Pool. Ice-making machine. Laundromat. Vibrating beds.

10 One day all this will be his. That's what DAD says.

11 The GARDEN COURT MOTOR MOTEL. Twenty-four rooms. Cable television. Telephone. Air conditioning. Video rentals. Breakfast coupons for the Heavenly Pie Pizza Palace.

12 Sonny swings the net deep and catches some cloud-shade on his shoulder. Here they come, he thinks to himself, and he forgets the bugs and looks up into the sky. But it's not a cloud. There are no clouds. Not even on the edges of the world, which he can see clearly from pool side, is there even the mention of a cloud.

13 Now, what the DING-DONG is that, he says to the dead bugs in his net.

14 It's surely not a cloud. But now half of him is in the shade, and he's standing in shadows with his net and the dead bugs, watching the pool water turn black and deep.

15 Whatever it is, it's coming fast. And he starts thinking fast, too. A meteor would be okay. Or a flying saucer. Or a dark-green garbage bag.

16 One thing is for sure. It's not the train.

17   Okay. Okay. He looks up because he's run out of things, and he's sorry now he didn't finish high school.

18   "DING-DONG," he says, even though he knows DAD doesn't like that kind of language.

19   "DING-DONG," he says, because he's excited. Not in a naughty, excited way, but in that excited way he gets when he watches someone get whistled with a phaser on Star Trek.

20   "Clear the way!"

21   Doesn't sound like a meteor.

22   "Look out below!"

23   Doesn't sound like a green garbage bag.

24   "MOVE IT!"

25   And that's when Sonny thinks about running. Getting the DING-DONG out of there. And he knows now that this is the right answer, and that he would have thought of it all by himself if he had just had a little more time, but now it's too late, and he knows that whatever it is that is falling out of the sky and screaming at him is going to hit the motel or the parking lot or the pool or—DING-DONG, DING-DONG, DING-DONG—him.

26   Before he can finish netting all of the bugs.

27   The way DING-DONG hits the fan.

28   POOOWLAAASH!

29   The explosion whips the net out of Sonny's hands and knocks him off his feet, and, as he goes down in a wet, lumpy heap, he finally figures it out. The video camera was the right answer. He should have run and got the video camera.

30   DING-DONG!

31   Instead he didn't finish high school and that's sure as DING-DONG one of the reasons he's soaking wet, flat on his DING-DONG, watching the waves break over the side of the pool. His ears are ringing, but when he opens his eyes he discovers that he can see fine, and what he sees when he looks is something floating to the surface of the water.

32   It's too big to be a bug.

33   "Hello," says the woman. "Hello," she says again.

34   All Sonny can see is the woman's head, but what he sees is disturbing. RED SKIN and BLACK HAIR. Okay, okay, okay. Sonny has to think. BLACK PEOPLE have BLACK SKIN and BLACK HAIR. And ASIAN PEOPLE have YELLOW SKIN and BLACK HAIR.

35   This is hard.

36   And HISPANIC PEOPLE have BROWN SKIN and BLACK HAIR. So the WOMAN WHO FELL FROM THE SKY must be … must be …

37   Sonny takes out his *Illustrated Field Guide for Exotic Cultures*, skips past Leviticus, and goes straight to the section with the pictures. Sonny thinks about asking the woman. Asking in a friendly manner. But he remembers that asking is against the law, and that if the WOMAN WHO FELL FROM THE SKY has the money or a valid credit card, he is legally required to rent her a room. Unless the GARDEN COURT MOTOR MOTEL is all booked up, which it always is when people from Exotic Cultures arrive at the front desk.

38   But he can guess. Guessing isn't illegal. And after looking at all the pictures, some of which are pretty graphic and revealing, he guesses that the woman in the pool is an INDIAN.

39   "You have to be a guest to swim in the pool," says Sonny.

40   "What happened to all the water?" says the woman.

41   "That's the rule." And now Sonny's feeling better. Now he's feeling in charge, again.

42   "Last time I was here;" says the WOMAN WHO FELL FROM THE SKY, "everything was water."

43   A meteor would have been simpler. Not the one that killed the dinosaurs. Something smaller. Dig it out, fill in the hole, patch the cracks, and get on with renting rooms to long-haul truckers bound for the coast. Too DING-DONG bad. Could have sold a meteor.

44   "What happened to the turtle?"

45   "We're all booked up," says Sonny.

46   "Why does the water smell funny?" The WOMAN WHO FELL FROM THE SKY gets out of the pool, and Sonny can see that his Exotic Culture tribulations are not over yet.

47   But Sonny has it figured out, now. The WOMAN WHO FELL FROM THE SKY fell out of a plane. You read about such things every day. She fell out of a plane. And the wind tore her clothes off.

48   That's why she's NAKED.

49   "DING-DONG," says Sonny, because he's excited and appalled at the same time.

50   "DING-DONG," he says again, because he didn't finish high school and can't think of anything else to say.

51   But most of all, Sonny says "DING-DONG" twice because the WOMAN WHO FELL FROM THE SKY has really big YOU-KNOW-WHATS and she's really hairy YOU-KNOW-WHERE.

52   And because she's PREGNANT.

53   Sonny looks up in the sky. But he doesn't see any sign of her INDIAN husband on the way down. Maybe he wasn't on the plane. Maybe he's driving out to meet her. Maybe he's on horseback. Maybe he's chasing buffalo. Maybe he's annoying a settler. Sonny knows what INDIANS do when no one is looking.

54   "You can't wait here," says Sonny. "You'll have to wait for him at the Heavenly Pie Pizza Palace."

55   "Who?"

56   "Your husband."

57   "What husband?"

58   DING-DONG, thinks Sonny. He was afraid of that. How many times has DAD warned him about something like this? As if there weren't enough women in the world already. As if we needed another one. And an INDIAN at that. And PREGNANT at that. Well, she can't go to the Heavenly Pie Pizza Palace. Now that Sonny thinks about it, he remembers that people eat there. People bring their families there.

59   "We're all booked up."

60   "There's supposed to be a turtle," says the WOMAN WHO FELL FROM HE SKY, and she crosses her arms on top of her tummy and underneath her YOU-KNOW-WHATS, so the water drips off THOSE OTHER THINGS.

61   "Where are all the water animals?"

62   Turtles? Water animals? Sonny doesn't like the sound of this.

63   "Who's going to dive in the water and bring up the dirt?"

64   All right! That does it. Sonny drops the pole by the side of the pool so it makes a CLANG-CLANG sound and gets the woman's attention.

65   "Dirt?" says Sonny. "Do you see any dirt at the bottom of my pool?"

66   The WOMAN WHO FELL FROM THE SKY walks to the edge of the pool and stares into the sky-blue water. And she looks at the GARDEN COURT MOTOR MOTEL. She doesn't look too happy now. She doesn't look too smug, either. Now she knows who's in charge.

67   "Not again," says the WOMAN WHO FELL FROM THE SKY

68   "As for any animals," says Sonny. "There's a pet-damage deposit of twenty-five dollars, cash or credit card," though Sonny doesn't know why he says this, since he can see that the WOMAN WHO FELL FROM THE SKY doesn't have any animals with her nor does she have any pockets in which to keep a credit card or enough money for a pet deposit, let alone a room.

69   It's a good thing Sonny's already made the beds and vacuumed the office and checked the licenses on the cars in the parking lot against the registration forms. It's a good thing he's collected the money from the vending machines and the washing machine and the dryer. It's a good thing he has nothing better to do than to stand by the pool and chat with an INDIAN who is NAKED and PREGNANT. It's a good thing DAD is having a nap. It's a good thing there's nothing on television.

70   "Why do you guys keep messing things up?" says the WOMAN WHO FELL FROM THE SKY. "Why can't you guys ever get things right?"

71   Sonny isn't sure the WOMAN WHO FELL FROM THE SKY knows the difference between right and not right. For instance, being NAKED is certainly not right. Being PREGNANT without a husband is definitely not right.

72   And being an INDIAN ... well Sonny isn't positive that being an INDIAN is not right, but ...

73   "Looks like we're going to have to fix it again," says the WOMAN WHO FELL FROM THE SKY.

74   We? What do you mean "we," Kemo Sabe? DAD taught him that one. No way, Jose. Sonny knows them all. Get a life. Hasta la vista, baby. Take a hike.

75   "Before it's too late."

76   Sonny knows better than to fall for that one. Only thing late around here is the train.

77   "Okay," says the WOMAN WHO FELL FROM THE SKY. "Pay attention. Here's how it's supposed to work. I fall out of the sky into the water and am rescued by a turtle. Four water animals dive to the bottom of the water and one of them brings up a bunch of dirt. I put the dirt on the back of the turtle and the dirt expands until it forms the earth. Are you with me so far?"

78   DAD says that people who sound as if they know what they're talking about are generally trying to sell you something.

79   "Then I give birth to twins, a right-handed twin and a left-handed twin. They roam the world and give it its physical features. Between the two of them, they help to create a world that is balanced and in harmony."

80   Encyclopedias. Sonny is pretty sure that the WOMAN WHO FELL FROM THE SKY is selling encyclopedias.

81   "But if I can't find the turtle, I can't fix the world."

82   The train doesn't pull onto the siding next to the Garden Court Motor Motel until evening.

83   "Three guys in a Chevrolet stalled on a level-crossing," Uncle HOLIE tells Sonny. "Drunk as skunks. Where's your DAD?"

84   "Sunday," says Sonny. "He's resting."

85   Uncle HOLIE and Sonny find the WOMAN WHO FELL FROM THE SKY a nice window seat.

86   "As soon as I find that turtle," says the WOMAN WHO FELL FROM THE SKY, "I'll be back."

87   Uncle HOLIE and Sonny stand by the side of the train and watch the sun set. "Don't worry," Uncle HOLIE tells Sonny, as he signals the engineer and steps onto the caboose. "It's what DAD would do. And there hasn't been a turtle on the coast for years."

88   Sonny watches the train chug-chug-chug off into the night, the lights of the caboose swaying back and forth in the dusk. Then he walks back to the GARDEN COURT MOTOR MOTEL. With its twenty-four air-conditioned rooms. Cable television. Ice machine. Vibrating beds. Breakfast coupons for the Heavenly Pie Pizza Palace.

89   Sonny gets a soft drink from the vending machine and stretches out on one of the aqua-green, plastic chaise lounges by the pool and closes his eyes. Fix the world? Just as well the WOMAN WHO FELL FROM THE SKY couldn't find a turtle, he thinks to himself. Just as well she didn't have a credit card.

90   The white stucco of the motel plumps up pink and then blue as evening spreads out across the land, and the big neon ball that says "GARDEN COURT MOTOR MOTEL" and "Welcome" twinkles like a star in the western sky.

Richard Ford

U.S.A. 1944–

Born in Jackson, Mississippi and raised in Mississippi and Arkansas, Richard Ford was educated at Michigan State University and the University of California at Irvine. Ford is wary of being labelled a "southern writer" and, indeed, an examination of his work shows that it is not dependent upon one specific locale or region. Instead, it is more profitable to examine the complexities of relationships, communication, and self-realization in Ford's work. Ford's fifth novel and sixth book, *Independence Day* (1996) was the first book to win both the Pulitzer Prize and the PEN/Faulkner Award for fiction. His story "Privacy" comes from his 2001 collection, *A Multitude of Sins*, which Ford describes as a series of stories about "the ways that people delude and fail each other."

Privacy   2001

1   This was at a time when my marriage was still happy.

2   We were living in a large city in the northeast. It was winter. February. The coldest month. I was, of course, still trying to write, and my wife was working as a translator for a small publishing company that specialized in Czech scientific papers. We had been married for ten years and were still enjoying that strange, exhilarating illusion that we had survived the worst of life's hardships.

3   The apartment we rented was in the old factory section on the south end of the city, the living space only a great, empty room with tall windows front and back, and almost no electric light. The natural light was all. A famous avant-garde theater director had lived in the room before and put on his jagged, nihilistic plays there, so that all the walls were painted black, and along one were still riser seats for his small disaffected audiences. Our bed—my wife's and mine—was in one dark corner where we'd arranged some of the tall, black canvas scenery drops for our privacy. Though, of course, there was no one for us to need privacy from.

4   Each night when my wife came back from her work, we would go out into the cold, shining streets and find a restaurant to have our meal in. Later we would stop for an hour in a bar and have coffee or a brandy, and talk intensely about the translations my wife was working on, though never (blessedly) about the work I was by then already failing at.

5   Our wish, needless to say, was to stay out of the apartment as long as we could. For not only was there almost no light inside, but each night at seven the building's owner would turn off the heat, so that by ten—on our floor, the highest—it was too cold to be anywhere but in bed piled over with blankets, barely able to move. My wife, at that time, was working long hours and was always fatigued, and although sometimes we would come home a little drunk and make love in the dark bed under blankets, mostly she would fall straight into bed exhausted and be snoring before I could climb in beside her.

6   And so it happened that on many nights that winter, in the cold, large, nearly empty room, I would be awake, often wide awake from the strong coffee we'd drunk. And often I would walk the floor from window to window, looking out into the night, down to the vacant street or up into the ghostly sky that burned with the shimmery luminance of the city's buildings, buildings I couldn't even see. Often I had a blanket or sometimes two around my shoulders, and I wore the coarse heavy socks I'd kept from when I was a boy.

7   It was on such a cold night that—through the windows at the back of the flat, windows giving first onto an alley below, then farther across a space where a wire factory had been demolished, providing a view of buildings on the street parallel to ours—I saw, inside a long, yellow-lit apartment, the figure of a woman slowly undressing, from all appearances oblivious to the world outside the window glass.

8   Because of the distance, I could not see her well or at all clearly, could only see that she was small in stature and seemingly thin, with close-cropped dark hair—a petite woman in every sense. The yellow light in the room where she was seemed to blaze and made her skin bronze and shiny, and her movements, seen through the windows, appeared stylized and slightly unreal, like the movements of a silhouette or in an old motion picture.

9   I, though, alone in the frigid dark, wrapped in blankets that covered my head like a shawl, with my wife sleeping, oblivious, a few paces away—I was rapt by this sight. At first I moved close to the window glass, close enough to feel the cold on my cheeks. But then, sensing I might be noticed even at that distance, I slipped back into the room. Eventually I went to the corner and clicked off the small lamp my wife kept beside our bed, so that I was totally hidden in the dark. And after another few minutes I went to a drawer and found the pair of silver opera glasses which the theater director had left, and took them near the window and watched the woman across the space of darkness from my own space of darkness.

10   I don't know all that I thought. Undoubtedly I was aroused. Undoubtedly I was thrilled by the secrecy of watching out of the dark. Undoubtedly I loved the very illicitness of it, of my wife sleeping nearby and knowing nothing of what I was doing. It is also possible I even liked the cold as it surrounded me, as complete as the night itself, may even have felt that the sight of the woman—whom I took to be young and lacking caution or discretion—held me somehow, insulated me and made the world stop and be perfectly expressible as two poles connected by my line of vision. I am sure now that all of this had to do with my impending failures.

11   Nothing more happened. Though, in the nights to come I stayed awake to watch the woman, letting my wife go off to sleep in her fatigue. Each night, and for a week following, the woman would appear at her window and slowly disrobe in her room (a room I never tried to imagine, although on the wall behind her was what looked like a drawing of a springing deer). Once her clothes were shed away, exposing her bony shoulders and small breasts and thin legs and rib cage and modest, rounded stomach, the woman would for a while cast about the room in the bronze light, window to window, enacting what seemed to me a kind of languid, ritual dance or a pattern of possibly theatrical movements, rising and bowing and extending her arms, arching her neck, while making her hands perform graceful lilting gestures I didn't understand and did not try to, taken as I was by her nakedness and by the sight on occasion of the dark swatch of hair between her legs. It was all arousal and secrecy and illicitness and really nothing else.

12   This I did for a week, as I said, and then I stopped. Simply one night, draped again in blankets, I went to the window with my opera glasses, saw the lights on across the vacant space. For a while I saw no one. And then for no particular reason I turned and got into bed with my wife, warm and smelling of brandy and sweat and sleep under her blankets, and went to sleep myself, never thinking to look through the window again.

13   Though one afternoon a week after I had stopped watching through the window, I left my desk in a moment of frustration and pointless despair, and stalked out into the winter daylight and up along the row of fashionable businesses where the old buildings were being restyled as dress shops and successful artists' galleries. I walked right to the river, clogged then with great squares of gray ice. I walked on to the university section, nearly to where my wife was at that hour working. And then, as the light was failing, I started back toward my street, my face hard with cold, my shoulders stiff, my gloveless hands frozen and red. As I turned a corner to take a quicker route back to my block, I found that I was unexpectedly passing before the building into which I had for days been spying. Something about it made me know it, though I'd never been aware of walking past there

before, or even seen it in daylight. And just at that moment, letting herself into the building's tall front door, was the woman I had watched for those several nights and taken pleasure and undoubtedly secret consolation from. I knew her face, naturally—small and round and, as I saw, impassive. And to my surprise though not to my chagrin, she was old. Possibly she was seventy or even older. A Chinese, dressed in thin black trousers and a thin black coat, inside which she must've been as cold as I was. Indeed, she must've been freezing. She was carrying plastic bags of groceries slung to her arms and clutched in her hands. When I stopped and looked at her she turned and gazed down the steps at me with an expression I can only think now was indifference mingled with just the smallest recognition of threat. She was old, after all. I might suddenly have felt the urge to harm her, and easily could've. But of course that was not my thought. She turned back to the door and seemed to hurry her key into the lock. She looked my way once more, as I heard the bolt shoot profoundly back. I said nothing, did not even look at her again. I didn't want her to think my mind contained what it did and also what it did not. And I walked on then, feeling oddly but in no way surprisingly betrayed, simply passed on down the street toward my room and my own doors, my life entering, as it was at that moment, its first, long cycle of necessity.

Salman Rushdie

India/England/U.S.A. 1947–

Salman Rushdie was born into a wealthy Muslim family in Bombay, India, but was educated at Rugby and Cambridge, where he received an M.A. in history. After briefly returning to the east to live with his family in Karachi, Rushdie returned to England and worked as an advertising copywriter until his second book, *Midnight's Children*, won him the Booker prize in 1981. Rushdie is most famous for *The Satanic Verses*, which caused the Ayatollah Khomeini of Iran to offer a one million dollar reward to anyone who killed Rushdie for what Khomeini felt was an attack on Islam. In 1998, the reward was increased to 2.8 million dollars. In 2000, Rushdie moved from England to New York. Rushdie's work is often a blend of eastern and western influences and shows the influences of both Indian and western popular cultures. However, neither culture escapes his wit. The story "Good Advice is Rarer Than Rubies," from his 1994 collection *East-West*, points out that what people value is often skewed by their faulty perception.

Good Advice is Rarer Than Rubies   1994

1   On the last Tuesday of the month, the dawn bus, its headlamps still shining, brought Miss Rehana to the gates of the British Consulate. It arrived pushing a cloud of dust, veiling her beauty from the eyes of strangers until she descended.

The bus was brightly painted in multicoloured arabesques; and on the front it said 'MOVE OVER DARLING' in green and gold letters; on the back it added 'TATA-BATA' and also 'O.K. GOOD-LIFE'. Miss Rehana told the driver it was a beautiful bus, and he jumped down and held the door open for her, bowing theatrically as she descended.

2   Miss Rehana's eyes were large and black and bright enough not to need the help of antimony, and when the advice expert Muhammad Ali saw them he felt himself becoming young again. He watched her approaching the Consulate gates as the light strengthened, and asking the bearded lala who guarded them in a gold-buttoned khaki uniform with a cockaded turban when they would open. The lala, usually so rude to the Consulate's Tuesday women, answered Miss Rehana with something like courtesy.

3   'Half an hour,' he said gruffly. 'Maybe two hours. Who knows? The sahibs are eating their breakfast.'

4   The dusty compound between the bus stop and the Consulate was already full of Tuesday women, some veiled, a few barefaced like Miss Rehana. They all looked frightened, and leaned heavily on the arms of uncles or brothers, who were trying to look confident. But Miss Rehana had come on her own, and did not seem at all alarmed.

5   Muhammad Ali, who specialised in advising the most vulnerable-looking of these weekly supplicants, found his feet leading him towards the strange, big-eyed, independent girl.

6   'Miss,' he began. 'You have come for permit to London, I think so?'

7   She was standing at a hot-snack stall in the little shanty-town by the edge of the compound, munching chilli-pakoras contentedly. She turned to look at him, and at close range those eyes did bad things to his digestive tract.

8   'Yes, I have.'

9   'Then, please, you allow me to give some advice? Small cost only.'

10   Miss Rehana smiled. 'Good advice is rarer than rubies,' she said. 'But, alas, I cannot pay. I am an orphan, not one of your wealthy ladies.'

11   'Trust my grey hairs,' Muhammad Ali urged her. 'My advice is well tempered by experience. You will certainly find it good.'

12   She shook her head. 'I tell you I am a poor potato. There are women here with male family members, all earning good wages. Go to them. Good advice should find good money.'

13   *I am going crazy*, Muhammad Ali thought, because he heard his voice telling her of its own volition, 'Miss, I have been drawn to you by Fate. What to do? Our meeting was written. I also am a poor man only, but for you my advice comes free.'

14   She smiled again. 'Then I must surely listen. When Fate sends a gift, one receives good fortune.'

15   He led her to the low wooden desk in his own special corner of the shanty-town. She followed, continuing to eat pakoras from a little newspaper packet. She did not offer him any.

16   Muhammad Ali put a cushion on the dusty ground. 'Please to sit.' She did as he asked. He sat cross-legged across the desk from her, conscious that two or

three dozen pairs of male eyes were watching him enviously, that all the other shanty-town men were ogling the latest young lovely to be charmed by the old grey-hair fraud. He took a deep breath to settle himself.

17   'Name, please.'

18   'Miss Rehana,' she told him. 'Fiancee of Mustafa Dar of Bradford, London.'

19   'Bradford, England,' he corrected her gently. 'London is a town only, like Multan or Bahawalpur. England is a great nation full of the coldest fish in the world.'

20   'I see. Thank you,' she responded gravely, so that he was unsure if she was making fun of him.

21   'You have filled application form? Then let me see, please.'

22   She passed him a neatly folded document in a brown envelope.

23   'Is it OK?' For the first time there was a note of anxiety in her voice.

24   He patted the desk quite near the place where her hand rested. 'I am certain,' he said. 'Wait on and I will check.'

25   She finished the pakoras while he scanned her papers.

26   'Tip-top,' he pronounced at length. 'All in order.'

27   'Thank you for your advice,' she said, making as if to rise. 'I'll go now and wait by the gate.'

28   'What are you thinking?' he cried loudly, smiting his forehead. 'You consider this is easy business? Just give the form and poof, with a big smile they hand over the permit? Miss Rehana, I tell you, you are entering a worse place than any police station.'

29   'Is it so, truly?' His oratory had done the trick. She was a captive audience now, and he would be able to look at her for a few moments longer.

30   Drawing another calming breath, he launched into his set speech. He told her that the sahibs thought that all the women who came on Tuesdays, claiming to be dependents of bus drivers in Luton or chartered accountants in Manchester, were crooks and liars and cheats.

31   She protested, 'But then I will simply tell them that I, for one, am no such thing!'

32   Her innocence made him shiver with fear for her. She was a sparrow, he told her, and they were men with hooded eyes, like hawks. He explained that they would ask her questions, personal questions, questions such as a lady's own brother would be too shy to ask. They would ask if she was virgin, and, if not, what her fiancé's love-making habits were, and what secret nicknames they had invented for one another.

33   Muhammad Ali spoke brutally, on purpose, to lessen the shock she would feel when it, or something like it, actually happened. Her eyes remained steady, but her hands began to flutter at the edges of the desk.

34   He went on:

35   'They will ask you how many rooms are in your family home, and what colour are the walls, and what days do you empty the rubbish. They will ask your man's mother's third cousin's aunt's step-daughter's middle name. And all these things they have already asked your Mustafa Dar in his Bradford. And if you make one mistake, you are finished.'

36   'Yes,' she said, and he could hear her disciplining her voice. 'And what is your advice, old man?'

37   It was at this point that Muhammad Ali usually began to whisper urgently, to mention that he knew a man, a very good type, who worked in the Consulate, and through him, for a fee, the necessary papers could be delivered, with all the proper authenticating seals. Business was good, because the women would often pay him five hundred rupees or give him a gold bracelet for his pains, and go away happy.

38   They came from hundreds of miles away—he normally made sure of this before beginning to trick them—so even when they discovered they had been swindled they were unlikely to return. They went away to Sargodha or Lalukhet and began to pack, and who knows at what point they found out they had been gulled, but it was at a too-late point, anyway.

39   Life is hard, and an old man must live by his wits. It was not up to Muhammad Ali to have compassion for these Tuesday women.

40   But once again his voice betrayed him, and instead of starting his customary speech it began to reveal to her his greatest secret.

41   'Miss Rehana,' his voice said, and he listened to it in amazement, 'you are a rare person, a jewel, and for you I will do what I would not do for my own daughter, perhaps. One document has come into my possession that can solve all your worries at one stroke.'

42   'And what is this sorcerer's paper?' she asked, her eyes unquestionably laughing at him now.

43   His voice fell low-as-low.

44   'Miss Rehana, it is a British passport. Completely genuine and pukka goods. I have a good friend who will put your name and photo, and then, hey-presto, England there you come!'

45   He had said it!

46   Anything was possible now, on this day of his insanity. Probably he would give her the thing free-gratis, and then kick himself for a year afterwards.

47   *Old fool*, he berated himself. *The oldest fools are bewitched by the youngest girls.*

48   'Let me understand you,' she was saying. 'You are proposing I should commit a crime ...'

49   'Not crime,' he interposed. 'Facilitation.'

50   ' ... and go to Bradford, London, illegally, and therefore justify the low opinion the Consulate sahibs have of us all. Old babuji, this is not good advice.'

51   'Bradford, England,' he corrected her mournfully. 'You should not take my gift in such a spirit.'

52   'Then how?'

53   'Bibi, I am a poor fellow, and I have offered this prize because you are so beautiful. Do not spit on my generosity. Take the thing. Or else don't take, go home, forget England, only do not go into that building and lose your dignity.'

54   But she was on her feet, turning away from him, walking towards the gates, where the women had begun to cluster and the lala was swearing at them to be patient or none of them would be admitted at all.

55   'So be a fool,' Muhammad Ali shouted after her. 'What goes of my father's if you are?' (Meaning, what was it to him.)

56   She did not turn.

57   'It is the curse of our people,' he yelled. 'We are poor, we are ignorant, and we completely refuse to learn.'

58   'Hey, Muhammad Ali,' the woman at the betel-nut stall called across to him. 'Too bad, she likes them young.'

59   That day Muhammad Ali did nothing but stand around near the Consulate gates. Many times he scolded himself, *Go from here, old goof, lady does not desire to speak with you any further.* But when she came out, she found him waiting.

60   'Salaam, advice wallah,' she greeted him.

61   She seemed calm, and at peace with him again, and he thought, *My God, ya Allah, she has pulled it off. The British sahibs also have been drowning in her eyes and she has got her passage to England.*

62   He smiled at her hopefully. She smiled back with no trouble at all.

63   'Miss Rehana Begum,' he said, 'felicitations, daughter, on what is obviously your hour of triumph.'

64   Impulsively, she took his forearm in her hand.

65   'Come,' she said. 'Let me buy you a pakora to thank you for your advice and to apologise for my rudeness, too.'

66   They stood in the dust of the afternoon compound near the bus, which was getting ready to leave. Coolies were tying bedding rolls to the roof. A hawker shouted at the passengers, trying to sell them love stories and green medicines, both of which cured unhappiness. Miss Rehana and a happy Muhammad Ali ate their pakoras sitting on the bus's 'front mud-guard', that is, the bumper. The old advice expert began softly to hum a tune from a movie soundtrack. The day's heat was gone.

67   'It was an arranged engagement,' Miss Rehana said all at once. 'I was nine years old when my parents fixed it. Mustafa Dar was already thirty at that time, but my father wanted someone who could look after me as he had done himself and Mustafa was a man known to Daddyji as a solid type. Then my parents died and Mustafa Dar went to England and said he would send for me. That was many years ago. I have his photo, but he is like a stranger to me. Even his voice, I do not recognise it on the phone.'

68   The confession took Muhammad Ali by surprise, but he nodded with what he hoped looked like wisdom.

69   'Still and after all,' he said, 'one's parents act in one's best interests. They found you a good and honest man who has kept his word and sent for you. And now you have a lifetime to get to know him, and to love.'

70   He was puzzled, now, by the bitterness that had infected her smile.

71   'But, old man,' she asked him, 'why have you already packed me and posted me off to England?'

72   He stood up, shocked.

73   'You looked happy—so I just assumed . . . excuse me, but they turned you down or what?'

74   'I got all their questions wrong,' she replied. 'Distinguishing marks I put on the wrong cheeks, bathroom decor I completely redecorated, all absolutely topsy-turvy, you see.'

75   'But what to do? How will you go?'

76   'Now I will go back to Lahore and my job. I work in a great house, as ayah to three good boys. They would have been sad to see me leave.'

77   'But this is tragedy!' Muhammad Ali lamented. 'Oh, how I pray that you had taken up my offer! Now, but, it is not possible, I regret to inform. Now they have your form on file, cross-check can be made, even the passport will not suffice.

78   'It is spoilt, all spoilt, and it could have been so easy if advice had been accepted in good time.'

79   'I do not think,' she told him, 'I truly do not think you should be sad.'

80   Her last smile, which he watched from the compound until the bus concealed it in a dust-cloud, was the happiest thing he had ever seen in his long, hot, hard, unloving life.

Lisa Moore

Canada 1964–

Lisa Moore, who lives in St. John's, Newfoundland, was educated at the Nova Scotia College of Arts and Design. "Melody" is from her latest collection of stories, *Open*, which was shortlisted for the Giller Prize for literature in 2002. *Open* follows an earlier collection of stories, *Degrees of Nakedness* (1995), in investigating the complexities of human behaviour and human relationships. "Melody," which contains a set of cryptic insights into women's lives, illustrates Moore's gift for ironic employment of a naïve narrator.

Melody   2002

1.

1   Melody lets the first half dozen cars go by; she says she has a bad feeling about them.

2   The trip will take as long as it takes, she says. There are no more cars for an hour. She pulls her cigarettes out of her jean jacket and some matches from the El Dorado. We had been dancing there last night until the owner snapped on the lights. The band immediately aged; they could have been our parents. They wore acid-washed jeans and T-shirts that said ARMS ARE FOR HUGGING, VIVA LA SANDINISTA, and FEMINIST? YOU BET!!!

3   Outside the El Dorado two mangy Camaros, souped up for the weekend Smash Up Derby, revved their engines and tore out of the parking lot. I watched their tail lights swerve and bounce in the dark. They dragged near the mall and sparks lit the snagged fenders. A soprano yelp of rubber and then near silence. I could smell the ocean far beyond the army barracks. The revolving Kentucky Fried Chicken bucket still glowing in the pre-dawn light. Waves shushing the pebble beach; Brian Fiander falling in beside me. He had been downing B52s. He

was lanky and discombobulated until his big hand clasped my shoulder and his too long limbs snapped into place like the poles of a pup tent.

૭

4   The clock radio in my dorm room came on in the early afternoon and I listened to the announcer slogging through the temperatures across the island. Twenty-nine degrees. Mortification and the peppery sting of a fresh crush. I'd let Brian Fiander hold my wrists over my head against the brick wall of the dorm while he kissed me; his hips thrusting with a lost, intent zeal, the dawn sky as pale and grainy as sugar. Brian Fiander knew what he was doing. The recognition of his expertise made my body ting and smoulder. My waking thought: I have been celebrated.

5   I felt logy and grateful. Also sophisticated. I'd had an orgasm, though I didn't know it at the time. I didn't know *that's* what that was. I could count on one hand the number of times I'd said the word out loud, though I'd read about it. I believed myself to be knowledgeable on the subject. I'd closed my eyes while Brian touched me and what I'd felt was like falling asleep, except in the opposite direction and at alarming speed: falling awake. Wildly alert. Falling into myself.

6   I made my way down the corridor to the showers, the stink of warming Spaghetti-Os wafting from the kitchenette. Wavy Fagan passed me in her cotton candy slippers and she smirked. I had a crowbar grin; his hand on my breast, slow, sly circles. Wavy smirked and I knew: *Oh that's what that was.*

7   The showers were full of fruity mist. Brenda Parsons brushing her teeth. Her glasses steamed. She turned toward me blindly, mouth foaming toothpaste. She had been going out with Brian Fiander.

૭

8   We can see anything that's coming long before it arrives, and nothing's coming. The highway rolls in the sulky haze of mid-afternoon and Melody and I are eternally stuck to the side of it. The night before comes back in flickers. A glass smashing, swimming spotlights, red, blue. Hands, buttons. The truck, when it appears, is a lisping streak, there and not there as it dips into the valleys. A black truck parting the quivering heat. A star of sunlight reaming the windshield.

9   I say, Do I stick my thumb out or what?

10   I'll do the thinking, says Melody. She ties the jean jacket around her waist in a vicious knot. We don't hitch but the truck pulls over. I run down the highway and open the door. Melody stays where she is, she just stands, smoking.

11   My friend is coming, I say. I climb up onto the bouncy seat. The guy is a hunk. A happy face on his sweatshirt. Smokey sunglasses. Brian Fiander barely crosses my mind. Brian is too willing and skinny; he's unworthy of me.

12   This guy tilts the rearview mirror and puts his hand over the stick shift, which vibrates like the pointer of a Ouija board. He has a wedding ring but he can't be more than twenty. A plain gold band. The fine hair on his fingers is blonde and curls over the ring, catching the light, and I almost lean toward him so he will touch my cheek with the back of his hand.

13   I've had too much sun, may still be drunk from the night before. Is that possible? I experience a glimmer of clairvoyance as convincing as the smell of

exhaust. I close my eyes and the shape of the windshield floats on my eyelids, bright violet with a chartreuse trim. I know in an instant and without doubt that I will marry, never be good with plants, suffer incalculable loss that almost, almost tips me over, but I will right myself, I will forget Melody completely but she will show up and something about her as she is now—her straight defiant back in the rearview mirror—will be exactly the same. She'll give me a talisman and disappear as unexpectedly as she came.

14   Melody is still standing with her cigarette, holding one elbow. She's looking down the road, her back to us, the wind blowing a zigzag part in her hair. A faint patch of sweat on her pink shirt like a Rorschach test between her shoulder blades.

15   She finally drops the cigarette and crushes it with her sneaker. She walks toward the truck with her head bent down, climbs up beside me, and pulls the door shut. She doesn't even glance at the driver.

16   Skoochie over, she says. My arm touches the guy's bare arm and I feel the heat of his sunburn, a gliding muscle as he puts the truck in gear.

17   We all set, the guy asks.

18   We're ready, I say. There's a pine-tree air freshener, a pouch of tobacco on the dash, an apple slice to keep it fresh, smells as pristine as the South Pole. It's going to rain. Melody changes the radio station, hitting knots of static. The sky goes dark, darker, darker, and the first rumble is followed by a solid, thrilling crack. A blur of light low and pulsing. The rain tears into the pavement like a racing pack of whippets. Claws scrabbling over the top of the cab. Livid grey muscles of rain.

&

19   Melody and I are working on math in my dorm room. She kisses me on the mouth. Later, for the rest of my life, while washing dishes, jiggling drops of rain hanging on the points of every maple leaf in the window, or in a meeting when someone writes on a flowchart and the room fills with the smell of felt-tip marker—during those liminal non-moments fertile with emptiness—I will be overtaken by swift collages of memory. A heady disorientation, seared with pleasure, jarring. Among those memories: Melody's kiss. Because it was a kiss of revelatory beauty. I realized I had never initiated anything in my life. Melody acted; I was acted upon.

20   I'm not like that, I say, gay or anything.

21   She smiles, No big deal. She twists an auburn curl around in her finger, supremely unruffled. Aplomb. She's showing me how it's done.

22   I like you and everything, I say.

23   Relax, she says. She turns back to the math, engaging so quickly that she solves the problem at once.

&

24   What I feel on the side of the highway, ozone in the air, the epic sky: I am falling hugely in love. Hank, the guy who picked us up in his black truck. Brian Fiander. Melody, myself. Whomever. A hormonal metamorphosis, the unarticulated lust of a virgin as errant, piercing, and true as lightning. A half hour later the truck hydroplanes.

25   Hank slams on the brakes. The truck spins in two weightless circles. I listen to the keening brakes of the eighteen wheeler coming toward us, ploughing a glorious wave of water in front of it. The sound as desperate and restrained as that of a whale exhausted in a net. I can see the grill of the eighteen wheeler's cab through the sloshing wave like a row of monster teeth. The transport truck stops close enough, our bumpers almost touching.

26   After a long wait, the transport driver steps down from the cab. He stands beside his truck, steely points of rain spiking off his shoulders like medieval armour. Melody opens her door and steps down. She walks toward the driver, but then she veers to the side of the road and throws up.

27   The driver of the transport truck catches up with her there. When Melody has finished puking he turns her toward him, resting his hands on her shoulders. She speaks and hangs her head. He begins to talk, admonishing, cajoling; once bending his head back and looking up into the rain. He chuckles. The thick film of water sloshing over the windshield makes their bodies wiggle like sun-drugged snakes. After a while he lifts her chin. He takes a handkerchief from an inside pocket and shakes it out and holds it at arm's length, examining both sides. He hands it to her and she wipes her face.

28   Hank whispers to me, I'm not responsible for this. He lays his hand on the horn.

29   Melody gets back in the truck. She's shivering. The other driver climbs into his cab. His headlights come on. The giant lights splinter into needles of pink and blue and violet and the rain is visible in the broad arms of light, and as the truck pulls out the lights dim and narrow, as if it has cunning. Then it drives away. Hank takes off his sunglasses and folds the arms and places them in a holder for sunglasses glued to the dash. He moves his hand over his face, down and up, and then he rests his forehead on the wheel. He holds the wheel tight.

30   What did you say to him, Hank asks. He waits for Melody to answer but she doesn't. Finally he lifts his head. He flings his arm over the back of the seat so he can turn the truck and I see the crackle of lines at the corners of his eyes.

ॐ

31   I watch Melody inside the Irving station a couple of hours later, her pink sleeveless blouse through the window amid the reflections of the pumps and the black truck I'm leaning against. She passes through my reflection and, returning to the counter, passes through me again like a needle sewing something up. Hank opens the hood and pulls out the dipstick. He takes a piece of paper towel from his back pocket, draws it down the length of stick, stopping it from wavering.

32   Melody comes out with a bottle of orange juice. It has stopped raining. Steam lifts off the asphalt and floats into the trees. Sky, Canadian flag, child with red shirt—all mirrored in the glassy water on the pavement at our feet. A car passes and the child's reflection is a crazy red flame breaking apart under the tires. The juice in Melody's hand has an orange halo. A brief rainbow arcs over the wet forest behind the Irving station.

33   You married, Hank? Melody asks. He's still fiddling with things under the hood.

34   I believe I met you at the El Dorado, Melody says.

35   Hank unhooks the hood, lowers it, and lets it drop. He rubs his hands in the paper towel and gives her a look.

36   I don't think so, he says.

37   I believe you bought me a drink, Melody says.

38   You're most likely thinking of someone else, he says.

39   Could have sworn it was me, Melody says, it sure felt like me. She laughs and it comes out a honk.

40   I'm going to carry on by myself from here, Hank says.

41   But you're probably right, Melody says, the guy I'm thinking of wasn't wearing a ring.

42   Good luck, he says. Melody hefts herself up onto a stack of white plastic lawn chairs next to a row of barbeques and swings her legs. Hank gets in his truck and pulls out onto the highway.

43   I can take care of myself, Melody yells. But now we've lost our ride, and it'll take a good hour to get to the clinic in Corner Brook from here.

⇛

44   The nurse leans against the examining table with her arms folded under her clipboard.

45   You'll need your mother's signature, she says. Anybody under nineteen needs permission from a parent or guardian. You'll need to sit before a board of psychiatrists in St. John's to prove you're fit.

46   Tears slide fast to Melody's chin and she raises a shoulder and rubs her face roughly against the collar of her jean jacket.

47   She wouldn't sign, Melody says.

48   The nurse turns from Melody and pulls a paper cone from a dispenser and holds it under the water cooler. A giant wobbling bubble works its way up, breaking at the surface. It sounds like a cooing pigeon, dank and maudlin. I can hear water rat-a-tatting from a leaky eaves trough onto a metal garbage lid.

49   My mother has fourteen children, Melody says.

50   The nurse drinks the water and crunches the cup. She presses the lever on the garbage bucket with her white shoe and the lid smacks against the wall. She tosses the cup and it hits the lid and falls inside. Then she wipes her forehead with the back of her hand.

51   You can forge the signature and I'll witness it, she says. She takes the top off the Bic pen with her teeth. She flicks a few pages and shows Melody where to sign. Melody signs and the nurse signs below.

52   I don't need to tell you, the nurse says.

53   I appreciate it, says Melody.

⇛

54   That year I live on submarine sandwiches microwaved in plastic wrap. When I peel back the wrap, the submarine hangs out soggy and spent; like a tongue after a strangling. The oozing processed cheese hot enough to raise blisters. I wear a lumber jacket over cheesecloth skirts, and red Converse sneakers. I learn to put a speck of white makeup in the outer corner of my eyes to give me an innocent, slightly astonished look. On Valentine's Day in the dorm elevator I tear an envelope; dried rose petals fall out and whirl in the updraft of the opening elevator

doors and there is Brian Fiander. I see I was wrong; he isn't skinny. If he still wants me, he can have me. I will do whatever Brian Fiander wants and if he wants to dump me after, as he has Brenda Parsons, he can go right ahead. He seems to go through girls pretty quickly and I want to be gone through.

☙

55   Melody and I get tickets on the CN bus into St. John's for the abortion. I wait for her outside a boardroom in the Health Sciences. I catch a glimpse of the psychiatrists, five men seated in a row behind a table. Melody comes out a half-hour later.

56   What did they say?

57   One of them commented on my hat, she says. He said I must think myself pretty special with a fancy hat. He asked if I thought I was pretty special.

58   What did you say?

59   The same smile as when she kissed me. Learning to smile like that will take time. The rainbow must belong to some other story. Stretching over the hills behind the Irving station, barely there.

60   After the abortion I hold her hand. She's lying on a stretcher and she reaches a hand out over the white sheet that is tucked so tightly around her shoulders that she has to squirm to get her arm free.

61   Not too bad, she says. She is ashen. Tears from the corners of her eyes to her ears.

62   Sometimes you have to do things, she says.

☙

63   During the rest of the winter I spend a lot of time with Wavy Fagan. She's marrying her high-school woodworking teacher; they have to keep the relationship secret. Wavy smokes, holding the cigarette out the window. I fan the fire alarm with her towel.

64   I don't spend much time with Melody; time together is exhausting. Wavy smokes, and she taps the window with her hard fingernail and tells me to come look. Six floors below, Melody is crossing the dark parking lot. It's snowing and a white circle of snow has gathered in the brim of her hat and it glows under the streetlight.

65   She's the one had the abortion for Hank Mercer, Wavy says.

2.

66   I am drunk and in profound pain, my tooth. I am a forty-year-old widow in someone else's bed. Whose bed? Robert turns on the bedside light. Primrose Place is where I am. Robert's new house with new everything. Big housewarming party. I can feel the throb of it through the floorboards. Wrought iron this and marble that. Where I've woken up for the last eleven months. He untangles his bifocals from the lace doily on the side table and comes over to my side and gets down, on his knees. He takes my cheeks in his hands. I can smell the alcohol in his sweat, on his breath.

67   Open up, he says.

68   I say, You have to take care of it.

69   It's five in the morning. He pays the taxi. I lean against the glass door of his office while he finds the keys. Everything behind the door leaps into its proper

place just before the door swings open. The fluorescent lights flutter grey, then a bland spread of office light. The office simulates an office. A sterile environment for extracting a tooth. Robert passes down a hall of convincing office dividers. Turns on the X-ray machine.

70 That's got to warm up, he says.

71 Just pull it out, I say.

72 Robert gets a small card from the receptionist's desk and slings himself into a swivel chair. The chair rolls and tips and he is flung onto the floor. He grips the desk and drags himself up and sits in the chair. He puts a pen behind his ear and feels around on the desk for it and remembers it behind his ear. The top of his head shines damply.

73 Any allergies, abnormal medical conditions, sexually transmitted diseases? He's slurring. I don't bother.

74 He leaves the room and I hear water running in a sink. The rip rip rip of paper towels from a dispenser. He comes back and pulls on a pair of latex gloves, letting them snap at his wrists, flexing his fingers.

75 Who was the man you were talking to, Robert says.

76 The gloves are the smell I've noticed on his hands, like the smell of freshly watered geraniums. He takes an X-ray and leads me to the chair.

77 Make yourself comfortable, he says. There's a poster of rotting gums— enlarged, florid gums oozing pus, the roots of the blackened teeth exposed and bleeding. Photographs of everyone who works in the office, the other dentists, the dental hygienists, and receptionists. I look for the redhead. A brief, uncomplicated affair, he said, terrific sex. Long after it was over Robert tidied away her student loan and Visa. Braids and a lab coat covered in teddy bears and balloons. I sink into the chair and a moment later feel myself sink into the chair. Robert prepares a syringe. He drops it. He picks it up and looks at the tip. He scrutinizes the tip of the needle for some time.

78 That man was all over you, he says.

79 I'm allowed to have a conversation.

80 He tosses the syringe toward the garbage bucket; it hits the wall and bounces end over end across the room. Robert holds up one finger.

81 I'll get another one.

82 You do that, Robert. I can hardly open my mouth. He puts his hands on my face and leans in to look, his entire weight rests on my sore cheek. He steadies himself and straightens up.

83 The infection is too severe, he says.

84 Coward, I say.

85 We should run a course of antibiotics first.

86 Robert, please.

87 This is unethical, he says, I love you. He begins to sob. He sobs silently with his mouth hanging open, his shoulders curled in, cradling himself. I don't care what position I've put him in. His house with the new, leakless skylights and cedar sauna. The spacious greenhouse, pong of aggressive rose bushes, dill, peat. Asking his dinner guests to pull the pearl onions from the earth. Orchids in aquariums with timed sprinklers. Philip Glass on the sound system, building tense, cerebral crescendos. Density of pixels this, lightweight that, gigs of this, surround sound. Pull my fucking tooth, you drunken idiot.

88   You are so remote, he says, wiping his eyes.

89   If you're crying about that guy.

90   Don't you feel anything?

91   He sticks the needle into my infected gum and I dig my nails into his wrist and my heel kicks the chair. The numbing spreads up my face and partway across my upper lip. My cheek is cold and stupid and the pain is gone in less than a minute. My nails break his skin.

92   We'll wait until you're good and frozen, he says. He leaves the room. I hear him walk into the reception area. He crashes into something. A coffee maker starts to grumble. The smell of coffee. He turns on a radio. A woman says, That's the reality of the situation, then static and classical music. He returns with the X-ray. He seems to have sobered.

93   The bacteria think they died and went to heaven, he says. He has become reverent.

94   Robert, I need to know you'll stop if I ask you to. He clips the X-ray to a light board. My teeth look blue and ghostly. The white jawbone: I think of my husband buried in the cemetery near Quidi Vidi Lake. Robert goes into the reception area, I hear him pour a coffee. He opens a filing cabinet drawer.

95   He shouts, Are you good and frozen?

❧

96   The toothache had been mild for weeks. I think I'm awake but the bed is facing in the wrong direction. Or I'm in the wrong bed. A toilet bowl filling continuously. Wet leaves and earth, is there a window? Stenographers on squeaky keyboards wait for a breath of wind and resume. A car unzips a skim of water. Hard fingernails clicking glass, the leaves, the skylight, keying data. Data dripping from leaf tip to leaf tip. A religious cult in the sewer can be overheard whispering in the toilet bowl. A conspiracy and the stenographers ache to crack it. Wind sloshes through the trees and the typing subsides. The trees are just trees. I am my tooth, a monolithic grief. A man beside me. Please be Des; please. It is Des.

97   The beach to ourselves, the park closed, early September. What heat, so late in the season. Each wave leaves a ribbon of glare in the sand as it withdraws. The sun is low and red, scissored by the long grass. Des strips to his underwear, trots toward the water. Stands at the edge of the ocean. High up, a white gull.

98   Des charges, arms raised over his head, yelling. The gull is silent. So high up it's barely there. Wide circles. It dips closer. The wave's crest tinged pink, fumbling forward. He dives through the falling crest. The soles of his feet. He passes through, bobs on the other side. Flicks water from his hair. His fist flies up, wing of water under his arm. The gull screeches. Metallic squawk, claws outstretched, reaching for the sand. The sun through the grass on the hill laserbeams the gull's eye, a red holograph. The gull's pupil is a long midnight corridor to some prehistoric crimson flash deep in the skull.

99   He calls, Water's great. My shirt, jeans, one sock stretches long. I have to hop. The sock gives up. I run hard. The wave is building beneath the bed. Except how cold. My body seizes.

100   Look at the one coming, Des says. The wave comes with operatic silence. Such surety, self-knowledge, so cold and meaningless and full of blasé might. I

reach out my hand. Here it comes. A wave full of light, nearly transparent, lacy webbing on the underside. The ocean sucking hard on my spine. The sandy bottom drops away.

101   It smashes us. The bed plummets and thumps the floor. The room makes itself felt. Dresser, a housecoat on a hook. Des died four years ago of heart failure. Peanut butter jar on the floor, fridge open. Holding the knife. Smoking toast in the stuck toaster. The red light of the ambulance on the walls of the hallway. Now I'm awake.

102   Tequila I drank, scotch. Elasticky top and sarong. Beer. Robert warned me, when he throws a party. Dancing. Slamming doors, laughter, the Stones. I have dated, since Des died, no one: an air traffic controller, a very young painter, no one, the reporter guy, absolutely no one, the carpenter. The tooth became unbearable two days ago. I didn't tell Robert. Pleased to meet you, hope you guess my name. You can't leave. How can you leave? Bodies pressed close, smoky ceiling. Blow the speakers. We took a cab. Hope you guess my. Get a taxi. If we dance. In the fridge door. Mine are the cold ones. Pleased to meet you. Have one of mine. The cold ones. I got laid. Tell me. I'll tell you after this. We need a toast. Our coats are where? Forget the coats. Don't leave, it's a party. Because the toilet. What happened to the tequila? Your own stupid fault. My wife took the traditional route. Does it have a worm in it? I'll put one in if you like. There have been women, yes. There have been women, I'll admit. We'll call ourselves the Fleshettes. The people impressed me most. I'm not responsible. Hope you guess my. We haven't talked. We're talking now. This is talking? Name. I love you. Don't say that. I love you, what do you think? I think more beer.

103   The sky is the deepest blue it gets before it begins to look black. The stars are blue. The trees roar with wind and become quiet. I lie flat on my husband's grave and look at the stars. Freshly mowed grass, a faint marshy smell, the ducks at the edge of the lake. This morning, resting my head against the hand dryer in the bathroom of Robert's office. Tears start this way: the bridge of my nose, my eyelids, the whole face tingling, the clutch of a muscle in the throat. The smell of burnt coffee—homey, unloved office coffee—makes me cry. Some songs: Patsy Cline. Bad blue icing on the birthday cake the girls bought for the boss. I cry at least four times a day. The tears catch in the plastic rims of my glasses. My eyelids like slugs. While waiting for the elevator I hear laughter inside, ascending, inclusive, sexual. I cry with jealousy. Marcy Andrews coming into the bathroom after me. Unclicking her purse, getting the cotton swab out of a pill bottle, tapping two pills into my hand. Marcy smoothing her thumbs over my wet cheeks. She turns me to the mirror and she looks hard at me.

104   She says, Lipstick will give you a whole new lease.

105   I can't be alone, I say.

106   The leaves in the graveyard smell leathery, pumpkinish. The branches creak when the wind rubs them together. Des's hands folded over a rose, his wedding

ring. When do the teeth fall away from the skull? Does that happen? It's beginning to get cold. Snow on his headstone makes me panicky.

107   A flashlight waves erratically through the shrubs, catching the bright green moss on a carved angel's cheek, her cracked wing. Another flashlight, soft oval bouncing in the leaves overhead, scuffle of feet. I'm surrounded by a circle of teenagers with baseball bats and fence pickets. They step, one by one, out of the trees and bushes. Or else they have always been standing there. All the headstones, tipping, lichen-crusted. I stand up, my legs watery. We stand like that, not speaking or moving.

108   You seen a guy run through here?

109   I whisper, No. I haven't seen anybody. Three policemen arrive and the teenagers flee. A policeman steps forward and puts an arm around my shoulder and I cry into his armpit.

❧

110   Robert lowers a tool into my mouth and I say, Stop.

111   I say, That was a test.

112   He says, That was a scalpel. I would just trust me if I were you.

113   I feel him cut the gum and fold the flesh back. His eyes full of veins blue and violet; my blood sprays dots on his glasses. He takes up another instrument and tugs at the tooth, twisting it, and I feel it tearing away. The hoarse, sputtering noise of the suction hose removing blood and saliva. Robert worked for nothing in Nicaragua after he graduated, teaching the revolutionaries to be dentists, the distant spitting of gunfire in the fields beyond his classroom. During the dot-com boom he invested—in and out—unspeakably rich.

114   My tooth hits a chrome bowl with a bright ping. He begins to sew the stitches. I feel the thread move through the gum and the sensation, though painless, nauseates me. Three tight stitches, the side of my mouth puckered. He gives me a wad of cotton and tells me to bite down. He peels the latex gloves. I worry the loose ends of the stitches with my wooden tongue. They feel like cat whiskers.

115   I've wanted to ask for some weeks, Robert says.

116   Maybe this is not the best time, I say.

117   I want to marry you, he says.

❧

118   The sound of the sliding metal rings when I rip open the shower curtain unnerves me. Waiting for the toaster to pop, a butter knife in my hand, I am aware of a presence. The washer shimmies across the laundry room floor until it works the plug from the wall and the motor goes quiet. The water stops slushing. An engrossing, animated silence. Every object—the vacuum cleaner, a vase of dried thistles—has become sensitive. The fridge knows. The unmade bed is not ordinary. I put a glass down and check. It's exactly where I set it down. Loving a dead person takes immense energy and it is making me cry.

❧

119   Robert works the champagne cork with his thumbs. The cork bounces off the ceiling and hits a mirror, causing a web of cracks. He hands me my glass and I can feel the fizz on my face.

120   He says, This is the happiest day of my life.

121   We twine arms and drink and the awkward intimacy of this, the complete lack of irony—I know instantly I've made a mistake.

❧

122   Robert is still at work and I'm watching the decorating channel. The camera slowly roves through a palatial, empty house in Vermont, a woman's chipper voice: Here we have an oak table, very countryish, but *workable* chairs, this dining room absolutely screams to be used. Use me, it's screaming!

123   I turn the TV off and listen to the shrill nothing that fills Robert's house. Leaves swirl off the lawn in twisting columns. A brown leaf hits the glass and sticks. The starlings are flying in formation over the university. A black cloud draws together and becomes thin as it changes direction. The sky is full of grey luster and the starlings seem feverish. I remember Des parking by the university once, just to watch them. It was late, we had groceries, ice cream in the trunk.

124   They're just playing, he said. I want to stay here, don't you? I want to watch all night.

125   I think: If you are there, get in touch with me now. I believe suddenly that he can, that it is just a matter of my asking.

126   The phone rings at exactly that instant. It rings and rings and rings. Then it stops. I put my hand on the receiver and I can feel a warm thrum. Then it rings again, loud. I go upstairs and brush my teeth. I rinse and start flossing. The phone rings again. It's ringing in all the rooms, terrifying me. I pour a bath and get in, and when it's deep enough I dunk my ears under the water.

❧

127   Robert gives me a glass of scotch and drops into the chair beside me. He presses his watch face so the dial glows, sending a circle of green light zigzagging across his face. The sale of my house has come through. A young couple with a dalmatian. Most of the furnishings went to the Sally Ann. A closet full of Des's shirts, a key ring with a plastic telescope, inside which there is a picture of Des and me on vacation in Mexico. It has to be held to a light. We are laughing, drinking from coconut shells. I'd let all the plants die. Robert has everything we need.

128   You're tired, I say, we're both tired.

129   What do you think of stem cell research, he says.

130   There are the dishes.

131   I could take a hair out of your head and make another you.

132   The laundry is—

133   Two of you. The real you and another you.

134   I know I'm tired.

135   One you is a roomful already.

136   I can't have sex with you tonight if that's what you're thinking, I say.

137   Why would I be thinking a thing like that?

138   I'm drifting to sleep while he talks. I dream I say I want my real husband, and I don't know if I've spoken out loud or not. I believe that Des is in the chair beside me and things are as they were five years ago, as if the past can do that. Lay itself down on the present. Cover it over. Become the present, even briefly. A pair of flip-flops, I'd stumbled and skinned my toe. Des had been hammering all day. The hammering had stopped, but the silent ringing of the hammer went on. It was late September and we went to the beach.

∾

139   In the morning I hear a car coming up the long driveway and I leap out of bed. A dark green minivan pulls up under the trees. The windshield is opaque with the shadows of the maple trees. The van parks and a man steps out. He's wearing cream-coloured pants and a pastel plaid shirt. He stretches and puts his hands on his hips. He helps a little girl out of the driver's side. She's wearing a white cotton dress and the skirt bells with the breeze. Finally the passenger door opens and a woman gets out. I'm standing in the upstairs window, struggling to get my jeans on. There is a wave rising inside me. It's full of light. It's dull and smart and hurting my throat. Robert rolls over in bed.

140   He says, Who would disturb us at this hour?

141   The woman has her hand over her eyes to block the sun and she's looking up into the bedroom window where I'm standing and I know it's Melody without even recognizing her. I run down the stairs and out the back without my shoes. I have never initiated anything in my life. I forgot her completely and here she is. She'll give me something.

142   She's exactly the same. The child is just like her. The guy holds out his hand. Melody says his name and I tell him I'm thrilled, but I forget his name. I forget the child's name but it's Jill.

143   I tried to call, she says, holding out her arms.

144   I say, I'm married. I start to cry. Melody kisses me.

145   I whisper, I've messed up, Melody.

146   She says, You'll just have to do something about it.

Appendix: An Introduction to Writing Literary Analysis

Assume you have reached the third week of classes in your English course, An Introduction to Literature. In class, the instructor hands you a set of topics for the first essay. It is worth 20% of your final mark, and you have two weeks to finish and submit it. This experience happens to students all over Canada, and you would be typical if you were worried about how you would fare on this standard assignment. The following introductory comments are intended to give you a firmer grasp of what you are being asked to do, the purpose of the assignment, and a method and approach that might help you to receive a satisfactory grade.

Step One: Choosing and Understanding a Topic

Let's start with the *assignment sheet*. Before doing anything else, you should be able to answer two questions: What am I being asked to do? Which of the topics appeals to me? For our purposes in this introduction, let's assume the following is the core of the handout.

1. Construct an analysis of the influence of gender loyalty on reading "The Boat."

2. Evaluate the discrepancy between the age of the narrator in "How I Contemplated the World from the Detroit House of Correction and Began My Life Over Again" and the quality of psychological and sociological insight achieved by that narrator.

3. Trace the contributions of irony and surprise to "A Good Man is Hard to Find" and "Happy Endings."

4. Explain the contributions of the narrative and imagery patterns to "Fern Hill" and "anyone lived in a pretty how town."

5. Compare the exploration of racial stereotypes in "Dear John Wayne" and "Pretty Like a White Boy: The Adventures of a Blue Eyed Ojibway."

6. Assess the influence of religion, class, and gender expectations on the action of "The Boarding House."

7. Develop a mythological reading of "The Ones Who Walk Away from Omelas" together with a consideration of contemporary instances of scapegoating.

Typically, such an assignment gives you a number of choices about what genre or genres you want to write about and about the particular angle or perspective you might adopt in your response.

The first action you should take is to *analyze each proposed topic*. Three aids to doing so are

- underlining the action word in the topic (if there is one) and ensuring you understand what that instruction entails;

- clarifying in your own mind what the topic expects you to do by isolating the angle of attack you are asked to follow;

- estimating what length of a response would be required to deal comprehensively with this topic.

Make notes on your responses to each of these questions; you may choose to keep those notes in your computer and to open a file entitled ENG100essay1, or, if you already have a file for this course, a separate file entitled "essay1." If you find you can't answer one of these questions, ask your instructor or a member of your study group about the element that is giving you difficulty. You should not proceed to the next step until you are certain that you understand what the topic expects you to do.

The second action we recommend you take is simpler. What text or texts— of the choices you have been given—are you most interested in writing about? Try to answer this question. If the answer comes quickly, also ask whether you are comfortable with the topic your instructor assigned for that text. If you are, you have completed the first important step in writing a literary analysis, *choosing your topic*.

Step Two: What is Literary Analysis?

You probably already have a fair understanding of literary analysis. You will have been doing it in one form or another for several years. A first year college or university course, however, will normally expect you to conduct your analysis at a more advanced level.

One facet of this assignment is what we might call a *demonstration essay*; you will be *demonstrating* that you can create and successfully structure an extended analysis. The dictionary will quickly tell you that to analyze is to break something into its constituent parts, its elements. This particular form of analysis is also related to *argument*. Basically, you are arguing that your response to the text is a valid and defensible response, and that you can demonstrate the reasonableness of your view with valid proofs. As such, then you have to write the essay as a kind of argument, with claims and supports for those claims.

These two steps, once finished, will bring you two thirds of the way through your pre-writing stage. You will have evaluated each of the topics and you will have chosen the one that attracts you and that you think you can write about successfully.

Step Three: What Do I Know/Need to Know in Order to Start?

The last of the pre-writing stages is also one of the most important. At this point, you need to discover and list the points and elements that will form the bedrock of your essay. Let's assume, by this point, that you believe the necessary length is one thousand to fifteen hundred words, or four to six pages. You can expect, then, to have ten to fifteen paragraphs, with as many as eight to thirteen of them being body paragraphs. By this juncture, you are beginning to form a picture, however thinly developed, of your essay in your mind, an essential part of the pre-writing phase.

You will already have developed your favourite pre-writing strategies for discovering what you know. You may prefer *free-writing*, with the screen turned off so that you can't see what you're writing. Or you may like starting with one of the *listing techniques*, followed by *sorting*. Others like using *trigger questions* or using the terms of the posed question as the cue to your internal search. Whatever you decide to use, remember the most critical element: you must have enough concrete examples, illustrations, proofs, supports to make your analysis credible and persuasive. Some students like to just start writing and hope it will all magically come clear in the actual process of writing. You may well make unexpected discoveries when you start writing, but we believe you should have a good road map before you start your journey.

Let's assume that you chose question 4 re the Cummings and Thomas poems. You like the poems, even if you're still a bit uncertain about the details of each, and you think the "compare" instruction is closest to other essays you have written. But you also need to have a sound understanding of the suggested angle of attack—"contribution of narrative lines and image patterns to"—and you may not have thought about the fact that you cannot look at elements in a poem without being able to relate them to the overall effect of that poem. So your problem is that your chosen essay has quite a few moving parts, and you will have to take more care than you normally might with organizing those thoughts before you begin.

Return to the discovery stage and use a listing technique. Write down "narrative line"/"anyone ..." as your first *header* and start listing all the elements of this Cummings poem that seem to tell a story. Then do the same for Thomas' "Fern Hill." In conducting this search, remember that progression and separate acts are essentials in a narrative and look to isolate these elements in each poem you re-read.

You should discover that what appears to be confusing diction and syntax in Cummings' poem evaporates once you concentrate on recovering the story line. From "anyone lived in a pretty how town" to "one day anyone died i guess/(and noone stooped to kiss his face)/busy folk buried them side by side," you will see the base elements of a couple's love for each other, a love that redeemed their lives. By concentrating on the narrative elements, the mystery of the unusual names, "anyone" and "noone," recedes, and you can focus on the language that insists on their union. With a little more investigation, you should also discover that the lives of these two lovers are opposite in every important way to the lives of the "someones" and "everyones," with the lesson slowly emerging that love can fulfil two lives in ways that all other activities cannot, even if those activities lead to being a "someone."

The story in "Fern Hill" discloses itself much more conventionally as you read about the magical summers of a child on a farm, with the emphasis on the newness and joy of each day, capped by the unanticipated concluding revelation of the "childless land" and the mortality of all, even of children.

Once your notes have captured the narrative patterns of each poem, use the same listing technique to isolate major image patterns. The key word, of course, is pattern; you can therefore begin by listing images that occur more than once. At this stage, all you have to do is list them; you don't need to explain what their recurrence might signify. When you have completed this task, you will probably have used up an evening, or at least all the time you can productively spend and still be fresh enough to do your collecting work successfully. So it's time for a break.

When you return to your task, ask yourself whether you have enough material to write your first draft. The most effective check on this is to look again at your assigned topic and see if you have handled all its requirements. You should immediately see that you haven't because the instruction part of the topic asks you to "explain the contributions of" the two elements you made all your notes on. Thinking about this instruction should also assist you to realize that explaining contributions will, in turn, require you to suggest what the poems are essentially conveying. That means you now have two elements in your analysis, and the second one—contributions—requires you to commit to an overall interpretation of each poem.

At this point, your investigation has led you to the point where you can construct a *provisional thesis*. Whether the term thesis is used or *central claim*, you need to know that an essay needs an engine or it becomes a survey of evidence only; evidence needs a purpose and frame before it can do its work, and your thesis/controlling claim provides that purpose. So take some time to build that provisional thesis before you start drafting. What do the concrete elements of the narrative lines and the image patterns do for these two poems?

You may decide to start with an assertion that the narrative lines develop a structure or sequence that works on a simple level to orient the reader. What about the image patterns then? What part do they play? You could begin simply and say they provide a commentary on the action that reveals its significance (in each case).

Once you have come up with a provisional thesis, test it to see if it fulfils the requirement of a thesis/controlling claim, which must have both a *subject* and a *particular perspective on that subject*. Are both of these elements present in your chosen thesis? Is there a subject? Have you taken a position or announced a perspective on that subject? In each case the answer is yes.

There is, therefore, only one thing left to do before you write your draft—make a *plan* you can follow. Few of us go to the trouble to write a formal outline. We are more likely to jot down a sequence of points we want to cover in our paragraphs, a sequence intended to be sufficient to respond comprehensively to our topic. As soon as you start to sketch your plan, you will discover that you have chosen a very busy topic, with quite a few moving parts.

At this point, you should consider *narrowing* your focus. You might consider meeting with your instructor to see if you could re-frame this topic so that it applies to one of the poems instead of to both. We include this point because students frequently try to be too ambitious with their essays, try to cover many things lightly instead of a few things comprehensively. Most instructors will value the latter approach more highly than the former. So let's assume you have met with your instructor, who has agreed that you can use one poem instead of two. You choose the Cummings poem. Now you have completed the last essential pre-writing act: you have *limited your subject to a manageable size*.

With your topic now successfully limited and focused, you can proceed to devise your *plan* or *sequence*. Do you want to deal with the narrative pattern first or start with imagery? When should you address the thematic intent of the poem, its core? Can you leave that until later and just start with the two patterns? Or do you have to get your general interpretation down early so that your discussion of the narrative and imagery patterns has a constant reference point. When do you want to deal with the "contributions" aspect? Developing your plan/outline/structure is really a matter of asking and answering strategic questions.

Gradually, therefore, you ask yourself structure questions and the answers create your sketch of the sequence you will use in writing your essay. At this point, the pre-writing phase is over, and another evening has passed.

You may think we have devoted too much attention to this third step, the real heart of the pre-writing phase. But we cannot emphasize too strongly how critical this stage is. Too often, writers begin before they have sufficiently defined their purpose and done the spade work to dig up the concrete supports they need to write a successful argument or inquiry and check whether their adopted focus is narrow enough to manage successfully. If you have done your pre-writing fully, your actual drafting should go well. Just be sure you know your subject well enough before starting that draft.

Let's review what you have done in this stage:

- asked yourself all the questions you need to answer before you can write on your chosen topic.

- answered those questions; if you can't answer them, get the help you need so that you can.

- listed in advance the concrete supports you will use later when you start writing paragraphs.

- defined the purpose of your essay more exactly.

- created a provisional thesis/controlling claim and checked to see if it has the two parts required of a thesis and if the thesis statement is sufficient to fulfil your purpose.

- sketched a basic order or sequence you can use to direct your response to the topic.

Step Four: Writing the First Draft

There's no magic to this step. You merely have to sit down at your computer with your plan and your notes and *start writing*. To do this, you may want to start a new file or simply expand the one you already have going. Obviously, you should observe the ritual that works for you as a trigger to write. We also recommend that you try to get a rough draft done in one sitting, especially for a relatively short essay. You will, however, be the best judge of when it's time to quit. Don't quit just because one segment is not coming to you when you could turn to another segment and find that you're ready to deal with it. You will probably find that you need to set aside two nights to complete a reasonable first draft.

Step Five: Editing the First Draft

Research into the writing habits of inexperienced and professional writers shows that the biggest single difference between the two groups is in the importance accorded re-writing. Published writers expect to spend at least 90% of their time editing, polishing, and reordering their work, while the novice writer is reluctant to devote even 10% of his or her time to the same activity. So we recognize you may well ignore the advice here but suggest you shouldn't.

Editing requires a method and a tight focus. For that reason, we recommend you edit for one feature of your essay at a time. We call it "sweeps editing" and believe it is far more effective than everything-at-once editing.

Once you have set aside your draft for at least a day, you can begin editing. Two simple edits to perform are the *coherence* and *special paragraphs* edits.

The *coherence edit*, remembering that "coherence" comes from the Latin word for "sticking together," is a detailed check to ensure that each paragraph has both internal and external coherence. You can conduct it by asking—and answering—the following questions:

1. Does each paragraph relate its claim to your larger claim? Highlight the sentence or part of a sentence that does that; don't worry if it took more than one sentence to make the necessary link. Remember that the connection may be to a concept that is part of a particular section of your essay or to the controlling claim of the essay.

2. Does each sentence link to the preceding sentence and/or to the claim that paragraph is developing? Highlight the key linking word or device that makes the connection. If you can't find any, revise the paragraph.

3. Can you find echo or transition words or phrases that bind the paragraph to the preceding paragraph? If you find none, you may have some rewriting to do.

The *special paragraphs edit* checks that the necessary work has been done by an introduction paragraph(s) and a concluding paragraph. Ask yourself:

1. Have I emphasized the overall purpose of my paper in a thesis or controlling claim? Can I use a highlighter to identify that sentence in my introduction?

2. Have I framed my controlling claim successfully? There should be multiple sentences devoted to establishing the context of your subject, defining any element that needs defining, laying the ground work for a higher level statement of purpose.

3. Have I offered any preview of how the paper will proceed? Is it acceptable to omit a preview? (In a short paper, a preview may be unnecessary.)

You may also include a final sweep or edit called the *format/ documentation* edit. In all likelihood, you have been asked to use MLA style, so you should take five to ten minutes to verify

- that your first page reflects *current MLA conventions,*

- that each essay page has a *running head* in the form recommended by the MLA Style Guide (current edition), and, finally,

- that your *documentation* and *handling of quotations* is correct. If you were asked to include a *Works Cited* page, check the correctness of that also.

Obviously, there are more sweeps you can make, but the above three will let you do a base edit and avoid losing marks needlessly.

Getting It Right: Formatting and MLA Conventions in Literary Analysis

It is difficult to cover all the aspects of writing a literary analysis in a short space, but we need to remind you that, when you use the ideas or words or rephrased versions of a writer's work, you have to *acknowledge* that borrowing.

Direct quotations are the most obvious source material, especially in a literary analysis. It is very hard to write about a text without referring directly to it. When you do use quotations from a work, make sure you *frame* them, that is, lead into them properly with an introductory phrase or sentence and integrate them into your analysis. In other words, don't drop them into your essay as if they say everything that needs to be said on the matter you are discussing. Remember that you are analyzing the literature. As such, you have to utilize a quotation as evidence or support that backs up your point of view. Similarly, if you are allowed to use critical commentary (*extrinsic support or secondary source material*) on the text or texts you are writing about, make sure that you give credit for the critics' ideas. There is nothing wrong with using the ideas of others. It shows that you have done some outside reading and considered various opinions on the topic at hand. It is dishonest, however, to offer their ideas or words as if they were your own. That is plagiarism.

There are also conventions for *presenting quotations* that you should observe when you are formatting your paper. The Modern Languages Association style is the one most of your instructors will insist you use. In MLA style, there are different conventions for using a *short quotation* and a *long quotation* from a poem. Similarly, there is a set of conventions for prose quotations as well. You should consult a handbook to make sure you understand and observe these conventions. Here are basic conventions you should understand:

- Four lines or less of prose are treated as a short quotation and integrated into the text of your essay, with quotation marks separating them from the sentences they appear in.

- More than four lines of prose are set up as a block quotation by indenting those lines ten spaces and double-spacing them. Do not place quotation marks around block quotations.

- Three lines of poetry are set up as a short quotation and integrated into the text of your analysis utilizing slash marks (/) to separate one line of poetry from another.

- More than three lines of poetry are set up as a block quotation and double spaced presenting the lines of poetry line for line as they were presented originally.

- In MLA style, quotations are followed by a reference, which uses as its minimum element the page number where the quotation was found: (57). If the author's name is not included in the introduction to the quotation or is not obvious for some reason, his or her last name is included with the page number in the parenthetic reference: (Smith 378). In a short quotation, the reference precedes the end punctuation, while, in a block quotation, the reference follows the concluding punctuation.

At the end of your paper, you will also need to list the works you cited in your analysis. The format for such an entry varies according to the source of the entry, but the standard convention in an MLA *Works Cited* list is to have the items entered in alphabetical order in the following manner:

> Author. "Title." *Book title* (if the entry is a part of a book). Place of Publication: Publisher, Date.

For instance:

> Page, P.K. "A Grain of Sand." *Planet Earth*. Erin, ON: Porcupine's Quill, 2002.

For more on all of these elements of presentation, you should consult a writing handbook such as *A Canadian Writer's Guide*.

There are several other elements that are worth reviewing, but let's settle for two, the *nature of proof* in the field of English and the inherent *structure* of both *special* and *body paragraphs* in analytical/argumentative writing.

The Nature of Proof in Literary Analysis

Every discipline has some limits to its truths. It is fair to say that English settles for probabilities rather than absolutes; the certainty of Mathematics would not be a legitimate goal in literary criticism. However, neither should you assume that leaves you free to assert whatever you choose about a particular text, simply because that's what you felt at the time. Even the Reader Response critics acknowledge that there must be limitations to what a reader can observe and expect to be believed by a general audience. This kind of question often arises in an introductory class as students think there is some particular magic to the art of interpretation when there really isn't. The onus is on you as the critic of a text or texts, however, to establish the *probability of your claims*.

In doing so, it may help you to know that there are two kinds of support you can present to your reader. The first is *intrinsic support*, the supports available to you from the texts you have studied and are writing about. With poems, imagery, form, diction, syntax, speaker, frame, and other considerations should provide you that intrinsic support. The narrative line you analyzed in Cummings' poem is a form of intrinsic support. Your understanding of syntax and parts of speech lets you assert that there is a love story in Cummings' poem. We can all read "anyone lived" and "noone loved him" and, later, "busy folk buried them side by side," and assert that this is one narrative line in the poem. That same understanding of syntax, diction, and verb tense will help you interpret a puzzling line like "little by little and was by was." In that case, you are using your general knowledge to assist your reading, but still applying it to what is intrinsic to the poem. One major source of establishing the credibility of your claims is therefore the text itself and all of its parts.

Your other source for achieving probability in your analysis is *extrinsic support*, proofs that you find outside the text and import into your act of interpretation. These sources range from other texts to history, sociology, biography, and mythology . . . an almost endless list. For our purposes here, one example might help. If you were reading Thomas' "Fern Hill," you could use biography to connect the title to Thomas' childhood; that would be a simple use of extrinsic support. However, ascertaining the source of the references in the poem to "apple" and "sabbath" and "Adam and maiden" and "grace" will offer you a more complex reading challenge. This "ghost" narrative line would have reminded the readers Thomas thought he was addressing that the Biblical account of what happened in Eden is a story about a fall from "grace." This becomes knowledge you will also need to read the poem. If you want to understand the reference more comprehensively, you need to get a Bible and read the Genesis narrative, or at least the first four to five pages. Then you will have *extrinsic support* for a *claim* that Thomas, in "Fern Hill," is repeating the story of the fall from innocence, with the child suddenly forced to wake from faith in his/her immortality to a realization of mortality and time's killing of us. In this fashion, extrinsic support can increase the probability of what we claim to be true in our interpretation of a text.

The Structure of Special and Body Paragraphs in Literary Analysis

This segment will appear to be suggesting that there is a formula that can be followed in writing the paragraphs of a literary analysis, but that is not our intention here. However, less experienced writers are often confused about what is expected of them in analytical writing, and the following is offered as one way of better understanding the kinds of expectations readers have when they begin to read what you have written.

Introductory paragraphs have a number of required elements:

- a typical first element is the naming of your subject field and is often a general statement that may also establish a context more specific than merely naming the field

- the second element involves narrowing and focusing, may require more than one sentence, and should lead to naming the text you are writing about

- the third element is optional and includes any backgrounding or definitional work you have to do to prepare for the next element

- the fourth element is the thesis or controlling claim; the statement of that thesis must be comprehensive enough to include all your later claims and supports for those claims

- the fifth element is the preview of your analysis/argument, optional in a short essay; try to avoid the stereotyped forms of "This essay will" or "I intend to address."

In a *concluding paragraph* at the end of your essay, the reader has every reason to expect three elements to be present—summary, restatement, and emphasis. The summary part is optional according to the length of your essay; the shorter it is, the less need there is for *summary*. But, if you do include some summary of your argument, it should come first. This will let you move naturally to an emphatic *restatement* of your controlling claim. You may even find you have to use several sentences to complete that restatement. If possible, you should also try to indicate the *wider significance* of that claim. Don't force this if it will not come, but see if it does. There are three elements potentially present, therefore, in a conclusion, and the last one (if it appears) is the sentence suggesting the most general significance of your thesis, the purpose of your essay.

Body paragraphs are the workhorses of your analytical writing. The description that follows offers one model that we think will help you at the beginning and know you will abandon as too formulaic once you are more experienced.

- the first element is optional and is the transition from what you were writing about in the previous paragraph to what you are going to assert in this paragraph. It forms the bridge from one essay unit to the next

- the second element is the claim for the paragraph; it is also possible to place the claim in the middle or at the end of the paragraph, but that is harder to do. We find it useful to remind writers that the paragraph has to have a point, a claim, if the analysis is to retain forward momentum

- the third element, which may, in fact, precede the second is any framing, definitional, contextual, or backgrounding points you need to set up the claim

- the fourth element is the proving or supporting sentence(s); this is the core of the paragraph and can include quotations (direct or indirect), illustrations, reasoning, or even extrinsic supports

- the fifth element would include any backing or elaboration needed to support your supports
- the final element establishes the relevance of your claim in this particular paragraph to your overall argument and especially to your thesis

Sample Paragraphs (for a paper on the Cummings poem)

INTRODUCTORY PARAGRAPH

Poetry demands of us a closer attention than does prose; reading a poem is always an act of interpretation as well as of reading (*naming the field*). This is particularly true of any poem by Edward Estlin Cummings because he employs an unconventional diction and syntax as one of his strategies to ensure we simultaneously read and discover his poems (*narrowing the field*). "anyone lived in a pretty how town" is an excellent example of this challenge Cummings poses for his readers (*the completed focus on a subject—one Cummings poem*). The title alone initially stumps the average reader with its unusual language and, more particularly, its use of "anyone" and "how" (*support for the abstract point about diction and syntax*). But Cummings offers us the help we need to interpret his unusual phrasing (*transition to the thesis statement*). If we pay attention to two simpler elements, the poem's story and the image patterns that comment on that story, we can read the poem successfully (*the thesis or controlling claim*).

BODY PARAGRAPH

Cummings said, "poetry is being, not doing" (Cummings 24), and it helps us to read the "anyone" poem if we first focus on the "being" that is the centrally celebrated action of this poem (*both transition and naming the poem's subject*). Action invokes plot, and we should start our reading by paying attention to the narrative line within the poem (*the central claim of this body paragraph*). The story in the poem is suggested immediately through its title, which gives us an agent, "anyone," an action, "lived," and a scene, "a pretty how town" (Cummings 94) (*first proof or support*). Having identified the agent, we simply track the particulars of "anyone"'s action (*bridge sentence*). In order, then, we read the next two actions: "he sang his didn't he danced his did" and "noone loved him more by more" (Cummings 94) (*proof, support*). If we have paid attention, we should know that "noone" is "anyone"'s lover; there is no other "him" that could be the reference here (*backing for our proof*). When we get to the seventh stanza, we have followed the intimate connection between these two (*bridge or transition sentence*). Now we discover that "anyone" has "died" and "noone" has "stooped to kiss his face" (Cummings 95) (*proof, support*). In short order, she dies also and they have been buried together. Their story has ended (*end of analysis/support for claim*). However, to grasp the significance of their life, their "being" together, we have to trace and understand the central image patterns in the poem that comment on the actions of the two lovers (*transition to next body paragraph*).

Glossary of Literary Terms

Accent: The additional stress given one syllable in a word over another. This property of language creates a repeating rhythm in accentual syllabic poetry. See also *prosody*.

Action: The events composing a narrative. Although action is often physical it may also be internal, as a character changes her or his understanding of another character, an event, or the nature of the world. See also *plot*.

Allegory: A text that functions on two levels at once: the literal, physical level and the symbolic, abstract level. For example, *Pilgrim's Progress*, an early allegory by John Bunyan, represents life as a journey. When Bunyan's Christian travels through the Slough of Despond, two levels of meaning are simultaneously conveyed to the reader.

Alliteration: A sound device in which the same consonant sounds are repeated, frequently at the beginning of words in the same line, to add emphasis to those words. See also *assonance*.

Allusion: A reference in a text to something outside the text, whether it be a person, a place, an event, a biblical scene or action, or a mythic character or action. An allusion asks the reader to take the meaning attached to that external reference and apply it to the text.

Ambiguity: The effect of suggesting multiple meanings in a word, phrase, gesture, or action, rather than a single meaning. Ambiguity makes a text more complex and rich.

Anagnorisis: The Greek word describing the central discovery made by the tragic hero, particularly the discovery of his or her responsibility for the reversal and fall that completes the action of a tragedy.

Anagram: A word or phrase made by rearranging the letters of another word or phrase.

Analysis: Interpreting a text or defending one's interpretation of a text by separating it into its parts. See also *literary analysis*.

Anapaest, anapaestic metre: See *prosody*.

Antagonist: The opposing force in a narrative, which may be a character, a circumstance, an inner weakness of the character, or an agent in the environment. The collision of the antagonist with the protagonist creates the conflict in a narrative, a conflict that may or may not be resolved at the end of the narrative. See also *plot*.

Anti-hero: A protagonist who is alienated from society and whose actions, therefore, are not intended to reform that society. Generally, the anti-hero can find no positive values or code to give allegiance to.

Approximate rhyme: See *rhyme*.

Archetype: A recurrent, universal symbol. The term comes from the psychology of Carl Jung, who believed that the instinctive energies of the body are expressed through autonomous symbols (in dreams, visions, synchronistic events). A journey is one example of a literary archetype, as it is an easily recognizable symbol of a quest.

Argument: One of the four major modes of prose. Argument attempts to convince the reader of the truth of a premise by means of logic and other forms of persuasion.

Assonance: The repetition of the same vowel sounds, usually inside words in a line or in contiguous lines. As with alliteration, assonance adds emphasis, links words, and creates a sound pattern.

Atmosphere: The emotional tone of a text.

Ballad: See *poetic forms.*

Bathos: A comic effect gained by suddenly dropping from an elevated to a low level in diction or imagery. Alexander Pope created bathos in the lines "Advance the fringed curtain of thy eyes, / And tell me who comes yonder."

Biographical criticism: See *literary analysis.*

Blank verse: See *poetic forms.*

Cacophony: A musical term describing the creation of discord on the reader's ear by employing sounds or sound combinations that are rough and unpleasant.

Caesura: A significant pause within a line of poetry, generally accomplished by full-stop punctuation or spacing.

Canon: The list of texts generally considered by academics, critics, and teachers to be worth reading and preserving. The list reflects cultural shifts, so, for example, Shakespeare may be part of the literary canon of one age but not of another. Some argue that the canon is biased toward white males and excludes works by women and by ethnic minorities.

Carpe diem: A Latin phrase that literally means "seize the day." Andrew Marvell advances this theme in "To His Coy Mistress."

Catastrophe: One name for the concluding action of a tragedy.

Catharsis: The Aristotelian idea that the audience gains relief from feelings of pity and fear for the tragic hero by witnessing his or her fall, discovery, and death. Their witnessing forces them to feel these emotions and thus purge them.

Character: An agent in an action. See also *plot.*

Characterization: The means employed by a writer to let us know a character in a text. Generally, we learn about character by what she or he does and says, by what others say about the character, and by such matters as dress and gesture. A writer may also allow the reader to enter the character's consciousness and share his or her thoughts.

Chorus: The group of people in a Greek play who comment directly on the action of the play and on the choices made by the central characters.

Classical unities: The belief of Renaissance critics reading Aristotle's poetics that a well-made plot observes three unities: the action must take place in one day, the action must be limited to a single scene, and the action must stick to one main plot. These were called the unities of time, place, and action.

Cliché: An expression that has been used so frequently that it has lost its ability to surprise or inform the reader. The word comes from the French name for a printing block; when the characters wore off the block, it would no longer print.

Climax: In a narrative, the high point at which the conflict is resolved.

Colloquial: Informal language reflecting the way people frequently speak.

Comedy: It is comedy's task to remind us that we are not so important or dignified as we might like to think we are. Like tragedy, comedy traces its roots to spring rituals pre-dating Greek drama. Comedies can be light hearted, as in romance and farce, as well as dark, as in irony and satire.

Comparison and contrast: A means of building an analysis or interpretation of a work. Comparison stresses similarities by examining two or more texts to see how they are different and how they are similar. Contrast stresses differences only.

Complication: An event that leads to ensuing action in a narrative, that renders the action more complex, or that leads the narrative in a different direction.

Conflict: A struggle between opposed forces. In fiction, that struggle is generally between the protagonist, or positive agent in the action, and the antagonist, or negative force in the action.

Connotation: The associative meanings a word carries that go beyond its literal meaning. *Lean* and *skinny*, for example, may have the same literal meaning, but their associative values are different.

Consonance: A form of slant rhyme in which consonant sounds in stressed syllables are repeated, especially at the ends of words (e.g., *roam* and *same*).

Convention: An accepted pattern or other device in a literary form, such as the conventions of the sonnet form.

Cosmic irony: See *irony*.

Couplet: Two lines of poetry, usually rhymed and sharing the same metre to establish them as a unit. A couplet may also form a single grammatical unit.

Crisis: The point in the plot where the action changes course; the major crisis of a plot is often called the *climax*.

Criticism: See *literary criticism*.

Dactyl, dactylic metre: See *prosody*.

Deconstructionism: See *literary criticism*.

Denotation: The fixed meaning of a word as given by a dictionary.

Dénouement: A French word for the conclusion of a prose plot following the climax. The word means "unknotting" or "unravelling." In a detective story, for instance, the dénouement explains all the previously unexplained actions of the characters. See also *resolution* and *falling action*.

Description: The physical presentation of an object or an event; one of the four modes of discourse.

Deus ex machina: The use of some special agency to conclude the plot and make things turn out favourably. In Greek theatre, the character of the god was literally lowered to the stage to rescue a character; the term now refers to a contrived means to bring the action to an end.

Dialect: A regional form of a language, with distinct diction, grammar, and vocabulary. Research has shown that there are nine dialects in Scotland, for instance; Newfoundland English can also be considered a dialect.

Dialogue: The direct exchange of speech by characters in a text.

Diction: In linguistics, *diction* means "word choice." Sometimes, diction is broken into two parts: vocabulary and syntax. When we discuss a writer's diction, we analyze any unusual features of diction in a text. Neoclassic writers believed different forms of poetry should have different levels and kinds of diction.

Didactic: A text described as didactic is one written with the clear intention to teach or instruct its readers, generally for a moral end.

Dimeter: See *prosody*.

Discovery: See *anagnorisis*.

Dramatic irony: See *irony*.

Dramatic monologue: See *poetic forms*.

Dynamic character: A character who is capable of change and, therefore, of surprising us.

Editorial omniscience: See *point of view*.

Effaced narrator: See *point of view*.

Electra complex: A psychoanalytic term used to describe the conflict of a daughter's unconscious competition with her mother for her father's attention and love; the female counterpart of the Oedipus complex. In Greek legend, Electra plotted the death of her mother to avenge the death of her father, Agamemnon.

Elegy: See *poetic forms*.

Elision: The omission of part of a word, as in *O'er* or *ne'er*.

End rhyme: See *rhyme*.

End-stopped line: A line that ends with an enforced pause, usually because it grammatically concludes there.

English sonnet (also Shakespearean sonnet): See *poetic forms*.

Enjambment: The continuation of the grammatical sense from one line into the next, reinforced by the absence of any punctuation or pause at the end of the first line.

Epic: A long narrative, usually in verse, conveyed in an elevated style. If the authorship is uncertain, it is called a *folk epic*.

Epigram: A pointed, compressed, and memorable statement, sometimes written in verse. The epigram originates in Greek and Latin literature.

Epigraph: A quotation or a motto that prefaces a text.

Episode: An incident in a larger narrative.

Epistle: A letter; the term is usually applied to a verse letter.

Escape literature: See *formulaic literature*.

Essay: A reasonably brief prose discussion of a single topic, usually employing either the expository or argumentative mode. The term was first used by the French philosopher Montaigne in his *Essais* and later adopted by Francis Bacon.

Euphony: Pleasing sounds; the opposite of cacophony.

Exact rhyme: See *rhyme*.

Explication: A method of reading a poem, originating in France, that requires careful, line by line analysis of a text, paying attention to the meanings and relationships of the words, phrases, images, and smaller units that compose that text.

Exposition: A prose text written to explain a subject; one of the four types of prose.

Fable: A brief story, often involving animals, that illustrates a moral.

Falling action: See *resolution* and *dénouement*.

Farce: A dramatic piece intended to elicit laughter from the audience, using improbable situations, rough wit, and physical comedy.

Feminine rhyme: See *rhyme*.

Feminist criticism: See *literary analysis*.

Fiction: Narratives invented by writers; the term can be expanded to apply to all imaginatively created texts.

Figures of speech: Using language in such a way that the reader knows the intended meaning goes beyond the literal meaning, such as referring to a car that is causing trouble as a *lemon*. See also *metaphor* and *simile*.

First-person narrator: See *point of view*.

Fixed form: A term applied to established patterns of line, stanza, and metre. See *strophic*.

Flashback: A scene in a narrative that interrupts the normal time progression to return to the past and narrate something that happened before the fictional time present.

Flat character: A one-dimensional character who cannot change and therefore cannot surprise the reader. See also *stereotype*.

Foil: A character in a narrative whose principal contribution is to illuminate some facet of the main character or characters by contrast.

Foot: See *prosody*.

Foreshadowing: Placing hints in a narrative about what is going to happen.

Formal criticism (also formalist criticism): See *literary analysis*.

Formulaic literature: Texts that follow a prescribed pattern to fulfil the reader's expectations (e.g., Harlequin romances).

Free verse: Poetry written in an open form without a repeating metre, rhyme scheme, or stanzaic form.

Genre: A French term for the types or categories into which literary texts can be grouped. The traditional genres are comedy, tragedy, epic, lyric, and pastoral; today, genres also include the short story, novel, essay, play, and film/television script.

Haiku: See *poetic forms*.

Half rhyme: An imperfect rhyme. See also *rhyme*.

Hamartia: The flaw in the tragic hero leading him or her to the unfortunate act that provokes the concluding catastrophe.

Hero, heroine: The older term for the leading agent in a literary text. In narrative and drama, the term *protagonist* is now more frequently employed.

Heroic couplet: Iambic pentameter lines rhymed in pairs.

Hexameter: See *prosody*.

Historical criticism: See *literary analysis*.

Hubris, hybris: The Greek term for excessive pride, the quality in some tragic heroes that leads to their downfall.

Hyperbole: Overstatement or exaggeration for effect.

Iambic metre: See *prosody*.

Image, imagery: A word, phrase, or figure of speech that makes a direct appeal to one or more of the senses; images may also work together to form a pattern that carries some part of the text's meaning.

In medias res: Literally means "in the midst of things." This term is used to describe the convention of beginning a plot in the middle of the action.

Internal rhyme: See *rhyme*.

Interpretation: The reader's conscious attempt to understand a text and explain it through reference to its parts as well as its whole.

Irony: The use of language to express a meaning different from or incongruous with the literal meaning. Irony is used in literature to create humour or to reveal hidden meanings to the reader.

Verbal irony refers to sarcasm or to some allied form in which what is said is not what is intended.

Dramatic irony occurs when the audience and one or more of the characters in the action know something or grasp an additional meaning that the character speaking does not.

Situational irony occurs when the contradiction or irony is embedded in the action or situation. The narrator of "The Boat," for instance, does not understand that his solitude and smoking in the opening scene show him to be his father's child.

Tragic irony occurs in drama when the action of the protagonist will lead to a disastrous result opposite to what the protagonist intended.

Cosmic irony occurs when the reader perceives that the times are "out of joint" and no amount of human effort can do anything about this radical disorder. In Thomas Hardy's novels, for instance, the human agents are dwarfed by the malign forces that operate against them.

Italian sonnet (also Petrarchan sonnet): See *poetic forms*.

Limerick: See *poetic forms*.

Limited omniscience: See *point of view*.

Literary analysis: Many approaches are available to the reader in responding to a text; literary analysis is a term for those possible perspectives. The following are some common approaches to literary analysis:

Biographical criticism is a narrower version of historical criticism. This approach purports that examining the life of the writer will assist us in understanding the writer's texts. Such an approach is hindered by its narrow assumption that writers create only from their actual experience.

Bisexual, Cross-gendered, Gay and Lesbian Studies, and *Queer Theory* come out of studies in disciplines such as literature, history, and sociology. While Gay, Lesbian, Bisexual, and Cross-gendered Studies are related to how work under study reflects the depiction of and questions related to gender and sexual orientation, Queer Theory resists definition. It challenges fixed definitions of sexual identity, and thinks that defining people by gender and a set of gender characteristics is wrong. In effect, Queer Theory has attempted to go beyond a study of sexual definitions in order to attempt to subvert traditional conceptions of normalcy and deviance.

Deconstructionism literally deconstructs the text. It starts from the assumption that language cannot create fixed or reliable meanings, nor can any construct made out of language. A text contains, within itself, the power to deconstruct itself. With a little effort, any number of "readings" of a text can be created, each with its own validity, if linguistic constructs can possess validity.

Feminist criticism focuses on the social construction of gender and identity. It has created a canon of female writers and critics and worked to supplement or replace what feminist critics see as a male-dominated critical perspective. It employs a large range of disciplines—especially history, psychology, and sociology—to assist in placing literature in a broad social context and in forging a criticism sensitive to feminist issues.

Formalist criticism takes an intrinsic approach, rather than the extrinsic approach of historical criticism. It focuses instead exclusively on the "form" of the text in the belief that everything necessary to understanding the text is inside the text itself. The most successful formalist school was the new criticism approach, which flourished between 1940 and 1970.

Historical criticism starts from the assumption that knowing more about the culture and times of a writer will help the reader understand the writer's texts. Historicism can include a scientific belief alluded to in a poem or the meaning of a word at the time the work was published. Historicism also extends to periods and their dominant spirit or culture or to the examination of movements such as romanticism or neoclassicism.

Marxist criticism takes an extrinsic approach to texts. Marxism had a strong influence on American writing in the 1930s, and a Marxist critic assumes some of the same stances we see in that literature. The Marxist critic is particularly interested in what might be called the political content of a text and in how the text advances the desired ultimate goal of a classless society.

Mythological criticism seeks to identify what is universal in a text, including archetypes of experience and action, and patterns that link the text to other texts or primary myths.

New Historicism still attempts to frame a writer within his or her time. It assumes, however, that no accurate history of a time exists—that we have only the present's version of that past. New Historicism focuses on the ideology of an age and how the literary text reflects or resists that ideology. This approach posits that the literature tells us something about the times, just as the times tell us something about the literature.

Psychological criticism seeks to meld intrinsic and extrinsic approaches and draws upon theories from psychologists, especially Sigmund Freud and Carl Jung. In its simplest form, for example, it would read *Hamlet* as an Oedipus complex plot; in more blended approaches, it uses what we know about the human unconscious, dream theory, and archetypes to further illuminate the actions, reactions, and motivations of characters. It may also analyze the motivations of the writer.

Reader-response criticism places the reader at the centre, rather than the text or the context out of which the text emerges. It tries to describe the reader's reception of the text and, therefore, rejects the notion of any single "correct" reading of a text. This approach still demands, however, that the reader have some defensible rationale for a reading.

Sociological criticism examines social groups, relationships, and values as they appear in a text (and what they tell us about that particular society) or the sociology of producing the text (literary schools and fashions, magazines and mass texts, and patterns of marketing and consumption).

Litotes: Understatement for effect. It generally employs negation to create an affirmative statement, as in Alfred, Lord Tennyson's *Ulysses*: "not unbecoming men who strove with gods."

Lyric poem: The lyric form was one of the ancient modes of poetry. The lyric poem carries the emotional and individual response of a speaker to an event or scene. The first collection of English lyrics dates from 1310; songs, elegies, sonnets, odes, and ballads are all lyric forms.

Marxist criticism: See *literary analysis*.

Masculine rhyme: See *rhyme*.

Melodrama: Originally applied to drama, this term refers to any work that relies on a romantic plot, stock characters, sensational action, direct emotional appeals to the audience, and other manipulative means to satisfy an audience.

Metaphor: A figure of speech that employs analogy to ascribe some features of one object to another. In a metaphor, unlike a simile, the comparison is simply asserted rather than prefaced with *like* or *as*. A special form of metaphor is *synecdoche*, in which a part is used to signify a whole, as in using *faces* to mean a crowd. Another special metaphor is *metonymy*, in which a close association with an object is used to stand for the object. For example, we might use *Ottawa* to mean the Canadian government or *the courts* to refer to the justice system.

Metonymy: See *metaphor*.

Metre: See *prosody*.

Monologue: Literally, a monologue is one person speaking. Conventionally, the term refers to a speech an actor delivers directly to an audience, unlike a soliloquy, which an actor delivers as if to him- or herself.

Mood: The overall emotional atmosphere of a scene or situation.

Motif: A pattern or theme that recurs in a text.

Motivation: The reasons and justifications behind what a character does. The term refers to the action taken by a character in response to circumstance. If we accept the motivation, we are inclined to describe the character as convincing.

Myth: A narrative usually involving supernatural events or persons as a way of interpreting natural events. Every literature has its supporting mythology, and English readers are most familiar with the Judeo-Christian, Greek, Roman, and Norse myths. Writers can create their own myths, as William Butler Yeats did in *A Vision*. Occasionally, they mix their myths for ironic effect, as in Thomas King's "The Garden Court Motor Motel."

Mythological criticism: See *literary analysis*.

Narrative: A story; also one of the four major forms of discourse, along with description, exposition, and argument.

Narrative poem: A poem that tells a story.

Narrator: The teller of the story.

New criticism: See *literary analysis*.

New historicism: See *literary analysis*.

Novel: An extended prose narrative.

Novella: A prose narrative of roughly forty to eighty pages in length; this form falls between the short story and the novel.

Objective point of view: See *point of view*.

Octave, octet: The eight-line opening unit of the Italian or Petrarchan sonnet; the volta or turn of the sonnet comes at the end of the octave/octet.

Octosyllabic couplet: A pair of rhyming lines each containing four feet.

Ode: See *poetic forms*.

Oedipus complex: A psychoanalytic term referring to the Freudian belief that the male child sees his father as a rival for his mother's attention and love, and competes with his father for that love.

Onomatopoeia: Words that have the special characteristic of suggesting their meaning by their actual sound, as in *buzz*.

Oxymoron: A combination of contradictory terms drawn from the Greek words meaning "sharp-dull" (e.g., jumbo shrimp, deafening silence).

Parable: A story created to illustrate a spiritual lesson.

Paradox: A statement that appears to contradict itself but that still contains truth. Robert Browning's character Andrea del Sarto, in the dramatic monologue of the same name, says, "less is more," and we understand the truth of his apparently contradictory statement.

Paraphrase: A restatement, in other terms, of an original text. We sometimes paraphrase a text to check our understanding of it or to compare our understanding to someone else's.

Parody: A deliberately humorous copy of an original work, often created to mock or criticize certain elements of the original.

Pathos: The quality in literature that arouses our pity, tenderness, or sympathy for a subject.

Pentameter: See *prosody*.

Peripeteia: The reversal of the protagonist's fortune, leading to fall and catastrophe in tragedy and to success in comedy. See also *reversal*.

Persona: The speaker of a poem. Literally, *persona* means "mask" and is a term applied to the narrator or speaker of a text to avoid confusion with the author.

Personification: A figure of speech that grants human qualities to nonhuman agents, whether they are objects, animals, nature or nature's properties, or ideas/abstractions.

Plot: Described by Aristotle as the "imitation of an action" and "the arrangement of incidents." Generally, plot means a sequence of events, which often includes an identifiable beginning, middle, and end. Plot traditionally involved a conflict between a protagonist and an antagonist, with the conflict being resolved or addressed by the events of the plot, but this expectation is not always fulfilled by the plots of contemporary stories.

Poem: A text composed of words; the text may be created or found. The first poems were sung by travelling bards in ancient times, before written language, and thus were characterized by their condensed and metaphorical language, rhyme, and rhythm, which helped the reciter to memorize the poem. Poems are often arranged in a sticchic pattern (one line following another) or strophic pattern (lines grouped into stanzas) and explore a subject in a personal or an impersonal way.

Poetic forms: The main styles and structures of poems are as follows:

Ballad: Traditionally, ballads are narrative poems that began as songs and were handed down orally. A ballad is a narrative poem employing quatrains with alternating four-beat and three-beat lines, and rhymes in the second and fourth lines. The ballad tradition has continued into our own time in folk music.

Blank verse: Verse written in unrhymed iambic pentameter. This is a common pattern in English narrative and dramatic poetry from Shakespeare to the twentieth century.

Dramatic monologue: A poem that one speaker recites to an audience of one or more listeners. The presence of the listeners and the situation surrounding the speech render the situation dramatic.

Elegy: A formal poem, originating in Greek and Latin literature, on the subject of death; an elegy is frequently provoked by the death of a particular person.

Ghazel: Originating in the Middle East in the eighth century, ghazels were originally related to love and wine and composed of five to eight couplets, all having the same rhyme. Contemporary poets have used the form to write about a variety of topics.

Glosa: In her 1994 collection *Hologram*, P.K. Page defines the glosa in this way: "The opening quatrain written by another poet; followed by four ten-line stanzas, their concluding lines taken consecutively from the quatrain; their sixth and ninth lines rhyming with the borrowed tenth. Used by poets of the Spanish court, the form dates back to the late 14th and early 15th century. It has not been popular in English."

Haiku: A Japanese form of poetry that employs three lines of five, seven, and five syllables to evoke a word picture with complex associations.

Limerick: A light verse form with a pattern of five anapaestic lines with three feet (and one rhyme) in the first, second, and fifth lines, and two feet (and another rhyme) in the third and fourth lines. Generally, the limerick is intended to create a comic effect.

Ode: A lyrical poem focused on a single theme or topic. The ode has its origins in Greek dramatic poetry, where it was choral. In English, the ode has three types. The Pindaric ode uses three stanzaic divisions: strophe, antistrophe, and epode. The Horatian or homostrophic ode uses one stanzaic pattern, as in Keats's, "Ode to a Nightingale." The irregular ode does not follow a set stanzaic pattern, as in Wordsworth's "Ode: Intimations of Immortality."

Prose poem: An open form of poetry presented as a prose passage but with the density and rhythm of poetry.

Rondeau: A verse pattern originating in France but popular in English literature, the rondeau characteristically has ten or thirteen lines, with the opening phrase repeated twice as a short refrain. Besides the refrain, the rondeau uses only two rhymes.

Sestina: A complex verse form, the sestina employs six six-line stanzas and a three-line envoy. Although usually unrhymed, the last words of the lines take on a fixed pattern. These end words must appear in each stanza, but their order is dictated by the fact that the last end word of one stanza becomes the first end word of the next stanza. Thus, if the first stanza of a sestina ended 1,2,3,4,5,6, the second would end 6,1,5,2,4,3, and the third pattern would be 3,6,4,1,2,5. The three-line envoy must use the end words 5,3,1, which are the end words of the sixth six-line stanza, and it must employ the other end words 2,4,6 in each of its three lines.

Sonnet: A fourteen-line poem written in iambic pentameter and generally following one of two rhyme schemes. The Petrarchan (Italian) sonnet creates an eight-line octave composed of two quatrains and a six-line sestet composed of two tercets, while the Shakespearean (English) sonnet employs three quatrains followed by a concluding couplet. The sonnet traces its roots to thirteenth-century Italy. The Petrarchan form plays the octave against the sestet; a tension or narrative is created in the octave and responded to by the sestet, with the turn (volta) coming at the end of the octave. In the Shakespearean sonnet, the response is left to the ending couplet, which may summarize or respond to the preceding quatrains.

Terza rima: Italian in origin, this form is composed of interlocking tercets in which the end word of the second line of one tercet forms the rhyme of the first and third line of the following tercet (aba, bcb, and so on). Sometimes terza rima ends with a different stanza form, such as a couplet or quatrain.

Villanelle: A nineteen-line poem using just two rhymes and repeating lines one and three. The first line recurs at lines six, twelve, and eighteen, and the third recurs at lines nine, fifteen, and nineteen. Lines one and three, in this pattern, also close the poem.

Point of view: As a literary term, point of view refers to the perspective from which the story is related. Point of view is one of the hidden yet deeply influential forces at play in a story. The choice of narrator has a great effect on the way readers receive and understand the story. Generally, a story is told by either a first- or third-person narrator.

First-person narrators are agents in the action and are therefore frequently called *inside narrators*. Because they are inside the story, they are limited in time and space and can relate only what they have directly witnessed or have been told by another character. The two principal kinds of inside narrators are *witness narrators* and *protagonist narrators*. The witness narrator is generally more reliable but less intimate as a narrator; with both narrators, however, we have to pay attention to any bias they may reveal in telling the story.

Third-person narrators are easily identified because there is no longer an "I" speaking directly to us. The narrator has now moved outside the story and relays what is happening from a much greater distance.

The most intimate kind of third-person narration is *limited omniscience*. This form of narration is limited to the perspective of one or more of the characters in the action; we occupy that character's consciousness and see from his or her perspective. Now we read, for example, "Lucy watched the man approach the bench. She wondered why he looked so anxious and why his approach was so tentative."

The most flexible form of third-person or outside narration is the *omniscient narrator*. This narrator has no time or space restrictions; she or he can go anywhere in time and space to observe and relay the action. We read, for instance, "The man, deeply troubled, slowly approached the couple on the bench." A variation originating in the eighteenth century is called *editorial omniscient*. In this form, the narrator not only has complete freedom but also uses it to directly address the reader about what was happening and even to express critical opinions from time to time. In this form, we might read, "Dear reader, try to imagine an anxious man, an uncertain man, approaching a bench and expecting rejection, and feel what he feels when he sees the couple look quickly away from his approaching form."

The most distanced of narrators is what has come to be called the *objective narrator* or *effaced narrator*. This narrator is analogous to a video camera recording the action, since only physical description is allowed. The narrator cannot enter any consciousness or relay anything that could not be physically witnessed.

Prologue: The introduction to a drama. The term has widened in application since its use in Greek and Roman drama and now can be applied to any formal introduction to a work.

Prose poem: See *poetic forms*.

Prosody: Prosody applies metrical analysis (scansion) to study the rhythm created by the poet. For many centuries, poetry written in English was dominated by the accentual syllabic tradition. Anglo-Saxon poetry was simply accentual, meaning the writer/singer had to create the right number of accents or stresses in each line. The accentual syllabic tradition also generally governed the number of syllables per line because, in English, the stress falls on the syllable.

To analyze the metre (pattern of stresses and syllables), you can simply follow these steps:

- Divide the lines of one stanza of the poem you are analyzing into syllables, using vertical lines to divide one syllable from another.

- Through reading aloud or some similar means, decide where the stresses fall in each line. Place the following mark above each syllable that is stressed or pronounced more loudly [/]. Then place this mark [∪] above all the unstressed syllables.

- Divide the lines you have analyzed into feet; a metric foot is a unit with one stressed syllable in it and one or more unstressed syllables.

- Use the following tables to decide what the metre of the poem is. Metrical analysis, or scansion, uses terms drawn from classical antiquity, so initially they are difficult to understand. However, the basic system is simple enough: metre is described by naming the type of foot that dominates the poem and then the number of feet in a typical line.

Kinds of Feet
iamb (iambic) ∪ / (afraid)
trochee (trochaic) / ∪ (beat it)
anapaest (anapaestic) ∪ ∪ / (from the tomb)
dactyl (dactylic) / ∪ ∪ (pottery)
spondee (spondaic) / / (dry rot)
pyrrhic ∪ ∪ (it was)

Number of Feet
One = monometer
Two = dimeter
Three = trimeter
Four = tetrameter
Five = pentameter
Six = hexameter
Seven = heptameter
Eight = octometer

If you were analyzing a sonnet, you would find that the typical foot was one unstressed syllable followed by a stressed syllable—in other words an iamb—and that there were five of these feet in each line. Putting the two elements together would let you name the metre of the poem, iambic pentameter.

Protagonist: The principal agent in a text; the term originally meant the first actor in early Greek drama. The Greek word *agon* meant contest, and the protagonist and antagonist are the chief agents in that contest.

Psychological criticism: See *literary analysis*.

Pun: A play on words taking advantage of similarities in sound or meaning between two words; for example, a dead person has reached "a grave destination."

Quatrain: A four-line stanza.

Reader-response criticism: See *literary analysis*.

Realism: The term generally means a presentation that is completely faithful to reality; more narrowly, it refers to a movement in the late nineteenth century to impart a higher degree of verisimilitude to fiction.

Recognition: The point in a plot at which the protagonist discovers previously unknown facts that influence a change of direction or attitude in him or her.

Refrain: One or more words repeated at regular intervals in a poem.

Resolution: The completion of a plot's complications, sometimes referred to as the *falling action*.

Reversal: The turning point in a plot when the protagonist's fortune changes. See *peripeteia*.

Rhetorical question: A question asked for rhetorical effect rather than to elicit an answer, which is implicit in the actual phrasing of the question: "Will the minister admit that his government is ethically bankrupt and must now call an election?"

Rhyme: True rhyme requires that the end sound or an internal sound of one line of a poem is the same as the end sound or an internal sound of another line; *slant* (approximate, near, half) *rhyme* occurs when the sounds are similar rather than identical. Identical end sounds are called *end rhyme*; identical internal sounds are called *internal rhyme*. End rhymes are called *masculine* if the end sound is a stressed syllable, and *feminine* if the end sound is an unstressed syllable. The rhyme scheme of a poem is stated by assigning the letter *a* to the first and any recurrent identical end sounds, the letter *b* to the next and any recurring identical end sounds, and so on. Using this scheme, the common rhyme scheme for a Petrarchan (Italian) sonnet is abbaabbacdecde.

Rhyme scheme: See *rhyme*.

Rhythm: The term applied to the patterning of stressed and unstressed syllables in lines of poetry; see also *prosody*.

Rising action: The action in a plot preceding the climax.

Romance: Fiction that features remarkable characters, exotic settings, dramatic events, supernatural or mysterious elements, and a strong love interest, or any fictional work free of the restraints of realism. Romance reinforces the value system of the society; in romance, the value system is triumphant in overcoming any challenge.

Round character: A character capable of surprising the reader and of change; a psychologically complex character. E.M. Forster said a round character "has the incalculability of life about it."

Run-on line: See *enjambment*.

Sarcasm: A mocking or bitter attack using language that contains a double meaning; verbal irony.

Satire: A work whose principal purpose is to amend or reform human action by mounting a humorous, witty, or ironic attack upon it. Satire enlists the audience's condemning laughter in opposing the satirized subject. Jonathan Swift, for example, caustically savages the English and Anglo-Irish in "A Modest Proposal" by inventing an Anglo-Irish speaker and having that speaker advance an inhuman proposal.

Scansion: A system for measuring the rhythm of an accentual-syllabic poem. It chiefly employs two marks to indicate whether a syllable is stressed or unstressed and then evaluates the pattern of stresses by category (iambic, trochaic) and quantity (dimeter, trimeter). See also *prosody*.

Scene: Either a unit of a play or the physical and/or human environment for the action of a plot.

Sentimentality: The attempt of the writer to make us feel more deeply than the action of the plot warrants.

Sestet: The six lines that end a Petrarchan (Italian) sonnet, usually rhymed cdecde.

Sestina: See *poetic forms*.

Setting: The time and place in which a story, play, or poem takes place, including the culture of the society the characters are part of.

Simile: A figure of speech that makes an explicit comparison between two things, usually introducing that comparison with the words *like* or *as*.

Sociological criticism: See *literary analysis*.

Soliloquy: A convention used in drama whereby a lone character speaks aloud but not to an audience; the soliloquy gives the audience insight into the character's mind and/or motivations.

Sonnet: See *poetic forms*.

Speaker: The voice that tells the story or the poem; see *persona*.

Spondee: See *prosody*.

Stanza: Any grouping of two or more lines in poetry; strophic poetry employs stanzas, while sticchic poetry does not.

Stereotype: A simplified, stock character, often dominated by a single characteristic. See also *flat character*.

Sticchic: Poetry without stanzaic divisions. See also *strophic*.

Stream-of-consciousness technique: A narrative that presents the random, sometimes disjointed, thoughts of a character as they come to the character.

Stress: The relative emphasis given a spoken syllable. See *prosody*.

Strophic: Poetry with stanzaic divisions. See also *sticchic*.

Structure: The general design of a work; the interaction of its parts and how they compose a whole.

Style: The characteristics of the narrative voice, composed of such elements as tone, diction, sentence structure, syntax, imagery, and rhythm.

Subplot: A subordinate plot connected to the main plot by character or theme.

Summary: A condensation of material into a form that includes only the critical matter.

Suspense: The writer's deliberate use of delay in the action to heighten the interest or anxiety of the reader concerning the outcome of a particular action or set of actions.

Symbol: An image, object, gesture, detail, or event that evokes in the reader a sense of an additional range of meaning beyond the literal. Literary symbols are of two types, *public* and *private*, with a public symbol being a concrete entity that has a clearly established meaning within a particular culture. Private symbols take their meaning exclusively or primarily from the text in which they appear. The author often uses the reference more than once in a text, and this multiple appearance also complicates the meaning of a symbol because of the associative meanings added through repetition in different contexts. Consider, for instance, the symbolic meaning of Aylmer's lab in Nathaniel Hawthorne's "The Birthmark."

Synecdoche: See *metaphor*.

Syntax: The order in which words are placed to make meaning; all languages require words to be correctly ordered in a successful statement. Syntax is often more unconventional in poetry than in prose.

Tale: A short and relatively simple narrative; *tale* is a more general term than *short story*.

Tercet: A three-line stanza.

Terza rima: See *poetic forms*.

Tetrameter: See *prosody*.

Theme: The central intent of a text; we have to test our notion of a text's theme by ensuring that it is sufficient to explain all parts of the text and not inconsistent with any individual part. In an essay, the term *thesis* is frequently employed to signify the subject of the essay and the author's perspective on that subject.

Thesis: See *theme*.

Third-person narrator: See *point of view*.

Tone: The reader's sense of what the writer's attitude is toward the subject and audience.

Tragedy: In drama, tragedy refers to a certain kind of play, a dramatic form that goes back to the Greeks and has a protagonist who falls, in part because of his or her own error, and who may be killed as a consequence of that error. As a literary form, tragedy bears witness to a predisposition in humans to struggle mightily but to fail and die, either through error or destiny.

Tragic flaw: The error of judgement or action referred to in *tragedy*. The tragic perception requires the audience to understand that the protagonist's doom is earned, in part, because of a flaw or lacking in the protagonist's character or judgement. Many Greek tragedies identify pride as the flaw. See also *hubris/hybris*.

Transition: A connection between one part of a text and the next.

Trimeter: See *prosody*.

Trochaic metre: See *prosody*.

Understatement (litotes): The opposite of overstatement (hyperbole); for instance, saying that Michael Jordan has decent basketball skills would be an understatement.

Unity: The concept that a text should have a unifying principle, together with the expectation that all parts of the text will contain that unifying principle and be successfully connected.

Verbal irony: Saying one thing while intending something opposite as signalled by tone; in writing, it is more difficult to send that signal. Verbal irony is usually softer than sarcasm though similar in kind.

Verse: A term applied generally to metrical composition and specifically to a single stanza of a poem.

Villanelle: See *poetic forms*.

Voice: Our sense of the character and attitude of the speaker or narrator of a text. In an essay, voice refers to how we want our reader to perceive us from our writing.

Index of Authors and Titles

Index of First Lines

Hence, Cupid! with your cheating toys, 28
Here we are all, by day; by night, we're hurled, 20
How vainly men themselves amaze, 25

I caught this morning morning's minion, kingdom of daylight's, 67
I have done it again, 143
I heard a Fly buzz—when I died—, 64
I imagine this midnight moment's forest, 140
I met a traveller from an antique land, 45
I plucked pink blossoms from mine apple tree, 65
I remember when the unicorns, 128
I sought a theme and sought for it in vain, 76
I walk through the long schoolroom questioning, 74
I wander thro' each charter'd street, 36
If all the world and love were young, 14
If I were a cinnamon peeler, 163
It seemed that out of battle I escaped, 90
It was my thirtieth year to heaven, 114
It was taken some time ago, 156

Jabbering double-crossing doubletalk, 190

Let us go then, you and I, 85
like a child lost, 177
Living in the earth-deposits of our history, 139

Much Madness is divinest Sense—,64
My mistress' eyes are nothing like the sun, 17
My religion makes no sense, 179
My wife and I lived all alone, 125

No. 176—*Copenhagen Market Cabbage*: 'This *new introduction*, 130
Nobody stuffs the world in at your eyes, 120
Nothing can take its place. If I write 'ostrich', 93
Now as I was young and easy under the apple boughs, 116

O Rose, thou art sick, 36
O sweet spontaneous, 92
Of all the causes which conspire to blind, 31
Of man's first disobedience, and the fruit, 20
Once I am sure there's nothing going on, 123
On either side the river lie, 50

Copyright Acknowledgments

POETRY

Robert Frost

"The Silken Tent," by Robert Frost in *The Poetry of Robert Frost*, edited by Edward Connery Lathem. Copyright © 1947, 1969 by Henry Holt and Co. Copyright © 1936, 1942 by Robert Frost. Copyright © 1964, 1970, 1975 by Lesley Frost Ballantine. "Neither Out Far nor In Deep," by Robert Frost from *The Poetry of Robert Frost*, edited by Edward Connery Lathem. Copyright © 1936 by Robert Frost. Copyright © 1964 by Lesley Frost Ballantine. Copyright © 1969 by Henry Holt and Co. Reprinted by permission Henry Holt and Company, LLC.

Wallace Stevens

"The Emperor of Ice-Cream" and "The Snow Man," by Wallace Stevens from *Collected Poems of Wallace Stevens*, by Wallace Stevens, Copyright © 1954 by Wallace Stevens and renewed 1982 by Holly Stevens. Used by permission of Alfred A. Knopf, a division of Random House, Inc.

William Carlos Williams

"The Red Wheelbarrow" and "The Last Words of My English Grandmother," by William Carlos Williams, from *Collected Poems: 1909–1939*, Volume One. Copyright © 1938 by New Directions Publishing Corp. Reprinted by permission of New Directions Publishing Corp.

E.J. Pratt

"The Prize Cat," by E.J. Pratt, from *Complete Poems*, Part One, edited by Sandra Djwa and R.G. Moyles, University of Toronto Press, 1989. Reprinted with permission of the publisher.

Ezra Pound

"The River-Merchant's Wife: A Letter," by Ezra Pound, from *Personae*. Copyright © 1926 by Ezra Pound. Reprinted by permission of New Directions Publishing Corp.

T.S. Eliot

"The Love Song of J. Alfred Prufrock," and "Little Gidding (Part V)," by T.S. Eliot, from *Collected Poems 1909-1962*, by T.S. Eliot. Reprinted by permission of Faber and Faber Ltd.

e.e. cummings

"anyone lived in a pretty little how town," by e.e. cummings. Copyright © 1940, 1968, 1991 by the Trustees for the e.e. cummings Trust. "O sweet spontaneous," by e.e. cummings. Copyright © 1923, 1951, 1991 by the Trustees for the e.e. cummings Trust. Copyright © 1976 by George James Firmage, from *Complete Poems: 1904–1962* by e.e. cummings, edited by George J. Firmage. Used by permission of Liveright Publishing Corporation.

Marilyn Dumont
"The White Judges" and "Letter to Sir John A. Macdonald," by Marilyn Dumont. Reprinted by permission of Brick Books.

Armand Garnet Ruffo
"Creating a Country," by Armand Garnet Ruffo, from *Opening in the Sky*, Theytus Books (1994). Reprinted by permission of the author.

George Elliott Clarke
"Casualties," by George Elliott Clarke, from *Fiery Spirits and Voices*, edited by Ayanna Black. Published by HarperCollins Publishers Ltd. Copyright © 1992, 1994, 2000 by Ayanna Black. All rights reserved. "Nu(is)ance," by George Elliott Clarke from *Blue*, published in 2001 by Polestar, an imprint of Raincoast Books. Reprinted by permission of Raincoast Books. "Blank Sonnet," by George Elliott Clarke from *Whyla Falls*, published in 1990 by Polestar, an imprint of Raincoast Books. Reprinted by permission of Raincoast Books.

ESSAYS

J.B.S. Haldane
"Some Enemies of Science," by J.B.S. Haldane, *from Possible Worlds*, by J.B.S. Haldane. Published by Chatto & Windus. Reprinted by permission of The Random House Group Ltd.

Northrop Frye
"Elementary Teaching," by Northrop Frye from *The Stubborn Structure*, Methuen. Reprinted with the permission of the Estate of Northrop Frye.

Basil H. Johnston
"One Generation from Extinction," by Basil H. Johnston. Reprinted by permission of the author.

Neil Postman
"Now ... This," from *Amusing Ourselves to Death*, by Neil Postman. Copyright © 1985 by Neil Postman. Used by permission of Viking Penguin, a division of Penguin Putnam (USA) Inc.

Gloria Steinem
"Sex, Lies, and Advertising," by Gloria Steinem. Reprinted by permission of the author.

David Suzuki
"The Pain of Animals," by David Suzuki from *Inventing the Future*. Copyright © 1989 by David Suzuki. Reprinted by permission.

W.H. New
"Giddy Limits: Canadian Studies and Other Metaphors," by W.H. New from *Borderlands: How We Talk About Canada*, by W.H. New, UBC Press, 1999. Used by permission of the Publishers. Copyright © 1988 University of British Columbia Press. All rights reserved by the Publisher.

SHORT STORIES